Droit commun

UNDERSTANDING BUSINESS LAW

Fifth Edition

R. Robert Rosenberg, Ed.D., C.P.A.

Educational Consultant
Former President of Jersey City Junior College
Jersey City, New Jersey

John E. Whitcraft, M.S.

Educational Consultant
Former Director, Division of Occupational Instruction
The State Education Department
Albany, New York

GREGG DIVISION/McGRAW-HILL BOOK COMPANY

NEW YORK   ST. LOUIS   DALLAS   SAN FRANCISCO
DÜSSELDORF   JOHANNESBURG   KUALA LUMPUR   LONDON
MEXICO   MONTREAL   NEW DELHI   PANAMA   RIO DE JANEIRO
SINGAPORE   SYDNEY   TORONTO

ACKNOWLEDGMENTS

Associate Editor: Sheila Furjanic
Senior Editing Manager: Mary Drouin
Copy Editor: Margarethe Aulehner
Production Assistant: Maria Winiarski
Designer: Graphicus, Inc.
Compositor: York Graphic Services, Inc.
Printer: The Murray Printing Company
Binder: Rand McNally & Company

419 825

PHOTO CREDITS

Martin J. Dain (Magnum Photos), p. 2; Strickler (Monkmeyer Photos), p. 28; Sebastian Milito, pp. 50, 108, 138, 168, 232 (all courtesy of Gimbels East, New York), p. 202 (courtesy of Walter Reade Organization), p. 408 (courtesy of Charles H. Greenthal & Company); Wide World Photos, p. 82; *The New York Times*, p. 260; Bruce Davidson (Magnum Photos), p. 284; Roy Pinney (Monkmeyer Photos), p. 312; The Chase Manhattan Bank Money Museum, p. 350; Rene Burri (Magnum Photos), p. 378; RCA Corporation, p. 442.

Library of Congress Cataloging in Publication Data

Rosenberg, Reuben Robert, date.
  Understanding business law.

  First ed., 1947, by R. O. Skar, A. E. Schneider, and B. W. Palmer, published under title: Personal business law.
  Fourth ed., 1967, by A. E. Schneider, J. E. Whitcraft, and R. R. Rosenberg, published under title: Understanding business law.
  1. Business law—United States. I. Whitcraft, John E., joint author. II. Schneider, Arnold Edward, date. Understanding business law. IV. Title.
KF889.6.R67 1973   346'.73'07   73-158
ISBN 0-07-053691-0

UNDERSTANDING BUSINESS LAW, Fifth Edition

23456789 MURM 7210987654

PREFACE

Law affects every phase of a person's life. Thus, every citizen, no matter what his role, should know what his legal rights are and how to protect them. But he must know that with these rights he has certain legal responsibilities. The objective of a business law course is to make students aware of both their rights and their responsibilities. *Understanding Business Law, Fifth Edition,* emphasizes business law as it affects young adults, and it provides them with practical guidelines for becoming effective citizens and consumers—both now and in the future.

Renting an apartment, buying and financing a car, opening a charge account, and finding a job are topics of particular interest to most young adults. *Understanding Business Law, Fifth Edition,* presents the legal aspects of these and many more important topics, and it presents the topics in a way that will motivate the students to learn. Short, easily-assimilated units encourage them to read their daily assignments. Each unit is followed immediately with a variety of application activities of interest to the students. The marginal terms throughout the book, which are a new feature in this edition, provide students with instant learning reinforcement. The photographs used throughout the book emphasize real-life situations, and introductory case problems, together with numerous examples in case-problem format, illustrate the importance of business law in everyday life.

Understanding Business Law presents the most recent legislation enacted in the area of business law. A few of the many updated areas include legislation affecting consumer affairs, automobile insurance, employment, and rental of real property. This edition also clarifies the effect of the Uniform Commercial Code on business law. Code references are presented in color throughout the book to highlight legal concepts that have been accepted by all states using the Uniform Commercial Code.

MOTIVATIONAL FEATURES

A variety of motivational features are built into *Understanding Business Law.* Each of these features plays an important part in making this edition easy for the student to read and understand.

MARGINAL QUESTIONS

Questions relating directly to the material covered in the text are color-highlighted in the left-hand margin of each page. These questions can be used as a series of pretests to determine a student's understanding of the specific text material before he reads the unit. They also serve to stimulate his interest in reading the material because they focus on the objective of the paragraphs. The marginal questions can also be used as post-tests to evaluate the student's comprehension of facts and information as he progresses from page to page.

Teachers can use the marginal questions as the basis for establishing performance goals. Since each question is directly related to the adjacent text material, the facts and information necessary to answer the question can be acquired by reading the corresponding text material. For example, the marginal questions "What is a void contract? How does it differ from a voidable contract?" could be used as the basis for developing a performance goal such as "Given five sentences that describe two voidable contracts and three void contracts, the student will accurately identify the two voidable contracts and the three void contracts."

LAWTOONS

More than a hundred lawtoons are used in this edition of *Understanding Business Law.* Every lawtoon is designed to reinforce an important legal concept or principle presented in the text material. Thus the lawtoons help the student to retain the new information and to recall it in the future.

INTRODUCTORY CASE PROBLEMS

Each unit begins with "What's the Law?"—two problem situations designed to interest young adults. Answers to these "stimulators" are located at the end of every unit.

UNIT ORGANIZATION

Understanding Business Law is organized into 16 parts, each consisting of three units—totaling 48. The units are designed to motivate the students to complete their daily assignments. Each unit is short and is followed by an interesting variety of end-of-unit activities.

LEARNING REINFORCEMENT FEATURES

Throughout the text, learning is reinforced by many special features. Each of these features helps to strengthen the student's understanding and increase his retention of important legal concepts and principles.

LEGAL DEFINITIONS AND MARGINAL TERMS

Approximately a thousand legal terms are presented to help the student increase his legal vocabulary. These selected terms are given in color in the right-hand margin where each word is defined. Thus a student has immediate word recognition and reinforcement when he reads a definition. The marginal terms also help the student to locate specific discussions and definitions needed to do the end-of-unit activities and the assignments in the activity guide.

CASE EXAMPLES

Each unit of the text contains numerous examples in a case format that illustrate important legal concepts and principles. These examples present a legal problem as well as its solution.

SUGGESTIONS FOR MINIMIZING LEGAL RISKS

This popular feature gives precautions that will enable the students to avoid costly and time-consuming legal mistakes in their personal and business affairs.

QUESTIONS AND PROBLEMS

The carefully selected questions and problems at the end of each unit provide topics for discussion and review. They also provide an informal measure of the students' understanding.

WHAT IS YOUR OPINION?

At the end of each unit are simple cases that are given to illustrate the legal principles and concepts developed in that particular unit. A discussion of these simple cases will give the teacher an indication of the level of the students' understanding of the facts related to the cases.

THE LAW IN ACTION

Interesting, real-life cases and accurate case citations are presented at the end of each unit. The cases involve situations which may be familiar to the students. The teacher's manual gives information on how to locate these cases in a law library.

A DIGEST OF LEGAL CONCEPTS

The important legal concepts and principles that affect people in their daily lives are summarized at the end of each part.

LAW DICTIONARY

An expanded glossary containing over 500 legal terms is presented at the back of the book. The glossary contains brief definitions of many of the legal terms that have been defined and explained in the text.

CORRELATED TEACHING AND LEARNING MATERIALS

The *Understanding Business Law* program includes the following correlated supporting materials.

ACTIVITY GUIDE

The *Activity Guide for Understanding Business Law* stimulates further study of business law concepts and principles through the use of activities and projects which are carefully correlated with the textbook. Included in the activity guide are completion, true-false, multiple choice, and matching exercises, short case problems, and projects utilizing professional legal forms.

ACHIEVEMENT TESTS

A set of tests is available for *Understanding Business Law.* The set contains 14 tests—12 of the tests cover the 16 parts of the textbook, and 2 tests are review tests covering Parts 1–8 and Parts 9–16.

TEACHER'S MANUAL AND KEY

The *Teacher's Manual and Key for Understanding Business Law* includes suggestions for teaching business law and for enriching the course with supplementary activities. Information on how to obtain valuable reference materials is also included. The manual and key contains answers to all end-of-unit activities, as well as the answers to the questions and problems presented in the activity guide and in the achievement tests.

ACKNOWLEDGMENT

The authors want to acknowledge the many contributions made to business law by the late Professor Edward A. Smith, of Syracuse University, that influenced the organization and tenor of *Understanding Business Law.*

R. ROBERT ROSENBERG

JOHN E. WHITCRAFT

CONTENTS

PART 1: The Meaning of the Law

WHAT'S THE LAW?

1. *Jamie Jackson is a muskrat trapper in a remote part of Alaska. He lives with his brother in a wooden cabin far from civilization and has no contact with other people for months at a time. Does Jamie have any contact with man-made laws?*

2. *Each spring, Jamie packs his muskrat furs and delivers them more than 100 miles to the nearest trading post. Under these circumstances would Jamie be concerned with man-made laws?*

△ UNIT 1: LAW IN EVERYDAY LIFE

The day you were born, the law stepped into your life. As long as you live, the law will be important to you. Does this thought startle you? Stop and think for a moment. The activities you have engaged in today, those of your parents, the local fire department, the police department, the public health department—yes, even the activities of your school officials—all are affected by law.

How are your activities affected by the law?

You aren't sure? Think about it. Did you buy a candy bar today? Did you ride on a bus? Did you drive a car? Did you ride a bicycle? Did you do part-time work for someone? In each of these situations, the law plays an important role. You cannot escape having legal dealings with someone every day unless you isolate yourself from the world entirely.

EXAMPLE 1   **When you buy groceries or pay to ride on a bus, you are governed by the law of contracts. When you drive a car, you are governed by motor vehicle laws. When you ride a bicycle, you are governed by local city ordinances and, in some cases, by state traffic regulations. When you work for someone, you are governed, in most cases, by one or more of the laws of contracts, agency, or state labor laws.**

It is clear, then, that you need to know something about law. The ordinary businessman and the average citizen can hope to learn only the basic rules. A knowledge of these basic rules, however, will help you over many rough spots when you are on your own.

LAW IN HUMAN RELATIONS

What does the law mean to you?

The phrase "the law" may have a different interpretation to different people. What does it mean to you? Do you think of a policeman? Do you think of "the law" as a set of rules designed to prevent you from doing

What is the real
purpose of laws?

the things you want to do? While it may seem that way sometimes, the real purpose of laws is to help you get along smoothly with other people in business and social relationships.

If you lived alone on an island and no other person ever came on your island, you might be free from man-made laws. You might stretch your imagination a little more and give yourself a smart sports car to drive on your island. Imagine also that you have a long, straight concrete highway running the length of your island. You could drive just as fast as you wished. You could drive on the right side of the road, on the left side, or down the middle. It would not make any difference. Let one other person come to your island paradise, however, with another automobile, and some man-made rules are going to be necessary—or someone is going to get hurt. This is but one example of why some rules of conduct are necessary if you are going to live in harmony and safety with other people.

Can we ever live
without
man-made laws?

LAW DEFINES RIGHTS AND DUTIES

Look around you—you are surrounded by people. You will probably always live among other human beings. You have your rights, but your rights must be adjusted so that the rights of others will be equally recognized. In other words, when you live among civilized people, you have many duties as well as many rights.

EXAMPLE 2   **While walking down the street, you were injured by a garden rake that a man was carrying under his arm. The passerby who hit you was not paying any attention to you or other sidewalk pedestrians. Even though both of you had a right to be walking on the sidewalk, each of you was required to respect the rights of the other. The man who injured you failed to safeguard your rights and is therefore liable for the injuries which you suffered.**

Throughout the study of business law, you will discover this interplay of rights and duties. The study of law will enable you to know your duties as well as to enjoy your rights. You will learn to see and understand the other fellow's point of view because of your knowledge of the law.

Knowing that the law establishes a system of rights and duties may not be sufficient. There will be occasions when you will need to know exactly what your rights are and exactly what your duties are. You may have heard it said, "If you do what is right, you will never have any legal

The private rights of an individual are often restricted in the interest of the overall public welfare.

problems." That is good advice, but it is not the whole story. It is true that the law tries to see that "justice" is done. But what is "right," and what is "justice"? In most lawsuits (court cases), each party thinks that he is right and the other fellow is at fault. This difference of opinion as to who is right and who is wrong in various legal situations is the real reason why we have so many lawsuits. Each party is attempting to use "the law" to prove that he is right. Let's look at this situation:

If we know our rights and duties, why are there so many lawsuits?

EXAMPLE 3   Ray Greene lent his typewriter to Tom Smith so that Tom could type a term paper. Tom kept the typewriter a week and then wrongfully sold it to Sam Archer. Sam thought the typewriter belonged to Tom because he had seen Tom carrying it home from school. Ray later discovered that Sam had his typewriter and demanded its return. Sam said that he paid good money for it and that he would not give it up unless his money was refunded.

Ray certainly has a right to the return of his typewriter. Sam certainly has a right to the return of his money. What would "justice" be here? How should the case of Ray and Sam be decided?

The problem is very old. It is, however, very common even today. Both parties have rights; a judge must decide which one of two innocent parties must bear the loss. Ray could probably reclaim his typewriter, and Sam would have to get the money from Tom, if Tom had it.

Both Ray and Sam are protected by certain legal rules developed over the years. Ray should have known these rules before he parted with his typewriter. Sam should have known these rules before he parted with his money. Had they known these rules, they could have protected their rights. A knowledge of law prevents foolish mistakes.

Again, it must be emphasized that no one can know all the law. A knowledge of a few basic rules, however, will enable you to avoid many costly errors. It is usually much less troublesome to avoid getting into legal difficulties than to pay for getting out of them.

LAW ENFORCES LEGAL RIGHTS

Do you know when you should go to a lawyer for help in legal matters? Many people do not. Furthermore, some people frequently do not know when their "legal toes" are being stepped on. Many times these people suffer losses because they do not know that the law will come to their aid. Take, for example, the situation involving Ray Greene, Sam Archer, and the typewriter that you read about above. Here is a situation that involves rights; but, if the rights cannot be resolved, it may be necessary to go to a lawyer in order to find a remedy.

How can a knowledge of certain basic legal rules help you throughout your life?

EXAMPLE 4   Assume that Ray Greene has an absolute right to his typewriter and asks for its return. Sam replies, "True, you have the right to the typewriter; but I have the typewriter. Try to get it." Ray's right is not going to be of much use to him unless he has some legal method to aid him in enforcing his right.

A *legal remedy* is a procedure or an action that may be used to enforce a right. You might consider it as a means of correcting a wrong. The ordinary citizen can do little for himself in the way of applying legal

LEGAL REMEDY

Civilized man has learned to use the force of law rather than physical force to protect his rights.

What is the best way to enforce your legal rights?

remedies. If he uses force to obtain his rights, he will probably find himself in conflict with the law. He must, therefore, go to a lawyer for help because only a lawyer can bring a case before a court. While, theoretically, it is possible for a person to act as his own lawyer at the trial of a case, it would not be advisable for him to do so, since he will not have a complete knowledge of legal procedure. In the case involving the typewriter, if Sam Archer refuses to give up the typewriter, Ray Greene should go to a lawyer and ask him to start a lawsuit in order that Ray may get back his typewriter. In a later unit various other remedies that might be available to Ray will be presented.

LAW PROTECTS THE CONSUMER

Everyone is a consumer. We buy things to use, to eat, or to enjoy. One of the major purposes of the law is the protection of the consumer. In your reading you will often find this protection of the consumer referred to as "public policy." *Public policy* is the aspect of law that makes unenforceable those acts that are injurious to the public good. Because of this principle of public policy, the "well-being of the public" is uppermost in the minds of lawmakers, public officials, and other persons who make and administer our laws and regulations.

PUBLIC POLICY

How does the principle of public policy protect you?

There are many laws, both written and unwritten, that are designed to protect the public and the consumer. Some of them are old laws rewritten to make them more suitable for current problems. The most ambitious modernization of these laws is to be found in the *Uniform Commercial Code,* which is the one law or code in which prior uniform acts or laws have been substantially revised or integrated in line with present commercial practices.

UNIFORM COMMERCIAL CODE

Some of the laws giving protection to the consumer are laws of the federal government. A recent example is the Consumer Credit Protection Act, which was passed in 1968. This act, popularly known as the Truth in Lending Act, will be discussed in a later unit. Some are the laws of various state governments. Some are the laws of city (municipal) governments; these laws are often called *ordinances*.

ORDINANCE

Consumers are protected not only by these special laws and their administration but also by certain private agencies. These sources include better business bureaus, newspapers, medical and dental associations, trade associations, legal aid societies, and many other associations working in the interest of the consumer.

 APPLYING YOUR LEARNING

QUESTIONS AND PROBLEMS

1. Do you think that Robinson Crusoe and his man Friday needed any man-made laws on Robinson Crusoe's island? Why?
2. What are some traffic laws that you must observe if you drive a car? What are some penalties that might result from breaking these rules?
3. Can you give some examples of situations that resulted in friction or the breaking of friendships among people you know because someone failed to observe the rules?
4. What are some rules that are necessary for the smooth management of a school? Why are these rules needed?
5. Can you name some rules or laws in your school that are designed principally to protect your health?
6. Can you describe some everyday situations where you may have a right to do something but also a duty to protect the rights of others?

WHAT IS YOUR OPINION?

In each of the following cases, give your decision and state a legal principle that applies to the case.

1. The health laws in one community require that all school children be vaccinated. Joe McIntee contends that these regulations are contrary to his personal rights. He maintains that he has the right not to be vaccinated and take the chance of becoming ill. What are the arguments favorable to Joe? What are the arguments favorable to the school? What rights and duties are involved here?
2. Gordon Wyatt boarded a bus marked "Downtown," paid his fare, and sat down. Midway on the trip, the bus driver told Gordon that he must get off and take another bus. Gordon contended that he had paid his fare and was entitled to ride all the way downtown on this bus. The driver contended that, since Gordon was the only passenger, it was not worthwhile for him to drive his bus all the way downtown. Does Gordon have any rights? If so, what are they, and how did he acquire them? Does Gordon owe any duties? What are they?

3. Howard Hull left an unattended trash fire burning in his backyard while he went to the grocery store. The fire spread; and Howard's neighbor, Bill Jackson, feared it might set fire to Jackson's garage. Would Bill Jackson have the right to enter Howard's yard and put out the fire? Would it be proper for Bill to enter the yard and put out the fire if Howard were still at home and tending the fire himself?

4. If in Case 3 there were a city ordinance that prohibited the burning of trash within the city limits, would it be proper for Bill to enter Howard's yard and put out the fire if Howard were carefully tending the fire himself? What remedy would you suggest under these circumstances?

5. George Carter bought a new television set on an easy-payment plan. He later discovered that the fine print in the purchase contract he signed contained many agreements that he would never have consented to if he had read the contract. Do you think it would be in the interest of public policy to have a state law requiring that all such contracts be printed in type of a given size? Would this protect the consumer's rights? Would this take away any rights of the seller?

THE LAW IN ACTION

1. The defendant, Nathan N. Seaman, maintained and operated a brick kiln in a certain village. Fumes and sulfurous acid gas produced by the burning of bricks killed more than one hundred scotch pine trees that were growing on the plaintiff's nearby property. The plaintiff, Samuel B. Campbell, brought an action for the damages suffered and also for an injunction against future operation of the kiln, claiming that its operation in that location was a nuisance. What were some of Seaman's rights and duties? What were some of Campbell's rights? Was there any public policy involved here? (Campbell v. Seaman, 63 N.Y. 568)

2. Mrs. Kehr desired to change her will. The original copy of her will, signed by her, was in the possession of her attorney; but she had a carbon copy of the will in her possession. She wrote "null and void" on the carbon copy and filed it with her personal papers. After she died, a court action was necessary to determine whether the original will had been canceled. Do you think Mrs. Kehr was wise in her action? Do you think she would have been wiser to call her attorney? Would a little knowledge of law have prevented a lawsuit in this situation? (In re Kehr's Estate, 373 Pa. 473, 95 A.2d 647)

KEY TO "WHAT'S THE LAW?" Page 3

1. *Jamie would have very little contact with man-made laws because his personal rights would not often be in conflict with the rights of other individuals. We must remember, however, that even in these remote surroundings, Jamie is living with his brother, and his relations with him are governed by the law. Jamie is also trapping in Alaska and is subject to both state and federal laws.*

2. *Yes. Jamie would now be in closer contact with other people. As his contacts with other people increase, his concern with man-made laws would increase.*

WHAT'S THE LAW?

1. *Michael Torres is flying his new airplane. Is he involved with natural laws, with man-made laws, or with both?*

2. *If Joe Nickler promised to sell you his snowmobile and later refused to do so, could you have him arrested for refusing to perform?*

▲ UNIT 2: DEVELOPMENT OF LAW

Laws may be broadly classified into natural laws, moral laws, and man-made laws. "It's the law." What does this expression mean to you? Law means different things to different people.

In your science courses you have heard of the "law of gravitation" and of the "law of action and reaction." In an economics course you may have heard of the "law of diminishing returns." These are called *natural laws* because they are derived from nature. Natural laws are important to all of us. The airplane, for example, flies because it conforms to certain natural laws. If the engine should stop, the law of gravitation would most certainly cause the airplane to come down.

NATURAL LAW

There are other laws that are also important because they pertain to your business and social behavior and will affect you and your friends throughout your lives. These are *moral laws*, rules of conduct that may not be actual laws. Sometimes they are only rules of good behavior, such as being truthful, being honest in one's dealings with others, and being considerate of others.

MORAL LAW

How do you distinguish between natural laws and moral laws?

EXAMPLE 1 **A man who was being attacked by several men yelled for help, but no one who witnessed the assault came to his aid. The law does not require a person to endanger his own life in order to help another. Although we have a moral duty to aid our fellow man when he is in trouble, legal requirements to do so are nonexistent.**

While, ordinarily, these moral laws are only rules of good conduct, they sometimes become the basis of enforceable laws passed by state legislatures or the federal government. At one time in the past, for example, there were no laws limiting the rate of interest that might be charged for lending money. The only limitation on the lender was moral law. Good moral conduct required the lender not to take unfair advantage of the borrower who was hard pressed for money, but there was no legal regulation. Today, in most states the rate of interest that may be charged for the loan of money is strictly regulated by state laws. Thus, a former moral rule has become an enforceable man-made law.

The laws governing man have developed over a long, long period of time. And new man-made laws are still being developed.

EXAMPLE 2   The automobile brought about the need for a whole set of new laws. Before there were any automobiles, there was no need for motor vehicle laws that would regulate their operation. Today, however, the use of automobiles creates serious problems that must be met by appropriate legislation for their control.

We are constantly changing and improving our laws to adapt them to our changing patterns of living. Laws will never be completed. New laws will be added or old ones amended as long as civilization continues.

What areas of human relationship are covered by the classification of laws?

Our man-made laws may be classified as international law or municipal law. *International law* is recognized as the law that deals with relations between nations. The term *municipal law* is used to indicate the law of your city, state or nation. Your first reaction to the term municipal law would undoubtedly be to associate it with the laws of your own town or city. That is correct, but the term also has a broader meaning.

INTERNATIONAL LAW
MUNICIPAL LAW

MUNICIPAL LAW

The earliest laws governing mankind probably sprang into existence when the cavemen first began to hunt together. These primitive men found that they could protect themselves better and find more game by working in groups. Some rules governing the hunt had to be worked out. As primitive men began to live in larger and still larger tribal groups, it became necessary to develop laws that would permit them to work, hunt, play, and get along together for their mutual benefit. They quickly learned that a man cannot be an "outlaw" and still be accepted in a social system. He must learn to conform to the rules that govern all the people.

You can readily see that the first laws were tribal laws. As time went on, larger units of government developed. Laws were expanded to regulate these larger units. Thus, municipal law developed. Today, in this country, we have several levels of municipal law—your city laws, or ordinances; your county, or possibly your township, laws; your state laws; and, over all, the federal laws. Municipal laws have their origins in the English common law and the Roman, or civil, law.

Trace the development of municipal law.

THE ENGLISH COMMON LAW

Laws in this country are virtually all based on the English common law. The story of the development of the common law is an interesting one.

You will remember from your study of history that England in medieval days was governed by the *feudal system*—a system in which the feudal lord

FEUDAL SYSTEM

reigned supreme within his domain. The feudal lord owned all the land surrounding his castle; this land was worked by serfs, who had few, if any, rights. Because the lords settled arguments over rights with their neighboring lords by fighting matters out and the serfs had few rights, little law was needed.

As the common man began to rise from serfdom to the status of tenant farmer, however, he began to acquire some rights. At this point the need for law began to arise in order that disputes might be settled in accordance with some sensible system. The rights of one tenant might come into conflict with the rights of another. The earliest of these disputes were probably settled by the feudal lord. He would hear the arguments of each tenant and then make his decision. There was no formal body of law to guide him. He followed his own reason and best judgment. Later, civil officers having judicial powers (*magistrates*) were appointed to hear and settle disputes; but still there was no law to guide them. Quite logically, a magistrate might say to himself, "Now I decided a case much like this one six months ago. How did I decide that one?" To refresh his memory, he began to write down his decisions so that he could refer to them. As relations and communications with neighboring magistrates became better, he might exchange notes and ideas with them.

MAGISTRATE

How did the English common law develop?

At the same time the central government of the king, which at first was very weak, was becoming stronger, and the king began to establish courts. The king's courts made decisions and kept records. All this took place before the English Parliament was sufficiently well established to draw up a complete set of written laws. Thus, by the time the central government of the king had become strong enough and sufficiently well developed to pass a code of laws, the laws regulating the rights of the common man were already well established by the day-to-day rulings of the early courts. This is called the law of precedent or the *common law.* Parliament did not disturb these common-law precedents but merely picked up where they left off. The new laws that were passed by Parliament changed or modified the common law as needed to meet new situations or filled needs that were not present in the early common-law days.

What is the law of precedent?

COMMON LAW

When our forefathers founded this country, they brought with them from England these common-law principles which formed the basis of the law in force in the Colonies. Our state legislatures today pass new legislation called statutes.

Our forefathers brought common-law principles with them from England.

Some of these statutes are passed to help solve problems that did not exist at common law, such as our motor vehicle statutes, which were mentioned previously. Other statutes may merely bring the common law up to date and adapt it to our present needs. The exchange of goods among people and business establishments has been in operation since the beginning of time. The basic principles governing the law of sales were developed under the common law. Today's merchandising methods have brought about changes. Under common law, purchases were paid for in cash. Much business today is conducted on the credit plan. Thus, new laws have been enacted in order to protect the rights of both businessmen and consumers.

How do our present-day statutes relate to the common law?

A more complete study of the common law would illustrate how customs may become law. Many of the early rulings of the court that became law were based on custom. One of the sources of these customs was the law of the church, known as *ecclesiastical law.*

ECCLESIASTICAL LAW

Another source was the customs of merchants and traders. These customs formed the basis of what is known as the *law merchant.* The law merchant has become a part of the common law. You see, it would be quite logical for a judge who had no written law to look to the customs of merchants and traders to find the answer in an argument between two businessmen. Once the judge rendered a decision on the point in dispute, the decision became a part of the way of doing things, or the common law.

LAW MERCHANT

Upon what was the law merchant based?

ROMAN, OR CIVIL, LAW

One of the great contributions of the Roman Empire was a system of laws. The Roman, or civil, law is another form of municipal law. Rome conquered almost all the known civilized world of her day. To administer this great empire, she needed many laws. Through the influence of Emperor Justinian and other emperors who followed him, a complete code of laws was drawn up. An attempt was made in this code to write down all the laws and regulations of every kind that were to govern the rights of the Romans and their subjects. Virtually all the laws of Europe have been built around this *Roman Code.* Colonists settling in the New World brought the code of laws of the particular European nation from which they came. Thus, all the Latin American countries follow the Roman Code. In this country the laws of the state of Louisiana are based on it because Louisiana was settled by the French, and France had developed its legal system after the pattern set by the Roman Code.

ROMAN CODE

Why is most of our law based on the English common law while all Latin-American countries follow the Roman Code?

To illustrate the difference between the development of the English common law and the codified Roman law, let us consider how the game of basketball developed. The first game of basketball developed informally. A gym teacher hung up a peach basket and had two teams of boys try to throw a ball into it. There were no formal rules. Each team simply tried to get the ball and throw it into the basket. You can see that a referee was soon needed. The referee began to make some decisions as to how the game should be played so that no one would get hurt. The next time

Can you imagine what would happen in a basketball game if there were no rules and regulations?

How does the English common law differ in origin and development from the Roman Code?

the boys played the game, the referee would recall his decisions of the previous day and would also make new decisions as problems developed. As the new game became increasingly popular, a set of formal rules developed along with it. Nearly every year, these rules have undergone some changes. That is similar to the history of the development of the English common law. If, on the other hand, before the game had ever been played, the gym instructor, who was familiar with other ball games, had proceeded to work out a set of formal rules, we would have a situation similar to the origin of the Roman Code.

You can readily see that, even though the instructor had worked out detailed formal rules in advance, some modifications would have to be made as the game developed. That has been true of all codified law. *Codified law* is law based upon a system of principles and rules. In like manner, even though the first rules of basketball were made "on the spot," they were written down later and became the rules of the game. The same has been true of the common law. Today, much of the common law has been rewritten in the form of codified laws passed by state legislatures.

CODIFIED LAW

STATUTE LAW

Another form of municipal law is called statute law. *Statutes* are laws specifically passed by a governing body created for that purpose. Thus, laws passed by the English Parliament, the United States Congress, the state legislatures, or local city councils can all be called statute law.

STATUTE

These laws consist of additions to or modifications of the original common law to meet modern situations. Also, modern living raises many problems that were never contemplated by the common law; therefore, much new legislation is necessary. These new laws, passed by legislatures, are found in state and federal statutes.

Trace the development of statute law.

While the laws of all states except Louisiana are based on the English common law, interpretation of them may differ from one state to another. This did not cause much trouble in the early days of our country because trade did not extend beyond the borders of a trader's own state. But as interstate commerce developed, a need developed along with it for more uniformity in state laws.

The federal statutes regulate matters that concern the nation as a whole, and they are based on the rights given to the federal government by our Constitution. In some instances both federal and state statutes may govern a situation, such as kidnapping, taxation, or narcotics control.

The Uniform Commercial Code   Various attempts have been made through the years to make the laws in the fifty states more nearly uniform. The resulting legislation concerning business transactions is known as *uniform acts* or uniform laws. These acts, revised and rewritten, are now included in a single statute, the *Uniform Commercial Code*. The Code was formulated by the National Conference of Commissioners on Uniform State Laws and the American Law Institute. It was first published in 1952. The Code, consisting of ten articles, has been revised and amended several times since the first official edition was issued. Its stated purpose is "to simplify, clarify, and modernize the law governing commercial transactions; to permit the continued expansion of commercial practices . . . ; and to make uniform the law among the various jurisdictions." U.C.C., Sec. 1-102

That the Code is meeting a need is evidenced by the fact that it has been adopted by all states and territories except Louisiana and Puerto Rico. Exact interpretations of its provisions will be found in court decisions to be made in the years ahead.

> UNIFORM ACTS
> UNIFORM COMMERCIAL CODE

> How has the Uniform Commercial Code contributed to the uniformity of law among the states?

The Uniform Commercial Code has been adopted in all states and territories except Louisiana and Puerto Rico.

CIVIL, OR PRIVATE, LAW

The law that affects the regulation of the rights and duties of individuals is called *civil*, or private, *law* because individuals only—not the state—are involved in any court actions taken.

Note that the term civil law is used to indicate two different classifications. In worldwide use the term indicates codified law, or Roman law, as contrasted with English common law. Within this country it is used as another name for private law as contrasted with public law.

> What is civil, or private, law?

> CIVIL LAW

PUBLIC LAW

The branch of law that pertains to the relationship between the state and private citizens is known as *public law*. The term *state* is used to indicate any unit of government—local, state, or federal. Public law is usually classified as criminal law, administrative law, or constitutional law.

PUBLIC LAW
STATE

Criminal Law   All levels of government—local, state, and national—pass laws that deal with the health, safety, good conduct, and preservation of society. If a person violates one of these laws, he is guilty of a crime and may be prosecuted by the proper authority—usually the state. The law of crimes and their punishments is called *criminal law*. An act may be both a crime and a private wrong. A *private wrong* is one that causes loss or injury to a private citizen, as contrasted with the harm that befalls the general public when a crime is committed.

CRIMINAL LAW
PRIVATE WRONG

EXAMPLE 3   Stephen Rogers, in violation of the Motor Vehicle Code, was driving his car at 70 miles an hour on the city streets. While so doing, he ran into Ronald Crossett's car and seriously damaged it. Stephen would find himself as the defendant in two court actions—one brought by the state or the city for violating the Motor Vehicle Code, which is part of the public law. In the second action Ronald would be suing for the damages done to his automobile, which would come under private law.

Administrative Law   In a complicated modern society such as ours, state and federal legislatures cannot always pass detailed laws to take care of every need. Instead, they may pass general laws and delegate to a board or commission the responsibility of making detailed rules for the administration of the law. These boards or commissions are called *administrative agencies*, and the rules they make are called *administrative law*. Some examples of administrative agencies are the Interstate Commerce Commission, Federal Trade Commission, Federal Communications Commission, and state public service commissions. Some of these agencies will be described in subsequent units in the discussion of particular problems.

ADMINISTRATIVE
AGENCY
ADMINISTRATIVE
LAW

EXAMPLE 4   The legislature of a certain state passed a law regulating the rates to be charged by express companies that were engaged in interstate commerce and had business offices within the state. A commission, appointed as a result of an act of Congress, had previously enacted regulations governing the rates of express companies. These regulations differed from those passed by the state. The control of interstate trade and any laws passed by Congress affecting such trade take precedence over state law. The state law on this subject would be void.

Constitutional Law   *Constitutional law*, which is part of our public law, is the branch of law that deals with the organization of the government and the exercise of its powers. The government may be that of a state or of a nation; laws in this category may be state laws or federal laws.

CONSTITUTIONAL
LAW

The Constitution of the United States is the broad, basic foundation for our laws in this country. It sets forth the fundamental rights of citizens, defines the limits within which the federal and the state governments may pass laws, and describes the functions of the various branches and divisions of our national government.

The law enables man to enjoy his rights and privileges and, at the same time, prevents him from interfering with the rights of other people.

State constitutions are patterned after the federal Constitution, which takes precedence. A state constitution lays down principles to guide the state legislature in making laws for conducting state business.

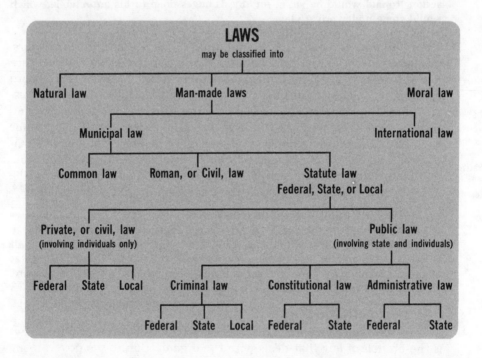

LAWS
may be classified into

- Natural law
- Man-made laws
- Moral law
  - Municipal law
  - International law
    - Common law
    - Roman, or Civil, law
    - Statute law — Federal, State, or Local
      - Private, or civil, law (involving individuals only)
        - Federal
        - State
        - Local
      - Public law (involving state and individuals)
        - Criminal law
          - Federal
          - State
          - Local
        - Constitutional law
          - Federal
          - State
        - Administrative law
          - Federal
          - State

INTERNATIONAL LAW

The nations of the world are *sovereign powers* and are, therefore, not subject to the laws of other nations. The mutual agreements nations enter into among themselves constitute *international law*. In our modern world we find it necessary to concern ourselves more and more with the affairs

SOVEREIGN POWER

INTERNATIONAL LAW

of other nations. The field of international law and international relations, therefore, becomes very important in these times when nations create tensions that affect the welfare and future of the entire world. In your social studies you have read about the World Court at The Hague, the United Nations, the Geneva Conference, and many other conventions that are primarily concerned with the field of international conduct and law. The advent of the space era and space flight has created urgent need for an international legal order. The law of force can be supplanted by the force of law only when the world's leaders resort to binding international lawmaking.

"International law comes into existence as a result of the mutual agreements entered into by sovereign powers." Explain what this means.

APPLYING YOUR LEARNING

QUESTIONS AND PROBLEMS

1. What natural laws have you studied or read about?
2. Name some important moral laws that might not be enforceable at law.
3. What might have been some early man-made laws? Why do you think so?
4. What are some administrative agencies that have the responsibility of administering broad general laws in your state?
5. Why is international law more important today than ever before?
6. A state law provides that a person must have a license to drive a car. How would you classify this legislation?
7. A state has adopted the Uniform Commercial Code. If there is a conflict between a provision in the Code and one of the specific laws governing bank deposits and collections in the state, which will take precedence? Why?

WHAT IS YOUR OPINION?

In each of the following cases, give your decision and state a legal principle that applies to the case.

1. Carl McGraw observed a roller skate—not his own—on a public sidewalk. He could have put it in a safe place with very little effort on his part. He did not do so; and an elderly lady following him stepped on the skate, fell, and was seriously injured. Did Carl have a legal duty to remove the roller skate? Did Carl have a moral obligation to remove the skate?
2. Henry Cook failed to stop at a stop sign and, as a result, crashed into Dale Anderson's automobile. Did Henry violate any public law? Did he violate any private law? Could Dale collect a fine from Henry if Henry violated a public law? Could a police officer force Henry to pay for the damage?
3. When Hawaii and Alaska were admitted as states, each had to adopt some new laws. Were these statutory laws, common laws, or both?

4. Wilson Hull said the local tax collector assessed him for excessive taxes. Would the settlement of this dispute be a matter of private law or public law?

5. A state law in one state prohibited the sale or serving of alcoholic beverages to people under the age of twenty-one. One town in the state unanimously voted to lower the drinking age to eighteen. Which law would take precedence? Why?

THE LAW IN ACTION

1. The defendant in a certain action was charged with the crime of operating a motor vehicle on a public highway without being of proper age and without a license. Would this be a breach of common law or statutory law? Would it be private law or public law? (People v. Grogan, 260 N.Y. 138, 183 N.E. 273)

2. The plaintiff in this case was injured because of a defective wheel on an automobile he had purchased from a local dealer. Would an action brought for his injuries be a matter of public law or private law? If the dealer had failed to properly inspect the car before delivery as required by law in his state, would this be a violation of public law or private law? (MacPherson v. Buick Motor Co., 217 N.Y. 382, 111 N.E. 1050)

KEY TO "WHAT'S THE LAW?" Page 9

1. *Both. Michael would be involved with the natural laws that cause the airplane to fly and with man-made regulations.*

2. *No. Arrest is used by public officers to enforce public laws. Your rights against Nickler would be created by private law, and they would be enforced by private action on your part.*

WHAT'S THE LAW?

1. *Arthur Troy threatens to strike you with a baseball bat. Will the law protect you from such injury, or must you bargain with Arthur for protection?*

2. *Sam Miller steals your new car, sells it, spends the money, and is then caught by the police. Will the police pay you the value of the car?*

▲ UNIT 3: PROTECTING YOUR RIGHTS

One of the primary purposes of the law is to protect you from the wrongful acts of other persons. This protection is given, first, by preventing or discouraging other persons from doing wrongful acts that might injure you; and, secondly, if you are injured by a wrongful act of another person, by giving you a remedy for that injury. The remedy usually given is the right to recover what you have lost or payment for your loss.

FUNDAMENTAL RIGHTS

The right to be protected from the wrongful acts of other persons is a very fundamental one. It comes from two sources. First, we are born with certain *natural rights*. We have these rights by virtue of being citizens in our country. They include (1) the right to be free from bodily harm, (2) the right to enjoy a good reputation, (3) the right to have our property free from damage, and (4) other rights to be discussed later.

NATURAL RIGHT

What are some of our basic natural rights? How are they protected?

Secondly, we voluntarily acquire rights by agreements with other persons. It is this second class of rights that constitutes the law of contracts and related subjects. These subjects will occupy a large part of our time in this course. However, we first need an understanding of our basic natural rights and how the law protects them.

VIOLATION OF RIGHTS

This study of our basic natural rights and the laws that protect them is divided into two parts: first, the law of crimes; second, the law of torts. A *crime* can be briefly defined as the breach of a duty, imposed by law,

CRIME

If you accidentally violate a traffic ordinance, you are guilty of a misdemeanor and may be punished by fine or imprisonment.

owed to the public. *Tort* may be defined as the interference with one's rights by another person, either by an intentional act or through negligence. You will note that both of these definitions relate to a duty to respect a natural right, not rights voluntarily acquired by contract.

TORT

You will recall an illustration described in Example 3, Unit 2, in which Stephen Rogers, while driving his car at 70 miles an hour on a city street, ran into and seriously damaged a car belonging to Ronald Crossett. Clearly, the rights of Ronald Crossett were not respected. The law will give him the right to recover the monetary value of the damage done to his car. In addition, the law may punish Stephen Rogers so that he will not be inclined to drive in this reckless fashion again. This example demonstrates the difference between wrongdoings that we call torts and wrongdoings that we call crimes. A tort is a personal injury. The person injured by a tort has a right to bring an action in court for the damages caused by the wrongful act. The injured party himself brings the action for damages; thus, tort actions fall within the category of private law.

Distinguish between the law of crimes and the law of torts. How do they differ? Can a wrongful act be both a crime and a tort? Explain.

In our illustration Stephen Rogers was guilty of a tort because he caused individual harm to Crossett. Stephen was also guilty of a crime because he was driving his automobile at a speed far in excess of that allowed by law and thus breached a duty owed to the public. As punishment for his crime, the state will prosecute him; and the action will be brought, not by Ronald Crossett, the injured party, but by the *district attorney*, who looks after the legal affairs of a specific judicial district. The district attorney might be called by another name, such as prosecuting attorney, county attorney, city attorney, state's attorney, or some other title.

DISTRICT ATTORNEY

CLASSIFICATION OF TORTS

There are many varieties of wrongful acts that may be classified as torts. The more common ones are given here.

How does assault differ from battery? Why do we refer to the tort as assault and battery?

Assault and Battery   An *assault* is an unlawful threat or attempt to do bodily harm to another person. *Battery* is the actual unlawful touching of another person, usually violently done. Assault and battery usually occur together and form the common tort of assault and battery.

ASSAULT
BATTERY

EXAMPLE 1 **If John Brown swung at or even threatened Joe Smith with a stick but did not strike him, this would be an assault. If John actually hit Joe with a stick, this would be a battery. The two together would be assault and battery.**

When we say that a person is liable in damages for his negligence, what do we mean?

Negligence *Negligence* is the failure to exercise the degree of care required by law. The degree of care required varies with the circumstances of each case, and the law of negligence can be quite complicated. In everyday language the tort of negligence occurs when a person is injured because of the careless conduct of another.

NEGLIGENCE

EXAMPLE 2 **If Stephen Rogers drove his car on a city street in a careless manner, the tort he commits would be classed as negligence. He would have to pay for any injury he caused by his carelessness.**

Differentiate between libel and slander. How may a person be injured by these torts?

Defamation (Libel and Slander) *Libel* is an untruthful written or printed statement that injures another person's reputation or reflects upon his character. *Slander* is similar to libel except that the untrue statement is made orally to a third person.

LIBEL

SLANDER

EXAMPLE 3 **Carlton in anger told Stewart that Young was a liar and a cheat when Young refused to return a valuable picture that Carlton had sold to him for a nominal sum. Young would be permitted an action in tort against Carlton for damages to his reputation on the tort of slander. If Carlton had made these charges against Young in writing, he would be guilty of the tort of libel.**

What does the term trespass mean in a legal sense?

Trespass *Trespass* is a wrongful injury to or interference with the property of a third person. This includes wrongful entry onto another's land and its unpermitted use.

TRESPASS

EXAMPLE 4 **Fred Nichols and his friends went fishing in a private lake, owned and stocked by Englehardt, without the owner's permission. Entering on Englehardt's property and fishing in his lake without proper authority to do so is a trespass. Englehardt, therefore, may bring a suit for damages against Nichols and his fishermen friends.**

Explain what fraud means.

Fraud *Fraud* consists of some deceitful practice used with the intent to injure another party. This tort is often referred to as *deceit*.

FRAUD

DECEIT

Nuisance *Nuisance* is an unlawful act that causes an unreasonable or unwarranted injury to the property of another person.

NUISANCE

If you harm another individual or damage his property, even though you did not intend to do so, you have brought about a tort for which you may be held liable.

EXAMPLE 5 Richard Ward built a wooden board fence on his side of the property line, separating his property from that of his neighbor, Norbert Davis. The wooden board fence was 10 feet high and 10 feet long. It was set up for the sole purpose of eliminating Davis's view from his new picture window. This particular move by Ward could be classified as a nuisance. The local court would probably order its immediate removal.

What would be considered a nuisance from a legal viewpoint?

Conversion A *conversion* is an unauthorized appropriation of the personal property of someone else for the use of the person taking it. This would include such actions as stealing property or using borrowed property in an unauthorized way.

What is a conversion?

CONVERSION

False Arrest *False arrest* is an unlawful physical restraint by a person of another's liberty, whether in prison or otherwise.

How would you explain false arrest?

FALSE ARREST

EXAMPLE 6 A customer in a store was suspected of shoplifting. She was restrained from leaving the store by a clerk, taken to the manager's office, questioned, and searched. If she was found to be innocent of the charge, this would be false arrest.

REMEDIES FOR TORTS

If a wrongdoer has injured you by committing a tort, your injury usually can be measured in terms of money damages.

EXAMPLE 7 When Stephen Rogers damaged Ronald Crossett's car by his negligent driving, Ronald's injury would be the cost in money of repairing his damaged car. If his car is properly repaired and Stephen pays the bill for the repairs, then Ronald's financial loss has been restored.

In a limited number of cases, however, money will not compensate the injured party for his injury.

EXAMPLE 8 Joe Jones had a beautiful locust tree on his lawn. Al Chambers, who lived next door, did not like the tree because it shaded his house. Chambers threatened to come onto Jones' property and cut down the tree. If Chambers did this, money damages would not properly restore Jones to his original position because a similar locust tree cannot be grown in a normal lifetime.

If Chambers' threat seemed serious, Jones could go to court and ask the judge to order Chambers not to trespass on his property and not to remove the tree.

The law affects almost everything we do—even our recreation.

What remedies
are available for
torts?

What do you
understand by
the expression "a
person who
refuses to obey a
court injunction
can be held in
contempt of
court"?

A court order issued by a judge ordering a person not to do a certain act is called an *injunction.* The remedy of injunction, however, is available only in special circumstances where money damages will not adequately repay the injured party for the wrong done.

INJUNCTION

If Wilson violated the judge's order and did cut down the tree, he would be guilty of contempt of court. *Contempt of court* is a deliberate violation of the order of a judge or a refusal to perform as ordered by a judge. Contempt of court is a crime, and Wilson could be sent to jail for his wrongdoing.

CONTEMPT OF COURT

CLASSIFICATION OF CRIMES

Crimes, which were defined earlier as the breach of a duty owed to the public, may be classified as felonies and misdemeanors. The person guilty of a crime has violated a state or federal statute or a municipal ordinance and may be prosecuted for his wrongdoing by a public official called the district attorney.

Felony   A *felony* is a serious crime such as murder, burglary, armed robbery, or arson, which is punishable by imprisonment in a state or federal penitentiary. Prior to a 1972 Supreme Court decision which ruled capital punishment unconstitutional, felonies were also punishable by death.

FELONY

EXAMPLE 9   Hill, who was in financial difficulties, set fire to his own house, which was heavily insured. If his intentions were to obtain insurance money, he was guilty of the crime of arson.

Misdemeanor   A *misdemeanor* is a less serious crime, usually punishable by fine or imprisonment in a county or local jail. Some examples of misdemeanors are theft of small sums of money, driving an automobile without a license, and serious traffic violations. There are many others.

MISDEMEANOR

EXAMPLE 10   Aubry was stopped by a policeman for driving in the wrong direction on a one-way street and for going through a red light. These wrongful acts are misdemeanors. Aubry will be subject to a fine on both counts. If his record shows that he is a frequent violator of traffic rules, he may also be given a jail sentence.

 APPLYING YOUR LEARNING

QUESTIONS AND PROBLEMS

1. Name and define several types of common torts.
2. Give some illustrations of wrongs that might be both crimes and torts.
3. What is the difference between slander and libel? Are they both types of defamation?
4. Distinguish between a felony and a misdemeanor.

5. Name several examples of crimes that would be classed as felonies.
6. Name several examples of misdemeanors.
7. What division of law (if any) exists, applies, or is needed for each of the following situations?
   a. A father forbade his son to stay outdoors after 10 p.m.
   b. A person was attacked, severely injured, and robbed of his valuables by a thug.
   c. Students in a certain state are required to attend school until they reach the age of sixteen.
   d. You made an appointment to meet someone for the purpose of attending the theater. He failed to keep the appointment.
   e. A sailor, the sole survivor of a shipwreck, saved himself by swimming to an island that was apparently uninhabited.
   f. A wholesaler informed several other wholesalers that one of his customers did not pay his bills. His statement was false and damaged the customer's reputation and credit.
   g. The wholesaler in the preceding situation conveyed the false information in writing.
   h. A state legislature passed a law taxing all interstate shipments of goods.
   i. A party to a contract refused to comply with the terms of the agreement.
   j. Fishermen of one country fished in the waters controlled by another country without the consent of that country.
   k. Several persons of a certain race were denied the right to vote in their home state.

WHAT IS YOUR OPINION?

In each of the following cases, give your decision and state a legal principle that applies to the case.

1. Roger Reed forged John Kahler's name on a check. He gave the check to Richard Taylor in payment for his radio. Reed was arrested for passing a worthless check and spent three months in jail. Must he also make good to Taylor the amount of the check?
2. Tom Winslow agreed to sell his automobile to Paul Saylor for $900. Later, Tom refused to sell and deliver the car. Would this be a tort?
3. In a certain community an elderly woman was beaten and robbed by an unknown person. Burk Simpson told several people that Sam Olsen was guilty of the crime. This was a false statement, and Sam sued Burk for slander. Was this a tort? If this was a tort, could Sam collect damages for the injury to his reputation?
4. Frank Reed parked his car at a supermarket and went inside to make a purchase. When he returned, he observed that the keys were in the car; so he started the motor and drove home. When he got home, he discovered that he had taken someone else's car that was just like his. Was Frank guilty of a crime? If so, what was it? Was he guilty of a tort? If so, what was the tort?

A DIGEST OF LEGAL CONCEPTS

1. The law influences the life of each person from the day he is born to the time of his death.

2. Law helps establish "rules of the game" that make it possible for people to live in peace and harmony with others.

3. People have certain rights under the law, but they also have the duty to respect the rights of other persons.

4. To enforce legal rights, one must have available some legal remedies.

5. A knowledge of legal rights and a recognition of legal duties will help one to avoid legal difficulties.

6. One should see a lawyer before acting in important matters because he is an expert in determining one's legal rights and duties.

7. Broadly speaking, laws may be classified into natural laws, moral laws, and man-made laws.

8. Man-made laws function as municipal laws or international laws.

9. Municipal law may be classified into common law; Roman, or civil, law; and statute law.

10. Statute law may be classified into private, or civil, law and public law.

11. Statute law may also be classified into local, state, and federal law.

12. Public law may be classified into criminal law, administrative law, and constitutional law.

13. Constitutional law may be either federal or state.

14. International law is the law that regulates those nations that have entered into mutual agreements.

15. The common law is the law of precedent based on the decisions of the early English courts.

16. The civil law, when distinguished from the common law, is based on the Roman codified law and is the basis of the laws of most of the continent of Europe, the Latin American countries, and the state of Louisiana.

5. Dennis Casey began to plant a hedge on his property line. His neighbor, Jeff Cooper, claimed that Casey was trespassing and planting the hedge two feet over the line on Cooper's property. What remedy should Cooper choose? Should he physically keep Casey away? Should he ask the court for an injunction, or should he wait until the hedge is planted and sue for damages?

6. Rodriguez, whose wife was critically ill, drove her to the hospital in his car at an excessive rate of speed, ignoring traffic signals and one-way streets. When arrested, he pleaded that the trip was a matter of life and death because of the condition of his wife's health. Do these facts, if proved correct, excuse him from the charges made?

THE LAW IN ACTION

1. The plaintiff in this case became ill while at work and desired to go home. The foreman of the mill where the plaintiff worked locked the doors and refused to let the plaintiff leave. Would the foreman's action be a tort, a crime, or both? Would you call this assault, battery, or false arrest? Davis & Allcott Co. v. Boozer, 215 Ala. 116, 110 So. 28)

2. The plaintiff bought a car on credit, making only a down payment. Later, while the car was being serviced by the dealer, the plaintiff's father paid the dealer the balance of the purchase price, took the car home, and refused to let the plaintiff have it. Was the dealer guilty of conversion? Was the father guilty of theft? (Sullivan & O'Brien, Inc. v. Kennedy 107 Ind. App. 457, 25 N.E.2d 267)

3. Hoffman and Armstrong were neighbors, and their properties were separated by a fence. A cherry tree on Hoffman's land had branches overhanging Armstrong's property. Hoffman's sister was standing on the fence picking cherries from the overhanging limb. Armstrong ordered her to stop, claiming that she was trespassing. Miss Hoffman refused, and Armstrong pushed her off the fence, causing her to break a leg. Try to bring out as many legal problems as possible from these facts. Suppose that Armstrong had also called Miss Hoffman "a dirty thief." What other legal problems might this make? What other facts can you add that might raise still more legal problems? (Hoffman v. Armstrong, 48 N.Y. 201)

KEY TO "WHAT'S THE LAW?" Page 19

1. *The law will protect you. If Arthur did strike you, he could be arrested. If he continued to threaten you, you could ask the judge for an injunction ordering him to stop his illegal activity.*

2. *No. The duty of the police is to arrest Sam for his crime. You would have to bring a private lawsuit against Sam for the conversion of your car.*

A DIGEST OF LEGAL CONCEPTS

17. Civil law may also mean private law as contrasted with public law.

18. Private law regulates the rights and duties of individuals to each other.

19. Public law deals with the relationship between the state and individuals.

20. Constitutional law is the law that establishes broad principles of government.

21. The Uniform Commercial Code simplifies, clarifies, and modernizes the laws governing commercial transactions.

22. The law protects individuals from the wrongful acts of other persons.

23. All persons are born with certain natural rights, and the violation of any one of these natural rights constitutes a tort.

24. All rights other than natural rights are acquired by agreement.

25. A tort is the breach of a duty owed to an individual relating to a natural right.

26. A person injured by a tort must bring a personal action against the wrongdoer to recover damages for his injury.

27. The compensation to the individual injured by a tort is usually in the form of money damages.

28. While an assault is an unlawful threat to do bodily harm to another person and battery is the actual unlawful touching of another person, the two usually occur together to form the common tort of assault and battery.

29. Although the torts of libel and slander are similar in that both result from the making of untrue statements that injure another person's reputation or reflect upon his character, slander results when the statements are made orally to a third person, while libel is the result of published written or printed untrue statements.

30. A crime is a breach of a duty owed to the public.

31. A person guilty of a crime is prosecuted by the district attorney.

32. A single wrongful act may be both a tort and a crime.

33. Crimes are classified into felonies and misdemeanors.

WHAT'S THE LAW?

1. *Bob Witherow owed Gene Bianco money for blueprint services rendered. Gene contended that his blueprint services were worth $200. Bob claimed they were worth only $100, but he offered to settle for $150. Should Gene sue Bob or settle for the $150?*

2. *Suppose that Gene sues Bob and gets a judgment against him for $200, but Bob still refuses to pay. Can Gene get his money?*

▲ UNIT 4: ENFORCING YOUR RIGHTS

When we speak of an action at law, what do we mean?

If a conflict of rights cannot be settled by agreement, the parties involved must ask the courts to settle their differences for them. You will recall Example 3 in Unit 1. In that example Tom Smith had wrongfully sold Ray Greene's typewriter to Sam Archer. Ray had demanded its return and Sam had refused. Both Ray and Sam had certain rights. A request made by Ray and Sam asking the courts to determine and enforce their rights is what we ordinarily call an action at law or *lawsuit*. **LAWSUIT**

Distinguish between substantive law and procedural law.

The courts do two things: first, they determine the rights of the parties; and second, they provide a remedy for the enforcement of these rights. The law relating to the determination of rights is called *substantive law*. The law relating to the remedies provided for the enforcement of rights is called adjective, or *procedural, law*. **SUBSTANTIVE LAW** **PROCEDURAL LAW**

If Ray Greene found it necessary to bring an action in court to get back his typewriter, he would have to hire a lawyer. The lawyer would then take the various steps necessary to bring the case before the courts. It is the process of moving the case through the courts that we shall study in this unit.

You should always ask yourself, "Is a lawsuit really necessary?" before you start a court action. You must remember that litigation may be a costly and time-consuming process. If you can possibly settle a dispute out of court or by arbitration you should do so. If court action can be prevented by some sort of compromise agreement, much time and money may be saved. Such an out-of-court settlement is known as a *compromise of a disputed claim*. **COMPROMISE OF A DISPUTED CLAIM**

EXAMPLE 1 If Ray and Sam in our illustration about the typewriter could use pressure on Tom Smith and force him to make good the loss caused by his wrongful act, no lawsuit would be required. If no agreement is possible, then some action through the courts is necessary.

SETTING THE STAGE FOR A LAWSUIT

The trial of a lawsuit in court can be very dramatic. In a courtroom there is action. People are doing things. This makes an excellent setting for a drama. We also can use this dramatic setting as a device for studying how a lawsuit is conducted. The following material will be set in the form of a script for a play in order that you may more effectively find out "who does what" in the trial of a lawsuit.

THE CAST OF CHARACTERS: (In Order of Appearance)

Plaintiff: Injured party who brings the action.

Plaintiff's Attorney: Lawyer conducting the lawsuit for the plaintiff in court.

Clerk of the Court: The person who receives and files all papers relating to the trial, sets up the trial calendar, and handles all other clerical matters for the court.

Process Server: A sheriff, marshal, other court official, attorney—sometimes the plaintiff himself—who gives notice to the various parties in a lawsuit by handing them official documents.

Defendant: Party being sued in court.

Judge: Person who presides over all actions in open court.

Jury: Group of private citizens systematically selected from citizens of the immediate community to decide the facts of the case. The trial jury is often called the *petit jury*.

Witnesses: Individuals called into court to testify with regard to the facts of the case.

Sheriff: The officer ordered by the court to enforce its orders.

ACT I: STEPS TO BE TAKEN BEFORE TRIAL

The action before trial takes place as follows:

Plaintiff: Asks his attorney to commence a lawsuit.

Plaintiff's Attorney: Files a document called a petition, or *complaint*, with the clerk of the court stating the plaintiff's side of the argument and asking the court to decide in his favor.

Clerk of the Court: Issues a *summons*, which is a formal notice to the defendant that he is being sued, and gives the summons to a process server.

Process Server: Hands the summons to the defendant or touches him with it as notification that action has been commenced.

REMEMBER: If you are ever served with a summons, grab your hat and run for a lawyer. The summons notifies you that a lawsuit has been started against you and the time for self-help is now past.

Defendant: Goes to his attorney, requests him to defend the action, and usually provides an *answer*, or statement of his side of the story.

Defendant's Attorney: May file a *demurrer* instead of an answer, saying in effect, "Even if your facts are true, the law does not give you a remedy."

Margin notes (left):

What do we call the parties involved in a civil lawsuit?
What function does the clerk of the court serve?

Who is a process server? What does he do?

How does a petition differ from a summons?

Who may file a demurrer in a lawsuit? What is its purpose?

Margin notes (right):

PLAINTIFF

CLERK OF THE COURT

PROCESS SERVER

DEFENDANT

JURY

PETIT JURY

WITNESS

SHERIFF

COMPLAINT

SUMMONS

ANSWER

DEMURRER

A summons must be served on a defendant personally. No one else is permitted to accept a summons for him.

EXAMPLE 2 If, in our illustration, Ray Greene brought an action against Sam Archer for possession of the typewriter, Sam might properly file a demurrer. There is no argument in this case over the facts. Actually, the only question is one of law: To whom will the law give the typewriter?

Clerk of the Court: After a demurrer is filed, refers the matter to the judge.

Judge: Calls the parties together to hear arguments as to the question of law raised by the demurrer. If he believes that the law is in favor of the plaintiff if the facts are proved, he overrules the demurrer and the defendant must file an answer or appeal to a higher court. If he believes the law is favorable to the defendant, he sustains the demurrer and the case is dismissed. If the plaintiff thinks that the judge should not have dismissed the case, he may appeal to a higher court.

Plaintiff: If the defendant's answer has raised a new problem or issue that must be decided by the court, the plaintiff will file a reply, responding to the new material presented by the defendant's answer and telling his side of the story on the new issues raised.

EXAMPLE 3 John Bogart sold a tape recorder to William Britton. Bogart had promised, or guaranteed, that the recorder was in perfect condition and contained all new tubes. The purchase price was $50 and was to be paid on the first of the following month. The purchase price was not paid, and Bogart brought an action against Britton to collect. In his answer, Britton admitted the sale and admitted that the money was due, but he defended on the ground that the tape recorder was not in good condition and did not contain new tubes as warranted. If Bogart filed a reply denying Britton's claim, then an issue would be raised.

Why are pleadings necessary before a case can go to trial?

These various documents filed with the clerk of the court before the case comes to trial are called *pleadings*. If these pleadings have been properly drawn, they have raised issues or questions that must be decided by the court and the jury, and the case is now ready to go to trial.

PLEADINGS

ACT II: THE TRIAL OF THE ISSUES

What is a court docket?

Clerk of the Court: Places the case on his calendar, or *court docket*, for trial. This is simply a list of cases to be tried, in order.

COURT DOCKET

Judge: On the day set for trial, calls the court to order and causes a jury to be drawn from a list of citizens provided by the clerk of the court. Supervises questioning by the attorneys of each juryman selected. (Questioning is designed to obtain a completely impartial, unbiased jury.) After selection of the jury, requests plaintiff and defendant to present their arguments to the court and jury so that there may be a determination of the facts and the law that is related to them. In most cases the facts are decided by a jury. If both parties agree before trial, however, the jury may be dispensed with and the judge may decide both facts and the law.

REMEMBER: The law and its application to the facts are decided by the judge.

Plaintiff's Attorney: Presents to the court and jury all his evidence, which may consist of signed sworn statements (*affidavits*), and documents, testimony of witnesses, etc., to prove the plaintiff's story. (The plaintiff is given the first opportunity to express his side of the case.) AFFIDAVIT

How does the testimony of lay witnesses differ from that of expert witnesses?

Witnesses: Lay or direct *witnesses* testify to facts within their personal knowledge and to those opinions that are based on the facts they have perceived, such as the opinion that a person was drunk. Sometimes *expert witnesses,* who do not testify as to the facts but give expert opinion on scientific facts or principles that apply to the case, are called to testify. LAY WITNESS EXPERT WITNESS

When may a person be declared in contempt of court?

EXAMPLE 4   A witness requested by a court order (subpoena) to appear at a trial failed to do so. Another refused to answer questions asked him during the trial. It was held that the presiding judge had the right to declare both witnesses to be in contempt of court and that he had the power to impose a fine or a jail sentence. A person may be declared by a judge to be in contempt of court when he has shown open disrespect of the court. SUBPOENA

Defendant's Attorney: Has the opportunity to cross-examine the plaintiff's witnesses to test further the truth of their statements and to bring out any related evidence that was not developed on direct examination. Also presents evidence favorable to the defendant, using witnesses and any other evidence important to the defendant's case.

Plaintiff's Attorney: Has an opportunity to cross-examine defendant's witnesses.

Defendant's Attorney: Presents his summary of arguments for the benefit of the jury. (The defendant's attorney presents his summary first.)

Plaintiff's Attorney: Has an opportunity to sum up the plaintiff's case in a final argument to the jury.

What are trial briefs? How are they used in an action at law?

Judge: Instructs the jury as to the law to be applied. The jury cannot vary from the laws that are expressly stated by the judge in his instructions. Arguments as to the law in question are seldom made in court but are, instead, presented to the judge as *trial briefs,* prepared by the attorneys prior to trial. In his brief the attorney presents his arguments as to the law involved and asks the judge to instruct the jury in a manner favorable to his client. After studying the requested instructions of both parties, the judge makes his decision as to what the law is and instructs the jury accordingly. TRIAL BRIEFS

Jury: Retires to a room especially provided to discuss facts secretly and

Never take the law into your own hands. For every wrongful act, punishment is prescribed by the law.

How does a jury arrive at a verdict in a lawsuit?

consider the evidence presented in court. The jurors determine the true facts of the case and render a verdict in accordance with these facts and the instructions as to the law given them by the judge. After reaching a verdict, the jurors return to the courtroom, and their *foreman*, or spokesman, makes their statement at the request of the judge.

FOREMAN

Judge: Pronounces *judgment*, which is the official decision of the court, in accordance with the verdict. If the jury has violated his instructions and returned a verdict contrary to the law, he may overrule the jury and give a judgment notwithstanding the verdict.

JUDGMENT

Who pronounces judgment in accordance with the verdict?

Clerk of the Court: Records the judgment. This is the final determination of the issues unless an appeal is taken to a higher court by the party losing the case in the trial court.

ACT III: SATISFYING THE JUDGMENT

Act III is concerned with the enforcement of the rights which have been determined in the two previous acts.

EXAMPLE 5 Suppose that Ray has sued Sam and that the judge has rendered judgment in favor of Ray, stating that the typewriter belongs to him and that Ray has a right to its return. Sam still has the typewriter, however. If he voluntarily returns it to Ray, the case is finished. But suppose that he doesn't; then what happens?

If the judgment is not honored by the judgment debtor, what individual remedies are available to the judgment creditor?

If the judgment debtor does not pay, then the judgment creditor (usually the plaintiff) must proceed further with (1) individual remedies or (2) collective remedies with other creditors.

Individual Remedies The more common individual remedies are (1) a writ of execution, (2) a writ of replevin, and (3) a writ of garnishment.

EXECUTION

Plaintiff's Attorney: Returns to the court and asks the judge for a *writ of execution,* or an order by the judge to the sheriff, ordering him to seize goods or property belonging to the judgment debtor, sell them, and use the money to pay the judgment debt to the plaintiff.

WRIT OF EXECUTION

Judge: Issues a writ of execution to the sheriff.

Sheriff: Seizes property belonging to judgment debtor, sells it at auction, and uses the proceeds to pay the judgment debt to the plaintiff. If the defendant's property is not sufficient to pay the judgment or if no property is available for seizure by the sheriff, the judgment usually remains enforceable for twenty years.

REPLEVIN

Plaintiff's Attorney: Returns to the court and asks for a *writ of replevin* if the plaintiff desires the return of a specific article. This is the judge's order to the sheriff to seize an item and return it to the true owner.

Judge: Issues a writ of replevin to the sheriff.

Sheriff: Seizes the item specified and returns it to the true owner.

WRIT OF REPLEVIN

GARNISHMENT

Plaintiff's Attorney. May ask the judge to issue a *writ of garnishment* if the judgment debtor has money in the bank or is owed money by some third party. This is an order to a third party who owes money to the judgment debtor, ordering him to pay the money to the judgment creditor and not to pay it to the judgment debtor.

WRIT OF GARNISHMENT

Judge: Issues the writ as requested. If the money owed or to be owed is for wages, most states limit the amount that can be seized or withheld.

If the judgment debtor is insolvent, what collective remedies are available to his creditors?

Collective Remedies The above remedies are successful where the judgment debtor has money or property. Where he is *insolvent*—that is, has more debts than he can pay—it is much better to have a cooperative action brought by all his creditors. The three most common of these are voluntary composition of creditors, state receivership actions, and bankruptcy proceedings. The aims of these actions are to try to retrieve the greatest possible amount of money from the debtor's assets, to distribute the money received from the sale of these assets evenly among all his creditors, and to give a release or discharge to the debtor as to any unpaid balances owed.

INSOLVENT

 ## APPLYING YOUR LEARNING

QUESTIONS AND PROBLEMS

1. Is it better to sue or to make a reasonably good settlement out of court?
2. Is it advisable to sue a person for a small amount? Why?
3. How would you determine whether or not to bring suit on a claim?
4. If your attorney advises you that you have a good chance of winning in a court action, what steps may he take before bringing suit?
5. Name and explain briefly the general steps in an ordinary lawsuit.

WHAT IS YOUR OPINION?

In each of the following cases, give your decision and state a legal principle that applies to the case.

1. Fred Beckwith fell on the sidewalk in front of Jordan Sampson's House. All agreed that the sidewalk was in good condition and that Jordan

had breached no duty. If Beckwith filed a petition and brought action against Jordan, should Jordan file an answer or a demurrer or take other action?

2. Ed Munson owed $100 to Joe Stone. He refused to pay the debt because he believed that Stone had cheated him. Stone waited until Munson left for a trip to Europe, then filed a petition to start a court action. He told the process server to leave the summons at Munson's house. Would a court render a judgment against Munson while he is away? Would this be fair?

3. Charles Baker owed ten creditors $20,000. He had no money; his only asset was a $10,000 building. Should each creditor ask for a writ of execution to be levied against the building?

4. Bill Kelly had wrongfully obtained possession of John Swan's automobile. Swan brought a court action for its return and was awarded judgment in his favor. If Kelly still refused to deliver the car, what should Swan do? Would a writ of execution, a writ of replevin, or neither be appropriate?

5. A witness requested by court order (subpoenaed) to appear at a trial failed to do so. Another witness refused to answer proper questions asked of him during the trial. Can either witness be held in contempt of court? What punishment, if any, can be given them?

THE LAW IN ACTION

1. A defendant was being prosecuted for burglary. In your opinion would it be proper for a person who had been robbed by burglars four different times to serve on the jury? (State v. Martinez, 220 La. 899, 57 So. 2d 888)

2. The only evidence in an action for damages resulting from a collision of two automobiles was the tire marks, the position of the cars when found, and measurements made by the state police. Both drivers were killed. Could this evidence be presented to the jury by the statement of lay witnesses? If inferences were to be drawn from this evidence, could they be drawn by lay witnesses? (Phoenix Refining Co. v. Powell, 251 S.W. 2d 892, Tex. Ct. of Civ. App.)

KEY TO "WHAT'S THE LAW?" Page 29

1. *Unless there were some very unusual circumstances, Gene should not sue. Gene could be wrong about how much his services are worth, and there is not enough money involved to make a lawsuit worthwhile.*

2. *Yes. Gene should return to the court and ask the judge to issue a writ of execution to the sheriff, ordering him to seize property belonging to Bob, sell it, and use the money to pay Gene's judgment.*

WHAT'S THE LAW?

1. *Pat Corrigan, who lives in Nebraska, has a claim for $150 against Alonzo Hickson, who lives in Iowa. Alonzo refuses to pay, and Pat wishes to bring an action against him in a federal court, maintaining that he would not get justice if he sued in Alonzo's state court. Can Pat bring his action in a federal court?*

---

2. *Bart Harris was indicted by a county grand jury. Joe Burroughs contends that Bart has been found guilty of a crime. Is this contention correct?*

⬩ UNIT 5: FUNCTIONS OF LAW COURTS

Primitive man had little use for law or for courts. In his role as family or tribal head, he decided all disputes in accordance with the customs of the times. Imagine, if you can, any attempt to dispense justice today in our highly developed civilization under such conditions. You will agree that it just cannot be done. With the development of civilized society, rules of action or conduct governing men in their relations with one another—prescribing what is right and prohibiting what is wrong—had to be formulated. These rules are called *codes of law*. The demand for places where impartial justice could be obtained on the basis of these codes led to the creation of courts.

CODE OF LAW

The establishment of courts and court procedures represents one of the great achievements of the human race. By providing peaceful means for the settlement of disputes between parties, courts make an important contribution to the preservation of law and order.

You learned in Unit 4 that, if you cannot get a satisfactory settlement of your claim by a voluntary agreement, you must bring an action and ask the court to enforce your rights. You may well ask, "In what court would I bring my action? There seem to be so many of them."

FEDERAL AND STATE COURTS

First of all, you have two court systems to consider: those of your own state and those of the federal government. Each has exclusive jurisdiction over certain specified types of controversies. *Jurisdiction* is the power and authority conferred on a court or a judge to try an individual or a disagreement and render a judgment. With exclusive jurisdiction, each court system has the sole right to try these specified cases. In other types of

What is meant by the term exclusive jurisdiction?

JURISDICTION

What are the
functions of the
state and federal
government
courts?

cases, however, you may have the choice of bringing your action in one
or the other of these two court systems.

REMEMBER: In either case, the functions of the court are the same. These
functions are (1) to find the facts of the case and (2) to apply the proper
law to the facts.

STATE COURTS

Each state has its own court system. Therefore, in order to learn about
the exact organization of all the courts in your own state, you must usually
consult a local attorney or judge. The general pattern, however, is the
same in all states. You might look at your state court system as a pyramid.
Many small local courts form the base of the pyramid. These local courts
support and feed into area, or county, courts, usually called courts of
general jurisdiction. Courts of general jurisdiction, in turn, support and
feed into appellate, or appeal, courts. At the top of the pyramid is always
one court of highest appeal, which makes final decisions on state cases.

Local Courts *Local courts* are called courts of limited jurisdiction. This
means that they have jurisdiction only in minor matters, petty crimes,
and civil actions involving small amounts of money.

LOCAL
COURTS

In order that the law may
be administered fairly and
equitably in justice of the
peace courts, able and
conscientious men must
be chosen as judges.

JUSTICE OF THE PEACE COURTS *Justice of the peace courts,* or magistrate's
courts, as they are sometimes called, were the only local courts in the
early days of our country. They were established to furnish a means of
trying small claims cases and punishing petty crimes in each local community. They continue to serve that function today in many communities.
The justice of the peace, or magistrate, hears both criminal and civil cases
without a jury, both to determine the facts and to apply the law. In most
states the defendant may appeal the justice's decision to the county court.

JUSTICE OF THE
PEACE COURT

MUNICIPAL COURTS In larger communities, justice of the peace courts
have been replaced by *municipal courts*. These courts serve the same function as justice of the peace courts, but in the larger cities these functions
may be divided among several specialized courts. These specialized courts

MUNICIPAL
COURT

Name several
specialized
municipal courts.

may be, for example, traffic courts, police courts, juvenile offenses courts, family courts, and courts of small claims.

SMALL CLAIMS COURTS   Many cities have courts for special cases, such as *small claims courts*. In most cases where these courts exist, actions for $500 or less can be filed. Small claims courts have their value in the fact that the parties (the plaintiff and the defendant) may act as their own attorneys. The trial proceedings in this court are conducted very informally. It is a relatively inexpensive means of obtaining justice in minor civil cases.

SMALL CLAIMS COURT

Why are courts of
small claims of
special
importance to
many people?

Courts of General Jurisdiction   In most states each county has at least one *court of general jurisdiction*. These courts are called by various names, such as county court, superior court, court of common pleas, circuit court, and, in a few states, supreme court.

COURT OF GENERAL JURISDICTION

What are some of
the special names
given to courts of
general
jurisdiction?

Usually, any case may be commenced in the court of general jurisdiction; but minor cases are commonly commenced in the more informal local courts. An appeal to the court of general jurisdiction is made if one of the parties feels that he has not obtained justice in the local court. All cases involving major crimes and large amounts of money must be commenced in the court of general jurisdiction.

It is in these courts of general jurisdiction that most important matters are tried. It is the duty of these courts both to determine the facts, usually with the aid of a jury, and to apply the appropriate law to these facts when they are determined.

Intermediate Court   The function of *intermediate courts* is to hear appeals from the courts of general jurisdiction. An appeal may be taken to an intermediate court by one of the parties if he believes that he did not have a fair trial in the lower court or that the judge in the court of original jurisdiction did not properly interpret the law. Intermediate courts hear appeals only on matters of law. The facts are finally, or conclusively, determined in the trial court; that is, the court of general jurisdiction. It is only when there is evidence that the jury had been prejudiced and had decided contrary to the evidence presented in the trial that the intermediate court will review the facts.

INTERMEDIATE COURT

Will intermediate
courts ordinarily
review the facts
or the law in an
appealed case?

EXAMPLE 1   **Slocum sued Archbold for injuries suffered in a two-car crash. The case was tried in a local county court, and the court supported the defendant. If Slocum's lawyer finds grounds for an appeal founded upon errors in the county court's interpretation of the law, he would then appeal to a higher court and ask for another trial.**

Intermediate courts are usually called *appellate courts*, district courts of appeal, or some similar term. Many states do not have intermediate courts. Instead, appeals are taken directly from the trial court to the highest court of the state.

APPELLATE COURT

What special
names are given
to intermediate
courts?

Highest Courts of Appeal   In forty states the highest court is called the *state supreme court*. In the others it is called court of appeals, court of errors, or some similar name.

It is the function of these high courts to make a final determination on matters of law that cannot be decided in the lower courts. Here, again,

STATE SUPREME COURT

they do not retry a case and redetermine the facts; they only decide whether an error was made in the lower courts in the determination of the law involved.

FEDERAL COURTS

Over what types of actions and cases do federal courts have exclusive jurisdiction?

The federal courts have exclusive jurisdiction over (1) all actions in which the United States or a state is a party, except those actions between a state and its own citizens; (2) all cases involving a violation of a federal law; (3) all admiralty, maritime, patent-right, copyright, and bankruptcy cases; and (4) cases involving citizens of different states where the amount of money in question is large. The federal courts also form a pyramid, but it is not so complicated as that of the state courts. .

What name is given to the courts of original jurisdiction in the federal system?

Federal District Courts At the bottom of the pyramid in the federal system are the *federal district courts*. The United States and its territories are divided into judicial districts. Many of the districts are subdivided into divisions. District courts are the courts of original jurisdiction in the federal system. Most federal cases are first tried in district courts.

FEDERAL DISTRICT COURT

EXAMPLE 2 **A local FBI office was broken into and robbed of a large sum of money. The thief was apprehended by the state police and turned over to the federal district court for trial. This was proper since the offense was committed against a federal agency.**

What is the function of the United States Circuit Court of Appeals?

Courts of Appeals The entire United States is divided into judicial circuits. In each circuit there is a *United States Court of Appeals*. It is the function of these courts to hear appeals from the federal district courts. A person convicted in the federal district court may, if he has grounds for appeal, have his plea heard in the proper court of appeals. If the appeals court reverses the conviction, the district court is required to give the accused a new trial before a new jury. Most appeals are given final determination in the United States Courts of Appeals because the Supreme Court of the United States hears only a selected number of appeal cases.

UNITED STATES COURT OF APPEALS

The United States Supreme Court has both original and appellate jurisdiction. What does this mean?

The Supreme Court The *United States Supreme Court* is the highest court in the land. It has both original and appellate jurisdiction. Its original jurisdiction is over important matters in which the federal government, states, or foreign governments may be a party. The cases selected by the Supreme Court for review on appeal from the courts of appeals are those provided for in the Federal Judicial Code and those involving very important public questions, such as the constitutionality of important legislation.

UNITED STATES SUPREME COURT

EXAMPLE 3 **On a busy street corner, Ray Swartz was delivering a political speech criticizing the current mayor and police force of the city. Several policemen arrested Swartz for blocking the pedestrian traffic flow on the sidewalks—a violation of a city ordinance. A city judge fined Swartz $10 for the violation. He then appealed his case to a higher court, claiming that the city ordinance interfered with his right of free speech.**

This case, even though the fine imposed was small, raises a question of a constitutional right and might possibly be appealed through all the courts, even up to the United States Supreme Court.

SPECIAL COURTS

There are often courts established by both the state and federal governments to handle very specialized cases. Among the more common of these are courts of claims by both state and federal governments and surrogate, or probate, courts by the states.

Courts of Claims Neither the federal government nor a state government may be sued by individuals, except by permission of the government. However, the federal government and most state governments have set up special courts, called *courts of claims*, in which cases may be brought by individuals who have claims against these governments.

COURTS OF CLAIMS

Probate courts, or surrogate courts In each county of most states will be found a special court known as a *probate*, or surrogate, *court*, to supervise the administration of the estates of deceased persons. The work of these courts will be discussed in Unit 45, where the distribution of property by wills and inheritance will be explained.

PROBATE COURT

CRIMINAL COURTS

Most of our courts in both the federal and state systems try both civil and criminal cases.

In the trial of criminal cases, the courts do the same two things that they do in civil actions; that is, they (1) determine the true facts and (2) apply the law to the facts. In criminal cases, however, the law is usually relatively certain. The big problem is to determine the facts. For this reason the honesty and judgment of the trial jury is exceptionally important.

Serving on a jury is a very responsible duty. Every citizen has a duty to serve when called. The jury is often the very heart of justice. If you shirk your duty and allow unqualified, dishonest, or prejudiced persons to sit on juries, considerable financial loss and irreparable personal harm may fall on innocent persons and a miscarriage of justice may then take place.

EXAMPLE 4 **Jenson, the defendant in a case, attempted to bribe a juror to insist on a verdict in Jenson's favor, or to "hang"* the jury. The juror reported Jenson's offer to the court. Jenson could be charged with contempt of court and could be tried by jury separately for this offense.**

What is the major difference between a criminal action and a civil action?

The major difference between a criminal action and a civil action is the way in which it is commenced. You will recall that the injured party begins a civil action by filing a petition. In a criminal case the action is usually originated by the district attorney.

It is the duty of the district attorney to make investigations to determine whether crimes have been committed and whether certain wrongdoers should be prosecuted. In doing this the district attorney often has the aid of a grand jury.

---

*A juror "hangs" the jury when he refuses to agree with the decision of the others, thus preventing the jury from rendering a verdict (unanimous decision).

Jury service is a most responsible citizenship duty. The honesty and judgment of the trial jury are extremely important.

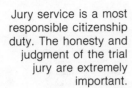

GRAND JURY

A *grand jury* is a jury of inquiry. It is a group of citizens called together by a proper court official to determine whether there is sufficient evidence to justify the accusing of certain persons of certain crimes. You should distinguish clearly in your mind the difference between a grand jury and a trial, or petit, jury. The trial jury is called a *petit jury* because it usually has a smaller number of jury members than a grand jury. The grand jury conducts a preliminary hearing only. Its hearings are held in secret, and it does not convict persons of crimes.

PETIT JURY

Distinguish between a grand jury and a petit jury.

Unlike a trial jury, the grand jury carries on its own investigations, usually under the leadership of the district attorney. The jury calls witnesses, makes investigations, and considers all other kinds of evidence. The members of a grand jury do not make final determinations of fact, however; they only indicate their suspicions. If the members of a grand jury believe, after hearing the evidence and listening to the testimony of witnesses, that a crime has been committed by the named individual or individuals, they issue what is known as an *indictment*, which is a written accusation issued by a grand jury, charging the individual or individuals named therein with a certain crime.

INDICTMENT

What is the legal significance of an indictment issued by a grand jury?

You should note carefully that an indictment does not mean that the named person is guilty of the crime. It only indicates the belief of the grand jury that a crime has been committed and that there is a possibility that the party named in the indictment is guilty of the crime.

The next step in the process is for the district attorney to bring an action in court, charging the indicted party with the commission of the crime. His guilt or innocence is then established by a trial in court. This trial of a criminal action in court is similar to that of a civil action. A jury is called; the attorneys present evidence, question witnesses, and sum up their arguments for the jury. Then the jury determines the facts indicating guilt or innocence, and the judge pronounces sentence.

REMEMBER: In the trial of a criminal case, the determination of the fact of the guilt or innocence of the accused is the most important matter to be determined. Criminal law is well defined in modern statutes, and there are usually few problems of law to be decided in the trial of a criminal case.

THE UNITED STATES COURT SYSTEM

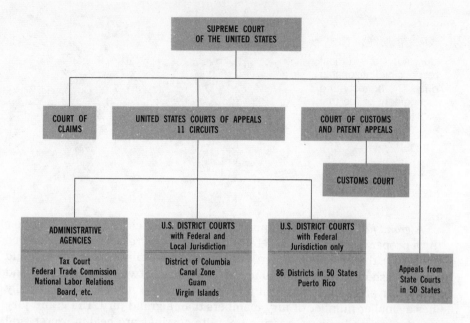

Source: Business Law Syllabus, University of the State of New York, State Education Department, Bureau of Secondary Curriculum Development.

 APPLYING YOUR LEARNING

QUESTIONS AND PROBLEMS

1. What two separate systems of courts do we have in this country?
2. What are the two principal functions of these two separate systems of courts?
3. It has been stated that, ordinarily, the intermediate courts hear appeals only on matters of law. What is meant by this statement?
4. Under what conditions might an intermediate court be willing to review the facts of a case?
5. What names are usually given to the highest court of appeals in the various states? What name is most commonly used?
6. What is the principal function of these highest courts of the states?
7. The United States Supreme Court has original jurisdiction over what types of cases? It has appellate jurisdiction over what types?
8. Why are special courts necessary? Name some special courts.
9. What is the principal function of the grand jury? the petit jury?

WHAT IS YOUR OPINION?

In each of the following cases, give your decision and state a legal principle that applies to the case.

1. James Parker was seriously injured on a state highway and threatened to sue the state for $50,000 damages. May Parker bring a suit against the state? If so, in which court must his claim be tried?

2. Bill Adams alleges that he suffered injuries as a result of an assault on his person by Harry Jackson. He seeks to recover the sum of $5,000 as damages. To save time and money, he desires to have the case tried before the court of appeals in his state. May he do so? Why?

3. Fred Wilson was arrested for a traffic violation. He was fined $100 by the local justice of the peace. Wilson maintained that this was excessive and unfair and stated that he would appeal the case to the federal courts where he could get a fair trial. May he do so? Why?

4. Joe Barnes, who lives in Pennsylvania, owes $15,000 to Thomas Carson, who lives in Ohio. Is Carson entitled to bring an action against Barnes for this amount in Pennsylvania? Would this case be tried in a federal court? Why?

5. The Missouri River, forming a boundary line between Missouri and Kansas, suddenly changed its course and cut a new channel several miles east of its old bed. Kansas claims all the land between the old and the new river beds. Will this controversy be tried in the first instance by the United States Supreme Court? Why or why not?

THE LAW IN ACTION

1. In a lawsuit brought in the federal district court, it was admitted by everyone that the parties were residents of different states. Would it be absolutely necessary to bring this action in a federal court? Would this be a factor used in deciding which court had jurisdiction? (Mitchell v. Nixon, 200 F. 2d 50, 5th Cir.)

2. The defendant in a certain action was convicted on a robbery charge in a state court. Part of the evidence used against him was obtained from a tapped telephone conversation. The defendant appealed to the United States Supreme Court, claiming that the Federal Communications Act forbids the use of evidence obtained by wire tapping. Ordinarily, would you expect federal laws to be interpreted in state courts? If the defendant's constitutional rights had been violated, would an appeal to federal courts be proper? (Schwartz v. Texas, 344 U.S. 199)

KEY TO "WHAT'S THE LAW?" Page 36

1. *No. The amount of money involved is small. His claim would have to be for several thousand dollars before a federal court would have jurisdiction. The exact amount is changed from time to time by federal laws.*

2. *No. The indictment by the grand jury means only that there are sound reasons to suspect that Bart might be guilty as charged.*

WHAT'S THE LAW?

1. *Richard Harvey is employed to teach auto mechanics for one year at the local high school. Does this involve business law? In what way?*

2. *Mr. Harvey and two students, Tom Adams and Bill Jasper, agree to repair the high school principal's car on a Saturday afternoon. Does this agreement involve business law?*

△ UNIT 6: BUSINESS LAW PAST AND PRESENT

Business law applies to all of us—you, your parents, your friends, your school, your community. Business law is not confined entirely to what we ordinarily think of as relationships between businessmen and among business firms. We come in contact with business law in many ways.

EXAMPLE 1 Mr. White owns a factory. As a manufacturer, he must know about patents, trade regulations, transportation of goods, and many other principles that involve business law. Mr. Brodie is a banker. He will be concerned with laws regulating money and finance—an important part of business law. Mr. Kent is a real estate broker. His problems may be different from those of Mr. White and Mr. Brodie; but business law is important to him in the handling of contracts, deeds, mortgages, and so on. Mr. Quigley is an accountant. Can you think of several ways in which business law is important to him? In almost every business transaction, some law is involved, and it may properly be called business law.

HISTORICAL DEVELOPMENT OF BUSINESS LAW

Actually, what we call business law has developed over a long, long time. In fact, it began to develop very early in history. You remember that in our discussion of the law merchant (Unit 2), we mentioned that merchants, out of necessity, set up their own rules for settling their problems and their differences of opinion. These traders started the practice of holding their own informal courts to settle their arguments. It was in these early English informal courts that some basic principles that are foundations of our modern business law were developed. Much of the law of contracts, sales, commercial paper, and other legal subjects had their beginnings in the law merchant. The common-law courts began to follow the rules of

Trace the development of business law from the law merchant to the Uniform Commercial Code.

the law merchant in settling differences between merchants and traders. These decisions of the common-law courts were recorded and became the precedents that form the common law relating to business transactions.

Business law has had the careful attention of our state and federal legislatures since the founding of our country. There are many important statute laws that deal with business matters. The Uniform Commercial Code, laws dealing with partnerships and corporations, and bankruptcy law are examples. It was not only important to have laws that were designed for business transactions; it was also important that these laws be uniform. You see, we really have fifty different sets of state laws in this country. Each state has the right to make its own laws, subject to the restrictions of the Constitution of the United States. All the states except Louisiana base their laws on the English common law, so the laws in most states are essentially the same. Through the years, however, slight differences have developed. This did not matter too much when there was little trade between states; but as trade between the states, or *interstate commerce*, began to develop, it became important that the laws of each state be alike.

Why is it desirable that laws governing business transactions be uniform among all the states?

What is meant by interstate commerce?

INTERSTATE COMMERCE

Can you imagine the confusion of the shipping clerk if he had to check transportation laws in each state to which he shipped a package?

DEVELOPMENT OF UNIFORM LAWS

About seventy years ago, the governors of the various states, recognizing the need for uniformity, met together and appointed commissioners on uniform laws. These commissioners, in turn, obtained the services of the best legal scholars and gave them the job of drafting model laws on various phases of business law. Within recent years a comprehensive Uniform Commercial Code has been drawn. This new Uniform Commercial Code is now the law in every state except Louisiana. Louisiana, a former French possession, has developed its legal system after the pattern set by the Roman Code. Its legislature is now considering adoption of the Uniform Commercial Code.

QUALITIES THAT MAKE FOR BUSINESS SUCCESS

Why is a good reputation essential for success in business?

Anyone working in the field of business will find that his reputation is one of his most valued assets. One cannot maintain a good reputation without following accepted ethical principles.

EXAMPLE 2   Tom Apple copied from his college classmate's examination paper. Other students were aware of Tom's copying procedures, but his instructors never noticed anything wrong. Tom Apple's name came up for discussion at a college class reunion thirty years later. It was discovered that none of Tom's former classmates did any business with him. They felt that if a man could not be trusted to be honest at examination time, the same would hold true in a business transaction. Tom's fellow students had remembered his dishonest examination procedures for thirty years.

Good conduct often requires more than sticking to the letter of the law. There are some businesses that, by their very nature, depend on the mutual trust of the parties engaged in them. The grain traders on the Chicago Board of Trade buy and sell millions of dollars' worth of grain each year. They make contracts by a nod of the head, a wave of the hand, or by other signals that make up their own signs of communication. Most of these contracts are so informal that they could not be enforced in court. The business of grain trading, however, requires such informality if the traders are to handle the large volume of transactions that flows through the exchange every day. These traders must trust one another if they are going to stay in business.

The same honesty and ethical conduct is required in all business. If it should become necessary for a businessman to sue in order to enforce his contracts or to collect his bills, he would be forced out of business.

You make your own business reputation. If you are consistently honest and completely dependable, if you are prompt in paying your bills, if you keep your word, you will soon win the respect of those with whom you must live and work. You will eventually establish a sound financial credit rating and a reputation for being ethical.

 ## APPLYING YOUR LEARNING

QUESTIONS AND PROBLEMS

1. How does business law touch on many areas of everyday life?
2. Why is it desirable to have uniform laws in the United States?
3. How might morality and legality differ in some common business situations?
4. What unethical business practices have you heard or read about?
5. What qualities of character and conduct would you look for in a person if you were planning on entering into a business partnership with him?

WHAT IS YOUR OPINION?

In each of the following cases, give your decision and state a legal principle that applies to the case.

1. The Bestever Supermarket operated within the limits of Cleveland, Ohio. What areas of law might affect the operation of this business?

2. Henry Barstow broke his leg in a school football game. He was rushed to the city hospital. Doctor Wilson was called by Henry's parents, and he went to the hospital and set Henry's leg. How many business transactions can you identify that might have legal consequences?

3. The First Methodist Church of Boville wished to sell their old church building and build a new one. In the accomplishment of these objectives, would they be more concerned with ecclesiastical law or business law?

4. The Super Cut-Rate Department Store consistently advertised brand-name goods at a very low cost, even though it had none of these items in stock. Its purpose was to get customers to come to the store. Once the customers were in the store the sales clerks would use high-pressure methods to try to sell the customers inferior goods. Would this be the morally right thing to do? Would it be good business practice? Do you think this is legal?

5. Bill Quigley, who is very wealthy, refused to contribute to the support of his poverty-stricken parents. Can he be required to do so?

THE LAW IN ACTION

1. The plaintiff purchased a box-seat ticket to the defendant's theater. While occupying the box and watching the performance, he hung his coat on a hook at the back of the box and it was stolen. The plaintiff sued for the value of the lost coat. Would this raise a problem of business law or some other kind of law? Can you see more than one business law problem in this case? Remember, in this case you are only looking for problems. The answers will come later in your study. (Kumsky v. Loeser, 37 Misc. 504, 75 N.Y. Sup. Ct. 1012)

2. The plaintiff purchased a coat from the defendant. The coat had a fur collar and the plaintiff had been assured by the defendant that it was not dyed fur. This was not true, and the plaintiff suffered injury from poisonous and irritating materials in the dye. Would this be a business law case? Do you see elements of moral obligation in this case? (Flynn v. Bedell Co., 242 Mass. 450, 136 N.E. 252)

3. "When the defendant, Clifford Witter, a dance instructor, waltzed out of the employment of the plaintiff, the Arthur Murray Dance Studios of Cleveland, Inc., into the employment of the Astaire Dancing Studios, the plaintiff waltzed Witter into court." Witter's contract of employment had specifically provided that he would not work for another dance studio if he quit working for the plaintiff. What points of business law can you find here? What were Witter's rights and duties? the studio's? (Arthur Murray Dance Studios, Inc. v. Witter, 105 N.E. 2d, 682, Ohio Ct. of Common Pleas)

KEY TO "WHAT'S THE LAW?" Page 44

1. *Yes. Richard Harvey would have a contract of employment with the school. Employment contracts are a very important part of business law.*

2. *Yes. This would be a contract for service. It might also involve the purchase and sale of some new parts. All of these would involve business law.*

A DIGEST OF LEGAL CONCEPTS

1. Courts determine the rights of parties when there is a conflict of interests.

2. Courts provide remedies for the enforcement of rights after the rights of the parties have been determined.

3. Civil actions are commenced through a court action by the injured party who is called the plaintiff.

4. The purpose of a lawsuit is to determine the true facts, to determine accurately the law that applies, and to give judgment in accordance with the law and the facts.

5. Each party to a lawsuit has the opportunity to tell his side of the story by filing written statements before trial. These statements are called pleadings.

6. The real points of disagreement between the parties are determined by the pleadings.

7. Each party who is being sued is entitled to notice of this fact. He is given this notice by being served with a document called a summons.

8. A demurrer is used to determine whether the law will provide a remedy if the facts stated prove to be true.

9. It is the responsibility of the jury to determine the true facts of the case.

10. It is the judge's responsibility to determine the law that applies to the case.

11. The judge may overrule the jury's verdict if the jury does not follow his instructions on matters of law.

12. The judgment given by the judge determines the rights of the winning party.

13. The winning party may have to return to the court and ask the judge to issue additional orders if the losing party does not voluntarily pay the judgment.

14. There are two systems of courts—the federal courts and the state courts.

15. The state courts are the local courts (courts of limited jurisdiction), courts of general jurisdiction, appellate courts, and the court of highest appeal, usually called the supreme court.

16. In the federal system, the courts are the federal district courts, the United States Court of Appeals for the circuit, and the Supreme Court of the United States.

17. The authority of a court to decide an action or suit is called its jurisdiction.

18. A court must have jurisdiction over either the subject matter or the persons involved before it can legally proceed to try a case.

19. A particular court may have exclusive, original, or appellate jurisdiction, depending on the nature of the case and the function of the court.

20. The basic responsibilities of the courts of original jurisdiction are to find the facts of the case and to apply the proper law to the facts.

21. Intermediate and highest courts of appeal hear cases ordinarily involving appeals on matters of law.

22. Some states do not have intermediate courts, and appeals are taken directly from the trial court to the highest court of the state.

23. Special courts have been set up by both the federal and state governments to hear specialized types of cases.

24. Cases are ordinarily tried before a jury where the facts are in dispute, although the parties may agree to try the case before a judge.

25. The grand jury makes an investigation to determine whether a crime may have been committed. If the evidence points to this conclusion, the grand jury issues an indictment against the party suspected of being guilty.

26. The petit jury evaluates the evidence presented in court and then attempts to establish the facts that are in dispute.

27. The Uniform Commercial Code has been developed to facilitate business transactions among people residing in different states.

28. Business law may be defined as a collection of basic legal principles that apply to business transactions.

29. Business law is not one subject but a combination of many different subjects.

30. Morality and legality are not always identical.

PART 3: Making Contracts

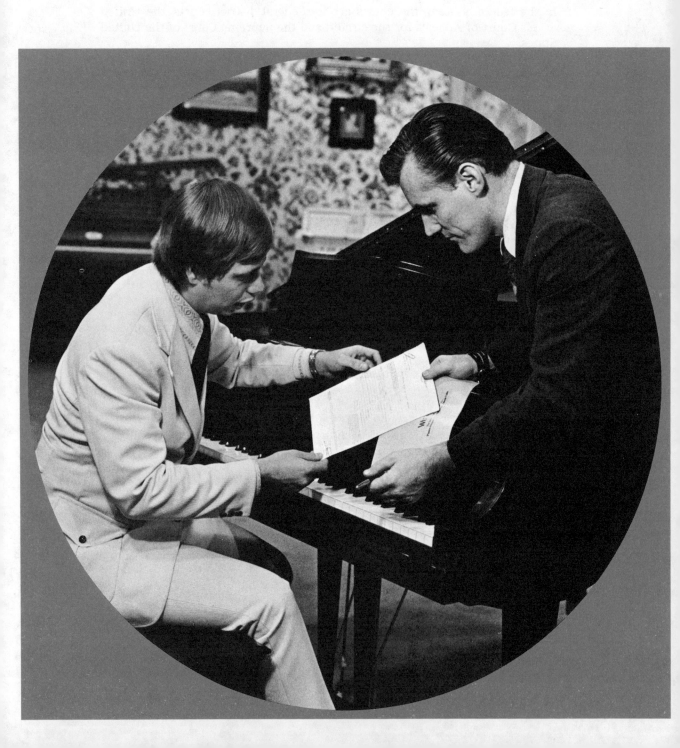

WHAT'S THE LAW?

1. *You go into a cafeteria, select what you intend to eat, get your ticket punched, take your tray to a table, and then sit down to eat the food. Nothing is said by anyone. Have you promised to pay for the food? Is this a contract? If so, what kind?*

---

2. *Mr. Paige offers to pay you $2 if you will mow his lawn. You say nothing, but you get your power mower and do the job. Does Mr. Paige owe you $2? Is this a contract?*

⬚ UNIT 7: CONTRACTS IN EVERYDAY AFFAIRS

Many people think of contracts as certain long and hard-to-read documents, poorly understood by all but experienced businessmen, lawyers, and other experts. While some contracts may fit this description, it is not an accurate picture of contracts in general. You have already made hundreds of contracts. You make a contract whenever you buy something at a store; travel by bus, plane, or train; engage some kind of personal service; or agree to perform a job for others.

TYPES OF CONTRACTS

Every business transaction and every act in our everyday lives involving an exchange of money values results in an agreement called a contract. A *contract* may be defined as "any agreement enforceable at law." Note that it is an agreement and that the agreement must be "enforceable at law." Some types of agreements are not enforceable at law. For example, Sarah Jones agrees to go to a movie with George Thomas; Mr. Barr accepts a dinner invitation from a customer; Ralph Cooke promises to call Edward Stone next Friday night at eight. Such agreements are social engagements. They are not contracts and are not enforceable at law.

CONTRACT

Are all agreements enforceable at law?

REMEMBER: From an ethical standpoint, you should live up to these social agreements, but the law cannot compel you to do so.

EXPRESS AND IMPLIED CONTRACTS

Contracts may be either express or implied. An *express contract* is stated in words and may be either oral or written.

EXPRESS CONTRACT

All parties to a contract should understand the language that is used.

EXAMPLE 1 Marty Dalton offers to wash Mr. Johnson's new automobile, and Mr. Johnson agrees orally to pay Dalton for his services. This is an example of an oral express contract and is enforceable at law.

Why should important contracts be put in writing?

An oral contract depends almost entirely on the memory and honesty of the parties. If one party dies, it usually is virtually impossible to prove an oral contract. If a contract is really important, therefore, it should be put in writing. This makes it easier to prove the contract should difficulties arise later.

A written contract may consist of a letter, memorandum, note, or other instrument that clearly states the intentions of the parties. The writing may be printing, typewriting, or any other form of "mark." No particular form need be followed, as long as the parties clearly express themselves in understandable language. U.C.C. Sec. 1-201(46)

Distinguish between express and implied contracts.

Many contracts are implied by the acts of the parties. Such contracts are known as *implied contracts*.

IMPLIED CONTRACT

EXAMPLE 2 You drop your fare into the coin box as you board a bus. Neither you nor the bus driver speaks. It is mutually understood by your acts of payment and boarding that the driver of the bus is to transport you to your desired destination.

REMEMBER: All important contracts should be in writing. Even writing simple contracts may at times prevent inconvenience and loss. Read all written contracts carefully! Ignorance of the contents of a contract that you sign will seldom, if ever, excuse you from fulfilling its terms.

SIMPLE AND FORMAL CONTRACTS

How does a formal contract differ from a simple contract?

Contracts may be either simple or formal. A *formal contract* is written and is under seal. All other contracts, written or oral, that are not under seal are known as *simple*, or parol, *contracts* (see example on page 53). Contracts under seal are discussed on pages 84 and 85.

FORMAL CONTRACT

SIMPLE CONTRACT

When is a contract considered an entire contract?

Contracts are also classified as executed or executory. In an *executed contract* the terms have been fully carried out by both parties. In an *executory contract* the terms have not been fully carried out by one party or by both parties.

EXECUTED CONTRACT

EXECUTORY CONTRACT

When each part of an agreement is dependent upon the other parts for satisfactory performance, the contract is considered an *entire contract*.

ENTIRE CONTRACT

A SIMPLE AGREEMENT

Troy, New York
August 1, 19—

Lawrence Rice and Clarence Drake hereby enter into the following agreement.

Lawrence Rice agrees to clean and paint the outside surface of the frame dwelling belonging to Clarence Drake, located at 1625 Hudson Avenue in the city of Troy, New York, using paint and materials supplied by Clarence Drake, and applying two coats of paint; said cleaning and painting to be completed on or before October 1, 19—.

In consideration of this, Clarence Drake agrees to pay Lawrence Rice the sum of $250 on the completion of the work according to customary standards of exterior painting of frame residences.

Lawrence Rice

Clarence Drake

Entire contracts are not performed until all the terms of the agreement have been executed.

EXAMPLE 3 **A tailor cannot demand payment for a new suit of clothes ordered by a customer until the suit is completely finished and ready for delivery. If the tailor demands payment for the trousers before starting to fashion the coat, the customer may refuse to accept partial delivery and may legally cancel the entire order.**

Failure to perform all the requirements of the contract not only relieves the other party of liability but also gives him a cause of action for damages because of such failure. All goods specified in a sales contract must be presented in a single delivery, and payment is due only on those goods at that time; but where the circumstances give either party the right to make or demand delivery in lots, the price—if it can be apportioned—may be demanded for each lot.

What is a
divisible contract?

Some contracts, known as *divisible contracts,* are made up of two or more independent items—that is, the items sold are used independently. A party to such a contract may recover for any part of the contract performed by him as agreed; that is, partial performance is permissible in this type of contract.

DIVISIBLE
CONTRACT

EXAMPLE 4   Scott ordered a radio and an electric toaster from the local appliance dealer. He wanted both shipped to his home at the same time. Because this order constitutes a divisible contract, Scott must pay the dealer if he delivers the radio but not the toaster. Failure of the dealer to deliver the toaster would not excuse Scott from liability for payment on the radio. Scott would have the legal right to complain about the nondelivery of the toaster and could seek damages in a suit based on the contractual terms.

ELEMENTS OF AN ENFORCEABLE CONTRACT

What are
the six basic
requirements that
make a contract
binding?

You will remember that a contract has been defined as "any agreement enforceable at law." A contract must meet certain basic requirements in order to be enforceable at law. These requirements are (1) offer and acceptance (agreement), (2) real consent, (3) competent parties, (4) valid consideration, (5) legal purpose, and (6) written form when required.

Every contract must fulfill every one of these basic requirements in order to be absolutely binding and enforceable at law.

THE CONTRACT AGREEMENT

EXAMPLE 5   Leroy Young placed the following advertisement in his high school newspaper: "For Sale, One Polaris Camera, $75." Donald Clark read the ad and then telephoned Leroy and stated, "I'll buy that Polaris camera if it's the model I'm looking for."

A contract may eventually result from these preliminary statements, but clearly there is no agreement between the two parties as yet. Leroy has not said he will sell, nor has Donald definitely said he will buy. There is no mutual assent or agreement by both to a clearly stated proposal. Without such an agreement, there can be no contract.

An agreement
usually results
from an offer and
an acceptance.
What does this
statement mean?

Agreements are usually arrived at by means of an offer and an acceptance. An *offer* is a definite statement by one party, called the *offeror,* of the terms under which he will contract. An *acceptance* is the unqualified assent of the other party, called the *offeree,* to the proposal stated. The offer and acceptance may be made orally in person, by telephone, by an exchange of letters or telegrams, by a formally drawn written agreement, or by a combination of these methods. The important thing is that the parties understand each other.

OFFER
OFFEROR
ACCEPTANCE
OFFEREE

REQUIREMENTS OF AN OFFER

What are the
three basic
requirements of
an offer?

There are three basic requirements of an offer: (1) It must be definite and certain, (2) it must be communicated to the offeree, and (3) it must be made with the intention of entering into an enforceable obligation.

A newspaper advertisement is generally considered an invitation to the public to make an offer. If a price error is made by the paper or if the merchandise is sold out, the merchant may refuse the customer's offer to buy.

Must Be Definite and Certain   Even though one or more terms are left open, a contract for sale does not fail for indefiniteness if the parties have intended to make a contract and there is a reasonably certain basis for giving an appropriate remedy. U.C.C. Sec. 2-204(3)

When we say that an offer must be definite and certain, do we mean that all terms must be spelled out in full detail? Explain.

EXAMPLE 6   Joe Vasquez was offered a position as account executive with the International Corporation. He was to receive $800 a month plus a "reasonable" commission on total sales. Do you think that this is a definite and certain offer?

It is not "definite and certain" because it would be difficult to determine exactly what a "reasonable commission" is. The court, however, could fix a reasonable commission based on acceptable practices in the trade.

REMEMBER: An offer should include the same points covered in the lead of a good newspaper story—who, what, when, where, how much—if it is to be clear, definite, and certain.

EXAMPLE 7   Oakes said to his friend Schelfe, "I am buying a new automobile. If you will buy my used car for cash, I will sell to you at a reasonable price and deliver it to you at once." Schelfe accepted the offer and asked Oakes to transfer title to him. Oakes delivered the used automobile to Schelfe, who refused it because he had changed his mind. Was Schelfe bound by the agreement?

In the above example, the court could fix a reasonable price based on the value of the car in the used-car market.

Does the acceptance of a newspaper ad always result in a contract?

Very often, an invitation to make an offer is confused with an offer. Most newspaper advertisements, price quotations, and display advertising fall within the "invitation" class.

EXAMPLE 8   A newspaper advertisement appeared in the evening paper and read, "Our Best Quality Suits on Sale for $99.50." Mike Petras walked into the store and said, "I accept your offer." What did Mike agree to do?

Actually, he agreed to nothing. The advertisement was merely an invitation to the public to come in, see the suits, and make an offer.

For the acceptance of a newspaper offer to result in a contract, what must it contain?

It is possible to make an offer to the general public by means of an advertisement, but all the terms must be set out in the advertisement. An example of a public offer is the advertisement or notice offering a reward for the capture of a criminal or the return of something that has been lost. A specific sum is offered in return for a specific act, and it is directed to the public at large. Anyone reading the notice may accept by doing the required act.

How may offers be communicated?

Must Be Communicated   Offers may be made in many ways—by telephone, by letter, by telegram, or by other methods. Generally, there is no problem as to the method of communication, although sometimes a letter or a telegram may go astray. It is in connection with reward offers that trouble arises in regard to the requirements of communication.

EXAMPLE 9   **Peter Jensen found a wallet on Main Street in his hometown. An identification card and address of the owner was in the wallet. Peter returned the wallet to its rightful owner. The owner thanked him but did nothing additional. Later in the evening, while reading the local newspaper, Peter discovered that the owner had offered a reward for the return of the wallet. Can Peter collect the reward?**

No, Peter cannot collect the reward. He may get peeved about it and consider it unfair, but he cannot collect. He did not know of the reward at the time he returned the billfold, so it cannot be said that he accepted the offer. There can be no agreement if the offeree does not know of the offer, even if he has done the act requested in the offer.

You cannot collect a reward for the return of lost property if you did not know about the reward prior to returning the property.

Must Intend an Enforceable Obligation   In the following example, words are used that sound as though an offer is being made when, actually, no offer is intended.

EXAMPLE 10   **Dick and Harry are taking parts in a play. Dick, reading his lines, says to Harry, "I will sell you my automobile for $500." Harry, also reading his lines, replies, "I accept your offer." Dick has stated a definite offer, and Harry has made a definite acceptance. Is there a contract?**

No, there is no contract. Each man was playing a part in a play. Neither intended to enter into legal relations to sell or buy a car. Similar situations arise when an offer is made to enter into a social engagement, or when an offer is made in the heat of anger, or when an offer is made as a joke. When these conditions exist, there is no legal offer.

You cannot expect a written contract for every agreement; but when the amount of money is large or the contract is important, insist on some written evidence of the bargain.

REQUIREMENTS OF AN ACCEPTANCE

As in the case of an offer, there are certain basic requirements for an acceptance.

Must Be Unconditional   The acceptance must be made without attaching any conditions to the original offer.

EXAMPLE 11   Ray offers to sell his boat to John for $45 cash. John replies, "I accept if you will allow me to pay $9 a week for five weeks." Edward, who is with John at the time, speaks up and says, "I'll accept your offer and pay the $45 cash right now." Is there a valid acceptance?

No, there is no valid acceptance. This situation illustrates two important requirements of a valid acceptance. An offer is completely within the control of the offeror. He may offer any terms he chooses and may make the offer to any person he chooses. No one else may change his terms, and no one but the offeree to whom the offer is made may accept. Thus, John is not making a valid acceptance because he is changing the terms. Edward is not making a valid acceptance because the offer was not made to him.

What are the basic requirements of a valid acceptance?

Communication of Acceptance   The time at which an acceptance takes effect may be very important because, when the acceptance has been communicated by the offeree to the offeror, the parties are in agreement, and a contract comes into being. There is no special problem of communication when the parties are dealing face to face. When one of the parties speaks, the other party hears him and the offer or the acceptance is communicated. When the parties live at a distance, however, and must negotiate by letter or telegram, some arbitrary rules must be made as to when the acceptance takes place.

Let's assume that Ray and John live in different cities. Ray has made an offer by letter to sell his boat to John. John decides to accept. There is no contract yet. He writes a letter, addresses it to Ray, and puts a stamp on it. Still no contract. He carries the letter across the street to a post-office mailbox, pulls down the slide, lays the letter in, but holds his finger on it. Still no contract. When he lifts his finger, however, and the letter slides down into the box beyond his control, a contract is formed.

When the offer
refers to the sale
of goods, how
must the
acceptance be
made?

The acceptance of an offer for the sale of goods may be made in any manner and by any medium that is reasonable in the circumstances. U.C.C. Sec. 2-206(1A) An acceptance made through an agency other than that used by the offeror results in a contract, even if it never reaches the offeror.

Ray could have stated the time and place of acceptance in his offer, indicating that a contract would not come into existence until he received the acceptance. In that case, there would be a contract only when Ray received the acceptance, provided that he received it within the specified time limit.

Sometimes an offer specifies that it must be accepted by an act. When that is true, then the act must be performed before there is an acceptance. A promise to do the act is not enough. Thus, if Larry Czonka promised to pay Floyd Little $5 if Floyd would climb to the top of the school flagpole, Floyd would have to climb to the top in order to accept the offer.

There is also the requirement that the promise or the act of acceptance must be positive. If Ray, in his letter to John, offering the sale of the boat, had concluded his offer by saying, "If I do not hear from you, I shall assume that you have accepted my offer," John's silence after receiving the offer would not bind him to pay. Ray has no right to try to force an acceptance through John's lack of action.

A person cannot be compelled to speak or to write in order to avoid a binding agreement and is under no obligation to reply to an offer.

May silence ever
indicate the
acceptance of an
offer?

Silence may indicate assent, provided both parties understand and agree that this is to be the means of acceptance.

EXAMPLE 12 **Dowd, a vacuum cleaner salesman, demonstrated one of his machines at Mrs. Milton's house. Mrs. Milton said she would have to consult her husband before deciding to buy it. Dowd then offered to leave the cleaner with Mrs. Milton, saying, "If I don't hear from you by the end of the month, I'll bill you for it." Mrs. Milton agreed. A month passed and the salesman's bill arrived. Has a contract making Mrs. Milton responsible for the price of the cleaner resulted?**

By her silence, Mrs. Milton accepted Dowd's offer and is liable under the agreement. Both parties had agreed that continued silence would be the manner of acceptance. A contract for sale of goods may be made in any manner, including conduct by both parties, that shows agreement. U.C.C. Sec. 2-204(1)

TERMINATION OF OFFER

In what ways may
an offer be
terminated?

By Lapse of Time Again, we may assume that Ray has offered to sell John his boat for $45. This time, Ray tells John that the offer will remain open until noon on the following day. A time has been specified, and John must accept within that time. If he does not come around until one o'clock, he will be too late; the offer ended at twelve.

If no exact time had been stated, John would have a reasonable time within which to accept. What is a reasonable time depends on the circumstances. U.C.C. Sec. 1-204 If Ray and John were dealing face to face, the offer would terminate when they parted company, unless the time was extended.

Where beginning a requested performance is a reasonable mode of acceptance, an offeror who is not notified of acceptance within a reasonable time may treat the offer as having lapsed before acceptance. U.C.C. Sec. 2-206(2)

EXAMPLE 13   **Jackson said to McGann, "If you will reshingle the roof of my house, I will pay you $450. McGann did nothing for three months and then decided to do the work. After the passage of such a long period of time, unless McGann informed Jackson of his intention, Jackson may treat McGann's acceptance by either word or act as not binding upon him.**

By Revocation or Withdrawal   With Example 11, let us suppose that John starts to Ray's house at ten o'clock the next morning with the intention of accepting Ray's offer. Ray, seeing John coming, runs into the house and closes the door. When John comes up on the porch, Ray calls to him and says, "I withdraw my offer." He may do so.

An offer may be withdrawn any time prior to acceptance, unless something has been paid to keep the offer open. (Payment of a sum to hold an offer open is known as an *option*.)

OPTION

What is a firm offer? How does it differ from an option?

This rule has been modified as it applies to *firm offers* (irrevocable offers). If a merchant makes a written and signed offer to buy or sell goods it is not revocable because of lack of consideration if it gives assurance that it will be held open for a stated time or, if no time is stated, for a reasonable time. U.C.C. Sec. 2-205

FIRM OFFER

A revocation becomes effective when it is received by the offeree.

By Rejection   Changing our facts again, suppose that, when Ray makes his offer, John replies, "I wouldn't have that boat as a gift." Ray's offer is terminated by this rejection, and, if John changes his mind two minutes later and tries to accept, he may not do so.

By Counteroffer   Prior to the advent of the Uniform Commercial Code, an acceptance which materially altered the terms of the offer did not ordinarily create a contract. It was regarded as a qualified or a conditional acceptance or *counteroffer* and acted as a rejection of the original offer.

COUNTEROFFER

If instead of flatly rejecting the offer, John had said, "I'll give you $37.50," his statement would constitute a counteroffer, and, like a rejection, it would terminate the offer. If Ray refused the $37.50, John could not go back and accept the $45 offer; it no longer exists.

Conforming to accepted business practice between merchants in the sale of goods, the law now provides that an expression of acceptance or written confirmation sent within a reasonable time acts as an acceptance, even though it states additional or different terms, unless acceptance is conditional, depending on assent to the new terms. U.C.C. Sec. 1-205

The additional terms are to be considered as proposed additions to the contract. Between merchants these terms become part of the contract

When, if ever, may an offer be accepted and result in a binding contract even though additional or different terms are stated by the offeree?

unless the offer expressly limits acceptance to the terms of the offer, unless these terms materially change the offer, or unless notification of objection to these terms has already been given or is given within a reasonable time. U.C.C. Sec. 2-207(2)

EXAMPLE 14 **A manufacturer offered by mail to sell Sheraton, a dealer, color television sets for $395 each. Sheraton mailed his acceptance as follows: "I accept your offer. Send three sets immediately on e.o.m. 10-day terms."**

This is a valid acceptance and results in a contract unless, within a reasonable time, the manufacturer objects to the terms of payment. If the offer had specified that payment must accompany the order, acceptance would be limited to these terms; a change such as that suggested in the example above would result in a termination of the offer.

Under what conditions may an offer be terminated by operation of law?

By Operation of Law The death or the insanity of either party would make the fulfillment of an agreement impossible; therefore, the offer is said to be terminated by the happening of these events.

SUGGESTIONS FOR MINIMIZING LEGAL RISKS

When you make an offer . . .

1. If the offer is important, decide whether to obtain legal counsel before sending or making the offer.
2. In sending a written communication, be sure that it is not subject to more than one possible interpretation.
3. To be safe, you should state, "This is an offer," or "This is not an offer, but rather an invitation (or request) for an offer."
4. It is desirable to specify in the offer the time and the manner in which the acceptance is to take place.
5. Be definite and clear as to the exact terms of the offer and any conditions that may apply to the terms.
6. If it becomes necessary to withdraw an offer, remember that the withdrawal does not become effective until it is received by the offeree.

When you make an acceptance . . .

1. Be sure that you understand clearly all the terms, conditions, and legal implications involved in accepting the offer.
2. If the contract is very important, determine whether you should obtain legal advice before accepting the agreement.
3. Keep a correctly dated carbon copy or duplicate or some written record of the acceptance, and indicate the date and time when the acceptance was communicated.
4. Set up a calendar showing the dates when all commitments, financial and otherwise, must be met according to the terms of the contract.

△ APPLYING YOUR LEARNING

QUESTIONS AND PROBLEMS

1. Give several reasons why a written contract is better than an oral one.
2. Generally, an advertisement is not considered to be an offer, although it could be under certain conditions. Give examples.
3. If you found a valuable article, what should you do if you wish to collect the reward offered for its return?
4. What are the essential requirements of a valid offer?
5. If the offeree uses a method of communication that is different from that used by the offeror, when does the acceptance take place?
6. If no manner of acceptance is indicated in the offer, how should the offeree plan to submit his acceptance?

WHAT IS YOUR OPINION?

In each of the following cases, give your decision and state a legal principle that applies to the case.

1. Nelson said to Carlson, "Meet me at the theater entrance tomorrow afternoon at two o'clock. I have two tickets to a musical comedy." Carlson agreed but failed to show up. Has Nelson a legal claim against Carlson?
2. Goodman orally agreed to buy ten clarinet reeds from Herman's stock for $15. When Herman delivered the reeds, Goodman refused to accept them, stating that he was not bound on his oral agreement. Was the agreement enforceable?
3. Archer mailed an offer to Miles, and Miles mailed a properly addressed and stamped letter of acceptance ten minutes before he received a revocation of the offer. Was the revocation effective?
4. Parker offered to sell Carter a carload of coal at $25 a ton. The letter offering the coal for sale was received by Carter on Thursday morning at ten o'clock. Carter mailed a letter of acceptance at four o'clock in the afternoon. Parker received the letter on Friday morning at eleven, an hour after he had mailed a letter to Carter revoking the offer. Is there a contract?
5. Hooper offered to sell his farm to Sawyer. Sawyer told his friend Wells of the offer and mentioned that he did not plan to accept it. He suggested to Wells that he might accept if he wished to do so. Wells wrote an acceptance, which Hooper received. Is there a contract?
6. A firm mailed a form letter to all its customers offering to sell 2,000 barrels of apples at $4 a barrel. Perkins ordered the entire lot at the price stated, but delivery was refused. Has Perkins a claim against the company?
7. Black's letter to Donovan contained an offer stating, "This offer subject to receipt of acceptance by June 10." Donovan wrote and mailed his acceptance on June 8, but it did not reach Black until June 11. Was there a valid contract?

8. Nichols offered to sell Fisk an antique piano for $200 and agreed orally to keep the offer open for five days. The same day, a neighbor told Fisk that he had bought the piano from Nichols. Has Fisk any rights against Nichols?

9. Carter ordered a sports jacket and a raincoat from the Duke Men's Shop. If the shop delivers only the raincoat, claiming that the jacket that was ordered had been inadvertently sold to another customer, must Carter accept and pay for the raincoat?

10. On June 2 Bristol wrote to Burton offering to sell his automobile for $1,000 and stated that the offer was "good for ten days." Burton received the letter on June 2 and wrote and mailed a letter of acceptance on June 11. Because Bristol received the letter of acceptance on June 14, he claimed that there was no contract. Is he right?

11. Myers received by letter from Whitney an offer, which he was asked to accept by return mail. Myers accepted in a telegram, delivery of which was delayed. Before receiving the telegram, Whitney notified Myers that he was revoking the offer. Was there a contract?

12. Morris made an offer by wire to Gordon, who accepted immediately by mail. Was there a contract at the time Gordon mailed the letter?

13. McGraw said to Wilson, "I'll give you $10 if you hit a home run in tomorrow's game." Wilson hit a home run in the fifth inning. Can Wilson demand that McGraw pay him $10?

THE LAW IN ACTION

1. The plaintiff agreed to sell and the defendant agreed to buy "5,000 gallons of Worthmore Motor Oil SAE 10-70 Base . . . @ 21-31 cents per gallon." Several other brand names of oil were listed in the same manner. The defendant repudiated the agreement and refused to take delivery on any oil. Was there a contract? (Willhelm Lubrication Company v. Brattrud, 197 Minn. 626, 268 N.W. 634)

2. The defendant ordered 25 carloads of coal from the plaintiff in such a form as to make the order a valid offer. The plaintiff replied, "You can be assured if it is possible to ship the entire 25 cars we will do so, but under the circumstances this is the best we can promise you." The plaintiff shipped 7 carloads under this agreement and then refused to ship any more. When sued for the purchase price of the cars shipped, the defendant entered a counterclaim for the 18 cars not shipped. Was there a good contract for 25 carloads of coal? (Guyan Coal & Coke Company v. Wholesale Coal Company, 229 Mich. 257, 201 N.W. 194)

KEY TO "WHAT'S THE LAW?" Page 51

1. *Yes. You have promised to pay for the food. This is an implied contract. The agreement was arrived at by the actions of the parties rather than by any spoken words.*

2. *Yes. This is an implied contract. The offer is accepted by doing the act requested.*

WHAT'S THE LAW?

1. *You buy David Todd's typewriter for $65. You think it is worth $90. Later you find it is worth only $40. Do you have any rights?*

2. *Before you bought the typewriter, you asked David whether it had pica type. David said, "Yes," honestly thinking it had. It turns out, after you have paid the $65, that the type is elite, not pica. Have you any rights?*

◭ UNIT 8: DEFECTIVE AGREEMENTS

There are times when people enter into agreements that are defective, and these cannot be enforced in a court of law. To be enforceable, agreements must be genuine.

EXAMPLE 1 **Grant Rollins, a Midwestern farmer, inquired about the price of a particular automobile in the used-car lot. Ray Sharkey, the used-car dealer, replied to Grant in the language of his trade, "I'll sell the car to you for just 650 potatoes." Grant said, "I accept." Grant went to his truck and returned with 650 potatoes in a sack and demanded the car. Ray Sharkey refused to sell because he thought everyone should know that "potatoes" meant dollars.**

Name a basic requirement of every valid contract.

In this case there is both an offer and an acceptance, but we know instinctively that something is wrong. The agreement between the parties is not a real one, because they do not have the same thing in mind. There is a defect in their mutual understanding. First and foremost in any valid contract is the requirement that it must be apparent that the parties understand each other. The term *valid,* when used in a legal sense, means "good or having legal force or authority."

VALID

Only when there is a "meeting of the minds" can there be a genuine agreement. What does this mean?

Only when there is a meeting of the minds can a valid contract be created. U.C.C. Sec. 2-204(1) A valid contract exists when both parties recognize the existence of such a contract, even though the exact time of the agreement cannot be pinpointed.

EXAMPLE 2 **Milton, a salesman for Machine Clean Solvents, sent several barrels of cleaner to Machinery Suppliers with the understanding that, after they had tested the product and if they were satisfied with it, Machinery Suppliers would bottle it under their own name and sell it to the trade.**

Machinery Suppliers notified Milton that the solvent met their standards and that they were having bottles and labels prepared with a view to offering the

cleaner for sale. Even though the exact time when the agreement was made cannot be determined, a valid enforceable contract for sale nevertheless resulted from the actions of the parties.

DEFECTIVE AGREEMENTS

Contracts that are not valid are either voidable or void.. *Voidable* means that, because of a defect, one of the parties may, at his option, declare the contract at an end. He may *avoid* or disaffirm it, that is, refuse to carry it out. Note that we did not say that both parties have the right to avoid, but only the party or parties injured. Voidable does not mean void. A so-called *void* contract is no contract at all. It is unenforceable by either party. A voidable contract, on the other hand, is a perfectly good contract up to the time it is disaffirmed or avoided. If the injured party chooses, he may give up his right to disaffirm and hold the other party to the contract as it stands.

VOIDABLE

AVOID

VOID

What is a void contract? How does it differ from a voidable contract?

Parties to a voidable contract may be led or forced into it in one of five ways: (1) mistake as to the identity of the parties, (2) misrepresentation, (3) fraud, (4) duress, or (5) undue influence. A void contract exists when the parties who enter into it are mistaken as to the identity of the subject matter or the existence of the subject matter.

MISTAKE

Mistake, as used here, is a misunderstanding of the terms of an agreement or of the identity of the parties to an agreement.

MISTAKE

EXAMPLE 3 If Jack has two typewriters, one an Underwood and the other a Remington, and if his offer to you does not designate which one he is selling, then there might not be a genuine agreement. If Jack has in mind selling the Remington and you have in mind buying the Underwood, there is no genuine agreement. If he says, "I will sell you my typewriter for $65," his offer is ambiguous. "My typewriter" could describe either equally well.

Not all mistakes, however, will cause an agreement to become either void or voidable.

EXAMPLE 4 If you buy Jack's typewriter for $40 because you think it is worth $75, you cannot complain later if it turns out to be worth only $20. You made a mistake as to its value, but that type of mistake will not set aside a contract.

What kinds of mistakes will ordinarily result in a void contract?

The type of mistake that will make a contract void, or unenforceable by either party, must be a mistake as to the identity of the subject matter, as in Example 3, or it must be a mistake as to the existence of the subject matter, as in the following example.

EXAMPLE 5 If Jack offers to sell you his Underwood typewriter and you accept, but if unknown to either of you the typewriter was destroyed by a fire in Jack's home an hour before, then the subject matter does not exist, and no contract has been made between you and Jack.

Always read contracts before signing them. You are responsible for agreements you sign even if you have not read them.

A mistake as to parties may prevent the formation of a valid contract.

EXAMPLE 6 **Suppose you send an offer by letter to your friend Jim Green, who lives in a nearby town. The postmaster delivers your letter to another Jim Green, who happens to reside in the same town. The wrong Jim Green likes your offer and accepts it. The contract would be voidable because he is not the person you had in mind.**

If, however, you are dealing face to face with a person that you think is Jim Green, but who really is not, your mistake as to his identity will not prevent the contract's being binding. You make the offer to the person facing you. He is the person who may accept it. Mistaken identity of this kind will not prevent a contract.

A mistake as to the nature of an agreement will not ordinarily prevent its binding the parties. Thus, if you sign a written agreement without reading it, you are bound, even though you may be mistaken as to what it says. By signing, you agree that the writing sets forth the terms of your agreement. It is your responsibility to know what the agreement says.

Most lawsuits involving mistake result from a careless use of language by the parties.

REMEMBER: Always state your offers and your acceptances in plain, clear, simple language. Be sure that the other party understands you.

MISREPRESENTATION AND FRAUD

What is the difference between fraudulent and nonfraudulent misrepresentation?

Misrepresentation is a misstatement of fact. Misrepresentation will make any contract voidable—whether the misrepresentation was unintentional (nonfraudulent) or intentional (fraudulent).

MISREPRESEN-TATION

Nonfraudulent misrepresentation may be either innocent or negligent. When the person making the statement has no way of knowing the statement is false, he is guilty of *innocent* misrepresentation. When the person making the statement is able to verify his information but does not do so, he is guilty of *negligent* misrepresentation.

NONFRAUDULENT

INNOCENT

NEGLIGENT

EXAMPLE 7 **Suppose that Jack, when he offers to sell his typewriter, says, "My uncle is giving me a Remington typewriter that he has had only a few months. It is a new-model machine and is in top-notch condition." Relying on Jack's statements, you buy the typewriter, only to find that Jack's uncle has not given him the good machine but an old one that needs repair.**

If it can be proved that Jack actually thought that his uncle was giving him the new-model machine, he would be guilty of nonfraudulent misrepresentation. You may recover the money you paid for the machine, but you may not sue for damages. Now, let us change the situation, as in the following example.

EXAMPLE 8   Jack knows that his uncle is giving him a used machine that needs a complete overhauling to put it in good condition. Nevertheless, Jack tells you that the typewriter is a new model and is in first-class condition. You take Jack at his word and buy the typewriter, only to find that it is not what Jack described it to be. What course of action is open to you?

Fraudulent misrepresentation would now be present because the statements were intentional misrepresentations of material facts. You may avoid the contract, and, if you suffered any loss, you may sue for damages.

How would you define fraud?

Fraud can be defined as (1) a false statement of material fact, (2) known to be false by the party making it, (3) made with the intention of inducing action from the person to whom it is made, (4) and actually inducing action from that person to his subsequent injury.

False Statement of a Material Fact   "The sales price of used cars will double within the next two months." "This is the best automobile ever built." "This car was owned by Mr. Silver, the local banker." "The brakes are in excellent condition. They were recently relined." Suppose that these statements were all made to Harold to induce him to buy a used car. All of them are false, but the first two could not be the basis of fraud. They are not statements of fact. They are the dealer's opinion only, and we must expect some "puffing" or "seller's talk" on the part of the dealer. The last two statements are not matters of opinion. The car either did or did not belong to Mr. Silver and the brakes either were or were not relined. These are statements of *material fact* or statements made to induce the other party to contract. Because they are false, Harold could avoid the contract.

Intent to Deceive the Injured Party   If the false statements of fact had not been made to Harold but to someone else, then Harold could not avoid the contract on the grounds of fraud. If these statements had been made to James Short by the dealer while he was trying to sell the same car to James, Harold could not rely on them just because he happened to hear

FRAUDULENT

FRAUD

MATERIAL FACT

No contract is in force unless the parties involved have identical subject matter in mind.

the conversation. The statements must have been made to Harold with the intention of inducing Harold to buy before they can become the basis of fraud.

Reliance by the Injured Party   Consider the following example.

EXAMPLE 9   **Suppose that before Charlie buys a car, the dealer allows him to try it out. Charlie drives it to show his good friend, Mike, who is a mechanic. Mike removes the left front wheel and points out the worn brake lining to Charlie. Further investigation finds the rest of the car to be in top condition. Mike recommends buying the car even though the dealer lied about the brakes.**

If Charlie relies on the recommendation of his friend and buys the car, he cannot under these circumstances later avoid the contract on the grounds of fraud.

If the false statement is not believed by the injured party and does not cause him to act, it cannot be the basis of fraud.

DURESS

EXAMPLE 10   **One evening while driving his car on a country road, Mr. Haywood picked up a hitchhiker, who stole Haywood's car. The hitchhiker then forced Mr. Haywood, at gunpoint, to endorse a bill of sale for the car. The car was found by police in a used-car lot some days later. The used-car dealer produced the bill of sale endorsed by Mr. Haywood, claiming that the bill of sale gave him good title.**

What is the effect of duress on a contract?

Mr. Haywood's agreement to sell was definitely voidable under these circumstances. The agreement was not his own but was forced on him by duress. *Duress* is overcoming the will of a person by a threat of physical force or bodily detention against a contracting party or a member of his immediate family.

DURESS

The threat must be a threat of physical harm or bodily detention. A mere threat of financial loss is not enough, although today many courts will hold that there is duress if the threat is one of physical destruction of a person's property.

UNDUE INFLUENCE

Undue influence may be defined as a personal or domestic pressure, usually exerted by one in a position of trust, on another person who normally could be expected to trust the person who exerts the pressure.

UNDUE
INFLUENCE

EXAMPLE 11   **Mrs. Sterling nagged at her husband day after day, week after week, and month after month to persuade him to convey title to the farm to her. Finally, reaching the point at which he would do anything to stop her nagging, he deeded the farm to her. Thereupon, she threw him out. Mr. Sterling claimed that the deed was induced by undue influence, and the court set the transfer of title aside.**

How does undue influence affect the validity of a contract?

Usually, the pressure is exerted by a strong person upon another who is weaker because of ill health, old age, or mental immaturity.

Contracts produced under duress are not enforceable.

EXAMPLE 12 **Mrs. Bernard, a childless widow in failing health, engaged a nurse-companion. As Mrs. Bernard's health worsened, she grew to rely on the nurse to an ever greater degree, even to the extent of entrusting confidential matters to her. Shortly before Mrs. Bernard's death, the nurse induced Mrs. Bernard to make a will, naming her as the sole beneficiary. Relatives contested the will on the grounds of undue influence.**

This would probably be a case involving undue influence. On the other hand, if additional evidence tended to show that this was what Mrs. Bernard wanted to do with her property, the court might hold otherwise.

Differentiate between duress and undue influence.

Duress may or may not be present along with undue influence. Usually, we think of duress as involving a threat. Undue influence usually does not involve a threat but rather a persuasive pressure exerted by one who is in a position of trust.

SUGGESTIONS FOR MINIMIZING LEGAL RISKS

As the offeror you should . . .

1. Do all in your power to avoid mistakes by making your offer as clear as you possibly can.
2. Be careful not to misrepresent innocently any material facts.
3. Never knowingly participate in a fraud by misrepresenting material facts with the intent to deceive the offeree.
4. Avoid any actions or words that might be construed as duress or undue influence in your business relationships.

As the offeree you should . . .

1. Check and recheck all possible material facts that are important.
2. Ask the offeror for further clarification on doubtful points.
3. If the contract is important, consult legal counsel.
4. Never rush into an important agreement.
5. If possible legal difficulties are anticipated, get a written statement signed by the offeror.

▲ APPLYING YOUR LEARNING

QUESTIONS AND PROBLEMS

1. What are the five ways that a party may be led or forced into a defective agreement?
2. What is the usual effect on a contract of a misunderstanding because of one's own neglect or carelessness?
3. How may a mistake be made regarding the value or quality of the subject matter?
4. What kinds of mistakes will render a contract void or not enforceable by either party?
5. If you fail to read the fine print on a written contract, may you later avoid the contract when you are injured financially as a result of your failure to do so? Why?
6. Would your answer to Question 5 be the same if you were blind and could not read the contract? Why?
7. How can you avoid making mistakes in your future contracts?
8. Give an example of nonfraudulent and of fraudulent misrepresentation.
9. What elements must be proved by the injured party to establish fraud?
10. What is meant by a false statement of a material fact?
11. Give an example of a contract that might come into being as a result of duress.
12. Give an example of a contract that might come into being as a result of undue influence.

WHAT IS YOUR OPINION?

In each of the following cases, give your decision and state a legal principle that applies to the case.

1. White agreed to buy from Wilson a boat that, without the knowledge of either party, had been destroyed by fire. Must White pay for the boat?
2. Ford sold an old chair to Pierce for $5. Later, to the surprise of both men, the chair was found to be a valuable antique. Can Ford recover the chair, claiming that there has been a mistake as to the subject matter of the contract?
3. Parker, a dealer in used cars, told Ames that a particular car "is a bargain at $600." Ames bought the car. Later, he discovered that the motor was in bad condition, that the radiator leaked, and that other used-car dealers had better cars for sale at $600 than the one he bought. Does Ames have any legal claim against Parker?
4. Mrs. Larkin selected and purchased kitchen furniture that she thought was maple but later discovered was pine wood. Because of this mistake, Mrs. Larkin demanded that the merchant take back the furniture. Must the merchant comply with Mrs. Larkin's demands?
5. Hill hurriedly signed a form that he assumed was a request for a sample or examination copy of an expensive reference book. Later it developed that he had actually signed an order for the book. When the book was

delivered, Hill refused to accept it and claimed he was not bound to the agreement because of the mistake. Is Hill legally bound to his agreement?

6. In a letter to Browning, Graves offered to sell a particular radio for $79. Browning immediately mailed a letter of acceptance. On receiving Browning's letter, Graves discovered that he had typed $79 instead of $97, as he had intended. Was there a valid contract to sell the radio for $79?

7. Adams finds a ring and shows it to Carter, who thinks it is worth $200. Carter offers Adams $60 for the ring, and Adams accepts. Later, Carter discovers that the ring is worth only $20 and refuses to pay Adams the amount agreed upon. Adams brings an action for the contract price. Is he entitled to judgment?

8. Dirk bought a tractor on the strength of a salesman's statement that it would lessen the cost of planting and harvesting his wheat. At the end of the season, Dirk found his cost had increased rather than decreased and sought to recover the price paid for the tractor. Is Dirk within his rights?

THE LAW IN ACTION

1. The plaintiff was injured while on the job and was unable to work for several weeks. During this period he was treated by the company physician, and he returned to work when the same physician certified that he was able to do so. His employer's insurance company settled his claim on the basis of the length of time he was unable to work; and the plaintiff signed a release, releasing the insurance company from any further liability. It later developed that the physician was mistaken in his diagnosis. The injury of the plaintiff was serious instead of slight, and he was unable to continue his employment. The plaintiff claimed that the release he signed was invalid because of the misrepresentation of the company doctor. Was he correct? (Gerald v. Liberty Mutual Insurance Company, 170 F. 2d, 917)

2. The plaintiff, Vargas, was an artist who had been under contract with Esquire magazine for several years. When presented with a new contract by the president of the defendant company, he signed it without reading it. The plaintiff then attempted to avoid the contract, claiming that it did not contain the terms he thought it did. He further claimed that he signed it only because he had relied upon the president of the company to look after his business affairs. Was this a case of undue influence? (Vargas v. Esquire, Inc., 166 F. 2d, 651)

KEY TO "WHAT'S THE LAW?" Page 63

1. *No. You made a mistake as to the value of the typewriter, but it was your own mistake and not induced by anyone.*

2. *Yes. In this situation you may avoid the contract on the grounds of misrepresentation.*

WHAT'S THE LAW?

1. Fred Smith, age seventeen, has an opportunity to buy a motorboat from John Hurd, an adult, for $300. Fred enters into an agreement to pay for the boat at $30 a month. Before making the first payment, he decides that the boat is no good and refuses to make the payments. May he do this?

2. Fred refuses to make payments or to return the boat to Hurd, stating that Hurd deceived him by saying it was a good motorboat worth at least $600. May Fred do this?

⬙ UNIT 9: CAPACITY OF PARTIES TO CONTRACT

Suppose that you walked into the corner drugstore, stepped behind the soda fountain, put on an apron, and announced to the proprietor, "I'm working here now." Would this mean that you now have a job? Of course not. It takes two people to make a bargain. That is an old, well-known expression, and it holds true with contracts. It takes two or more parties having capacity to act to make a contract that is binding upon both.

What do we mean by capacity to contract?

Even if the proprietor said, "O.K. It's a deal. You have a job," there would still be only one party who has the full capacity to contract. You, as a *minor* (under legal age) cannot be bound on a contract if you choose to avoid it. This does not mean that you cannot enter into contracts at all, because you can and do. Because you lack full contractual capacity, however, many of your contracts are voidable.

MINOR

INCOMPETENT PARTIES

Name several of the most common classes of persons who lack capacity to contract.

Two of the most common classes of persons who lack capacity to contract are minors, sometimes called infants in legal language, and those who are mentally ill. Other classes of persons lack capacity to enter into certain types of contracts. In time of war enemy aliens are denied certain legal capacity, and even in time of peace some states prevent aliens from entering into some types of contracts by law. Convicts also have certain limitations put on their contracting powers in a few states.

Intoxicated persons are sometimes classed as incompetents. The contracts of intoxicated persons are sometimes treated in much the same way as the contracts of the mentally ill.

It is primarily for their own protection that minors and the mentally ill are declared incompetent.

An intoxicated person is liable for the reasonable cost of necessities of life purchased by him.

EXAMPLE 1 Suppose that Barry, who is sixteen years old, inherits $150,000, which he may spend as he desires. A group of fast-talking, experienced operators surround Barry and attempt to get some of his inherited money.

Why does the law give incompetent persons the right to avoid or disaffirm many of their contracts?

Barry may be a fairly smart boy, but he just has not had the experience necessary to be able to spend the $150,000 wisely. To protect him from being taken advantage of by more experienced persons, the law gives him the right to disaffirm, or avoid, many of his contracts. This same right to disaffirm contracts is also given to the mentally ill and for the same reason. Also, if the mentally ill person has been declared insane by a court action and a guardian has been appointed to look after his affairs, the mentally ill person's contracts are void, not just voidable.

What effect does a declaration by a court action that a mentally ill person is insane have on his contracts?

You should note that, in general, the contracts of incompetent persons are voidable only, not void. When one of the parties to a contract is incompetent, it is only the incompetent person who can avoid the contract. If he chooses to enforce the contract, he may do so. Usually, such contracts are carried out by both parties, and it makes little difference that the contracts are voidable. It is only when the incompetent person chooses to be released from his promise that the contract terminates.

REMEMBER: An incompetent's contracts are voidable for his protection only. The law does not intend that an incompetent person shall use the right to avoid his contracts to injure other people.

CONTRACTS OF MINORS

EXAMPLE 2 Clinton Barker, on his seventeenth birthday, received $50 as a gift from his uncle. Clinton was in a buying mood. The first thing he saw was a movie camera. It was a $75 camera on sale for one day only at $50. After he got it home, he realized that it was of no use unless he had film. Furthermore, he would also need a projector to enjoy his purchase. However he could not buy these items because he had no more money.

Clinton, by acting in haste, had made a poor investment. Because he was only seventeen years old, he could return the camera, disaffirm his contract, and ask for the return of his money. Why should this be so?

The law protects a minor if he is taken advantage of by an unscrupulous person.

The law is very practical here. For hundreds of years, young people of high school age have been doing impulsive things. The law gives them a second chance when they have used poor judgment. Until they have reached a mature age, they may avoid their contracts.

When do minors reach the age of legal majority?

● The age at which minors reach legal maturity, usually called *majority* in legal language, is fixed by statute in each state. In most states it is still twenty-one years, but since the legal voting age was lowered to eighteen years in 1972, several states have lowered the age of majority accordingly.   **MAJORITY**

| Legally, you become eighteen or twenty-one years old on the day before that birthday. |

In some states, for example, a minor may enter into a binding contract for life insurance at a much earlier age. The reason is that it is to a minor's advantage to take out a life insurance policy at an early age. Furthermore, insurance companies are usually closely supervised by the state, and there is very little chance that a minor will be taken advantage of. You should consult the statutes of your own state to learn the legal age at which you will attain majority and thus have full capacity to enter into all types of contracts. Also find out, if possible, what types of valid contracts can be entered into in your state by minors prior to the general age of legal majority.

MINORS' CONTRACTS FOR NECESSITIES

EXAMPLE 3   Clinton, in Example 2, might have spent his money more wisely. Suppose that, instead of a camera, he had bought a warm coat, a sweater, a cap, and a pair of overshoes. These are things he actually needs. They are what the law calls necessaries, or necessities. Clinton would be bound to keep them and pay a reasonable price for them.

You will note, however, that Clinton must actually need this clothing. In addition, it must be shown that he was not being adequately provided for by his parents or guardian. If he already had plenty of winter clothing or if his parents were willing and able to supply his needs, then the items would not be necessities and he could disaffirm his contract for them in the regular way.

NOTE: *The bullet indicates that there may be a state statute that varies from the law discussed here. Whenever you see this bullet, find out, if possible, what the statute is in your state covering this point or principle of law.*

FUNDAMENTAL
NECESSITIES

What are the
fundamental
necessities of
life?
What is meant by
one's station
in life?

The *fundamental necessities* are food, clothing, shelter, and medical care. In addition, other things might be classified as necessities if they were needed by a minor in a given "station of life." A college education, for example, might be declared a necessity for a minor who had plenty of money to pay for such an education.

| A minor's station in life determines what are necessities for him. |

MINORS' CONTRACTS FOR OTHER THAN NECESSITIES

"Infancy is a
shield, not a
sword." What
does this
statement mean
to you?

If the contract of a minor is not for necessities, he may avoid it if he chooses and he will not be bound to live up to his agreement. A long time ago, however, a famous judge made the statement, "Infancy is a shield, not a sword." The law does not intend to give the minor the right to take advantage of other persons wrongfully. To protect the minor fully, however, his right to disaffirm must be an almost absolute right. *Disaffirm* means to indicate by a statement or by some act an intent not to abide by the contract. Thus there are times when a minor may legally take unfair advantage of an adult. To prevent a minor from using his infancy as a sword, the law applies several rules.

DISAFFIRM

Sometimes minors well able to pay try to use infancy to defraud others.

EXAMPLE 4   Ron Luther, a minor, has a $150,000 savings account in his name. He is planning a party for his friends and contracts to pay Rinaldo Catering Services $250 if they will prepare and serve the food and refreshments for the party. Rinaldo Catering Services handles the entire affair, but when their bill is presented, Ron Luther disaffirms his contract and refuses to pay.

A court might hold in this case that giving parties was a necessity for a minor in Ron's station in life, and, if so, Ron would have to pay the reasonable value of the party.

A minor arrested for stealing may be held criminally liable. The law protects a minor against his own inexperience, but not against his own wrongdoing.

| If a minor has the consideration he received, he must return it. |

There is a real problem when the minor does not have the consideration to return. States solve this problem differently according to their own statutes.

EXAMPLE 5   A minor bought a typewriter on credit. He sold it and spent the money. When sued, he defended on the grounds that he was a minor.

Many courts would hold that he cannot be forced to pay. If, however, the minor paid cash for the typewriter, sold it, spent the money, and then sued the seller to get the purchase price back, most courts would refuse his claim. In many states, however, even if he cannot return the goods, he can get his money back.

| If a minor makes an untrue statement about his age, he must pay damages for his fraud. |

Even when a minor who is twenty years of age but looks older tells the other party that he is twenty-two years old, he can still avoid his contract in most states. He is guilty of fraud, however, and must pay damages for any loss that results.

EXAMPLE 6   Adam Thomas, a minor falsely representing that he was twenty-three years of age, purchased a sports car. His sports car was involved in a two-car accident shortly thereafter. Adam then attempted to avoid the contract and receive a return of the money he spent.

Adam may avoid his contract, but he must pay for the damage to the car. The loss to the dealer was the direct result of the fraudulent misrepresentation and the minor must make good the loss.

What rules does the law apply to prevent a minor from legally taking advantage of an adult?

| A minor may not affirm the parts of a contract favorable to him and disaffirm the unfavorable parts. He must disaffirm all or none. |

A minor may, however, disaffirm one of two separate contracts.

EXAMPLE 7   Milton Orio contracted to purchase a fishing boat and an outboard motor for $650. Later, Milton decides that he would like to keep the outboard motor, but not the fishing boat.

Milton cannot keep the motor and disaffirm the contract to buy the boat. If he had entered into two contracts—one to buy the boat for $550 and another to buy the motor for $100—he could disaffirm one and ratify the other.

| If a minor executes a deed that actually transfers title of houses, land, etc., to a new buyer, the deed may not be avoided until after the minor becomes of legal age for the transfer of real estate. |

The reason for such a rule is this: Deeds to land must be recorded in a public office, and future buyers of the property depend on this record. To allow a minor to sell and disaffirm at will would put the records in a state of hopeless confusion.

RATIFICATION OF MINORS' CONTRACTS

How may a minor ratify his executory contracts after he reaches majority?

After a minor reaches majority, he may ratify, or approve, his executory contracts if he chooses. After ratification, he may no longer disaffirm them. He may ratify in words, in writing, or by his actions.

EXAMPLE 8 **Dick Green, who was twenty years of age, bought a car. He made a down payment and promised to pay a certain amount each month for eighteen months. After he reached twenty-one, he continued to make payments for two months.**

If a minor fails to disaffirm an executed contract or affirm an executory contract after reaching the age of majority, is he bound by the contract?

Dick's action is a ratification. If he later wrecked the car, he could not return it and demand the return of his money. Even if he made no payments, he would be bound if he kept the car an unreasonable length of time after reaching majority without paying anything.

A minor must disaffirm his executed contracts within a reasonable time after reaching majority, or he will be held liable for the contracts. However, a minor must positively affirm his executory contracts before they will be binding on him after he reaches the age of majority.

SPECIAL STATUTORY RULES

● Many states have made statutory changes in the capacity of minors to enter into contracts. It is quite common, for example, for girls to be given the capacity to marry at eighteen. Many states have given minors the capacity to enter into contracts for life insurance. Some states give limited capacity to minors over eighteen who are engaged in business in their own names to make contracts essential for the conduct of the business. These are but a few of the statutory changes; there are many, many more. You should consult the statutes of your own state to determine what special contractual capacities your home state has given to you.

REMEMBER: You, as a minor, have the capacity to enter into only those contracts that are specifically mentioned in the statutes of your state.

SUGGESTIONS FOR MINIMIZING LEGAL RISKS

Minors . . .

1. Just prior to becoming of legal age, make an inventory of all your contractual obligations—those for purchases or sales, services, money payments, or important agreements of any kind. Decide just what you should do about each contractual obligation when you reach legal age—whether you should affirm or disaffirm each agreement.

2. Follow the legal procedure for disaffirmance approved by the laws of your state. Within a reasonable time after reaching the age of majority, disaffirm those contracts you do not wish to ratify.
3. To be safe, it is desirable to get a written statement of the other contractual party's agreement to the disaffirmance.
4. If the obligation is important or extensive, obtain legal counsel as to the manner of disaffirmance to ensure that the obligation is discharged.

Adults . . .

1. Don't rely on a person's appearance in judging age or competency. Find out about the age, mental illness, insanity, or any other possible incompetencies of the other party or parties to a contract.
2. When dealing with a minor, if the contract is for something other than the reasonable value of necessities, insist that one of the parents or a guardian sign the agreement.
3. Become familiar with the special statutes of your state, particularly those that permit minors to enter into certain types of legal contracts prior to the age of majority.
4. If there is a question as to the possible interpretation of necessities for a particular minor in his station in life, consult legal counsel before concluding a sales agreement with the minor.

△ APPLYING YOUR LEARNING

QUESTIONS AND PROBLEMS

1. What is meant by competent party?
2. Who is considered to be a minor, or infant?
3. Technically, when does a minor become of age for most contracts?
4. Why does the law give special rights to persons having certain incapacities to contract?
5. What classes of persons have these incapacities?
6. What risk does an adult run if he contracts with minors?
7. How can an adult reduce the risk involved when he contracts with a minor?
8. Name several things that a minor might contract for that he could be held liable for.
9. Name several items a minor might buy that he could *not* be held liable for.
10. Why may a minor avoid a contract, even though he has misrepresented his age?
11. What is meant by affirmance, or ratification? Give an illustration of the ratification of a contract.
12. What is meant by disaffirmance, or avoidance? Give an illustration of the avoidance of a contract.

13. May a minor avoid a contract even if he is unable to return the consideration or property received?
14. May a minor affirm part and disaffirm part of the same contract? Explain.
15. What is the legal difference between a contract made with a mentally ill person and one who has been judicially declared insane?
16. What is the possible legal effect of a contract made with an enemy alien? an alien in peacetime? a drunkard? a convict?
17. What four general rules can you give governing minors' contracts for things other than necessities?

WHAT IS YOUR OPINION?

In each of the following cases, give your decision and state a legal principle that applies to the case.

1. Jordon, nineteen years of age, purchased a television set for $500 and told the dealer he was twenty-three years of age. Two months after the purchase, he returned the television set and demanded the return of his money. The merchant refused to comply with Jordon's demands and claimed that Jordon was liable on the contract because he had stated that his age was twenty-three. May Jordon avoid the contract?
2. While on a fishing trip, Larkin, a minor, broke his arm and engaged the services of a physician. Claiming infancy as a defense, he refused to pay the physician. Was Larkin legally bound to pay the physician?
3. Carr, while a minor, bought a radio for $75. The day after his twenty-first birthday, he sought to return it, claiming that it did not satisfy his needs. Can Carr force the seller to accept the radio and return the purchase price to him?
4. Brown, aged twenty, owns and operates a radio repair shop. Claiming infancy as a defense, he seeks to avoid a contract made for the purchase of supplies necessary for his shop. Is this a good defense?
5. Two months before becoming of age, Smith purchased a motorboat for $3,000, paying cash. Three years later, he sought to avoid the contract, claiming that he was a minor at the time of the purchase. Was he legally bound to the contract?
6. Hart, seventeen years of age, paid $50 for a portable radio. Before he received the radio, Hart asked for the return of his money. Is he legally entitled to it?
7. Hudnet, a minor, conveyed a tract of land to Black. While still a minor, Hudnet sought to avoid the agreement and to recover the land. Was he entitled to do so?
8. Kepler was declared by the court to be insane, and a guardian was appointed to take care of him. Later, Kepler made an agreement to purchase certain clothes from a merchant. Was the agreement binding on Kepler?
9. Garson sues Harris for breach of contract. Harris proves he was intoxicated when the agreement was executed. Does this fact affect the validity of the contract?

THE LAW IN ACTION

1. The plaintiff, a few months under the legal age of majority, bought from the defendant, a broker, certain common stocks of various corporations. A few weeks later, the stock market dropped, and the stocks purchased became almost worthless. The minor returned the stocks to the broker and demanded the return of the purchase price. Can he get his money back? (Joseph v. Schatzkin, 259 N.Y. 241, 181 N.E. 464)
2. The defendant, a boy just under the legal age of majority, contracted to buy a correspondence course, "Complete Steam Engineering," from the plaintiff company. When the defendant became twenty-one, the contract was still completely executory. He had paid nothing and had received nothing. He disaffirmed his contract shortly afterward, and the company sued, claiming that this was a contract for an education and was therefore a necessity. Was the correspondence course a necessity in this case? (International Textbook Company v. Connelly, 206 N.Y. 188, 99 N.E. 722)

KEY TO "WHAT'S THE LAW?" Page 71

1. *Yes. As a minor, Fred may disaffirm his contract and refuse to pay for the boat.*
2. *No. He must return the boat so that he owes nothing and has received or retained nothing. He is in the same position financially that he was in before the deal.*

A DIGEST OF LEGAL CONCEPTS

1. To be considered a valid contract, an agreement must be enforceable at law.

2. To be enforceable at law, a contract must contain a genuine agreement, be supported by valid consideration, be entered into between competent parties, and be for a legal purpose. Sometimes a contract must be in writing to be enforceable.

3. A genuine agreement must contain a valid offer and a valid acceptance.

4. A valid offer is definite and certain, it must be communicated, and it must be made with the intention of creating an enforceable obligation on acceptance.

5. Even though one or more terms are left open, a contract does not fail for indefiniteness if the parties have intended to make a contract and if there is a reasonably certain basis for giving an appropriate remedy.

6. A merchant's written and signed offer to buy or sell goods is not revocable because of lack of consideration if it gives assurance that it will be held open for a stated time or, if no time is stated, for a reasonable time.

7. To be valid, an acceptance must be definite, it must not materially alter the terms of the offer, it must be made by the party to whom the offer was made, and it must be made within the time and in the manner stated or indicated.

8. To be valid, an acceptance must be made before the offer is terminated.

9. When the offer refers to the sale of goods, the acceptance may be made in any manner and by any medium reasonable under the circumstances.

10. A price quotation, a circular letter, or an advertisement is often not definite and certain enough to be an offer. They are usually considered to be merely invitations to make an offer.

11. A general offer to the public may be made by advertisement if all the necessary elements of an offer are contained therein.

12. Generally an offer may be withdrawn at any time before it is accepted.

13. The withdrawal of an offer is not effective until it reaches the offeree.

14. An acceptance usually cannot be implied from silence on the part of the offeree unless these terms were previously agreed upon or unless the parties had entered into mutually acceptable agreements of that type in the past.

15. Social agreements are not contracts; they are not enforceable at law.

16. An offer that specifies that it must be accepted by an act is not accepted until the act is performed.

17. A written contract may consist of a letter, memorandum, note, or other instrument that clearly states the intentions of the parties.

18. An agreement is not genuine if induced by misrepresentation, fraud, duress, undue influence, or certain types of mistakes.

19. An agreement induced by misrepresentation, fraud, duress, or undue influence is voidable at the option of the injured party.

20. A mutual mistake as to the identity or existence of the subject matter prevents a genuine agreement; therefore, no contract exists. An agreement of this type can be set aside by either party.

21. A mistake that results from one's own neglect or carelessness is not sufficient to avoid a contract.

22. A mistake as to value, nature of the agreement, or extent of the liabilities incurred ordinarily will not set aside a contract.

23. A mistake as to the identity of the parties will not prevent the formation of a contract if the mistake is due to carelessness.

24. One may avoid a contract by claiming misrepresentation or fraud only when one actually relied on it and was influenced by it to his injury.

25. Expressions of opinion are not to be considered misrepresentations.

26. A mistake that causes the delivery of the offer to the wrong party ordinarily will prevent the formation of a contract.

WHAT'S THE LAW?

1. *Cora Holiday became discouraged with her schoolwork and decided to quit school. Her Uncle Ronald wrote a letter and promised her $1,000 if she would stay in high school until she graduated. Cora concurred and finally did graduate, but her uncle made no effort to give her the $1,000. Can Cora do anything?*

---

2. *Assume that you like school and that you have made the honor roll regularly for the past two years. Your uncle says that he will give you $1,000 for having been such a bright student. Months go by, and your uncle forgets the promised award. Can you do anything?*

△ UNIT 10: CONSIDERATION IN BUSINESS CONTRACTS

What is consideration? When is it said to exist?

What may a detriment consist of?

One of the basic elements of an enforceable contract is that an agreement must be supported by consideration. *Consideration* may be defined as a benefit received by the party making the promise (the promisor) or a detriment suffered by the party to whom the promise was made (the promisee). A *detriment* may consist of making a promise, doing an act, or refraining from doing something that one has a legal right to do. Consideration exists when a person does something that he is not legally required to do, or when he refrains from doing something that he has the legal right to do. This act of refraining is called *forbearance*.

CONSIDERATION

DETRIMENT

FORBEARANCE

EXAMPLE 1 **Pete Robertson's favorite uncle, Steve, who possesses full capacity to contract, promises Pete a gift of $200 cash with no strings attached. Steve tells Pete, "You are an honorable young man. Your high school grades are excellent. You have also been a great help to your parents at home. Next Tuesday I am going to give you $200 as a reward for your achievements. Is that acceptable to you?" Pete promptly replied, "Yes!"**

In this example there is no consideration for the uncle's promise. Pete and his uncle have an understanding. The understanding is definite and certain, and both Pete and his uncle understand it in the same way. If Pete's uncle changes his mind, however, and refuses to give the Pete the money, Pete cannot sue his uncle for breach of contract. The uncle received no benefit from his promise, and Pete did not give up anything at his uncle's request.

REMEMBER: Valid consideration may consist of money or other property, services, a promise, or a sacrifice or the giving up of some right.

Why do the courts ordinarily refuse to enforce a promise made without consideration?

Unless there is consideration to support a promise, the courts will not enforce the promise, and it cannot be called a contract. The theory is that, if you gave up nothing in reliance on a promise, then you have not been injured if the promise is not kept. Something which is given for which no consideration is received is called a *gift*.

GIFT

EXAMPLE 2 **Hilton, a furniture salesman, sold a sofa to Clark for $150. After Hilton prepared the bill of sale and accepted a $25 deposit from Clark, the proprietor claimed that an error had been made in placing a much lower price tag on the sofa than it was actually worth and demanded that the sale be canceled.**

A valid enforceable contract resulted from the $25 deposit by Clark. The proprietor could be held on the contract entered into by Hilton and Clark. Hilton had acted within the scope of his duties. His employer was bound.

Can a donor of a gift that has already been made have the contract set aside for lack of consideration and obtain the return of the article?

If a contract has been fully performed by both parties, no consideration is required. Thus, if Pete's uncle, in Example 1, actually gave Pete the $200, it would be a valid gift and he could not demand its return.

REMEMBER: An executed contract will not ordinarily be set aside for lack of consideration.

NECESSITY FOR CONSIDERATION

The detriment suffered—that is, what one gives up—may take many forms. In like manner, the benefit received may be very small. However, one or the other—the detriment or the benefit—must be present. Otherwise, with very few exceptions, the courts will not enforce the promise. The most common exception to the rule that consideration is required applies to contracts under seal. The word *seal* refers to a private seal attached by one or both of the parties. A seal on a written instrument gives it formality and a presumption of consideration, unless the contrary can be proved. Contracts under seal are also called *formal contracts*.

SEAL

FORMAL CONTRACT

How would you explain the origin of a private seal?

Historically, contracts under seal were used when common man could not read or write. In order to indicate that he agreed to contracts which he dictated to someone else, he would melt wax on the paper and press his own private seal into the wax.

EXAMPLE 3 **Bartlett requested payment from Hughes upon the following written statement: "I promise to pay Zachary Barlett $250 on demand." This statement was signed "Henry Hughes (Seal)."**

Since a sealed instrument carries the presumption of consideration, it is unnecessary for Bartlett to prove that consideration was exchanged to make the demand for the $250 valid. Hughes, however, has a right to prove that no consideration was given. This is usually rather difficult to do.

The original need for contracts formalized by a seal has long since passed. In those cases where the seal is still used, as in the case of contracts for the sale of real estate, it is no longer necessary to melt wax and to impress it with a signet ring or other private seal. It is sufficient if the person signing the contract attaches a red paper wafer, or simply writes the word *Seal* after his signature, or even simply the letters *L. S.* The letters *L. S.* stand for *locus sigilli,* meaning "the place of the seal." LOCUS SIGILLI

In the case of contracts for sale of goods, affixing a seal to a contract for sale or an offer to buy or sell goods does not constitute a sealed instrument, and the law with respect to sealed instruments does not apply. U.C.C. Sec. 2-203

What is a notary public?

Entirely apart from this use of the seal is the use, sometimes, of seals to indicate genuineness or authority. Such seals are the seal of a corporation, the seal of a public official, or a seal attached by a *notary public* (an official who certifies that the person signing an instrument is the person he purports to be). These seals indicating genuineness or authority should not be confused with the private seals we have been discussing that are used to create a formal contract. NOTARY PUBLIC

A PROMISE AS CONSIDERATION

EXAMPLE 4 **Suppose that you agree to sell your transistor radio to Carl Adams for $25. Carl agrees to buy it at that price. You have made a promise to sell. Carl has made a promise to buy. Each promise is consideration for the other.**

Why are mutual promises considered valid consideration?

When you agreed to sell, you placed a legal obligation upon yourself. That legal obligation is consideration for Carl's promise. In like manner, Carl assumed a legal obligation with his promise to buy, and that obligation is consideration for your promise to sell. This is the most common type of contract, and it causes very little trouble because the mutual promises automatically assume the nature of consideration and so provide that essential element of an enforceable contract.

PLEDGES AND SUBSCRIPTIONS

● Citizens and business firms are frequently asked to sign pledges or subscriptions to support worthy community projects. As these community projects are usually charitable in their nature and, therefore, working in the public interest, the courts will usually try to find some way in which

NOTE: *The bullet indicates that there may be a state statute that varies from the law discussed here.*

In most states, promises to make gifts to charitable institutions are enforceable if the institution makes commitments relying on the promised gift.

to enforce these pledges or subscriptions, even though technically they are promises to make a gift and are, therefore, not based on a formal consideration. Not all courts find consideration for these pledges or subscriptions in the same way. Some courts hold that the promises of other persons who have subscribed to the same fund amount to consideration. Others hold that, if the charitable institution has been injured through relying on such subscriptions, they are enforceable. Still others hold that there is an implied promise on the part of the institution to use the funds in the manner designated, and this amounts to consideration.

In what ways do the courts interpret pledges or subscriptions as promises?

ADEQUACY OF CONSIDERATION

EXAMPLE 5   Suppose that William Turner sees a statuette in an antique shop belonging to Henry Powers. He thinks that the figure is a rare piece worth a large sum of money. He offers Henry $250 for the statuette and Henry accepts. Later, William discovers that he was mistaken and that the figure is a cheap import worth not more than $10. He refuses to keep his bargain, claiming that there was no consideration for his promise.

William will have to pay. He got what he asked for. If, for example, Henry had falsely represented to William that the statuette was a genuine antique and very valuable, the inadequacy of the consideration could be used along with other evidence to show fraud on Henry's part. The contract would be set aside on the grounds of fraud.

How would you define unconscionable?

A court may refuse to enforce a contract or any clause of it that it deems *unconscionable;* that is, where the consideration is ridiculously inadequate. If a court as a matter of law finds a contract or any clause of a contract to have been unconscionable at the time it was made, the court may (1) refuse to enforce the contract, or (2) it may enforce the contract minus the unconscionable clause, or (3) it may so limit the application of any unconscionable clause as to avoid any unconscionable result. U.C.C. Sec. 2-302

UNCONSCIONABLE

What may a court do if it deems a contract to be unconscionable?

When it is claimed or appears to the court that the contract may be unconscionable, the parties are given a reasonable opportunity to present evidence as to the commercial setting, purpose, and effect of the contract in order to aid the court in making a decision.

A purchased article need not be adequate in value to the price paid. If the court finds the purchase contract to have been unconscionable at the time it was made, however, the court may refuse to enforce it.

Doing something you are already legally bound to do does not constitute consideration for a new contract.

SPECIAL APPLICATIONS OF CONSIDERATION

"A promise must create a new obligation." What does this mean?

Each promise made as consideration for another promise must create a new obligation. If you promise to do something you are already legally bound to do, your promise does not create a new obligation and is not valid consideration.

PART PAYMENT OF A DEBT

EXAMPLE 6   Roger Bolton owes Guy Light $200. Roger admits that the money is owed honestly and that payment is overdue. Guy is pressuring Roger for payment and states, "If you will pay me $175, I will cancel the debt for $200." Roger paid the $175 because he relied on Guy's promise. The following day Guy sued Roger for the remaining $25.

Roger will have to pay the $25. Guy's promise to forgive the balance is not binding on him because there was no consideration for it. "Why not?" you ask. "Roger paid the $175 relying on Guy's promise." The answer is that Roger already owed the $175. He was not doing anything that he was not already legally bound to do.

Is a promise by a creditor to forgive the balance of a debt ever valid?

If the release had been in writing and signed by Guy, it would have been valid. Most state laws hold that a promise to forgive the balance of a debt is valid if it is in writing and signed by the creditor. U.C.C. Sec. 2-209(1)

SETTLEMENT OF DISPUTED CLAIMS

Suppose, however, that there is an honest difference of opinion as to how much is owed.

EXAMPLE 7   Clarence claims that Terry owes him $100 for services, but Terry maintains that he owes only $50. Clarence thinks that his services were worth $100. Terry thinks that they were worth only $50. If Terry compromises on $75, each has given up something and the agreement is binding.

This happens many times, particularly in contracts for services. When you call a plumber or take your car to a garage for repairs, unless a price is agreed on before the work is done, you are implying that you promise to pay the reasonable value of the services.

EXTENSION OF TIME FOR PAYMENT

EXAMPLE 8 **Assume that Terry owes an agreed amount of $100. Assume also that it is now due and payable but that Terry does not have the money. Clarence promises to extend the time of payment thirty days if Terry will agree to pay at that time. Terry gives his promise, but the next day Clarence sues him anyway.**

Clarence is not bound by his promise to extend the time of payment. Terry promised nothing new, and thus there is no consideration for the promised extension. Some states have changed this rule by statute. Learn whether your state has a special statute on this.

CONSIDERATION IN YOUR EVERYDAY LIFE

The promises, acts, and forbearances that occur in your everyday life and that amount to consideration are endless. The following are examples that pertain to the application of consideration to everyday situations:

A debt is paid in advance for a lesser amount than is due. Is the earlier payment considered valid consideration for the reduced payment?

1. To amount to consideration, the act done or promised must be legal and not contemplate the violation of the law.
2. If a person pays a debt in advance, he is doing something he is not legally bound to do, and this would amount to consideration for settling the debt for a lesser amount.
3. If a person has made a gift in the past, has performed services in the past as a gift, or has been paid for past services, he may not use these past performances as consideration for a new promise.

SUGGESTIONS FOR MINIMIZING LEGAL RISKS

1. Carefully analyze all your contractual obligations to determine whether the requirement of valid consideration is present.
2. Consult legal counsel on important agreements when you are in doubt about the nature or validity of the consideration.
3. If you are promised a gift, do not rely on getting it unless you promise something or do something that can be interpreted as a new obligation on your part.
4. Obtain a statement in writing, signed by the promisor, in case (1) a promise to pay extra compensation is given, or (2) an agreement is reached on settling a disputed claim for less than the full amount.
5. Obtain a written statement, signed by the creditor, in case (1) you agree to settle a past-due debt for less than the full amount, or (2) you are promised additional time in which to pay an existing debt, and you do not provide additional consideration.

△ APPLYING YOUR LEARNING

QUESTIONS AND PROBLEMS

1. What is meant by consideration? What are the most common forms of consideration?
2. Illustrate an agreement that is not enforceable due to lack of consideration.
3. Why is a promise of a gift not enforceable? What is the legal status of a gift that has already been given? Can one be forced to return a gift?
4. Ordinarily, are the courts interested in the value of the consideration to see that it is equal to the promise in value? Under what circumstances may a court refuse to enforce a contract on the grounds of inadequacy of consideration?
5. In what types of contracts might the courts inquire into the value of the consideration? Give an illustration of such a contract.
6. Under what conditions may a debt be discharged by paying an amount less than the original debt?
7. What is the legal effect of a seal?
8. How may one bind an oral agreement to extend the time payment of a debt? Explain.
9. Under what conditions are pledges or subscriptions usually held to be enforceable promises?

WHAT IS YOUR OPINION?

In each of the following cases, give your decision and state a legal principle that applies to the case.

1. Corning promised to give his daughter a watch as a birthday present. Was this a legally enforceable promise?
2. Harper delivered a colt to Dorr as a gift but later demanded its return on the grounds that Dorr gave no consideration. Can Harper recover the colt?
3. Waring accepted a used automobile from Grant in full settlement of an $800 debt. Waring found out shortly afterward that the automobile was worth no more than $500. Did he have a claim against Grant for $300 on the basis of fraud?
4. Johnston became annoyed at his neighbor Burnside and offered a hoodlum $1,000 if he would steal and wreck Burnside's automobile. The hoodlum wrecked the car, as agreed, and then demanded the $1,000 from Johnston. Johnston refused to pay. Can the hoodlum collect the $1,000 through legal proceedings?
5. Strong claimed that Perkins owed him $250, but Perkins claimed that the debt was only $220. Finally, Strong agreed to accept $235 in full settlement. After Perkins had paid the $235, it was found that the true debt was $250. Was Strong legally entitled to an additional $15?
6. Burton accepted $100 from Larkin in full settlement of a past-due note

of $150 and gave him a signed release of the entire debt. Is the debt entirely canceled? Would your answer be different if there were no signed release?

7. Porter owes Watson $200. When the debt is due, Porter offers Watson $150 in cash and a watch worth about $25 in full settlement. Watson accepts. Is the entire debt canceled?

8. Miller, who had been injured by Wilson's automobile, agreed not to sue Wilson if Wilson would promise to pay him $1,000. Wilson promised. Was he legally bound to his promise?

9. Carson's car ran out of gas. Grover, driving by, saw Carson's predicament and offered to tow him to the next filling station. Carson accepted the offer; and after they reached the filling station, Carson said he would send Grover a check for $5 for his kindness. Is he legally bound to do so?

10. Lowe left his car at the Browning Garage for a motor tune-up and agreed to pay $20 for the job. Before the job was completed, Lowe said to the proprietor, "I'll pay you $10 extra if you do a good job." Is Lowe bound on his promise?

11. Pratt promised his son $2,000 if he would enter and complete medical school. The son completed the course. Was he legally entitled to the $2,000?

12. Baker's debt to Martin was due on June 1, 1973. Martin signed a written promise on May 20, 1973, to give Baker an additional two months to pay the debt. Was this promise binding?

THE LAW IN ACTION

1. An aunt made the following statement to her nephew: "I want you to come to my funeral. If you will agree to come and attend my funeral, if you outlive me, I will give you $500 and pay all expenses." The nephew promised to do so and lived up to his promise. The executor of the aunt's estate refused to pay the $500, claiming that there was no consideration for the promise. Was there consideration for the aunt's promise to pay $500? What was it, if any? (Earle v. Angell, 157 Mass. 294, 32 N.E. 164)

2. The plaintiff had cared for the defendant's adult son at a time when the son was ill and far from home. After the care had been gratuitously given, the defendant promised to pay the plaintiff for his services. Later the defendant refused to pay, claiming that there was no consideration for his promise. Is the defendant correct in his contention? (Mills v. Wyman, 3 Pickering [Mass.] 207)

KEY TO "WHAT'S THE LAW?" Page 83

1. *Yes. Cora could sue for breach of contract. This might not be the wisest procedure under the circumstances, but she has entered into a valid, enforceable contract with her uncle. Her continuance in school and graduation were consideration for her uncle's promise.*

2. *No. You cannot do anything. Your uncle's promise was a result of past performance on your part. You gave no new consideration for his promise.*

WHAT'S THE LAW?

1. *Jack Michaelson needed money. It was four days before payday, and he had an important date. Jack offered to give his friend Edward Everhardt $1 if Edward would lend him $10 until payday. Was there anything illegal in this transaction?*

---

2. *Art Buckley offered a pair of skis for sale to four of his friends, stating that he would sell them to the highest bidder. Tom Rich went to the others and offered each of them $1 not to bid on the skis. Tom then bid half their value. Was this a legal agreement?*

▲ UNIT 11: LEGALITY OF SUBJECT MATTER

EXAMPLE 1 **Mason and Tompkins agreed to rob a bank and split the proceeds. Mason was to stand guard, and Tompkins was to blow the safe. Tompkins, however, double-crossed Mason. Mason brought an action, asking the court to force Tompkins to split up the "loot," as he had promised.**

Of course, this is a simple case to solve. The courts are established to enforce the law. They will not give any aid to the enforcement of an agreement the object of which is to violate the law.

LEGALITY OF PURPOSE

Legality of purpose is one of the basic requirements of a contract. An agreement that requires the performance of an act that is illegal is not enforceable as a contract. The subject matter of a contract must be legal.

What different meanings are given to subject matter in the law of contracts?

The term *subject matter* is used in different ways in the law of contracts. Sometimes subject matter means a *tangible object* (something you can touch or that occupies space). An automobile is an example of tangible subject matter. At other times subject matter may mean an act done or to be done, for example, the act of selling the car. At still other times, it may mean the promise or promises that constitute the bargain. As discussed in this Unit, subject matter will usually mean an act.

SUBJECT MATTER

TANGIBLE OBJECT

You have learned that one of the basic requirements of a valid contract is that the purpose of the agreement must be legal. It must be based on legal subject matter. An agreement that requires the performance of an act that is illegal is not enforceable as a contract.

REMEMBER: Subject matter may be a tangible object, a completed or uncompleted act, or a promise. The subject matter of a contract must be lawful, definite, and physically possible to perform.

ILLEGALITY OF PURPOSE

Contract agreements that propose to violate statute law are illegal. Contracts that the courts believe to be contrary to the general public interest are also illegal.

CONTRACTS THAT VIOLATE STATUTE LAW

Common types of contracts that violate statute law are usurious agreements, gambling agreements, agreements to violate licensing laws, and some Sunday agreements.

What is a usurious agreement?

Usurious Agreements If you agree to pay a higher rate of interest than the law permits, your agreement is usurious. Most states specify the maximum rate of interest that may be charged for the loan of money. Collecting more than the maximum legal rate is *usury*. A pressing need for money may make some people easy victims of loan sharks. Usury laws are designed to protect the public from this danger.

USURY

EXAMPLE 2 **Linda Chavez wants to purchase an automobile just after she becomes twenty-one years of age. In order to make the down payment, Linda borrows $200 from Robert Lightner. Linda promises to pay Robert $20 per month for 15 months, representing a payment of $300 for the use of $200—a ludicrously high interest rate.**

The law would not require Linda to pay the full $300. She has promised to pay a higher rate of interest than the law permits. The bargain is illegal, and the courts would not enforce it.

The legal rate of interest varies for different kinds of loans. The reason is that the risk taken by the lender may be different for different types of loans. For example, look at the difference between loans made by banks, personal-loan companies, and pawnshops. Always verify the most recent statute of your own state for recent changes or revisions in interest rates allowable for ordinary loans.

● Bank loans are usually made only when some guarantee, such as a mortgage or other collateral, is given to secure the repayment of the loan. As the bank's risk is small in such cases, the rate of interest is relatively low. Personal-loan companies demand less security and charge a higher rate of interest. A legal rate of $2\frac{1}{2}$ percent a month is quite common on loans made by these companies. Pawnbrokers run a greater risk and are allowed to charge higher interest.

Do usury laws apply to credit sales or installment sales?

Usury laws do not fully protect the consumer when goods are bought on credit or are purchased on time-payment plans. You should understand that usury laws apply only to a loan of money. However, the Truth in Lending Act, which will be discussed more fully in Unit 21, is one step taken by the federal government to make the consumer aware of the cost of credit. The merchant or lender must now indicate the annual percentage rate charged on each installment sale or loan.

NOTE: *The bullet indicates that there may be a state statute that varies from the law discussed here. Whenever you see this bullet, find out, if possible, what the statute is in your state covering this point or principle of law.*

Do not jump to the conclusion that all banks and merchants who extend credit are robbing you. Remember that they are entitled to a fair return for the use of their money. Also remember that there are risks involved. Sometimes people do not return money borrowed or do not pay for items purchased on credit. Before you sign any credit or loan agreement, be sure to take advantage of the protection provided by the Truth in Lending Act and look for a statement of the true rate of interest.

Gambling Agreements   Another type of illegal agreement prohibited by statute is a gambling agreement. If you bet on the results of a basketball game, you know without being told that you could not collect in court if you won your bet.

Do any states permit some types of gambling?

● Some types of gambling have been licensed in a few states, for example, parimutuel betting in New York State, Illinois, California, and some other states. This does not mean that all gambling is legal in these states. It is only the licensed types that are legal and then only when conducted strictly in accordance with the license. Lotteries are a form of gambling and are considered illegal in many states, although legalized lotteries have been gaining acceptance. Of course, as untapped sources for additional revenue are sought by governmental bodies, other states may follow the lead of these states in making some types of gambling legal.

Wagering contracts are illegal in most states, and the courts will not aid in the collection of a debt which has been incurred as a result of a wager.

Agreements to Violate Licensing Laws   To engage in certain trades or professions, a person is required by law to have a *license*—a legal document stating that the holder has permission from the proper authorities to carry on a certain business or profession. To engage in such a business or profession without a license is illegal.

LICENSE

EXAMPLE 3   Walter Jarvie went to work as a plumber. He purchased some new plumbing tools and contracted to install a new shower for Joe Smith. Jarvie installed the shower exactly as the contract required. He believes he has completed a good job adhering to all specifications. Smith, however, refuses to pay Jarvie.

● Jarvie cannot collect for his work. The law requires that a person have a license in order to engage in the plumbing business, and Jarvie did not have such a license. His contract was illegal, and the courts will not aid him in the collection of his money.

For the protection of the public, a license is required to engage in some trades and professions. A contract to give such service when you do not possess such a license is unenforceable.

Is an agreement made on Sunday illegal even if the work is to be done on some other day in the week?

● **Sunday Agreements**   In many states it is illegal to do certain types of work on Sunday. An agreement to perform the prohibited work on Sunday would be illegal. If the agreement is made on Sunday but the labor is to be done on some other day in the week, the contract is enforceable.

CONTRACTS CONTRARY TO PUBLIC POLICY

An agreement that requires the performance of an act that is detrimental or harmful to the public welfare is considered to be *contrary to public policy*, even though the act in itself may not be illegal. Such agreements are unenforceable.

CONTRARY TO PUBLIC POLICY

Agreements in Unreasonable Restraint of Trade   *Restraint of trade* means the elimination of competition with the intent to control prices.

RESTRAINT OF TRADE

OUTRIGHT CONTRACTS NOT TO COMPETE   Even though outright contracts not to compete are illegal, in some cases a reasonable restraint is allowed. In the sale of a business, for example, it is quite common to restrain the seller from engaging in a competitive business for a reasonable period of time. This is understandable. The buyer often pays a substantial price for the *goodwill* (the public approval and patronage) of the business. The buyer of the business is entitled to the protection of that goodwill. The seller may not be restrained from business activity for a longer period of time than is necessary to protect the sale, nor can he be restrained over too great an area. If the restraint is unreasonable considering the nature of the business sold, then the restraint is illegal and unenforceable.

What is goodwill?

GOODWILL

AGREEMENTS TO DEFEAT COMPETITIVE BIDDING   In auction sales and in certain other types of contracts, competitive bidding is vitally important, If, before the bids are made, the bidders get together and agree not to bid more than a certain price, they are not playing fair. The resulting contract is not enforceable. It is not a result of open and competitive bidding. The bidders' agreements are also not enforceable.

Agreements Interfering With Operation of the Courts   Any contract that tends to interfere with the administration of justice is illegal. Thus, an agreement to pay a lay witness to testify at a trial is unenforceable. A *lay witness* is one who testifies as to the facts of the case. Witnesses are paid a regular fee by the courts to compensate them for their time. An agreement by one of the parties to pay the witness an additional amount might color the witness's testimony. *Expert witnesses* are sometimes called

LAY WITNESS

EXPERT WITNESS

to testify as to technical matters. These witnesses are paid by the party calling them, and they may testify only on general principles, not on the facts of the case.

Agreements Inducing Breach of Private or Public Duty Many persons hold positions of trust. This means that they have a responsibility for the well-being of other people. Your congressmen, your state representative, and all other public officials come within this class. They owe a duty to work for the best interest of the public. Any contract that attempts to influence these public officials to use their position for private gain is unenforceable. This rule applies to private persons in positions of trust as well as to public officials.

Agreements Tending to Defraud Another An act committed with the intention of injuring someone is a *civil wrong,* or a tort, even though the act itself may not be a crime. A tort, or a civil wrong, is any violation of a person's rights. For example, a contract to defraud a third person or to injure him in other ways would be a civil wrong, or a tort. The courts will not enforce such wrongful agreements.

CIVIL WRONG

Will the courts ever enforce a contract that results in a civil wrong?

Agreements Interfering With Marriage The law encourages marriages and protects family relationships. A contract that would have the effect of discouraging or interfering with good family relationships may be illegal and, therefore, unenforceable in the courts.

EXAMPLE 4 **If a father promises to give his daughter $1,000 if she does not get married, the contract would not be enforceable. The same would be true if the father promised $1,000 to a married daughter if she would leave her husband.**

THE EFFECT OF ILLEGALITY

You have already learned that the courts will not enforce an illegal agreement.

Where illegality appears, the court will take no action in the interest of either party.

Thus, if you have paid money under an illegal agreement, you cannot get it back. However, if one of the parties is ignorant of the facts that make the bargain illegal, the courts may hear his case.

EXAMPLE 5 **Martin Reston sold some cattle to Bob Richardson. The cattle were all diseased, which would prohibit the sale of such animals under the state health laws. Richardson did not know that the cattle he purchased were diseased.**

This would be an illegal contract; but, since Richardson did not know that the cattle were diseased, he can probably get his money back.

There might be a case in which only part of the contract is illegal. If the legal part can be separated from the illegal part, the legal part can be enforced. In the illustration given about the plumbing job, for example, the sale of the plumbing equipment and materials would be legal; and the seller could collect for the selling price of these things. It was the labor contract that was illegal because the plumber had no license; so this part would be uncollectible.

REMEMBER: Don't take chances. If an agreement is illegal, don't get involved in the agreement.

SUGGESTIONS FOR MINIMIZING LEGAL RISKS

1. When in doubt regarding the legality of the subject matter of an important agreement, consult an attorney before you sign.
2. Remember that virtually all gambling and wagering agreements are illegal in most states and that the courts will not enforce such agreements.
3. Become sufficiently familiar with the statutes of your own state so that you will know which types of agreements are considered illegal in your state.
4. Where a license is required to perform services, obtain the license; otherwise, you may not be able to enforce a claim for your services.
5. You run a grave risk of losing your reputation or possibly becoming a subject for blackmail if you enter into an agreement to commit a crime or into one that is contrary to public policy. Don't take such chances!

 # APPLYING YOUR LEARNING

QUESTIONS AND PROBLEMS

1. The subject matter must meet certain requirements in order to have an enforceable contract. What are these requirements?
2. Name several types of agreements that would not be enforceable because the subject matter is in violation of statute law.
3. What is meant by usury? How may this differ in the various states?
4. Name several types of gambling agreements that are not enforceable in your state. Are there any types that are legal in your state? If so, name them.
5. What are some trades or professions that require a license in your state or community?
6. What is meant by agreements that are contrary to public policy? Name several types of agreements that fall into this class.
7. What is meant by unreasonable restraint of trade? Give an example.
8. Give several examples of agreements that might interfere with the operation of the courts. Why are these frowned upon and rightly so?
9. What is meant by the breach of a private or a public duty? Give some examples of agreements that would not be enforceable.
10. What do the courts generally do regarding agreements that are illegal?
11. Under what conditions may the court assist someone even though an agreement is illegal? Give examples.

WHAT IS YOUR OPINION?

In each of the following cases, give your decision and state a legal principle that applies to the case.

1. Seaton purchased some illegal drugs from Parker, giving Parker a promissory note for $500 in payment. Could Parker enforce payment of the note in the courts?

2. Armstrong agreed to sell Karper an automobile for $2,000 and a sub-machine gun for $500. There is a law that prohibits the sale of sub-machine guns. If Armstrong fails to carry out his promises, what rights does Karper have?

3. Smith promised to pay Wilson $10,000 if Wilson would destroy some evidence needed in a criminal case against Smith. Wilson destroyed the evidence. When Smith refused to pay the $10,000, Wilson sued for the amount promised. Is he entitled to judgment?

4. A state statute requires real estate brokers to obtain a license. Burke, without getting a license, engages in buying and selling real estate for others. He sues one of his clients for a fee. Is he entitled to judgment?

5. Beam promised $10,000 to an assemblyman if he would influence the legislature to enact a certain law. Was this an enforceable agreement?

6. Hope sold Ames his camera repair shop located in Rochester, New York. In the contract Hope agreed never to engage in a similar business in New York State. Two years later Hope opened a camera repair shop in New York City. Was he liable for breach of contract?

7. Mower, a defendant, promised to pay $300 to Dorsey if he would testify falsely for Mower at his trial. Dorsey testified as agreed. Was he legally entitled to the $300?

8. Perkins promised his daughter $10,000 if she would never marry. Was she entitled to collect this amount from his estate when he died if she had not married?

9. Long sold his retail drugstore in Buffalo, New York, to Rand. In the contract he agreed not to engage in the same type of business in the state of New York for a period of ten years. Was this agreement binding?

10. Beecher purchased some wild game from Webster in violation of a state statute prohibiting such sales. Beecher decided several hours later that he had made a bad bargain and asked Webster to refund his money. Webster refused. Could Beecher expect the aid of a court in obtaining a return of the purchase price?

11. Black, a manufacturer, entered into an agreement with Weston, a retail merchant, whereby Weston was not to sell Black's product at less than a given price. Weston cut the agreed price, and Black sued him for breach of contract. Weston contended that the agreement was illegal. Was his defense valid?

12. Gardner, a 4-H member, bought from Park a calf that was supposed to have been vaccinated, according to state statute, against certain

diseases. When Gardner discovered that the calf had not been vaccinated, he demanded the return of the purchase price, in turn offering to return the calf to Park. Park refused. Will the courts help Gardner get back his purchase money?

THE LAW IN ACTION

1. The plaintiff sold intoxicating liquors to the defendant on credit in a state where such a sale was legal. The defendant shipped the liquor into a dry state where its sale was illegal. The defendant did not pay for the goods. When sued, the defendant claimed that the contract of purchase was illegal because the plaintiff could have suspected that the liquors were to be resold illegally. Was the defendant correct? (Graves v. Johnson, 156 Mass. 211, 30 N.E. 818)
2. The defendant leased certain property to the plaintiff and warranted that there were no zoning laws that would prohibit the use of the premises for manufacturing purposes. There actually were zoning laws that would prohibit such use, and the plaintiff sued the defendant for damages arising from the defendant's breach of warranty. The defendant claimed as a defense that he could not be sued because the contract was illegal. What is your opinion? (Municipal Metallic Bed Mfg. Corp. v. Dobbs, 253 N.Y. 313, 171 N.E. 75)

KEY TO "WHAT'S THE LAW?" Page 91

1. *Yes. This transaction is usurious because the interest rate is 10 percent. This is higher than most statutes allow.*
2. *No. This was an attempt to interfere with competitive bidding and thus was contrary to public policy.*

WHAT'S THE LAW?

1. *Pete Jurges orally contracted to buy Bill Barto's bicycle for $40. Is it necessary that this contract be in writing in order that the agreement may be enforced?*

2. *Suppose that in the preceding situation it was an automobile instead of a bicycle and that the price was $600. Would your answer be different?*

◮ UNIT 12: FORM OF AGREEMENT

"You can't sue me. Our agreement was not in writing." This was Pete's answer when Bill threatened to sue him for breach of contract. Was Pete right or wrong? It depends on the nature of their contract.

DESIRABILITY OF WRITTEN AGREEMENTS

Why should all important contracts be in writing.

All important contracts should be in writing. You realize, of course, that it would be foolish to demand a written instrument for every trivial agreement, but that is not the case with important agreements. Here are some reasons why your important agreements should be written and expressed in clear language: (1) There can be no argument later as to the terms or your misunderstanding them, (2) you are more likely to consider all the terms more carefully, and (3) it is much easier to prove your case in court in the event of a lawsuit.

Why is it important that all written contracts be made definite and certain?

When you put your contracts in writing, remember to make them definite and certain. This is important because, when an agreement is put into writing, the parties to the agreement are bound by its terms.

THE PAROL EVIDENCE RULE

If a lawsuit is brought on a written contract, the parties cannot change the terms by means of oral evidence that is contradictory to the terms in writing. *Evidence*, in this instance, means proof presented at a court trial. The rule that disallows the introduction of oral evidence is known as the *parol,* or oral *evidence rule.*

EVIDENCE

PAROL EVIDENCE RULE

REMEMBER: You may not change the terms of a clearly written agreement by oral statements. U.C.C. Sec. 2-202

EXAMPLE 1 **Suppose that you enter into a clearly stated, definite written agreement with Ralph McAuliffe. You agree to sell your deer rifle to him for $75, and he agrees to buy the rifle for your price. The written statement confirms this and no more. You cannot later on contend that McAuliffe had orally promised to pay you an extra $15. You are bound by the written agreement.**

Under what conditions may oral evidence be introduced?

Oral evidence may be introduced if its sole purpose is to clarify some point that is not clear in a written agreement. Terms may not be contradicted by oral evidence but may be explained or supplemented. U.C.C. Sec. 2-202

EXAMPLE 2 **The Standard Music Company sold a color television set and included in its written agreement a 90-day guarantee of the set. Within the guarantee period, two of the tubes burned out, and the purchaser sought their replacement under the guarantee. The seller refused, claiming that the guarantee covered only the set, not the tubes.**

What is meant by custom of the marketplace?

Oral evidence may be introduced in an attempt to determine whether the written guarantee covers both the set and the tubes or only the set. The general practice of persons engaged in the sale of television sets may be introduced to indicate the *custom of the marketplace.* U.C.C. Sec. 2-202(a) If it is found that the custom of the business is to guarantee only the set, the tubes would not be covered. The terms of an agreement may be interpreted and applied in accordance with business custom, but when such interpretation is unreasonable, express terms control performance. U.C.C. Sec. 2-208(2)

CUSTOM OF THE MARKETPLACE

REQUIREMENT FOR WRITTEN AGREEMENT

All contracts are easier to prove in court if they are in writing. To prove some types of contracts, the courts require written evidence.

You may ask, "Why some types of agreements and not others?" The answer is somewhat historical. The early English courts learned that contracting parties were more likely to commit *perjury*—to make false statements in court under oath—in proving certain agreements. Therefore, an early English statute provided that five types of agreements must be proved by written evidence. This statute, called the *Statute of Frauds,* has been adopted, with modification, in all fifty states.

What is perjury.

PERJURY

STATUTE OF FRAUDS

● Some states have added other types of agreements to the original five classes. You should consult the statutes of your own state to find out what additional classes of contracts must be in writing.

Under the Statute of Frauds, what types of contracts must be proved by written evidence?

CONTRACTS THAT MUST BE IN WRITING

The five classes of contracts that must be in writing are (1) contracts to pay the debts of others, (2) contracts in consideration of marriage, (3) contracts to sell an interest in real property, (4) contracts requiring more than a year to perform, and (5) some contracts to sell personal property.

NOTE: *The bullet indicates that there may be a state statute that varies from the law discussed here.*

If you make an original promise to pay for something and it is expected that you and you alone will pay, your promise does not have to be in writing to be enforceable.

Contracts to Pay Debts of Others   An oral promise to pay the debts of someone else is not enforceable.

EXAMPLE 3   Roland Jackson's uncle took him into a clothing store and said to the merchant, "If you will sell this young man a suit of clothes on credit, I will pay you if he doesn't."

The merchant would be wise to get such a promise in writing. If he does not, Roland's uncle could not be sued to enforce his promise. This is a promise to pay the debt of someone else, and the law would require written evidence to prove the promise in court.

If Roland's uncle had said, "Give this young man a suit of clothes and charge it to me," no writing would be required. This would be the uncle's own debt from the beginning. It was never implied that Roland would pay. Thus, the uncle is not promising to pay someone else's debt, and no writing is required.

Contracts in Consideration of Marriage   Contracts in consideration of marriage are not common in our modern American law. They are a holdover from old English customs and rarely arise today.

EXAMPLE 4   James Goble orally promised Martha Brooks $10,000 if she would marry him. Is this an enforceable contract?

No. The contract would have to be in writing to be enforceable. When two persons, however, mutually agree to marry without consideration, they do not need to put their agreement in writing. Such agreements to marry do not, and never did, require a written contract.

Contracts to Sell an Interest in Real Property   *Real property* may be loosely defined as land and the things that are permanently attached to it. Agreements that deal with real property must be in writing. Real-property contracts are important. Many times, these contracts must be filed in a public office in order to protect the owner's rights. An oral agreement just will not do.

REAL PROPERTY

Contracts Requiring More Than a Year to Perform   The law requires all contracts to be written if they cannot be performed within one year from the date of their making.

Will the courts enforce an oral agreement that can be performed in six months? in eighteen months?

EXAMPLE 5   Suppose that on the first day of May you entered into an oral contract with Amos Tucker. The contract provided, among other things, that you were to work for one year and that you were to begin work on the first day of the next month.

This contract must be in writing. It is obvious that you cannot completely perform it in less than thirteen months from the day you entered into your agreement. You must remember, however, that the written requirement applies only to contracts that cannot possibly be performed within a year of their making.

EXAMPLE 6   If you had contracted to work for Amos Tucker for "as long as Tucker remains president of the Tucker Company," your agreement would not have to be in writing.

The time here is uncertain. Tucker might continue to be president of the Tucker Company for many, many years; on the other hand, he might be president for only a few months longer. The contract, therefore, could be completed in less than a year. It is the possibility of performance within a year that is the deciding factor.

Some Contracts to Sell Personal Property   *Personal property* consists of movable property, such as furniture, books, livestock, cultivated crops, stocks, bonds, and all personal effects of any kind. A contract for the sale of goods (personal property) for the price of $500 or more is not enforceable unless there is some writing indicating that a contract of sale has been made between the parties and signed by the party against whom enforcement is sought or by his authorized agent. U.C.C. Sec. 2-201(1)

PERSONAL
PROPERTY

Is an oral contract to sell goods valued at $600 enforceable?

EXAMPLE 7   Hilton entered into an agreement with a friend for the purchase of the friend's automobile for $950. This agreement was "a gentleman's agreement" and was not in writing. A short time later, Hilton changed his mind and so notified his friend. Although seriously intended and made with mutual assent, the agreement was not enforceable because there was no written contract.

WHAT THE WRITING MUST CONTAIN

What are the essential parts of a contract that must be reduced to writing?

The entire contract is not required to be in writing—only the essential parts. Usually, it is sufficient if the writing identifies (1) the subject matter, (2) the parties, (3) the price and terms, if any, and (4) the respective intent of the parties to contract. Furthermore, it must be signed by the party

All written contracts should be definite and certain. The concerned parties to the agreement must then abide by its terms. If any essential part is not included, the contract will not be valid.

against whom it is to be used as evidence. U.C.C. Sec. 2-201(1) U.C.C. Sec. 2-204(3) This means that, if you were seeking to enforce your contract with Amos Tucker, it would have to be signed by him. If, however, Tucker were seeking to enforce the contract against you, the writing would have to be signed by you.

Who must sign the written agreement?

You must remember that here we are talking about the written evidence necessary to prove a contract. It is common practice, of course, when a contract is completely reduced to writing, to make two copies and have each copy signed by both parties.

REMEMBER: Get your important contracts in writing if you wish to avoid difficulty and expense in enforcing them.

SUGGESTIONS FOR MINIMIZING LEGAL RISKS

1. Remember that certain types of contracts must be in writing to be enforceable. If in doubt about a particular contract, consult a lawyer for legal advice if the contract is important to you.
2. Because the sale or purchase of real property is ordinarily an important contract, be sure to have a lawyer draw up the contract so that it will specify all necessary details and terms for your protection.
3. Determine the minimum legal requirements in your state for written contracts involving the sale of personal property and endeavor to obtain written memoranda in each case involving more than the legal minimum.
4. If at all possible, obtain some written evidence of important agreements, even though the law does not require it. Written evidence will help you to prove your case if a future controversy arises.

APPLYING YOUR LEARNING

QUESTIONS AND PROBLEMS

1. What is the parol evidence rule?
2. Name at least five types of contracts that must be in writing.
3. Does your state specify certain additional types of contracts that must be in writing? Explain.
4. Give an illustration indicating how you might make a contract to pay the debt of another person. Under what circumstances would you be willing to carry out such an agreement even though the agreement was not in writing?

5. Can you think of possible illustrations of contracts in consideration of marriage? List and explain.

6. Give several illustrations of property that you believe would be classed as real property. Would all these require written contracts for purposes of sale or purchase? Explain why or why not.

7. Give several illustrations of property that you believe to be personal property. Under what conditions would a contract for the sale of these items have to be in writing.

8. Must the writing be a formally drawn instrument? What must the writing contain to be used as evidence?

9. Explain why many oral contracts that should have been in writing are honored by businessmen in their business dealings.

WHAT IS YOUR OPINION?

In each of the following cases, give your decision and state a legal principle that applies to the case.

1. On July 15, Trimble orally agreed to work for Burke until June 1 of the following year. Is this a valid contract?

2. By telephone, Bailey agreed to act for two years as manager of a store owned by Kline at a salary of $12,000. Is this a binding contract?

3. Cooper, meeting Ames on the street, orally agreed to sell him his summer home for $5,000. Was this an enforceable contract?

4. During a telephone conversation, Cook agreed to buy Rice's house for $8,000. Is this an enforceable agreement?

5. Ruth agreed in writing to sell Rich a piece of land adjoining the latter's factory. When the delivery date came, Ruth refused to convey the land and offered to pay Rich any reasonable money damages. As Rich needed the land to expand his plant, he refused to accept money damages and brought suit for specific performance. Will he succeed?

6. Larson promised Little $10,000 if he would marry Larson's niece. Little married the niece, but Larson refused to pay the promised sum. Could Little enforce the promise against Larson?

7. Norton orally agreed to sell his farm to Dillon for $10,000. He gave Dillon a written memorandum as follows: "On this date I hereby agree to sell my farm to E. J. Dillon for $10,000, A. R. Norton." Dillon later refused to carry out the agreement. May Norton begin an action for breach of contract?

8. Beck made an oral agreement to purchase a building lot from the Bitner Realty Company. At the same time he wrote a memorandum of the agreement, which he signed and gave to the realty company, although the company did not sign. When Beck failed to purchase the property as agreed, the Bitner Realty Company brought an action for damages. Was the realty company entitled to judgment?

9. On December 22, Black, a sales manager, orally agreed to work for Jones for one year, beginning January 1, at a salary of $14,800, payable in monthly payments. He worked for one month and then left of his own accord. Is he liable for damages?

THE LAW IN ACTION

1. The plaintiff had requested the defendant to extend credit to a certain employee of the plaintiff for meals. The plaintiff's words were, "Go ahead and let him continue to have meals, and I will pay for them if he doesn't." The plaintiff now contends that his promise is not enforceable because it was not in writing. Is he correct? (Johnson Co. v. City Cafe, 100 S.W. 2d 740)

2. The defendant had entered into an oral contract to marry the plaintiff after the plaintiff's son finished high school. The son was a freshman in high school at the time the agreement was made. Would this contract be enforceable? (Brock v. Button, 187 Wash. 27, 59 P. 2d 761)

KEY TO "WHAT'S THE LAW?" Page 99

1. *No. Contracts for the sale of goods must be in writing where the purchase price is $500 or more.*
2. *Yes. Here the purchase price would be more than $500.*

A DIGEST OF LEGAL CONCEPTS

1. In general, an agreement must be supported by consideration in order to be enforceable as a contract.

2. Promising to do or doing what one is already legally bound to do is not considered valid consideration.

3. Where a contract has been fully performed, evidence of consideration is not required.

4. A court may refuse to enforce a contract or any clause of it that it deems unconscionable.

5. The doing of or the promising to do an illegal act cannot be used as proof of sufficient consideration to support a contract.

6. An act previously performed, known as past consideration, will not support a promise as sufficient consideration.

7. Ordinarily, a promise to make a gift is not enforceable because of lack of consideration.

8. A promise is not sufficient consideration for another person's promise unless both promises impose new legal liabilities on the two promisors.

9. If a debt is not yet due, a mutual agreement to pay less than the full amount will ordinarily bar an action to recover the unpaid portion.

10. A settlement of a disputed claim for less than the full amount is ordinarily binding on the parties.

11. When property of uncertain value, or partial payment of money plus property, is taken in full payment of a debt, the debt is ordinarily considered paid in full.

12. A promise to pay extra compensation is binding by statute in some states if such promise is made in writing and signed by the party assuming the obligation, even without consideration.

13. The refraining, or forbearing, from bringing suit on a claim is valid consideration for a promise to pay money in settlement of such claim.

14. If a debt is already due, payment of less than the full amount will not bar recovery of the unpaid balance unless there is a state statute to the contrary.

15. The subject matter of a contract may be a tangible object, an act, or a promise.

A DIGEST OF LEGAL CONCEPTS

16. Contracts in violation of statute law are illegal and void.

17. Usurious contracts are unenforceable because they demand a greater rate of interest than is allowed by law.

18. Usurious contracts apply only to a loan of money.

19. The law usually allows a higher rate of interest on small unsecured loans.

20. Gambling agreements are illegal in most states. Some exceptions may be permitted by state statute.

21. Contracts to perform certain acts, if performed without a license where a license is required by law, are not enforceable.

22. No act that the law classifies as a crime can be the subject matter of a contract.

23. Contracts contrary to public policy are unenforceable.

24. Contracts in unreasonable restraint of trade are contrary to public policy and are unenforceable.

25. A contract for reasonable restraint of trade can be enforced if it deals with the sale of a business.

26. Outright contracts not to compete are contrary to public policy and are unenforceable.

27. Agreements to defeat competitive bidding are unenforceable.

28. A contract that tends to interfere with the administration of justice is illegal and is unenforceable.

29. Agreements inducing the breach of a public or private duty are illegal.

30. Agreements to commit a civil wrong, or tort, are unenforceable.

31. Agreements that interfere with marriage or family relationships are unenforceable.

32. The courts will not aid either party to an illegal agreement if both are equally wrong.

33. The courts will usually aid an innocent party who is defrauded by an illegal agreement.

34. Money paid under an illegal agreement cannot be recovered by court action if the parties are equally in the wrong.

PART 5: How Contracts Work

WHAT'S THE LAW?

1. *Seth Green owed John Hale $10. Can John sell his right to collect the money to Tom Carter?*

---

2. *Ben Cooper sold Peter Karnes a watch for $25 on credit. Ben stated that the watch was only one month old and had a 14-karat gold case. This was not true. The watch was many years old and virtually worn out. Ben assigned his right to collect the $25 to David Wilson, and David tried to collect from Peter. Can David collect the $25 from Peter?*

⏹ UNIT 13: OPERATION OF CONTRACTS

RIGHTS AND OBLIGATIONS

Ordinarily, only the original parties in a contract acquire rights. No one else has any right or interest.

EXAMPLE 1   Harold Hoover enters into a contract with Joe Nelson. The contract stipulates that Harold is to mow Nelson's lawn at least once a week and that Nelson in turn will pay Harold $7.50 per week. Nelson leaves for a vacation and is gone for a month, but he has paid Harold for mowing the lawn prior to his departure. Harold, however, does not mow the lawn. Sam Lovell, Joe Nelson's neighbor, threatens to sue Harold for not fulfilling his contractual agreement with Nelson.

Harold has broken his contract with Nelson, and Nelson may sue, but the matter is no concern of Lovell's. Lovell might argue that he received some benefit from a neatly trimmed yard next door, but this would be only an incidental benefit. Nelson did not have that in mind when he hired Harold, and Lovell did not acquire any enforceable rights by the contract.

May a third party ever acquire rights in a contract made by others?

Sometimes, a third person, who is called the *third party beneficiary*, may enforce a contract when it is made specifically for his benefit.

THIRD PARTY BENEFICIARY

EXAMPLE 2   Suppose that you owe Ralph Carter $25 for a radio you bought from him. Later, you sell your typewriter to Arthur King for $25. You and Arthur agree that, instead of Arthur's paying the $25 to you, he would pay it to Ralph. This arrangement would settle your account with Ralph as well as Arthur's debt to you.

Ralph now has a claim against Arthur as well as against you. He was not a party to your contract with Arthur, but it was made specifically for his benefit. If Arthur fails to pay the $25, Ralph can sue him.

If a father pays his son's college expenses with the understanding that the son will return the money to his younger brother when he is ready for college, the younger brother may enforce the contract.

ASSIGNMENT OF RIGHTS

How may a person acquire rights under a contract by assignment? Do these rights have monetary value?

People who are not parties to the original contract may sometimes acquire rights by assignment. The rights acquired under a contract have monetary value, and under certain circumstances, they may be sold and conveyed to someone else.

EXAMPLE 3   **If you buy a radio for cash from Ralph Carter, you get complete title to it. It is yours. You may do with it anything you choose. If you no longer want it, you may sell it, give it away, or exchange it for something you do want. Ralph no longer has any control over the radio.**

EXAMPLE 4   **On the other hand, suppose that you did not pay cash for the radio. Instead, you promised to pay Ralph $25 on the first of next month. Ralph now also owns something. He owns the right to collect $25 from you. He may sell this right, give it away, or exchange it for something he wants.**

What is meant by a notice of assignment? Is any special form required?

If a person who owes money receives notice that the debt has been assigned, will he be discharged from his obligation if he pays the debt to the assignor?

This transfer of a right, as contrasted with a transfer of goods, is called an *assignment*. The party who sells and transfers the right is called the *assignor*. The party who receives the right is called the *assignee*. U.C.C. Sec. 2-210(4)

ASSIGNMENT
ASSIGNOR
ASSIGNEE

How Rights May Be Conveyed   The law requires no particular form to convey a right by means of an assignment, but usually it should be in writing. An oral assignment might be legal, but it would be hard to prove.

Perhaps the most important reason for a written statement is this: The party who owes the money or other duty of performance is entitled to notice of the assignment. If he is not notified, he may pay the debt to the assignor. If he does pay the debt to the assignor, his obligation is terminated. If he has been notified of the assignment or, better still, if he is shown the written assignment, then he is legally bound to pay the assignee only, and payment to the assignor will not discharge his debt.

Some assignments are made automatically because of the provisions of certain statutes. All states have laws that deal with the settlement of a person's estate after his death.

Statute law also provides that when a person is adjudged a bankrupt, his property is automatically assigned to a trustee.

What Rights May Be Assigned Most rights are assignable, but some are not. Remember, there are three parties to an assignment: the assignor, the assignee, and the third party who owes the debt or obligation.

May the rights of
a third party be
changed by an
assignment?

REMEMBER: You may not change the rights or obligations of the third party by an assignment.

If the rights of the third party would be changed in any way, the contract is not assignable. If his rights would not be changed, the contract is assignable. U.C.C. Sec. 2-210(2)

EXAMPLE 5 **Suppose that, in Example 1, Joe Nelson decides at the last minute that he does not wish to have his grass cut while he is on his vacation. He might contend that, because he has a right to Harold's services, he can sell those services to his neighbor, Lovell.**

This he cannot do. Harold's obligations would be changed. He had agreed to mow Nelson's yard only. Lovell's yard might be bigger. Also, Harold has a right to choose his employer, and he may not wish to work for Lovell. This is a contract for personal services, and such contracts are never assignable.

May contracts for
personal services
ever be assigned?

But you ask, "Suppose that it is all right with Harold? Maybe he would like to work for Lovell." If it is all right with Harold, then a three-party deal may be worked out in which Lovell is subsituted for Nelson. An agreement of this kind is called a *novation*. A novation is the substitution of a new obligation for an old one, which thereby invalidates the old obligation. The term novation may also apply to a substitution of a new type of performance. Nelson and Harold, for example, might agree that, instead of mowing the grass, Harold might spade up the garden and get the agreed amount of pay.

What type of
agreement results
in a novation?

NOVATION

Contracts involving personal services are not assignable with the sale of a business.

EXAMPLE 6 When Ralph Carter sold you the radio in Example 4, he guaranteed it to be in perfect shape. He further promised that he would pay for any repairs necessary within the next thirty days. Within the 30-day period, two tubes burned out. It cost you $5 to replace these tubes.

You now have a claim against Ralph for $5, and you may rightfully deduct this from your debt and pay Ralph only $20. If, before the purchase price was due, Ralph assigned his right to collect the $25 to Lester Thomas, you could deduct the $5 when Lester came to collect. Ralph had a net claim of only $20; thus, all he could sell to Lester was a net claim of $20.

| You can never assign a greater right than the right that you possess. |

DELEGATION OF DUTIES

May duties ever be transferred to someone else? What is meant by a delegation of duties?

In every contract there are duties as well as rights. Harold Hoover had a right to collect $7.50 a week for his labor, but he also owed a duty to cut the grass. Nelson had a right to have his grass cut, but he also owed a duty to pay Harold $7.50 a week. Duties may at times be transferred to someone else. This transfer of a duty is called a *delegation*.

DELEGATION

| You may not delegate a duty if it will change the other party's rights. |

Thus, Harold cannot delegate his duty to cut the grass to Tom Allen. Nelson contracted for Harold's services. Allen might cut the grass faster, but not so well as Harold.

It is not often that a duty may be delegated, because a duty usually requires personal performance. It is possible, however, in some contracts.

EXAMPLE 7 Killbasa is in business for himself as a contractor only. He does not promise Thomas that he will mow the lawn himself; he promises only that he will guarantee the mowing of the lawn for $7.50 per week. Killbasa is a busy contractor. He enters into similar contracts with many people. His hired men then perform the lawn-mowing labor.

If this fact is understood by the property owners, it is perfectly all right to delegate the duty of doing the work to someone else. This is really a form of subcontracting and occurs many times in business contracts. It is quite common, for example, in building contracts.

An assignment of a contract is an assignment of rights and is a delegation of performance of the assignor's duties, and its acceptance by the assignee constitutes a promise by him to perform the assignor's duties. This promise is enforceable by either the assignor or the other party to the original contract. U.C.C. Sec. 2-210(4)

When the offeror and the offeree include in their contract an agreement that the contract may not be assigned, both parties are restrained.

EXAMPLE 8 Ryan contracted to build a garage for McGovern. The contract stipulated that Ryan would do the work himself and that he would not assign the contract to any outside third party. Although such a contract could, under ordinary circumstances, be assigned to another competent builder, the restricting clause would invalidate any attempt to do so.

Unless the circumstances indicate differently, a provision in a contract prohibiting its assignment is interpreted as barring only the delegation of the assignor's duties. U.C.C. Sec. 2-210(3)

Continuing Responsibility You remember that the rights of the other party may not be changed by an assignment or a delegation. Thus, when you delegate a duty and sometimes when you assign a right, you cannot completely transfer your obligation to perform or pay.

Does the assignment of a right or delegation of a duty relieve a person of responsibility of performance?

When you assign a contract, by your act you guarantee the work or promises that you have assigned to another. You still have the duty to see that the job is done. You also become a guarantor of payment to the assignee from the other party to the original contract. Likewise, if you sell an article that you bought before you have paid for it, you might delegate to the buyer the duty of paying the purchase price to the original seller. If, however, the buyer does not pay for it, you would have to pay. The original seller relied on your credit, and you cannot completely escape your liability by the delegation to the buyer.

You must remember that delegating performance of a contract does not relieve the party delegating of any duty to perform or any liability for breach. U.C.C. Sec. 2-210(1)

EXAMPLE 9 **The Phillips Construction Company agreed to build a new plant for Woolrich Woolen Mills. Phillips assigned the plumbing contract to Jones, a local contractor. Phillips, by this sublet assignment, makes itself liable for the plumber's work and also guarantees the plumber that Woolrich Woolen Mills will pay the amount due for his plumbing work. The guarantee remains in force until both sides of the agreement have been duly executed.**

The assignor of a contract conveys or transfers all the rights he has. He no longer retains any control over the rights, nor does he have any right to collect, if the right is to collect money or goods. He may delegate his liabilities to someone else, but he must stand ready to make good if the party to whom he delegates does not perform.

The assignee gets whatever rights the assignor had, but no more. He will be liable for any deductions from the assigned claim that would have been good against the assignor (see Example 6).

SUGGESTIONS FOR MINIMIZING LEGAL RISKS

1. Since a few states do not permit a third party to enforce a contract made for his benefit, consult an attorney should you become a third-party beneficiary under a contract.
2. To be safe, you should put a notice of assignment in writing and see that the third party receives a copy.
3. As you may be held liable where a duty is delegated and the third party fails to perform, you should keep in touch with the third party and check on his performance.

4. It may be to your advantage to assign your housing lease if you are required to move on short notice. Read the lease carefully to make sure that it contains a clause permitting you to do this.

 # APPLYING YOUR LEARNING

QUESTIONS AND PROBLEMS

1. Do third parties ordinarily acquire any rights under a contract between the two principal contracting parties? Explain.
2. Under what conditions may a third party acquire enforceable rights under a contract, even though not a party to the original contract?
3. What is meant by an assignment? How can other parties sometimes acquire rights by means of an assignment?
4. Why is it desirable to have the notice of assignment in writing?
5. Under what circumstances might an assignment be made automatically?
6. What general rule can be stated that will signify what rights may be assigned?
7. What is meant by a novation? How does it relate to an assignment?
8. What is meant by a delegation? How is it different from an assignment?
9. Give an example of a delegation, preferably from your own knowledge or experience.
10. May one get completely rid of his liabilities through an assignment or a delegation? Explain.

WHAT IS YOUR OPINION?

In each of the following cases, give your decision and state a legal principle that applies to the case.

1. Ransom contracted to sell his automobile to Meeker for $500. Meeker was to pay $100 down and $50 a month for the next eight months. Before the car was delivered or any money paid, Meeker assigned his rights under the contract to Watson. Can Watson demand the automobile from Ransom on the same credit terms? Can Watson demand the car if he gives Ransom $500 in cash?
2. Murray entered into a contract to work as a mechanic for Larkin for one year. Three months later, Larkin transferred his right to Murray's services to Titus. Murray refused to work for Titus. Will he be liable for damages?
3. Melon engaged Carr, a well-known artist, to paint for him. Before the picture was completed, Carr died. The executor of the estate engaged a former assistant in Carr's studio, an artist of outstanding ability, to finish the picture. Can Melon, knowing the facts, be required to accept and pay for the picture?

4. Kerper was under obligation to pay certain rentals on property to Smith. Smith assigned his rights to Parker. Kerper was not notified, and he made a settlement with Smith. Was Parker entitled to collect from Kerper?

5. Barr assigns a claim for $200 against Drake to Burke. Burke calls Drake on the telephone and tells him of the assignment. Later, Drake pays Barr, and Burke brings suit against Drake for the $200. Drake defends on the grounds that he was not properly notified. Is this a valid defense? Would your answer be the same if Burke had notified Drake's wife of the assignment over the telephone while Drake was away from home on business and the wife forgot to tell Drake on his return?

6. Taub assigned to Richards a claim for wages due under an employment contract. Proper notice of the assignment was given. Is Richards entitled to collect the amount due?

7. The Turner Company sold goods to Reed on credit. After waiting for several months after the account should have been paid, the Turner Company notified Reed that it was assigning its rights to a collection agency. Is this legally permissible?

THE LAW IN ACTION

1. The Chicago Tribune Syndicate & Press Service, Inc., had a contract to furnish the old Washington Post Company with the following four comic strips for publication: The Gumps, Gasoline Alley, Winnie Winkle, and Dick Tracy. The Washington Post was adjudged a bankrupt, and the court-appointed trustee assigned the right to receive the above comic strips to the reorganized company, Meyer, the plaintiff in this case. The Tribune Syndicate claimed that the contract was not assignable, canceled it, and sold the rights to the same comic strips to the Washington Times. Was this contract to furnish comic strips assignable? (Meyer v. Washington Times Co., 76 F. 2d 988 D.C. Cir.)

2. The wife of the defendant had executed a will leaving all her property to the defendant. During her last illness she asked the defendant to draw another will for her so that she might leave certain property to the plaintiff. Because of the extreme illness of the wife, the defendant suggested that, if she would let the old will stand as it was, he would convey the designated property to the plaintiff. After the death of the wife, the plaintiff brought action to enforce the husband's promise. Is this a third-party beneficiary contract? (Seaver v. Ransom, 224 N.Y. 233, 120 N.E. 639)

KEY TO "WHAT'S THE LAW?" Page 109

1. *Yes. The right to collect money is impersonal and is therefore assignable.*
2. *No. Ben cannot assign a right greater than he possesses. He did not possess the right to collect $25 and, therefore, could not assign this right to David.*

▲ UNIT 14: DISCHARGE BY ACTS OF PARTIES

The discharge or termination of contracts is quite as important as their formation and operation.

TERMINATION OF CONTRACTS

Differentiate between the termination and the cancellation of a contract.

Contracts, like everything else, eventually come to an end. A contract is considered *terminated* when either party puts an end to the contract for reasons other than for its breach. It is considered canceled when either party ends the contract because of breach by the other party. U.C.C. Sec. 2-106(3)b(4)

TERMINATED

DISCHARGE BY AGREEMENT

Contracts may be terminated by mutual agreement of the contracting parties.

EXAMPLE 1 Suppose that Lawrence Langham has contracted to sell his tractor to Jerry Reid for $1,200. Both Lawrence and Jerry have reached the legal age. Lawrence suddenly changes his mind. He decides not to sell the tractor. Lawrence visits Jerry prepared to defend his decision but finds out that Jerry has changed his mind also. Jerry decides not to purchase the tractor. Each man agrees to call the agreement off. Lawrence and Jerry shake hands amiably after agreeing to terminate the original agreement, and the contract no longer exists.

This is as it should be. Whatever the parties agree to do in the first place, they may later mutually agree not to do. The agreement to terminate a contract may take any one of several forms.

Mutual Release The agreement entered into by Lawrence and Jerry terminating their agreement was a *mutual release*. Each released the other from his obligation. Each gave up something, so the agreement to terminate is binding. The release must be mutual, however; otherwise, there would be no consideration for the promised release.

What do we mean when we say that an agreement was terminated by mutual release?

EXAMPLE 2 **Suppose that Lawrence had delivered the tractor; but before Jerry had paid the $1,200, the tractor was destroyed by a fire in Jerry's garage. Because he feels sorry for Jerry, who lost many other things in the fire, Lawrence says to him, "Just forget about the $1,200. We will call off the deal, and the tractor is my loss."**

This would not be an enforceable release. There is no consideration for Lawrence's promise. He has already performed his part of the bargain, and his release is only a promise to make a gift. Lawrence could later sue Jerry for the $1,200 if he changed his mind and decided to enforce the contract.

Novation You have already learned about novations in Unit 13. In the following example of a novation, a new agreement is substituted for the old one.

EXAMPLE 3 **If, in Example 1, Jerry decided that he did not want to buy the tractor, he might find another buyer for Lawrence. Jerry brings George Adams over to Lawrence's house, and the three of them agree that George is to buy the tractor at the same price and that Jerry is to be released from his promise.**

Accord and Satisfaction Another way in which an existing contract can be discharged is by substituting another contract for it. This is called an *accord and satisfaction*.

EXAMPLE 4 **Suppose, in Example 1, that Jerry still wants the tractor but does not have the money to make good on his agreement. He goes to Lawrence, explains the situation, and offers to give Lawrence his expensive camera and color television instead of the $1,200. If Lawrence agrees and accepts the camera and the television, Jerry's promise to pay the $1,200 is discharged.**

It should be noted in the above example that Lawrence must actually accept the items. His promise to accept would not be binding.

How does an accord and satisfaction terminate a contract?

For all practical purposes, a novation and an accord and satisfaction are considered much the same, since they discharge the original agreement by substituting another agreement for it. The technical difference lies in the fact that a new executory agreement comes into existence in a novation, whereas an accord and satisfaction must be completely executed in order to be binding.

● **Arbitration Agreements** Sometimes the parties may disagree as to the interpretation of their contract. They may agree to accept the interpretation of an impartial third person or persons. If they do so, this is called *arbitration;* and the agreement, as interpreted by arbitrators, is substituted

NOTE: *The bullet indicates that there may be a state statute that varies from the law discussed here. Whenever you see this bullet, find out, if possible, what the statute is in your state covering this point or principle of law.*

What effect do arbitration agreements have on existing contracts in some states?

for the old agreement. Arbitration agreements are not enforceable in all states. Check your own state statutes to determine whether arbitration agreements are enforceable in your state.

Merger Sometimes an existing contract is merged with a new one.

EXAMPLE 5 Suppose that the tractor was delivered to Jerry on the first of June and that he had agreed to pay the $1,200 on the first of July. On the first of July, Jerry did not have the money; however, he gave Lawrence his promissory note for $1,200.

The contract to buy is now merged with the promissory note. If Lawrence later has to sue to get his money, he would sue on the promissory note.

What five different forms may a mutual agreement to terminate a contract take?

REMEMBER: If you enter into a mutual agreement to discharge or terminate a contract, it may be in the form of a mutual release, a novation, an accord and satisfaction, an arbitration, or a merger.

DISCHARGE BY LAPSE OF TIME

Sometimes the termination of a contract is provided for in the terms of the original agreement.

EXAMPLE 6 Suppose that Tom Dickson agreed to work for Mr. Sawyer for one month, beginning on the first day of July and ending on the thirty-first day of July. Or suppose that Tom agreed to work until Mr. Sawyer left for his summer vacation.

There would be no question as to the termination of the contract in either one of these situations. In the first situation the contract ends on the thirty-first of July; in the second, the contract ends when Mr. Sawyer leaves for his vacation.

DISCHARGE BY PERFORMANCE

Full Performance Most contracts are completely performed by both parties. This full performance discharges the contract. Nothing short of full performance will discharge a contract in most cases.

If both parties have fully performed their parts of a bargain, the contract is terminated by performance.

A bill in any amount may be paid in United States coins.

Under what conditions is substantial performance sufficient to discharge a contract?

Substantial Performance Sometimes, however, a very special situation will make substantial performance sufficient to discharge a contract. This special situation is limited almost exclusively to construction or labor contracts, and then only when work has been done or improvement has been made on someone else's property.

EXAMPLE 7 **Suppose that Mr. Bell agreed to build a house for Mr. Hill. It was to be built according to certain plans and specifications on land owned by Mr. Hill. The specifications called for "Reading Pipe," but the subcontractor who did the plumbing for Mr. Bell overlooked the word "Reading." The pipe he installed was just as good, but it was not "Reading Pipe." When the house was finished, Mr. Hill refused to pay any of the contract price, claiming breach of contract.**

Mr. Hill must pay. He may deduct any damages suffered from the breach, but he cannot get the house for nothing because of the mistake.

You will note several important facts in this example. First, the land belonged to Mr. Hill, so the house belonged to Mr. Hill. If the land had belonged to Mr. Bell and Mr. Hill had only contracted to buy the house when completed according to the plans and specifications, Mr. Hill would not have to take the house. Substantial performance would not be sufficient here. Mr. Bell would have to sell his house to someone else. The second fact to remember is that it would not be sensible to rip out perfectly good plumbing and replace it with pipe that was no better.

Substantial performance serves as a practical way of solving difficult problems that occasionally arise in certain types of contracts. Remember that it does not apply to ordinary contracts. Usually, if a contract can be performed readily, nothing short of full performance is sufficient.

What is the effect of tender of performance on the liability of the offeror?

The Effect of Tender The offer by one party to perform his part of the agreement is known as *tender of performance*. Usually, mere tender of performance will not discharge the contract, even if the tendered performance is refused. Tender will, however, discharge the offeror from any further penalties for failure to perform. U.C.C. Sec. 3-604

TENDER OF PERFORMANCE

EXAMPLE 8 **Suppose that Hanson owed Miller $100, which was due on the first of July. Hanson did not tender payment until the first of August. Miller refused to take the money at that time and said, "You didn't pay the money when it was due. Now I'm going to sue you and make it cost you plenty."**

Hanson still owes Miller $100. However, if Miller did sue, he could collect $100 plus interest on the $100 at the legal rate for the one month between the due date of tender and the tender of performance.

Waiver Sometimes, when tender has been made, a contract may be discharged by the other party's waiving his right to demand performance. To waive one's rights means to give them away or to relinquish them voluntarily. Usually, a waiver must be supported by consideration, or it must be in the form of a valid gift; otherwise, it may not be effective.

What is a waiver? What forms may a waiver take?

EXAMPLE 9 **Goldberg entered into a contract to wash and wax Mr. Silver's new car one week from Saturday. Mr. Silver paid Goldberg $2 in advance for the job. Goldberg arrived on the assigned Saturday prepared to wash and wax Mr. Silver's car. Mr. Silver, however, said, "Goldberg, I have an important out-of-town business trip to make today, and I need my car. Keep the $2 I gave you for your inconvenience, and we will terminate the original agreement."**

Goldberg's obligation is discharged, and Silver may not later demand that Goldberg polish his car. Silver waived his right to performance by his gift of $2 to Goldberg.

REMEMBER: Tender of performance may save you additional costs in penalties.

DISCHARGE BY BREACH

When is a contract considered breached? What remedy is available to the injured party?

When a party refuses to fulfill his obligations either by failure to carry them out or by carrying them out in a negligent and unsatisfactory manner, he is said to have breached his contract and the injured party has the right to demand damages.

Anticipatory Breach When a party to a contract announces to the other his intention of renouncing his liability (not going through with the contract), he is said to have made an *anticipatory breach*. He has, in other words, breached (violated) the agreement even before he has been required to act. Modern decisions permit the injured party to bring an action for damages at once rather than requiring him to wait until the date of performance has arrived and passed.

When is a party to a contract said to have made an anticipatory breach?

ANTICIPATORY BREACH

EXAMPLE 10 **Suppose that you made a contract with a carpenter to build a playroom in the basement of your house. The carpenter was to begin work on June 20, but on May 9 he called you and said that he would not do the job as agreed. You have the right to bring an action for damages against the carpenter for an anticipatory breach.**

When either party repudiates a contract, the performance of which is not yet due, and the loss of which will substantially impair the value of the contract to the other, the injured party may await performance by the other party for a commercially reasonable time or he may resort to any remedy for breach of contract. U.C.C. Sec. 2-610

If one party breaches a contract, should the other party continue to perform the contract?

Once a party has received notice of cancellation of an agreement by the other, he is not permitted to continue with the execution of the work or service covered by their contract. To do so would only increase the amount of damages resulting from the breach. He may, however, proceed on the seller's right to set goods aside for the contract in spite of the breach or to salvage unfinished goods.

EXAMPLE 11 **A manufacturer of educational toys received a contract for 10,000 jigsaw puzzles for a large department store. After only 1,000 of the puzzles had been manufactured, the store canceled the order. Continued production of the other puzzles would be at the manufacturer's own risk.**

Does the principle of anticipatory breach apply to promises to pay money at some future date?

The principle of anticipatory breach does not apply to promises to pay money at some future date. One who renounces his obligation on a promissory note payable at a future date cannot be sued on the note until after the payment date of the note.

Impossibility of Performance There are four instances in which impossibility of performance is an acceptable excuse for nonperformance.
1. When performance becomes illegal after the contract has been formed.
2. When death or illness prevents one of the parties from performing a personal service.
3. When the exact subject matter of the contract has been destroyed.
4. Where an essential element of the contract is missing and has been assumed present by both parties to the contract.

A contract is also considered to be breached and terminated if the party to whom an obligation is due makes it impossible for the other to perform.

EXAMPLE 12 **Manning entered into a contract to paint the rooms in Stapleton's home. When Manning arrived with his painting equipment, Stapleton prevented him from entering. Stapleton thus breached the contract by making Manning's performance impossible.**

Failure to Perform When performance of the contract is due, a party may wholly or partially fail to perform what he promised. Such failure to perform constitutes a breach of contract and gives the injured party the right to bring an action for damages.

Very often, when one party has done part of what he promised or part of the contract has been carried out, the question arises as to whether the entire contract is discharged or whether only the part of the contract not performed is terminated. The answer depends entirely on whether the contract is entire or divisible.

Distinguish between an entire and a divisible contract.

The real intent of the parties governs. The courts will not decide that a contract is divisible merely because it is to be carried out at stated periods if it was intended by the parties to be one contract (an entire contract). This question arises, for example, in an agreement to deliver and pay for goods in installments at different times.

How may a divisible contract be treated where full performance is not possible?

If the contract is divisible (that is, if the promise to be performed by one party consists of several distinct items, with the consideration apportioned to each item), the agreement has the effect of a group of contracts joined together. In such a case recovery is permitted for each completed portion, even though the whole agreement may not be performed. The innocent party may sue for damages caused by the breach of the uncompleted portion of the contract.

The party against whom a breach of contract is committed may terminate the contract if he chooses.

REMEDIES OF INJURED PARTY

What remedies are available to the injured party because of a breach?

The injured party may choose to consider the contract terminated or discharged. In either event the agreement is called off and neither party is obliged to perform. If the injured party has suffered no loss, this may be the best choice for him to make.

If the injured party has suffered a loss, he might better stand ready to perform his part of the bargain and then sue the offending party for damages that resulted from the breach.

Sometimes the injured party may bring an action for specific performance, but only if money damages will not repay him for the loss he has suffered.

EXAMPLE 13   If Russell contracted to sell Keller a rare book, the only one of its kind in existence, and Russell then breached his contract and refused to deliver, Keller might have a right to specific performance.

Under what conditions might a court require performance of a contract according to the original terms?

Money damages would not be enough in this case. Keller can get the benefits of his agreement only by getting the book from Russell. He cannot go out and buy another book just like it from someone else. If, however, there was another copy of the book that he could buy at a higher price, he could not force Russell to perform. His remedy would be to buy the other book and sue Russell for additional costs.

Specific performance may be granted in situations where the purchaser is not able to obtain the goods elsewhere. U.C.C. Sec. 2-716(1)(2)

EXAMPLE 14   Hartford's Department Store contracted with the Spray-Proof Shower Curtain Company for the delivery of one gross of patented plastic curtains on or before a date fixed in the contract. When the shower curtain company notified the store that they would not deliver under the terms of the contract because of an unexpected rise in the cost of raw materials, Hartford's sued for specific performance. The court will grant Hartford's plea. Hartford cannot obtain the curtains elsewhere. Spray-Proof holds the patent and is the sole manufacturer; the court would decree specific performance.

SUGGESTIONS FOR MINIMIZING LEGAL RISKS

1. Most legal risks can be minimized by entering into contracts only with persons who have a reputation for being trustworthy, thoroughly competent, financially responsible, and permanently established in the community.
2. Before entering into an important contract, give very careful consideration to the possible extent of your loss should the other party fail to perform.
3. When an important contract is entered into that might lead to considerable loss of time or money in case of a dispute over carrying out its terms, it is wise to have a clause inserted in the contract providing for arbitration in case of dispute.
4. If possible, avoid contracts involving "conditions" where performance on your part is subject to the "approval or satisfaction" of the other party, particularly where the conditions are under the control of the other party.
5. In case of a breach of contract, explore the possibilities of arriving at an acceptable settlement through negotiation out of court before starting court action.

 APPLYING YOUR LEARNING

QUESTIONS AND PROBLEMS

1. From your own experience, can you recall an agreement that was discharged by a mutual release? How did the mutual release come about? Explain.
2. Why is consideration by both parties necessary for an enforceable release?
3. Explain the difference between a novation and an accord and satisfaction.
4. Are arbitration agreements enforceable in your state? Describe a contract that might be terminated by substituting a new contract reached through arbitration.
5. Illustrate from your personal experience some of your contracts that were terminated by full performance.
6. Substantial performance may in special cases discharge a contract. Explain the reason for this ruling by the courts.
7. How does tender of performance affect a contract that has not been performed?
8. What may the injured party do if the other party refuses to perform on his promise?

WHAT IS YOUR OPINION?

In each of the following cases, give your decision and state a legal principle that applies to the case.

1. Jack Carson and Ruth Horton became engaged to marry, and Jack gave Ruth a beautiful diamond ring. Later, they had an argument. Ruth returned the ring and said, "I wouldn't marry you if you were the last man on earth." Jack replied, "That's O.K. with me." Has their contract been terminated? If so, on what basis?

2. O'Brien contracted to purchase a horse from Burke for $200. He took possession of the horse and promised to pay the amount on the first of the following month. The date arrived and O'Brien did not have the money, so he offered Burke a promissory note for $200, payable in six months. Burke accepted. Did this discharge the original contract? If so, on what basis?

3. When Gerald Smith was fifteen, his father promised him $1,000 if he would not smoke until he was twenty-one. Just before Gerald became twenty-one, his father had a heart attack and was unable to work. He tendered Gerald the $1,000 on his twenty-first birthday, but Gerald refused to accept. Does this discharge the contract? If so, on what basis?

4. Suppose in Case 3 that Gerald said, "Dad, you may need the money now. Give it to me later on when you can spare it better." Gerald's father then died soon after. Has the contract been discharged? Can Gerald bring an action against his father's estate to collect the money?

5. Spaulding, a concert violinist, contracted to purchase a rare old Italian violin from the Freeman Music Store for $15,000. The music store learned that the violin was worth much more and refused to deliver the violin to Spaulding upon tender of the money. The store then tried to get him to accept another violin. Spaulding refused. What can Spaulding do?

6. Turner was employed on July 1, 1972, by the Work-Right Business School to teach accounting for a period of one year. Turner's work was entirely satisfactory, and nothing further was said about future employment. On September 1, 1973, Turner reported for work and was told there was no job for him. He threatened to bring action. Will he succeed?

7. Paul Doran agreed to buy an expensive camera from Martin Hershey when he received his inheritance from his aunt's estate. When the will was read, it was discovered that the will had been changed and that Paul had been left out of the new will. Has the contract between Paul and Martin been discharged? If so, on what basis?

8. Ralph Liston agreed to plow a large cornfield for Joe Davis. The agreement called for payment of $100 out of the proceeds when Joe sold his corn crop in the fall. A flood destroyed the entire crop of corn. Would this result in the discharge of the contract? If so, on what basis?

9. Larson contracted to buy a house trailer from Richards for $1,000 when he thought he was going to Florida. He became ill and could not make

the trip, so he got Barnes to agree to buy the trailer from Richards by agreement among the parties. Was Larson's contract discharged? If so, on what basis?

10. Barnes, in the preceding case, found it impossible to raise the $1,000, so he offered to give Richards a car worth $1,500 in lieu of the $1,000. Before the car was delivered, however, Richards brought an action for the $1,000. Barnes pleads that the offer to give the car bars the right of action. Is this a valid defense?

11. Decker contracted to paint Beck's barn for $100. Decker arrived with his ladders and paint, but Beck refused to let him paint because he said the weather was too cold. Later, Decker became very busy and was unable to return as soon as Beck wanted him to. Beck threatened to sue him on the contract. Will he succeed?

12. Assume that in the two weeks after Beck's objection to letting Decker paint the barn, in Case 11, Decker telephoned Beck and asked him whether he was ready to have the barn painted. Beck told him that he had changed his mind and had decided to paint the barn himself. Has the contract been discharged? Can Decker bring an action for breach of contract?

THE LAW IN ACTION

1. The plaintiff brought an action to collect the final balance owed for the construction of a theater. The defendant refused to pay, claiming that certain small items in the contract had not been performed, although he admitted that the cost of completing the omitted items would be small. The plaintiff's action was for the final balance less the cost of finishing the omitted items. Is this an example of substantial performance? (Cassinelli v. Stacy, 238 Ky. 827, 38 S.W. 2d 980)

2. The plaintiff brought an action for the purchase price of certain ladies' clothing. The defendant admitted that he had contracted for the clothing, but claimed that his contract to accept the clothing had been discharged by the failure of the plaintiff to deliver within the specified time. It was understood by both parties at the time the contract was entered into that the clothing was for sale on the fall market. The plaintiff did not deliver the goods until six weeks after they were promised and after all chance for resale on the fall market had passed. Was the contract discharged by the lapse of time? (Sunshine Cloak & Suit Co. v. Roquette 30 N.D. 143, 152 N.W. 359)

KEY TO "WHAT'S THE LAW?" Page 116

1. *No. The agreement to buy the brown suit was discharged by agreement.*
2. *No. This is a case of substantial performance. He must pay the agreed price, less the cost of changing the buttons.*

WHAT'S THE LAW?

1. *In January Ray Hunter contracted to sell Harry Owens $10 worth of fireworks on July 1. On March 1 a state law was passed that prohibited the sale of fireworks. Can Harry sue Ray for breach of contract if Ray fails to deliver according to the contract?*

2. *Dave Anderson contracted to pitch with the Blue Stars Baseball Team. Dave was injured in an automobile accident and was unable to walk for the next year. What happens to the contract?*

◬ UNIT 15: DISCHARGE BY OPERATION OF LAW

Your agreements are enforceable contracts only when they meet the requirements set by law.

EXAMPLE 1 **Joe Martinez had contracted to build a new service station on a busy corner lot for Ed Volk. When Martinez visited the corner lot to begin construction, he was halted by a city policeman who told him, "You cannot build a service staton on this lot because City Council voted a change in zoning laws at last night's meeting. Service stations are hereby prohibited in this residential neighborhood." Is Martinez still duty-bound by his contract to build?**

Martinez is no longer bound by his contract because the new law has made the performance of the contract illegal. The law sometimes takes a hand in the discharge of contracts.

TERMINATION BY OPERATION OF LAW

How are contracts sometimes terminated by operation of law?

The law may also declare your contracts terminated if certain conditions are not met. The law is practical. There are times when performance becomes impossible. There are other times when the best interests of society demand that your contract be terminated. Under these circumstances, the law declares your contracts discharged by *operation of law*.

OPERATION OF LAW

IMPOSSIBILITY OF PERFORMANCE

Sometimes we think of performance as being impossible when actually it is only difficult. It is only actual impossibility of performance that will discharge a contract.

Personal-Service Contracts   If you contract to do a job yourself, you and you alone can fulfill your obligation. You cannot transfer that obligation to someone else without the consent of the other party to your contract. This you learned in Unit 13 on assignments. It then reasonably follows that if you die or become so physically disabled that personal performance by you is impossible, the contract will be discharged.

Every contract involving service, however, must be examined carefully to see whether you are promising personal performance or whether you are merely promising that a certain job will be done. *Personal-service contracts*, which promise personal performance, may not be assigned if they are dependent on an individual's unique talent or made by a member of a profession. Doctors, musicians, artists, athletes, and members of the other arts and professions may not assign their contracts. Tradesmen are not included in this classification. The skills possessed by tradesmen are recognized as being standardized with little difference resulting if the work is done by any skilled person in the same trade.

PERSONAL-SERVICE CONTRACT

What type of personal-service contracts are not assignable? What types are assignable?

EXAMPLE 2   **An artist is engaged to paint a mural in the rotunda of a new arts building because of his interpretive abilities in the type of painting desired. This is a personal-service contract and may not be assigned. The contract need not contain the usual restrictive clause against assignment.**

EXAMPLE 3   **Suppose the arts building had contracted with plasterers who were to prepare the surfaces of the rotunda walls for the artist's work. Although this contract is for personal service, it may be assigned because it is related to a trade and not to a profession or an art.**

What are the determining factors that are considered where personal performance is required?

Delegation of performance does not relieve the delegating party of any duty to perform or any liability for breach. U.C.C. Sec. 2-210(1) Usually, when the performance demands skill, judgment, or personal satisfaction, personal performance is indicated. Such a contract may not be assigned, nor can its performance be delegated to another.

Where Conditions Cannot Be Met   Agreements involving personal service are not the only types of contracts that may be terminated by impossibility. Performance of other conditions may become impossible.

A contract to put a new roof on a house is terminated by impossibility of performance if the house burns down before the work is started.

EXAMPLE 4 Suppose that Jack Daley, a roofer, contracted to replace the roof on Ray Good's home for $1,400. Two days before Daley was to begin the job, Good's home was completely destroyed by a tornado.

How may destruction of the subject matter make it impossible to perform a contract?

The contract is discharged. Performance is impossible. One cannot put a roof on a house that is not there. All building contracts, however, are not necessarily terminated by the destruction of the subject matter.

EXAMPLE 5 Suppose that Mr. Daley had contracted to build a new house for Mr. Good instead of replacing the old roof. The contract provided that Mr. Daley was to build the house for $25,000 according to certain architectural plans. Daley worked on the house until it was near completion, and a fire suddenly destroyed it at that point.

The contract is not terminated in this case. Performance is not impossible. Mr. Daley can still build the house as provided for in the contract. He will lose money, yes, but performance is still possible.

How may changes in the law make it impossible to perform a contract?

Where Performance Is Illegal Another type of impossibility arises when performance of the contract becomes illegal. You have already learned that a contract whose performance would be illegal at the time it was entered into is void. The same general rules apply when performance becomes illegal after the contract is entered into.

EXAMPLE 6 Suppose that Harvey Jones, who is fourteen years of age, contracted to work for Mr. Carlino for three months. At the time the agreement was made, such employment was perfectly legal. Shortly afterward, however, a new child-labor law that prohibited the employment of anyone under sixteen years of age took effect.

Harvey and Mr. Carlino have no choice in the matter. The contract is terminated. Legal performance has now become impossible.

ALTERATION

How may alteration of the terms of a written contract discharge the contract?

Sometimes other wrongful acts of one of the parties will discharge a contract by operation of law. One of these wrongful acts is altering a contract.

EXAMPLE 7 A written contract provided that Peter Merkle was to buy Bart Little's canoe for $25. Bart secretly inserted a "1" in front of the "25" and then attempted to collect $125 from Peter. Bart has outsmarted himself. The contract is discharged by his wrongful alteration. Not only may he not collect $125, but also he cannot enforce the original contract.

The contract, however, is not discharged if Peter chooses to enforce it. If Peter still wants the canoe at $25, he can get it or can collect damages if Bart will not deliver.

STATUTES OF LIMITATIONS

When your contract has been breached by the other party, you ordinarily have a right to sue him. Under some circumstances, however, this right to sue may be taken away from you. The law may specify the time within which a contract may be enforced.

You may not sleep on your rights. Action must be commenced within the time specified by law, or the right of action is lost.

● In all states there are statutes that specify the length of time within which a legal action may be brought on a contract. These statutes are called *Statutes of Limitations.*

STATUTE OF LIMITATIONS

EXAMPLE 8 **Suppose that Lee Wells owed Warren Barrett $100. Lee did not pay, and Warren did not bring any action to collect for more than ten years.**

Warren probably cannot collect. He has waited too long. You may not "sleep on your rights" and then expect the law to help you collect.

The Statute of Limitations for breach of contracts for sale of goods is four years in most states. This means that an action must be commenced within four years after the cause of action has become an enforceable right. By the original agreement, the parties may reduce the period of limitations to not less than one year, but they may not extend it. U.C.C. Sec. 2-725(1)

What happens to the computation of the time period if a debtor leaves the state or becomes incapacitated?

The time begins to run at the very moment a breach occurs, but a "time out" is called if the debtor leaves the state or if the creditor is incapacitated.

EXAMPLE 9 **Suppose that Al Briggs breached his contract and refused to pay Jim Hamilton the $100 he had borrowed from him. A month later Briggs went out of state and did not return until ten years later. Prior to the time of Briggs's return, Jim Hamilton was found to be insane and was committed to a state mental hospital. Even though he may remain in the mental institution for ten additional years, Hamilton could still bring suit for the money due him as soon as he is released from the hospital and declared sane again.**

The time of Briggs's absence from the state and the time of Hamilton's mental incapacity would not be counted in the statutory limitation period.

What effect does the admission by the debtor of the existence of a debt have on the statutory limitation period?

● Also, if something is paid on account or if the debtor admits the existence of the debt after the time period has elapsed, the debt is renewed for another statutory period. In New York State and some other states, such a new promise must be in writing.

The following table illustrates some of the more common statutes of limitations. Remember, there are many special statutes of limitations in every state. In order fully to protect yourself in important business relationships, you should refer to the most recent statutes in your state.

NOTE: *The bullet indicates that there may be a state statute that varies from the law discussed here. Whenever you see this bullet, find out, if possible, what the statute is in your state covering this point or principle of law.*

SELECTED STATUTES OF LIMITATIONS*

STATES	OPEN ACCOUNTS	CONTRACTS IN WRITING			JUDGMENTS
		NOTES	SIMPLE CONTRACTS	SEALED CONTRACTS	
Alabama	3	6	6	10	20
Alaska	6	6	6	10	10
Arizona	3	6	6	6	5
Arkansas	3	5	5	5	10
California	4	4	4	4	5
Colorado	6	6	6	6	20
Connecticut	6	6	6	17	No limit
Delaware	3	6	3	20	10
Florida	3	5	5	20	20
Georgia	4	6	6	20	10
Hawaii	6	6	6	6	10
Idaho	4	5	5	5	6
Illinois	5	10	10	10	20
Indiana	6	20	6	20	20
Iowa	5	10	10	10	20
Kansas	3	5	5	5	5
Kentucky	5	15	15	15	15
Louisiana	3	10	10	10	10
Maine	6	6	6	20	20
Maryland	3	3	3	12	12
Massachusetts	6	6	6	20	20
Michigan	6	6	6	10	10
Minnesota	6	6	6	6	10
Mississippi	3	6	6	6	7
Missouri	5	10	10	10	10
Montana	5	8	8	8	10
Nebraska	4	5	5	5	5
Nevada	4	6	6	6	6
New Hampshire	6	6	6	20	20
New Jersey	6	6	6	16	20
New Mexico	4	6	6	6	7
New York	6	6	6	20	20
North Carolina	3	3	3	10	10
North Dakota	6	6	6	6-10 real estate	10
Ohio	6	15	15	15	21
Oklahoma	3	6	5	5	5
Oregon	6	6	6	10	10
Pennsylvania	6	6	6	20	20
Rhode Island	6	6	6	20	20
South Carolina	6	6	6	20	10
South Dakota	6	6	6	20	20
Tennessee	6	6	6	6	10
Texas	2	4	4	4	10

cont.

* The Uniform Commercial Code specifies a four-year period for actions on contracts for sales of goods.

SELECTED STATUTES OF LIMITATIONS (Continued)

| STATES | OPEN ACCOUNTS | CONTRACTS IN WRITING | | | JUDGMENTS |
		NOTES	SIMPLE CONTRACTS	SEALED CONTRACTS	
Utah	4	6	6	8	10
Vermont	6	6	6	8	8
Virginia	3	5	5	10	20
Washington	3	6	6	6	6
West Virginia	5	10	10	10	10
Wisconsin	6	6	6	10–20	20
Wyoming	8	10	10	10	26
District of Columbia	3	3	3	12	12

BANKRUPTCY

Sometimes people get hopelessly in debt—so hopelessly that they cannot meet the demands of their creditors. The debtor and his creditors are faced with the problem of how to realize the largest possible amount of money from the sale of the debtor's property and how to distribute that money fairly among the creditors.

Sometimes these problems can be worked out informally by cooperative action of the parties concerned. More often, however, some legal way is needed to force the cooperation of all the creditors. It is to provide a legal way of solving these problems that the Federal Bankruptcy Act was passed. Bankruptcy actions are always brought in the federal courts.

Who May Become a Bankrupt Any individual and any corporation, except certain ones specified in the federal statute, may become a voluntary bankrupt. A *voluntary bankrupt* is a person or corporation that asks to be adjudged a bankrupt. The same classes of persons may be adjudged *involuntary bankrupts*—that is, bankrupts against their will—unless they are wage earners or farmers. The financial difficulties of wage earners and farmers are provided for by special parts of the federal statute.

VOLUNTARY BANKRUPT

INVOLUNTARY BANKRUPT

How is one adjudged a bankrupt?

To be adjudged an involuntary bankrupt, a person (or corporation) must (1) be insolvent—that is, owe more money than he can pay; (2) owe debts of $1,000 or more; (3) have committed an act of bankruptcy.

According to the Federal Bankruptcy Act, any of the following six acts, when committed by an individual or a corporation, is considered an act of bankruptcy.

1. To transfer or conceal any part of his property with the intent to defraud or delay payment to his creditors.

2. To transfer while insolvent any part of his property to one or more creditors with intent to prefer them over other creditors.

3. To permit a creditor to obtain a lien by means of a judgment through legal proceedings while he, the debtor, is insolvent.

What are the six
acts of
bankruptcy listed
in the Bankruptcy
Act?

4. To make a general assignment of all his assets for the benefit of all his creditors.

5. To permit the appointment of a receiver or trustee to take charge of his property while insolvent or while unable to pay debts as they mature.

6. To admit in writing his inability to pay his debts and his willingness to be adjudged a bankrupt.

How is a
bankruptcy
proceeding
brought before a
federal court?

Discharge in Bankruptcy A bankruptcy action is commenced by three or more creditors* filing a petition in a federal court asking that the debtor be declared an involuntary bankrupt. The general procedure followed by the court is to cause all the bankrupt's property to be turned over to a trustee. The trustee is required to sell the property at the highest possible price and to distribute the money received equally among all the creditors. There are a few preferred claims, such as taxes and wages.

EXAMPLE 10 **If a debtor owes $10,000 to all his creditors and the trustee can get no more than $5,000 by selling all his property, each creditor would get 50 percent of his claim. The debtor would be discharged from paying the balance.**

Does a discharge
in bankruptcy
terminate all of
one's outstanding
contractual
obligations?

For all practical purposes, this discharge terminates all the bankrupt's outstanding contractual obligations. Technically, these obligations still exist; but the remedy for enforcing them in court no longer exists. The Bankruptcy Act has modified the common law so that a person who becomes hopelessly in debt may be relieved of further obligation on his contracts if the court adjudges him a bankrupt. However, debts tinged with fraud or wrong are revived even after the debts have been discharged in bankruptcy.

SUGGESTIONS FOR MINIMIZING LEGAL RISKS

1. When you contract for services, have clearly in mind whether you expect to demand personal services or not. Remember, where time is an important factor, that impossibility of personal performance discharges the contract and this may create a hardship on you. There are advantages and disadvantages involved, so calculate your risks carefully. Many times it is an advantage not to require personal service where equally satisfactory service will suffice.

2. When you plan to enter into an important contract wherein you might suffer a sizable loss in case of impossibility of performance due to the destruction of subject matter, it would be prudent to discuss the potential risks with the other party and come to an understanding as to the sharing of risks and losses and make that understanding a part of the original contract.

*If there are fewer than twelve creditors, any one creditor may file the petition.

3. Consider seriously the risks involved in entering into important long-term contracts that might later be declared illegal, particularly if these contracts necessitate a heavy financial investment on your part. Examples of such contracts include the following: building, amusement, fireworks, radio stations, television stations, distribution and sale of liquors, and race tracks.

4. Prepare all written instruments, particularly negotiable instruments, so that there is little possibility or danger of alteration of the original instrument.

▲ APPLYING YOUR LEARNING

QUESTIONS AND PROBLEMS

1. What is meant by impossibility of performance? Give an example.
2. What is meant by personal performance?
3. How can you tell whether personal performance is expected or required?
4. What is the result of inability to perform personally on the contract? Give an example.
5. Explain how a contract for personal service might be discharged because of the destruction of the subject matter. Give an example.
6. The destruction of the subject matter does not always discharge a contract for personal service. Explain.
7. What is the effect on the contract when a condition becomes impossible to perform?
8. How may a contract be terminated by the prevention of one of the parties? Give an example.
9. What is meant by statutes of limitations? What are the limitations for different types of contracts in your state?
10. Under what conditions may the time be extended for an additional statutory period?
11. What is bankruptcy? Who may be a bankrupt?
12. Why is it desirable to have bankruptcy laws?
13. What is the distinction between a voluntary bankrupt and an involuntary bankrupt?
14. What is meant by an act of bankruptcy?
15. Are bankruptcy actions brought in a state or a federal court?

WHAT IS YOUR OPINION?

In each of the following cases, give your decision and state a legal principle that applies to the case.

1. Norbert contracts to build a wooden garage for Wilson. Before work is begun, a local law is passed prohibiting the erection of wooden garages in the city. Is Wilson liable to Norbert on the contract?

2. Curry contracted to grade a roadbed for a new paving for the village of Hopewell. The first morning on the job, his road grader struck a large stone and was broken. Curry claimed that this resulted in impossibility of performance that terminated the contract. Is his contention sound?

3. Murray agreed to sell Burns all the peaches grown this year in his orchard. A severe frost ruined the peach crop, and Murray was unable to deliver any peaches. Was he liable to Burns for breach of contract?

4. Martin entered into a contract with Deitrick whereby he agreed to erect a commercial garage on a plot of ground owned by Deitrick. Before the garage could be erected, a zoning ordinance was passed making illegal the use of the land for such purposes. Was the contract terminated? Were the parties to it discharged from all liability by such change in law?

5. Burke was judicially declared a bankrupt. In discussing his financial problems with his friend Ames, Burke stated that this is an illustration of the discharge of contracts by operation of law. Ames disagreed and said that Burke's statement is not technically correct. Do you agree with Burke or Ames?

6. Dennis agreed to sell Arner 10 bushels of apples at $3 a bushel. A severe hailstorm ruined all Dennis's apples in his orchard, so he claimed that he could not sell Arner the apples. Could Arner bring action against Dennis for breach of contract?

7. Mandel entered into a contract with the Hewlett Lumber Company for the purchase of 50,000 feet of yellow pine lumber. Mandel intended, as the lumber company knew, to use the wood in the manufacture of pin games. After the contract was made, a law was passed making the manufacture and sale of these games anywhere in the state illegal. Did this new law relieve Mandel from liability on the contract?

8. A statute states that no action on a debt may be brought four years after the debt is due. Simpson had owed Kerr $200 for four years, but six months later he gave Kerr $50 on the account. Simpson later refused to pay the balance, claiming that the Statute of Limitations bars recovery. Is this a valid defense?

9. Baer was a salesman selling automobile parts on a commission basis for his firm. Adamson, a customer, ordered 5 dozen bolts of a certain type. Baer, wishing to increase his earnings for that period, wrote up the order for 5 gross. When the shipment came through, Adamson refused to pay for the bolts. Baer tried to persuade Adamson to keep 5 dozen and pay for them, telling him that it was just a mistake on the part of the shipping clerk. Adamson refused, stating that the contract was discharged. Can Adamson refuse to pay for the bolts? Must Adamson return all the bolts to Baer?

10. The junior class of Brownsville High School engaged Steve Morgan and the Intruders, a well-known band, to play for the annual Junior Prom. Morgan later had an opportunity to book a more profitable engagement on the date of the Junior Prom. He offered to send the

Blue Boys to Brownsville instead. Morgan claimed that it was impossible to be in two places at the same time and did not appear. Has the contract been discharged because of impossibility of performance? What rights are available to the junior class?

11. Johnston took his television set to Jones for repairs. Jones agreed to repair it for $10. After a more careful inspection, Jones discovered that he could not repair the set without a sweep generator, an expensive electrical instrument that he did not have. Jones contended that the contract was discharged because of impossibility of performance. Is his contention sound? If Jones does not repair the set, can Johnston bring suit for breach of contract?

12. Fox gave his 90-day note for $600 to Hoffer. He left the state a short time after and did not return until five years later. When Hoffer learned of Fox's return, he immediately brought suit on the note. The Statute of Limitations operating in his state provides that an action not commenced within four years from the date that payment was due on a sale of goods shall be barred or outlawed. Would Hoffer be successful in his suit? Explain.

THE LAW IN ACTION

1. The defendant had contracted to construct a theater for the plaintiff. He had obtained a building permit and commenced work on the building when he was stopped by order of the Commissioner of Buildings under the authority of a local ordinance that prohibited the construction of a theater within 200 feet of a church. The plaintiff sued for breach of contract, and the defendant claimed that the contract was terminated by impossibility. Is the defendant correct? (Fisher v. United States Fidelity and Guaranty Co., 313 Ill. App. 66, 39 N.E. 2d 67)

2. The plaintiff was a salesman employed to sell flour for the defendant. The defendant's mill was destroyed by fire, and the defendant was unable to fill many orders for flour that had been obtained by the plaintiff. The plaintiff contends that he was entitled to his commission on the sales whether the orders were filled or not. Each order taken by the plaintiff contained a clause excusing the defendant from performance in case the mill was destroyed by fire. Was the plaintiff entitled to his commission? (Maidment v. Krause Milling Co., 225 App. Div. 492, 233 N.Y.S. 621 Sup. Ct.)

KEY TO "WHAT'S THE LAW?" Page 126

1. *No. The contract is now illegal and impossible to perform.*
2. *The contract would be terminated by impossibility of performance.*

A DIGEST OF LEGAL CONCEPTS

1. Rights acquired under a contract may be enforced only by the original parties, unless the promises were made specifically for the benefit of a third party.

2. A third party may enforce a contract that was made specifically for his benefit.

3. If the third party is only an incidental beneficiary, he may not enforce the contract.

4. Most rights acquired under a contract may be transferred to a third party by means of an assignment.

5. No particular form is required by law to transfer rights by assignment.

6. When a person dies, his contracts are assigned to his executor or his administrator by operation of law.

7. When a person is adjudged a bankrupt, his contracts are assigned to a trustee by operation of law.

8. Rights acquired under a contract may not be assigned if the rights of the other party will be changed by the assignment.

9. Contracts for personal services are not assignable because they cannot be assigned without changing the rights of the other party.

10. If the assignor, the assignee, and the third party all agree, any rights or duties may be transferred, modified, or changed by means of a novation.

11. The assignor may assign only the rights that he himself possesses.

12. No delegation of performance under a contract relieves the party delegating of any duty to perform or any liability for breach.

13. After an assignment is made, the assignor has no further claim or interest in the contract.

14. Notice must be given to the third party before the assignment is binding upon him.

15. A contract may be discharged by a new enforceable agreement in which each party agrees to discharge the other from further performance on the former contract.

16. A contract may be discharged by substituting a new agreement for the former contract. If a new obligation is assumed, the substituted agreement is called a novation. If the new agreement merely discharges the old, it is called an accord and satisfaction.

17. A contract may be discharged by being merged with a new enforceable agreement.

18. If a contract provides by its own terms that it is to end at a certain time, the contract is discharged when that time arrives.

19. If a contract provides that it is to terminate on the happening of a certain event, the happening of the event discharges the contract.

20. A contract is discharged if it has been fully performed by both parties.

21. Sometimes, in special cases where justice can be done in no other way, contracts may be discharged by substantial performance.

22. Tender of performance will release the tendering party from any additional penalties for nonperformance.

23. When a party to a contract announces that he does not intend to go through with the contract, he is said to have made an anticipatory breach.

24. A breach of the contract by one party will discharge the contract only if the other party so desires.

25. The party against whom the breach is committed may, if he wishes, declare the contract still binding and sue for any damages he suffered from the breach.

26. Specific performance may be decreed when the purchaser is not able to obtain the goods elsewhere.

27. Contracts may be terminated by operation of law.

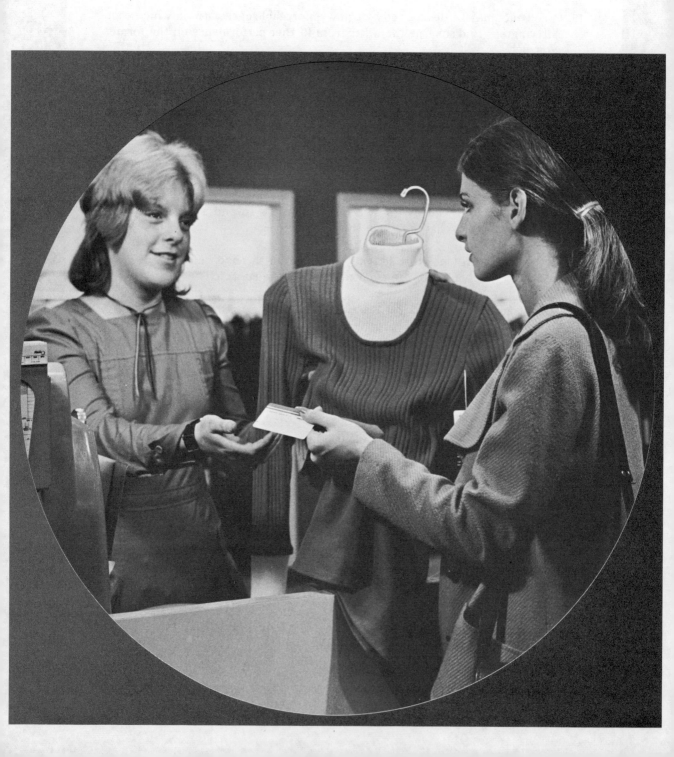

WHAT'S THE LAW?

1. *Tim Larson contracted to sell his farm to Ellis Drake. Would this transaction be regulated by the Uniform Commercial Code?*

---

2. *Fred Dawson ordered some ornamental iron railings for his porch. The railings were to be made by the Warren Iron Works according to specifications furnished by Dawson. Was this a sale?*

▲ UNIT 16:
CONTRACTS FOR THE
SALE OF GOODS

Sales follow the law of contracts; but because they are so frequent, so varied, and so much a part of our daily living, they merit our special attention. A *sale* is a contract whereby property is transferred from one person to another person for a price.

SALE

EXAMPLE 1 **Tom Thompson wanted to purchase a new power lawn mower and entered into a contract with the Clymer Hardware Store, provided he could sell his old hand mower. Harry Foster was interested in buying a used mower so Tom pushed his used hand mower down the street to Foster's house and offered the mower to Foster for $20. Foster said, "Sold. Here is your $20. Please roll the mower into the garage."**

We have two contracts in this example. In one, Tom Thompson disposed of something he no longer needed. In the other, he agreed to buy something he very much wanted. Millions of transactions like these are entered into every day. Sales are the most common type of contracts.

Look at the example again. These two contracts are not alike. In one, Thompson actually sold and transferred the ownership of his old lawn mower to Foster. In the other, Thompson only promised to buy a new mower at some future time. The new mower still belongs to the hardware store, but a *contract to sell* has been made, in which the ownership of goods will be transferred by the seller to the buyer for a price at some future time. There is an important difference between a sale and a contract to sell, and this difference is carefully considered under the special rules pertaining to sales transactions. The Uniform Commercial Code heeds this difference and provides guidelines to be followed.

CONTRACT TO
SELL

Who is considered
a merchant under
the Uniform
Commercial
Code?

Today, more than ever before, the law governing commercial transactions recognizes the fact that customs and usage are important practices that must be considered in the creation of sales contracts, especially as these business customs and practices relate to merchants. A *merchant* is a person who deals in goods and who holds himself out as having special knowledge or skill peculiar to the practices or goods involved in the business transaction. U.C.C. Sec. 2-104(1)   MERCHANT

UNIFORM LAWS GOVERNING SALES

Visualize, if you can, the confusion that would result if the laws pertaining to sales were not reasonably precise and understandable. Virtually everybody buys or sells something every day. Moreover, most people buy from and sell to many different people in many different parts of the country in the course of a year.

For this reason, we need some special rules with regard to sales. The general rules of contracts apply, but to make sure that the rights and duties of the parties are clear, certain rules have been changed. These special laws pertaining to sales are not new. Many of them originated in the law merchant, which was the name given to the customs and precedents based on commercial usages that were recognized by early businessmen, merchants, and mariners in their dealings with one another. They became part of the common law when the early courts began to apply the rules of the law merchant to court cases. In recent years these same special rules have been modernized and restated.

What is your
understanding of
the term law
merchant?

What does the
term "goods"
mean?

The law of sales deals with the sale of goods. *Goods*, according to the Code, means all things (including specially manufactured goods) which are movable at the time of identification to the contract for sale. Goods also includes the unborn young of animals, growing crops, and other identified things attached to realty such as timber, minerals, and the like—all of which may be removed. However, neither the money in which the price is to be paid nor investment securities such as stocks and bonds are considered "goods." U.C.C. Sec. 2-105(1) Sec. 2-107(1)   GOODS

To be valid subject matter of a contract for sale, goods must be tangible personal property. By *tangible* we mean something that occupies space—something that you can touch and put your hands on. Thus, the law of sales does not apply to the sale of land, nor does it apply to the assignment of rights that are not tangible. An *intangible right* is the right to collect money, stocks, bonds, or any similar things that have value but are not tangible. The right to collect money has value, but inasmuch as it does not occupy space or is not capable of being touched, it cannot be classed as "goods." Therefore, it is an intangible right.   TANGIBLE

INTANGIBLE
RIGHT

EXAMPLE 2 Remember the example in Unit 13 in which you bought a radio from Ralph Carter and promised to pay him $25 on the first of next month? The radio would be classed as "goods." The agreement by which the title passed to you would be a sale. The right of Ralph to collect the $25 would be an intangible right. If he transferred that right to someone else, that would be an assignment.

The assignment of a right must be in writing if the amount of money involved is $500 or more.

CONTRACTS NOT COVERED BY LAW OF SALES

The law of sales does not apply to the sale of real property. *Real property* is land, buildings, and anything affixed either naturally or artificially to the land. The transfer of real property is correctly or technically called a *conveyance*.

REAL PROPERTY

CONVEYANCE

CONTRACTS FOR LABOR AND MATERIALS

Suppose that you wish to buy a suit, and you go to the Wearwell Clothing Store to choose one from stock. You find a suit that you like, and you buy it. This is a sale of goods; the law of sales operates.

On the other hand, you may decide to have a suit made especially for you by a tailor. This would not be a sale of goods, and the law of sales would not operate. The suit is being made especially for you; therefore, if you refuse to accept it when it is finished, it could not be put in stock for sale to another customer—at least, not without alterations and additional expense. In other words, you have made a *contract for labor and materials*. The law of sales does not apply to contracts for labor and materials, but only to the sale of goods. It is sometimes very important to distinguish between a sale and a contract for labor and materials because some sales must be in writing, while contracts for labor and materials need not be. A contract for labor and material is not considered a sale of goods because it is not suitable for sale to the general public.

The law of sales does not apply to all sales contracts. Name two contracts to which it does not apply.

CONTRACT FOR LABOR AND MATERIALS

EXAMPLE 3 **Lowry, the owner of an expensive imported camera, placed a special order for a telephoto lens designed especially for him. At a later date prior to delivery of the lens, he notified the manufacturer that he had changed his mind and did not want the lens. He claimed that he was not obligated to take the lens because the contract was not in writing. Lowry was liable on the oral contract. The lens was a special one made to Lowry's specification and was not suitable for sale to the general public. This was a contract for labor and materials and did not have to be in writing to be enforceable.**

When goods are made to order and cannot be resold to the seller's regular customers, the contract is for labor and materials and the law of sales does not apply.

Contracts need not be in writing "if the goods are to be specially manufactured for the buyer and are not suitable for sale to others in the ordinary course of the seller's business." U.C.C. Sec. 2-201(3)(a)

OTHER BUSINESS CONTRACTS

CONTRACTS TO SELL

A contract for sale includes both a present sale of future goods and a contract to sell goods at a future time. A sale consists of the passing of title from the seller to the buyer for a price. A *present sale* is a sale that is accomplished when the contract is made. U.C.C. Sec. 2-106(1) Before an interest in goods can pass, the goods must be both existing and identified (set aside for the buyer, labeled, or otherwise identified) in the contract. Goods which are not both existing and identified are *future goods*. A present sale of future goods or an interest in them is like a contract to sell. U.C.C. Sec. 2-105(2)

What is a present sale?

PRESENT SALE

What are future goods?

FUTURE GOODS

EXAMPLE 4 If you contract to transfer title to your transistor radio to Jacob Boyd and it is understood that the title is to pass as soon as the agreement is binding, the transaction is a sale. If you contract to pass title to Jacob Boyd next Tuesday, the outcome is only a contract to sell.

For an agreement to be a sale, title must pass at the time the agreement is made. That is the fundamental element of a sale. Title to goods passes from the seller to the buyer in any manner and on any conditions explicitly agreed on by the parties.

You may contract to sell all the fish you expect to catch, but you cannot actually sell the fish until they are caught and you can transfer title.

CONDITIONAL SALES AND CHATTEL MORTGAGES

It is common practice today for people to buy things on monthly time payments. When they do, they usually sign an agreement that provides that the seller is to retain title until the goods are paid for, although the risk of loss during the installment-payment period is on the buyer. This sort of transaction is not a sale because title does not pass. It is called a *conditional sale*, which is a contract that provides that the title shall pass when the purchase price is paid. Conditional sales have a set of rules all their own. These rules are not the same as the rules that control sales agreements.

CONDITIONAL SALE

Sometimes, when you buy on monthly time payments, you sign a chattel mortgage instead of signing a conditional sales agreement. A *chattel mortgage* is a mortgage on personal property. Technically a chattel mortgage

How does a chattel mortgage differ from a conditional sale?

CHATTEL MORTGAGE

is different from a conditional sales contract, but the legal effect as to the title is just the same.

Title to the goods is transferred by the seller to the buyer as a result of the sale, and then it is immediately transferred back to the seller through the chattel mortgage. The seller then retains title until the full payment is made. A conditional sale and a chattel mortgage are both considered security interests. U.C.C. Sec. 1-201(37) An interest in personal property which secures payment or performance of an obligation is known as a security interest.

BAILMENTS

When you lend goods to another person and expect to have the same goods returned to you at a later time, the act is called a *bailment.* You do not give up title to the goods, only possession; therefore, the transaction is not a sale.

BAILMENT

EXAMPLE 5 **When you lend your golf clubs to Bill Tate, you give up possession of your property, but you retain title. You expect to get the golf clubs back. This transaction is then a bailment and not a sale.**

SALES CONTRACTS THAT MUST BE IN WRITING

Where the sales price is low, the sales contract does not have to be in writing. You have learned that almost all states have statutes that require a written instrument to prove a sale where the sales price is $500 or more.

What evidence may you submit to prove sales contracts and contracts to sell?

The entire contract need not be in writing. It is required only that some evidence be in writing that will prove the existence of the contract. A written memorandum signed by the party to be held liable on the contract is sufficient; the writing does not have to be in any particular form. The Statute of Frauds is satisfied if the memorandum proves the existence of a contract obligation to buy or sell goods and contains enough of the terms to enable a court to make a judgment in case of breach of contract.

Can a sales contract for more than $500 be proved without some written evidence?

An admission or statement in court by the party being sued that he entered into an oral contract with the other party for the sale of goods in an amount of $500 or more will make the contract enforceable. The contract is enforceable only for the quantity of goods admitted. U.C.C. Sec. 2-201(3)(b) This rule applies to nonmerchants as well as to merchants.

In proving sales and contracts to sell, other types of evidence may be used instead of a written instrument. These may be a partial or a full payment that has been accepted by the seller or partial or full delivery which has been accepted by the buyer.

EXAMPLE 6 **George Hunter purchased a motion picture camera, projector, and screen for $825. He took the camera with him and requested that the projector and screen be sent to his home. Even though this was an oral contract, the contract would nevertheless be enforceable because Hunter had accepted partial delivery of the subject matter.**

The law provides that "acceptance of a part of any commercial unit is acceptance of that entire unit." U.C.C. Sec. 2-606(2)

EXAMPLE 7 **If George Hunter did not take any part of his purchase with him but he did pay all or part of the purchase price, then again, no writing is required.**

The general rule is that when all or part of the price is paid no written instrument is required. Even if the goods are not delivered, no writing is required if something is paid to bind the bargain.

REMEMBER: A written instrument may save you considerable trouble and expense later.

SUGGESTIONS FOR MINIMIZING LEGAL RISKS

When you are the purchaser . . .

1. Be sure that the seller has a clear title to the goods before paying for them. Make sure that the seller did not find, borrow, steal, or purchase on an unpaid conditional sales contract the goods offered for sale.
2. Demand adequate proof of the seller's ownership of the goods before paying for them.
3. Minimize your risks by buying goods from a responsible seller who is known to be financially able to make good if called on as a result of a breach of contract.
4. Avoid buying goods by mail from a seller if you are unable to determine in advance that he is completely responsible.
5. Make a very careful inspection of the goods when you are purchasing, and determine the financial responsibility and character of the seller before making the purchase.

 APPLYING YOUR LEARNING

QUESTIONS AND PROBLEMS

1. Have you been a party to a sales contract today? Explain.
2. What are the requirements of a valid sales contract? Do the same general rules of contracts apply to sales contracts?
3. Distinguish between personal property and real property. Does the law of sales apply to real property? Explain.
4. Differentiate between the sale of goods and the assignment of a right.
5. Does the law of sales apply to a contract for labor and materials? Explain.
6. Explain the difference between a sale and a contract to sell. Give an illustration of each.

7. How can you distinguish between a sale and a conditional sale?
8. Will an oral agreement be adequate for all sales? If not, which ones must be in writing?
9. What are the conditions under which a written agreement or a memorandum will not be required to prove the sale?
10. What are the requirements of a writing that will be sufficient to prove a sale in order to satisfy the requirements of the law?
11. If you ordered an expensive boat built to your specifications, would it be necessary to have the agreement in writing? Why?

WHAT IS YOUR OPINION?

In each of the following cases, give your decision and state a legal principle that applies to the case.

1. Maris innocently purchased from Newton goods that had been stolen. Did Maris get a legal title?
2. Kerper orally agreed to furnish the materials and make a suit of clothes for Merkle for $90. The clothes were made to Merkle's individual measurements. Was this an enforceable contract?
3. Verdon orally agreed to buy a quantity of flour from the Avon Milling Company for $100. Verdon received part of the flour, which he immediately resold. A few days later, when the milling company attempted to deliver the remainder of the flour, Verdon refused to accept it, contending that under the Statute of Frauds there had never been a valid contract. Is Verdon liable?
4. Collins bought a new $75 suit on credit. The jacket fitted perfectly, so he took it with him. The trousers, however, required alteration, and he left them with the seller. Would this contract have to be written to be enforceable?
5. Kane was planning to take a fishing trip. Before he left, he agreed to sell all the fish he caught on the trip to Laird for $10. Is this a sale? Explain.
6. The Topeka Furniture Company sold its business, including all its customers' accounts, to the Archer Furniture Company. All customers were properly notified of the assignment. Carr, one of the customers, refused to pay his account to the Archer Company, claiming he was indebted to the Topeka Furniture Company only. Is he correct?
7. A salesman for a shoe manufacturer was given a telephone order by Merlin for $1,000 worth of shoes of the type regularly sold by the company. Later, when the manufacturer requested Merlin to confirm the order, Merlin refused, stating that he was not bound by an oral order. The manufacturer held that the agreement was for labor and materials and was not governed by the Statute of Frauds. Who is right?
8. Webster contracted to buy a new television set for $300. He paid North, the seller, $100 at the time the contract was made. It was agreed that title to the set would pass to Webster when he paid the balance. Before Webster paid the balance, North's creditors seized the set. Can Webster get the set from North's creditors?

9. Mrs. Simpson "borrows" a cup of sugar from her neighbor, Mrs. Black. By implication, it is understood that Mrs. Simpson will return a cup of sugar after she goes to the store and replenishes her own supply. Technically, is this a sale or a bailment?

THE LAW IN ACTION

1. John Pew gave the plaintiff the following written statement just before he sailed on a fishing trip: "We hereby sell, assign, and transfer to Alfred Low & Co. all the halibut that may be caught on the present fishing trip of our schooner, at $5\frac{1}{4}$ cents per pound." John Pew was adjudged a bankrupt before the ship returned, and it was necessary for the court to decide whether the above agreement was a sale or a contract to sell. What do you think should be the decision? (Low v. Pew, 108 Mass. 347)

2. The plaintiff contracted to buy and the defendant contracted to sell 100,000 sets of paint-can ends per day for a specified period. The defendant breached this agreement and, when sued, claimed that because the agreement was oral, it could not be enforced. The can ends were made to the specifications provided by the plaintiff and could not be sold for any other purpose. Do you think this agreement was a sale? Did the agreement come within the Statute of Frauds? (Canister Co. v. National Can Corp., 63 Supp. 361)

KEY TO "WHAT'S THE LAW?" Page 139

1. *No. This would be a sale of real property and would not come within the scope of the Uniform Commercial Code.*
2. *No. This would be a contract for labor and materials.*

WHAT'S THE LAW?

1. Alan Jones rented a power saw from the Webster Hardware Store for two weeks. A week later he wrongfully sold it to Don Richards. Did Don get any title to the saw?

---

2. Scott Mitzner shipped goods to Sam Adams on a straight bill of lading. He kept the original copy of the bill of lading in his own possession and insisted that title to the goods did not pass to Sam until he delivered the bill of lading. Is this correct?

◢ UNIT 17: PASSING TITLE TO GOODS

What does ownership imply?

Let us assume that you received a wristwatch for Christmas last year. You say you own this watch. Just what do you mean when you say you own it? Did you ever stop to think about the nature of ownership and what rights ownership gives? First, of course, you have a right to possess the watch, but you might have a right of possession even if you had just borrowed the watch. There is more to ownership than mere possession. You have a right to do with the watch as you choose. You can give it away; you can sell it; you can leave it to someone in your will. You can even destroy it if you wish. No one else has any right to the watch unless you give it to him. These are the usual characteristics of ownership. *Title* technically is the means by which you prove ownership, but in the ordinary use of the term, it means essentially the same thing as ownership.

TITLE

WRITTEN EVIDENCE OF OWNERSHIP

BILL OF SALE

What is a bill of sale?

There are several other types of evidence that are better than possession for proving title. The sales slip and the invoice which you receive when you purchase merchandise provide acceptable evidence of ownership. When you buy goods that involve a considerable amount of money, it is always well to get a written statement that the seller is transferring ownership to you. Such an instrument is called a *bill of sale*.

BILL OF SALE

A bill of sale, however, proves only that you once had title. It does not prove that you still own the goods.

Example 1 Bob Brown bought a 12-gauge shotgun from Fred White and received a bill of sale. Bob then sold the shotgun to Steve Bobick. The day after this sale, Bob wrongfully contracted to sell the same shotgun to Jim Johnson. In making the sale to Jim, Bob presented the bill of sale from Fred White as proof of his ownership.

The bill of sale meant nothing because Bob no longer had title.

BILL OF LADING

It is sometimes important to have a written instrument, the possession of which is considered conclusive evidence of ownership. Such an instrument is called a *negotiable document of title*. Title may be transferred from one person to another through the transfer of this instrument. There are two types of negotiable documents of title. One is an order bill of lading, and the other is a negotiable warehouse receipt. U.C.C. Sec. 7-503 — NEGOTIABLE DOCUMENT OF TITLE

A *bill of lading* is a receipt for shipment of goods. It is given by a transportation company (known as a carrier) to a shipper when goods are accepted by the carrier for shipment. There are two kinds. One is a *straight bill of lading*, which is a receipt only. It is an acknowledgment by the carrier that the goods have been received, and that is all. The other is an *order bill of lading*. In addition to acknowledging receipt of the goods, an order bill of lading provides that the goods will not be delivered to anyone unless the original bill of lading is presented to the carrier when the goods are demanded by either the shipper or someone else to whom the shipper has transferred it by endorsing his name on the back of the document. Thus, possession of the order bill of lading is evidence of ownership of the goods. U.C.C. Sec. 7-303 An order bill is often used in the following way.

Margin: Distinguish between a straight bill of lading and an order bill of lading.

Margin: How does an order bill of lading prove ownership?

Margin: BILL OF LADING — STRAIGHT BILL OF LADING — ORDER BILL OF LADING

EXAMPLE 2 Suppose that Dan Walters, who lives in Pittsburgh, sells a freezer to John Bowser, who lives in Detroit. Dan arranges to deliver the freezer by air freight and receives an order bill of lading. Dan then sends a letter to John informing him that the bill of lading will be mailed when John's check for the purchase price arrives. In this way, Dan is assured of receiving the money due him.

John cannot get delivery of the freezer from air freight until he produces the order bill of lading. He cannot get the order bill of lading until he pays for the freezer. An order bill of lading is really a credit instrument, but its use is important in many sales transactions.

Warehouse Receipts A warehouse receipt operates like a bill of lading. Again, there are two kinds. A *nonnegotiable warehouse receipt* operates like a straight bill of lading; it is only a receipt for the goods. A *negotiable warehouse receipt* operates like an order bill of lading; the original copy must be presented to the warehouseman before the goods will be delivered. U.C.C. Sec. 7-104(1,h) — NONNEGOTIABLE WAREHOUSE RECEIPT — NEGOTIABLE WAREHOUSE RECEIPT

EXAMPLE 3 Suppose that John Bowser pays for the freezer, receives the order bill of lading, and picks up the freezer at the air freight station. He then stores the freezer in the Acme Warehouse and receives a negotiable warehouse receipt. Next day, he sells the freezer to Tom Wilson and negotiates the warehouse receipt.

Goods shipped on an order bill of lading must be held by the carrier until the original order bill is presented by the consignee.

What uses are often made of credit instruments?

Wilson can rely, in most cases, on Bowser's possession of the negotiable warehouse receipt as being conclusive evidence of title. Like order bills of lading, however, negotiable warehouse receipts are more often used as credit instruments. U.C.C. Sec. 7-104 Both carriers and bills of lading will be explained more fully in Unit 31.

EXAMPLE 4 Instead of selling the freezer, John Bowser might use the warehouse receipt as security for a loan. To do this, he would give the negotiable warehouse receipt to the bank when it lent him money. The bank would then hold the warehouse receipt as security until the loan was repaid.

PASSAGE OF TITLE

It is sometimes very important to determine the exact moment at which title passes to the buyer.

EXAMPLE 5 You agree to sell your transistor radio to Joe Roberts. Joe immediately pays you for the transistor radio, stating that he will pick it up in a day or two. A robber steals the transistor radio that night. Whose transistor radio was stolen by the robber, yours or Joe Roberts'?

The law says that loss follows title, but who had title? If title passed with the agreement, it is Joe's loss. If title did not pass until delivery, then it is your loss.

The law states that in a contract to sell specific goods, title shall pass at the time the parties intend it to pass. If the parties specify a certain time, title passes at that time. Unfortunately, the parties often do not say anything about the passing of title. To meet this problem, the law lays down certain rules for determining the intent of the parties.

When does title pass to specific goods that are sold on an unconditional contract?

Where there is an unconditional contract to sell specific goods that are ready for delivery, title passes at the time the agreement is made. The time of payment and the time of delivery are not important.

EXAMPLE 6 When you agreed to sell your transistor radio to Joe, title passed to Joe when the contract was completed. Therefore, the theft of the transistor radio is Joe's loss. If you had agreed to replace a transistor before Joe picked it up, title would not pass until the new transistor had been installed. Goods must be in a deliverable state.

When goods are unascertained at the time of the contract (that is, they are nonspecific goods), title does not pass until specific goods have been appropriated to the buyer's order.

EXAMPLE 7 **Suppose you are a transistor radio salesman, and you agree to sell Joe a particular make and model of transistor radio. None of this particular make and model is in stock presently, but you expect to receive shipment and to deliver the transistor radio in one day. Title does not pass until the radios are received, and one is selected to fill Joe's order.**

GOODS PURCHASED WITH PRIVILEGE OF RETURN

Suppose that it is agreed that Joe is to take the radio home, with the privilege of returning it within ten days if he is not satisfied. Two days later, Joe's house burns down and the radio is destroyed. Whose loss is it? This is a puzzling question. If the agreement was a sale, then title passed and the loss is Joe's, even though he did have the privilege of returning the radio and revesting the title in you. Until he returned it, it was his. This is one of the features of a purchase in which the goods are bought with the privilege of return. Under a sale or return, unless otherwise agreed, the option to return the goods extends to the whole or any salable part of the goods while in their original condition, but the return must be made within an agreed or reasonable time. Also, the return is at the buyer's risk and expense. U.C.C. Sec. 2-327(2)(a)(b)

Upon whom does the risk of loss fall when goods are sold on a sale or return basis?

GOODS PURCHASED ON TRIAL OR ON APPROVAL

If, however, Joe did not agree to buy the radio at once but only took it home with the understanding that he would buy the radio if he liked it, then no title passed. Title would not pass until Joe signified his approval, either by saying so or by keeping the radio longer than agreed upon. Under these circumstances, then, the loss would fall on you if the radio were destroyed in the fire. Under a sale on approval, even though the goods are identified to the contract, the risk of loss and the title do not pass to the buyer until acceptance, unless there has been an agreement to the contrary. U.C.C. Sec. 2-327(1)(a) The use of the goods consistent with the

Upon whom does the risk of loss fall when goods are sold on approval?

Goods sold on "sale or return" may be seized by the buyer's creditors because the goods belong to the buyer until they are returned.

purpose of trial is not acceptance, but failure to notify the seller of one's decision to return the goods in the agreed time or within a reasonable time is acceptance. If the goods conform to the contract, then acceptance of any part is acceptance of the whole. U.C.C. Sec. 2-327(1)(b)

REMEMBER: You should be very careful to understand your contract when you take goods out on trial or on approval.

The seller will usually try to set up the transaction as a "sale or return," so that title passes to you. You should make it quite clear that you are not buying until you give your approval. U.C.C. Sec. 2-326(1)(b)

SALE BY AUCTION

At ordinary auction sales, you, as the bidder, are making the offer. The auctioneer is only soliciting offers. The acceptance of your offer occurs and the sale is made when the auctioneer brings down his gavel and cries, "Sold." Title passes at that time. You may withdraw your bid at any time prior to acceptance, but your retraction does not revive any previous bid. U.C.C. Sec. 2-328(2)

At ordinary auction sales, the acceptance of the offer occurs when the auctioneer brings down his gavel and cries, "Sold!"

How does an auction sale without reserve differ from one with reserve?

In an auction sale without reserve, the auctioneer is offering to sell the goods to the highest bidder; thus, he becomes the offeror. He may not withdraw the goods after putting them up for bidding unless no bid is made within a reasonable time. Sales with reserve give the auctioneer the right to withdraw goods if reasonable bids are not made. He may do so at any time until he announces completion of the sale. U.C.C. Sec. 2-328(3)

What does by-bidding at an auction sale mean?

The unauthorized practice of placing an accomplice in the crowd to make bids for the purpose of raising the bids of bona fide purchasers is known as *by-bidding*. The practice is illegal and, if proved, the resulting sale may be set aside on the ground of fraud.

BY-BIDDING

EXAMPLE 8 After Norm Canfield bought an antique vase at an auction sale, he discovered that the man against whom he was bidding was an agent of the auctioneer placed in the crowd merely to encourage the raising of the other offers. Proof of this fact would give Canfield the right to have his agreement set aside and bring an action for damages.

F.O.B. SALES

When does title pass when goods are shipped f.o.b. shipping point?

The abbreviation f.o.b. means "free on board." When a price is quoted for goods *f.o.b.* (*shipping point*), the buyer must pay the freight charges from the shipping point to the destination. Thus, "f.o.b. Detroit" means that the seller will put the goods on freight cars or trucks at Detroit, but the buyer pays all expenses from there. At that point the goods become the responsibility of the buyer; title passes when the seller delivers the merchandise to the carrier (transportation company) for shipment. When the term is f.o.b. (shipping point), the seller must take the goods to that place in the manner provided and bear the expense and risk of putting them into the possession of the carrier. U.C.C. Sec. 2-319(a)

F.O.B. SHIPPING POINT

EXAMPLE 9 **A machine is shipped to a customer f.o.b. St. Louis, the home city of the seller. Title to the machine would pass to the customer as soon as the seller delivered it to the freight depot in St. Louis and it was accepted by the carrier.**

In the event of loss, the customer would be permitted to make an owner's claim against the carrier. He would not, however, be relieved of his responsibility to pay the seller, even though the machine never reached him. This is always true even in those cases where the seller has requested the carrier to refuse to make delivery until the full purchase price has been paid, as would be the case in a typical *c.o.d.* (collect on delivery) *shipment*.

C.O.D. SHIPMENT

When does title pass when goods are shipped f.o.b. destination?

Goods sold under the terms *f.o.b. destination* remain the property of the seller, and he continues to have the risk of ownership until the merchandise reaches its destination. When the term is f.o.b. the place of destination, the seller must at his own expense and risk transport the goods to that place and there tender delivery of them in the manner provided. U.C.C. Sec. 2-319(b)

F.O.B. DESTINATION

Tender of delivery requires that the seller hold the goods for the buyer and give the buyer any notification reasonably necessary to enable him to take delivery. The manner, time, and place for tender are determined by the agreement. U.C.C. Sec. 2-503(1) Sec. 2-504(b)(c)

EXAMPLE 10 **If the customer in Example 9 had not wished to accept the risk of ownership during the shipment of the machine, he could have designated that delivery would have to be made f.o.b. shipping point. The destination would be the city in which he lived. If he lived in Chicago, the terms would have been f.o.b. Chicago, Illinois.**

If the terms are "f.o.b. (shipping point), c.o.d.," title passes to the buyer at the shipping point, but the carrier retains possession of the buyer's goods until the carrier receives the money due the seller.

STOLEN GOODS

It is a fundamental rule of law that a thief acquires no title to the goods that he steals and, therefore, cannot convey a good title. You cannot lose title to your goods except through some action of your own. The true owner never relinquishes title to the stolen goods, and even an innocent

May lost or
stolen goods ever
be regained by
the true owner
from an innocent
purchaser for
value?

purchaser who acquires the goods in good faith and for value would be obliged to return the goods to the owner. The true owner can always regain possession when and if the goods are found, no matter in whose possession they may be.

EXAMPLE 11 Kline bought a jeep from Madison, paying a fair price for it. Later, Hanna demanded that Kline return the jeep to him with the claim that Madison had previously stolen the jeep from him. Hanna provided an auto registration to prove his ownership. Kline must return the jeep to Hanna. Kline can acquire no better title than Madison possessed. Madison could not convey title to Kline when he possessed no title himself.

LOST GOODS

With goods that you find, the situation is a little different. Between you and the true owner, the true owner always has a right to recover the goods. Between you and everyone except the true owner, however, you, as a finder, have absolute right of possession. You may even sell such rights as you have, as long as it is understood by the buyer that you do not claim to have title, but only possession. The true owner may recover the goods even from a purchaser who bought the goods from the finder in good faith and for value.

UNORDERED GOODS

When a person receives unordered merchandise, he need not keep it or pay for it. The recipient may treat the unordered merchandise as a gift from the seller, and he may retain or dispose of it as he sees fit. He is under no obligation to the seller unless a prior agreement exists.

EXAMPLE 12 Chester Marcus received a leather wallet through the mail just prior to the Christmas holidays with a request either to send $3 for it or return it at the company's expense. Marcus refused to do either. He was acting within his rights.

No one may force a person to perform a duty that he is not legally required to perform.

BULK SALES

The sale of an entire inventory to one buyer is occasionally made by a merchant for the purpose of defrauding the wholesale firms with which he does business. Also, a dishonest merchant sometimes buys up a large quantity of merchandise without paying for it and then sells it to third parties and makes off with the proceeds.

EXAMPLE 13 Suppose that Jerry French owns a small grocery store. He owes a number of bills, but his creditors feel secure. Jerry has a good business and a good stock of merchandise. They know that if Jerry does not pay, they can have some of his merchandise seized and sold to pay their claims. Jerry, however, fools

them. He makes a quick sale of his entire business for cash, puts the money in his pocket, and leaves the state.

When does a bulk sale result?

BULK SALE

A *bulk sale* is any transfer in bulk and not in the ordinary course of the transferor's business of a major part of the materials, supplies, merchandise, or other inventory of an enterprise. U.C.C. Sec. 6-102(1) Although all bulk sales are not made with this intent, the rights of creditors are protected under the law. A buyer under a bulk sale may lose all ownership rights to the goods purchased if he does not abide by the provisions of the Bulk Sales Act and the Uniform Commercial Code. Creditors who have suffered damage may demand the return of all goods bought, with no obligation to reimburse the purchaser. The requisites of the Bulk Sales Act are as follows.

1. The seller shall (a) give the buyer a detailed inventory of the merchandise, including cost price, at least ten days before the sale is made; and (b) give the buyer a list, sworn to be correct, of his creditors and the amount owed to each. U.C.C. Sec. 6-104(1)(2)(3)

2. The buyer (transferee) shall (a) retain the inventory and list of creditors for six months, subject to the inspection by any of the seller's creditors, or file them in a public office, and (b) notify the seller's creditors (either by registered or certified mail or personally) of the proposed sale and the terms of the sale at least ten days before taking possession of the goods or paying for them, whichever happens first. The buyer must give notice to any party who is known to him to have any claim against the seller, even though he is not included in the list of creditors supplied by the seller.

What is the purpose of the Bulk Sales Act?

If, after observing these regulations, the buyer pays for and takes title and possession of the inventory, the creditors may not thereafter interrupt his rights to the property. U.C.C. Sec. 6-105, 107(3)

EXAMPLE 14   **Montgomery owned a local souvenir store, and he advertised the store for sale. Greer purchased the store, which included a $20,000 merchandise inventory. Later, Greer learned that Montgomery had sold the store to defraud his creditors. The creditors claimed the entire inventory shortly thereafter.**

Had Greer followed the requirements of the law without receiving any notice from the creditors within the stated period, his final purchase would have assured him of uninterrupted ownership of all the inventory received.

SUGGESTIONS FOR MINIMIZING LEGAL RISKS

When you are the purchaser . . .

1. If there is any doubt as to when the title is to pass, obtain a written statement, if possible, stating the time at which the title is to pass.
2. Should the purchase be one that comes within the provisions of the Statute of Frauds, obtain a written contract signed by the seller or his agent.

3. If there is a possibility of loss due to fire or theft of valuable goods purchased and not yet delivered and still under the control of the seller, either enter into a contract that the loss will be borne by the seller or take out insurance to cover the possible loss.

4. When you are trying out or considering goods for possible purchase, try to purchase on trial or on approval rather than with the privilege of return.

 APPLYING YOUR LEARNING

QUESTIONS AND PROBLEMS

1. Does possession of goods always mean that one has ownership of the goods? Explain.
2. Does possession of a bill of sale prove that you own the goods?
3. What is meant by a negotiable document of title? What are the two types of negotiable documents of title?
4. What is meant by a warehouse receipt? How is it used?
5. What are the two types of warehouse receipts? Distinguish between them.
6. Why is it very important to know the exact moment that title passes in a sale of goods?
7. Explain when title passes in each of the following cases:
    a. Nonspecific or unascertained goods are sold.
    b. Goods are sold with the privilege of return.
    c. Goods are sold "on trial" or "on approval."
    d. Goods are sold at a public auction.
8. What is the practice with respect to the passing of title in each of the following cases:
    a. An f.o.b. (destination) sale; an f.o.b. (shipping point) sale.
    b. A sale of stolen goods.
    c. A sale of lost goods.
    d. A bulk sale without due notice to creditors.
9. What part does an auctioneer play in the making of contracts at an ordinary auction sale?

WHAT IS YOUR OPINION?

In each of the following cases, give your decision and state a legal principle that applies to the case.

1. Berne, of Rochester, sold goods to Williams, of Cleveland, the contract stated that the price was $150, f.o.b. Rochester. While the goods were being transported by railroad from Rochester to Cleveland, they were damaged. Did this loss fall on Williams?

2. Lutz made a contract to buy a used car from the White Motor Company. According to the terms of the contract, the company agreed to repaint the car. Before the car could be painted, it was destroyed through no fault of the White Company. The company sued Lutz for the contract price. Would the White Company win?

3. Norton, of Topeka, Kansas, ordered from Gardner, in Warren, Ohio, electrical equipment according to specifications given in Gardner's catalog. The equipment was shipped f.o.b. Topeka. If the equipment were damaged en route, through no fault of the common carrier, who should stand the loss, Norton or Gardner?

4. Sumner sold and delivered a washing machine to Richards. Sumner told Richards that he had the privilege of returning the washing machine at any time within fifteen days if it proved unsatisfactory. Ten days after Richards received the machine and while it was in his home, it was damaged by fire. Must Richards stand the loss?

5. Horne was thinking of buying an adding machine from Perkins but was not certain that it would do his work efficiently. Perkins told him to take the machine on "ten days' trial or approval." After Horne had had the machine in his office for six days, it was destroyed by fire through no fault of his. Must Horne pay for the machine?

6. Irvin bought a hunting dog from Smith, on approval, and agreed either to pay $200 for the dog if it suited him or to return it within five days. The dog was kept seven days and died of colic. Smith sued Irvin for the price of the dog. Can Smith collect?

7. Good visited a furniture store and selected a chair priced at $45. The store and all its contents were destroyed by fire before Good had returned to pay for the chair and take it home. The merchant billed Good for $45, the price of the chair. Can he collect?

8. Sandy Jameson and Anna Dianopolis, owners of a small beauty salon in San Jose, California, owed $5000 for the installation of hair dryers and for a large assortment of beauty supplies. Both girls decided that they would rather live in Portland, Oregon, so they sold their business and used the money to take an extended vacation before moving to Portland. Do Sandy and Anna have any responsibilities as required by the Bulk Sales Act? Does the Bulk Sales Act impose any responsibilities on the buyer of the beauty salon?

THE LAW IN ACTION

1. The plaintiff sold an automobile to Jack Wortham, who paid the purchase price by check. The check proved to be worthless; but, before this fact was discovered by the plaintiff, Wortham had sold the car to Shepherd, who purchased it in good faith and for value. Could the plaintiff recover the car from the defendant? Why or why not? (Pingleton v. Shepherd, 219 Ark. 473, 242 S.W. 2d 971)

2. The defendant bought a stack of hay located on the plaintiff's farm. It was agreed that the defendant should leave the hay in the stack, removing a load at a time as he needed it, and that the hay should be

weighed at the time it was taken from the stack. The price was fixed at so much per ton. Before any hay was removed, the stack was destroyed by fire. Who must bear the loss? Why? (Allen v. Elmore, 121 Iowa 241, 96 N.W. 769)

KEY TO "WHAT'S THE LAW?" Page 147

1. *No. Alan could not pass any title to Don because he did not own the saw.*
2. *No. A straight bill of lading is a receipt for the goods shipped only. It does not indicate title or ownership of the goods.*

WHAT'S THE LAW?

1. *Eric Anderson bought a suit of clothes on 30-day credit. At the end of the 30 days, the seller demanded the money or the return of the suit. Does the seller have a right to take back the suit if Eric does not pay?*

---

2. *Gene Harris bought a radio on a conditional sales contract. Before the radio was paid for, it was destroyed by fire. Gene contends that he does not have to finish paying for the radio. Is he correct?*

◢ UNIT 18: BUYING ON CREDIT

You need not always pay cash for the things you buy. Sometimes credit is necessary to make a much-needed purchase. This is the basis of installment sales, in which you buy on time or on credit.

EXAMPLE 1 Suppose that you are offered an after-school job. The job will pay you $20 a week, but you must have a bicycle to do the work. You do not have a bicycle, and you do not have the cash to buy one. If, however, you can made an arrangement with a sporting-goods store to buy a bicycle on credit and pay for it out of your $20 a week, everyone will profit. Your employer will get a helper, you will have a job, and the dealer will sell a bicycle.

Multiply your personal situation several million times, and you will see how important consumer credit is to American business.

CONDITIONAL SALES

The basic problem involved in granting consumer credit may be illustrated as follows:

EXAMPLE 2 Suppose that you bought the bicycle in Example 1. It was sold to you on credit in the regular fashion. It was a sale, and title passed to you. That is the nature of a sale—title passes at once. Then, suppose that at the end of the first week you quit your job, sold the bicycle to Bob Rizzo for cash, and spent the money to go to summer camp.

When does title pass on goods sold "on time"?

You still owe the seller the purchase price, but you do not have a job, you do not have any money, and Bob Rizzo now owns the bicycle. Where is the seller going to get his money? If you are honest, you may eventually pay, but the seller may have to wait a long time for his money.

It was to avoid situations of this kind that the conditional sale was developed. In a *conditional sale*, the goods are sold with the express condition and understanding that title shall remain with the seller until the purchase price is paid. Thus, the conditional buyer cannot sell the goods to someone else. He does not have title, and, having no title himself, he cannot pass good title to a subsequent buyer. Furthermore, because the original seller still owns the goods, he can get them if they are not paid for according to the terms of the agreement.

CONDITIONAL SALE

PASSAGE OF TITLE

The fundamental difference between a sale and a conditional sale is the time when title passes. In a sale, title passes when the contract is made. In a conditional sale, title is retained until the goods are paid for. If this is so, who suffers a loss if the goods are stolen or destroyed?

If you bought the bicycle in Example 1 on a conditional sales contract, you would not get title until the bicycle was fully paid for. You must note, however, that the seller would retain title for security purposes only. In all other respects you are the owner. You have the right of possession and use. It is your duty to keep the bicycle in repair, and you have the risk of loss. If the bicycle is stolen or destroyed, you must continue to make the payments until the purchase price is fully paid.

Who bears the risk of loss in a conditional sale?

While the general idea of conditional sales exists in all states, there is considerable difference in the way different states work out the details. It would be well for you to consult with local banks, finance companies, merchants, and better business bureaus to learn something about the possible ways that conditional sales are handled in your locality.

FILING CONDITIONAL SALES CONTRACTS

You recall the discussion in which you might have bought the bicycle on a conditional sales contract and then wrongfully sold it to Bob Rizzo. You learned that title would not pass to him because you had none to give. You learned also that the seller could repossess the bicycle. But what about Bob's rights? He knew that you had bought the bicycle. You

The conditional seller has a string on the goods sold. He retains title for security purposes and may repossess the goods if they are not paid for.

CONDITIONAL SALES CONTRACT

Date __February 13__ , 19__   Buyers' Name __Maurice Crandall__

To __Ray G. Schmidt__   Residence
<u>   Seller   </u>   Address __1202 Maple Drive__

__843 Elm Street__
<u>   Street   </u>

__Palo Alto, California__   __Palo Alto, California__
<u>City   State</u>   <u>City   State</u>

I (meaning the undersigned buyer or buyers, jointly and severally) hereby buy from
you the following goods.

Article	Model No.	Serial No.
Stereo-HiFi	Premier 63	P81-73021

Use This Schedule If Monthly Payments Are Unequal		

Use This Schedule
If Monthly Payments Are Unequal

$____on____19____ | $____on____19____
$____on____19____ | $____on____19____
$____on____19____ | $____on____19____
$____on____19____ | $____on____19____
$____on____19____ | $____on____19____

Cash price .... $ __229.95__
Sales tax .... $ __6.90__
Credit service charge....... $ __6.00__
Total purchase price........ $ 242.85
Down payment
(a) Cash .... $ __42.85__
(b) Allowance for
    trade-in ...... $ __none__ $ __42.85__
Balance .... $ 200.00

which is payable in installments of $____20____ on the ____10th____ day of
each ____month____ , commencing on ____April 10____ , 19__ .

Title to goods purchased under this contract is retained by you until payment
of full purchase price. I agree to keep the goods safely and free from all other liens
and at the above address unless you consent in writing of their removal.

The full balance shall become due on default, together with a 15% attorney's
fee if then placed with an attorney for collection. In case of default, you shall also
have the right to retake the goods wherever located, hold and dispose of them and
collect expenses, and I shall have the right to redeem the goods or require their
sale at public auction, all as provided by the law of the State of California.

This is our entire agreement, subject to any written guarantee or service contract duly delivered by you and cannot be changed orally. If I shall be given written
notice that you have assigned this contract, you shall continue responsible for all
of your obligations, but your assignee's rights shall be independent of my claims
against you.

THIS IS A CONDITIONAL SALES CONTRACT

Ray G. Schmidt   *Maurice Crandall*
<u>Accepted Seller's Signature</u>   <u>Buyer's Signature</u>

I have received an executed copy of
this contract. No other extension of
credit exists, or is to be made, in connection with this purchase.

By __J. C. R. Supt.__   *Maurice Crandall*
<u>   Title   </u>   <u>Buyer's Signature</u>

had the bicycle in your possession, and he paid cash to you for it. Is he going to be left the loser.

Rights of Third Parties How can we protect the rights of innocent third parties? The innocent third party might be either the unsuspecting buyer or another creditor who had extended credit, relying on the possession of the goods by the conditional buyer.

Why should the seller record every conditional sales contract?

● To protect the interests of third parties, a conditional sales contract or a "financing statement" must be recorded (filed) by the seller in a public office. If the seller fails to do so, he cannot recover the goods from one who innocently purchases them from the buyer. The public office may be that of the county clerk, the city clerk, the recorder, or some other designated office in the town or county where the buyer resides. Each state specifies the appropriate office. U.C.C. Sec. 9-401

In conditional sales, how are the rights of the innocent third parties protected?

Now you know how Bob might have protected himself. He knew you had recently bought the bicycle. He could have gone to the proper office and checked to see whether a conditional sales contract had been recorded. These records are open to the public. Anyone has the privilege of examining them. Unfortunately, many people do not know this, and thus they lose the protection that the law gives them. U.C.C. Sec. 9-407

DEFAULT ON SALES CONTRACTS

Another problem raised by conditional sales is how to protect the rights of both the seller and the buyer in case the goods are not paid for.

In case of default, what rights does the seller have?

Rights of the Seller All states agree that the conditional seller may repossess (take back) the goods if the payments are not met.

● Some states hold that the seller may repossess the goods and that he must then sell the goods at a fair price. If this resale does not cover the amount still owed plus collection costs, the seller may bring an action for the remaining balance.

Rights of the Buyer The buyer has the right to keep the goods under the terms of the contract. If he fails to make the payments, then he loses his basic right and the seller may repossess.

Sometimes, the buyer may have almost fully paid for the goods when some misfortune makes it impossible for him to pay the balance. It is for this reason that many states require that the goods must be resold, especially if more than 50 percent of the purchase price has been paid. Any excess over the unpaid balance is returned to the conditional buyer.

CHATTEL MORTGAGES

What is a chattel mortgage?

While the theory of chattel mortgages is a little different from the theory of conditional sales, chattel mortgages and conditional sales contracts operate much the same way in practice. A *chattel mortgage* is a mortgage on personal property. The basic purpose of both is to give the seller a right to retake the goods if the purchase price is not paid.

CHATTEL MORTGAGE

NOTE: *The bullet indicates that there may be a state statute that varies from the law discussed here.*

Goods repossessed under authority given by various credit devices usually must be resold at a fair price. This is to protect the interests of both the creditor and the debtor.

EXAMPLE 3   If you had purchased the bicycle under a chattel mortgage contract, you would have signed over to the store the title to the bicycle. In the event of any default by you, the creditor would have the legal right to seize the bicycle and sell it, applying the money realized to your obligation. If the resale does not bring enough money to cover your debt, a "deficiency judgment" may be entered against you or an action brought by the creditor for the balance owed on your contract.

The first chattel mortgages were the same as real property mortgages, using the word "personalty" rather than "realty." They gave the seller the right to go into court and have the mortgage ordered foreclosed. Foreclosure was followed by seizure and sale of the goods by the sheriff. Conditional sales contracts were created originally to get around this necessity for court action and make it possible for the seller to seize the goods himself.

● In some states the procedure for foreclosing chattel mortgages has been changed so that the modern form is very frequently close to a conditional sales contract.

BAILMENT LEASES

Bailment leases are used in only a few states. Where they are used, they operate very much like a conditional sales contract. The theory is that the seller only rents the goods to the buyer with the understanding that, when the amount of the rental paid equals the purchase price, the buyer (lessee) will be permitted to take title to the property on the payment of some token amount, usually $1.

BAILMENT LEASES

EXAMPLE 4   Had you followed this plan, you would have rented the bicycle for a specified number of months. When all rent had been paid, you would then purchase the bicycle for $1 and receive full ownership rights.

When does title generally pass in a bailment lease?

● The courts in many states have held that such an agreement is really a sale, and they rule that title passes when the contract is made.

TRUST RECEIPTS

To illustrate trust receipts, let us assume that the buyer is an automobile dealer. When he buys a carload of automobiles, he must pay cash for them. Sometimes, he finds it necessary to borrow money at the bank in order to raise the cash. He could, and often does, execute chattel mortgages on the cars to obtain the loan. The bank now has title to the cars until the loan is paid. This makes it awkward when he attempts to resell a car because he does not have title, and he must get a release from the bank before the sale can be made.

How may trust receipts be used as security for bank loans?

To meet this special need, a credit instrument called a *trust receipt* is sometimes used. By executing a trust receipt, the dealer declares that he holds title to the goods, not for himself, but for the benefit of the bank, thus, he can convey good title to the new buyer, but the money he receives automatically becomes the money of the bank. Again, you see that we have a problem of protecting the rights of third parties.

TRUST RECEIPT

EXAMPLE 5 **Suppose that another creditor extends credit to the car dealer because he knows that the dealer has a warehouse full of new automobiles. If, unknown to this creditor, trust receipts had been issued on all these cars, the creditor would be misled.**

● Some form of notice is required to protect third parties. Many states require that trust receipts be recorded.

SUGGESTIONS FOR MINIMIZING LEGAL RISKS

1. Read the fine print on the conditional sales contract to determine what additional costs may be added in case of a default of a payment.
2. If goods are repossessed on a conditional sales contract, make a written demand on the seller within ten days that the goods be sold and the proceeds be applied to the unpaid balance.
3. If financial difficulties make it impossible for you to keep up payments on a conditional sales contract, try to work out some alternative plan with the seller—either for a new contract with lower payments or for a mutual assignment of your contract to some other person. This avoids the possible risk of having to pay the difference between the amount returned on a forced sale and the unpaid balance on your conditional sales contract.
4. It is wise to take out insurance against risk of loss by fire, theft, and other possible risks on sizable purchases made on conditional sales contracts, chattel mortgages, or other credit devices.
5. When purchasing goods that you suspect may have been originally bought by the seller under a conditional sales contract or other form of credit instrument, check the public records to see whether the credit instrument and a subsequent release have ever been recorded.

▲ APPLYING YOUR LEARNING

QUESTIONS AND PROBLEMS

1. What is the fundamental difference between a sale and a conditional sale? Explain.
2. What is the theory behind the conditional sales contract? Why do such contracts tend to stimulate and increase sales?
3. What is meant by the statement that "the seller retains title for security purposes only"? Explain.
4. Do all states follow the same laws governing conditional sales contracts?
5. What may happen when the purchaser defaults in keeping up payments on a conditional sales contract?
6. What are the buyer's rights under a conditional sales contract?
7. What are some other credit devices frequently used in selling goods on a time basis?
8. What are the advantages to a businessman in using a trust receipt rather than a conditional sales contract or a chattel mortgage when purchasing goods on a time basis? Explain.

WHAT IS YOUR OPINION?

In each of the following cases, give your decision and state a legal principle that applies to the case.

1. You buy a radio on a 12-month installment plan. After you have made four of the twelve monthly payments, a fire breaks out in your home and destroys the radio. Does the merchant bear the loss?
2. Light sold a radio to Green on an installment plan of ten monthly payments and recorded the sale in the proper public office. After Green had made two monthly payments, he sold the radio to Burke. Did Burke obtain good title?
3. Hall wished to borrow $300 from the First National Bank. He offered to use his new car as security. Would he execute a chattel mortgage, a conditional sales contract, or some other instrument?
4. Newton owned an electrical appliance store. He wished to borrow $500 from the First National Bank and use his merchandise as security. Would he execute a chattel mortgage, a conditional sales contract, a trust receipt, or some other instrument?
5. Norton sold Weston a power mower on 30 days' credit. At the end of the 30 days, Weston failed to pay the purchase price. May Norton go to Weston's house and take back the mower? Explain.
6. Norton rented Weston a power mower at a rental of $2 a week. It was agreed that at the end of 30 days Weston could buy the mower if he wished and that the four weeks' rental could be applied on the purchase price. At the end of 30 days, Weston did not return the mower, nor did he offer to pay for it. Can Norton go to Weston's house and take back the mower? Explain.

7. Norton sold Weston a power mower on a conditional sales contract, Weston promising to make weekly payments of $2. Weston made the first payment, but no more. At the end of 30 days, can Norton go to Weston's house and take back the mower? Explain.

8. If Norton took back the mower after Weston's first and only payment, could Weston demand the return of his $2?

THE LAW IN ACTION

1. Allen borrowed money from the plaintiff and had a chattel mortgage executed on his tobacco crop to secure the repayment of the loan. The plaintiff failed to record the chattel mortgage. After the crop was harvested, Allen wrongfully delivered the tobacco to the defendant as a pledge to secure the payment of his rent. The plaintiff demands the tobacco from the defendant. Should he get it? (Mason & Moody v. Scruggs, 207 Ky. 66, 268 S.W. 833)

2. The defendant sold an automobile to the plaintiff on a conditional sales contract. The conditional sales contract contained the usual provision that the defendant could repossess the car if payments were not made on time. The plaintiff did not keep up his payments, and the defendant repossessed the car from a lot beside the plaintiff's house without the knowledge or consent of the plaintiff. The plaintiff sued the defendant for conversion. Is he entitled to a judgment? (Ikovich v. Silver Bow Motor Car Co., 117 Mont. 268, 157 Pac. 2d 785)

KEY TO "WHAT'S THE LAW?" Page 158

1. *No. Title to the suit passed to Anderson at the time the sale was made. The only action available to the seller is for the purchase price.*

2. *No. In a conditional sales contract the title is retained by the seller for security purposes only. The risk of loss falls on the buyer.*

A DIGEST OF LEGAL CONCEPTS

1. Sales agreements require all the basic elements of a valid contract to be enforceable.

2. The law of sales applies to transactions in goods only.

3. The term goods, means all things (including specially manufactured goods) which are movable at the time of identification to the contract for sale other than the money in which the price is to be paid.

4. In a sale, title passes immediately after the contract is made.

5. In a contract to sell, title does not pass until a later time.

6. In a conditional sale, title is retained by the seller for security purposes until the goods are paid for.

7. Contracts need not be in writing if the goods are to be specially manufactured for the buyer and are not suitable for sale to others in the ordinary course of the seller's business.

8. Exceptions to the rule that a written contract is required are as follows:
   a. Where the goods are delivered or partially delivered.
   b. Where the purchase price is paid or partially paid.
   c. Where some money has been paid to bind the bargain.
   d. When the party being sued admits in court that he entered into an oral contract.

9. A sale is not complete until title passes from the owner to the purchaser.

10. The seller usually does not retain title or have a claim on goods sold on ordinary credit.

11. Evidence that will satisfy the writing requirements of the law may be a written contract or a memorandum, properly signed by the party to be charged or his agent, containing evidence of a contract for the sale of goods and specifying the "quantity of the goods mentioned in the writing." A memorandum may be a letter, a telegram, a sales slip, an order form, or other paper.

12. To be the subject matter of a sale, goods must be in existence and owned by the seller. The seller can contract to sell goods that he reasonably expects to own in the future.

13. Ownership gives to the owner of goods the exclusive rights to possess, control, and resell them.

14. Possession of goods is not conclusive evidence of ownership.

15. Goods delivered to a carrier in return for an order bill of lading may not be reclaimed at their destination unless the original order bill is presented to the carrier.

16. Goods delivered to a warehouseman in return for a negotiable warehouse receipt may not be reclaimed unless the original negotiable warehouse receipt is presented to the warehouseman.

17. Title to existing goods passes to the buyer when the parties agree that it shall pass.

18. Where there is an unconditional contract to sell specific goods in a deliverable condition, title passes when the contract is made. Where there is a contract to sell unascertained goods, title passes when goods are appropriated to the contract.

19. In a sale or return agreement, title passes at the time of sale, but the buyer may return the goods and revest the title in the seller.

20. The title to goods sold on approval does not pass to the buyer until the buyer's approval is given.

21. The owner of goods does not lose his title to them if they are stolen.

22. The buyer of stolen goods gets no title to them, because they may be reclaimed by the original owner.

23. The rights of a finder are good against everyone except the true owner.

24. In a sale at auction, title passes when the gavel falls and the auctioneer says, "Sold!"

25. In an f.o.b. (shipping point) sale, title passes to the buyer when the goods are delivered to the carrier by the seller.

26. In an f.o.b. (destination) sale, title passes to the buyer only when the merchandise reaches its destination.

27. In a conditional sale, title does not pass until the goods are paid for.

WHAT'S THE LAW?

1. *Anthony Alvarez was shopping for a new clock. The store manager stated, "This clock is absolutely guaranteed." How much reliance can Anthony place on this statement?*

2. *Jack White walked into a drugstore and said, "I want a bottle of 'Indian Joe's Cure-All.' I have a bad cold." The druggist sold him the product, but it did not cure his cold. Could Jack sue the druggist for breach of warranty?*

◢ UNIT 19: WARRANTIES IN SALES AGREEMENTS

EXAMPLE 1 Suppose that you wish to buy a new color television set. You know nothing about television electronics. You have no skill that enables you to determine by looking at a set whether it is good or bad or whether it will work satisfactorily in your home.

Even if you had such a skill, the set delivered to your home ordinarily will not be the floor sample you looked at. It will probably be another set just like the floor sample.

Ordinarily, a television set will be delivered to your home sealed in its original carton. You see the actual set you buy for the first time when it is unpacked in your own home. In making such a purchase, you must rely on the respresentations and promises of the seller. The representations and promises of the seller, used to induce you to buy, are called *warranties*. **WARRANTY**

There are two kinds of warranties: (1) express warranties and (2) implied warranties. Express warranties by the seller in contracts for sale are created by affirmation, promise, description, or sample. Any affirmation of fact or promise made by the seller to the buyer which relates to the goods and becomes part of the basis of the bargain creates an express warranty that the goods shall conform to the affirmation or promise. Any description of the goods or sample or model which is made part of the basis of the bargain creates an express warranty that the goods shall conform to the description or sample or model. U.C.C. Sec. 2-313(1)(a)(b)(c) An **EXPRESS** *express warranty,* as the name implies, is a statement of fact expressed by **WARRANTY** the seller for the purpose of inducing the buyer to purchase. An *implied* **IMPLIED** *warranty* is not stated in words but is implied from the nature of the sale **WARRANTY** and the surrounding circumstances. In ordinary usage, the term *"guarantee"* **GUARANTEE** is often used in place of "warranty."

How do you distinguish between an express warranty and an implied warranty?

EXPRESS WARRANTIES

It is not necessary to the creation of an express warranty that the seller use formal words such as "warrant" or "guarantee." U.C.C. Sec. 2-313(2).

One nationally known manufacturer, in advertising its products, decided to substitute the simple term "promise" for the more legal sounding language frequently used, and has now revised practically all its consumer product guarantees. One guarantee now reads: "[We] promise to replace any . . . product that ever breaks from extreme temperature." This trend to use simple language will likely cause future warranties, or guarantees, to be written in less formal legal language.

The express warranty may be (1) a representation of a present or a past fact, or (2) a promise as to performance in the future. The following example illustrates the first type of express warranty.

EXAMPLE 2   If the seller tells you that the television set has 26 tubes, he has made a statement of fact. The set either has 26 tubes or it does not. If it does not, a false statement of fact exists and there is a breach of warranty.

The example below illustrates the second type of express warranty.

EXAMPLE 3   If, in addition, the seller states that he will warrant (guarantee) the set to give good reception in your home, this is a promise. No one knows, until the set has been installed and tested whether it will so perform or not. Therefore, the warranty is not a statement of fact. But if the set does not give good reception, there is a breach of warranty because the seller promised that it would, and you relied on his promise.

How can you minimize your risks with respect to warranties?

An express warranty is limited to the words used by the seller. It is imperative that you demand a warranty that is stated in clear, precise, and unambiguous terms if you desire to minimize your risks. Suppose that the seller says, "This set is warranted," or, "This set is guaranteed." That is all he says. Can you assume a promise that the set contains 26 tubes or that it will give good reception in your home? Absolutely not! The only thing that the seller is warranting by his words is that the item is a television set.

May oral evidence be used to clarify a written warranty?

There is another precaution that is very important if you wish to avoid trouble later. Always get a warranty in writing if possible. If, for example, you enter into a written contract to buy a television set, insist on a written warranty to support the contract of sale. Written instruments usually cannot be modified by oral testimony. However, statements having a bearing on a written contract may be introduced as further clarification of the contract unless expressly excluded by the written agreement. The sole purpose of such oral evidence must be to clarify some point in a written agreement. U.C.C. Sec. 2-202(b)

EXAMPLE 4   Suppose, when you buy a television set, the seller gives you a written guarantee reading, "This television set is guaranteed for six months from date of delivery." Nothing more was said. A short time after the set is delivered, you request the seller to send a repairman to make some needed minor adjustments. The seller refuses, saying that the guarantee covered only replacement of defective parts due to manufacturing.

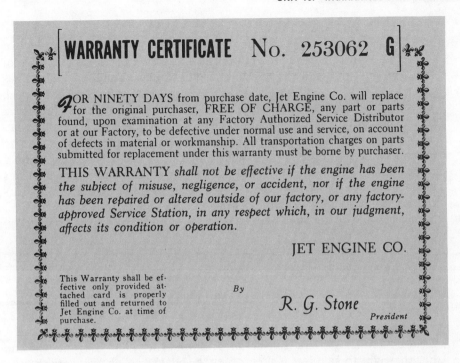

WARRANTY CERTIFICATE No. 253062 **G**

*F*OR NINETY DAYS from purchase date, Jet Engine Co. will replace for the original purchaser, FREE OF CHARGE, any part or parts found, upon examination at any Factory Authorized Service Distributor or at our Factory, to be defective under normal use and service, on account of defects in material or workmanship. All transportation charges on parts submitted for replacement under this warranty must be borne by purchaser.

THIS WARRANTY *shall not be effective if the engine has been the subject of misuse, negligence, or accident, nor if the engine has been repaired or altered outside of our factory, or any factory-approved Service Station, in any respect which, in our judgment, affects its condition or operation.*

JET ENGINE CO.

This Warranty shall be effective only provided attached card is properly filled out and returned to Jet Engine Co. at time of purchase.

By

R. G. Stone

President

The written guarantee in this situation is such that the court would permit the introduction of oral evidence to clarify the meaning of the word "guarantee" in this particular case. The *rule of the marketplace*, or what that term usually means in the sale of such instruments, would be applied by the court.

RULE OF THE MARKETPLACE

An agreement modifying or rescinding a contract needs no consideration to be binding.

Modification or rescission is treated as a matter of good faith rather than as a matter for consideration. Thus, a cabinetmaker who requests compensation above the agreed price for work that he is doing because of an increase in cost of materials need give no additional consideration if the other party to the contract agrees to pay the additional sum.

Factual statements and warranties are often made by the seller after a sales contract has been entered into. These statements and warranties are binding without consideration. U.C.C. Sec. 2-209(1)

EXAMPLE 5   Mrs. Murphy bought lace curtains from a home furnishings dealer. Some time later, she asked the dealer if washing the curtains would shrink them. He assured her that the curtains were guaranteed against shrinkage. This is considered an express warranty and, although made after the contract was completed, is binding even without consideration.

The requirements of the Statute of Frauds must be satisfied if the contract as modified is within its provisions. U.C.C. Sec. 2-209(3)

REMEMBER: In reference to an express warranty, (1) see that it is definite and certain and (2) get it in writing if possible.

IMPLIED WARRANTIES

May a seller ever
avoid implied
warranties?

Implied warranties are implied by the acts of the parties, the nature of the transaction, or the surrounding circumstances. They are guarantees given buyers by operation of law. They may be classified as (1) general, applying to all sales (implied warranties of title); and (2) special, applying to special circumstances (implied warranties of quality). The seller may avoid these warranties only by an agreement or a notice given to the purchaser at the time of the sale. Manufacturer's warranties usually contain limiting statements that protect them from additional warranties made by the seller or his agent. The statement usually reads, "No warranties, either express or implied, unless contained in this agreement, will be enforceable by the purchaser against the manufacturer." U.C.C. Sec. 2-316(1)

GENERAL IMPLIED WARRANTIES OF TITLE

What does the
seller warrant in
an implied
warranty of title?

Unless a contrary intention appears, the seller warrants that he either owns the goods or that he has a right to sell them. This is called an *implied warranty of title*. Normally, there are three things warranted as to title.

IMPLIED WARRANTY OF TITLE

RIGHT TO SELL If the transaction is a sale, the seller warrants that he has the right to sell; if it is a contract to sell, the seller warrants that he will have the right to sell by the time title is to pass.

RIGHT OF QUIET POSSESSION The seller warrants that no one else may rightfully take the goods away from the buyer in the future.

EXAMPLE 6 **Oliver sold a diamond watch to Bardley for $100. A short time later, Bardley had to surrender the watch to Lardner who proved that he was the true owner. The watch had been stolen from Lardner's room and sold to Oliver, who knew nothing of the theft. As Oliver did not possess a good title, he could not transfer a good title to Bardley. He was, therefore, liable for breach of the implied warranty of title. Of course, Oliver may sue the person who sold the watch to him for breach of the same warranty.**

TITLE FREE OF ENCUMBRANCES The seller warrants that there are no conditional sales contracts, chattel mortgages, or any other charges outstanding against the goods. U.C.C. Sec. 2-312(1)

SPECIAL IMPLIED WARRANTIES

There are some warranties applying to special circumstances. These are known as *implied warranties of quality*.

IMPLIED WARRANTY OF QUALITY

Sale by Inspection If the buyer has examined the goods, there is no implied warranty as to defects he should have seen. The law specifically states that "when the buyer before entering into the contract has examined the goods or the sample or model as fully as he desired or has refused to examine the goods, there is no implied warranty with regard to defects which an examination ought in the circumstances to have revealed to him." U.C.C. Sec. 2-316(3)(b)

This set is marked "unconditionally guaranteed." For what—reception? operation? quality of construction? This warranty is unenforceable because it is vague and indefinite.

EXAMPLE 7   Suppose that the seller offers to sell you the floor-sample television set that you are looking at. You look it over quickly and decide to buy it. In your haste to buy, you overlook a deep scratch that you should have seen.

You cannot claim a breach of warranty when you discover the scratch.

Sale Without Inspection   There are certain implied warranties that apply when the buyer does not have the opportunity to inspect the goods before purchasing.

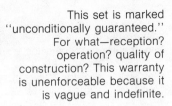
Name the implied warranty that applies in a sale by sample.

SALE BY SAMPLE   Usually, in making a purchase, you do not buy the floor sample. You do not want the shopworn sample. Even where items are much smaller than a television set, the merchant usually says, "I'll give you a fresh article, packed in a box." Under these circumstances, there is an implied warranty that the article you receive will be just like the sample you looked at. You have the right to refuse the merchandise if it differs from the sample. U.C.C. Sec. 2-317(b)

SALE BY DESCRIPTION   There are many times when you do not even see a sample before you buy. You order from a catalog, an advertisement, or a verbal description given you by the seller. Here, again, there is an implied warranty that the goods will conform to the description. U.C.C. Sec. 2-317(a)

What is the double warranty in a sale by sample and description?

SALE BY SAMPLE AND DESCRIPTION   When a sale is made through the use of both samples and description, the sale carries a double warranty that the merchandise will conform to both the description and the sample. The law gives such a warranty the weight of an express warranty, providing that any sample or model or any description of goods which is made part of the basis of the bargain creates an express warranty that the whole of the goods shall conform to the sample, model, or description. U.C.C. Sec. 2-313(1)(a)(b)(c)

Implied Warranties of Fitness for Purpose   The general rule is that there is no implied warranty of fitness for any particular purpose. This general rule, however, is subject to an important exception.

Are there exceptions to the general rule that there is no implied warranty as to quality or fitness for any particular purpose?

WHERE THE BUYER RELIES ON THE SELLER'S SKILL   Consider the following examples.

EXAMPLE 8   Suppose that you walk into the store and say to the seller, "I want to buy a Model 147 Zilco television set with a 21-inch screen." The seller sells you the exact set you order. After the set has been installed, you discover that it is of poor quality and does not perform well in your locality.

There may be an implied warranty of fitness for a particular purpose if the buyer relies on the skill and knowledge of the seller and this fact is known to the seller.

There is no breach of warranty here. The seller made none. You asked for a certain model Zilco television set, and that is what you received.

EXAMPLE 9   Krafchick purchased a Vervex electric lawn mower from a local department store. When the lawn mower was delivered, Krafchick found that it did not work properly because of a defective part. The store was liable because of a breach of an implied warranty of fitness for a particular purpose.

The law provides that when the seller knows about any particular purpose for which the goods are required and the buyer is relying on the seller's skill or judgment to select or furnish suitable goods, there is—unless it is excluded or modified—an implied warranty that the goods shall be fit for such purpose. **U.C.C. Sec. 2-315**

This warranty exists even when the seller is a nonmerchant, if he knows the purpose for which the article is bought or if the buyer relies on his skill and judgment. Suppose you approached the seller and said, "I am interested in a television set that will perform well in my home. Will you come out, make some tests, and recommend a set of good quality that will perform well in my location?" If, afterward, you buy, relying on the recommendation of the seller, there is an implied warranty.

> There is always an implied warranty of fitness, unless it is excluded or modified by the seller, when the buyer makes known his needs to the seller and then buys, relying on the seller's recommendation.

To exclude or modify any implied warranty of fitness for a particular purpose, the exclusion must be in writing and be conspicuous, that is, written so that it will readily be noticed by the buyer. **U.C.C. Sec. 2-316(2)** The statement may simply be that "there are no warranties which extend beyond the description on the face thereof." An implied warranty can also be excluded or modified by course of dealing or course of performance or usage of trade. **U.C.C. Sec. 2-316(3)(c)**

May a seller ever modify or exclude his implied warranty of fitness?

Implied Warranty of Merchantable Quality   Where goods are bought from a merchant who customarily sells like or similar goods, there is an implied warranty of *merchantable quality* or merchantability. Merchantable quality is hard to define. It is often stated that, for goods to be merchantable, the buyer must be able to resell the goods by the same description. If, for example, a dealer sold wheat, it must be resalable as wheat.

How would you define merchantable quality?

MERCHANTABLE QUALITY

If the wheat delivered turned out to be mixed with corn, the dealer could not say, as a defense, that it was merchantable as chicken food. The law provides that, unless excluded or modified, a warranty that the goods are merchantable is implied in a contract for their sale if the seller is a merchant of goods of that kind. **U.C.C. Sec. 2-314(1)** To exclude or modify this warranty, merchantability must be specifically mentioned and, in case of a writing, written so that a reasonable person will notice it. **U.C.C. Sec. 2-316(2)**

Under what conditions are goods considered merchantable?

To be merchantable, goods must (1) pass without objection in the trade under the contract description; (2) be fit for the ordinary purposes for which such goods are used; (3) be adequately contained, packaged, and labeled as the agreement may require; (4) conform to the promises or affirmations of fact made on the container or label, if any; and (5) in the case of fungible goods, be of fair average quality within the description. **U.C.C. Sec. 2-314(2)** The implied warranty of merchantability does not apply in the case of a sale by a nonmerchant or by a casual seller.

Implied Warranty of Fitness for Human Consumption In recent years, a rule has developed that goods sold as food must be fit for human consumption. Should you suffer damage from the purchase of harmful or adulterated foods, the law will usually provide a remedy. The serving of food or drink to be consumed either on the premises of the seller or elsewhere is a sale and is included under the implied warranty of merchantability as well. **U.C.C. Sec. 2-314(1)**

CAVEAT EMPTOR TODAY

In the early days, before our law had developed to its present status, buying and selling were conducted under conditions very different from those found in today's markets. *Caveat emptor,* which means "Let the buyer beware," was the rule of the marketplace. Then, the buyer and the seller usually had the goods right before them. Then, too, both the buyer and the seller were usually about equally skilled in judging the value and usefulness of the goods. Most goods at that time were purchased "as is." The buyer could examine the goods and determine their value for himself. By careful inspection, he could also determine whether they would suit his purpose. The seller made no promises at all with respect to the quality or the usefulness of the goods.

CAVEAT EMPTOR

If you buy something "as is" the only warranty in effect is the implied warranty of title.

What effect do
expressions like
"as is" and
"with all faults"
have on implied
warranties?

Under present law, all implied warranties except the implied warranty of title are excluded by expressions like "as is," "with all faults," or other language which, in common understanding, calls the buyer's attention to the exclusion of warranties. U.C.C. Sec. 2-316(3)(a)

EXAMPLE 10   Quigley bought for cash a mahogany desk from a retail furniture dealer. The red sales tag attached to the desk read: "Reduced from $198 to $75, sale final, with all faults." When the desk was delivered to Quigley's home, he found that the drawers stuck and that one side was badly marked and scratched. Quigley has no recourse. By the terms of the sale, he has assumed all risk as to quality. He is protected only by an implied warranty of title.

The opinion of the seller is not a warranty. You must expect a certain amount of "puffing," or "seller's talk." On this point the law specifically states that an affirmation of the value of the goods or a statement that is merely the seller's opinion or commendation of the goods does not create a warranty. U.C.C. Sec. 2-313(2)

THIRD-PARTY BENEFICIARIES OF WARRANTIES

A seller's warranty whether expressed or implied extends to any natural person who is in the family or household of his buyer or who is a guest in his home if it is reasonable to expect that such person may use, consume, or be affected by the goods and may be injured in person by breach of the warranty. A seller may not exclude or limit the operation of this provision of the law. U.C.C. Sec. 2-318

If the buyer of
contaminated
food becomes ill
after eating it,
may he sue the
seller?

If food is sold for human consumption, the buyer, members of his family, and his guests are protected by the implied warranties of merchantability and fitness for a particular purpose. The seller can be sued by the buyer and anyone who partakes of the food at the buyer's invitation and suffers injury as a result.

SUGGESTIONS FOR MINIMIZING LEGAL RISKS

When you are the purchaser . . .

1. Examine carefully all goods for sale on an "as is" basis because goods purchased on this basis ordinarily carry no express or implied warranties as to quality.
2. If you are purchasing from a producer or a manufacturer goods to be resold to customers, be sure that the goods are of proper quality, not harmful or adulterated. Otherwise, the customers will have a right of action against you as the middleman, even though you are not responsible for the improper quality or defect.

3. Rather than purchase goods by description alone, specify to the seller exactly what the goods are to be used for, and let the seller select the goods to be used for your specific purpose, relying on his expert skill and knowledge of the goods.

4. When buying expensive goods for a special need by trade name, try to obtain an express warranty from the seller; that is, ask the seller to warrant that the goods will fit the purpose for which they are to be used.

5. When you purchase goods by supplying the plans and specifications, request the seller to agree that the goods will meet the specifications and be suitable for your specific needs.

 # APPLYING YOUR LEARNING

QUESTIONS AND PROBLEMS

1. What conditions exist today that make it more difficult to buy goods by inspection as compared with conditions a hundred years ago?
2. What is meant by a warranty? Give a simple definition of a warranty in your own words.
3. What are some important things you should consider in asking for an express warranty from the seller?
4. What is meant by a general implied warranty? Explain and illustrate.
5. What is meant by a special implied warranty? Explain and illustrate.
6. Name several items that are ordinarily sold by sample and several items that are ordinarily sold by description.
7. What is meant by an implied warranty of fitness? Explain and illustrate.
8. Do you believe that the law will provide a legal remedy in case you are sold some food that makes you seriously ill? Why?
9. What is meant by the rule of caveat emptor? Does this rule apply today?

WHAT IS YOUR OPINION?

In each of the following cases, give your decision and state a legal principle that applies to the case.

1. In selling drapes to Mrs. Turner, Woods said their colors would not fade. The drapes faded when laundered. What rights has Mrs. Turner?
2. Mrs. Turner purchased some curtains from Woods that she did not examine. Later, she discovered that the fringe was poorly attached. What legal obligation does Woods have to her? What might Woods, a reputable businessman, do?
3. Parker purchased from North a quantity of lumber that was piled in North's lumberyard. Later, Parker found that the boards were not so straight or free from knots as he had thought. Did he have any claim against North?

4. Sutton bought an automobile from a used-car dealer. Horner proved that the car had been stolen from him and demanded its return. Can he recover it?

5. When selling cloth to Storm, Hart stated that it was all-wool cloth. Later, Storm found it was only 70 percent wool. Is this a breach of warranty?

6. When Martin was buying an electric motor, he stated that he wanted a motor to operate a certain piece of machinery. The motor proved incapable of doing so satisfactorily. Is there a breach of warranty on the part of the seller?

7. "This machine is guaranteed by the manufacturer for a period of one year from date of purchase," was printed on the tag attached to the washing machine Bailey purchased. The machine did not wash clothes so quickly as the salesman had led him to think. Is the manufacturer obliged to refund Bailey's money?

8. Horton bought a television set from Dudley. The following day, Horton returned and complained about the reception he was getting. Dudley said, "Don't worry about that. I'll warrant the set to give good reception after it is adjusted." Even after adjustment, Horton continued to get poor reception. Can Horton bring an action for breach of warranty? Explain.

THE LAW IN ACTION

1. The plaintiff sold a stove to the defendant. In making the sale, the plaintiff stated, "The stoves . . . are first class . . . the best and finest oil stoves on the market . . . and would give first-class satisfaction." Would this be a warranty or is it just "seller's talk"? (Detroit Vapor Stove Co. v. Weeter Lumber Co., 61 Utah 503, 215 Pac. 995)

2. The defendant Zimbalist purchased two violins from the plaintiff. In discussing the violins prior to the purchase agreement, both parties had referred to one of them as a "Stradivarius" and to the other as a "Guarnerius." In the bill of sale, they were also described as a "Stradivarius" and a "Guarnerius." Both violins proved to be copies and not originals. Zimbalist refused to pay the purchase price, and the plaintiff brought action, claiming that the violins had been sold after a careful inspection by the buyer and that there had been no warranty as to their origin. Do you think there was a warranty in this case? Why or why not? (Smith v. Zimbalist, 2 Cal. App. 2d 324, 38 2d 170)

KEY TO "WHAT'S THE LAW?" Page 169

1. *Very little. An express warranty must be definite and precise.*
2. *No. There is not always an implied warranty of fitness when the buyer selects merchandise and does not seek the advice or assistance of the seller.*

WHAT'S THE LAW?

1. *Bill Rovan ordered three gallons of paint from the Bright Color Paint Shop. Four gallons were delivered. Does Bill have to accept and pay for the extra gallon? May he keep the extra gallon if he wants to? If he keeps it, how much will he have to pay?*

2. *The new radio purchased by Art Walker had a defective tube. This amounted to a breach of warranty. Can Art do anything about it?*

▲ UNIT 20: BREACH OF SALES CONTRACTS

Explain how competitive conditions affect dealer-customer relationship.

Particularly in the field of retail merchandising, the slogan "The customer is always right" sometimes takes the place of the old idea of caveat emptor— let the buyer beware. Competitive conditions are such that dealers are forced to favor their customers. This is often carried to such lengths that the seller is far from exercising the possible legal rights that he has against the buyer.

EXAMPLE 1 A woman bought a new dress for $45 and returned it for a refund shortly thereafter when she found a dress in another store which she preferred over the original purchase. The store accepted the return even though it was not legally bound to do so.

Many merchants follow the plan of accepting the return of any article that the customer, for any reason or no reason, sees fit to return. Unless the amount involved is great, the dealer permits the customer to cancel orders for goods with no particular questions asked.

DUTIES OF BUYER AND SELLER

What duties does the law impose on both the buyer and the seller?

Regardless of what the common practice is, the law imposes certain duties on both the buyer and the seller. It is the duty of the seller to transfer to the buyer goods of the quantity and quality agreed on. It is the duty of the buyer to take the goods and pay for them. U.C.C. Sec. 2-301

If one or more of these points are violated, there arises the occasion for a *remedy* (the legal means of obtaining redress, or correcting a wrong) against the party committing the wrong.

REMEDY

REMEDIES OF THE BUYER IN CASE OF BREACH

How much should a person seek from the one who has breached an agreement? May he seek an arbitrary figure? Are there guidelines?

In all claims for breach of contract, the party bringing the suit must determine the damages in terms of money. Actions for breach of contract result in money damages, which are fixed according to the losses suffered by the injured party.

There may be two situations when a buyer has grounds for complaint:
1. The seller may refuse to let the buyer have the goods that he has bought.
2. The buyer may receive the goods but may suffer from the breach of an express or an implied warranty.

Action for Nondelivery If the seller refuses to give the goods to the buyer, the buyer's remedy usually depends on whether or not he has title to the goods. If he has title to the goods, the goods are his and he can demand them. If he fails to receive the goods when he requests them, the buyer may start a *replevin action,* an action to obtain possession of personal property. The court issues a *writ of replevin,* ordering the wrongful holder of goods to deliver them to the rightful owner. If the goods cannot be obtained elsewhere, the buyer need not have title to the goods to exercise this right of replevin. U.C.C. Sec. 2-716

Where the seller fails to make delivery of the goods purchased or breaches the contract, the buyer may "cover" by purchasing goods to substitute for those due from the seller. U.C.C. Sec. 2-712(1) The buyer may then recover from the seller the difference between the cost of the goods he purchased and the contract price, together with any incidental or consequential damages. But he must subtract any money he saved by substituting. U.C.C. Sec. 2-712(2)

If the buyer prefers, however, he can allow the seller to keep the goods and sue for damages.

EXAMPLE 2 **Kretz bought some black angus cattle from Semple. Both men considered that title had passed at once. However, when Kretz came to the cattle range to take the cattle, Semple decided not to release them.**

Kretz could demand the cattle, as they were legally his. On the other hand, if title has not yet passed to the buyer, all that the buyer can do is to sue for damages for breach of contract. He cannot demand the goods because the general rule is that a person cannot be compelled to perform a contract. A breach merely gives rise to a claim for damages.

ACTUAL AND INCIDENTAL DAMAGES In actions for breach of contract, the injured party is permitted to recover the *actual damage* caused by the other's failure of performance.

EXAMPLE 3 **You make a contract with a bookstore for the purchase of an encyclopedia set offered at a price of $250. The store fails to deliver the set of books according to the agreement. After investigation, you learn that the same set of books will cost you $300 at any other bookstore. You are entitled, therefore, to sue for your actual damage, which is the difference between $250 and $300, or $50, the amount of money you stand to lose by purchasing elsewhere.**

Margin notes:

Under what circumstances would a buyer start a replevin action?

"The buyer may cover where the seller fails to make delivery." Explain.

REPLEVIN ACTION
WRIT OF REPLEVIN

ACTUAL DAMAGE

How are damages measured in a breach of contract suit brought by the buyer?

The law provides that the "measure of damages for non-delivery or repudiation by the seller is the difference between the market price at the time when the buyer learned of the breach and the contract price together with any incidental and consequential damages, but less expenses saved in consequence of the seller's breach." U.C.C. Sec. 2-713(1)

What are incidental damages?

The law lists as *incidental damages* "expenses reasonably incurred in inspection, receipt, transportation, and care and custody of goods rightfully rejected, any commercially reasonable charges, expenses or commissions in connection with effecting cover and any other reasonable expenses incident to the delay or other breach." U.C.C. Sec. 2-715(1)

INCIDENTAL DAMAGE

What are liquidated damages?

LIQUIDATED DAMAGES   Parties sometimes include in their contract a statement of agreed damages, should either one breach the contract. They agree that these will be the damages sought in the event of a suit. The law provides that "damages for breach by either party may be liquidated in the agreement but only at an amount which is reasonable in the light of the anticipated or actual harm caused by the breach, the difficulties of proof of loss, and the inconvenience or non-feasibility of otherwise obtaining an adequate remedy. A term fixing unreasonably large liquidated damages is void as a penalty." U.C.C. Sec. 2-718(1)

EXAMPLE 4   **The Young Supply Company ordered a machine for its new plant, which was being constructed in Sacramento. The machine was a vital link in the production of a new product, and the Young Company had inserted in its contract with the seller the following terms: "The Young Company will be paid $250 each day beyond the date agreed upon for delivery of said machine." Considering the profits that might be lost through delay in delivery, the liquidated damages provision would, no doubt, be considered reasonable and proper.**

NOMINAL DAMAGES   If a seller refuses to deliver the goods and the purchaser could buy the same goods in the open market at a price equal to or less than the contract price, his legal right to receive delivery under the contract has, nevertheless, been breached, even though he has suffered no loss. In case of suit, the courts would usually award him nominal damages, often fixed at six cents or a dollar.

SPECIFIC PERFORMANCE   If the agreement covers an article of rare value, especially one of a sentimental nature, specific performance may be enforced. The buyer's right to specific performance, or replevin, may be

If the property bought and sold is unique in character, the buyer may demand specific performance on a contract to sell.

When may the
buyer sue for
specific
performance?

decreed where the goods are unique, in cases involving real estate, or in other proper circumstances. The decree of specific performance may include such terms and conditions as to payment of the price, damages, or other relief as the court may deem just. U.C.C. Sec. 2-716(1)(2)

Specific performance may also be decreed in cases where the buyer is unable to obtain the product elsewhere.

Action for Breach of Warranty   Express and implied warranties usually center around either title or quality. If the title is not clear and if, for this reason, the buyer has to give up the goods to the true owner or to pay the true owner some money, the buyer has a claim against the seller for any amount he has paid out. This means, for instance, that, if the true owner takes the goods, the buyer may recover the full purchase price.

What remedies
are available to
the buyer when
there is a breach
of warranty as to
the quality of the
goods?

When the breach of warranty refers to the quality of the goods, the buyer has the choice of various remedies. He may accept and keep the goods, and he may put in a claim for the damage suffered by the breach of warranty. If he has not yet paid the price, he may make a proper deduction from it. The law specifically states that when the buyer has accepted the goods and given notification to the seller that the goods do not conform to the contract, the buyer may recover as damages for any breach of warranty the loss resulting from the seller's breach. U.C.C. Sec. 2-714(1), 607(3)(a)

EXAMPLE 5   An air-conditioning unit was incorrectly installed in an office. A service company called in to make the necessary adjustments charged the firm $35. This amount may be deducted from the original bill because it was reasonable under the circumstances.

If the buyer has not yet received the goods, he may refuse to accept them, and he may also sue for the damage he has suffered, if any.

He may return the goods and demand a refund of the purchase price. If the seller refuses to accept the return of the goods or to return the money received for them, the buyer may hold the goods for the seller and sue for the purchase price plus incidental damages.

EXAMPLE 6   A grocer ordered a neon sign for the front of his store. Upon its delivery, the grocer discovered that the name of his grocery store had been misspelled.

The grocer could sue on the breach of the implied warranty that the sign would be the same as ordered. He could return the sign and demand the return of any money paid. This last method is, perhaps, the one most commonly practiced in our day.

There is also an implied warranty that the seller will deliver the right amount of goods. Delivery of a smaller quantity than ordered gives the buyer the right to reject the goods and sue for damages for breach.

EXAMPLE 7   Jackson, the owner of a new motel, made an agreement with the Tru-Color Television Company for the purchase of 60 table-model television sets to be delivered in thirty days. If the company delivered only 35 of the 60 sets promised, Jackson would have the right to refuse the entire shipment and bring an action against the television company for damages.

What are the three remedies available to the buyer when a greater quantity of merchandise than ordered is delivered?

The delivery of a greater quantity than ordered gives the buyer a choice of three remedies: (1) He may reject the entire shipment; (2) he may accept only what was ordered and reject the rest; (3) he may accept the entire shipment and pay for it at the contract price. U.C.C. Sec. 2-601

If the buyer accepts the order as delivered, he must pay the contract price for each unit delivered.

REMEDIES OF THE SELLER IN CASE OF BREACH

If the buyer refuses to accept and pay for the goods, the seller may choose one of several courses of action. His choice will depend on the facts of the case and the surrounding circumstances. If the buyer is solvent, the seller would usually prefer to enforce the sale and collect the purchase price. U.C.C. Sec. 2-703 If the buyer is insolvent or hard pressed for money, the seller might prefer to keep the goods.

Action for the Purchase Price If title to the goods has passed to the buyer, the seller may bring an action for the purchase price. The goods now belong to the buyer, and the seller has a right to collect the price.

When may a seller cancel a sale and resell the goods?

The seller may cancel the sale and resell the goods (1) if the goods are of a perishable nature, (2) if the right of resale was reserved in the contract, or (3) if the buyer has been in default for an unreasonable length of time.

If the goods are resold, the seller must make a fair sale at a fair price. U.C.C. Sec. 2-706 If he does this, he may then bring an action for any difference between the resale price and the contract price, together with any incidental expenses, but less expenses saved in consequence of the buyer's breach. U.C.C. Sec. 2-709 If the buyer fails to pay the price, the seller may recover, together with incidental expenses [U.C.C. Sec. 2-710] the price (1) of goods accepted or of similar goods lost, damaged, or destroyed within a reasonable time after risk of their loss has passed to the buyer; and (2) of goods identified to the contract if he is unable to resell them at a reasonable price.

When the seller sues for the price, he must hold for the buyer any goods which have been identified (set aside, labeled, or tagged) to the contract and are still in his control. However, if resale becomes possible, he may resell them at any time prior to the collection of the *judgment* (court order for the buyer to pay for the goods). The net proceeds of any such resale must be credited to the buyer, and payment of the judgment entitles him to any goods not resold. U.C.C. Sec. 2-709

JUDGMENT

Action for Damages for Nonacceptance If title to the goods has not passed, the measure of damages for nonacceptance by the buyer is the difference between the market price at the time the buyer breached the sales agreement and the unpaid contract price, together with any incidental damages, but less expenses saved as a result of the buyer's breach.

How are damages measured in a breach of contract suit when the buyer refuses acceptance of the goods?

If this is inadequate to put the seller in as good a position as performance would have done, then the measure of damages is the profit (including reasonable overhead) which he would have made from full performance by the buyer, together with any incidental expenses which he incurred, such as commissions or shipping charges in making the sale. U.C.C. Sec. 2-708

If the buyer has no money, the seller may prefer to have the goods back rather than bring action for the purchase price.

If the goods are of such a nature that they cannot be sold to anyone else, the seller may notify the buyer that he now holds the goods as the bailee or agent of the buyer and then bring an action for the purchase price.

Holding the Goods If the credit of the buyer is not good, the seller may retain possession of the goods until they are paid for or he may *rescind* (cancel) the sale entirely. If title to the goods has passed to the buyer, the seller can hold possession provided (1) that the goods were originally sold for cash and the cash purchase price has not been paid, or (2) that the goods were sold on credit and the credit period has expired. This right is called an *unpaid seller's lien* and is completely dependent on the possession of the goods by the seller. The lien is lost by the delivery of the goods, either to the buyer himself or to a carrier for delivery to the buyer.

RESCIND

UNPAID SELLER'S LIEN

What is an unpaid seller's lien?

Occasionally, after the unpaid seller has shipped the goods, he discovers that the buyer is insolvent. Under these circumstances the seller has the right to stop the goods in transit and demand that the carrier not deliver them to the buyer but hold them for the benefit of the seller. This right of *stoppage in transit* is provided for under the law which states that "the seller may stop delivery of goods in the possession of a carrier when he discovers the buyer to be insolvent, and may stop delivery of carload, truckload, planeload, or larger shipments of express or freight when the buyer repudiates or fails to make a payment due before delivery or if for any other reason the seller has a right to withhold or reclaim the goods." The seller's right to stop delivery of the goods may be exercised even when the goods are in the possession of a warehouseman. U.C.C. Sec. 2-705(1)

STOPPAGE IN TRANSIT

Explain what is meant by a stoppage in transit.

The seller must accept all responsibility for any charges or damages that may result to the carrier if shipment is interrupted because the carrier as well as the seller may be subjected to a suit for damages if the insolvency information is unfounded.

EXAMPLE 8 **Suppose the Tru-Color Television Company had ordered 50 color television sets from the Instrument Manufacturing Company. En route, the shipment was held up by the Instrument Company when word reached it that**

Tru-Color had become insolvent. The rumor was without foundation; Tru-Color was in excellent financial condition at the time of the stoppage. Tru-Color may sue the Instrument Company and the carrier for damages and also file a claim for damages to its credit reputation.

The law further provides that when the seller discovers the buyer to be insolvent, he may refuse delivery except for cash including payment for all goods theretofore delivered under the contract, and may stop delivery of goods in transit.

"Where the seller discovers that the buyer has received goods on credit while insolvent, he may reclaim the goods upon demand made within ten days after receipt, but if misrepresentation of solvency has been made to the particular seller in writing within three months before delivery, the ten day limitation does not apply." U.C.C. Sec. 2-702(1)(2)

Not only *insolvency* (inability to pay one's debts as they become due) but fraud or breach of contract by the buyer is reason enough for the seller to stop the goods in transit.

INSOLVENCY

What is the legal effect on a contract that has been rescinded by the seller?

An unpaid seller who has transferred title to but not possession of goods may rescind the sales contract if the purchaser repudiates the contract or does something that shows he is unable to perform or is in default of payment for an unreasonable time. A rescinded contract is always treated as if it had never been made.

MINIMIZING THE DAMAGES

Upon whom does the responsibility for minimizing damages in a breached contract rest?

An injured party must take all available steps to minimize the damages that might accrue from the other party's failure of performance. At all times he will be obliged to protect the other party from any unnecessary losses.

SUGGESTIONS FOR MINIMIZING LEGAL RISKS

1. If the seller breaches the contract, you, as the buyer, should consider carefully the various remedies available to you. Select the one that will be the most advantageous to you.

2. Sometimes buying on credit is advantageous to the purchaser because it may be easier to obtain an adjustment on a purchase where there is a breach of warranty by the seller.

3. The unpaid seller should carefully consider the credit standing of the purchaser in determining the remedies available to him. If the buyer is solvent, the seller will want to confirm the sale and receive the purchase price. If the purchaser is on the verge of insolvency, it would be better for the seller to try to get the goods back.

4. If the buyer breaches his contract and refuses to accept the goods, the seller should again consider the available remedies. If the market price of the goods has gone up, the seller will benefit by avoiding the sale and keeping the goods. If the market price has gone down, he will benefit by confirming the sale and bringing an action for the purchase price.

 ## APPLYING YOUR LEARNING

QUESTIONS AND PROBLEMS

1. Do you think that the merchants in your community are liberal in accepting returned goods sold to customers? Explain your views on this point.

2. Do you think that customers in your community take unfair advantage of some merchants because of their liberal policies in accepting returned goods? Explain your views on this point.

3. Under what two conditions may the buyer have grounds for complaint against the seller? What remedies are available to the buyer?

4. What remedies are available to the seller if the buyer refuses to accept the goods?

5. What remedies are available to the seller when the buyer refuses to pay for the goods and the goods are still in the possession of the seller?

6. Under what conditions may the seller exercise the right of stoppage in transit?

7. Assume that you are the seller and that you sold goods to a solvent buyer who refused to accept and pay for the goods. How could you enforce your sale and make your profit on it? Explain how you would do this.

8. Assume that you sold goods to a buyer who was on the verge of insolvency. Explain what you should do to protect yourself in a transaction where the buyer refused to accept and pay for the goods.

WHAT IS YOUR OPINION?

In each of the following cases, give your decision and state a legal principle that applies to the case.

1. Burns received two boxes of Christmas cards, with an invoice enclosed, from the Bright Company, although he only ordered one. He used all the cards. Can the Bright Company compel Burns to pay for both boxes?

2. On March 1, Rich signed a contract agreeing to make and deliver to Abel, on or before October 1, 100 men's overcoats. Rich had difficulty in getting some of the necessary materials and notified Abel on September 28 that he would be unable to make delivery. Did Rich have a valid excuse that freed him from being liable for damages for failure to live up to the contract?

3. Conklin contracted to sell a radio of a specified make and model to Torme for $100. When Torme came in to pay for and pick up the radio, he found that Conklin had sold the radio they had in mind to someone else. Torme threatened to sue for breach of contract; but later in the day, he found that he could buy exactly the same radio from the Appliance Store for $90. What should Torme do?

4. Zerke sold goods to Winters with no stipulation as to credit. Zerke sent his deliveryman to Winters' house with the goods but instructed him not to leave the goods unless they were paid for. The deliveryman violated his instructions, however, and left the goods without collecting. Zerke demanded the return of the goods, claiming he had an unpaid seller's lien. Is he correct? Explain.

5. On June 5, Dart sold and delivered an electric motor to Firman, terms net 30 days. Firman was given the privilege of returning the motor any time within 15 days. On June 12, the motor was damaged by fire through no fault of Firman's. Must Firman stand the loss?

6. On April 10, 1965, Burke bought some goods from Maris on credit. On February 5, 1968, Burke paid a small amount on the bill. On May 1, 1971, he informed Maris that he would pay no more on the account because it had become outlawed. Was Burke correct?

7. Murray contracted to sell a stove to Kent. Kent later breached his contract and refused to accept delivery. Murray brought an action for the contract price. Is this action proper? If not, what should Murray do?

THE LAW IN ACTION

1. The defendant purchased a television set from the plaintiff. The set did not give satisfactory service even after numerous service calls by the seller. The defendant refused to pay the purchase price and offered to return the set. The plaintiff refused to accept the set and brought an action for the purchase price. Pending the outcome of the trial of the case, the defendant continued to use the set. Was the plaintiff entitled to a judgment for the purchase price? (Wagner v. Guy et al., 252 S.W. 2d 420 Ky.)

2. The plaintiff manufactured and sold a special order of Christmas cards to the defendant. The defendant attempted to cancel the order before delivery and refused to accept the cards when they were offered for delivery. The plaintiff brought an action for the purchase price, claiming that the cards could not be sold on the open market. The defendant claimed that the only action valid against them would be for damages for breach of their contract. Who is correct and why? (Illustrated Postal Card & Novelty Co. v. Holt, 85 Conn. 140, 81A 1061)

KEY TO "WHAT'S THE LAW?" Page 179

1. *No. The contract was for three gallons only. Yes, he may keep the additional gallon if he wishes and pay the contract price per gallon.*
2. *Art may return the radio and demand either another one that is in good condition or the return of his money. He might also keep the radio he has, replace the defective tube, and deduct the cost from the purchase price.*

1. *Paul Johnson applied for a charge account at Charleston Dry Goods Store. His application was turned down because of a bad credit rating that the store received about Paul from a local credit bureau. Does Paul have a right to learn what was included in the bad credit rating?*

2. *Noah Simpson and Harry Jones owned the only two laundries in a small town. They contracted not to compete with each other. Is this a legal agreement?*

▲ UNIT 21: CONSUMER-BUYER PROTECTION

Why is this considered the age of consumer protection?

The 1970's ushered in what may well be considered the age of consumer protection. Today, more than ever before, the federal government is forcing manufacturers and retailers to deal fairly and openly with the consumer. Never in the history of the world have consumers had so much money to spend, and never in the history of the world has there been such a glittering array of products to be bought. The competition for the consumer's dollar is tremendous. Most of this competition is honest, but some of it is not. Many times, the consumer gets his money's worth but discovers later that he has been "high-pressured" into buying something he does not really need. How to spend your money wisely and get the best value for it—that is one of the biggest problems that you, as a consumer, have to face.

Basically, this is not a problem of law but of consumer education. The law will not make your contracts for you. No government agency is going to step in and solve your problems for you when you have made a foolish purchase. This does not mean, however, that the law leaves you completely at the mercy of the unscrupulous seller. For many years there have been consumer protection laws. Until recently, however, they have not always been easy to understand, and information has been difficult to locate. Some consumer protection laws are federal, some are state laws, and some are local city ordinances.

An important step toward making consumer protection laws and information easier to find and understand was the creation of the federal Office of Consumer Affairs in 1971. The major activities of this office are as follows.

OFFICE OF CONSUMER AFFAIRS

1. Help to develop and put into practice federal programs to aid the consumer.

LITTLE GIANT LAWNMOWERS LAST A LIFETIME

Honest merchants will usually make good on products that prove to be of grossly inferior quality. If the merchant fails to do so, shop somewhere else.

2. Insure that consumer interests are considered in the formulation of government policies and the operation of federal programs.

3. Conduct investigations, conferences, and surveys concerning the consumer.

4. Submit recommendations to the President on improving existing federal programs.

5. Take action on individual consumer complaints.

6. Assist in making product information available to the public.

7. Promote and coordinate research to improve consumer products, services and information.

8. Help state and local governments to promote consumer interests.

9. Help private enterprise to promote and protect consumer interest.

What are the major activities of the Office of Consumer Affairs?

THE DEVELOPMENT OF CONSUMER PROTECTION

Suppose that, in your shopping for a radio, you discovered that all the radio dealers in town had entered into an agreement not to compete with one another and to sell only at agreed fixed prices. This would be *price fixing*. Such practices are contrary to public policy, and the agreements of the dealers would be unenforceable. You have many times heard the expression "Competition is the life of trade." It is one of the basic principles of economic life in this country. Keep it in mind as you study the material that follows.

PRICE FIXING

ANTITRUST LAWS

Antitrust laws are laws that have been passed by the federal government to prevent the formation of a *monopoly,* or a business without competition, as well as other types of restraint of trade in any given industry. Major antitrust legislation which was passed as far back as the turn of the century is still very much in effect today.

MONOPOLY

The Sherman Antitrust Act, passed in 1890, has prevented the merging of competing companies into one giant organization that could control an entire industry and has prevented any business agreements that would have the effect of restraining trade.

SHERMAN ANTITRUST ACT

EXAMPLE 1 Four large milk distributors entered into an agreement to sell milk at a price to be determined by a committee appointed by them. When one of the distributors cut the price to his customers, the other distributors sought to recover damages because he had violated the agreement. It was held that this agreement was not enforceable at law because it resulted in an illegal monopoly.

The Federal Trade Commission Act of 1914 created the FTC for the purpose of eliminating unfair methods of competition. The main emphasis of the FTC at this time was to protect one business firm from another rather than to protect consumers.

FEDERAL TRADE COMMISSION ACT

The Clayton Act, also passed in 1914, has strengthened the Sherman Antitrust Act and prohibited certain specific activities which tended to substantially lessen competition or create monopolies.

CLAYTON ACT

The Robinson-Patman Act, passed in 1936, amended and brought up to date the provisions of the Clayton Act. The most important provision of this act strengthened the section of the Clayton Act that dealt with price discrimination.

ROBINSON-PATMAN ACT

Name several federal antitrust laws. What purpose do they serve?

PROTECTION AGAINST UNFAIR TRADE PRACTICES

The 1938 Wheeler-Lea Amendment to the Federal Trade Commission Act gave the FTC the power to deal with cases in which unfair trade practices injured the consumer. The FTC also gained the authority to act against false advertising of food, drugs, and cosmetics. Enforcement of the Wheeler-Lea Amendment does not in any way depend on whether the advertiser knows or does not know an advertisement is false.

WHEELER-LEA AMENDMENT

EXAMPLE 2 A toothpaste is advertised as preventing cavities when, in fact, it has no preventive power. This would be in clear violation of the Wheeler-Lea Amendment to the Federal Trade Commission Act.

Even under early common law, certain unfair trade practices were considered wrong. One of these is the practice of intentionally passing off your goods as those of another person. It is on this principle that the law of trademarks is founded.

Any business agreement that tends to eliminate competition constitutes an unreasonable restraint of trade and is illegal.

EXAMPLE 3   Ray Segal was a weaver. He made a very high grade of cloth that he called "Weavecloth." Because of its excellent quality, "Weavecloth" was soon in great demand among consumers. Jay Underwood, an early-day "fast-buck artist," began to sell a competing cloth, which he also called "Weavecloth." Underwood's cloth was of inferior quality, but consumers bought it because they thought it was the same high-grade cloth manufactured by Segal.

In our illustration "Weavecloth" had become a *trademark* of Ray Segal. Trademark law is old, but it is still very important in modern business law. When a consumer buys trademarked goods, he at least knows the name of the manufacturer or distributor who stands behind the goods.

In more modern times the law has moved to eliminate many more types of unfair trade practices. One of these practices is *business defamation* which is the circulating of false or damaging rumors about a competitor or his business. If the false or damaging rumors are by word of mouth, they are called *business slander*. If they are written, they are called *business libel*.

TRADEMARK

BUSINESS DEFAMATION

BUSINESS SLANDER

BUSINESS LIBEL

What constitutes business slander and libel?

EXAMPLE 4   Harry Benson and Jack Hogan were competing funeral directors in their hometown. Benson desired to arouse public indignation against Hogan, so he sent letters to relatives of those people who were ill. He solicited the business of the relatives in case any ill person passed away. Benson signed Hogan's name to each of the letters.

Another unfair trade practice which has been eliminated is *malicious competition*. This practice consists of competing and cutting prices solely for the purpose of driving a competitor out of business.

MALICIOUS COMPETITION

EXAMPLE 5   George Ford, a wealthy man, became so enraged at Tony Randolph, a masonry contractor, that he wanted to put Randolph out of business. Ford organized his own contracting company, hired an experienced contractor to operate it, and charged only one-half the price Randolph charged. Ford was determined and willing to operate his new business at a loss.

Ford's actions would be considered unfair competition because Ford's sole purpose was to do harm to Randolph. He admitted to friends that he expected to close up his shop as soon as he caused Randolph to become insolvent.

Most states and the federal government have regulations against such unfair trade practices as false and misleading advertising and dishonest labeling and branding. Those statutes vary widely but the purpose of each one is to protect the consumer from being mislead or injured.

LAWS REGULATING THE TYPE AND QUALITY OF GOODS SOLD

The federal government employs a variety of controls designed to restrain, discourage, or penalize the sale of certain commodities thought to be harmful to health or morals. These controls may take the form of (1) unusually high taxes, as in the case of the special excise taxes on liquor and tobacco; (2) labeling requirements, as proposed by the Federal Trade Commission and enacted into law by Congress in 1965, regarding the marketing of cigarettes (all package labels and all advertisements are required to warn the public that smoking is a health hazard); and (3) outright prohibition, as in, for example, the banning of all cigarette advertising on television after January 1, 1971.

EXAMPLE 6 **Jim Clark had straight, unruly hair. He bought a highly advertised product at the drugstore that promised to make his hair curly and keep it well groomed. After using the product Clark discovered that not only was his hair not curly but most of it came out. Also, Clark's scalp and face became irritated by the product. In addition, the bottle was labeled 12 ounces, but it contained only 8 ounces.**

Clark certainly was entitled to protection from this kind of product. Laws protecting the consumer from harmful or adulterated products are not new. As early as 300 B.C., a law in India prohibited the adulteration of grain, scents, and medicines. In England a law was passed in 1597 providing for the forfeiture of spoiled fish to the Crown. Even though laws of this kind had early beginnings, it was not until comparatively recent years that extensive laws have been passed for the specific purpose of protecting the consumer. Again, both the federal and state governments have passed laws to protect the consumer against the sale of adulterated, spoiled, poisonous, or mislabeled products. The most important of these many laws will be discussed here.

What does the Federal Food, Drug, and Cosmetic Act seek to accomplish?

The most outstanding federal law in this field is the Federal Food, Drug, and Cosmetic Act. This is a very comprehensive act prohibiting the manufacture and shipment in interstate commerce of any food, drug, cosmetic, or device for health purposes that is injurious, adulterated, or misbranded. Basically, an *adulterated food* is one which contains any poisonous or harmful substance that may make it injurious to health. A food is *misbranded* if its labeling or packaging is false or misleading in any respect.

FEDERAL FOOD, DRUG, AND COSMETIC ACT

ADULTERATED FOOD

MISBRANDED

The Federal Food, Drug, and Cosmetic Act requires that packaged drugs bear the name and address of the manufacturer and a statement of the quantity or weight of the contents. Labels on nonprescription drugs must give the common name of the drug if a trade name is used, directions for its use, caution against use that may prove unsafe for children or harmful to the consumer, and a warning if the drug contains habit-forming

The federal, state, and local governments have regulations to help prevent the sale of injurious, adulterated, or misbranded products.

properties. The law imposes criminal penalties on firms and individuals responsible for a violation, even if they were unaware of the adulterated or misbranded character of the goods involved.

EXAMPLE 7   Through an oversight, the label on the container of a widely used sleeping pill did not contain a warning that the drug used in the pill contained habit-forming properties. A consumer who suffers injury as a result of the omission of this warning may hold the manufacturer liable for damages.

What are the provisions of the Wool Products Labeling Act?

WOOL PRODUCTS LABELING ACT

Another act of importance administered by the Federal Trade Commission is the Wool Products Labeling Act. This act provides for the accurate labeling of all wool products and products containing wool. The label must show the amount of wool fiber in the fabric, the percentage by weight of new wool fibers, percentages of reprocessed or reused fibers, and the percentage of each fiber other than wool if such fibers make up 5 percent or more of the total. Reprocessed wool is remanufactured from unused wool materials. Reused wool fiber is salvaged from used goods.

EXAMPLE 8   Woolen dresses were sold by a manufacturer in interstate commerce. The manufacturer had attached a label to each dress giving his name and Federal Trade Commission registration number, in compliance with the labeling requirements of the Federal Wool Products Labeling Act. He was held to be in violation of the act because the label did not also show the percent and kind of wool used.

What are the provisions of the Fur Products Labeling Act?

FUR PRODUCTS LABELING ACT

The Fur Products Labeling Act has for its purpose the proper labeling by a retailer of all furs sold by him. Every tag, sales ticket, or advertisement used on furs must contain the true name of the fur. The act provides that the retailer must securely attach a tag to every fur and fur-trimmed article sold by him containing the true name of the animal from which the skins were taken, the name of the country in which the animal originated if the skins were imported, whether the fur has been changed by dyeing or bleaching or whether it contains pieces of less valuable parts of the animal, and the name of the retailer or his place of business.

This information must also appear on the sales check that the retailer issues to his customers. Failure to fully comply with these requirements makes the retailer subject to severe penalties that may be imposed by the Federal Trade Commission.

If goods are manufactured and sold within the boundaries of one state, the federal government has no control. Thus, all states have their own pure-food laws that apply to intrastate sales. In addition, there are many other state health laws such as: (1) licensing laws controlling establishments that sell food; (2) meat- and milk-inspection laws; (3) laws regulating the processing and canning of food; (4) laws licensing individuals whose work affects the public health, such as physicians, dentists, pharmacists, accountants, chiropractors, and restaurant workers.

What areas do state consumer protection laws cover?

Other laws adopted by states and cities provide additional consumer safeguards. They (1) regulate weights and measures, (2) require theaters to maintain adequate fire and safety equipment, (3) forbid false and misleading advertising, and (4) regulate state banks, insurance companies, finance companies, and savings and loan associations.

MODERN TRENDS IN CONSUMER PROTECTION

Now is the time to keep constantly on the alert for changes in consumer protection laws. This age of consumer protection has brought about many changes which can directly affect you as a consumer. As a result of the work of the Office of Consumer Affairs and other such consumer protection agencies, newspapers, radio, television, and magazines frequently report the latest news in consumer protection information. In your own community there are private agencies that aid you as a consumer. Local merchants' associations, Better Business Bureaus, and your local newspapers do much to assure fair trade practices. National associations, such as the Better Business Bureau, and insurance, banking, and trade associations, also lend their aid in protecting the consumer. In recent years independent testing associations, often working with the United States Department of Agriculture and state universities, have published reports on the testing of consumer products. You, as a consumer, should look to these agencies for help. Many of these consumer reports will be found in your school library or local public library. In this unit only some of the more important consumer protection laws are mentioned. Your own investigation should reveal more laws which relate directly to you.

What are the main provisions of the Truth in Lending Act?

TRUTH IN LENDING ACT

The Consumer Credit Protection Act, popularly known as the Truth in Lending Act, was already mentioned in Unit 11. This 1968 act requires all persons who either extend or make arrangements for the extension of consumer credit in the regular course of business to inform any would-be debtor of (1) the amount of the financing charges in dollars and (2) the finance charges shown as an annual percentage rate. The act also provides that any merchant, lending company, or service agency offering credit terms must include the annual percentage rate in any advertisement which states a rate of finance. When credit terms are expressed in an advertisement, the advertisement must also include the cash price for the same merchandise or service.

EXAMPLE 9 **Penney Brown applied to open a charge account at Bandon's Department Store. Either before or at the time of credit approval, Bandon's was required to inform Penney of the annual percentage rate she would be paying for the privilege of using her charge account.**

TRUE RATE OF INTEREST

Although the Truth in Lending Act requires interest to be expressed as an annual percentage rate, it may be useful for you to know how this rate is determined. If you repay a loan or buy goods on the monthly payment plan, you may be paying for the use of money which you have already returned. This may happen most often in the case of bank loans and on purchases of large, expensive items.

EXAMPLE 10 **Lois Owens borrowed $300 from the bank for six months at 6 percent interest to buy the necessary equipment to begin a candle-making business. She agreed to pay it back to the bank in six equal payments of $50 a month. The true rate of interest that Lois is paying is 12 percent instead of 6 percent.**

Let's examine the reason for this larger interest rate. When Lois's loan was approved, the bank subtracted the six percent interest for six months' use of the money from her $300. This practice is called *discounting*. The interest amounted to $9, which left Lois only $291. Although she was being charged for the use of $300, she never actually received the whole $300. Each month as Lois paid back more of the money, the amount of her debt went down. This means that each month she had less of the borrowed money to work with. The average debt that Lois had, which is the average amount of borrowed money she had to work with, was only $150.

DISCOUNTING

MONTH	DEBT	
First	$ 300	
Second	250	
Third	200	$ 150 average debt
Fourth	150	7)$1050
Fifth	100	
Sixth	50	
Seventh	0	
	$1050	

An easier way to compute the average debt is to divide the whole debt by 2 ($300 ÷ 2 = $150)

As you remember, the actual amount of interest subtracted by the bank was $9. The number of months of the loan was six months, and the average debt was $150. With this data, you can estimate the *true rate of interest* Lois paid by using the following simple formula.

TRUE RATE OF INTEREST

$$\frac{\text{Estimated true}}{\text{rate of interest}} = \frac{\text{amount of interest}}{\text{average debt}} \times \frac{12}{\text{number of months of loan}}$$

$$\frac{\text{Estimated true}}{\text{rate of interest}} = \frac{9}{150} \times \frac{12}{6} = \frac{108}{900} = .12 = 12\%$$

The same basic principle applies when you buy goods that are paid for in monthly installments. For example, if 10 percent interest (commonly known as a *carrying charge* in installment buying) is added to the purchase price of an item, and if the item is paid for in six monthly installments, the yearly interest rate is 20 percent. Because you are paying some of the money owed each month, the true interest rate is approximately 40 percent.

CARRYING CHARGE

What remedy do you have against untruthful credit reports which harm your credit rating?
A new federal act, the Fair Credit Reporting Act, passed by Congress in 1970, is another consumer-protection device provided by the government. This act prohibits the abuse of a very valuable asset of the consumer—his credit.

FAIR CREDIT REPORTING ACT

The Fair Credit Reporting Act deals with unfavorable reports issued by credit bureaus. These reports, which often contain much personal data, character studies, etc., are frequently issued to insurance companies, businesses, or prospective employers. When rejecting an applicant, the company must supply the applicant with the source of its credit report, thus giving such a person the right to challenge the report. The applicant then has an opportunity to offer and support his side of the story.

The Fair Credit Reporting Act also provides that the credit reporting agency must tell you the nature of the information that they have on file for you. If the information is incorrect or incomplete, you have a right to correct the report and provide supporting information to prove your contentions. If the report is proven inaccurate, the reporting agency must delete it and send deletion notices to businesses and others who have received reports containing the erroneous information. In cases of erroneous reports, you have a right to know who received your credit record in the past six months. If the report was given to companies in which you were seeking employment, you must be advised of the distribution of such erroneous information during the past two years.

EXAMPLE 11   George Keegan was a successful businessman in Minnesota. He and his family moved to Arizona for his wife's health. When George tried to get a job, he had no luck. After he applied to many firms and was turned away from each one, he found out that a credit bureau in Arizona had received incorrect information that he had a very undesirable personal life which included incidents of wife beating and disorderly conduct. George had the right to find out the source of this incorrect information. He also had the right to support his side of the story and correct the mistaken information.

How would the provisions of the Economic Stabilization Act help you in your everyday shopping?

The Economic Stabilization Act of 1970 and the amendments of 1971 could aid the consumer every time he goes shopping. The act authorized the President to stabilize prices, rents, wages, and salaries through 1973. As a result of price stabilization, retailers were prohibited from increasing their prices until a list of base prices, or those which were in effect at a prior time in 1970, were readily available for customer inspection. **ECONOMIC STABILIZATION ACT**

What must a care label tell the consumer?

A recent regulation by the Federal Trade Commission requires that all finished articles of wearing apparel have a *care label* permanently attached to them. This label must give instructions as to how to wash, dry, iron, bleach, dry-clean, and otherwise regularly care for and maintain a particular article. The label must also warn the purchaser as to any unusual care and maintenance procedures which are necessary. This applies to clothes which appear to be washable but should, in fact, be dry-cleaned. The regulation also requires that the label be readily seen by the user. **CARE LABEL**

The Federal Trade Commission also helps inform the consumer who is going to make his own wearing apparel about fabric he has purchased. A tag with care instructions must be included with every fabric purchase.

SUGGESTIONS FOR MINIMIZING LEGAL RISKS

1. Find out as much as you can about the recent developments in consumer protection and about the agencies in your own community which can help you protect your rights.

2. Read carefully all credit documents and know how much interest you are really paying.

3. Where you believe unfair business practices are being followed, make specific complaints to the seller or dealer. If you get no satisfaction, report the facts to the Better Business Bureau or your local Chamber of Commerce.

 # APPLYING YOUR LEARNING

QUESTIONS AND PROBLEMS

1. Explain how competition serves to protect the consumer.
2. Explain the reasoning behind this statement: "In reality you are the most important factor in consumer protection."
3. Do you believe that we should have stricter antitrust laws? Why?
4. What is meant by unfair trade practices? Give several examples of unfair trade practices.
5. Name several agencies that enforce regulations designed to protect the consumer.
6. What are some aids that are available in your community for consumer protection?
7. What appears to be the trend in consumer protection?
8. What new legislation do you believe should be passed to give further protection to the consumer? Explain why.

WHAT IS YOUR OPINION?

In each of the following cases, give your decision and state a legal principle that applies to the case.

1. Clark and Grey were competitors in the dairy business. As they had the only two dairies in town, they agreed to divide the territory, raise the price of milk, and no longer compete. Clark breached this agreement, lowered the price of milk, and began to solicit business all over town. Could Grey sue Clark for breach of contract? Explain why this is a consumer problem.

2. Again assume that Clark and Grey were competitors in the dairy business. Clark began to circulate false rumors that Grey's cattle were infected with tuberculosis. Can Grey bring an action against Clark? Explain why this is a consumer problem.

3. Referring to Case 2, would Grey bring his action in a federal court or a state court? Is it likely that the Federal Trade Commission would be involved in this action? Explain.

4. Marino shipped a power shovel from California to New York. He contended that the railroad charged his shipment at too high a rate. Would he take his complaint to a federal or a state commission for settlement? Why?

5. Judy Mitzner went shopping at Heidner's Boutique. When she asked where the care label was located in a particular dress, she was told that Heidner's had a policy of removing the labels because they cause skin irritation when clothing is tried on. Would Heidner's be violating a law by removing these labels?

6. Jerome contended that fair-trade laws were a benefit to the consumer. Lahr contended that they were not. Present arguments supporting the position of each.

7. Lehman decided to modernize his automobile repair shop. He bought the most efficient new equipment he could find, studied up-to-date labor-saving methods of repair, and began aggressively to go after new business. Soon he had all the business in town, and his competitors became insolvent. Has Lehman violated any laws or been guilty of unfair trade practices?

8. Hale owned a small factory producing novelty goods. His entire output was sold through a retail store at the factory. To what extent would his business be controlled by the Federal Trade Commission?

9. Dressler was in the market for some household goods. He contended that there were federal laws controlling the quality of all goods sold. Do you agree with him?

THE LAW IN ACTION

1. The defendant, Charles Amador, assumed the stage name of "Charlie Aplin" and proceeded to make motion pictures in imitation of the well-known Charlie Chaplin character. The plaintiff, Charles Chaplin, the originator of the well-known movie character, brought an action asking the courts to restrain the defendant from further imitation of the name or the character. Was he entitled to judgment? (Chaplin v. Amador, 93 Cal. App. 358, 269 P. 544)

2. The plaintiff ordered a roll and a cup of coffee at the defendant's lunch counter. The roll was taken from a container by the waiter and served to the plaintiff. The roll contained a pebble and caused the plaintiff to break a tooth. The plaintiff sued for breach of an implied warranty. The defendant claimed that he could not be held because he had no way of knowing that the roll contained a pebble. Could the plaintiff collect? (Cushing v. Rodman, 65 App. D.C. 258, 82 F. 2d 864)

KEY TO "WHAT'S THE LAW?" Page 189

1. *Yes. He may not only find out but also may take steps to have incorrect material corrected.*
2. *No. This is a contract in restraint of trade.*

A DIGEST OF LEGAL CONCEPTS

1. Any seller who induces a buyer to buy as a result of certain statements of fact or promises warrants the goods sold.

2. Every sale made by the seller carries with it certain express or implied warranties.

3. An agent who, in making a sale, makes known the true name of the owner usually does not make any personal warranty of title.

4. An express warranty is a statement in words by the seller as to the quantity, quality, fitness, or soundness of the goods sold.

5. An implied warranty is not stated in words but is implied by law from the actions of the parties, the nature of the sale, or the surrounding circumstances.

6. Words of the seller that are only voluntary statements of opinion, commonly referred to as "sales talk" or "puffing," are not interpreted as warranties.

7. Where the contract is in writing, warranties are also usually required to be in writing.

8. An implied warranty of title, which, by the mere act of selling, is inherent in every sales contract, warrants that the seller has a good title to the goods, that the goods are free from the claims of other persons, and that the buyer will not be disturbed in his possession of them.

9. In a sale by sample or model, there is an express warranty that the goods will conform to the sample or model.

10. In a sale by description, there is an express warranty that the goods will conform to the description.

11. There is an implied warranty of fitness for the named purpose where the buyer has made known the use to which the goods will be put and has relied on the skill of the seller in their selection.

12. There is an implied warranty of merchantable quality where the goods are bought by description or by sample from a dealer who customarily sells like or similar goods.

13. Where the buyer has had an opportunity to inspect the goods, there is no implied warranty as to defects that the inspection would ordinarily disclose.

14. In the sale of food, there is an implied warranty that the goods are fit for human consumption.

15. All implied warranties except the implied warranty of title are excluded by expressions like "as is," "with all faults," and similar language.

16. An agreement modifying or rescinding a contract needs no consideration to be binding.

17. Modification or rescission is treated as a matter of good faith rather than as a matter for consideration.

18. It is the duty of the seller to transfer to the buyer goods of the quality and quantity agreed on.

19. It is the duty of the buyer to accept the goods and pay for them.

20. If title to the goods has passed to the buyer and the seller wrongfully refuses to give up the goods, the buyer may bring an action for the possession of the goods if they cannot be obtained elsewhere, or the buyer may allow the seller to keep the goods and then sue for the amount by which he has been damaged because of the failure of the seller to deliver.

21. If the seller has breached a warranty, the buyer may accept and keep the goods and bring an action for the damage resulting from the breach, refuse to accept the goods if they have not been delivered and sue for damages for the breach, or return the goods and demand a refund of the purchase price.

22. Where the seller discovers that the buyer has received goods on credit while insolvent, he may reclaim the goods upon demand made within ten days after receipt.

23. If the goods have been delivered to a carrier, an unpaid seller may stop them in transit if the buyer becomes insolvent.

24. The seller's right to stop delivery of the goods may be exercised even if they are in a warehouseman's possession.

25. If title has already passed to the buyer and he refuses to accept the goods, the seller may bring an action for the purchase price. The seller may also cancel the sale and resell the goods if they are of a perishable nature, when such a right is reserved in the contract or when the buyer has been in default an unreasonable length of time.

PART 8: Agency

WHAT'S THE LAW?

1. *Ronald Burns is sent to the store by his mother to buy groceries. Is Ronald an agent?*

2. *Harvey Wilson has a paper route. He is hired by the newspaper to solicit customers, to deliver papers, and to collect the subscription price. Is he an agent?*

▲ UNIT 22: CREATION OF AN AGENCY

There may be occasions when you yourself cannot do all the things that are necessary. You may have to call on someone else to get a job done.

EXAMPLE 1 Andy Burkett went into business for himself by opening a small hamburger stand. Initially, Burkett performed all the work requirements by himself; but as his business began to grow, he soon found that he needed some assistance. He then hired Frank Cataldi to work for him and found that this additional help allowed him to be more efficient in serving customers. Burkett offered Cataldi an opportunity to work longer hours and earn more revenue.

When Burkett hired Cataldi, he probably did not realize that he had entered into certain new legal relationships. When Burkett leaves Cataldi in charge of the business, Cataldi is theoretically taking Burkett's place, as he is dealing with third persons in Burkett's name. Cataldi is then an agent.

What is an agent? An *agent* is often defined as a person who acts for and in behalf of another **AGENT** in dealing with third persons and is subject to the control of the person for whom he is acting. There are three parties necessary in an agency relationship: (1) the principal, Burkett; (2) the agent, Cataldi; and (3) one or more third persons, the customers.

What is a principal? To be a *principal*, one must have the legal capacity to enter into valid **PRINCIPAL** contracts. Any person who has the right to perform an act for himself may delegate its performance to another, and the contracts made for him by an agent will be as valid and enforceable as if he had made them himself.

A minor may be a principal, but all his contracts and those entered into for him by his agent are voidable unless the agreements are enforceable under the rule of necessities. A minor may, however, act as an agent with

When may a
minor serve as
an agent? a
principal?
all the rights and obligations of an agent because he is actually an intermediary and not a party to a contract. He is merely creating a contractual relationship between the principal and the third party.

EXAMPLE 2 **During a serious illness, Manning, seventeen years old, requested a friend to purchase certain medicines prescribed for him by a physician. He also asked his friend to rent a color television set to be installed in the sickroom during his illness. Manning would be fully liable for the cost of the medicines, but the contract for rental of the television would be voidable because it does not constitute a necessity to a minor.**

AGENCY RELATIONSHIPS

EMPLOYER–EMPLOYEE

It may have surprised you that we called Cataldi an agent in Example 1. You might have said, "Why he is just an employee!" And so he is part of the time. In modern business relationships it is often difficult to distinguish between an employee and an agent. The same person may at times be an agent and at other times be an employee. Take Cataldi, in Example 1. Burkett may tell Cataldi to go into the kitchen, wash the dishes, and make up a new supply of hamburgers. While Cataldi is doing that, he is an employee. He is doing what he is told to do without using any discretion of his own, and he is not in contact with third parties. When Cataldi is out in front waiting on customers, however, especially when he is left alone in charge of the business, he is an agent.

Distinguish
between an agent
and an employee.
The distinction, then, is this: An *agent* deals with third persons for the principal and uses some discretion or judgment of his own; an *employee* does what he is told to do and does not deal with third persons.

EMPLOYEE

INDEPENDENT CONTRACTOR

EXAMPLE 3 **Burkett decided to enlarge his hamburger stand. He entered into a contract with Leo Gibbs. The terms of the contract provided that, for the sum of $5,000, Gibbs was to build an addition to the stand according to certain plans and specifications. Is Gibbs an employee or an agent?**

In home situations as well as in business—whether you are an agent or an employee—you are subject to the authority of the person for whom you perform your duties.

How is an independent contractor different from an agent?

INDEPENDENT CONTRACTOR

Gibbs is neither an employee nor an agent; he is an *independent contractor.* He is not working under Burkett's direction. He has promised to achieve a certain result, but the manner in which he proceeds to achieve that result is left to him. An independent contractor is responsible under the terms of the contract, but he is not to be considered an employee or an agent, and the law of agency does not apply to him. Thus, for example, an independent contractor probably assigns all or part of his duties, but an agent or employee could not, since each renders personal services.

Can an agent assign his duties?

HOW AGENCIES ARE CREATED

Modern business could not be carried on without agents. One man does not have enough time, nor usually does he have enough skill, to carry on even a small business enterprise by himself. He must delegate some of the work to others. This creates legal risks because, when someone else is doing your work for you, you are responsible for his actions.

BY ORAL OR WRITTEN AGREEMENT

Most agencies are created by agreement. Most of these agreements are contracts, but some are not.

EXAMPLE 4 **Sometimes you offer to help a friend without thought of compensation. You are doing the job "for free." There is no consideration, so there is no valid contract. But if you do the job, you are an agent.**

Usually the agency agreement does not have to be in any particular form. Like other contracts, an agency agreement is sometimes oral, sometimes written. A few types of agreements, however, need some special explanation so that you may better understand them.

Equal Dignities Rule   The Statute of Frauds specifies that certain contracts must be in writing if they are to be enforceable. The *equal dignities rule* specifies that a contract of agency must be in writing if the contracts that the agent is to make with third parties in behalf of the principal are to be in writing. Likewise, if the agent is to enter into contracts under seal, his agency must be created by authority under seal.

EQUAL DIGNITIES RULE

Power of Attorney   A principal who wishes to supply the agent with positive proof that he has authority to act may execute a *power of attorney.* This is a formal written statement of the specific acts that the agent may do for the principal. It must be signed by the principal and usually must be notarized. A power of attorney is often used by persons who, because of ill health or extended absence from home, wish to appoint others to transact their business. A power of attorney is absolutely necessary if the agent is to execute deeds, mortgages, or other documents that are to be recorded in a public office.

POWER OF ATTORNEY

What is a power of attorney? When is it absolutely needed?

Statute of Frauds   You will remember that contracts that cannot be performed within a year from the time of making must be in writing. Thus, if, by the terms of the agreement, the agency is to last more than a year, the agreement must be in writing in order to be enforceable.

POWER OF ATTORNEY

Know all Men by these Presents,

THAT I, Robert L. Anderson, of the City of Sacramento, in the County of Sacramento, and State of California

have made, constituted and appointed, and by these presents do make, constitute and appoint Franklin M. Townsend, of the City of Sacramento, in the County of Sacramento, and State of California

my   true and lawful attorney for me and in my name, place and stead

to represent me in the purchase and sale of canned fruits and vegetables

in the State of California   giving and granting unto my said attorney full power and authority to do and perform all and every act and thing whatsoever requisite and necessary to be done in and about the premises, as fully, to all intents and purposes, as I   might or could do if personally present, with full power of substitution and revocation, hereby ratifying and confirming all that my said attorney   or his substitute   shall lawfully do or cause to be done by virtue hereof.

In Witness Whereof, I have hereunto set my   hand   and seal the twenty-third   day of   June   in the year one thousand nine hundred and seventy-three

Sealed and Delivered in the presence of *Robert L. Anderson*

Lawrence A. Hart
Maxwell D. Harson

State of California
County of Sacramento }ss.: **Be it Known,**   That on   the twenty-third   day of   June   one thousand nine hundred and seventy-three before me Katherine C. Fraley a Notary Public in and for the State of California   duly commissioned and sworn, dwelling in the City of Sacramento   personally came and appeared

Robert L. Anderson   to me personally known, and known to me to be the same person   described in and who executed the within Power of Attorney, and   he

acknowledged the within Power of Attorney to be   his act and deed.

In Testimony Whereof, I have hereunto subscribed my name and affixed my seal of office, the day and year last above written.   *Katherine C. Fraley*
                                    Notary Public

BY IMPLICATION

The acts of the parties may clearly indicate, or imply, that an agency exists.

EXAMPLE 5   Suppose that, in Example 1, Cataldi had been hired at first strictly as an employee. He was to sweep, wash dishes, and work in the kitchen only. One day, Burkett called Cataldi out to the counter and said, "I have to go downtown for a few hours."

When does an agency by implication come into existence?

Was Cataldi an agent? Yes, even though he was not specifically delegated to carry out the assignment of looking after the business during Burkett's absence, he was, by implication, expected to do so, and, therefore, Cataldi became an *agent by implication.*

AGENT BY
IMPLICATION

BY ESTOPPEL

An *agent by estoppel* is one who is falsely represented to be an agent when he actually is not. The false representation must be made by the alleged principal, and it must be relied on by the third person to his subsequent injury.

AGENT BY ESTOPPEL

EXAMPLE 6 **Suppose that Ellis Carter makes a sales call on Burkett. Carter is a salesman for a bakery and wishes to sell Burkett a new kind of hamburger roll. Burkett does not want to be bothered, so he says to Carter, "Go out and talk with Ike Harris; he is my agent and does all the buying for me." Actually, Ike is not Burkett's agent. He is just a person loafing in front of the hamburger stand. Burkett simply wanted to get Carter out of the door. Carter, however, talked with Ike, and Ike gave Carter an order for 100 dozen rolls in Burkett's name. When the rolls were delivered, Burkett refused to take them claiming that Ike was not his agent. May Burkett do so?**

No, Burkett will have to pay for the rolls. He had represented that Ike was his agent. Carter had relied on that statement to his injury, so Burkett is now estopped from denying the agency relationship.

Agency by implication and agency by estoppel look very much alike. Technically, however, they are different. An agency by implication is a real agency. Its existence is proved by the acts of the parties rather than by spoken words. An agency by estoppel, so called, is really not an agency at all. The alleged principal has falsely represented that an agency exists, and the law forces him to live up to his representation.

Distinguish between an agency by implication and an agency by estoppel.

BY RATIFICATION

How is an agency by ratification created?

At times, a person may act as an agent when he has no authority to do so. If the principal, with full knowledge of all the facts, accepts the benefits of the unauthorized act, there is an *agency by ratification*.

AGENCY BY RATIFICATION

EXAMPLE 7 **One day while Cataldi was in charge of the hamburger stand, a man came in who had a used dishwasher for sale. Cataldi did not have the authority to buy such an item, but he knew that Burkett had been looking for just such a machine. Rather than lose the chance for a bargain, he contracted to buy the dishwasher in Burkett's name.**

If you represent someone as your agent when he is not, you will be held responsible by estoppel for his actions.

Agent for CLIPYOU DATA PROCESSING SCHOOL

If a principal refuses to ratify any unauthorized contracts made by his agent, is he liable for them?

Burkett will not be bound by such a contract if he does not want to be bound; but if he ratifies the bargain and accepts the dishwasher, he must pay for it. A principal's failure or refusal to ratify the unauthorized acts of his agent makes the agent personally liable in damages to a third party. An agent who fails to point out that he is working for a principal or refuses to disclose the identity of his principal will be liable on the contracts he makes with third parties to the same extent as though he were acting for himself.

EXAMPLE 8 **Gross, an attorney, was authorized to purchase a certain property for Lincoln Associates. Gross was instructed not to disclose for whom he was working and to make the purchase as though he were making it for himself. Under this arrangement Gross may be held personally responsible on any contract he may make with the owners of the property.**

BY NECESSITY

EXAMPLE 9 **Burkett needed a vacation, so he left Cataldi in charge of the business and went to Canada on a fishing trip. While he was away, a severe wind blew off part of the roof of the hamburger stand. The wind was followed by heavy rains, and to prevent serious injury to the stand and its contents, Cataldi called in Leo Gibbs to make emergency repairs.**

Under ordinary circumstances Cataldi would not have the authority to order repairs made on the roof, but here he would be an *agent by necessity*. This type of agency is sometimes necessary to prevent loss to the principal.

Certain relationships imply the creation of agency rights, although, in fact, they may not actually exist. The wife and children of a man who fails to provide the essentials of life will be declared agents of the man by necessity for the purpose of purchasing food and clothing. The man will be responsible for the contracts made in his name as long as the purchases are reasonable.

AGENT BY NECESSITY

The wife of a man who has deserted his family has the right to purchase necessities of life for herself and her children and charge them to her husband. She is considered an agent by necessity.

KINDS OF AGENTS

GENERAL AGENT

Who is a discretionary agent?

A *general agent* is a person who has been given authority to do any act that is within the scope of the business. The general manager of a department store, for example, would be a general agent.

General agents are sometimes called *discretionary agents*, having the right to use their judgment in all matters pertaining to the agency.

GENERAL AGENT

DISCRETIONARY AGENT

EXAMPLE 10 Otto Lakeland was appointed manager of a new service station for the River Gas and Oil Corporation. On a busy holiday weekend, Lakeland hired two extra men to work in the station. A motor on one of the gas pumps stopped running, and Lakeland decided to call an electrician to make the pump repairs. As the service station manager, Lakeland was granted the authority to make these types of decisions and to bind his employer to these decisions.

SPECIAL AGENT

A *special agent* is employed to accomplish a specific purpose or to do a particular job. A salesman is a special agent. He has authority to take orders or, perhaps, to sell and pass title to specific goods sold, but that is the extent of his authority. He cannot buy in the principal's name, nor is he usually authorized to collect the purchase price unless he actually delivers the goods sold.

SPECIAL AGENT

FACTORS AND DEL CREDERE AGENTS

Sometimes an agent may act more or less independently as a middleman. A commission merchant, for example, may have his own place of business, to which farmers may bring their produce. The produce is left with the commission merchant for sale. Customers who come to purchase do not care who the owner of the goods is. The customers deal directly with the commission merchant, and they look to him to make good if the goods are not satisfactory. Such an agent is usually called a *factor*. A *del credere agent* is a selling agent who guarantees payment of his customers' accounts. For this guarantee, a del credere agent usually receives higher commissions than do other agents.

FACTOR

DEL CREDERE AGENT

EXAMPLE 11 Canfield employed Judson to act as his agent in selling merchandise for him. The contract of agency was made for one year and included a guarantee by Judson that Canfield would not suffer any loss because of sales on credit that Judson might make. Merchandise valued at $650 was sold to Drew, who failed to pay for the goods. Canfield sued Judson. It was held that Canfield could collect from Judson on his contract of guarantee. Judson was a del credere agent, and his promise is enforceable.

What are the relationships that result from a functioning agency?

An *agency relationship* results from a contract between the principal and the agent (as explained in this unit). A *contractual relationship* between the principal and the third party results through an act of the agent (to be explained in Unit 23). A *legal relationship* between the agent and the third party results when the agent represents his principal (to be explained in Unit 24).

The diagram below summarizes the three relationships that result when an agency is functioning.

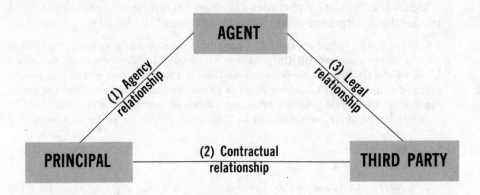

SUGGESTIONS FOR MINIMIZING LEGAL RISKS

1. When you enter into an agency contract either as a principal or as an agent, be sure that the terms of the contract are clear, particularly with respect to the duties of the agent and the extent of his authority.
2. When you work for someone else, be sure that the nature of your relationship is understood by you and the other party. Trouble may result if you think you are an agent and the other party thinks you are an independent contractor.
3. When you contract with an independent contractor, be sure that he understands that he alone is responsible for any liabilities he incurs.
4. If you, as a principal, authorize an agent to act for you away from your place of business, provide him with written evidence that he is your agent. The written evidence should also clearly state the nature and the extent of his authority.
5. Use great care in appointing a general agent. It is usually much better to limit an agent's authority to the specific acts you expect him to do. Remember that a general agent has the potential power to cause you serious financial difficulties—possibly insolvency and eventual bankruptcy.

APPLYING YOUR LEARNING

QUESTIONS AND PROBLEMS

1. What is an agency?
2. Name the parties in an agency and describe their functions or obligations.
3. What are the legal and personal qualifications needed by one to be an agent? a principal?
4. How can you determine whether a person is acting as an agent rather than as an employee?
5. What is an independent contractor?
6. How do agency agreements ordinarily come into existence?
7. What is the effect of the equal dignities rule on a contract of agency?
8. Name several types of agency agreements that must be in writing.
9. What do we mean by the creation of an agency by implication? by estoppel? by ratification? by necessity?
10. What are the distinguishing characteristics of a general agent? a special agent?
11. How would you describe the functions of a factor? of a del credere agent?

WHAT IS YOUR OPINION?

In each of the following cases, give your decision and state a legal principle that applies to the case.

1. Ames appointed Rice, a minor, as his agent. Rice made a contract for Ames with Perkins. Claiming the infancy of Rice as a defense, Perkins sought to avoid the contract. Can Perkins do so?
2. Dugan appointed Berg, a minor, to be his purchasing agent. Berg contracted with West to buy merchandise for Dugan. Is Dugan bound on the contract?
3. Without authority to act, Vasquez falsely represented himself to be an agent for Dorr and contracted to buy goods from Silver. Dorr refused to accept the goods. Could Silver hold Vasquez liable?
4. Mesler had a five-year contract as sales agent for Nord. After working for three years, Mesler became ill and assigned his uncompleted contract to Mack. Mesler mailed a letter to Nord, telling of the assignment. Is Nord bound by the assignment?
5. Mahar was employed by Knott in his store. When Knott was out of the store, he always left Mahar in charge, authorizing him to make sales and limited purchases. Knott, however, always referred to Mahar as an employee and contended that Mahar was not an agent. Was he correct? Why?
6. Irving sold a large radio to Heath. Giles, who owned a station wagon and was a friend of Irving's, offered to deliver the radio for Irving just as a personal favor. Is Giles an agent? Why?

7. Butler fell from a ladder in his store and was knocked unconscious. He was taken to a hospital for treatment but did not regain consciousness for six weeks. While Butler was in the hospital, his wife took over the operation of the business without any authority to do so. Was the wife an agent? If so, what kind?

8. Klees appointed Hunt as his agent, with full authority to sell his house and execute a deed. Would Klees have to execute a power of attorney to make it possible for Hunt to sign a contract to sell the house? Would the same be true with reference to the execution of the deed?

THE LAW IN ACTION

1. An agent of the plaintiff contracted for fire insurance in the name of the plaintiff, and a policy was issued by the defendant company. The agent did not have authority to enter into such a contract, and the plaintiff did not even know of the existence of such a policy until after the goods covered by the insurance were destroyed by fire. When the plaintiff learned of the policy, he immediately ratified his agent's act. The insurance company refused to pay the loss, contending that the plaintiff's right to ratify was terminated by the fire. What is your opinion? (Marqusee v. Hartford Fire Insurance Company, 198 F. 475)

2. The defendant company operated a large department store. Space in the store was leased to a dentist by the defendant. The dentist was in reality an independent contractor operating his own office under a professional license. The defendant did advertise to the public, however, that the dentist was a part of the store's operation, furnished as a service to its customers. The plaintiff was injured by the carelessness of the dentist in working on the plaintiff's teeth. The plaintiff sued the defendant and the defendant denied liability, claiming that the dentist was not its agent but only a tenant. Is the defendant liable for the injury? (Hannon v. Siegel-Cooper Company, 167 N.Y. 244, 60 N.E. 597)

KEY TO "WHAT'S THE LAW?" Page 203

1. *Yes. Ronald is acting for and in behalf of his mother and subject to her control in buying the groceries.*

2. *Yes, in this case. Newsboys, however, often buy their own newspapers and act as independent contractors. Each case must be decided on its own facts.*

WHAT'S THE LAW?

1. *Norman Tyre was an agent of Jerome Murphy. Jerome sent Norman to buy a certain radio for him for $25. Norman liked the radio so well that he bought it for himself and refused to give it to Jerome. May Jerome demand the radio from Norman?*

---

2. *Burns had full authority to buy goods for Green. Burns bought goods from Lacey and charged them to Green. Lacey relied solely on Burns' representation that he was an agent. Green refused to pay, saying Burns had no apparent authority to act. Is this correct?*

◭ UNIT 23: RELATIONSHIP OF PARTIES

In an agency there are three relationships, each of which has its particular rights and duties. These relationships are (1) the relationship between the principal and the agent, (2) the relationship between the principal and the third person or persons, and (3) the relationship between the agent and the third person or persons. Each must be studied separately, because the rights and duties involved are not the same.

OBLIGATIONS OF PRINCIPAL AND AGENT

PRINCIPAL TO AGENT

"The laborer is worthy of his hire" is a well-known expression, and the same concept applies to most agency relationships.

Compensation The agent is working for and in behalf of the principal, and he is entitled to be paid for his services unless the agent is a *gratuitous agent* (one not legally obligated to fulfill his promise). The principal must pay the agent the compensation agreed upon in the contract. If no specific amount has been stated, a reasonable sum must be paid for any authorized acts performed by the agent in behalf of the principal. The principal's duty to pay the agent exists whether the agency resulted from contract or from ratification. If a person acts as agent for the two parties to a contract with their knowledge, he is entitled to receive compensation from each of the parties involved.

What is a gratuitous agent?

May a person ever act as an agent for the two parties to a contract and collect compensation from each?

GRATUITOUS AGENT

An agent may retain in his possession property belonging to his principal if the principal refuses to compensate him for his services. The *right of lien* is terminated when the agent has been compensated.

Reimbursement If the work done requires that the agent spend his own money in his principal's interest, he is entitled to reimbursement.

EXAMPLE 1 **John Clawson desires to have his auto greased and washed. He tells his agent, Hank Heinz, to drive the auto to the service station and have it greased and washed. Heinz drives the car to the station as instructed and pays for the service with his own money. Clawson must repay Heinz for the expenses he incurred.**

Indemnity Indemnity differs slightly from reimbursement. If an agent suffers a loss or damage as a result of obedience to his principal's instructions, he is entitled to be paid the amount of the loss or damage. This right is known as *indemnity*.

EXAMPLE 2 **Suppose, in Example 2, that Mr. Clawson had removed the license plates from his car to clean them. He had intended to have Heinz replace them, but he forgot to tell him about it. On the way to the service station, Heinz was arrested for driving a car without license plates and was forced to pay a fine.**

Heinz has suffered a personal loss through following the instructions of his principal, and Mr. Clawson must indemnify him for this loss.

Responsibility of Principal for Torts A *tort* is a private or civil wrong other than a breach of contract that arises from the breach of a right or duty owed to another for which a court of law will grant damages. A tort does not arise from the breach of a contract but, rather, from the violation of a duty imposed by law. A principal is always held liable for his agent's torts if they are committed while the agent is doing what he was instructed to do. Thus, a fraudulent statement made by an agent within the scope of his authority binds his principal on the contract.

Is a principal
ever liable for
torts committed
by his agent?

Whether a tort is committed willfully or negligently has no effect on the degree of the principal's liability.

EXAMPLE 3 **Henry Olsen and Pat Palmer hitched a ride on the back of Mr. Rankin's truck. The truck was being driven by Rankin's agent, James Rhodes, who had given the boys permission to ride on the tail gate. Rhodes drove the truck in a negligent fashion and, while trying to pass another truck, caused an accident that seriously injured Henry and Pat. Can Henry and Pat hold the principal, Mr. Rankin, liable for their injuries?**

The answer would be "Yes." Rhodes was guilty of two negligent acts. One was within the scope of his employment. The other was not. Since driving the truck was within the scope of his employment and his negligent driving was the cause of the injury, the boys may recover damages from the principal for their injuries.

If we change the facts and assume that Rhodes was driving carefully, but, while he was driving over a rough road, the boys were thrown off the rear of the truck, our answer would be different. In this situation the injury to the boys would be traceable only to the negligence of Rhodes in allowing them to ride on the rear of the truck. The principal, Mr. Rankin,

A principal is held liable for his agent's torts if they are within the scope of the agent's employment.

would not be liable because this negligent act of Rhodes was not a part of his job. Rankin would be liable for only such acts as were within the scope of Rhodes's employment.

When can an agent be held personally liable for his torts?

The agent himself will be liable for those torts committed outside the scope of his employment or authority. In such cases the agent is said to be "on an excursion of his own," carrying out some act unrelated to his duties or authority.

● Under the motor-vehicle laws of most states, the employer is held liable to third parties for the negligence of an employee while driving a vehicle on business for the employer. The laws usually provide that "every owner of a motor vehicle operated on a public highway shall be liable for death or injury to a person or damage to property resulting from the negligence of a person to whom he gave his express or implied permission to use such vehicle on the business of the owner or otherwise." You should remember, however, that this is a special statutory liability and has nothing to do with the law of agency.

AGENT TO PRINCIPAL

Can a gratuitous agent ever be held liable for any loss resulting from his failure to follow instructions?

Obedience   The agent must obey all reasonable orders and instructions within the scope of his agency contract. A great many lawsuits result from the failure of the agent to do so. He becomes personally liable to his principal for any loss resulting from violation of orders, even though he can show that he exercised great care and forethought. Even a gratuitous agent who undertakes to perform a promise must follow instructions or become responsible for any loss resulting from failure to do so.

EXAMPLE 4   **Suppose that Mr. Clawson (from Example 1) had told Heinz to have the car washed and greased only and to pay cash for the job. Instead of following instructions, Heinz also had the oil changed, ordered a new oil filter installed, and charged the entire bill to Mr. Clawson's account.**

NOTE: *The bullet indicates that there may be a state statute that varies from the law discussed here. Whenever you see this bullet, find out, if possible, what the statute is in your state covering this point or principle of law.*

Naturally, when the filling-station operator presents his bill to Mr. Clawson, there is likely to be an argument. Clawson must pay the extra charges, but he can collect this amount from Heinz. Heinz is liable for the extra charges.

What is a
fiduciary
relationship?
Good Faith   An agency is a *fiduciary relationship.* That means that the relationship is of highest trust and confidence. It exists when one person assumes the responsibility of acting for another person, handling his property, or spending his money. An agent is in a position to do his principal great harm if he acts carelessly or willfully, contrary to the principal's interest. The principal often entrusts the agent with his business, his property, his money, and sometimes even his good name. This places on the agent the highest duty of special care and good faith. The Uniform Commercial Code stipulates that every contract or duty imposes an obligation of good faith in its performance or enforcement. U.C.C. Sec. 1-203

FIDUCIARY
RELATIONSHIP

A principal is responsible for all the acts of an agent done within the scope of employment.

EXAMPLE 5   Seiken requested Trayner to invest a large sum of money for him in stocks and bonds. Trayner was an account executive for a large stock-brokerage company and was considered to be an expert in that business. He purchased securities that, a short time later, proved to be worthless. Seiken sued Trayner and the firm that employed him.

In order to hold Trayner and his employers liable, Seiken would be obliged to prove gross negligence, lack of good faith and loyalty, or disobedience of orders and instructions. If Trayner used prudence and skill, he cannot be held liable as an insurer of the investment.

"A servant cannot
be loyal to two
masters." What
does this
expression mean?
Loyalty   The agent must be loyal to his principal and must at all times act in his interest. He may not work for someone else in competition with his principal. "A servant cannot be loyal to two masters." An agent is considered disloyal if he himself makes a profit at the principal's expense or gives false reports or information to the principal.

EXAMPLE 6   Many years ago, Smiling Jack of the comic strips had an agent named Mr. Brotherly. Smiling Jack needed a certain piece of land to use as an airport, so he sent Mr. Brotherly out to buy it for him. Mr. Brotherly, instead of following instructions, bought the land for himself and tried to resell it to Smiling Jack for several times what he paid for it. The comic-strip artist solved the problem in a very unbusinesslike way. He had someone shoot Mr. Brotherly and then forgot about the whole affair.

A much less violent remedy, however, was available to Smiling Jack. He could have brought a legal action and asked the court to order Mr. Brotherly to reconvey the land to him for the exact amount Mr. Brotherly had paid for it.

Judgment and Skill   An agent, in performing his work for the principal, must use all the skill and judgment of which he is capable. The agent, however, will not be held liable for an honest mistake in judgment nor for a lack of skill when he has done the best he can.

EXAMPLE 7   Michael Morris worked in Mr. Bloom's service station each day after school. Michael was a diligent worker who was willing to learn even though he did not know much about the service station operation. While he was alone at the station one day, a customer asked Michael to grease the wheel bearings. Michael approached the task enthusiastically, but he used ordinary grease in place of the special grease required by the wheel bearings. The brake linings were ruined.

Even though Mr. Bloom might have to pay for the damage, Michael would not be held liable because he had done the best he could. If, on the other hand, Michael had indicated to Mr. Bloom at the time of his employment that he was an experienced car greaser, he would be liable because an experienced worker would know better than to do the job in the way that Michael did.

Is an agent liable for a mistake in judgment?

Duty to Account   When an agent is handling money that belongs to someone else, he is acting in a highly fiduciary capacity. As an agent, he must account for every cent of his principal's money that he handles. He must keep it separate from his own, keep it safe, and turn it over to the principal in accordance with the principal's instructions. If, because of the careless way in which the agent carries money, it is impossible for him to tell how much belongs to him and how much belongs to the principal, the agent loses all claim to the money. The entire amount is considered as belonging to the principal.

Do all profits that result from the contract of agency belong to the principal?

EXAMPLE 8   Hilman worked on a laundry truck, making deliveries for the Standard Laundry Company. On one day in which he made a number of deliveries, Hilman made cash collections and placed the funds in a pocket containing money of his own. If, upon checking in at the end of the day, Hilman could not correctly account for his funds and accurately list which of the money was his and what amount belonged to his employer, the employer would have a right to demand the total sum. Since the confusion of the funds was due to Hilman's negligence, he is fully responsible.

Does an agency
relationship
always involve a
contract for
personal services?

Duty of Personal Performance   Usually, an agency relationship involves a contract for personal services. As you learned in your study of contracts, the performance of such a contract may not be delegated to someone else. An agent must do the job himself, unless the contract specifically or by implication provides for delegation. This rule applies to a minor as well as to an adult.

EXAMPLE 9   Suppose that you have a check drawn on a bank in a distant city. You take the check to your own bank and ask the bank to collect it for you. By your act you are appointing your bank as an agent for the collection of the check. You do not, however, expect the cashier of the bank to get on the plane and personally go to the distant city to collect the money. You expect the bank to send the check through regular clearinghouse channels and thus delegate the responsibility of collection.

OBLIGATIONS OF PRINCIPAL AND THIRD PARTIES

PRINCIPAL TO THIRD PARTIES

If the agent follows his principal's instructions and acts within the scope of the authority given him by his principal in dealing with third parties, the contract that results is a binding obligation between the third party and the principal.

> The principal is bound on all contracts entered into by the agent in the principal's name if the agent is acting within the scope of his actual or apparent authority.

Actual Authority   *Actual authority* means the authority given to the agent by the principal. Such actual authority may be expressed in words, or it may be implied from the acts of the parties or the nature of the transaction.

When is an agent
said to be acting
within the scope
of his authority?

If the agent has actual authority to act for his principal, it makes little difference whether the third party knows he is dealing with an agent or not. If the agent has actual authority, he can make a binding contract in the principal's name.

EXAMPLE 10   Julie Thompson appointed Paul Nash as her agent for the sale of Julie's automobile. She gave Paul full authority to sell. She gave him the car and the necessary papers properly signed, so that Paul could give good title. Julie authorized Paul to collect the purchase price. Paul sold and delivered the car to Ray Pold, giving him the necessary title papers, but put the money in his own pocket and left town. Can Julie recover her car?

No. Ray has a good and valid title to the car, and Julie may not recover it. Paul was acting within the scope of his actual authority up to the time that he put the money into his own pocket and absconded.

Apparent Authority   When an agent stays within the scope of his actual authority, there is not much chance for trouble. When the agent goes beyond the scope of his actual authority in entering into contracts in his principal's name, a great deal of trouble usually results. The problem is then to determine whether the principal has clothed the agent with apparent authority to act.

EXAMPLE 11   If, in Example 10 Julie Thompson had given Paul Nash the car and the necessary title papers but had told Paul not to make a final sale without first consulting her, we should then have a more difficult problem. Suppose, also, that Julie had instructed Paul that he was not to accept cash in payment, but only a certified check made out to Julie. If Paul then sold the car for cash without consulting with Julie and absconded with the money, what would your answer be concerning the title to the car?

It is still a valid sale to Ray if he does not know of the limitations on Paul's authority. When Julie gave Paul the car and the title papers, she gave him apparent authority to sell and deliver title. The secret limitations on Paul's authority would not be binding on anyone who did not know about them. From the facts of the case, Ray had the legal right to suppose that Paul was acting within the scope of his authority.

Implied Authority   When an agent is carrying out the duties assigned to him by his principal, he is clothed with the implied authority to do everything necessary to bring to satisfactory completion these expressly authorized duties.

EXAMPLE 12   Jackson, an agent for a manufacturer of dolls and doll accessories, sold a complete assortment of doll clothes to a retail toy dealer. Unless the contract with his principal provided otherwise, he had the implied authority to sell the goods on credit or to collect cash for the goods at the time of the sale.

THIRD PARTIES TO PRINCIPAL

May an agent sue a third party for breach of an agreement that the agent made on behalf of his principal?

The third party who deals with a principal through an agent is actually contracting with the principal. Once the contract is made, the agent drops out of the picture. The contract and the obligations and duties that follow are those of principal and third party. The third party owes the principal the duty of living up to his agreement. If the third party breaches his contract, the principal has a right to sue. If the agent brings the action, he brings it in the principal's name, not his own.

EXAMPLE 13   Chesler was employed by Hamm as a general agent to perform any duties necessary in the conduct of his wholesale merchandising business. Chesler contracted with the Royal Novelty Corporation for a large order of merchandise manufactured by Royal Novelty. The company knew that Chesler was making the purchase as Hamm's agent. If it became necessary to sue because of the corporation's failure to comply with the terms of the contract, Hamm would have to bring the action.

After the contract was made, Chesler was no longer a party to it. His place as principal was taken by Hamm whom he legally represented. The novelty corporation's breach of contract gave Hamm the right to sue. The suit cannot be brought in Chesler's name.

SUGGESTIONS FOR MINIMIZING LEGAL RISKS

1. If you are an agent, have a clear understanding with your principal on the matter of spending your own money in his interest. Do not assume an authority that you do not have. You might not get your money back.
2. Failure to live up to your duties as an agent amounts to a breach of contract. If your principal sustains a loss, you might have to make good the loss.
3. When serving as an agent, never represent yourself as having a skill that you do not possess. It may cost you money.
4. If you are a principal, make every effort to convey the specific scope or extent of your agent's authority to third parties with whom he does business.
5. As a principal, never allow your agent to develop habits that might lead to injury to others. Damage suits could bankrupt you.

 APPLYING YOUR LEARNING

QUESTIONS AND PROBLEMS

1. The principal has certain obligations to his agent. What are they? Explain and illustrate each.
2. What are the agent's obligations to his principal? Explain and illustrate each.
3. What are the principal's obligations to third parties? Explain.
4. What is meant by the agent's actual authority? Give a typical example.
5. What is meant by the agent's apparent authority?
6. Under what conditions is the principal liable for the torts of his agent?

WHAT IS YOUR OPINION?

In each of the following cases, give your decision and state a legal principle that applies to the case.

1. Sears, Tidings' salesman, sold a used car to Rapp for $600. Tidings had told Sears not to sell the car for less than $650. Is Tidings bound on the contract?
2. Newbury, while driving on business for his principal, was fined $25 for speeding. Is the principal legally bound to reimburse Newbury?
3. Noble gave Meskil authority to sell a truck for him for $900. Meskil sold the truck for $950. He gave Noble $900 and kept the additional $50 for himself. May Noble, on learning the facts, recover the $50?

4. Henzel, who was a real estate agent for Gray Brothers, was authorized by his firm to buy a certain piece of real estate. He bought the property for himself for $30,000 and then sold it to Gray Brothers for $40,000. Later, when Gray Brothers discovered what Henzel had done, they demanded his profit. Were they entitled to recover the $10,000?

5. Frear, sales agent for Doran, sold some furs to Crider, stating that they were from China. When it was discovered that the furs came from Alaska, Crider sued Doran. Doran stated that he had not authorized Frear to make such a statement concerning the furs. Is Doran liable for damages?

6. With the knowledge of the principals, McCabe acted as sales agent for Long and also as buying agent for Jonas in the sale of an expensive painting. Is McCabe entitled to compensation from both parties?

7. Burg, the owner of a wholesale drug business, specifically instructed his salesman, Bain, to sell for cash only. In this type of business, it is customary to sell goods on a credit basis. Bain sold a quantity of drugs on credit to Amato, who was not aware of Burg's instructions. Burg refused to deliver the goods to Amato on the grounds that Bain had no authority to sell goods on credit. Was Burg bound on the contract?

8. Yager, a restaurant owner, employed Foster to manage the business and gave him specific orders not to buy supplies on credit terms. Shaw, not knowing of Yager's orders to Foster, sold supplies to the restaurant on thirty-day terms. Can Shaw hold Yager liable for the payment?

THE LAW IN ACTION

1. The defendant was an agent of the plaintiff. He was employed as a traveling salesman to sell a line of high-priced knit goods. Unknown to the plaintiff, the defendant also acted as a salesman for a line of inexpensive knit goods. When sued for violating his duty to the plaintiff, the defendant contended that he only sold the cheaper line to customers who would not buy the plaintiff's high-priced goods. Was this a good defense? Why? (Robert Reis & Company v. Volck, 151 App. Div. 613, 136 N.Y.S. 367)

2. The plaintiff ordered the defendant, who was an agent of the plaintiff, to buy 100 shares of Pacific Mail stock for the plaintiff. Instead of buying the stock on the market, the defendant sold the plaintiff 100 shares of Pacific Mail stock that the defendant owned. The plaintiff did not discover this fact until after the stock depreciated in price. After learning the true situation, the plaintiff repudiated the transaction, tendered back the stock, and demanded the return of his money. In your opinion, could the plaintiff get his money back by returning the stock? Why? (Taussig v. Hart, 58 N.Y. 425)

KEY TO "WHAT'S THE LAW?" Page 213

1. *Yes. An agent cannot compete with his principal.*
2. *No. The agent had the actual authority to buy, and that was all that was necessary.*

WHAT'S THE LAW?

1. *Gordon Fox operated a department store in his own name, although actually he was only an agent for the real owner, Jack Farr. Bill McKnight sold goods to Fox on credit; but later, when he discovered that Farr was the true owner of the business, he tried to collect from Farr. Could he do so?*

2. *If instead of trying to collect from the real owner, Farr, McKnight had tried to collect from the agent, Fox, could Fox defend on the grounds that he was only an agent?*

◬ UNIT 24: AGENCY RELATIONS AND TERMINATION

OBLIGATIONS OF AN AGENT AND THIRD PARTIES

The agent is the go-between who brings the contracting parties together and "stands in the shoes of the principal" in making the contract.

AGENT TO THIRD PARTY

May an agent ever be held personally liable on contracts that he enters into on behalf of another?

If the agent makes known to the third party that he is dealing as an agent only and if the agent acts strictly within the scope of his authority, he assumes no liability as to the resulting contract. There are two special situations, however, in which the agent may be held liable. These are (1) when the agent does not disclose his principal and (2) when the agent wrongfully exceeds his authority.

When Principal Is Not Disclosed An *undisclosed principal* is one whose identity is not revealed, even though the third party knows that the agent is acting for someone else. When the principal is undisclosed at the time of the contract and the third party later ascertains his identity, he has the option of holding either the agent or the undisclosed principal, but not both. If, however, his acts are subsequently ratified by the principal, the principal assumes the liability, thus releasing the agent from responsibility for any damage.

UNDISCLOSED PRINCIPAL

When the agent pretends in his negotiations that he is dealing in his own name and does not disclose the fact that he is working for a principal, the third party may, if he chooses, hold the agent personally liable on the contract. U.C.C. Sec. 3-403(2a)

EXAMPLE 1   **Mike Mitchell managed a produce stand for Seaside Markets. Mike was very popular in town, so the business was named "Mike Mitchell's Produce Stand," and Mike operated the business as though it was his own. The Wholesale Produce Market extended credit to the business. When the invoices were not paid, the Wholesale Produce Market brought an action against Mike. Mike defended himself on the grounds that he was only an agent.**

The Wholesale Produce Market could hold either Mike or Seaside Markets responsible for the payment. Ordinarily, a creditor will choose to hold the principal because the principal usually has more money, but if Mike had more money than Seaside Markets, the Wholesale Produce Market might elect to hold Mike responsible for the bill.

When Agent Exceeds His Authority   The agent can bind his principal to a contract only when the agent is acting within the scope of his actual or apparent authority. If the agent violates his instructions and enters into contracts he has no authority to make, the third party may usually hold the agent liable. The main thing to remember is that, if the agent exceeds his authority, he may be held liable for the injury that results.

Who may be held liable in damages if an agent violates his instructions and injuries result?

EXAMPLE 2   **The Thurston Printing Company instructed Heller to purchase an electric typewriter for not more than $595. Heller found that he could buy the desired typewriter for $425, which he did. He used the $170 that he saved to purchase a duplicating machine for the office. The employer refused to accept the duplicator which Heller had no authority to buy. Heller would be required to pay the Thurston Printing Company $170 and could either return the duplicator to the seller for a cash refund or keep it for himself.**

THIRD PARTY TO AGENT

Does a third party in an agency relationship owe a contractual duty to the agent?

Ordinarily, the third party owes no contractual duty to the agent because no contract exists between them. The third party, however, does owe a duty not to cause injury or loss to the agent wrongfully. The third party, for example, must not interfere with the contractual relations that exist between the principal and the agent.

EXAMPLE 3   **Dick Oliver was employed as an agent for Arthur McLean. Joe Lewis did not like Dick, and he wrongfully caused Dick's discharge by making false statements to Arthur McLean about Dick. Dick would have a cause of action against Joe for interfering with his contractual relations.**

EXAMPLE 4   **Bert Lyons wished to sell his house and employed Roy Ivers on a commission basis to sell the house. Ivers showed the house to Elmer Havens and actually convinced Elmer that he should buy it. Elmer pretended that he was not interested. Later, he went to Bert Lyons and made a deal. The purpose of the direct deal was to defraud Ivers of his commission for making the sale.**

Ivers would have a cause of action against Elmer for any damages arising from this wrongful act.

Practically, it is sometimes difficult to tell whether a real estate agent has earned his commission or not. To earn his commission, he must actually sell the house within the time stated in his contract. If the agent has had his opportunity to sell but does not convince the buyer and the

If a third party wrongfully causes a principal to breach his contract with an agent, the third party must pay damages for any loss caused by the breach.

negotiations come to an end, he cannot complain if the buyer and the seller later get together. It is possible for the buyer and the seller to do so provided that the buyer honestly is not convinced and that he is not simply pretending not to be sold so as to get a better price by dealing direct with the seller-principal.

TERMINATION OF AGENCY RELATIONSHIP

Most agencies are based on contracts. The ordinary rules for the termination of contracts, therefore, apply to agencies.

TERMINATION BY CONTRACT

Performance If an agent is appointed to accomplish a certain purpose, the agency terminates when the purpose is achieved. If an agent is appointed for a specified period of time, the agency terminates when that time elapses. In other words, when the contract is performed, the agency is at an end.

Agreement As in contracts, the principal and the agent may mutually agree to terminate the agency. Termination may be predetermined by the passing of a specified period of time or by the completion of certain designated tasks.

Discharge of Agent Contracts of agency containing no terms as to duration are said to *exist at will*. The principal has the right to revoke the agency agreement and discharge the agent for incompetence, disloyalty, or similar shortcomings. If the principal exercises his right of revocation, he must pay the agent what is due him under the agreement.

What do we mean when we say that a contract of agency exists at will?

EXIST AT WILL

EXAMPLE 5 **An extra salesman was employed by Barclays to help out during the holiday season. When the salesman's services were no longer needed, Barclays revoked the agency by notifying the salesman that he was no longer needed and paying him for his services. As no duration was mentioned in the original contract agreement, the agency was said to exist at will.**

The principal may terminate an agency by discharging the agent, except where the agent has an interest in the subject matter. When an agent is discharged in violation of a contract, the principal will be liable for his breach, but the agency will, nevertheless, terminate.

Where the agent has an interest in the subject matter of the agency, he cannot be discharged. This is known as an *irrevocable agency*.

IRREVOCABLE AGENCY

EXAMPLE 6   Frank Girtler borrowed money from the First National Bank for the purpose of remodeling his office building. To secure the repayment of the loan, Frank appointed the bank as agent for the collection of the rents from tenants. The understanding was that the rent money was to be applied to the repayment of the loan and that the agency was to last until the loan was repaid.

What is an agency contract coupled with an interest?

This agency would be irrevocable until the loan was paid. This is often called a situation in which the power is coupled with an interest.

Breach by Agent   The agent may terminate the agency by quitting his job. Here, again, if the agent breaches a contract by his act, he may be liable for damages as a result of his act; but he cannot be forced to work against his will. He may, however, under some circumstances, be prevented from working for someone else in the same type of enterprise.

EXAMPLE 7   Charlie Mulligan contracted to play baseball through a given season for the Blue Sox. After the first two weeks of the season, Charlie quit the Blue Sox team and began playing with a rival team called the Railroaders. Can Mulligan be required to play for the Blue Sox?

May an agent ever be forced to complete his contract if he does not desire to do so?

No, he cannot be forced to play for the Blue Sox, but he may have to pay damages for his breach of contract. He could be prevented, by legal action, from playing with the Railroaders.

TERMINATION BY OPERATION OF LAW

Death of Principal or of Agent   Death of the principal or of the agent will terminate the agency unless it is irrevocable. This is understandable because an ordinary agency is based on a contract for personal services. An irrevocable agency situation is really a security device and follows a different set of rules.

Must third parties be notified of the termination of an agency if the principal or the agent dies?

Notice to a third party of the termination of the agency is not necessary, as the law assumes notice to all at the time of death.

An agent may not be forced to work for a principal, but if the agent breaches his contract of employment, he may under some circumstances be prevented from working for a competitor of his employer.

Bankruptcy   The bankruptcy of the principal will also terminate the agency because bankruptcy cancels all the bankrupt's ordinary contracts and vests title to his property in a trustee for the benefit of creditors.

The bankruptcy of the agent sometimes terminates the agency for the same reasons, but the principal and the agent may continue the relationship if they choose. In most cases the bankruptcy of the agent will not prevent the agent from doing his job in the regular way, and there is no reason to terminate the agency.

Impossibility of Performance   The destruction of the subject matter or the incapacity of the agent makes performance impossible. Therefore, the agency is terminated.

Subsequent Illegality   If after an agency contract has been entered into, the purpose of the agency is declared an illegality, the agency is considered terminated by operation of the law.

NOTICE TO THIRD PARTIES

Why should a principal give notice to third parties when an agency relationship is terminated?

Third parties who have done business with the principal through the agent and third parties who knew of the agency relationship are entitled to notice of its termination. A principal who fails to notify the third party may be estopped from denying a continuing agency should a third party enter into an agreement with the agent believing that he is still associated with the principal.

EXAMPLE 8   **Bancroft, a salesman, was discharged from the Metropolitan Suppliers, Inc., because of several misunderstandings he had with the sales manager. Shortly thereafter, Bancroft visited one of the accounts that he had serviced for his former employer and accepted a payment of $125 that the debtor expected Bancroft to turn over to Metropolitan Suppliers, Inc. No notice had been given to this other company concerning Bancroft's discharge. If Bancroft absconded with the $125, Metropolitan Suppliers, Inc., would have to give credit to the customer for the payment because of the company's failure to give notice.**

The type of notice required depends on how the former business relations were carried on. There are three situations to be considered.

1. When the third party has extended credit to the principal through the agent, the third party is entitled to actual notice. Notice by registered mail is perhaps the surest way to give such notice. This is possible because the names of the creditors are known to the principal.

2. When the third party has never extended credit but has done a cash business with the agent or knows that other persons have dealt with the principal through the agent, notice by publication in a newspaper is sufficient. Look in the classified advertisement section of your own local newspaper, and you may find notices of this kind.

3. When the third person has never heard of the agency relationship, no notice of any kind is required. The third party who is dealing with an agent for the first time has a duty to investigate for himself the extent of the agent's apparent authority.

SUGGESTIONS FOR MINIMIZING LEGAL RISKS

1. If you, as a third party, are dealing with an agent, always demand satisfactory evidence of his authority. It is your responsibility to determine the extent of the agent's apparent authority.
2. If you are acting as an agent, never assume authority you do not have. Remember that if your principal fails to ratify your unauthorized act, it is your personal obligation to make good on the contract.
3. Never act as an agent for an undisclosed principal if your credit is better than his. The creditors are sure to hold you responsible.
4. Never terminate an agency contract that you have agreed to perform unless your principal agrees to release you. Even though your principal probably would not exercise his right to sue you for breach of contract, it would still be bad business practice.
5. In terminating an agency relationship when you are a principal, be sure that all parties have proper notice of the termination.

 APPLYING YOUR LEARNING

QUESTIONS AND PROBLEMS

1. Does the third party in an agency relationship owe a duty to the agent or to the principal? Explain.
2. Under what two conditions may the agent be held liable to the third party?
3. Assume that an agent fails to disclose his principal and that the third party later learns the true identity of the principal. May the third party hold the agent liable? May he hold the principal liable? Why may he wish to hold the agent liable in some cases and hold the principal liable in others?
4. What can the third party do when the agent exceeds his authority?
5. Could the third party become liable, under certain conditions, to the agent? If so, explain how this might happen.
6. Name the various ways in which an agency agreement might be terminated.
7. What does the termination of an agency agreement by operation of law mean?
8. May an agent who has been declared a bankrupt continue to serve as an agent if it is agreeable with the principal? Explain your answer.

WHAT IS YOUR OPINION?

In each of the following cases, give your decision and state a legal principle that applies to the case.

1. Curtis advanced $500 to Dorr with the understanding that he (Curtis) would deduct that amount from the proceeds of the sale of Dorr's house, which Curtis was authorized to sell. Does Dorr have a legal right to revoke the agency contract?

2. Nixon owed Beam $95. Not knowing that Beam had discharged Amos, his collection agent, Nixon paid the debt to Amos, as he had customarily paid previous debts. Did this payment legally cancel Nixon's debt to Beam?

3. Bass, acting strictly within his authority as an agent of Stein, bought goods from Merlin. The goods were charged to Stein, and Merlin knew that Bass was acting as an agent. Before the goods were paid for, Stein became insolvent and Merlin brought an action against Bass for the purchase price. Can he collect from Bass?

4. Would the answer to Case 3 be the same if Bass had not disclosed the fact that he was buying as an agent for Stein?

5. Lester, purchasing agent for Nesbitt signed a contract on July 7 to buy goods from Yates. Neither Lester nor Yates knew at the time the contract was signed that Nesbitt had died on July 6. Was the contract binding?

6. Engle was employed by Justin as a sales agent under a written contract for a two-year period. Seven months after beginning the agency work, Engle sold certain merchandise for $1,400, even though Justin had given him orders not to sell it for less than $1,600. When Justin learned of the sale, he discharged Engle. Was Engle entitled to collect damages for his discharge?

7. Gedrow was appointed as a sales agent for Barrett. Gedrow contracted to buy an adding machine from one of his customers because he knew that Barrett, his principal, was in the market for one, and this one seemed a bargain. Barrett refused to ratify the contract and accept the machine. Can Gedrow, the sales agent for Barrett, be held liable for any loss suffered by the customer? Why?

THE LAW IN ACTION

1. The defendant contracted to buy certain goods from the plaintiff. In negotiations, the defendant represented himself to be an agent for the South Dakota Panama-Pacific Exposition Commission, an unincorporated association. The goods were not paid for; and the plaintiff sued the defendant, contending that the defendant must pay because he represented himself to be the agent of a nonexisting principal. Can the agent be forced to pay for the goods in this case? Why? (Robbins & Company, v. Cook, 42 S.D. 136, 173 N.W. 445)

2. The defendant was a tenant of a landlord who died. The defendant had customarily paid his rent to a properly authorized agent of the landlord.

Notice of the landlord's death was not communicated to the tenant, and he continued to pay the rent to the designated agent after the principal's death. The agent stole the rent money and left town. The estate of the deceased landlord then brought action to collect the rent a second time, claiming that all authority of the agent to collect rent was terminated at the landlord's death. What is your opinion? Why? (Farmers' Loan & Trust Company v. Wilson, 139 N.Y. 284, 34 N.E. 784)

KEY TO "WHAT'S THE LAW?" Page 222

1. *Yes. An undisclosed principal can be held when he is discovered to be the real principal.*
2. *No. The third party can elect to hold the agent of an undisclosed principal if he chooses to do so.*

1. When a person acts by consent for and in behalf of another and is subject to the second party's control, an agency relationship can ordinarily be assumed to exist.

2. Anyone who has the capacity to enter into a valid contract may be a principal.

3. An agent need not have contractual capacity, but he must have the physical or the mental capacity to do his job.

4. An agent deals with third persons in the name of his principal and uses some discretion or judgment of his own.

5. An employee does as he is told and does not enter into agreements with third persons.

6. An independent contractor agrees to accomplish a named result based on the terms of the contract. He may use any means he chooses to accomplish that result.

7. An agency may be created by agreement, implication, ratification, and sometimes necessity.

8. The equal dignities rule specifies that a contract of agency must be in writing if the contracts that the agent is to make with third parties in behalf of the principal are required to be in writing. Also, if an agent is to enter into contracts under seal, his appointment must be created by authority under seal.

9. If an agent is to execute documents that must be filed for public record, his appointment must be by a formal power of attorney. The power of attorney also must be filed for record with the document.

10. An agency by implication is proved by the acts of the parties; that is, by the principal and the agent.

11. An agency by estoppel exists when the principal falsely represents the status of the agent and the third person relies on the false representation to his injury.

12. If a principal, with full knowledge of all the facts, accepts the benefits of an unauthorized act done in his interest, an agency by ratification is created.

13. A state of emergency may sometimes make it necessary for an unauthorized person to act for a principal in order to prevent loss. This usually will create an agency by necessity.

14. A selling agent who guarantees payment of his customers' accounts usually receives higher commissions than do other agents. He is known as a del credere agent.

15. An agent has a right of lien on property in his possession belonging to his principal if the principal refuses to pay him for his services.

16. The principal must compensate the agent for his services unless the circumstances indicate a gratuitous agency.

17. The principal must reimburse the agent for all necessary expenses paid by the agent in carrying out the duties for his principal.

18. The principal must indemnify the agent for all injuries suffered as a result of following the instructions of the principal.

19. The agent must follow the instructions given by the principal.

20. The agent owes a duty of utmost good faith in his dealings with the principal.

21. The agent may not compete with or make a profit at the expense of the principal.

22. The agent must strictly account for all money of the principal that comes into his hands.

23. An agent may not delegate his duties to another unless his contract with the principal gives him such a right either expressly or by implication.

24. The principal is bound on all contracts entered into by the agent in the principal's name if the agent is acting within the scope of his actual or apparent authority.

25. A person who acts as agent for the two parties to a contract with their knowledge is entitled to receive compensation from each.

26. The principal is liable for all torts of the agent committed within the scope of the agent's employment.

27. The agent is liable to the third party only when he does not disclose his principal or when he wrongfully exceeds his authority.

WHAT'S THE LAW?

1. *Charles Pinkett was the executive vice-president of the Northern Label Corporation. Would his job be covered by the laws of employment?*

---

2. *Alan Burns, while on the job and acting within the scope of his employment, was negligent in the operation of an automobile. By his negligence, he injured Tom Herter. If Alan were an agent, would his employer have greater liability than if Alan were an employee?*

⚠ UNIT 25: CONTRACTS OF EMPLOYMENT

How would you distinguish between an employee and an agent?

Most of the broad laws of employment cover all persons who work for another, regardless of the nature of their duties. The president of a large corporation and the man who sweeps the floors are both employees. Laws usually are passed for the protection of employees in the lower income brackets because they have the greater need for protection. Most corporation presidents can look out for themselves. Nevertheless, anyone who works for a salary is an *employee*. When an employee, acting for his employer, enters into a contract with a third person, he is an *agent*.

EMPLOYEE
AGENT

EXAMPLE 1 Mr. Edward Oligher was hired as the manager of the Topline Men's Store. Because he was the manager, he entered into many contracts with third parties as an agent of the store. In his contractual dealings, Mr. Oligher was an agent. However, he was hired by the Topline Men's Store; therefore, in his relations with the store, he was an employee.

CREATION OF EMPLOYMENT CONTRACTS

Contracts of employment are not new to you. Many of the illustrations used in the three parts on contracts involved contracts of employment.

ORAL CONTRACTS OF EMPLOYMENT

Many contracts of employment are oral.

EXAMPLE 2 Patrick Mullin agreed to work in Mr. Levinson's supermarket on Saturdays at an agreed wage of $12 per Saturday. This contract would not have to be written. Length of employment was not discussed. Employment could last one week or perhaps several years. Either Patrick or Mr. Levinson could terminate the agreement at any time.

You can have an enforceable oral contract with a specified period of employment if the period of employment is for less than a year.

EXAMPLE 3 **If, in Example 2, Patrick Mullin had promised to work for Mr. Levinson for the next fifty Saturdays, the agreement would be an enforceable oral contract because it could be performed in less than one year from the time of making.**

WRITTEN CONTRACTS OF EMPLOYMENT

Must a lifetime contract always be in writing to be enforceable?

If the contract of employment is for a period of more than a year, it comes within the Statute of Frauds and must be in writing to be enforceable. As you learned in Unit 12, however, the written requirement applies only to contracts that cannot possibly be performed within a year of their making.

EXAMPLE 4 **The Business Computer Company discovered a young man of unusual scientific talent in its organization. The company offered to send the youth to engineering school for four years of advanced training if he would agree to work for the company for five years after graduation. Since this agreement would not terminate for more than nine years, a written contract would be required under the provisions of the Statute of Frauds.**

The president of a large corporation is an agent because he acts for and in behalf of the corporation. He is also an employee because he works for a salary and is not the owner.

Are oral contracts of employment ever as valid as written contracts?

This does not mean that there must be a formal written contract. Very often the contract is created by an exchange of letters. If these letters contain written evidence that will satisfy the requirements of the Statute of Frauds, that is all that is necessary. Also, many times the parties will agree orally to a long-term contract and later write down a memorandum of their agreement. Usually, they will make two copies of the memorandum, and each party will sign both copies.

Unreasonable Restraint of Employment Employment contracts are enforceable only when they are free from unreasonable restraints.

EXAMPLE 5 **When Mark Stevenson went to work as a clerk for the Business Computer Company, he had to sign an agreement containing the following terms: "For the duration of this contract and for three years thereafter, I agree not to accept employment with any other firm engaged in the manufacture, maintenance, or repair of computers." Because of the unreasonable restraint placed upon Stevenson, with no sound reason for it, this section of his contract would probably be held unenforceable.**

Reasonable Restraint of Employment Persons employed by firms engaged in research and development and persons to whom trade secrets are divulged in connection with their employment may be restrained from accepting employment with other firms engaged in the same work for a reasonable time after the termination of their employment. These agreements are considered to be for the public good, since they provide a measure of protection to the employers.

The restraint should not be so extensive, however, as to take away a former employee's right to seek employment. Such wide restraint is permitted only concerning employment in competitive situations.

Distinguish between reasonable and unreasonable restraint of employment.

EXAMPLE 6 **The Business Computer Company is engaged in the development of a new ground-control system. Elders was hired as an electronics engineer to design circuits to be installed in the system. His contract contained terms similar to those Stevenson had agreed to in the preceding case. Because of the confidential nature of Elders' work and the financial loss that might be suffered if details were given to a competitor, the terms would be valid and enforceable.**

COLLECTIVE-BARGAINING CONTRACTS

You may possibly contract with your employer as a member of a group of fellow employees. Today, in many industries, employment contracts are negotiated, not by individuals, but by groups of employees called *bargaining units*. A bargaining unit is usually a union, selected by a vote of the employees to represent them in working out conditions of employment with their employers. This is called *collective bargaining*, and the process is now firmly established as an institution for the improvement of working conditions and industrial relations. Collective-bargaining contracts now determine the wages and other working conditions of employment for millions of workers in the United States.

What is collective bargaining?

BARGAINING UNIT

COLLECTIVE BARGAINING

EXAMPLE 7 **Karl Stuchell was hired to work for the Classic Automotive Company. As an employee of the Classic Automotive Company, the terms of his employment would be covered by a collective-bargaining contract between the Classic Automotive Company and the local union representing automotive employees.**

Governmental Control of Collective Bargaining A hundred years ago, collective bargaining was held by the courts to be an illegal conspiracy. Just why the courts so ruled is difficult to understand. Times have changed, however. The belief gradually developed that collective bargaining was a matter to be determined by the employers and their employees. As time went on, there developed the concept that government should encourage collective bargaining. Still later came the theory that government should exercise an element of regulation and control in the process.

Today, especially in the trades and in industry, the worker is represented by union agents whose knowledge of the law and of employees' rights assures the employee the full benefit of his rights under the law. A *labor union* is a bargaining agent in behalf of the workers it represents. Any negotiations with employers by union representatives must be approved

LABOR UNION

Collective bargaining is not an innovation brought about by the employer. It is a hard-fought-for right acquired by employees.

Do labor union representatives usually have authority to enter into binding employer-employee agreements on behalf of the members?

by the rank-and-file members before they become the workers' agreement. Approval is by a vote, conforming to government regulations.

EXAMPLE 8 **All employees of the Metropolitan Transit System were members of a union. In seeking better terms for its new employment contract, the union was instructed to ask for an across-the-board increase of 96 cents an hour. The union was able to get an offer of only 40 cents an hour from Metropolitan's representatives. The acceptance of the 40-cent increase would require a vote of the union members before it became binding upon the employees.**

The first general federal statute dealing with collective bargaining was the National Labor Relations Act, sometimes called the Wagner Act, passed in 1935 and declared by the Supreme Court to be constitutional in 1937. The purpose of the act was to encourage collective bargaining, discourage certain unfair labor practices, and provide aid from the federal government in obtaining fair bargaining. The *National Labor Relations Board* was established to enforce the provisions of the act.

WAGNER ACT

NATIONAL LABOR RELATIONS BOARD

The Wagner Act was thought by many people to give too great an advantage to the union bargaining units; therefore it was amended in 1947 by the Labor-Management Relations Act, commonly known as the Taft-Hartley Act. This new act reaffirmed the policy of the federal government in encouraging collective bargaining but proposed to limit the scope of such bargaining and to provide control of unfair practices by the unions as well as by the employers.

TAFT-HARTLEY ACT

The Taft-Hartley Act has, in turn, been criticized by many people. It is to be expected that other changes will be made in the future pertaining to this very important subject of collective bargaining.

THIRD-PARTY RELATIONSHIPS IN EMPLOYMENT CONTRACTS

In the part on agency, you studied about the rights, duties, and responsibilities resulting when an employee acts as an agent for his employer. You also learned in that part about the liability of the employer, or principal, for the negligent acts of his agent. Here we shall give some consideration to the liability of the employer for the negligent acts of any employee, whether he is an agent or not.

Employer's Liability for Employee Negligence The employer is liable for all the negligent acts of his employee that are committed within the scope of his employment. This is the same rule we learned in agency except for the differences that arise in the nature and scope of employment.

EXAMPLE 9 **Louis Jaffe was employed as a carpenter for the Acme Construction Company. One day, while working on a scaffold over a sidewalk doing a job he was hired to do, he carelessly dropped his hammer and hit Victor Kelley on the head. The Acme Construction Company would be liable for Kelley's injury because Louis was negligent in doing a job he was hired to do. Angry over being hit on the head, Kelley picked up the hammer and threw it in an open manhole where it could not be retrieved.**

EXAMPLE 10 **Louis could not work without a hammer; so he abandoned his job and went down the street to buy a new hammer. On his way back, holding the hammer in his hand, he carelessly dropped it and broke Henry Kuhn's toe. The Acme Construction Company would not be liable for Kuhn's broken toe. Louis was outside the scope of his employment when he went for the new hammer.**

What is meant by scope of employment?

If Louis had been the foreman on the job with authority to buy any tools necessary to get the work done, then he would have been within the scope of his employment when he went for the hammer and the Acme Construction Company would have been liable for Kuhn's injury.

A special group of statutes imposes a liability on the employer for injury done by an employee to a fellow workman. These are called workmen's compensation laws, and they will be discussed in the next unit.

Some states also impose a special liability on the employer when the work being done by the employee is highly dangerous to other people. An example would be work involving blasting and the use of dynamite.

SUGGESTIONS FOR MINIMIZING LEGAL RISKS

1. Remember that a contract of employment is an important contract. It is important that the terms of the agreement are clear and thoroughly understood by both parties.
2. Always remember that your negligent acts as an employee may cause injury to other persons. Your negligent acts may cause financial loss to you as well as to your employer because you are not relieved from personal responsibility for such acts. The injured party may be able to recover from both you and your employer.
3. If you become employed under a collective-bargaining contract, be sure that you personally understand the nature of the agreement.
4. If you should join a bargaining unit, concern yourself with the organization and efficient management of your bargaining unit. Do your part in trying to achieve a democratic and efficient organization. Attend meetings regularly and vote for your representatives.

▲ APPLYING YOUR LEARNING

QUESTIONS AND PROBLEMS

1. How has the modern concept of employer-employee relationships evolved over the past few centuries?
2. In your own words give a definition of an employer and an employee.
3. Explain how one might be both an agent and an employee. Give an illustration of a position of this type in your own community.
4. Name several occupations in your locality in which the contract of employment is probably only an oral contract. Do some people working in these occupations work for more than a year? Explain how this is possible.
5. Name several occupations in your locality in which the contract of employment is probably covered by a written contract. How do you account for this?
6. Are there some industries in your locality in which the employees are organized and the contracts of employment are governed by collective-bargaining agreements? If so, name the collective-bargaining units representing the employees.
7. Do you believe that the trend in the future will be toward more or fewer collective-bargaining agreements? Give reasons for your answer.
8. What are the correct names and the popular names given to the federal statutes that encourage collective bargaining under certain controls?
9. Explain and illustrate how an employer might be held liable for the acts of an employee. What conditions must ordinarily exist before the employer can be held liable?
10. Assume that you are driving a car belonging to your employer and that you have an accident that seriously injures a pedestrian. If you are not to blame for the accident, do you think your employer could be held liable? Explain. Does your state have a special motor-vehicle owner's liability statute?
11. When is an employment contract considered in unreasonable restraint of trade?
12. Under what conditions are some employment contracts that restrain employees from working for other firms considered valid?

WHAT IS YOUR OPINION?

In each of the following cases, give your decision and state a legal principle that applies to the case.

1. While in Larson's store, Marlow, a customer, was injured by falling boxes that had been carelessly stacked by a salesclerk. Is Larson liable to Marlow for the damages?
2. An employee of a dry-cleaning company, through carelessness, used the wrong cleaning fluid and ruined Mrs. Sanford's dress. Was the company liable for the damages?

3. Payne borrowed his employer's station wagon to use on a fishing trip. While on the trip, Payne negligently injured Wilkes by his careless driving. Could the employer be held liable for the injury under the laws of agency or employment?

4. Hurst was employed as a truck driver for the Burke Machinery Company. While driving the company's truck on the wrong side of the road, he ran into and damaged Lawton's automobile. Was the Burke Machinery Company liable for the damage?

5. Meier, a contractor, employed Lynch as a carpenter. It was understood in the contract of employment that Lynch was to be employed "as long as Meier remained in the contracting business." Would this contract have to be in writing?

6. Hunter was appointed manager of Hagen's store and given full authority to act as a general agent for Hagen. Would Hunter be protected by the statutory laws of employment even though he could be classified as an agent?

7. McKay was employed by Porter and given a one-year contract at a salary of $7,800 a year. After a few weeks McKay began to be very careless in the performance of his job. He was consistently late to work. He refused to follow Porter's instructions and caused Porter to lose a great deal of business. McKay was discharged at the end of six months. Can he bring an action for breach of contract?

THE LAW IN ACTION

1. The plaintiff was a baseball player employed by the defendant ball club. The plaintiff's contract gave the employer the right to fine or suspend any ball player who was delinquent in the performance of his duties. The plaintiff was fined and suspended for using profane language in a private argument with the team manager. Was this fine and suspension proper under the terms of the contract? (Cross v. Detroit Baseball Club, 84 Mo. App. 526)

2. Mrs. Fleming was attacked by a man who was delivering her groceries. The deliveryman had been hired by the defendant without any references and with little investigation of his character. The defendant knew, however, that the employee was an alcoholic and had been fired from a previous job for drunkenness. Was the employee within the scope of his employment when he attacked the plaintiff? Was the plaintiff entitled to a judgment? (Fleming v. Bronfin, 80 Atl. 2d 915)

KEY TO "WHAT'S THE LAW?" Page 233

1. *Yes. Everyone who works for another and is paid for his services is covered by some laws of employment.*

2. *No. The liability would be the same in either case if the agent or employee was acting within the scope of his employment.*

WHAT'S THE LAW?

1. *Fred Burton was employed by the Drake Manufacturing Company. One day, he was injured on the job and was unable to work for a period of four months. If he had no money and no family to assist him, would he be able to support himself through this period?*

2. *Herbert Clark applied for a job in a factory that manufactured goods to be shipped in interstate commerce. Would the amount of Herbert's wages be determined entirely by agreement between Herbert and his employer?*

◭ UNIT 26: LAWS AFFECTING EMPLOYMENT

Society has an interest in you and your job. Your health, your safety while on the job, and the care you receive if you are injured are all matters of public concern. These are not matters to be determined by individual contract between employer and employee; special laws regulate these things.

LAWS RELATING TO WORKING CONDITIONS

Name two broad classifications of laws that relate to working conditions.

We can broadly classify laws relating to working conditions as (1) laws designed to prevent industrial accidents and occupational diseases and (2) laws to provide for the care of injured workmen. In addition to these laws, many industrial concerns have very strict safety codes of their own.

EXAMPLE 1 Robert Hackman accepted a job with the Easternhouse Electronic Corporation. He was given a copy of the corporation's safety code when he reported for work the first time and was told to read the code. Hackman was informed that he would be discharged immediately for any code violation.

Thousands of dollars are spent every year by some firms in the search for safer and less fatiguing methods of doing jobs. These companies find it pays off, not only in better employer-employee relations but also in money. Strange as it may seem, statistics show that large industrial concerns usually have a better safety record than small concerns and that self-employment has the poorest record of all. In other words, safety often depends on you; and working by yourself may be the most dangerous occupation in the world as far as you are concerned.

WORKMEN'S COMPENSATION LAWS

In spite of all our laws and safety codes, accidents do happen and workmen are injured. When a workman is injured, he has to be cared for.

At common law the injured workman had little chance of collecting from his employer for his injury. Even if he were injured through the failure of the employer to furnish safe tools or a safe place to work, he could not collect if (1) he himself had contributed to his injury by his own negligence, (2) he had been injured by a fellow workman, or (3) he had known the risks of the job and had voluntarily assumed them. In addition, he frequently was not in a financial position to sue his employer even if none of the foregoing defenses were available to the employer.

EXAMPLE 2 Back in 1840 Hiram Strang was hired to work in a textile mill. His employer explained to him, when he went to work, that his job was highly dangerous. One day, he turned his head for a moment to talk to a fellow worker, and his hand was crushed in the machine he was operating. Hiram could recover no damages from his employer for his injuries. He would be barred by his own contributory negligence and his own voluntary assumption of the risks involved.

How does the protection provided employees today by statute law for injuries suffered on the job differ from that provided at common law?

Today, the law follows an entirely different philosophy with regard to injured workmen. The cause of injury or death does not matter, provided that it was not the intentional, drunken, or grossly careless act of the workman. The injured workman is compensated for all expenses incurred in the care and treatment of the injury.

EXAMPLE 3 If, in Example 2, Hiram's injury had occurred today instead of in 1840, he would receive a definite compensation for his injury. The amount of his compensation would be calculated on the basis of the workmen's compensation laws of the state in which he is employed.

Who pays for the cost of caring for injured employees?

Of still greater importance, the law now adopts the policy that the cost of caring for injured workmen is one of the costs of producing goods. The employer must bear this cost, but he in turn passes on the cost to the consumer by a slight increase in the price of the goods.

● Laws passed to accomplish this purpose are called *workmen's compensation laws*. Every state in the Union now has workmen's compensation laws of some kind, but they differ widely in form and application.

What must a workman do to qualify for benefits under workmen's compensation laws?

WORKMEN'S COMPENSATION LAWS

Although the provisions are not uniform in all states, workmen's compensation laws usually provide that the employer must be notified of an accident within the time specified by law. Such notice reduces the possibility of an employee's making a claim for injuries which may not have been caused on the job.

EXAMPLE 4 Louis Burroughs complained to his company physician about a painful back injury. He claimed that the injury occurred when he was loading bushel baskets of peaches into the produce cooler more than two months previously. Louis may not receive any workmen's compensation because of the delay in reporting his complaint and injury.

NOTE: *The bullet indicates that there may be a state statute that varies from the law discussed here.*

The laws also provide that the employee shall not be eligible for compensation unless his disability continues for an extended period, ranging from six days to three weeks; that he shall be paid a fixed amount for any given injury, usually a certain proportion of his weekly salary for a given period; and that he shall be entitled to medical, surgical, and hospital care required by his injuries.

Ordinarily, what benefits are received by an injured employee?

Workmen's compensation laws provide for the payment of benefits to all workmen in covered employments injured in the line of work, regardless of how the injury occurs.

EXAMPLE 5   James O'Toole lost the index finger of his left hand in an accident while he was operating a hydraulic press. By state law the compensation granted for the loss of this finger was $250. O'Toole will, therefore, receive $250 plus reimbursement for all other expenses incurred in the care and treatment of the injury as well as weekly payments while he is away from his job.

In case of death due to an accident on the job, a percentage of the deceased workman's wages will be paid to his family for a specified number of weeks.

The employee may appeal to the state compensation commission if he believes that he has not received all that he is entitled to under the workmen's compensation law. Further appeal to the courts may be made should the compensation commission's ruling seem unfair.

EXAMPLE 6   One of the Carlton Manufacturing Company's production workers suffered a serious injury, which he reported to the plant safety department. The manager would not certify the injury for compensation, claiming that the worker had been negligent. An appeal to the compensation commission would probably reverse the company's decision and result in an order to the firm to certify the man for compensation.

The employer usually protects himself by taking out insurance known as *workmen's compensation insurance*. He adds the annual cost of this insurance to his cost of doing business.

WORKMEN'S COMPENSATION INSURANCE

Compensation is sometimes provided by law to employees who become ill because of certain occupational diseases.

EXAMPLE 7   Eric Westmore, a lead burner, developed lead poisoning. Lead poisoning is an occupational disease and is covered by workmen's compensation in most states. Westmore was entitled to reimbursement for medical and other expenses and losses resulting from his illness.

MINIMUM WAGE LAWS

FEDERAL FAIR LABOR STANDARDS ACT

Laws dealing with minimum wages are another example of society's interest in you and your job. The hardships growing out of the depression period in the 1930s strengthened the feeling that the government must, in the interest of public health and safety, set minimum standards for wages and working conditions. This led to the passing of the Federal Fair Labor Standards Act, in 1938, known also as the Wage and Hour Law.

What are the chief provisions of the Federal Fair Labor Standards Act?

FEDERAL FAIR LABOR STANDARDS ACT

WAGE AND HOUR LAW

The chief provisions of this act are (1) a minimum hourly wage rate, (2) time and a half for all overtime work in excess of forty hours a week, (3) control of child labor, and (4) control of industrial homework.

Originally, the federal law covered only workers who *produced* goods for shipment in interstate commerce. Amendments have extended coverage to many more workers including certain hospital, retail, hotel, restaurant, and school employees by broadening the definition of interstate commerce. The most recent amendment, effective in 1968, increased the minimum hourly wage to $1.60. A proposed increase to $2.20 hourly may become effective in 1974.

EXAMPLE 8 Ben Tucker went to work as a production workman in the Wearwell Shoe Factory. The shoes manufactured by Wearwell were shipped to all parts of the United States for resale. Ben's contract with his employer would thus be controlled by the Federal Fair Labor Standards Act.

EQUAL-PAY RULE

In 1964 Congress passed legislation making it mandatory for employers who were engaged in interstate commerce of any kind to pay women the same rate of pay as men holding the same type of job. This is known as the Equal-Pay Rule. A proposed amendment to the constitution, which was sent to the states in 1972 for ratification, says, "Equality of rights under the law shall not be denied or abridged by the United States or by any state on account of sex." State governments are also beginning to pass similar laws dealing with strictly intrastate employment.

What is the Equal-Pay Rule?

EQUAL-PAY RULE

EXAMPLE 9 Mary Larkin was employed as a laboratory research assistant for the Chemical Manufacturing Center. Her monthly salary was $600. Donald Dixon was paid a monthly salary of $700 for performing the same duties as Mary within the same department. The Chemical Manufacturing Center would be required to pay both Mary Larkin and Donald Dixon the identical salary every month.

SOCIAL SECURITY LAWS

The first attempt made in this country to help individuals meet the loss of earnings due to sickness, accident disability, unemployment, old age, and death came in 1935 with the passage of the Social Security Act. The act, as amended in 1967 and by the tax revision laws of 1969, provides financial aid through federal grants to state agencies and provides direct

SOCIAL SECURITY ACT

federal aid to insured workers who are retired or disabled as well as to their dependents or survivors. The Social Security Act also provides automatic medical insurance for almost all Americans over sixty-five, whether or not they are eligible for other social security benefits, and makes provisions for low-cost voluntary medical insurance for the aged.

Explain the two major purposes of the Social Security Act.

The purposes of this act and its amendments made over the years are (1) to encourage everyone to provide for his own old age and period of unemployment through a system of national social insurance; and (2) to provide for those who are unable to work by a system of public assistance. These two purposes are achieved through the many divisions of the Social Security Act. The three major divisions of the Act are concerned with (1) old-age, survivors, and disability insurance, (2) unemployment insurance, and (3) public assistance. Do not confuse these separate coverages with one another.

OLD-AGE, SURVIVORS, AND DISABILITY INSURANCE

How are the funds provided for old-age, survivors, and disability insurance? How do the contributions to social security of employees and self-employed persons compare?

You should think of this division of social security as strictly insurance. By having a certain percentage of his wages deducted from every paycheck, the employee is contributing toward the future support of himself after he retires and for the support of those dependent on him after he dies. His employer contributes an equal amount for the same purpose. The tax is also paid by most self-employed persons. They pay approximately $1\frac{1}{2}$ times the rate paid by an employee.

EXAMPLE 10 **In Example 1, Robert Hackman went to work for the Eastern-house Electronics Corporation. His employment was covered by social security; so it was necessary for him to make application for a social security number. Once he was assigned a number, all his contributions and those of his employer would be credited to that number, whether he changed jobs or not.**

Here are some significant things to remember about old-age, survivors, and disability insurance.

1. It is a federal system. State and local governments do not take any part in this division of social security.

2. It and other public retirement plans now cover almost all the employed.

3. It provides for a monthly income for the retired employee after age sixty-five. However, if the employee elects to do so, he may retire at age sixty-two and receive a slightly smaller income.

At what age may a nonworking wife of a retired worker receive 50 percent of his benefits?

4. The nonworking wife of a retired worker receives monthly benefits equal to one-half the amount received by her husband when she reaches age sixty-five. If she chooses, she may claim a smaller benefit when she reaches age sixty-two. Insured female workers may retire at age sixty-two.

5. The widow of an insured worker gets full monthly payments for herself upon reaching the age of sixty-two or at any age if she has dependent children. Payments are also made for all unmarried dependent children until they reach age eighteen, or age twenty-two if they are still in school. Payments for the widow end when her youngest child reaches eighteen, but they will start again when the widow reaches sixty-two. She may also receive her payments at age sixty if she will accept reduced benefits.

EXAMPLE 11 Mrs. Gerber was forty-two years old when her husband was killed in an automobile accident. He had been fully insured under social security. The couple had two dependent children, twelve and fifteen years old. Mrs. Gerber will receive benefits until she is forty-eight years old, when her youngest child becomes eighteen. Payments will then cease until she reaches her sixty-second birthday, or age sixty if she is willing to accept reduced benefits. If her youngest child remains unmarried and a full-time student, he can continue to receive his benefits until age twenty-two.

If children of a deceased insured worker are still in school, until what age may they receive benefits?

6. Dependent children of a deceased insured worker receive monthly benefit payments until they reach the age of eighteen or twenty-two if they are still in school or until they marry, whichever occurs first.

7. An insured worker who becomes totally disabled may receive payments for himself and dependents after he has qualified for social security benefits. These payments continue until his sixty-fifth birthday, when he begins to receive benefits under the old-age insurance provision of the act.

EXAMPLE 12 At the age of thirty-eight, Walsh suffered injuries which totally disabled him. He applied to the local social security office for benefits provided by the federal disability insurance provision of the act. Proof of total disability would entitle Walsh to disability benefits to be paid monthly until he reaches the age of sixty-five, when he is automatically covered by old-age insurance.

Recent amendments allow disability benefits for a worker whose disability has continued for twelve months; payments begin immediately if the disability is expected to last at least twelve months. Prior to this amendment, benefits were allowed only when a worker's disability was expected to last for a long or indefinite time or to result in death.

8. On the death of an insured worker, a lump-sum death benefit payment not exceeding $255 will be made to the widow or widower, if she or he lived in the same household or if she or he paid the burial expenses. The exact amount received will depend upon the amount of coverage held by the worker at the time of death.

9. The rates of contributions and benefits are specified by the tax revision laws of 1969 and 1972 and can be amended again to meet changing needs.

EXAMPLE 13 West was employed as an accountant for Standard Electrical Supplies while preparing for his examination as a certified public accountant. Both West and his employer were taxed 5.85 percent of $10,800 of his income. After passing his examination for C. P. A., West opened an office of his own. As a self-employed person, he was then taxed 8.0 percent of his income from his practice up to $10,800. This is the maximum. Payments based on income over $10,800 would not increase his retirement benefits.

MEDICARE

At what age may people become eligible for Medicare?

As of July 1, 1966, nearly all Americans sixty-five and over became eligible for two kinds of health insurance protection under social security: (1) hospital insurance and (2) additional voluntary medical insurance for those who chose to take it. These are known as the *Medicare* provisions of the Social Security Amendments of 1965.

MEDICARE

The purpose of hospital insurance is to help pay the bills when a person is hospitalized. The program also provides payments for nursing care and other services in an extended-care facility after hospitalization, outpatient hospital diagnositc services, and home health services.

The purpose of medical insurance is to help pay bills for doctor's services and for a number of other medical items and services not covered under the hospital insurance program.

The medical insurance program is voluntary. Those eligible decide whether to enroll for protection under the medical insurance program. They can have this important added protection at a low cost ($5.30 monthly) because the federal government will pay an equal amount toward the cost.

UNEMPLOYMENT INSURANCE

Jobs are not always plentiful. There have been times when jobs were almost impossible to find. When people have no jobs, they cannot buy goods. When goods are unsold, the factories that make goods shut down, and then more people are out of jobs. This is the vicious circle that causes *depressions*. To help combat this vicious circle and also to provide food for **DEPRESSION** the families of people who are out of work, we have unemployment insurance.

What is meant by unemployment insurance? The Unemployment Insurance division of the Social Security Act provides for a joint federal and state system of unemployment insurance. It is the theory of the Social Security Act that each state should operate its own unemployment insurance system, subject to certain conditions imposed by the federal government. The following are some of the general features of state unemployment insurance systems:

1. The state systems are administered through public employment offices that try to find jobs for the unemployed.

2. Benefits are paid only to those who genuinely desire work and cannot find it.

3. A worker is disqualified if he refuses suitable work without cause, has been discharged for misconduct, or has quit a job without good cause.

You cannot collect unemployment insurance if you refuse to work when employment is offered.

EXAMPLE 14 Max Reid was employed by the Parker Company. He was late to work every day and refused to follow the instructions of his boss. As a result, he was discharged. He applied for unemployment insurance at his state employment office. There, he was offered similar employment with another company, but he refused it, claiming that he had a right to unemployment insurance and that he wanted to take a vacation. Max would receive no unemployment insurance benefits.

4. A worker also may be disqualified for a limited period if his unemployment arises out of a strike or lockout. Individual states determine the period of a worker's disqualification.

EXAMPLE 15 Employees in the shipping and receiving departments of a company went on strike when their demands for additional wages were refused by their employer. The strike lasted for six months. The disqualification period in this state was forty-nine days. Workers would be eligible for unemployment benefits on the fiftieth day.

The amount of benefits received vary from state to state. The following fundamental principles are found in almost all state systems.
1. The benefit is related to the workman's rate of pay.
2. The benefit is related to his family need.
3. The benefit is not large enough to remove his incentive to work.

REMEMBER: If you need a job, or information about unemployment insurance, go to your nearest state employment office. It has been established to assist you.

PUBLIC ASSISTANCE

What is the nature of public assistance under the Social Security Act?

The Public Assistance divisions of the Social Security Act provide for the care of the needy who are unable to work or look after themselves and who are not covered by the old-age benefits of the act. This responsibility is shared by the federal, state, and local governments. Most of this responsibility rests in the state and local governments, but the federal government does assume substantial responsibility for public assistance to the needy aged, the blind, dependent children, and, since 1950, permanently and totally disabled persons.

EXAMPLE 16 John Rand was unable to work because of physical infirmities and advanced age. He had never been covered under the old-age insurance provision of the Social Security Act because his kind of employment was exempt under the act. Upon application to the proper state office, Rand may be eligible to receive an old-age pension.

CIVIL RIGHTS

What does the Civil Rights Act attempt to do?

Congress enacted in 1964 and updated in 1968 what is known as the Civil Rights Act. The law provides uniform legislation in areas which had previously been administered under the laws of the states rather than under federal legislation. The Civil Rights Act bans discrimination in

CIVIL RIGHTS ACT

What are the
most significant
provisions of the
Civil Rights Act?

voting, schools, hiring, firing, and promotions, as well as union membership, and bars bias and discrimination in the use of such public accommodations as hotels, restaurants, and theaters. It also provides that there will be no discriminatory practices followed in state and local programs where federal funds are provided for such projects.

The provision against job discrimination applies to all employers who employ twenty-five or more persons.

EXAMPLE 17   **The Progressive Converters Company employed twenty-four men and women. When the personnel department turned down a particular application for employment, the firm was threatened with prosecution under the Civil Rights Act. The Progressive Converters Company claimed that they did not come within the provisions of the bill since their total number of employees was under twenty-five. The company was correct.**

SUGGESTIONS FOR MINIMIZING LEGAL RISKS

1. Acquaint yourself with the location of your local state employment office so that you can get information on current employment laws. Remember that these laws change from time to time; so keep in touch with this office for up-to-date information.
2. Consider your health and the safety of working conditions in any job you accept. The hazards of the job may be greater than the benefits can actually justify.
3. If you are injured on a job, take immediate steps to protect your rights to obtain workmen's compensation benefits.
4. If you should lose your job through no fault of your own, get in touch with your state employment office at once in order to protect your rights for unemployment insurance.

APPLYING YOUR LEARNING

QUESTIONS AND PROBLEMS

1. Why is it better to have special laws governing working conditions rather than to leave these matters to an individual contract between employer and employee?
2. Under common law what was expected of an employer by way of protecting his employees from injury on the job?
3. What are some of the employment conditions that are regulated by special statutes in many states?

4. Why do many industrial concerns find it to their advantage to set up special safety codes of their own?

5. What are the provisions commonly found in modern workmen's compensation laws in the various states?

6. Why is it desirable to have minimum-wage laws? Does your state have any minimum-wage laws covering certain selected occupations? If your state has such laws, what are some of the covered occupations?

7. What is meant by social security? How has this concept changed during the past few centuries?

8. Explain the purposes of the division of the Social Security Act that provides for old-age, survivors, and disability insurance.

9. How are a workman's benefits determined under employment insurance? What is the source of funds needed to carry on this service?

10. What is meant by public assistance? How are the funds obtained for carrying on this service?

11. Explain the health insurance provisions of the Medicare provision of the Social Security Amendments of 1965.

WHAT IS YOUR OPINION?

In each of the following cases, give your decision and state a legal principle that applies to the case.

1. Stanley owned an old, rundown factory. He employed Rowe and put him to work on a machine that Stanley knew was virtually worn out. He also knew that the machine had some cracked and defective parts that made it dangerous to use. Rowe was injured because of these known defects. Could Stanley be held liable for Rowe's injury under common-law rules?

2. Suppose, in Case 1, that Rowe's injury had been partly caused by his own negligence. Could he then recover damages from Stanley?

3. Suppose that Rowe had not been negligent, but that a fellow workman had caused his injury. Could he then recover from Stanley?

4. Knox was employed by the Morgan Machine Tool Company as an expert machinist. Nash was employed by the same company to sweep the floors. If both were injured at the same time, in the same accident, would they draw the same workmen's compensation benefits? Why?

5. Pelzer was not very ambitious. He had a small income from property he had inherited, and he preferred to live on that rather than work. After he was past sixty-five years of age, however, a period of inflation made it difficult for him to live on his income; and he made application for benefits under old-age, survivors, and disability insurance. Would he get the benefits? Why?

6. If, in Case 5 Pelzer were ill, as well as being aged, could he get help of any kind? If so, what?

7. Nesbit was employed by the Corner Grocery Store as a clerk. He contended that his wages should be determined by the Federal Fair Labor Standards Act. Was he correct? Explain.

8. In appreciation of long hours of overtime put in by Sherwin in the service department of the Home Supply Company, the company gave him a gift of $25. Sherwin had actually worked thirty hours overtime. Under the provisions of the Fair Labor Standards Act, was the employee amply compensated for his services?

THE LAW IN ACTION

1. The plaintiff, while on the job and working for the defendant company, playfully threw a small piece of rubber tubing at a fellow employee. To avoid detection in his prank, he ducked behind a hand truck. In so doing he struck his nose on the truck and was painfully and permanently injured. The plaintiff filed a claim for his injuries, alleging that he was injured in doing acts growing out of his employment. Do you think the plaintiff should be paid? (Ognibene v. Rochester Mfg. Co. et al., 298 N.Y. 85, 80 N.E. 749)
2. The plaintiff brought an action for overtime wages alleged to be due him under the Fair Labor Standards Act. The defendant, who manufactures and sells ice, contends that the act did not apply to his business because most of his business was local. The defendant in addition to his local business did furnish ice to both freight and passenger trains operating in interstate commerce. Do you think the defendant was correct in his contention? Why? (Wagner v. American Service Co., 58 Fed. Supp. 32)

KEY TO "WHAT'S THE LAW?" Page 240

1. *Yes. Workmen's compensation laws would most likely provide for his care.*
2. *No. Federal laws would impose some regulations in this case.*

WHAT'S THE LAW?

1. *Ira Evans was fifteen years old. He felt he was as well informed as most people ever get; therefore, he decided to terminate his schooling and obtain a job. Do you think his chances of getting a job are very good? Why?*

2. *Jacob Knight lives on a farm and does farm work for his father. Does this violate any child-labor laws?*

◬ UNIT 27: MINORS AND EMPLOYMENT

In a primitive society everybody works, the very young, the very old, and all ages between. They have to. The combined labors of all are required to supply the barest necessities for existence. In our modern society this is not necessary. One of the earmarks of modern civilization is the ability to produce the necessities of life, and many of the luxuries, with a minimum expenditure of effort on the part of the workmen in our society.

Before the development of the machine age, children worked, but they worked in the home. The family income was earned in the home and on the farm. Each member of the family had his job to do. Early manufacturing industry began in the home. A boy could learn his father's trade in his own home, or he might be apprenticed to a master craftsman and live in the master's home while he learned his trade.

EXAMPLE 1   In 1750 Ezra Perkins worked in his father's shoemaking shop while learning the shoemaker's trade. Ezra did not need the protection of child-labor laws because he was working at home for his own parents.

The invention of the steam engine and the Industrial Revolution changed all this. The wage earners of the family began to go out of the home and into the factories to earn their living. Using the simple machines of the factories, the unskilled workman could now do the work formerly done only by skilled craftsmen. The machines were relatively simple. They were not the automatic machines you see in factories today. They required many hand operations that could readily be done by even very young children. As a result, thousands and thousands of children were soon being employed in factories, working long hours under very dangerous and unhealthy conditions.

How did the industrial revolution affect the employment of minors?

PROTECTION OF MINORS

Do labor unions generally look with favor on the employment of children?

Very early, several factors began to work against this revolting exploitation of child labor. Church and social leaders protested on a humanitarian basis. As a more democratic type of government developed here and abroad, more formal school education for children was needed if they were to become useful adults and citizens. Adult workmen soon began to see that child labor worked directly against their efforts to improve their own wages and working conditions. Labor unions very early joined the social and humanitarian groups that were working against the evils of child labor.

Ordinary home chores done by children for their parents are not covered by child-labor laws.

What states were the early leaders in developing legislation regulating child labor?

Child-labor legislation, however, developed very slowly. In 1842 Massachusetts passed a law limiting the work of children under twelve years old to ten hours a day. Connecticut in the same year passed a similar law, but these two states were far ahead of their times. By 1880 only a few states had laws limiting the work of children in factories, and only one regulated the hours for children in "any gainful occupation." By 1930 all but four states had child-labor laws dealing with manufacturing, and two-thirds of the states had laws dealing with nonmanufacturing occupations. You will note that all these early laws were state laws. Early attempts had been made to obtain a constitutional amendment making child-labor laws a federal matter, but these efforts met with little success.

The 1930s mark the beginning of our present-day progress in child-labor laws. The *National Recovery Administration,* established in 1933, prohibited child labor in industries engaged in interstate commerce, specifying a minimum age of sixteen in most cases. The NRA was declared unconstitutional two years later, but the standards set during its short life have had a definite influence on state legislation since that time. **NATIONAL RECOVERY ADMINISTRATION**

In 1934 the annual Conference on Labor Legislation adopted a set of standards for state child-labor legislation, and these standards have had a great influence on child-labor laws since that time. The table shown on page 253 sets out these recommendations and lists the states that meet each standard.

CHILD LABOR LEGISLATION AND THE EXTENT TO WHICH STATE CHILD-LABOR LAWS MEET THESE STANDARDS

AREAS OF REGULATION	RECOMMENDED STANDARDS	EXTENT TO WHICH STATE CHILD-LABOR LAWS MEET RECOMMENDED STANDARDS
Minimum age	16 years in any employment in a factory; 16 in any employment during school hours; 14 in nonfactory employment outside school hours.	24 states and Puerto Rico approximate this standard in whole or in part (AL, AK, CO, CT, GA, IL, KY, LA, ME, MD, MA, MT, NJ, NY, NC, OH, PA, RI, SC, TN, VA, WV, WI, WY)
Hazardous occupations	Minimum age 18 for employment in a considerable number of hazardous occupations.	Few, if any, states extend full protection in this respect to minors up to 18 years of age, though many state laws prohibit employment under 18 in a varying number of specified hazardous occupations.
	State administrative agency authorized to determine occupations hazardous for minors under 18.	25 states, the District of Columbia, and Puerto Rico have state administrative agencies with such authority (AK, AZ, CO, CT, FL, HI, KS, LA, ME, MD, MA, MI, NE, NJ, NY, NC, ND, OH, OR, PA, UT, VA, WA, WY, WI)
Maximum daily hours	8-hour day for minors under 18 in any gainful occupation.	17 states, the District of Columbia, and Puerto Rico have an 8-hour day for minors of both sexes under 18 in most occupations (AK, CA, CO, KY, LA, MT, NJ, NY, ND, OH, OR, PA, TN, UT, VA, WA, WI) 5 other states have this standard for girls up to 18 (AZ, IL, IN, NV, NM)
Maximum weekly hours	40-hour week for minors under 18 in any gainful occupation.	5 states (AK, KY, NJ, TN, VA) and Puetro Rico have a 40-hour week for minors under 18 in most occupations. In addition Wisconsin has a 40-hour week for 16-year-olds in a school week, and Washington has a 40-hour week for minors under 16 when school is not in session.
Work during specified night hours prohibited*	13 hours of night work prohibited for minors of both sexes under 16 in any gainful occupation.	7 states and Puerto Rico meet this standard, at least for most occupations (HI, IA, KS, NJ, NY, NC, OK). In addition Kentucky and Utah meet this standard for minors under 15; Ohio for girls under 16 and for boys under 16 on nights preceding schooldays; Oregon for minors under 16, except on special permits; and Virginia for minors under 16 on nights preceding school days. 11 states and the District of Columbia prohibit 12 or 12½ hours of night work for minors under 16 (AZ, IL, MD, MA, MN, MO, NM, ND, PA, RI, TN). Missouri prohibits 12 hours of night work on nights preceding school days; Tennessee prohibits 12 hours of night work for minors under 16 attending school.
	8 hours of night work prohibited for minors of both sexes between 16 and 18 in any gainful occupation.	10 states, the District of Columbia, and Puetro Rico meet or exceed this standard, at least for most occupations (AR, CT, KS, KY, LA, MA, MI, NJ, OH, TN); Maryland meets the standard for those attending school.
Employment certificates	Required for minors under 18 in any gainful occupation.	23 states, the District of Columbia, and Puerto Rico require employment or age certificates for minors under 18 in most occupations (CA, CT, DE, FL, GA, HI, IN, KY, LA, MD, MA, MI, MT, NJ, NY, NC, OH, OR, PA, UT, VA, WA, WI) New Hampshire requires such certificates for minors between 16 and 18 in occupations subject to the provisions of the Federal Fair Labor Standards Act. Two other states (AL and NV) require certificates for minors under 17.

* 14 states and Puerto Rico prohibit work of children under 16 after 6 p.m., 18 states and the District of Columbia prohibit work after 7 p.m., and 15 states after 8 p.m. or later. Of those prohibiting work after 6, 7, or 8 p.m., 11 permit work until 9 or 10 p.m. under certain circumstances, usually during vacations or on nights preceding nonschool days. SOURCE: *U.S. DEPARTMENT OF LABOR, Bureau of Labor Standards, March, 1966.*

FEDERAL LEGISLATION

The most progressive step in federal child-labor legislation is the child-labor portion of the Federal Fair Labor Standards Act of 1938, as amended in 1949. This act prohibits the shipment, in interstate commerce or in foreign trade, of any goods produced in factories in which "oppressive child labor" has been used within thirty days of the removal of the goods. *Oppressive child labor* is generally defined in the act as any employment of minors under the age of sixteen in any of the occupations covered by the act and the employment of minors under eighteen in occupations declared by the Secretary of Labor to be particularly hazardous.

What is the federal act that prohibits "oppressive child labor"?

OPPRESSIVE CHILD LABOR

EXAMPLE 2   Two hundred years after Example 1, one of Ezra Perkins' descendants, Eugene Perkins, aged fourteen, applied for a job in a shoe factory. He did not get the job because the shoes being manufactured were to be shipped in interstate commerce, and Eugene's employment would be illegal under the Federal Fair Labor Standards Act. It is highly probable that the child-labor laws of his own state would prohibit his employment also, even if the goods were not to be shipped in interstate commerce.

Minors between the ages of fourteen and sixteen may be employed in other occupations if the Secretary of Labor determines that their employment does not interfere with their schooling. Exceptions are (1) children working in agriculture after school hours, (2) child actors, (3) children working for their parents in occupations other than manufacturing, and (4) children delivering newspapers to the consumer.

EXAMPLE 3   Charles Brush, fifteen years old, was employed as a newsboy for a local paper. He worked 4 hours a day, 6 days a week, and was paid $18. A social worker investigated to learn whether the Federal Wage and Hour Law was being violated. It was held that the law was not being violated because it applies to persons engaged only in interstate commerce and not in intrastate commerce. Therefore, the minimum-wage provisions and maximum number of hours of employment provided by the law were inoperative in this case. Of course, any violation of state or local laws would be prosecuted by other authorities.

The greatest contribution of the Federal Fair Labor Standards Act probably has been the placing of some measure of control of child labor under a federal agency that can thoroughly study its operation.

INDUSTRY-EDUCATION COOPERATION

Effective regulation of child labor requires the cooperation of industry and educational institutions. Legislation cannot do the whole job alone. Many industries have their own child-labor codes and restrict child labor to an even greater extent than do the laws. Other industries, however, require laws to make them conform.

Education and the child-labor problem are closely connected. One of the great evils of child labor is its interference with the education of future citizens. Public schools work hand in hand with the enforcement officers of child-labor acts. Work permits, for example, are usually issued by the public school system.

Well-educated citizens are necessary for the world of tomorrow. The education of young people should not be sacrificed by allowing them to go to work too soon.

EXAMPLE 4 **Albert Jansen wanted to work in Mr. Walker's grocery store after school. Even though Albert was only fourteen years old, he discovered that the laws of his state would permit him to work at this job if he obtained a work permit from the local school board.**

The development of child-labor laws has been slow and in many cases irregular. Much progress has been made in recent years, however; and the prospects for the future look bright. The administration of the Federal Fair Labor Standards Act is making many advances. More and more, powerful organizations are supporting the child-labor movement. The need for better-educated citizens is becoming increasingly recognized. State legislation is constantly improving; and, on the practical side, factories are becoming more automatic, and the economic need for child labor is becoming less with each new advance in industrial production methods.

What evidence indicates that child-labor conditions are improving?

SUGGESTIONS FOR MINIMIZING LEGAL RISKS

1. Remember that laws regulating the employment of minors are passed for your protection. Do not risk injury to your future health or security by violating these laws.
2. Become familiar with the current laws of your state regulating the employment of minors. As these laws are subject to change at every session of your legislature, obtain reliable information from your local state employment office just prior to employment.
3. Do not misrepresent your age in seeking employment; it is likely to be discovered later. Even though you may not lose your job as a result of the misrepresentation, your reputation for honesty will be impaired.
4. Report promptly to your employer every injury that you may have, no matter how trivial it may seem at the time. This is essential in order that your employer can protect your health and can, if necessary, make an accurate record of the injury, which will establish evidence that may be needed later in filing a claim for the injury.

5. If injured on a job where there is not a company nurse or physician, get the best available medical attention as soon as possible. Follow your doctor's orders to the letter. This may save expensive and time-wasting complications.

APPLYING YOUR LEARNING

QUESTIONS AND PROBLEMS

1. What changing conditions have been largely responsible for the current child-labor laws in this country?
2. In your opinion, why have some states made further advances in child-labor legislation than others?
3. Do you think that child-labor legislation should be made uniform throughout all the states through the passage of some federal statutes? Explain your reasons.
4. What exceptions in the Federal Fair Labor Standards Act permit minors between fourteen and sixteen years of age to work, even though the product of their labors may be sold in interstate commerce?
5. Do you think that additional child-labor legislation is needed in your state? Explain why or why not.

WHAT IS YOUR OPINION?

In each of the following cases, give your decision and state a legal principle that applies to the case.

1. Jim Phelps, fourteen years of age, lived on a farm and did the usual farm chores for his father. Would his work be controlled by the child-labor provisions of the Federal Fair Labor Standards Act?
2. Suppose that Jim Phelps lived in the city and worked after school hours in his father's grocery store. Would the Federal Fair Labor Standards Act now apply to his employment?
3. Suppose that Jim Phelps's father owned a steel mill instead of a grocery store. What further information do you need now to determine whether the Federal Fair Labor Standards Act applies?
4. If all the products of the steel mill in Case 3 were used in local building construction, would the Federal Fair Labor Standards Act apply to Jim Phelps's employment? Why?
5. Even though the Federal Fair Labor Standards Act might not apply, is it likely that a state statute would prohibit Jim Phelps, a fourteen-year-old minor, from working in a steel mill? Why?
6. Ruth Pitts, seventeen years of age, was offered a position as a waitress in a summer resort during her summer vacation. The hours were to run from 7 a.m. to 7 p.m. six days a week. Do you think that Ruth would be permitted by law to accept the offer if she lived in your state? Give a reason for your answer.

7. Would your answer be the same if the hours of employment were from 7 p.m. to 7 a.m. in an all-night restaurant? Why?

8. Edward Reed, sixteen years of age, was told by a friend that he might need a work permit to obtain a job that was available in a local filling station. If Edward Reed lived in your state, would he be required to get a work permit?

9. Sarah Thomas, fifteen years of age, put in an application for employment at the local five-and-ten-cent store. She stated on her application that she was eighteen years old. Would the store be violating any special state statutes in your state by employing Sarah? Explain.

10. Suppose that Sarah Thomas, in Case 9, had been required to work from 9 a.m. until 9 p.m. on Saturdays. Would this be in violation of any special state statutes if Sarah lived in your state?

THE LAW IN ACTION

1. The defendant employed children to assemble tomato and cabbage crates. These crates were to be used as the containers for the shipment of products in interstate commerce. Do you think this employment would be controlled by the Fair Labor Standards Act? (Lenroot v. Hazlehurst Mercantile Co., 59 F. Supp. 595 S.D. Miss.)

2. The Western Union Telegraph Company contended that the Fair Labor Standards Act did not apply to it because it did not "produce" goods as defined by the statute and "shipped" nothing in interstate commerce. What do you think? (Western Union v. Lenroot, 323 U.S. 490)

KEY TO "WHAT'S THE LAW?" Page 251

1. *No. Education and training are important in getting a job today.*
2. *No. Child-labor laws do not apply in this case.*

A DIGEST OF LEGAL CONCEPTS

1. The broad laws of employment apply to all legally competent persons who hire others to work for them (employers) and to all persons who work for hire for others (employees).

2. Agents are employees, and their relations with their principals are covered by the laws of employment.

3. The general laws of contracts apply to employment contracts.

4. Oral contracts of employment are enforceable if they can be performed within a year from the time of making.

5. A contract of employment that cannot be performed within a year from the time of making must be supported by a note or memorandum in writing.

6. A contract of employment in which no length of time is specified is a contract at will and may be terminated at any time by either party.

7. A contract that specifies the length of the employment may not rightfully be terminated without cause by either party until the end of the specified period. A wrongful termination before the end of the period would be a breach of contract.

8. Either party may terminate an employment contract before the end of the period for justifiable cause without being guilty of breach of contract.

9. Collective-bargaining contracts are valid agreements and may be enforceable as contracts.

10. When an employee, acting for his employer, enters into a contract with a third person, he becomes an agent with respect to this contract.

11. An employer is liable for all the negligent acts of his employee that are committed within the scope of his employment.

12. A labor union is a bargaining agent acting in behalf of the workers it represents.

13. Employees to whom trade secrets are divulged in connection with their employment, may be restrained from accepting employment with other firms engaged in the same work for a reasonable time after the termination of their employment.

14. Workmen's compensation laws provide for the care of all workmen injured on the job in covered occupations, regardless of the cause of their injuries.

15. A workman's compensation for injury is usually calculated on the basis of his rate of pay and the number of weeks he was unable to work because of his injury.

16. The Federal Fair Labor Standards Act as amended in 1949 provides for minimum rates of pay and maximum working hours for all workmen producing goods for shipment in interstate commerce.

17. In 1964 the Equal-Pay Rule was passed by Congress, making it mandatory for employers engaged in interstate commerce to pay women the same rate of pay as men holding the same type of job.

18. Social security laws provide for the care of individuals who are unable to provide for themselves because of a loss of earnings due to sickness, accident, disability, unemployment, old age, or death.

19. The Social Security Act provides for (a) old-age, survivors, and disability insurance; (b) unemployment insurance; and (c) public assistance.

20. Old age, survivors and disability insurance is a system of insurance that was set up and is administered by the federal government and that is paid for by contributions from both employer and employee.

21. The Social Security Amendments of 1965 provide automatic hospital insurance for almost all Americans over sixty-five, whether or not they are eligible for other social security benefits.

22. The Social Security Act as amended in 1965 also provides for low-cost voluntary medical insurance for the aged.

23. The Medicare provisions of the amended Social Security Act consist of these hospital and medical insurance benefits.

24. Unemployment insurance is a system of insurance jointly operated by state and federal governments. Administration is under the control of the state, but standards set by the federal law are followed.

25. The Civil Rights Act bans discrimination in voting, schools, hiring, firing, promotions, and in the use of hotels, restaurants, and theaters.

PART 10: Bailments

WHAT'S THE LAW?

1. *Joe Oliveras borrowed his neighbor's lawn rake. The rake was old and worn; the handle was so rotten that it snapped off through no fault of Joe's. Must Joe replace the broken rake handle with a new one?*

---

2. *Willie Sands borrowed ten sheets of notebook paper from his friend Art Dorsey and promised to return an equal number of sheets the next day. Is this a bailment?*

▲ UNIT 28: NATURE OF BAILMENTS

You may be a bailee or a bailor right this minute. If you have in your possession something that belongs to someone else, you are a *bailee*. If someone else has some of your belongings in his possession, you are a *bailor*. A *bailment* exists any time personal property is in the possession of and under the control of someone who is not the rightful owner.

BAILEE
BAILOR
BAILMENT

EXAMPLE 1 Merle Strong had a term paper to write for his English class and thought the paper would appear neater if it was typewritten. However, Merle did not own a typewriter. Harold Barr, a good friend of Merle's, had just purchased a new typewriter. Merle borrowed his friend's new typewriter. Was this a bailment?

Yes, this was a bailment. Merle would be the bailee and Harold would be the bailor. Even in this simple transaction, basic legal rights and duties exist.

A bailment is one of the most common business and personal transactions. It occurs thousands of times every day. It may be the simple act of a housewife borrowing her neighbor's vacuum cleaner, or a student borrowing a book from the school or public library, or the deposit of a million dollars' worth of bonds with a bank for safekeeping.

BAILMENTS AND AGREEMENTS

When is a bailment considered a contract?

Most bailments in business transactions are based on contracts, but many bailments in personal relationships are not based on contracts. If the bailment agreement is supported by consideration, then, in all probability, a contract exists. But, if no consideration is present, then you know from your study of the laws of contracts that there can be no contract.

When personal property is placed in the hands of someone other than the owner, a bailment exists.

EXAMPLE 2   **Barbara Bailey placed her mink coat in storage for the summer with the Cleveland Fur Salon. Barbara promised to pay the $10 service charge for storage. The Cleveland Fur Salon agreed to store the mink coat safely and return it to Barbara early in the fall. What would you call this transaction?**

This would be a bailment because the Cleveland Fur Salon has in its possession the coat belonging to Barbara. It would also be a contract because of the presence of consideration—Barbara's promise to pay the service fee of $10.

EXAMPLE 3   **George Popson offered the use of his motorcycle to his friend Andy Harvilla. This was a friendly gesture on George's part with no thought of remuneration. Andy accepted George's offer and borrowed the motorcycle to ride to a neighboring town.**

Explain what is meant by a gratuitous bailment.

This would be a *gratuitous*—that is, a free—*bailment,* and no contract would be involved. By accepting the gratuitous offer, however, Andy has made an implied promise to use the motorcycle with great care.

GRATUITOUS BAILMENT

Sometimes, we may have a bailment even when there is no agreement at all.

EXAMPLE 4   **John Tracy found a watch lying on the sidewalk. He picked it up, put it in his pocket, and later advertised in the local paper to find the true owner. Was this a bailment?**

Yes, this was a bailment. John was the bailee because he had in his possession a watch that belonged to someone else. There was no contract. He had made no agreement with anyone.

TRANSACTIONS THAT ARE NOT BAILMENTS

There are several types of transactions that look somewhat like bailments but actually are not. Examples of these might be sales, loans of money, and conditional sales. In drawing a distinction between bailments and these similar transactions, however, you should keep in mind that, in a bailment, personal property is in the hands of someone who is not the owner. Furthermore, in a bailment it is always understood that the bailed goods will be returned to the true owner. In a bailment there is not even a temporary passing of title.

EXAMPLE 5 Hugh Burton visited his brother's farm to hunt quail. After two days of unsuccessful hunting, Hugh went home, saying, "I'll leave my gun here, since I won't be needing it in the city. You might have better luck with it than I've had."

In a situation like this, trouble could develop in the interpretation that might be placed upon Hugh's words. Did he give the gun to his brother? Or did he intend to create only a bailment, in which case he would return to get the gun? The similarities are so great that only a jury might determine whether Hugh's intention was to pass title or merely possession. A clear expression of intention would eliminate problems of this kind.

SALES

Can a bailment also be a sale?

It is easy to distinguish a sale from a bailment in most cases. In a sale, title passes to a new owner. In a bailment, possession passes to the bailee, but title remains with the bailor. U.C.C. Sec. 2-106(1) It is only in special cases that you may have trouble in distinguishing between bailments and sales. Such a special case is illustrated in the following example:

EXAMPLE 6 Mrs. Wenzel borrows a cup of sugar from Mrs. Truax. This is not a bailment. Mrs. Truax does not expect to get the same sugar back. She expects to pass title to this cup of sugar to Mrs. Wenzel in return for the implied promise of Mrs. Wenzel to return another cup of sugar just like the borrowed sugar.

Legally, then, it is a sale because title passes. In everyday language we would call this type of sale a *barter*.

BARTER

LOANS OF MONEY

Does loaning money constitute a bailment?

When you lend money, you do not expect to have the identical pieces of money returned to you. Title to, or ownership of, the money is transferred to the borrower in return for his promise to return a like amount.

EXAMPLE 7 Suppose that you deposit $20 in the bank. You might now say to yourself, "I have money in the bank." Actually, you do not have the $20 you deposited in the bank. In reality, you lent the money to the bank. You do not expect to get the same money back. You passed title to the bank and expect the bank to return a similar amount to you on demand. This, then, is not a bailment.

The deposit of money in a bank is not ordinarily a bailment because you do not receive the same money back.

CONDITIONAL SALES

You will remember from your earlier study that a *conditional sale* is one in which the title to the goods is retained by the seller. This makes a conditional sale look very much like a bailment. A study of the following example, however, should show a distinction between a conditional sale and a bailment.

CONDITIONAL SALE

EXAMPLE 8 **Suppose that you bought a new tape recorder, paying $10 down and promising to pay $10 a month for the next 10 months. You would probably sign a conditional sales contract giving the seller the right to hold title until the tape recorder is paid for. This appears to be a bailment, but usually it is not.**

You will remember that in a conditional sale the seller retains title for security purposes only. In all other respects, the title would be yours, and the expected final result of the transaction would be for you to acquire absolute title when the goods are finally paid for. U.C.C. Sec. 2-401 Sec. 9-113

This, then, makes a conditional sale different from a bailment. In a bailment it is expected that the goods shall remain only temporarily in the hands of the bailee and that ultimately they will be returned to the possession of the bailor.

IMPORTANCE OF BAILMENTS

Bailments are common business and personal relationships, and they are extremely important. Both the bailor and the bailee have certain rights and assume certain duties. The greater duty is usually on the bailee because he has someone else's (the bailor's) goods in his possession. The bailee, however, is not absolutely responsible for any and all losses that might befall the goods. He must exercise the degree of care required by the particular facts of each bailment. The care required of the bailee is defined as *reasonable care* under the circumstances; that is the degree of care which a reasonable man would exercise in the situation in order to prevent the happening of foreseeable harm to the goods. If he fails to exercise the necessary care, he is regarded as negligent and liable for any loss or damage to the goods.

What is meant by reasonable care?

REASONABLE CARE

Also, the bailee must strictly comply with the terms of the bailment. If the bailee violates the terms of the agreement in any way, he becomes an *insurer* and is absolutely liable for any loss.

How can a bailee become absolutely liable for any loss sustained?

INSURER

Different kinds of bailments require different degrees of care. In order that you may better understand this rule, bailments have been classified into several groups in the next two units, and the rights and duties pertaining to each group are discussed separately.

SUGGESTIONS FOR MINIMIZING LEGAL RISKS

1. Give some thought to the risks involved before you entrust your goods to the possession of someone else, as you automatically assume certain risks in so doing.
2. When you take goods to a repairman, look for one who not only has a good reputation but also has the physical facilities for protecting your goods.
3. If you store your goods for any length of time, it may be wise to protect them by insurance rather than to depend on the legal liability of the bailee for protection.
4. If you buy goods on a conditional sales contract, remember that, if they are destroyed, it is your loss, even though title is retained by the conditional seller for security purposes. If the goods are valuable, you should consider insuring them at the time the contract is signed.
5. Do not lend your goods to a friend unless you are convinced that he knows how to give them proper care and will be responsible in caring for them.

 APPLYING YOUR LEARNING

QUESTIONS AND PROBLEMS

1. How would you define a bailee? a bailor? a bailment?
2. Give an example of a bailment that is based on a contract. Give an example of a bailment in which there is no contract.
3. How would you distinguish between a bailment and a sale?
4. Does title pass in a bailment? Explain your answer.
5. Does title pass in a conditional sale? Is a conditional sale a bailment? Why or why not?
6. Is a bailee an insurer of the goods left in his care? Explain.

WHAT IS YOUR OPINION?

In each of the following cases, give your decision and state a legal principle that applies to the case.

1. York entered the Jacques Café and checked his hat and coat at the checkroom. Would this be a bailment? Explain.
2. Suppose that York had kept his hat and coat with him and had hung them on a hook beside the table. Would this be a bailment?
3. Suppose that, when York went to his table, a waiter took York's hat and coat and hung them up in a remote part of the room. Would this be a bailment? Explain.

4. Wade saw his neighbor Warner trimming his hedge by hand. Wade took his power trimmer over to Warner and said, "Use my trimmer if you wish." Warner accepted; but said nothing except, "Thank you." Is there a bailment? Is there a contract?

5. Suppose that, in Case 4, Wade had said, "I will let you use my power trimmer if you will trim my side of the hedge also." Would this be a bailment? Would it be a contract?

6. Rector borrowed $100 from the First National Bank. Would this be a bailment? Why or why not?

7. Suppose, instead, that Rector had deposited $100 in the First National Bank. Would this be a bailment?

8. Tripp allowed McGee to store hay in his barn. Through no fault of Tripp's, the barn burned down. Would Tripp have to pay McGee for the hay destroyed?

THE LAW IN ACTION

1. The defendant, M'Divani, leased a furnished appartment from the plaintiff. The defendant promised to return the furnishings, listed in the lease, in as good a condition as they were when he received them, ordinary wear and tear excepted. A valuable rug was stolen from the apartment. To determine the possible liability of the defendant, it was necessary to decide whether the law of real property or the law of bailments would control the loss. What do you think? Why? (Kaye v. M'Divani, 6 Cal. App. 2d 132, 44 P2d 371)

2. The plaintiff placed a valuable package in a public locker in a railroad station. He inserted a quarter as required, locked the locker, and took the key. When he returned, the package was gone. The plaintiff contends that his actions constituted a bailment and that the locker company was liable as a bailee. Do you agree? Why? (Marsh v. American Locker Company, 7 N.J. Super. 81, 72 A2d 343)

KEY TO "WHAT'S THE LAW?" Page 261

1. *No. Even though the borrower must be very careful in using the lawn rake, he is not liable if it is broken through no fault of his own.*

2. *No. Title passed to the paper borrowed, and different paper would be returned the next day.*

WHAT'S THE LAW?

1. *Casey Brock took his shotgun to a gunsmith for repairs. While in the gunsmith's possession, the shotgun was stolen through no fault of the gunsmith. Must Casey bear the loss?*

2. *Suppose that the gunsmith suspects that Casey does not own the gun. May he refuse to return the gun to Casey when Casey demands its return?*

△ UNIT 29: MUTUAL BENEFIT BAILMENTS

CLASSIFICATION OF MUTUAL BENEFIT BAILMENTS

Who benefits in a mutual benefit bailment?

A *mutual benefit bailment* is one in which both the bailor and the bailee receive some benefit; it is based on a contract in which each party receives and gives some consideration. Most bailments arising out of business transactions are mutual benefit bailments.

MUTUAL BENEFIT BAILMENT

HIRING LABOR OR SERVICE ON PERSONAL PROPERTY

When hiring labor or service on personal property, what type of legal relationship is created?

Agreements where property is transferred to another for work, repairs, or services for which the owner agrees to pay a fee are mutual benefit bailments.

EXAMPLE 1 **Suppose that you took your radio to a serviceman to have it repaired. By implication you would be promising to pay him for his service, and he would be promising to repair your radio satisfactorily. This would be a bailment for the mutual benefit of you and the repairman.**

When property is left with a serviceman for repairs, who is the bailor? the bailee?

Rights and Duties of the Bailor As a bailor, you have certain rights and you owe certain duties. Your most common rights are (1) to have your radio repaired with the skill the repairman says he has, (2) to have your radio protected from harm by the use of reasonable care on the repairman's part, and (3) to have your radio returned when the job is done and you tender payment.

Your duties are (1) to pay the repairman for his services; (2) to warn him if there is a hidden defect that makes the radio dangerous to handle; and (3) to call for the radio when the job is done, unless it is agreed that the repairman will deliver it to your home.

A mutual benefit bailment exists when personal property is left in the shop of a serviceman for repair.

Rights and Duties of the Bailee The rights of the bailee, who in this case is the repairman, are (1) to receive payment for his services; (2) to be warned of inherent dangers in the goods; (3) to have you, as bailor, pick up your goods without undue delay after the work is completed; and (4) to have what is called a *mechanic's lien*, that is, a right to hold the goods until the service charges are paid. He would, however, lose this right if he gave up possession of the radio. He might also lose this right if he agreed to accept payment at a later date. U.C.C. Sec. 7-209(4)

MECHANIC'S LIEN

His duties are (1) to use the skill in performing the work that he represents himself to have, (2) to use reasonable care in protecting the goods, and (3) to return the goods on demand when payment is tendered.

EXAMPLE 2 **The French Dry Cleaners completed cleaning and pressing Stager's suit and placed it on the rack with other finished work. Before Stager called for the suit, a burglar stole it. The store had not been negligent, and the loss was not due to lack of reasonable care. Stager will have no rightful claim against the French Dry Cleaners for his loss.**

Losses by fire, theft, or other causes beyond the control of the bailee do not excuse the bailor from paying for the bailee's services if the work had been completed prior to the time of loss and if the bailor had been notified that the property was ready for delivery.

STORING ANOTHER'S GOODS

EXAMPLE 3 **In Example 2, Unit 28, Barbara Bailey stored her mink coat for the summer with the Cleveland Fur Salon. This would be a mutual benefit bailment, but of a slightly different kind. The rights and duties of the parties are similar to those in a service bailment.**

Rights and Duties of the Bailor In the example, Barbara's rights would be (1) to have her coat kept safely by the use of reasonable care. Reasonable care varies with the nature of the goods stored; the care required of a fur coat would be quite different from that required of a piece of furniture or a live animal. The circumstances determine the nature of the care. U.C.C. Sec. 7-204(1) Barbara would also have the right (2) to have her coat returned to her when she calls for it at the end of the agreed storage period or at any other suitable time.

Barbara's duties would be (1) to pay the storage costs, (2) to give notice to the bailee of any special care required of these goods, and (3) to call for the coat at the end of the period unless there was an agreement for delivery.

Rights and Duties of the Bailee The Cleveland Fur Salon, the bailee, would have the right (1) to its storage charges; (2) to be given notice by the bailor of any special care required; and (3) to have the goods picked up at the end of the storage period.

The Cleveland Fur Salon would owe a duty (1) to store the goods according to the terms of the contract, (2) to use reasonable care in protecting the goods against loss, and (3) to return the goods to the bailor when demanded.

If a fur store agrees to store a coat in a specific place, storage elsewhere will make them fully responsible for all damages that may result from any cause whatsoever.

Storing your possessions for a fee is a mutual benefit bailment based on a contract in which each party (the bailor and the bailee) gives and receives some consideration.

HIRING THE USE OF ANOTHER'S GOODS

Today, it is a very common practice to rent goods when you need an article for only a limited time. If you made a survey in your own locality, you would probably find the following, and many other items, for rent by the day or by the week: floor sanders, power tools, lawn mowers, garden tractors, trailers, automobiles, trucks, power shovels, and contractor's equipment. Hiring the use of another's goods is another type of mutual benefit bailment.

EXAMPLE 4 **Suppose that you have started a lawn-mowing business, contracting to cut the grass of various people in your neighborhood. You find that you can get more business than you can handle with your "push-it-yourself" lawn mower. You find also that you can rent a power mower from a neighborhood hardware store for a nominal sum. Being a young, astute businessman, you rent the mower, and, with it, you find you can cut twice as many lawns. This is a mutual benefit bailment.**

Rights and Duties of the Bailor The rights of the bailor, or hardware store, in Example 6 would be (1) to collect the rental charges for the mower, (2) to have the mower used with reasonable care, and (3) to have the mower returned at the end of the period of rental.

When hiring use of another's goods, what rights has a bailor? what duties?

The duties of the bailor would be (1) to furnish you with a mower that was in sufficiently good repair to be safe to use and (2) to warn you of any dangers involved in the use of such equipment.

What are the rights and duties of the bailee when hiring use of another's goods?

Rights and Duties of the Bailee   You, as a bailee, would have the right (1) to receive reasonably safe equipment, (2) to be warned of any dangers involved in its use, and (3) to use the bailed goods according to the terms of the contract.

Your duties would be (1) to pay the rental charges for the mower and (2) to use the mower with reasonable care. This would not mean that you would be absolutely liable for the loss, destruction, or breakage of the mower. You would be liable only if the loss, destruction, or breakage resulted from a failure on your part to use reasonable care. If you violated the terms of your contract and used the goods in a manner other than that agreed on, you would be liable as an insurer for any loss or damage to the goods. You would also have the duty (3) to return the mower to the bailor.

EXAMPLE 5   Roth rented a formal suit from the Youngline Valet. While wearing the suit, Roth crawled under his car to make an adjustment. The resulting damage to the suit would make Roth liable to the Youngline Valet. He did not use the bailed property with reasonable care.

BAILMENT AS SECURITY FOR A LOAN (PLEDGE)

Many times, a bailment is coupled with the loan of money. The goods of the borrower in such a bailment are turned over to the lender to hold as security for the loan. This is a special type of transaction, but it is a bailment for the mutual benefit of both parties.

Where a pledge is made as security for a loan, who is the pledgor? the pledgee?

The property left as security is called the *pledge*, or *pawn*. The borrower, or debtor, is the *pledgor*, or bailor. The lender, or creditor, is the *pledgee*, or bailee, and may be a bank, a loan company, a credit union, a pawnbroker, or another person.

PAWN
PLEDGE
PLEDGEE
PLEDGOR

EXAMPLE 6   Suppose that you urgently need $50 to meet a sudden emergency. You have a $100 United States Steel Corporation bond, but you do not want to give it up. The bond is a good investment, and you feel sure that you could repay a loan of $50 in sixty days if the bank will lend you the money. You might find that the National Bank would lend you the money if you deposit your bond with them to hold as security.

The pledgor, or owner, gives an implied warranty of title of property pledged as security. Implied warranty of title also applies to a bailment of property pledged as security for the repayment of a debt.

What are the rights and duties of the pledgor? the pledgee?

Rights and Duties of the Pledgor (Bailor)   Even though you have handed over your bond to the bank to hold until the loan is repaid, you have (1) the right to demand the return of the same bond when you tender repayment of the loan and (2) a right at the same time to any interest on the bond that may have been collected by the bank.

Your duties would be (1) to repay the loan with interest and (2) to tender repayment and demand the bond's return at the proper time and place.

The failure of the bank to return the bond gives you the right (1) to bring an action of replevin to recover your property or (2) to bring an action of trover. *Trover* is a common-law action which allows the owner of personal property to demand payment for its value. This action is used by someone who would rather receive the value of his property than the property itself.

TROVER

Rights and Duties of the Pledgee (Bailee) The rights of the bank would be (1) to have repayment of the amount of their loan with interest and (2) to hold your bond until repayment was made.

The bank's duties would be (1) to use reasonable care in keeping your bond safely and (2) to return your bond to you when you tender repayment of the loan with interest.

If pledged property is destroyed or stolen due to the negligence of the pledgee, is the pledgor released from his debt?

If pledged property is stolen goods, the pledgee will be required to give up the article to the real owner without the owner reimbursing the pledgee.

Surrender of the pledged property by the pledgee before he receives payment of his loan does not cancel the debt.

If the pledged property is destroyed or stolen and the pledgee is in no way negligent, the pledgor would not be released from his debt.

EXAMPLE 7   Rankin pledged a diamond ring with a pawnbroker as security for the repayment of a loan. The pawnbroker put the ring in his safe. The safe was robbed and the ring stolen.

It was held that the pledgee (pawnbroker) is required to exercise only reasonable care and is liable only for ordinary negligence. The pawnbroker was not liable for the loss and would not be barred from an action against Rankin on the debt.

BAILMENTS BY NECESSITY

A common type of mutual benefit bailment, implied by law, is the *bailment by necessity*. This type of bailment arises in situations where a customer is required to give up possession of property for the benefit of both parties, such as when one purchases a suit and is required to give up possession of his own property while being fitted, or when one receives services in a barber or beauty shop, where he must give up possession of a hat or other articles of apparel; and in such cases the bailee is required to accept the other's property and to exercise reasonable care in its protection.

BAILMENT BY NECESSITY

EXAMPLE 8   Suppose you and your friend attended a formal dinner at the Chilton Hotel. Because of bad weather, both of you wore overcoats and hats. There was no checkroom in the hotel dining room, and outer clothing had to be left on racks near the door. The formality of the dinner necessitated the removal of wraps. A bailment by necessity would arise, placing a burden of reasonable care upon the hotel management.

Loss of the property due to the hotel's negligence or lack of care would give you and your friend a rightful claim for damages.

SUGGESTIONS FOR MINIMIZING LEGAL RISKS

1. If you rent goods from someone, inspect them carefully before taking possession. Do not accept defective goods unless the defect is pointed out by the bailor before you take possession. You take certain risks unless you do this.
2. If you rent goods to someone, be sure that they are in good condition and safe to handle before you deliver them.
3. When you are in possession of another's goods by virtue of a bailment contract, be sure you do not do anything that would violate the terms of the agreement. If you do, you become an insurer of the goods.
4. When storing goods with another, be sure that the bailee can give them proper care. Take out insurance if you wish to protect yourself fully.

 # APPLYING YOUR LEARNING

QUESTIONS AND PROBLEMS

1. If you take your radio to a repairman, are you a bailor or a bailee? What are your rights?
2. What duties do you owe to the man who services your radio in his shop?
3. If you store your goods in a warehouse, what are your rights as against the warehouseman?
4. What would be the rights of the warehouseman in his relations with you?
5. What is meant by a mutual benefit bailment?
6. What is a pledge? How does it differ from a bailment for storage?
7. How is a pledge different from a conditional sale?
8. What is the general degree of care required in a mutual benefit bailment?
9. What is the pledgor's warranty of title?
10. Explain when a bailment by necessity arises.

WHAT IS YOUR OPINION?

In each of the following cases, give your decision and state a legal principle that applies to the case.

1. Milne borrowed $25 from Monaco, giving his watch as pledge. If the watch is stolen, will Monaco have to pay for its loss?
2. When Nestler rented a car from A-1 Rental Agency, he was told that it used an excessive amount of oil and should be checked every 100 miles. He drove 50 miles and burned out a bearing through lack of oil. Is he liable for damages?

3. Ryder rented a power saw from Salman Hardware. He left it out in the rain, and it was badly damaged. Will he have to pay for the damage done?

4. Worth agreed to pasture Tegler's cattle at an agreed weekly price. Is this a bailment? What degree of care is required in looking after the cattle?

5. If Worth knew there were poisonous grasses in his pasture, would he be liable if Tegler's cattle became ill from eating the grass?

6. After Hall bought a tire from Reliable Auto Supply on credit, the salesman said, "If you leave your car, we will mount the tire for nothing." He left his car, and the new tire was put on. Was this a bailment of the car? of the tire?

7. Before Hall called for his car, Reliable discovered that his credit was not good. Could the company hold the car until the tire was paid for? the tire?

THE LAW IN ACTION

1. The plaintiff's goods were stolen from the defendant's warehouse by the defendant's employees. The plaintiff contends that the defendant is liable. The defendant had no reason to suspect that its employees were dishonest. Can the plaintiff recover for the loss? Why? (Firestone Tire & Rubber Co. v. Pacific Transfer Co., 120 Washington 665, 208 p. 55)

2. Wallace parked his car in the defendant's garage and got a claim check. Later, a thief walked into the office while it was unattended, picked up a new check with a stub attached, substituted it for the one on Wallace's car, and walked out. When the attendant returned, the thief presented the fraudulent check and requested the car. The attendant, unaware of the fraud, delivered the car to the thief, who drove off. When sued, the defendant said he was not liable because the attendant had used ordinary care in protecting the car. Wallace claimed that there still is an action for breach of contract because the attendant had promised by implication to deliver the car to no one except himself. Does Wallace have an action for breach of contract? (Potomic Insurance Co. v. J. W. Nickson, 64 Utah 395, 231 p. 445)

KEY TO "WHAT'S THE LAW?" Page 267

1. *Yes. The gunsmith is liable only if he does not use reasonable care in protecting the gun.*

2. *No. He received it as a bailee and must return it to the bailor on demand.*

WHAT'S THE LAW?

1. When Ned Porter borrowed his neighbor's lawn mower, he was told that one blade was weak and that he should be careful. Ned was in a hurry and pushed the mower too fast. The blades stuck; and because Ned was pushing hard, one blade snapped. Ned says he is not liable because he was using reasonable care. Is he correct?

2. Bill Carter offered to care for Walter Robin's silver while Walter was away. He stored it carefully, but it tarnished. Was he obliged to have it polished.

▲ UNIT 30: GRATUITOUS BAILMENTS

CLASSIFICATION OF GRATUITOUS BAILMENTS

What is a gratuitous bailment? *Gratuitous bailments* are those in which either the bailor lends the goods to the bailee for his use without charge, or the reverse, those in which the bailee takes possession of the goods for the bailor and keeps them safely without charge. When the bailor lends the goods without charge, the bailment is for the sole benefit of the bailee. When the bailee cares for the goods without charge, the bailment is for the sole benefit of the bailor.

GRATUITOUS BAILMENT

EXAMPLE 1 If your friend John Heran lent you his typewriter for a week expecting nothing from you in return, the bailment would be for the sole benefit of the bailee. John, in this case, is the bailor and you are the bailee.

EXAMPLE 2 If your friend John Heran, who was going away for a week, asked you to look after his dog as a personal favor while he was away, then a bailment for the sole benefit of the bailor would be created, provided that you agreed and took possession of the dog.

GOODS LENT WITHOUT CHARGE

You might ask, "What's the difference whether the goods are lent without charge, or whether you pay for their use? The bailee has to take care of them in either case." Again, you are right. It is a very similar situation, but there are some important differences in the rights and duties involved.

Rights and Duties of the Bailor In a bailment in which goods are lent without charge, the bailor has a right (1) to the return of his goods at the end of the agreed period, (2) to demand the return of the goods before

What are the
rights of a
gratuitous bailor?
What are his
duties?

the end of the period, unless some consideration can be found to make the agreement a contract, and (3) to have a very high degree of care applied in the use and preservation of his goods. This is the big point of difference between free use and use for hire.

REMEMBER: When the use is paid for, a mutual benefit bailment exists, and only ordinary care is required. But, when the use is free of charge, a gratuitous bailment exists, and a very high degree of care by the bailee is required.

The duties of the bailor are the same as before: (1) to furnish the bailee safe equipment and (2) to warn the bailee of inherent or hidden dangers. The bailor who is lending goods free of charge does not have to put them in perfect condition or in even reasonably good condition; but if they are so defective as to be dangerous to use, he must warn the bailee of the danger.

What are the
rights of a
gratuitous bailee?
What are his
duties?

Rights and Duties of the Bailee The bailee, in a bailment for his sole benefit, has the right (1) to specific notice of any hidden dangers relating to the goods and (2) to the use of the goods according to the terms of the agreement. The bailee would owe a duty (1) to exercise a very high degree of care in using the goods, (2) to use the goods only as specified in the agreement, and (3) to return the goods at the end of the agreed period.

If the bailee uses a high degree of care and the goods are lost or damaged through no fault of his, he is not liable for the resulting damage. If, however, the goods are damaged through even slight negligence on his part, he is liable. Also, if he uses the goods in a manner contrary to the agreement, he becomes absolutely liable as an insurer for any damage whether it is his fault or not.

EXAMPLE 3   **Suppose that, in Example 1, you kept John's typewriter longer than the agreed week, even though John had asked for its return. Then, suppose that three days after the typewriter should have been returned it was stolen from your home through no fault of yours. You would be liable to John for its loss because you had violated the terms of the agreement and thus had become an insurer of the goods.**

STORAGE AND CARE OF GOODS AS AN ACCOMMODATION

Here, again, the rights and duties of the parties are very similar to those discussed in Unit 29 relating to goods stored for hire. Again, the difference is largely in the degree of care required of the bailee.

EXAMPLE 4   **George Hibbard, a friend of yours, was sent on a three-week business trip to ten states. He asked you if you would be willing to take care of his car while he was away. You agreed to do George a favor and drove his car into your two-car garage. This was a bailment created solely for the benefit of George Hibbard, the bailor.**

Rights and Duties of the Bailor The rights of the bailor where the bailment is soley for his benefit are (1) to have the goods stored in the manner and in the place agreed upon, (2) to have at least slight care used

When the bailment is for the sole benefit of the bailee, he is required to use a high degree of care in the use of the bailed goods.

in looking after them, and (3) to have the goods returned to him when he calls for them at the end of the bailment.

It is his duty to warn the bailee of any dangers involved in handling the goods.

EXAMPLE 5   Hibbard, who knew that the engine of his car was leaking oil, did not inform you of this leakage. The oil ruined your newly painted cement floor. Hibbard would have to accept responsibility for cleaning and repainting expenses.

Where goods are stored for another as an accommodation, what are the bailor's rights? the bailor's duties?

It is also the duty of the bailor to call for the goods and relieve the bailee of their care at the end of the agreed time. In addition the bailor is responsible for reimbursing the bailee for any necessary expenses that the bailee might have in the care of the bailor's property.

EXAMPLE 6   You discover that the ignition lock on Hibbard's car is damaged. To prevent a theft, you hire a locksmith to make the necessary repairs to the ignition lock and pay him $15 for labor and parts. Hibbard would then be obligated to reimburse you for expenses incurred because the lock repairs were necessary and the charges were reasonable.

Where goods are stored for a friend free of charge, what are the bailee's rights? The bailee's duties?

Rights and Duties of the Bailee   The bailee has the right (1) to goods that are safe to handle and store; (2) to warning as to any danger involved in handling the goods; and (3) to have the bailor pick up the goods at the agreed time, unless there is a contract as to delivery.

The duties of the gratuitous bailee are (1) to use at least slight care in looking after the goods, (2) to store the goods in the manner and in the place provided for in the agreement, and (3) to return the goods to the bailor at the end of the period on demand.

EXAMPLE 7   If Hibbard's car was stolen through no fault of yours, you would not be held liable. Neither would you be liable for rust damage if your garage was unusually damp and the roof leaked. George asked you to store the car in your garage and you complied with his request.

EXAMPLE 8   Suppose, however, that the car was in the way in your garage; so you took it over to your neighbor's and stored it in his garage. You would now be an insurer and absolutely liable to Hibbard for any loss if the car were damaged or stolen.

EXAMPLE 9 If the weather turned very cold during Hibbard's absence, you should add antifreeze to the water in the radiator of Hibbard's car. If you failed to do so, any damage resulting to the car as a result of your negligence might make you liable for all necessary repairs.

The bailee has no implied right to use the bailor's property. Should the bailee use the property in his possession, he would become fully liable for any damages that might result, even though he had used great care and was not guilty of negligence.

Does the bailee who stores the goods of a friend as an accommodation ever have an implied obligation to use the property without the consent of the bailor?

EXAMPLE 10 Suppose you used Hibbard's car one morning when your own car would not start. Although you were extremely careful, the car skidded on the icy highway and was badly damaged. You would be fully liable for the damages.

Some property, however, requires use or exercise to maintain its value. If the property is of a type that might depreciate from nonuse, the bailee would have an implied obligation to perform the services necessary to maintain the property in proper condition.

LOST PROPERTY

Under what conditions may a person become an involuntary bailee?

One of the most common ways in which you may become an *involuntary bailee*—that is, a bailee without an agreement of any kind—is to find an article. As a finder, you are considered to be a bailee for the true owner. You have certain rights and duties in this capacity.

INVOLUNTARY BAILEE

Misplaced Property There is an exception to the rule that the finder holds the property until the true owner can be found. If the lost property is found on the counter of a store or on a table in a restaurant or hotel or on a chair in a washroom or in some similar public or semipublic place, it is considered not to be lost but to have been misplaced. It is reasonable to suppose that the owner will recall where he left it and return for it. For this reason, the finder may not keep the article in his possession but must leave it with the proprietor or manager to hold for the owner. If the property is found on the floor or in the corridor or any other place that would indicate that it was not placed there intentionally, the finder may retain possession of the article as it is not likely that the owner would recall where he lost it.

Distinguish between lost property and misplaced property.

EXAMPLE 11 Mrs. Luster, a customer, found a purse on a small shelf in a fitting room of the Fashion Dress Shop. She gave the purse to the owner of the store but later, when she learned that it had not been claimed, sued the store for its return.

Mrs. Luster could not regain possession of the purse. It was found in an area used only by customers of the shop. The proprietor owed his customers a duty of guarding any property that was left there. He was, therefore, entitled to retain possession of the purse until it was claimed by the true owner.

LOCAL ORDINANCES It would be well, however, to make some inquiry as to whether your state or your city has any special laws with regard to lost articles. Some states and cities do provide for the special handling of lost articles. These regulations differ rather widely, but the general

The rights of the finder are good against the whole world except the true owner, but good conscience and sometimes the law require that diligent effort be made to find the true owner.

purpose of each is to aid in the restoring of the lost article to the true owner. Local regulations may, for example, require you to advertise for the true owner or to deposit the article with a named public official. Persons who have lost things would naturally go to the designated public official to see whether their goods had been found and deposited with him.

Duties of the Finder Suppose that while you are walking down the street you find a watch lying on the sidewalk. You pick it up and take it home with you. Your duties as a finder would be (1) to try to find the true owner, (2) to use at least slight care in protecting and keeping the watch safely, and (3) to return it to the true owner if he can be found and identified.

What must the finder of a lost article do?

Rights of the Finder Your rights are a little greater than those of an ordinary bailee. As stated by a judge a long time ago, "The rights of the finder are good against the whole world, except the true owner." In other words, you can use the watch as your own until the true owner is found.

What are the finder's rights if the true owner cannot be found?

The finder of lost property is entitled to any reward offered if he has not surrendered possession of the property prior to the time that he learns of the reward. Thus, if after returning a lost article, the finder learns that a reward had been offered for its return, he may not legally enforce the payment of the reward. He returned the article without expectation of reward. On the other hand, if the finder of lost property learns of the offer of a reward before he has returned the property to its owner, he is entitled to the reward. If a reward has not been offered, he is entitled to be reimbursed for any expenses that he may have incurred in connection with the possession of the property.

If, after returning a lost article, the finder learns that a reward has been offered for its return, is he legally entitled to the reward?

TORTIOUS BAILEES

If you knew who was the owner of the watch and refused to return it to him, you would be considered a *tortious bailee*. One who wrongfully retains possession of the lost property of another or is in possession of stolen property or uses a bailed article for a purpose other than agreed upon or refuses to return property at the termination of the bailment may be considered a tortious bailee.

Who may be considered a tortious bailee?

TORTIOUS BAILEE

EXAMPLE 12 Fisher found a wallet belonging to Chasan and intentionally and knowingly refused either to return the wallet or to contact Chasan about the matter. Fisher placed himself in a vulnerable position from his failure to return Chasan's property and would be fully responsible for the wallet and contents, regardless of the circumstances under which Fisher himself might either lose it or destroy it. Such failure to act would also make him criminally liable on a complaint made to the police.

Tortious bailees are fully and unconditionally responsible for any and all damage that results to property in their possession, regardless of the degree of care that they might exercise or the cause of the damage.

SUGGESTIONS FOR MINIMIZING LEGAL RISKS

1. When a friend lends you his property without charge, use the property with great care and only within the terms of the agreement.
2. If a friend agrees to store your goods free of charge, make sure that the goods are in proper condition for storage. You cannot expect the friend to give the goods anything more than slight care. If you do not adequately prepare the goods for storage, you cannot expect your friend to do it for you.
3. If you lend goods to a friend, be sure to warn him of any inherent dangers involved in the use of the goods. If the goods are not in first-class condition, be doubly careful to warn him of the defects.
4. If you find a lost article, use all reasonable means to find the true owner. Investigate any special statutes or ordinances that might impose special duties on you. Some statutes impose a penalty on the finder if he does not conform to statutory requirements.

 ## APPLYING YOUR LEARNING

QUESTIONS AND PROBLEMS

1. How does a gratuitous bailment differ from a mutual benefit bailment?
2. If a friend lends you an article, must you use greater or less care in its use than if you paid him a rental charge?
3. If you lend to a neighbor an article that is potentially dangerous to use, must you warn him of the danger?
4. Must the article you lend always be in perfect condition before you lend it to someone?
5. If you agree to store goods for a friend free of charge, are you obliged to give the goods any care? If so, how much?
6. What is an involuntary bailment? Give an example.

7. What are the rights of a finder of a lost article?
8. May a finder hold an article if it is claimed by the true owner? Explain.
9. If you find a lost article, what should you do with it?
10. What is the general degree of care required of a gratuitous bailee?
11. What is a tortious bailee?

WHAT IS YOUR OPINION?

In each of the following cases, give your decision and state a legal principle that applies to the case.

1. Gorman lent his automobile to Cutler, giving him permission to drive to a neighboring town. On the trip the car was damaged in an accident through no fault of Cutler's. Must Cutler pay for the repairs?
2. Suppose that Cutler drove 5 miles beyond the specified town and had an accident that again was not his fault. Would he in this case have to pay Gorman for the damage?
3. Dale borrowed a ladder from Conrad. When Conrad gave Dale the ladder, Conrad told Dale that it was old and that some of the rungs might be rotten. Dale assured him that he would use it with care. The ladder broke while in use and Dale was seriously injured. Could he sue Conrad because the ladder was unsafe?
4. Chase offered to store Burg's television set in his living room free of charge. In return, Burg told Chase to use the set any time he wished. Would this be a gratuitous bailment or one of mutual benefit?
5. If the television set in Case 4 burned out a tube while in use, would Chase have to replace it?
6. If Chase used the set without permission, would he have to replace the tube?
7. Carlson found a dog and, after making a reasonable effort to locate its owner, sold the animal to Linder. About six months after Linder had purchased the dog, O'Rourke, the true owner, saw the dog and demanded that Linder return it to him. Would Linder have to give the dog to O'Rourke?
8. Wardell asked Spencer, the proprietor of a lunchroom, for permission to leave a package that he was carrying behind the counter until he returned from a visit to a neighboring store. Spencer consented. When Wardell returned, the package was missing. Was Spencer liable for the loss?
9. Brandow found a watch on the sidewalk and took it to Brooks for repair. Brooks repaired the watch, but refused to give it back to Brandow because he knew that Brandow had found it. Could Brandow bring an action against Brooks?
10. On the day after Halloween, Baker found a chair on his front porch that had been placed there by pranksters. Was Baker a bailee? What duties does he owe to the owner of the chair?

THE LAW IN ACTION

1. The plaintiff handed the defendant a pair of valuable diamond earrings in the crowded lobby of a theater. The defendant had agreed to inspect, examine, and appraise them as a friendly act and without reward. The defendant was jostled by a third person and dropped one of the earrings. The earring was never found. What degree of care was owed by the defendant in this case? (Rubin v. Huhn, 229 Mass. 126, 118 N.E. 290)

2. At the defendant's store the plaintiff made some purchases that he was to pick up at the loading dock. While loading the goods in his car, he set his briefcase containing $589.71 down on the loading dock and forgot it. The briefcase was picked up by the defendant's employee and taken inside. The next day the briefcase was returned to the plaintiff, but the money was gone. The plaintiff contends that the defendant is liable because, as a bailee, he should have locked the briefcase in a safe place. Would this be a mutual benefit bailment? Do you think the defendant used the proper degree of care under the circumstances? (Mickey v. Sears, Roebuck & Co., 196 Md. 326, 76 A2d 350)

KEY TO "WHAT'S THE LAW?" Page 274

1. *No. In a gratuitous bailment for the benefit of the bailee, the bailee must exercise a very high degree of care in protecting the bailed goods from harm. In this case, the bailee had been warned that the blade was weak, but he did not abide by that warning.*

2. *No. This was a gratuitous bailment for the benefit of the bailor. Bill, as bailee, owed a duty of only slight care.*

A DIGEST OF LEGAL CONCEPTS

1. A bailment exists any time personal property is in the possession of someone who is not the true owner.

2. Most bailments that arise in business transactions result from a contractual agreement between the bailor and the bailee.

3. Most bailments that arise in an ordinary personal relationship result from an agreement that may or may not be a contract.

4. For a bailment agreement to be considered a contract, there must be sufficient consideration to support a contract.

5. There may be times when an involuntary bailment exists in which there is no agreement at all.

6. In a sale title passes; but in a bailment, only possession passes to the bailee and the title remains in the bailor.

7. In an ordinary conditional sale, title is retained by the seller for security purposes until the goods are paid for. For all other purposes, however, title passes to the conditional buyer. Thus the transaction is not a bailment.

8. In a mutual benefit bailment, both the bailor and the bailee give and receive some benefit.

9. The bailor who pays for services on his goods has a right (a) to expect reasonable skill in their repair, (b) to expect ordinary care of the goods, and (c) to receive the goods when he calls for them and tenders payment.

10. The bailor who purchases service on his goods has a duty (a) to pay for the services, (b) to warn the bailee of any inherent dangers in the goods, and (c) to pick up his goods when the job is done.

11. The bailee who receives pay for labor done on goods has a right (a) to collect for his services, (b) to be warned of any dangers involved in handling the goods, (c) to have the goods picked up when the work is done, and (d) to hold the goods on a mechanic's lien until he has been paid if the original agreement implied a cash transaction.

12. The bailee who receives pay for labor done on goods owes a duty (a) to use the skill he represents himself to have, (b) to protect the goods by the use of ordinary care, and (c) to redeliver the goods to the bailor on demand when called for.

13. A bailor who pays for storage of his goods has a right (a) to expect that his goods will be protected by the use of ordinary care and (b) to have his goods returned to him at the end of the storage period or at any other suitable time.

14. A bailor who buys storage of his goods owes a duty (a) to pay the storage costs, (b) to give notice to the bailee of any special care involved in handling, and (c) to pick up his goods at the end of the storage period.

15. A bailee who receives pay for the storage of goods has a right (a) to his storage charges, (b) to notice of any special care or handling, and (c) to have the goods picked up at the end of the storage period.

16. A bailee who receives pay for the storage of goods owes a duty (a) to store the goods in accordance with the terms of the contract, (b) to use ordinary care in the protection of the goods, and (c) to redeliver them to the bailor when he tenders the storage costs and demands them.

17. When a bailor rents the use of his goods to another he has the right (a) to collect the rental charges, (b) to have the goods used with ordinary care, and (c) to have the goods returned to him at the end of the period.

18. A bailor who rents the use of his goods to another owes a duty (a) to furnish reasonably safe goods and (b) to warn the bailee of any dangers involved in the use of the goods.

19. The bailee who hires the use of another's goods has the right (a) to expect reasonably safe goods, (b) to be warned of any dangers involved in their use, and (c) to use the goods according to the terms of the agreement.

20. A bailee who hires the use of another's goods owes a duty (a) to pay for their use, (b) to use ordinary care in using the goods, (c) to use them only according to the terms of the agreement, and (d) to return them at the end of the period.

21. If a bailee violates the terms of his agreement in the use of the bailed goods, he becomes an insurer for any loss or injury to the goods.

22. A bailor who bails goods as a pledge for a loan has a right to the return of the same goods on the repayment of the loan with interest.

PART 11: Buying Services

WHAT'S THE LAW?

1. *Nancy Baran wishes to ship an organ from Boston to Baltimore. Nancy's friend has a pickup truck and offers to haul the organ at a fair cost. Nancy could also ship the organ by rail or motor freight. What are some things she should consider?*

---

2. *In addition to shipping her organ by rail, Nancy also purchased a ticket and traveled to Baltimore by mainliner train. If Nancy chooses to ship her organ by rail, does the railroad have a greater responsibility for Nancy or for her organ?*

▲ UNIT 31: REGULATION OF COMMON CARRIERS

Statistics show that nearly one-fourth of the national income is spent on the transportation of persons and commodities. This is by no means a wasted expense. Raw materials are valuable only when they are moved to the point of processing; finished goods, only when they are moved to the place of consumption. Also, the need of a person to be at a certain place at a given time frequently outweighs the cost of getting there.

COMMON AND PRIVATE CARRIERS

A person or a company that undertakes to transport either persons or goods or both for a consideration is called a *carrier*. Carriers are of two kinds—common and private.

CARRIER

COMMON CARRIERS

What is a common carrier?

A *common carrier* is a company or a person who undertakes to carry persons or goods for hire. A common carrier is a bailee because he is in temporary possession of goods belonging to others. He is, however, a special type of bailee. A common carrier is different from other bailees in the following respects: (1) he is not free to choose his customers, and he must treat everybody alike; (2) he is, for all practical purposes, an insurer of the goods in his care; (3) he is subject to specific government regulations. Examples of common carriers are railways, express companies, steamship lines, airlines, and public trucking companies.

COMMON CARRIER

Name several examples of common carriers.

MOVING, HAULING AND JUNK COLLECTED

Contract haulers are not common carriers.

PRIVATE CARRIERS

What type of bailment is created when a private carrier accepts goods for shipment? What are its duties as a bailee?

A *private carrier*, sometimes referred to as a contract carrier, hauls goods for others under special arrangements. He does not purport to serve the public in general and is free to accept or reject any offers of transportation that are made to him. A private carrier is governed by the rules that we have already learned in our study of the bailee. The acceptance of merchandise by him creates a bailment for mutual benefit. He is required to exercise ordinary care, as in all other mutual benefit bailments.

PRIVATE CARRIER

EXAMPLE 1 Your neighbor has a truck. You employ him to transport a piano for you. In this transaction he is a private carrier and is governed by the rules of ordinary care. He may also do similar jobs for others, but this does not make him a common carrier as long as he leaves himself free to accept or reject any offers of transportation submitted to him.

REGULATION OF CARRIERS

All business concerns are more or less regulated by the general rules of law. Common carriers, however, are regulated by special laws.

INTERSTATE COMMERCE COMMISSION

What government agency regulates common carriers engaged in interstate commerce?

If a carrier operates in more than one state, the rates, the quality of service, employee relationships, and other matters are governed by the *Interstate Commerce Commission*, often referred to as the ICC.

Rate and schedule changes, whether for passenger or freight service, must have ICC approval. If the schedules filed by the carriers are not followed, the carrier may be called before the ICC for a hearing on a complaint, resulting either in a penalty or in a dismissal of the charge.

INTERSTATE COMMERCE COMMISSION

EXAMPLE 2 Ray Shore found that the passenger train he desired to travel on was removed from the train schedule. When Shore complained to the station agent about the removal, the agent called his attention to a change-of-service notice indicating the suspension of service granted by the ICC which was posted on the bulletin board. Shore had to comply with the ruling of the ICC.

The ICC also has jurisdiction over trucks operating as common carriers between states. The drivers of such equipment must carry logbooks in their truck cabs showing the number of hours they have been driving, points of departure and destination, trips made, and other information pertaining to operation and safety of heavy truck movement.

STATE COMMISSIONS

How are common carriers engaged in intrastate commerce regulated?

Almost all states have set up commissions that are responsible for the regulation of intrastate common carriers. Bus companies, short-line railroads, other public carriers, pipelines, and toll bridges come within their jurisdiction. Rulings of the state commissions, such as the Intrastate Commerce Commission and the Public Service Commission, as well as those of the ICC may be appealed to the courts if they do not satisfy the complainants or the carriers.

EXAMPLE 3 The Blue Star Bus Line carried employees of Machines, Inc., to the plant. Regular schedules were followed under a franchise granted the bus company by the state. Without the approval of the state commission, Blue Star reduced the number of trips by half. The employees at Machines, Inc., would have the right to petition the state commission for redress or even to appeal to the courts if the decision were not in their favor.

SHIPPING GOODS BY COMMON CARRIER

A common carrier is compelled to render universal and impartial service. His liability for universal service is limited, of course, by the type of transportation that he professes to offer and by the capacity of his equipment. Furthermore, he is not compelled to transport goods without receiving the full scheduled compensation. In fact, he is entitled to receive payment in advance. In practice, he does not always insist on this right.

Treating everybody alike means that he must charge the same rate to all persons and render them the same services under the same circumstances. He cannot charge a good customer a low rate and a poor customer a higher rate for the same transaction.

EXAMPLE 4 A public trucking company, operating between Minneapolis and Kansas City, charged a rate of $1.50 per 100 pounds on a certain type of merchandise shipped in lots of 1,000 pounds or over. The trucking company offered to give a 10 percent refund to an exceptionally heavy shipper. This was a violation of ICC rules that preferential rates are illegal.

LIABILITY FOR GOODS

A common carrier has far greater responsibility than an ordinary bailee for the property entrusted to his care. His liability may well be designated as that of an insurer of all goods accepted for shipment. The common carrier, however, is relieved of responsibility if the goods are damaged or destroyed by any of the following causes:

ACT OF GOD   An *act of God* is a circumstance beyond human control, such as a flood, tornado, or earthquake.

ACT OF GOD

EXAMPLE 5 A certain truck line was operating between cities about 300 miles apart. Bailey shipped some perishable goods that could have reached their destination in good condition if the truck had arrived at the scheduled time. Because of a serious flood, the truck was delayed three days; and the goods were spoiled. The trucking company could not be held liable, as the flood was classed as an act of God.

PUBLIC ENEMY   The term *public enemy* includes only the military forces of a country at war with us.

PUBLIC ENEMY

PUBLIC AUTHORITY   *Public authority* refers to the legal process of taking goods. The seizure of goods by an inspector or a legal agency owing to illegality, unsanitary conditions, or similar justifiable reasons exempt a carrier from any liability for failure to deliver the goods shipped.

PUBLIC AUTHORITY

EXAMPLE 6 Included in a shipment received at Los Angeles were four crates labeled "Machinery," consigned to a firm in Lima, Ohio. Detectives searched the car carrying these crates and, upon opening the cases, discovered that they contained illegal slot machines. The machines were confiscated by the police. The Eastern Railroad is exempt from liability for the confiscated property and cannot be held responsible for the value of the machines by either the shipper or the consignee.

FAULT OF THE SHIPPER   Mistakes in addressing and labeling and improper packing or misrepresentation of the nature of the goods are among conditions considered to be the fault of the shipper.

EXAMPLE 7 In the hope of saving on freight charges, Ben Brooks packed some strawberries in crates and labeled them "Potatoes." The berries spoiled. He could not collect damages because the spoilage was due to his own misrepresentation.

INHERENT LIMITATION OF GOODS   An example of an inherent limitation of the goods is unavoidable spoilage of perishable goods.

In all other cases besides these five, the common carrier is liable as an insurer. A common carrier is not excused from liability for losses due to strikes, mob violence, fire, and similar causes. He may also limit his liability by special contract; but, even if he makes such a contract, he is not excused from loss resulting from his own negligence.

Valuation   A common carrier's liability is limited to any valuation placed on the goods by the shipper. The rate charged by the carrier is to a large extent determined by the valuation on the article. Because of this rule, there is a temptation on the part of the shipper to place a low valuation on the goods in order to obtain a lower rate.

Under what conditions may a common carrier be relieved of liability?

What determines the valuation placed on goods for which the carrier will be liable?

EXAMPLE 8 Martin Chipp shipped a $500 musical instrument by express. In order to save charges, he placed a valuation of only $200 on the shipment. The instrument was lost in transit, and he collected only $200. The fact that the instrument was worth $500 was irrelevant, since he could not collect more than the declared value.

Bills of Lading—Straight and Order   When a person ships goods by a common carrier, he receives a paper that is known as a *bill of lading*. A bill of lading is a combination contract and receipt. It is a receipt because it describes the goods that are shipped and acknowledges that the goods

A common carrier has full control of the goods being transported and therefore is liable as an insurer for the safe delivery of the goods.

Why is it correct to say a bill of lading is a combination contract and receipt?

have been received by the carrier. It is a contract because it sets forth the terms of the shipment.

A bill of lading is issued by a person engaged in the business of transporting or forwarding goods.

A bill of lading is made out in triplicate. The shipper receives two copies, one for himself and the "original", or top, copy to send to the person to whom the goods are shipped. This person is called the *consignee*. The consignee must present the original copy of the bill of lading to the freight agent at the point of destination. This copy serves as notice to the carrier that the holder is entitled to receive the goods. The third copy is kept by the transportation company.

CONSIGNEE

How many copies of a bill of lading are made? What disposition is made of them?

If a shipment is sent *prepaid*, the shipper has paid the transportation charges. If the shipment is *collect*, the consignee must pay the transportation charges. Note that the terms "prepaid" and "collect" do not refer to any agreement covering the purchase price of goods between the seller and buyer; they merely refer to the agreement as to who will pay the transportation charges.

PREPAID
COLLECT

How are c.o.d. shipments handled?

"Collect on delivery" is abbreviated *c.o.d.* The feature of all such shipments is that the shipper can collect the money for his goods (and possibly for transportation) before they are turned over to the buyer. Payment may be made through the U.S. Postal Service or by express.

C.O.D.

Shipments via the post office or express companies are simplified since these agencies make c.o.d. collections for the shipper. Shipments by the ordinary freight companies are slightly more complicated because these concerns refuse to serve as collectors. In actual practice, c.o.d. shipments are often made on an *order bill of lading*, also called a sight draft bill of lading because a negotiable instrument, called a *sight draft*, is attached to it. The shipper can wait for the consignee to send his payment, or he can send the order bill of lading to a bank in the consignee's town. The bank will collect on the sight draft for the shipper and turn over the bill of lading to the consignee.

ORDER BILL OF LADING
SIGHT DRAFT

What type of bill of lading is negotiable?

EXAMPLE 9 **Dan Polanski of Benton, Illinois, wishes to ship goods valued at $125 to William Hayes in Williamsburg, Virginia. From the railway company,**

Polanski receives an order bill of lading. Polanski makes out a sight draft for $125, payable to himself and drawn on Hayes. The draft is attached to the bill of lading, and both are sent to a designated bank at Williamsburg. Before Hayes can obtain the bill of lading, he must pay the bank. The bank will then remit to Polanski.

An order bill of lading is made out to "the order" of the consignee and can be endorsed and passed on to others. A transfer of an order bill of lading transfers title to the goods described therein.

A *straight bill of lading* is not negotiable. The consignee may transfer his rights to another, but the transferee would be like the assignee in a contract, having no better title than either shipper or consignee has. U.C.C. Sec. 7-301(1)

STRAIGHT BILL OF LADING

EXAMPLE 10   Colonial Appliance Company delivered a bill of lading, describing ten cases of radio parts, to the agent of Eastern Railroad. The agent did not check to see if the Colonial Appliance Company's agent had deposited the cases on the freight platform, which he had not actually done. The carrier's agent signed the bill of lading and returned the shipper's copies to Colonial's agent. Should the bill be negotiated and transferred to a third party for value, the railroad would be responsible to the transferee for any loss resulting from its negligence or that of its agent.

Often an innocent party relies upon a bill of lading signed by an agent of the common carrier even though he has not actually received the goods described. If the carrier or his agent misdates a bill or issues a bill of lading for goods without having actually received them, he is held liable to one who has accepted the bill in good faith. U.C.C. Sec. 7-301

The ICC and some state commissions have approved certain limitations on liability that were sought by carriers and have included them in the printed bill of lading. Provision is also made on a bill of lading for other limitations which the carrier and the shipper may agree upon. U.C.C. Sec. 7-309(2)

Although permitted to limit its liability, the carrier is prohibited from absolving itself from liability for damage resulting from negligence. The carrier must exercise as much care in relation to the goods as a reasonably careful man would exercise under like circumstances. U.C.C. Sec. 7-309(1)

TERMINATION OF LIABILITY

When does the common carrier's liability end?

The common carrier's liability ends when the goods reach their destination and the consignee has had reasonable time to take them away.

In order fully to protect your rights, you should call for goods shipped to you as soon as you conveniently can after they have arrived at your local freight depot or express office. As a matter of fact, this whole question has lost much of its former importance because shipments of less than a carload are now usually delivered to your door by the carrier.

What are the rights of a common carrier?

Rights of a Common Carrier   A common carrier has two rights: (1) the payment of fees agreed upon for shipment and (2) the right of lien on all goods shipped for the amount of the shipping charges. This latter right terminates when payment is received by the carrier.

A carrier has a lien on the goods covered by a bill of lading for charges subsequent to the date of its receipt of the goods for storage or transportation, including demurrage and terminal charges. U.C.C. Sec. 7-307(1)

If the consignee does not call for the shipment within a reasonable time (usually forty-eight hours), the carrier may charge an additional fee, known as a *demurrage charge,* for storage.

DEMURRAGE
CHARGE

PUBLIC CARRIERS OF PASSENGERS

A common carrier that engages in transporting passengers is often called a *public carrier* in order to distinguish it from carriers of goods. Public carriers include all transporters of passengers, either persons or companies, who purport to serve the public in general. Examples are railroad companies; streetcar companies; and operators of buses, taxicabs, steamboats, ships, ferries, and airplanes. The same general rules apply to all these carriers, but their application may vary somewhat with the different circumstances involved.

PUBLIC
CARRIER

What are public
carriers? Name
several types of
public carriers.

EXAMPLE 11   John Swango and Bert Lampert were licensed cab drivers in a small town. Their licenses indicated that they were to meet all arriving trains at the station. One train arrived at 2:30 a.m., two hours after the previous train. Swango and Lampert would frequently fail to meet the 2:30 a.m. train. When questioned about the matter, the two drivers defended themselves on the ground that few passengers ever arrived on the 2:30 a.m. train. This was held as not a valid excuse.

A person may be ejected from a train or other conveyance for any reason that would have prevented the carrier from accepting the person as a passenger in the first place.

Perhaps the most common reason for ejecting a passenger is failure to pay the fare. The carrier is not compelled to carry a passenger without compensation. If the fare is not paid for a person requiring the assistance of a companion, both he and the companion may be ejected, even if the latter has paid the fare.

EXAMPLE 12   Mrs. Powell bought a ticket for herself but failed to get a ticket for her eight-year-old daughter, Ethel. She refused to pay her daughter's fare, maintaining that she had paid for her own ride and that it would be dangerous to eject poor innocent Ethel in a strange place alone. The conductor solved the problem by ejecting them both.

Any person may be ejected if he is a serious nuisance or danger to the other passengers or threatens the interests of the carrier. The carrier must exercise considerable caution in enforcing this rule because ejecting a passenger without sufficient cause is a serious offense.

If a passenger is to be ejected, it must be done as gently as possible, and the conveyance must come to a complete stop. The passenger must be put off at a place where he will not suffer danger or serious privation.

EXAMPLE 13   Howard LeRoy, while in a railway coach, started a disturbance that was displeasing to all and possibly dangerous to some. As the coach passed through a small town, the train slowed to about 5 miles an hour and LeRoy was ejected. He suffered an injury and collected damages from the railroad company. It was held that the train should have come to a full stop before LeRoy was ejected.

A common carrier has an obligation to accept all persons who may seek passage. There are, however, some exceptions. Common carriers may refuse passengers (1) when all available space is occupied or reserved, and (2) if they are disorderly, intoxicated, insane, or infected with a contagious disease.

EXAMPLE 14   One man attempting to board the train was intoxicated. He used loud and abusive language to the conductor, who refused to let him get on. The man's condition was a threat to the other passengers. The conductor acted within his rights.

PASSENGER

A person is, of course, a *passenger* as long as he is on board the train or other conveyance. A person, however, does not begin to be a passenger merely when he boards the conveyance, nor does he cease to be a passenger merely because the conveyance has reached its destination. He is, for legal purposes, a passenger when he arrives at the station a reasonable time before the scheduled departure of the train if he has the intention of becoming a passenger. It is not essential that he has bought a ticket. Similarly, on reaching his destination, he continues to be a passenger until he has been allowed a reasonable time within which to leave the station.

When is a person considered a passenger by a carrier?

A person who escorts someone to a train or who is at the station to meet someone is under the protection of the carrier in somewhat the same manner as a passenger. Such protection, however, is not afforded people who come to the station to loiter or merely to satisfy their curiosity.

EXAMPLE 15   For about forty years Edgar Hancock, who lives in a small town, has gone to the railway station almost every evening just to see a certain train come in. One evening, while there, he was injured through nobody's fault. Hancock did not, in any sense, have the status of a passenger and, therefore, was unable to collect damages from the railway company.

Under what circumstances may a public carrier be relieved of liability for injuries to passengers?

A public carrier has a very high responsibility for the safety of his passengers. There are strict and specific requirements regarding the means to be employed for safeguarding them. The carrier is responsible for any damage or injury caused by failure to provide proper safeguards or for harm arising from the negligence or torts of employees. A public carrier has no responsibility for accidents caused by forces beyond his control, such as an act of God, legal intervention, or a public enemy.

EXAMPLE 16   John Sutter tried to impress his friends by riding on top of the boxcar of a train. Sutter lost his balance and was badly injured when he fell. He could not collect damages because the accident was due entirely to his own improper actions.

A public carrier is not liable if a passenger is harmed chiefly because of his own negligence or if the harm results from a violation of the carrier's reasonable rules.

Common carriers are responsible for injuries caused passengers through carelessness of their employees.

EXAMPLE 17 Elmer Ward was well acquainted with Karl Joslin, the engineer of a train. While a passenger on the train and in spite of Joslin's vigorous protests, Ward insisted on riding in the cab with Joslin. While so riding, Ward was badly injured. He had no claim because he had violated the company's regulations.

PASSENGERS' BAGGAGE

If a passenger checks baggage with the carrier or if he otherwise leaves the baggage entirely within the carrier's control, the carrier becomes liable in the same manner as any carrier of goods. Technically and legally, *baggage* includes only such articles as the passenger intends for his own personal use. The fact that no extra compensation is given when baggage is checked is immaterial, although it is required that the checker must be a passenger. If the passenger carries his own belongings into the train, he himself has the main responsibility. Even in this case, the company may be held liable for failure to exercise reasonable care. **BAGGAGE**

If a person uses his trip on a public carrier as an excuse for gratuitous conveyance of "miscellaneous freight," the carrier is relieved of responsibility for such goods.

EXAMPLE 18 Gilbert Dwyer was making a hurried trip to a nearby city and back. He filled a trunk with nuts to be sold in the market and took it with him as baggage. The trunk and contents were badly damaged. Dwyer failed to collect from the railway company, as this constituted fraudulent transportation of freight.

May a public carrier limit his liability for loss of baggage?

The *Carmack Amendment* to the Interstate Commerce Act expressly permits the public carrier to limit his liability in connection with baggage carried in interstate commerce. U.C.C. Sec. 7-309 **CARMACK AMENDMENT**

EXAMPLE 19 Williams checked his sample cases and a large suitcase with the baggage agent. He kept with him a small traveling case containing things he might need while on the train. The Eastern Railroad would have to exercise ordinary care with this traveling case, but it would be an insurer for the things that had been left with the baggage agent.

OBLIGATIONS TO PASSENGERS

If a carrier claims that he furnishes special comforts, he must live up to his claims. This refers particularly to common conveniences and special accommodations, such as meal service. The carrier must either provide opportunities for refreshments on board the conveyance or must make proper stops to make the periodic procurement of nourishment possible.

The carrier must have a certain schedule and must follow this with reasonable accuracy. He must never leave a station ahead of time, and he must use great efforts to reach each station on schedule. The carrier must give the passenger ample time to get on and off the conveyance, and he must use great diligence in directing the passenger to get off at the proper destination indicated by his ticket.

What obligations has the public carrier to its passengers?

EXAMPLE 20   Bruce Foster boarded a train at 7 a.m. He reached his destination at 10 a.m. but did not get off the train because he had fallen asleep. The trainmen excused themselves by saying that all stations had been announced distinctly and that they did not expect any passenger to be sleeping at that time. It was held that this was not a valid excuse, that the conductor was negligent in the performance of his duties, and that Foster should be reimbursed for any losses he suffered.

SUGGESTIONS FOR MINIMIZING LEGAL RISKS

1. When you ship goods by freight, always obtain a bill of lading and keep it in a safe place. It is your receipt for the goods shipped and may be needed as evidence that the carrier received the goods.
2. When shipping goods, always pack them carefully. If they are fragile or perishable in nature, give proper notice to the carrier of the need for special handling.
3. If you pay shipping charges in advance, always get a proper receipt for your money and file it in a safe place. You may have to prove that charges were paid in case of a dispute later.
4. If you are notified of the arrival of a shipment of goods, pick the goods up at once. This will not only save you extra charges but will also protect you against possible loss, as the carrier remains an insurer for only a reasonable time after you receive notice.
5. If you are a passenger on a public carrier, be sure to comply strictly with all the safety rules of the carrier.
6. If you wish to make the carrier an insurer of your baggage, you should check your baggage rather than carry it with you.

▲ APPLYING YOUR LEARNING

QUESTIONS AND PROBLEMS

1. How is a common carrier different from an ordinary bailee?
2. How important is transportation in our national economic development and progress?
3. What are some of the different ways in which goods may be shipped?
4. How is a common carrier different from a private carrier?
5. Why do common carriers need special regulation? Who regulates them?
6. What are some of the special obligations of a common carrier?
7. What is the liability of a common carrier for goods received for shipment?
8. At what point does the common carrier's liability begin? At what point does it end?
9. How is an order bill of lading different from a straight bill of lading?
10. Does the carrier have a greater liability when he is carrying goods or when he is carrying passengers?
11. When may a passenger be ejected from a train or other conveyance?
12. What is the liability of the carrier for the safety of its passengers?
13. What is the liability of the carrier for the passengers' baggage?
14. Does it make any difference whether the baggage is checked or carried by the passenger?
15. What are the exceptions to the common carrier's obligation to accept all goods offered for shipment?
16. What are the exceptions to the common carrier's duty to accept all persons as passengers?
17. What is the law in cases where a carrier issues a bill of lading for goods not received by the carrier or its agent?

WHAT IS YOUR OPINION?

In each of the following cases, give your decision and state a legal principle that applies to the case.

1. Perry Durfee, on short notice, demanded that the railroad furnish him with stock cars in which to ship his cattle to market. The carrier was unable to furnish the cars at the time specified because of the heavy demand for stock cars at that time of year. Is the carrier liable for any loss caused by the delay?
2. Don Fowler requested a carrier to ship a piano for him. The carrier refused because the piano was not properly boxed or properly protected for shipment. Was this a proper action on the part of the carrier?
3. Alton Davis shipped perishable goods by freight but did not give the carrier notice of the perishable nature of the goods. Will the carrier be liable if the goods spoil because of delay in delivery?
4. Claude Lane shipped goods by freight and stated their value was under $100 in order to get a lower rate. The goods were destroyed in shipment

and Lane now claims that their value was $500. How much can he collect?

5. Clint Kaiser enters a railroad station in a very intoxicated condition. He demands the right to buy a ticket and board the train. Must the carrier accept him as a passenger?

6. John Cavanaugh deposited goods for shipment at a railroad freight house on Wednesday and asked for immediate shipment. The goods were not shipped at once and were still in the freight house when it was destroyed by fire on the following Monday. Is the railroad liable for the loss?

7. Walter Irish was given the opportunity to check his baggage on his ticket and have it carried in the baggage car on his train. He refused to do so and carried his baggage with him. Was the carrier an insurer of Irish's baggage?

8. A shipment of grain was lost when the lake steamer on which it was shipped collided with another boat and sank. Would the carrier's claim that the loss was caused by an act of God excuse him from liability?

9. Merchandise shipped by Alan Roth was destroyed in a train wreck. The railroad company was not negligent. Can Roth collect from the carrier for damages?

THE LAW IN ACTION

1. The plaintiff tried to get off a railroad train, carrying a bag in her right hand and her purse and knitting bag under her left arm. She held on to the rail with her left hand but misjudged the final step, which was 17 inches high, and fell. She brought an action against the railroad company for injuries. Was she entitled to damages? (Ellis v. Southern Pacific Co., 50 N.M. 76, 169 P.2d 551)

2. The plaintiff entered into a contract with the defendant for transporting theatrical properties. This special agreement provided that the railroad would not be liable for any loss, even though caused by the railroad's negligence. The goods were damaged, and the plaintiff contends that the special contract would not prevent him from recovering damages. What do you think? (McKeon v. N.Y., N.H. & H.R.R. Co., 177 App. Div. 462, 164 N.Y.S., 312, Sup. Ct.)

KEY TO "WHAT'S THE LAW?" Page 285

1. *Rail and motor companies are common carriers. The friend is a private carrier. The responsibility and liability of each type of carrier should be considered.*

2. *The railroad has a greater responsibility for the organ. It is absolutely liable for any damage to the organ, but is only liable for personal injury arising from a failure to use a high degree of care.*

1. *James Monroe rented a room by the month at the Pompey Hotel. His friend George Dean, who was in the city for an overnight stay, rented the room next to James's. Do James and George have the same relationship with the hotel in the eyes of the law?*

2. *In Question 1, would the hotel have a lien on James Monroe's baggage if he did not pay his monthly room rent? Would the hotel have a lien on George Dean's baggage if he did not pay for the one night's room charge?*

⧉ UNIT 32: RESPONSIBILITIES OF HOTELKEEPERS

In our modern age, hotels and motels are indispensable. If it were not for hotels and motels, a traveler would have to search until he could find someone who was willing to provide him with a lodging place. If there is a hotel or motel in town (and there usually is), the traveler usually goes right to it, knowing full well that he will be received. In fact, as we shall see later, the hotel or motel cannot refuse him except for excellent reasons.

HOTELKEEPERS AND THEIR GUESTS

Who is a motelkeeper or hotelkeeper?

A *hotelkeeper* or *motelkeeper* is an individual, partnership, or corporation that will lodge all respectable transients who will pay the usual price.

MOTELKEEPER
HOTELKEEPER

EXAMPLE 1 Robert Ashley, who lives on a transcontinental highway, occasionally takes in people who apply for lodging. He is not classed as a hotelkeeper because he does not profess to serve the public in general.

What is a transient? When does a transient become a guest?

A *transient* is one whose stay is more or less uncertain in duration; he seeks temporary lodging, and is called a *guest*. "Temporary" does not mean necessarily a short time. The essence of the relationship of hotelkeeper and guest is that the person who is staying at the hotel retains his character as a transient. He may stay a long time; but it is understood that he may leave at any time. He is considered a guest as soon as he enters the hotel premises, and the same duty of care is owed to him then as though he had registered and had been assigned a room.

TRANSIENT
GUEST

EXAMPLE 2 Harry Sherman, a traveling salesman, rented a single room by the day at a particular hotel. Since he never knew when his company would send him away, he made no permanent arrangements with the hotel. His business commitments caused him to remain at the hotel for seven months. During the seven-month period, Sherman was classified as a transient because he was renting his room on a daily basis.

EXAMPLE 3 Rod Hill was able to secure a comfortable room at the Mainliner Motel. After three days' residence, he decided that the Mainliner was ideally located for his business. Accordingly, he made arrangements to rent the room for six months at a special discount rate. While Hill was originally a transient guest, the new arrangement changed his status to that of a roomer, or lodger.

A *roomer* is any person staying at a hotel, motel, or rooming house for a definite period of time. Thus, the arrangement between a rooming-house keeper and a roomer is of a more permanent character than the relationship between a hotel or motel and a guest. For example, a rooming-house keeper may accept or reject persons according to his own judgment, and he may usually make any bargain that he sees fit. Except for certain statutes in some states and provisions of the Civil Rights Bill of 1964, rooming-house agreements are governed only by the general laws applying to contracts and personal behavior. **ROOMER**

What is a business guest? A person not living at a hotel but entering it to enjoy the other facilities offered to the public is a *business guest*. A business guest is one who comes on the premises with the intention of transacting some business with the hotel or its occupants. **BUSINESS GUEST**

EXAMPLE 4 Rod Hill arranged a dinner party for several purchasing agents of firms that traded with his company. While occupying the dining room, the group would be considered business guests. The Mainliner would be obligated to provide safe surroundings for such persons.

DUTIES, LIABILITIES, AND RIGHTS OF HOTELKEEPERS

May a hotelkeeper ever refuse to accept a guest? **Duty to Receive Guests** Since a hotelkeeper, by definition, is one who has undertaken to keep a public lodging place to accommodate all transients, he has by implication promised to take all respectable guests who are able to pay for their lodging if he has room for them. This has been the rule of the law for hundreds of years. It dates back to a time in history when travel was not safe. Robbers and highwaymen abounded, and it was not safe to stay on the road overnight. Thus hotels, or inns, were places of refuge; and to refuse a guest lodging was to leave him at the mercy of those who would rob him. Travel is comparatively safe today, but the genuine need for the convenience of overnight accommodations has caused the rule to remain.

EXAMPLE 5 Freytag sought accommodations at the Mainliner Motel but was refused. The clerk could give no reason for his refusal other than his personal dislike for Freytag's political affiliations. Freytag was a member of a minority political group holding a convention in the town at the time. Freytag could hold the motel liable for any damages he might show had resulted from the motel's failure to accept him as a guest.

A hotel is not obliged to accept a guest who is financially unable to pay for his lodging or who is so disreputable as to injure the hotel's reputation.

What act of Congress makes it a criminal act if a hotelkeeper refuses accommodations to any transient on the grounds of race, creed, or color?

The United States Congress passed the *Civil Rights Bill* in 1964; this makes it a criminal act if a hotelkeeper refuses accommodations to any transient on the grounds of race, creed, or color. Such discrimination in any form is thus barred by federal law, and many state laws that were in conflict with the Civil Rights Bill have been invalidated.

CIVIL RIGHTS ACT

Liability for Invasion of Guest's Privacy A hotelkeeper must guarantee a guest's exclusive right of occupancy and privacy of the room to which he has been assigned. Any unpermitted intrusion upon the guest's privacy by hotel employees or others gives the guest a right of action for *invasion of privacy*.

INVASION OF PRIVACY

EXAMPLE 6 **A few hours after occupying his room, Smith was embarrassed by the appearance of a bellboy and another guest, who entered the room with a passkey. Investigation proved that the room clerk had negligently assigned Smith's room to another guest, who arrived at a later hour. Such entry would be an invasion of privacy, for which Smith could seek damages from the Mainliner Motel.**

Liability for Property of Guest Under the common law, a hotelkeeper was considered an insurer of the property of the guest unless the damage to the goods resulted from an act of God, legal intervention, a public enemy, or the inherent nature of the goods. Acts of God include floods, tornadoes, cyclones, earthquakes, hurricanes, and other unpredictable natural phenomena.

EXAMPLE 7 **A hurricane struck the town in which the Mainliner Motel was located, breaking several windows in the upper floors of the motel. The accompanying rains caused considerable damage to property belonging to Smith and the other guests. Losses were the direct result of an act of God, and the Mainliner Motel will not be obligated to reimburse the guests for the damages claimed.**

How has the common law liability of a hotelkeeper for the safekeeping of the guest's property been changed by statutes in many states?

● **STATUTORY RULE** The common law rule has now been changed by statutes in many states. Most statutes provide that the hotelkeeper must keep a safe place for storing valuables belonging to the guest and must post notices in a conspicuous manner to that effect. If the guest fails to avail himself of this opportunity, the hotelkeeper is relieved of his common-law liability as an insurer. He is not excused, however, for failure to exercise

NOTE: *The bullet indicates that there may be a state statute that varies from the law discussed here.*

A hotel is not usually liable for the loss of valuables left in its rooms if a vault for the safekeeping of such valuables is provided in the hotel office.

reasonable care. If goods are stored with the hotelkeeper, or if the hotelkeeper fails to make proper provisions for safekeeping, his status as an insurer is retained.

EXAMPLE 8   Richard Coburn took a room at the Evergreen Hotel. He had in his possession a valuable diamond ring, which was lost during the night. The hotel proved that there was a good lock on the door and that all reasonable precautions had been made to protect the hotel against thefts. On the basis of these facts, the hotel escaped liability because Coburn should have put his jewelry in the hotel vault for safekeeping.

A reasonable interpretation of the law permits a guest to keep in his room valuables that he would ordinarily have on or about his person, such as watch, cuff links, rings, and a reasonable amount of cash.

Hotelkeepers are held by law to be insurers of the guest's property, which includes all property brought into the hotel for the convenience and purpose of the guest's stay. In the event of a loss, the hotelkeeper may be held liable, regardless of the amount of care exercised in protecting the guest's property.

EXAMPLE 9   Smith's room at the Mainliner Motel was entered by a thief, who stole two suits of clothing and valuable samples used in Smith's business. The motel is responsible for the loss, although it was in no way negligent in its effort to protect Smith's property.

Would a hotelkeeper be liable for damage to a guest's belongings in case of an accidental fire?

An exception is made in case of accidental fire, in which no negligence may be attributed to the hotelkeeper. In such instances the hotelkeeper is not liable as an insurer. This provision includes fires caused by other guests at the hotel at the same time. Such persons, even though on other floors, are called *fellow guests*.

FELLOW GUEST

EXAMPLE 10   A fire broke out on the second floor of the Mainliner Motel. Although the fire was confined to that floor, several guests on the first floor reported losses to their property due to fire and water. The motel was able to prove that the fire had started from a cigarette dropped on a bed by one of the guests. Such careless smoking violated both a city ordinance and a rule of the motel. The motelkeeper was not responsible for the losses caused by the fire.

Liability for Safety and Comfort of Guest   Places recognized as hotels and motels must provide a minimum standard of comfort, safety, and sanitation. Minimum standards include reasonable heat and ventilation, clean beds, reasonably quiet surroundings, and freedom from disturbances by hoodlums, criminals, and persons of immoral character.

Hotelkeepers are required to exercise reasonable care in the protection of their guests. Damages may be sought for injuries resulting from the negligence of the hotelkeeper or his agents.

What is considered "reasonable care" in the protection of guests?

EXAMPLE 11   **A section of carpeting in the hall outside Smith's room had torn loose, and the motel housekeeper had neglected to make the necessary repairs for several days. Smith tripped over the torn carpeting, suffering painful injuries. The Mainliner Motel had been negligent and may be held responsible by Smith for damages resulting from his injury.**

A hotelkeeper is liable to his guests for injuries suffered as a result of his negligence.

Liens on Property of Guest   Hotels may demand payment in advance, but frequently this right is waived in favor of people with luggage. If the guest does not pay his bill, the hotel has a lien on whatever articles the guest has with him, with the exception of clothes worn. The lien entitles the hotel to hold these goods until the guest pays his bill. The hotel, however, loses its lien if it permits the guest to take the property away.

What is a lien on a guest's property? How may a lien be lost?

EXAMPLE 12   **When Smith completed his business and was about to leave the city, he discovered that he did not have sufficient cash to pay his bill at the Mainliner Motel. The motel would not accept his check and took possession of his luggage as security until the bill was paid. After cash had been wired to Smith by his firm, he paid the bill. This terminated the motel's right of lien on his property.**

● Except as otherwise provided in the statutes of a few states, a lien on the property of a roomer is not permitted. Perhaps the reason for this is that a roomer's arrangements are of a more permanent nature than a guest's, and the proprietor takes less risk of a roomer leaving without paying his bill.

NOTE: *The bullet indicates that there may be a state statute that varies from the law discussed here.*

OBLIGATIONS OF GUESTS

What obligations do guests owe the hotel or motel?

Proper Use of Facilities   Under no circumstances may a guest give lodging to a visitor overnight without the express consent of the management. Since a visitor is not paying the hotel for accommodations, his stay may well be considered petty theft.

EXAMPLE 13   **Frank Gillette rented a room at the McCord Hotel. The rental price for the room was $18 for a single room and $22 for a double room. Gillette felt that two persons would not cause any more work in a room than one person and invited his friend to stay with him overnight. Gillette's plan was practically the same as stealing $4 from the McCord Hotel.**

A hotel is within its rights in preventing a person from entering the halls where guest rooms are located, unless he wishes to see someone for a legitimate purpose.

What is meant by checking in at a hotel or motel?

When you wish to get a room at a hotel, you must register at the desk. This *checking in* is necessary for the records of the hotel and also makes it possible to locate you if you are called.

CHECK IN

When you pay your bill to date, have you checked out of the hotel or motel facility?

When you are ready to leave, you must *check out*. This means that you turn in your key and give up further claim to the room. Paying your bill to date does not necessarily mean checking out. Definite checking out is needed in order to settle any dispute as to the time you vacated the room.

CHECK OUT

REMEMBER: You become a guest when you enter a hotel with a definite intention to register. You cease to be a guest when you check out and have had reasonable time within which to leave the premises.

SUGGESTIONS FOR MINIMIZING LEGAL RISKS

1. If you plan to stay overnight in a certain hotel, it is desirable to make reservations in advance, as this will ordinarily insure that you get a room at a reasonable rate.
2. It is desirable to establish credit in advance with a hotel in which you plan to stay. This might save you future embarrassment, inconvenience, and possible expense if you ran out of money and needed to cash a check.
3. Always deposit your valuables in the hotel safe if you wish full protection. Also, lock your luggage when you leave your room. Hotels are often the victims of petty thieves.
4. Be sure to register immediately on arrival at a hotel, and be sure to check out when you leave. Do not forget to turn in your key.
5. Report any loss of valuables or any accidents incurred in the hotel promptly to the hotel management. Keep a written record of the date, time, person to whom the report was made, and all other pertinent information needed to establish a legitimate claim for loss or damages.

▲ APPLYING YOUR LEARNING

QUESTIONS AND PROBLEMS

1. Why are hotels important to our modern way of life?
2. What is the difference between a hotel and a rooming house?
3. What is the difference between a guest and a roomer?
4. Why were inns important to travelers in early common-law days?
5. When, if ever, may a hotelkeeper refuse to accept a guest?
6. What was the liability of the innkeeper for the safekeeping of the guests' property at common law?
7. How may this liability be modified by modern statutes?
8. What is the liability of the hotelkeeper for the safety and comfort of the guest?
9. How does the guest enter into a contract with the hotelkeeper?
10. May the hotelkeeper demand payment for the room in advance?
11. Does the hotelkeeper have a lien on the goods of the guest for the payment of his bill?
12. Does a rooming-house keeper have the same lien as that of a hotelkeeper?
13. Explain invasion of privacy. How does this affect the obligation of a hotelkeeper to his guests?
14. Is a person who enters a hotel dining room considered a hotel guest? What is his legal status?

WHAT IS YOUR OPINION?

In each of the following cases, give your decision and state a legal principle that applies to the case.

1. Paul Kroth owned and operated a rooming house. He decided to enter the hotel business and proceeded to accept transient guests. Has Kroth taken on new responsibilities? What are they?
2. Hugo Holstein was severely burned while using the sun-lamp facilities of a hotel. The overexposure occurred when the automatic timer failed to operate. Was the hotel liable?
3. One night a guest in the Liverpool Hotel was taken ill with an infectious disease. The guest was removed to a hospital the next day, and his room was rented to Russel Trimble. Trimble contracted the disease because the room had not been properly disinfected. Is the hotel liable for Trimble's illness?
4. Leon Swartz was a duly registered guest at the Oswego Hotel. He had a large sum of money with him, which he kept in his room, although a safe was provided for the use of guests by the management. If the money were stolen, would the hotel be liable for the loss under most modern state statutes? Would the hotel be liable by common-law rules?
5. James Polito entered a hotel and deposited his baggage near the door and went to the desk to register. While he was registering, his baggage was stolen. Will the hotel be liable for the loss?

6. Kenneth Costello was a guest at a hotel for a period of three days. He attempted to leave without paying his bill, asserting that his employer would pay the bill if properly billed. If Costello is employed by a reputable company, may the hotel claim a right of lien on his baggage?

7. Sam Perron agreed to meet a friend in the lobby of a hotel. While there, Sam's luggage was stolen. Would he be considered a guest of the hotel? Could he hold the hotel liable for his loss?

THE LAW IN ACTION

1. The Ridgely Operating Company operated an apartment hotel, accepting both transient guests and permanent residents. White rented an apartment on a long-term basis and moved in. After unpacking his trunk, he placed his trunk in the hall to be picked up and taken to a storage room by the porter. The trunk disappeared. White contended that the company had an absolute liability for the loss of the trunk. Do you think this was correct? Why? (Ridgely Operating Co. v. White 227 Ala. 459, 150 So. 693)

2. The plaintiff gave his suitcase to a porter employed by the defendant hotel at the railroad station. The porter customarily met the train and carried the baggage of prospective guests to the hotel in this fashion. The plaintiff had been a guest of the hotel many times in the past, but this time he did not intend to register as a guest. He intended only to have his bag taken to the hotel. Later in the day he changed his mind, registered at the hotel, and asked for his bag. The bag had disappeared and was never found. The plaintiff contended that he became a guest as soon as the porter took his bag and that the hotel was liable for the loss of his bag. Was this a correct contention? Why? (Parker v. Dixon et al., 132 Minn. 367, 157 N.W. 583)

KEY TO "WHAT'S THE LAW?" Page 297

1. *No. Monroe is a roomer. Dean is a transient guest.*
2. *No—not on Monroe's luggage because, in most states, a lien on the luggage of a roomer is not permitted. Yes. Since Dean is a guest, the hotel has the right to hold his baggage until the room rent is paid.*

◢ UNIT 33: PUBLIC UTILITIES AND THE CONSUMER

What are public utilities? Would you classify common carriers and hotels as public utilities?

Public utilities are often defined as businesses "charged with a public interest." Historically, common carriers and hotels were the first public utilities—but no longer. Today, this term is used for certain businesses that bring services to our homes. Your local electric company, telephone company, gas company, and perhaps water company—these are the businesses you usually think of as public utilities. In addition, there are telegraph companies, bus lines, ferryboat companies, dock companies, pipelines, and sometimes others.

PUBLIC UTILITY

Name at least five kinds of businesses classified as public utilities.

Certain features are common to all of these businesses: (1) The company enjoys some kind of favorable business position; (2) the public has a definite interest in the operation and control of the utility company; and (3) the companies are engaged in selling you services, not goods.

How do public utilities differ from other businesses?

Your relations with your public service companies are not the same as your relations with your corner grocer. If you do not like the canned peas you bought at the corner grocery store, you may go farther down the street and buy where you think the quality is better or the price is lower. But there is only one company furnishing electricity to your neighborhood. You have no choice but to take the service offered and pay the prescribed rate. Nor does the company have a choice as to whom it will serve. Your electric company, since it is a public utility, must accommodate all who ask for service.

Must a public utility extend its services to all who request it?

Since the utility's service must be extended to all—the rich and the poor, those with good credit and those with bad—the law allows the utility to

Public utilities must service all customers within their franchise areas.

demand a deposit before rendering service. The amount of the deposit is usually calculated on the basis of the expected monthly light, gas, telephone, or water bill.

GOVERNMENTAL CONTROL OF UTILITIES

OPERATION BY FRANCHISE

What is a franchise? From whom is a franchise obtained?

Most public utilities operate under a franchise. A *franchise* is a special privilege conferred by a government to an individual or a corporation. Your electric-power company, gas company, and telephone company all have such a privilege or contract granted to them by your local or state government. This special franchise gives them the exclusive right to operate in your locality.

FRANCHISE

REGULATION OF SERVICES

Special privilege carries with it special responsibilities. Public utilities must be supervised and regulated to insure the performance of these special responsibilities. This is another form of consumer protection.

In your study earlier you learned that much consumer protection depends on competition. We have no competition, however, in the utility field. Utilities are *natural monopolies*. By that we mean that the public is better served if only one company is operating in a given area. Can you imagine, for example, two competing telephone companies in your town or two competing electric companies? This would mean a duplication of wires, poles, and equipment, with no better, and possibly poorer, service. Where one company is given a monopoly, however, that one company must be strictly regulated for the protection of the consumer.

NATURAL MONOPOLY

What state commission is responsible for making and enforcing state regulations to control public utilities?

State Public Utility Commissions State regulation is usually imposed by a state *public service commission*. These commissions are established by an act of the state legislature. The legislature creates the commission and delegates to it the responsibility of making and enforcing rules for the control of public utilities. These rules prescribe the kinds and types of

PUBLIC SERVICE COMMISSION

services and to whom they must be extended and determine the rates that may be charged. If the utility wants to increase rates or make a change in the service rendered, it must make an application to the public service commission. The commission examines the application very carefully to determine whether the increased rate is justified. If it is, the increase may be allowed; if it is not, the application will be refused. Many times, public hearings are held by the commission in connection with these applications. At these hearings, the individual consumer may express his opinions as to the proposed changes.

How may the individual consumer express his opinions about public utilities?

The individual consumer does not often have cause for complaint concerning individual transactions with utility companies. The utilities usually adhere strictly to the rules of the state commission in their dealings with individual consumers. In case a disagreement does arise, however, the consumer may appeal directly to the public service commission for relief. Collectively, the consumers of an area may take a complaint to the commission if they have a common complaint as to rates or service.

The state public service commission examines applications for rate increases and may conduct public hearings to determine whether they are justified.

What agency supervises and regulates radio and television stations?

Federal Control If a utility is doing business in interstate commerce, it is subject to state and to federal control, usually through the Interstate Commerce Commission. Telephone and telegraph companies, pipelines, and power transmission lines are examples of utilities that may be engaged in interstate commerce.

While not strictly public utilities, radio and television broadcasters, because of the great public interest involved, are very closely regulated by the federal government through the Federal Communications Commission.

SUGGESTIONS FOR MINIMIZING LEGAL RISKS

1. Utility bills should always be paid promptly. A penalty is often charged for overdue bills. If bills are long overdue, your service can be shut off. This may result in inconvenience and financial loss.

2. Do not tamper with your electrical equipment or gas equipment. If it is discovered that the equipment is not in proper condition, your service may be discontinued. If you are injured as a result of tampering with property belonging to the utility company, you probably could not collect for damages sustained.

3. Notify your utility company immediately if you discover a broken power line or gas leak. If you cannot get notice to the company, notify your local fire department or police department.

 APPLYING YOUR LEARNING

QUESTIONS AND PROBLEMS

1. What do you ordinarily think of when the term public utility is used?
2. What are the most common features found in companies classed as public utilities?
3. Why is it necessary to have some element of public control of public utilities?
4. May your local telephone company refuse to service you if it wishes? Why or why not?
5. Can the electric light company in your city refuse to give you service without justifiable cause? Explain.
6. What is a natural monopoly? How would you differentiate between a natural and an ordinary monopoly?
7. Why is a public utility justified in demanding a deposit before it extends service to a customer?
8. What is a franchise? What privilege does it confer?
9. What utilities can you name that would be controlled by your state public service commission?
10. What utilities are also controlled by the federal government?
11. To whom in your state would you complain if your local electric company refused to give you service? How about telephone service?

WHAT IS YOUR OPINION?

In each of the following cases, give your decision and state a legal principle that applies to the case.

1. The East Amboy Gas Company had a franchise with Johnstown under which it agreed to furnish gas to all the inhabitants of the city. New factories built in the city caused a 20 percent increase in the population which the gas company was not equipped to service efficiently. Would the company be required to furnish gas to these new customers?
2. If the East Amboy Gas Company mentioned in Case 1 brought gas into the city from out of state, might there be additional governmental agencies concerned with its regulation? Explain.

3. Louis Ahern built a summer cottage on a nearby lake. He requested the local power company to extend their power lines a quarter of a mile in order to give him service at his cottage. The power company insisted they were not compelled to extend their lines for so little business. To whom would the problem be submitted for solution?

4. The Williamstown Telephone Company contended that they were losing money and insisted on a raise in telephone rates. What would the company have to do in order to raise the rates?

5. George Barzee owned a house that was such a fire hazard that no insurance company would issue a policy of insurance on it. Barzee contended that insurance companies are public utilities and that he is entitled to insurance. What is your opinion?

THE LAW IN ACTION

1. The Missouri Pacific Railroad Company operated a bus line between Lynbrook and Wesbury under a franchise granted by the Public Service Commission with approval of the state legislature. During the winter months the buses were heated with an exhaust-type heater, which the passengers believed was hazardous to their safety. The Missouri Pacific refused to change the heaters. Norwood, one of the riders, brought an action against the company. What do you think would be the outcome of this case? (Norwood v. Missouri Pac. R. Co., 51 S. Ct. 458)

2. The defendant company was in the business of supplying electric power under a franchise granted from the city. It was also in the private business of wiring houses. The company adopted a policy of furnishing a transformer free to houses that were wired by it, but making an extra charge for transformers where the house was wired by other electricians. The transformers were absolutely necessary before service could be commenced. Could the company validly do this? (Snell v. Clinton Electric Light, Heat & Power Co., 196 Ill. 626, 63 N.E. 1082)

KEY TO "WHAT'S THE LAW?" Page 305

1. *No. A state public service commission created for that purpose by a state legislature determines the rates.*

2. *Yes. The pipeline would be interstate commerce and would be subject to federal regulations.*

A DIGEST OF LEGAL CONCEPTS

1. A carrier can be classed as a "common carrier" when he holds himself out as being ready and willing to sell his services to the general public.

2. Private, or contract, carriers are free to accept or reject any offers of transportation that are made to them.

3. A common carrier must accept goods offered for transportation by anyone. A private carrier may choose his customers.

4. A common carrier's liability for service is limited by the type of transportation that he professes to offer and by the capacity of his equipment.

5. A common carrier is an insurer of the goods shipped. He must make good for any loss or damage to the goods from any source whatever, except damage resulting from (a) an act of God, (b) an act of a public enemy, (c) an act of a public authority, (d) the fault of the shipper, or (e) an inherent fault in the goods.

6. The terms of the contract between the common carrier and the shipper are usually contained in the bill of lading, which acts as a receipt for the goods.

7. A carrier becomes liable for the safety of the goods as soon as he comes into possession of them, and his liability ends when the goods reach their destination and the consignee has had a reasonable time to take them away.

8. A carrier operating in more than one state must submit to the rulings of the Interstate Commerce Commission on rates, quality of service, employee relationships, and similar matters.

9. If a carrier or his agent issues a bill of lading for goods without having actually received them, he is liable to anyone who accepts the bill in good faith.

10. A carrier has a lien on the goods covered by a bill of lading for storage or transportation charges.

11. A carrier is prohibited from absolving itself from liability for damage resulting from negligence. A carrier must exercise as much care in relation to the goods as a reasonably careful person would exercise under like circumstances.

12. A common carrier has an obligation to accept all persons who may seek passage. However, common carriers may refuse passengers (a) if they are disorderly, intoxicated, insane, or infected with a contagious disease, and (b) when all available space is occupied or reserved.

13. A public carrier of passengers is held to a very high degree of care in providing for their safety.

14. A public carrier is not liable if a passenger is harmed chiefly because of his own negligence or if the harm results from a violation of the carrier's reasonable rules.

15. A common carrier may usually limit his liability to the shipper by contract, subject to the following limitations: (a) he may not impose limitations contrary to statutes, and (b) he may not completely relieve himself from liability for his own negligence or that of his employees.

16. A public carrier must never leave a station ahead of time and must try to reach each station on schedule.

17. A hotelkeeper, or motelkeeper, must accept all respectable guests who are able to pay for their lodging if he has room for them.

18. At common law an innkeeper had an absolute liability for the safekeeping of the guest's property.

19. Modern statutes usually allow a hotelkeeper to limit his liability if he provides a place of safekeeping for the guest's property.

20. Although hotels may demand payment in advance, they frequently waive this right in favor of a lien on the guest's luggage.

21. A hotel has the right of lien against the property of a guest and may hold the guest's property until the room rent is paid.

22. In most states the property of a roomer may not be held for unpaid room rent.

23. Public utilities, which enjoy a special, favorable business position because of their monopolistic nature, are charged with a public interest. They deal in services instead of goods.

24. Public utilities must extend their services to all consumers.

25. Public utilities may demand a reasonable cash deposit before giving service.

PART 12: Buying Protection

WHAT'S THE LAW?

1. *Tom Hall owned his own house. He objected to paying premiums on a fire insurance policy; instead of carrying insurance on his home, Tom opened a savings account and deposited in the bank the amount he would have had to pay in premiums. Is Tom wise to do this or not?*

---

2. *Would the plan followed by Tom in No. 1 be advisable for a corporation that had assets of $1,000,000? Why or why not?*

▲ UNIT 34: NATURE OF INSURANCE

What is the purpose of insurance?

Our lives are crowded with risks. These risks include loss of property, loss of health, loss of jobs—and the loss of our very lives. Of course, insurance cannot prevent losses. The purpose of insurance is to spread the losses among a greater number of people.

EXAMPLE 1 Fifty homeowners, each owning a house valued at $25,000, formed a community group to cover fire damage loss to any of the fifty homes. One year a fire gutted the home of one of the group causing $5,000 damage. Each homeowner paid $100 to cover the total loss.

This is a purely hypothetical case. Most people purchase protection from reliable insurance companies. Nevertheless, the principle is the same—a large number of people spread the risk.

You can limit your losses, of course, by being careful. But we are not so careful as we might be. Even if we were, there would still be risks, and unavoidable losses are bound to occur.

Approximately when did the idea of risk sharing begin in Italy? in England?

The idea of risk sharing, or insurance, is not new. *Marine insurance*—that is, insuring ships at sea against loss—began sometime prior to the year 1400 in the Italian mercantile cities of Venice and Genoa. The idea was introduced in England by Italian merchants and traders about the year 1500. By 1700 marine insurance was a flourishing business, centering around the famous Lloyd's Coffee House in London, which was the forerunner of today's corporation of Lloyd's, insurance underwriters.

MARINE INSURANCE

When did fire insurance begin in England? life insurance?

The cooperative sharing of fire losses did not develop until a hundred years later, following the great London fire of 1666, which destroyed 80 percent of the city's buildings. Life insurance began to develop shortly afterward, the first known company being the Society for the Assurance of Widows and Orphans, which was organized in 1698.

Insurance may be defined as a contract whereby one person, called the *insurer,* agrees to reimburse another person, called the *insured,* if the latter suffers a specified monetary loss.

INSURANCE
INSURER
INSURED

UNDERSTANDING INSURANCE TERMS

Certain terms are common to most forms of insurance. The most important of these terms are as follows:

The *policy* is the written instrument containing the insurance agreement.

POLICY

The *premium* is amount paid periodically by the insured for insurance.

PREMIUM

The *risk* is the event insured against, such as fire, theft, death.

RISK

The *subject matter* is the thing insured, such as a house, life, or car.

SUBJECT MATTER

The *binder* is an oral or written statement putting the insurance into force until the regular policy can be issued. As a matter of fact, insurance is usually considered as being in effect as soon as the application is accepted by an authorized agent of the insurance company.

BINDER

The *beneficiary* is the person who is to receive *indemnification* (compensation or reimbursement) under the policy. Except in life insurance, the beneficiary is usually, but not always, the insured.

BENEFICIARY
INDEMNIFICATION

EXAMPLE 2 **The Merchants Bank loaned Gardner $4,800 for the purchase of a sports car. Gardner signed an installment note, and the bank took out insurance on Gardner's life to protect its investment. Gardner was the insured; the insurance company was the insurer; Merchants Bank was the beneficiary of the policy. The bank received a binder from the agent of the insurance company and later received a regular policy. The policy would provide coverage until the loan was totally repaid. Thus, if Gardner were to die before repaying the loan, the Merchants Bank would recover $4,800 from the insurance company.**

A *representation* is a statement made by either party in connection with the issuing of the policy.

REPRESENTATION

A *warranty* is a statement that becomes a part of the policy.

WARRANTY

The *insurable interest* is the financial interest that a person has in the object insured. You cannot take out insurance unless the destruction of the subject matter would cause you a financial loss, and you may take insurance only to the extent of such a possible loss.

INSURABLE INTEREST

EXAMPLE 3 **Chandler owned a house next door to a beautiful $50,000 home belonging to Foland. Chandler attempted to take out a $10,000 fire insurance policy on Foland's house. Chandler contended that having such a beautiful house next door made his own house worth $10,000 more. It is hardly necessary to state that Chandler could not do this. He had no financial interest in Foland's house and, therefore, no insurable interest.**

What is the difference between a valued policy and an open policy?

A *valued policy* is one in which the amount of indemnification is definitely stated.

VALUED POLICY

An *open policy* is one in which the amount of indemnification is to be determined when the loss occurs.

OPEN POLICY

EXAMPLE 4   Gardner purchased a cabin cruiser and took out insurance to the amount of $10,000 to cover loss from storms or accidental sinking. The policy was an open policy. During a heavy windstorm and high tide, the boat broke away from its moorings and was sunk. An insurance investigator found that the boat could be replaced for $8,200. This is all that Gardner will receive, although the face of the policy reads $10,000.

KINDS OF INSURANCE COMPANIES

STOCK COMPANIES

Stock companies are corporations in which the stockholders own the company. The corporation underwrites the losses; and the profits, if any, are shared by the stockholders.

STOCK COMPANY

MUTUAL COMPANIES

What is the basic difference between stock and mutual insurance companies?

Mutual companies are those companies in which the policyholders insure themselves by paying premiums to the management, which, in turn, operates the company and pays the losses. Any profits are added to the company's reserves or returned to the policyholders as dividends.

MUTUAL COMPANY

EXAMPLE 5   Samler purchased fire insurance from the All Town Mutual Insurance Company. His premium was $108 per year. At the end of the first year he was assessed an additional $6.90 due to excessive claims experienced by the company. Samler refused payment of this added amount. The company may increase the premium in this way. This was a mutual company in which the policyholders insured themselves. They share profits in the form of dividends. If, however, premiums are not sufficient to pay losses, the policyholders must increase the amount of the premium payments.

MIXED COMPANIES

Mixed companies have some of the characteristics of each of the previously discussed insurance companies. There is usually a small group of stockholders who furnish the initial capital and who get some return on their investment by way of dividends. The policyholders also share in the profits if the profits are over a specified amount. The policyholders in mixed and mutual companies may elect to accept this profit in the form of an annual dividend, to apply it on the payment of the next year's premium, or to leave it with the company to purchase additional paid-up insurance.

MIXED COMPANY

How are profits distributed to policyholders in mixed and mutual companies?

FRATERNAL SOCIETIES

Fraternal societies are mutual fraternal organizations, usually organized to spread the loss of one member among the entire membership. Very often the proportionate loss is collected from the members by way of assessments after the loss has occurred.

FRATERNAL SOCIETY

INSURANCE COVERAGE

Most of the insurance that people take out may be grouped into general classes, such as those given below.

PERSONAL INSURANCE

One general class of insurance is personal insurance which includes a considerable variety of insurance contracts. These are briefly described below.

Loss of Life   The purpose of *life insurance* is to provide money for dependents in the event of the death of the person insured.   LIFE INSURANCE

Health and Safety   The purpose of personal *health and safety insurance* is to provide money in the event that a person loses his earning power through ill health or accident; it is sometimes called loss-of-income insurance.   HEALTH AND SAFETY INSURANCE

How does health and safety insurance differ from major medical insurance?

Major Medical Expenses   *Major medical insurance* provides for the needs of those who are hospitalized for long periods and whose surgical bills exceed amounts provided in the schedule of surgical insurance policies. It also provides for those who require extensive medical treatments.   MAJOR MEDICAL INSURANCE

Liability   The purpose of *liability insurance* is to provide a person with protection against probable claim for damages brought against him by a third party as a result of an accident involving property or personal injury.   LIABILITY INSURANCE

What is the purpose of liability insurance? fidelity insurance?

Fidelity   The purpose of *fidelity insurance* is to provide indemnity for a person or a company against another person's dishonesty. This insurance against dishonesty is often called *bonding*.   FIDELITY INSURANCE / BONDING

EXAMPLE 6   The All-American Loan Corporation protected its funds by providing fidelity insurance on all employees who handled funds. Ackerson, a cashier, embezzled $10,000 of the corporation's money, left town, and could not be located. Fortunately, the fidelity insurance policy covered the All-American Loan Corporation's loss from theft.

Unemployment   An *unemployment insurance* agreement compensates a person in the event that he loses his job.   UNEMPLOYMENT INSURANCE

Unemployment insurance provides financial relief only for those who lose their jobs.

PROPERTY INSURANCE

In addition to personal insurance, you may take out insurance against the loss or destruction of property. The common types of property insurance are briefly described as follows:

Fire The purpose of *fire insurance* is to help pay for loss of property destroyed by fire. It is possible to get fire insurance on any personal or real property.

FIRE INSURANCE

What is public liability insurance?

Public Liability The purpose of *public liability insurance* is to repay your losses if other persons are injured on your property as a result of your carelessness or neglect and you have to pay them for the injuries.

PUBLIC LIABILITY INSURANCE

Every homeowner should carry public liability insurance. If a guest is injured on your premises and you have to pay for his medical expenses, public liability insurance will reimburse you for your losses.

Automobile *Automobile insurance* may be of various kinds. Its purpose is to protect you against the loss of your car through fire, theft, or damage from the elements or other causes. In addition, you may carry automobile liability insurance to cover the cost of injury to other persons who may be injured through the operation of your car.

AUTOMOBILE INSURANCE

Marine *Marine insurance* is one of the oldest forms of insurance and covers losses suffered from shipping goods by water.

MARINE INSURANCE

Robbery and Theft The purpose of *robbery and theft insurance* is to repay your losses when your goods have been stolen.

ROBBERY AND THEFT INSURANCE

What is title insurance?

Title *Title insurance* is a special type of insurance that applies to real property and protects you if you should lose your real property because of a defect in your title.

TITLE INSURANCE

EXAMPLE 7 Young bought a house and, as a protective measure, purchased a title policy on his new property. Three years after the purchase, it was discovered that a third party had placed a lien against the property which had never been satisfied. Young's title policy would cover any payment due on the lien without expense to Young.

Casualty *Casualty insurance* covers many different situations in which negligence, chance, or accident may result in loss. In New York State, for example, casualty insurance includes glass, boiler and machinery, animal,

CASUALTY INSURANCE

Casualty insurance covers many types of risks in many states. Name the most common forms of risks covered by this type of insurance.

Give at least four reasons why some risks cannot be covered by insurance.

elevator, burglary and theft, personal-injury liability, property-damage liability, workmen's compensation and employer's liability, and credit insurance.

UNINSURABLE RISKS

Some risks, called *uninsurable risks*, cannot be covered by insurance for several reasons: (1) The probability of loss cannot be predicted with sufficient accuracy; (2) the extent of loss cannot be accurately determined; (3) proof of loss is too difficult to determine; and (4) the temptation to be careless would be too great. You cannot, for example, insure against failure in business, failure to get a particular job, failure in a career, inability to get married, or lack of success in marriage.

EXAMPLE 8   **The firm of Flynn and Higley was very liberal about extending credit. They attempted to take out insurance against business losses on bad debts. They found that they were unable to obtain this type of insurance. The reason is fairly obvious. These are risks that no insurance company could calculate. They are not risks arising from events beyond the control of the parties; they are risks created by the parties themselves by reason of their liberal credit policy.**

THE INSURANCE POLICY CONTRACT

An insurance policy is a contract. As a contract, it follows the ordinary rules governing contracts, which you studied earlier. There are a few special rules and statutes that apply to insurance contracts only. For the most part, however, you should think of an insurance policy as an important written contract.

FORM REQUIREMENTS

As the insurance agreement is a contract, it follows the same rules as any other valid contract. The insurance laws in the various states require that the contract be in writing. Many states require a standard policy form, specify that print on the policy must be of a certain size or larger, and permit insurance to be written only by accredited insurance companies. The insurance companies must strictly follow certain rules administered by the state insurance commission.

Who makes the offer in an insurance contract? How is the acceptance made?

What is a binder?

Offer and Acceptance   The offer in an insurance contract is made by the party who desires insurance by his filling out an application form for insurance and presenting it to the company's agent. The acceptance is made by the company's issuing of an insurance policy. The policy sets forth in detail the terms of the contract agreed on. Sometimes insurance companies will authorize their agents to issue a temporary acceptance called a *binder*. The purpose of a binder is to protect the applicant between the time the application is filed and the time the policy is issued. If the company decides not to accept the application, the binder is terminated.

UNINSURABLE RISKS

BINDER

You may not take out an insurance policy on the outcome of a horse race. The purpose of insurance is to protect the insured against loss, not to aid him in securing a speculative profit.

In an insurance contract, who is the insured? the insurer?

Parties   The party to whom the policy is issued is called the insured. If you personally take out a policy of insurance, you would be the insured. The insurance company that issues the policy is called the insurer.

What constitutes the consideration in an insurance contract?

Consideration   The consideration given by the insured is the payment, usually called the premium, or sometimes just the promise to pay the premium. The consideration given by the insurer is the promise of assuming the risk of loss. In other words, the company is promising to repay your losses as provided under the terms of the policy. This repayment of losses is usually called *indemnity*.

INDEMNITY

Insurable Interest   An insurable interest is an interest in the subject matter that would cause an actual loss to the insured. If there is no insurable interest, the contract would be illegal.

OTHER CONSIDERATIONS

EXAMPLE 9   Jorgenson knew that an electric wire in his home was defective but still applied for a fire insurance policy without indicating this fact. The home caught fire some time later and was completely destroyed because of defective wiring. Would the fire insurance company be justified in refusing to settle Jorgenson's claim for his loss?

All contracts require a certain degree of honesty and good faith. This is true to an exceptionally high degree in insurance contracts. Any important misstatement that you make may result in the invalidation of the policy. Not only must you truthfully answer all questions asked, but you must also reveal all material facts that may have a bearing upon the risk. Concealment of any important material facts will void the policy if you know about this fact or should be in a position to know.

The information that you give on your application for insurance is relied on by the insurance company in determining whether it wishes to accept the risk of issuing a policy to you. If you make misrepresentations in your application, you mislead the company. The company may later avoid its liability if you made any serious misrepresentations.

When will a misrepresentation void a policy?

A statement may be either a representation or a warranty. A representation is an oral or a written statement made before or at the time of closing the contract of insurance. It is usually not made a part of the policy. It must be substantially true but need not be literally true. It will not void the policy, even though untrue, unless it is also material to the risk. If, however, it is a statement that induces the insurer to accept the risk, it is considered material to the risk.

EXAMPLE 10   Dexter applied to All Town Insurance Company for a public liability policy on his car. When asked his age, Dexter answered that he was twenty-five years old, although he was only twenty-four, his twenty-fifth birthday being several months away. Dexter's statement was made without intent to defraud the company. Premiums for persons under twenty-five were much higher than those for persons twenty-five or over. All Town has the right to void the policy on the grounds of Dexter's representation of a material fact that induced All Town to issue the policy.

A warranty is a statement, usually incorporated into the insurance policy, that must be literally true, no matter how unimportant or immaterial.

EXAMPLE 11   A special liability and property damage policy for automobiles was offered by All Town Insurance Company at reduced premiums to all car owners who signed a statement that they did not drink alcoholic beverages and would not do so during the life of the policy. Lister, a light drinker, applied for such a policy and received it after signing the special statement contained in the application. His car was later involved in an accident and demolished. All Town proved that Lister was returning from a cocktail party at the time of the accident and that he had drunk a few cocktails. All Town would not have to reimburse Lister for his loss.

EXAMPLE 12   Suppose Dexter had been asked by the agent how many miles he usually drove each year and he replied "Not more than 5,000." In fact, as a salesman, Dexter drove the car an average of 20,000 miles each year. Considering the increase in risks, this great difference placed a much heavier burden upon the insurance company. All Town would, therefore, have the right to void Dexter's policy because of his intentional misrepresentation of the facts as he knew them.

SUGGESTIONS FOR MINIMIZING LEGAL RISKS

1. Do not rely too much on the insurance agent's oral statements. Oral statements seldom, if ever, bind the insurance company. Most companies will be bound only by the specific provisions of their written policies.
2. If oral statements have been entered into to take out an insurance policy, record in writing the date, time, amount, and agent's name. It is desirable to send a copy of this memorandum to the insurance company while waiting for a binder. If possible, obtain a written confirmation of the oral agreement from the agent.

3. Maintain an accurate calendar record of the expiration dates on all insurance policies. Review this record periodically. Agents are not legally required to remind you of pending expiration dates. This will protect you if your agent fails to notify you of a pending expiration date.

4. Check your insurance policies, especially your liability policies, to see that all names are spelled correctly and all persons to be covered are mentioned.

5. Read all the fine print in your policies in order to understand any limitations, exceptions, and conditions that may limit the coverage or nullify the insurance policy. Make a written list of all the possible circumstances under which the policy is not going to be effective.

 APPLYING YOUR LEARNING

QUESTIONS AND PROBLEMS

1. Name several risks that one might encounter in a lifetime. Explain.
2. What is the basic purpose of insurance?
3. What is the connection between risks and insurance?
4. Define insurance.
5. Name the four general types or classes of insurance companies, and explain the distinguishing features of each.
6. Insurance may be grouped into a number of classes. What are the two principal ones? Name several types of insurance contracts under each.
7. What are some risks that one cannot cover by insurance? Explain why this is so.
8. May insurance companies carry on business in any way they choose? Explain.
9. Explain what might result if you make a false statement when you take out insurance.
10. What is the difference between a valued policy and an open policy?
11. What is a premium, and how do you think it is determined?
12. What is the effect of a binder? Illustrate.
13. Must an insurance contract be made in writing? Explain.
14. What is meant by *insurable interest?* Explain.

WHAT IS YOUR OPINION?

In each of the following cases, give your decision and state a legal principle that applies to the case.

1. Kent purchased a house for $8,000 and tried to take out a fire insurance policy for $12,000, stating that the house was worth that much. Do you think Kent should be allowed to do this? Why or why not?

2. Larkin stored several barrels of gasoline in his garage but did not disclose this fact when he filled in an application for insurance on the garage. An explosion and fire destroyed the garage. The insurance company refused to settle on the policy. Can Larkin collect? Why or why not?

3. Murphy and Sands were former college classmates and good friends. Sands, without any request from Murphy, took out a fire insurance policy on Murphy's lake-shore cottage. A month later Murphy's cottage was destroyed by fire. Will the insurance company have to pay Sands? Why or why not?

4. Welsh telephoned an automobile insurance agent and stated that he had just purchased a $3,000 new car and desired to take out a $50 deductible collision insurance policy on the car. After answering all the agent's questions over the telephone, the agent told Welsh he was insured and the policy would be mailed in a few days. The next day Welsh ran into a truck and his car was totally demolished. Will the insurance company have to settle?

5. Lewis received several threatening messages that he would be killed if he did not pay some of his outstanding obligations. He took out an insurance policy without disclosing these threats. Within two months, his body was found floating in the river under very suspicious circumstances. When the facts came out, the insurance company refused to settle. Do you think that the insurance company is justified in refusing to pay the claim? Why or why not?

6. Whitney purchased a television set from the Berne Television Company on a time-payment plan. He decided to take out a fire and theft insurance policy on the set. Before the set was paid for, it was stolen. Must the insurance company pay Whitney? Why? What happens to the Berne Television Company?

7. Manion, a farmer, received an anonymous letter threatening the destruction of his farm by fire. He became alarmed and insured his property without disclosing to the insurance company the threat contained in the letter. May the company void the policy on learning these facts?

8. In the written application of fire insurance, Fuller stated that the building was twelve years old. This statement was made a part of the policy by reference. The building was, in fact, twenty years old. The company refused to indemnify Fuller for fire damages to the building, claiming that the statement as to the age of the building was a warranty, the falsity of which voided the policy. Was the company right in its contention?

THE LAW IN ACTION

1. Read owned a place of business that was insured by the Boston Insurance Company. The business was described in the policy as a café and cold-drink stand. The building was destroyed by fire, and Read brought an action for his loss. The insurance company contended that the policy was

void because Read illegally sold intoxicating liquor on the premises, creating an increased hazard in violation of the contract. What do you think? (Boston Insurance Co. v. Read, 166 F. 2d 551)

2. The insured stated in his application for insurance that he had not been treated by a physician within five years. This statement was not true, and the insured had made frequent trips to a physician within the previous year. Before a policy was issued, however, the insured had been examined by the company's own physician and approved. Do you think the policy was valid? Why? (Sambles v. Metropolitan Life Ins. Co., 158 Ohio St. 233, 108 N.E.2d 321)

KEY TO "WHAT'S THE LAW?" Page 313

1. *No. Tom is taking a greater risk than an ordinary person can afford to take.*
2. *Very large corporations sometimes "carry their own insurance," but unless their assets are very large, they cannot afford the risk.*

WHAT'S THE LAW?

1. *Thomas Sewak was twenty-three years old, married, and had one child. He wanted to purchase some life insurance, so he went to an older friend for advice. The friend said, "I have taken out a terrific life insurance policy. You should have one just like it." Is this good advice?*

---

2. *George Burns said, "You can't lose on life insurance. You always get back more than you put in—it costs you nothing." Robert Carr said, "You have to die to win on life insurance policies." Who is correct, George or Robert or neither of them?*

◬ UNIT 35:
LIFE INSURANCE

Life is uncertain. Only a few persons who have dependents accumulate enough to provide for these dependents in case they should die. Most men would find it very difficult to save up a sum of, say, $20,000, which they could leave in a bank or invest to provide for their dependents. "Death and taxes" are considered to be the only two certainties in life. Because death is certain to man but uncertain as to the time it will occur, the need for life insurance becomes evident.

If every person were sure of living seventy-five or eighty years, there would be no market for life insurance. In such a case the individual might better provide some kind of savings plan for himself. Unfortunately, we have no such assurance. Life insurance comes to the rescue by providing a plan whereby a person may create an estate as soon as he takes out the insurance. When a person takes out a $10,000 policy, he knows that from then on his dependents will have that much money at their disposal if he should die.

Why do we say that a person has created an estate as soon as he buys a life insurance policy?

EXAMPLE 1 **When Poland was twenty years old, he took out an ordinary life insurance policy for $10,000. He later married and raised a family. When he was seventy years old, after paying the premiums on the policy for fifty years, Poland contended that he would have been better off if he had invested his money in some other way. While this might seem logical, since he is still alive, it is a very shortsighted point of view. His family had had the protection of the policy while it was needed. If he had died when he was thirty, leaving a wife and small children, his insurance would have been a vital necessity.**

The ordinary laws of infancy apply to a minor's contract of life insurance except as changed by state statute. Many states have statutes that permit minors to enter into binding contracts for life insurance. The age at which minors may validly contract for life insurance is specified in the

May minors ever
enter into binding
life insurance
contracts?

What is meant by
the protective
feature of life
insurance?

What is meant by
double
indemnity in
case of death by
accident?

state statutes. Because the age varies from state to state, you should check the laws of your own state on this point.

A life insurance policy usually is delivered and becomes effective when the first premium is paid. The essential feature of life insurance is the promise by an insurance company that it will pay the beneficiary the stated amount in case of the death of the insured. This is known as the *protective feature* of life insurance. Sometimes, the policy may contain other protective features. Frequently, *double indemnity* is provided in case of death by accident. This means that, in the event of the accidental death of the insured, the beneficiary receives double the amount of the face value of the policy. The policy may also provide for the payment of a certain monthly sum in case of total and permanent disability. This latter feature may be combined with *waiver of premium,* which means that premium payments are stopped as long as the insured is disabled. Naturally, any of these provisions increases the cost of the premium.

PROTECTIVE FEATURE

DOUBLE INDEMNITY

WAIVER OF PREMIUM

EXAMPLE 2   Lorvan took out a $20,000 life insurance policy that included a $100-a-month provision for total disability and also waiver of premium. After ten years, he began to suffer from an illness that prevented him from working. These extra provisions would make it possible for him to support his family and to keep the much-needed insurance policy still in force.

LIFE INSURANCE CONTRACTS

Some people want protection only. Some are interested chiefly in investment. Between these two extremes, we have people who want both protection and investment in varying degrees written into one policy. This is the main reason why so many kinds of policies are offered. The basic question everyone should ask himself is: Am I seeking protection mainly, or am I seeking protection coupled with investment?

Term policies are entirely for protection and have no investment value. Endowment policies are chiefly for investment. If a person has no need for the immediate protective feature of an insurance policy, he may purchase an annuity, which will regularly pay out a certain sum once the purchaser reaches retirement age. It is impossible to set up a satisfactory insurance program that will fit everyone's needs. The insurance plan one adopts will depend on such factors as age, responsibilities, income, and the purpose the insurance is to serve. For convenience, group life insurance policies are divided here into four general types. They are listed below in the order of their cost to the insured.

TERM

A *term policy* is one that is payable by the insurance company only if the insured dies before a certain date—that is, the date on which the life of the policy expires. Such a policy is frequently issued for five or ten years. This type of policy, because of its low premium rate, has neither cash surrender value nor loan value and is taken out purely for protection.

TERM POLICY

What are some
characteristics of
term policies?

The breadwinner of a large family is well advised to carry term insurance.

EXAMPLE 3 The Business Loan Company stipulated that all policies taken out on the lives of those receiving loans would be term insurance. This provided the company with maximum security without the cash value and loan benefits for which it had no need. A loan of $5,000 to Custer would be secured by a term policy for the time stipulated in the loan. Should Custer die before full payment had been made to Business Loan Company, the balance would be fully repaid from the benefits provided in the term life insurance policy on Custer's life. Custer's estate would, thereby, be relieved of the obligation to repay the loan.

At the end of each surrender period, the premium is raised because the insured is older and, therefore, is a greater risk.

ORDINARY LIFE

Under the terms of an *ordinary,* or straight, *life policy,* the insured continues to pay premiums as long as he lives, unless he discontinues the policy. After the second or third year, this type of policy begins to accumulate a *cash surrender value.* This means that, if the insured wishes to discontinue the policy, he may draw out the specified amount of cash value. To this extent, such a policy has an investment feature, because the cash surrender value increases from year to year as the policy remains in force. The amount the holder can draw out is much less than the amount he has paid in, which means that he has been paying chiefly for protection.

ORDINARY LIFE POLICY

CASH SURRENDER VALUE

What are some characteristics of ordinary life policies?

LIMITED-PAYMENT LIFE

A *limited-payment life policy* provides that the payment of premiums will stop after a designated length of time, usually ten, twenty, or thirty years. The amount of the policy will be paid to the beneficiary upon the death of the insured, whether the death occurs during the payment period or after. Such a policy makes it possible for a person to complete the premium payments on his policy while he still has a high earning power. The cash surrender value of a limited-payment life policy is much greater than that of an ordinary life policy.

LIMITED-PAYMENT LIFE POLICY

What are the usual features of limited-payment policies?

EXAMPLE 4 **Lombardo took out a policy that provided that he should continue paying premiums until he was sixty years old. From that time on he would not have to pay any premiums, and the amount of the policy would be payable to his beneficiary. This is an example of a limited-payment life policy.**

ENDOWMENT

How does an endowment policy differ from a term policy? an ordinary life policy? a limited-payment policy?

An *endowment policy* provides protection for a stipulated time, generally twenty to thirty years. The face of the policy is paid to the insured at the end of the agreed period; or if he dies during the period, the full amount is paid to the beneficiary. The premium is higher because the policy builds up cash values more rapidly. For example, a twenty-year endowment policy purchased at age twenty-one would require annual premiums of approximately $43 per $1,000 of insurance.

ENDOWMENT POLICY

EXAMPLE 5 **Figueroa purchased a $10,000 twenty-year endowment policy, naming his wife as beneficiary. He died after the policy had been in force only three years. It was held that Figueroa's wife was entitled to the face of the policy, $10,000. If Figueroa had lived until the policy had been in force twenty years, the insurance company would have paid the $10,000 to him.**

ANNUITY

Most life insurance companies sell annuities. While an annuity is not strictly a life insurance contract, it is based on the age and probable length of life of the policyholder, so it is discussed here.

What is an annuity?

An *annuity* is a guaranteed retirement income which a person secures by either paying a lump-sum premium or by periodically paying a set amount to an insurer. The insured may choose to receive an income for a certain number of years, with a beneficiary receiving whatever is left of the annuity at the insured's death, or he may choose to receive payments as long as he lives and, at his death, lose whatever is left of the annuity (if anything). An insurer may tailor arrangements to suit an annuity purchaser; it may vary payment schedules, the allocation of proceeds, the date benefits begin, and the sum of each benefit payment.

ANNUITY

Another advantage of an annuity is that the contract usually provides that the depositor must leave the money in the hands of the company until the maturity date to get the full benefit of his investment. There is usually a certain deduction for drawing out the accumulation at an earlier date. If this were not the case, there would be a strong temptation to "cash in" whenever a person felt that he needed the money.

What are the advantages of an annuity?

The arrangement for monthly deposits is a great convenience. A person will gauge in advance what he thinks he can invest, and after a while, such deposits become a habit.

EXAMPLE 6 **Lotz is a man fifty years of age with no dependents. He made an agreement with an insurance company to deposit $100 a month for the next fifteen years, at which time he will begin drawing an annual amount based on his deposits plus interest. This is an example of an annuity. If Lotz should die sometime within the fifteen years, his heirs will collect only the accumulation based on the provisions in the contract.**

People engaged in
hazardous
occupations must
pay higher
premiums for life
insurance.

STANDARD CLAUSES

Standard clauses are found in most policies. Some of these clauses may be required by state statutes. The most common clauses found in life insurance contracts are the following:

STANDARD
CLAUSE

Change of Beneficiary The beneficiary is the person who will receive the money on the death of the insured, and thus he has a certain amount of interest in the policy from the time the policy is written. Most policies, however, have a provision permitting the insured, who is paying the premiums, to reserve the right to change the beneficiary if he chooses. If the policyholder fails to do so, the vested right of the beneficiary to the benefits of the policy cannot be taken away without his consent.

*Why is it
desirable to
reserve the right
to change the
beneficiary?*

EXAMPLE 7 Mann, Ross, and Lubin were partners, and a policy was purchased by the partnership on the life of each, with the partnership named as the beneficiary. The right to change beneficiary was not reserved by the partners. Mann withdrew from the partnership and requested the insurer to change the beneficiary of his policy. The request could not be granted. The policy must be continued in its original form.

● **Incontestability Clause** If the insurer has been misled in issuing the policy by false statements of the insured, the policy may later be canceled. It would be unjust, however, to allow the insurer to collect premiums for many, many years and then, on the death of the insured, refuse to pay because of some minor misrepresentation. For this reason, most policies provide that after a specified number of years—usually two or three—the policy becomes incontestable. This means that the insurer must pay, regardless of former defenses that might have been good prior to the expiration of the contestable time period. Many states provide for an incontestability clause by statute.

*What is the
reason for
including an
incontestability
clause in a life
insurance policy?*

EXAMPLE 8 Lindsley applied for a $50,000 ordinary life insurance policy but did not disclose that he had suffered severe injuries during combat in Viet Nam which had seriously affected his heart. He made a misrepresentation when questioned on these matters, and the policy was thereafter issued. Four years later

NOTE: *The bullet indicates that there may be a state statute that varies from the law discussed here.*

the insured died, and the misrepresentation was offered by the company as a defense against paying the policy. Since the policy had been in force for more than two years, such a defense was not admissible and the policy had to be paid.

Misstatement of Age Premium rates are based on the age of the insured at the time the policy was issued. If the insured misrepresents his age, he may get a lower premium rate than he deserves. Most policies provide, however, that this misrepresentation will not void the policy. If a claim must be paid on a policy on which the insured has misstated his age, the insurance company is required to pay only the amount of insurance that could be purchased by the premiums figured on the basis of the true age of the insured.

What is the effect on the insurance policy of a misstatement of age?

EXAMPLE 9 **Dixon applied to All Town Insurance Company for a $10,000 ordinary life insurance policy. To secure the benefit of a lower premium, he told the agent that he was thirty-eight years old, although he was forty-four. The annual premium at age thirty-eight for that amount of insurance was $268 a year. Had Dixon given his right age, the premium would have been $339 a year. Dixon died at the age of sixty-three, at which time All Town learned his real age. The beneficiary will receive only the amount that a $268 annual premium would have bought for a person taking out the policy at age forty-four.**

Suicide Most policies provide that the insurer will not pay if the insured commits suicide within a specified time, usually one or two years, after the policy is issued. After the specified time period, however, the insurer will have to pay.

Violation of the Law Most policies provide that the insurer is not liable if the insured dies or is killed while trying to evade capture because of a violation of the law.

Default All policies provide that the policy will lapse if the premiums are not paid within a specified period of time after they are due.

● The period (usually thirty or thirty-one days) allowed after the premium is due and before the policy will lapse for nonpayment of the premium is called *days of grace*. The number of days varies; so you should check the statutes of your own state on this point.

What is meant by days of grace?

DAYS OF GRACE

EXAMPLE 10 **All Town Insurance Company mailed a premium notice to one of its policyholders whose premium was due on May 1. The premium was not received by May 1. All Town must allow a thirty-day grace period during which time the policy would remain in force. The policy could not be canceled during this grace period without the consent of the insured.**

Lapse and Reinstatement When a premium is not paid, the policy is said to have *lapsed*. This does not mean that the policy is not good; it means that the company may, at its option, void the contract. Generally, the company will require you to take a physical examination in addition to paying the premium due before a lapsed policy can be reinstated. A policy is reinstated when the insured (1) pays the premium and any interest that may be due and (2) gives proper evidence to the insurance company that he is an insurable risk.

LAPSE

What must one do to reinstate a lapsed policy?

Cash Surrender Value After a life insurance policy (except term insurance) has been in force for a certain length of time, it has a *cash surrender value.* Now the insured can collect on his policy if it were canceled for one reason or another. The cash surrender value increases from year to year as the policy remains in force.

Loan Value If the insured does not wish to surrender his life insurance policy, he may, in case of financial need, borrow from the insurance company an amount equal to the cash surrender value of the policy at the time he applies for the loan. He must, of course, pay interest on the loan; but he need not surrender his policy. The amount that may be borrowed under these circumstances is called the *loan value* of the policy. Like the cash surrender value, the loan value increases from year to year.

What effect on the existence of a life insurance policy does the borrowing of the loan value have?

LOAN VALUE

EXAMPLE 11 **Haskin took out a $10,000 ordinary life insurance policy twelve years ago and paid his premiums regularly. When he needed $1,200 immediate cash, Haskin was able to borrow the money on his policy at the legal rate of interest because the policy had an immediate cash value of more than $2,000. Borrowing on the policy would keep it in force, and his beneficiary would receive the face amount of $10,000, less the amount of the loan, should the insured die before repaying the debt.**

THE INSURABLE INTEREST REQUIREMENT

What is meant by insurable interest in life insurance?

You may take out life insurance on someone else if you have an insurable interest in that person, but only to the amount of the insurable interest. *Insurable interest* means that you would suffer a money loss if the person died. You may, for instance, take out insurance on a debtor for the amount of the debt.

INSURABLE INTEREST

EXAMPLE 12 **You lend $1,000 to a friend, to be repaid at the end of three years. You now have an insurable interest in your friend's life to the extent of $1,000 for a three-year period. You should be able to get an insurance policy on your friend's life for $1,000 if your friend can pass the required physical examination and meet all the other requirements.**

The requirement of insurable interest is different in life insurance contracts as compared to fire insurance contracts. In life insurance contracts, for example, one must have an insurable interest at the time the policy is taken out. In fire insurance one must have an insurable interest at the time of the loss.

If, in Example 12, your friend repaid the loan at the end of three years, you would no longer have an insurable interest in his life. However, if you continued to pay regular premiums on the insurance contract, the insurer would have to pay the amount of the policy on your friend's death.

EXAMPLE 13 **Before her divorce, Mrs. Kane had taken out $10,000 life insurance on her husband, making herself responsible for the payment of all premiums and naming herself as sole beneficiary. This was done with the husband's consent, as required by law. Following their divorce, Mrs. Kane continued to pay the premiums. Mrs. Kane would be entitled to the $10,000 death benefit upon her ex-husband's death, even if it occurred many years after the divorce.**

ASSIGNMENT OF POLICY

Are life insurance policies usually assignable? Under what conditions might one wish to assign his policy?

A life insurance policy can usually be assigned to others. Some policies, however, require the consent of the insurance company for such assignment. The beneficiary's consent may also have to be obtained, unless the insured has reserved the right to change the beneficiary.

Assignments are most frequently made for the purpose of loans on the policy. After a given time, as has been explained, a policy has a certain loan value, and this amount may be borrowed from the insurance company itself or from anyone else who is willing to take the policy as security.

TERMINATION OF LIFE INSURANCE POLICIES

The most common cause of termination of an insurance contract is its complete execution. All policies terminate on the death of the insured and the payment of the benefits to the beneficiaries. Term policies expire at the end of the term specified. Investment-type policies terminate when settlement is made with the insured before his death.

How are life insurance policies terminated?

In addition, policies may lapse on nonpayment of the premium where there is no provision made for reinstatement. Also, policies that have a cash surrender value may be canceled by the insured on the surrender of the policy. Policies may be canceled by the insurer on the grounds of misrepresentation and fraud at any time prior to the time at which the policy becomes incontestable.

SUGGESTIONS FOR MINIMIZING LEGAL RISKS

1. As a copy of the application is usually made a part of the insurance policy, any misstatement is an invitation for trouble and possible expense later in trying to force settlement of an insurance claim. Therefore, be accurate and complete in your application statements. This principle holds true in making out applications for all types of insurance policies.
2. Beware of inexpensive policies sold through the mail, unless you know that these policies have been approved for sale in your state by your state insurance department or commission. You usually get protection in direct proportion to the costs of the insurance.
3. Life insurance companies usually require proof of age before final settlement is made on their policies. To save time and expense to your heirs, it is wise to affix to your policies before your death a copy of your birth certificate or other acceptable evidence of date of birth. Consult your insurance agent for further advice on this point.

4. The decision to take out life insurance is a very important one that may greatly affect the lives of those who may be dependent on you. Do not rush into it without very careful study and analysis. Consult several people who are competent to advise you on life insurance matters before making your final decision. In determining your insurance needs, include among those whom you consult some unbiased persons who do not profit from the sale of life insurance policies. It may even be desirable to read several books on life insurance before making your final decision.

5. As you may desire to change the beneficiary-at-will someday, check your policy to make sure that it provides for this possibility. It is usually desirable to name your beneficiary or beneficiaries rather than to have the insurance made payable to your estate, as this simplifies the payment of the face of the policy.

 APPLYING YOUR LEARNING

QUESTIONS AND PROBLEMS

1. What is the primary purpose of life insurance?
2. What is meant by the investment feature of life insurance?
3. Under what circumstances should a person consider taking out life insurance mainly for protection?
4. Under what circumstances might a person consider taking out life insurance for investment purposes?
5. Name and explain briefly four types of life insurance contracts.
6. What are the advantages and disadvantages of a term policy? a renewable term policy?
7. Under what circumstances may you take out a life insurance policy on someone else's life?
8. What is meant by insurable interest in life insurance?
9. What advantages, if any, does an endowment policy have over an ordinary life policy?
10. Why does a limited-payment life policy cost more than a term policy?
11. When may it be necessary to get permission of a beneficiary if one desires to change the beneficiary?
12. Give several examples of changing conditions that might cause one to desire to change the beneficiary in his policy.
13. Name several standard clauses of life insurance contracts. Explain briefly the meaning of each feature.
14. Are life insurance policies usually assignable? Under what conditions might one wish to assign his policy?
15. What are the regulations in your state regarding minors' rights to take out life insurance?

16. What are the advantages of an annuity?
17. What is the grace period in your state? the incontestability period?
18. How are life insurance contracts terminated?

WHAT IS YOUR OPINION?

In each of the following cases, give your decision and state a legal principle that applies to the case.

1. Keneston, a single minor, took out an insurance policy on his own life, naming his mother as beneficiary. He reserved the right to change the beneficiary-at-will according to the terms of his policy. Ten years later Keneston married and changed the beneficiary to his wife. On his death, both his wife and his mother claimed the insurance. To whom must the insurance company pay the insurance?

2. On May 1, 1972, Hilton, in an application for life insurance, stated that he had never been treated for tuberculosis. The policy was issued. Eighteen months later Hilton died of tuberculosis. On finding that Hilton had been treated prior to filing the application for insurance, the company refused to pay the beneficiary the face value of the policy. Does the insurance company have a legal right to refuse?

3. In the application that was made a part of the life insurance policy, Grover stated that he was a salesman; but, in reality, he was a guard on an armored truck that carried large sums of money. Six months later he was killed during a holdup of the truck. The insurance company refused to pay the face value of the policy to the beneficiary. Is the insurance company within its legal rights in refusing?

4. Gould, in his written and signed application for life insurance, answered "No" to the question, "Have you within the past five years had medical or surgical treatment or any departure from good health? If so, state when, and what, and duration." As a matter of fact, Gould had had a heart attack only six months previously. One year after receiving the policy, Gould died of a heart attack. May the insurance company avoid paying the policy?

5. An insurance policy was issued on the life of a person who was killed six months later while participating in an attempted bank robbery. The insurance company refused to pay the face of the policy to the named beneficiary. May it legally do so?

6. Kalter stated in his application for life insurance that he was twenty-two years of age, when, in fact, he was twenty-eight years old. After paying the premiums for five years, he died. At the time of death the insurance company discovered the correct age of Kalter and refused to settle on the policy, claiming that this was a material misrepresentation. Will the insurance company have to pay the claim?

7. Hacker took out a $5,000 twenty-year term policy on the life of Glander, his business partner. The partnership was dissolved after ten years; but Hacker continued to pay the premiums for two more years, when Glander died. Was the insurance company obligated to pay the face value of the policy to Hacker?

8. In September, 1965, the Goodwin Corporation insured the life of its president, J. B. Goodwin, for $25,000 under a twenty-year endowment policy. Six years later the company suffered a heavy loss, and President Goodwin committed suicide. Is the Goodwin Corporation entitled to collect the insurance?

THE LAW IN ACTION

1. The plaintiff corporation took out life insurance policies on the lives of the corporation president and the corporation secretary-treasurer, naming the stockholders as beneficiaries. The insurance company later contended that there was a lack of insurable interest and that the policy was invalid. Was this a correct contention? Why? (Mickelberry's Food Products Co., Inc. v. Haeussermann, 247 S.W.2d 731, Mo.)
2. The insured held an insurance policy issued by the defendant company, providing for double indemnity in case of accidental death. The insured died as a result of a brain hemorrhage that resulted from a violent sneeze caused by sniffing chopped whiskers into his nose while cleaning his electric shaver. The plaintiff contends that this was an accidental death and met the requirements of the double-indemnity clause. Do you think this would be a proper interpretation of the contract? Why? (Hughes v. Provident Mutual Life Insurance Co., 258 S.W.2d 290 [Mo. Ct. of App.])

KEY TO "WHAT'S THE LAW?" Page 324

1. *This might not be good advice. The young man might well need the greatest amount of protection for the least amount of money. The older man might be looking for a good investment.*
2. *Neither. The money you get back is the interest on your investment. Protection from risk always costs something. You do not have to die to collect on many types of life insurance.*

WHAT'S THE LAW?

1. *Jack Vernon argued, "Fire insurance is an investment."
Allan Roberts stated, "That isn't so. Fire insurance is an expense." Tim Rafferty commented, "You're both wrong. It is the
purchase of protection." Who is right?*

2. *When Bob Turner bought a new automobile, he said, "I'm
going to protect it and myself by obtaining every possible type
of insurance." How many types of insurance do you suppose
he would have to buy? Name them.*

▲ UNIT 36:
FIRE INSURANCE AND
AUTOMOBILE INSURANCE

FIRE INSURANCE

The owner of real estate constantly faces the possibility of having his
property destroyed by fire. When this happens, his loss may be very great.
The risk involved is somewhat different from that of life insurance. All
of us know that we are going to die sometime; and, by taking out life
insurance, we make systematic preparation for providing for those dependent on us. Fire insurance is different. In buying fire insurance, you
are protecting yourself against a financial loss that may never happen.

*How does the
risk in fire
insurance differ
from the risk in
life insurance?*

A *fire insurance policy* is a contract whereby the insurer promises, for a
stipulated premium, to pay the insured a sum not exceeding the face
amount of the policy if a particular piece of real or personal property is
damaged or destroyed by fire. Even before a policy is issued, a written
or even an oral binder is valid and may make fire insurance effective. The
policy covers losses to specific property located at the place stated in the
policy. The policy itself becomes effective as soon as the application is
accepted by the insurer, even though the insured has not yet paid the
premium.

FIRE
INSURANCE
POLICY

INSURABLE-INTEREST REQUIREMENT

*How does the
insurable interest
requirement in a
fire insurance
policy differ from
a life insurance
policy?*

Before you can take out fire insurance, the law requires you to have
an insurable interest in the property, during the risk, and at the time of
the loss. An insurable interest is not necessarily absolute ownership; you
are required to have only an interest sufficient to cause you monetary
loss in case the property is destroyed.

EXAMPLE 1   A house owned by Fred Quinn was insured against fire. Quinn sold the house to Thomas Clark. Quinn had paid a premium to All Town Insurance Company which would have continued the policy in force for seven more months subsequent to the sale. One month after the sale, the house burned to the ground and Quinn sought to collect on the policy. All Town did not have to pay because Quinn did not have an insurable interest in the house at the time of the fire. His interest ceased when he sold the house to Clark.

STANDARD POLICIES

Fire insurance policy contracts are far more standardized than life insurance contracts. That is, the fire insurance policies issued by various companies are very similar. Practically all states have adopted the New York standard fire insurance form with only slight modifications. Only the fire insurance policies of California, Maine, Massachusetts, Minnesota, and Texas contain provisions somewhat different from those contained in the New York standard form. The standard form is comparatively simple, and a sample copy can be obtained from almost any fire insurance agent.

Coinsurance-Clause Policy   Under a *coinsurance-clause policy,* the insurance company expresses the relationship between the insurance a client wishes to carry and the actual value of his property as a fraction. The client receives this fractional part of a loss as his indemnity payment. Thus, if a house valued at $10,000 is insured for $6,000, only 6,000/10,000, or three-fifths, of the loss can be recovered by the insured, since only three-fifths of the value of the property was insured.

COINSURANCE-CLAUSE POLICY

EXAMPLE 2   Suppose Svenson's summer house, valued at $20,000 and insured for only $12,000, had a fire loss of $10,000. Under the provisions of the coinsurance-clause policy, Svenson would receive only $6,000 in full payment.

$$\frac{12,000}{20,000} \text{ of } \$10,000 = \$6,000, \text{ amount recoverable}$$

The premise is that the insured is a coinsurer with the insurance company if he insures the property for less than its actual value. The difference between the value of the property and the amount of insurance is considered to be the personal risk of the insured. Of course, if the insurance carried is far more than the value of the property, only the actual fire loss will be paid.

What is a coinsurance clause policy? an 80 percent coinsurance clause policy?

80 Percent Coinsurance-Clause Policy   Under an *80 percent coinsurance-clause policy,* the insurance company will pay that part of a loss that the insurance carried bears to 80 percent of the value of the property. Thus, if a house valued at $10,000 is insured for only $6,000, only

80 PERCENT COINSURANCE-CLAUSE POLICY

$$\frac{\$6,000}{80\% \text{ of } \$10,000}, \quad \text{or} \quad \frac{\$6,000}{\$8,000}, \quad \text{or} \quad \frac{3}{4}$$

of the loss can be recovered by the insured, since only three-fourths of the 80 percent of the value of the property was insured. If, on the other hand, $8,000 insurance had been carried, the full loss up to $8,000 could have been collected from the insurance company, since this amount is 80 percent of the value of the property.

A fire insurance policy covers fire damage even if the insured causes the fire through negligence.

The 80 percent clause in a policy does not mean that only 80 percent of the value of the property is the maximum amount collectible. If the property is insured for its full value, the full amount could be collected.

EXAMPLE 3   Suppose that Svenson, in Example 2, had insured his $20,000 summer home for $12,000 under an 80 percent coinsurance-clause policy. The fire loss was determined to be $10,000 by an insurance adjuster. Under this policy, Svenson would recover three-fourths of his $10,000 claim, or $7,500.

$$\frac{12,000}{80\% \text{ of } 20,000} \times \$10,000 = \$7,500, \text{ amount recovered}$$

This type of policy simply provides that not less than 80 percent of the property shall be protected by insurance and that the insured shall bear the difference between the actual insurance carried and 80 percent of the value of the property. Here, as in the other two types of fire insurance policies, no more than the actual loss nor more than the actual amount of insurance carried can be collected.

HOMEOWNER'S POLICIES

Many of the leading insurance companies offer a combination policy known as the *homeowner's policy*. This policy covers protection for all types of losses and liabilities related to home ownership. Among the kinds of protection covered are losses from fire, windstorm, and related damage; burglary; vandalism; and injuries caused other persons while on the property. Homeowner's policies are issued in which the insured and his family are protected not just on the premises but anywhere in the world and for almost any cause. The rates are much lower than if each protection offered were covered by a separate policy.

HOMEOWNER'S POLICY

What is a homeowner's policy? What protection does it give?

EXAMPLE 4   All Town sold a homeowner's policy to Mackin. During a vacation trip, Mackin learned that his house had caught fire and has been extensively damaged. After the fire other losses resulted from vandalism and theft. All of these risks were covered in the one policy, and Mackin had no difficulty in computing his losses as he would have had if he had carried separate policies covering each specific loss with different insurers.

RIDERS, OR ENDORSEMENTS

What are riders or extended coverage endorsements in fire insurance policies? What protection do they provide?

If the coverage offered by a standard policy does not give you all the protection you desire, additional coverage is available. These provisions for additional coverage are called *riders*, or endorsements. They are written on special additional blanks and usually are pasted to your basic policy. The most common of these special contracts are called extended or *special-extended coverage endorsements*. Such endorsements ordinarily provide for protection against losses resulting from windstorm, hail, explosion, riots and other civil commotions, aircraft, vehicles, smoke, and often water.

RIDER

SPECIAL EXTENDED COVERAGE ENDORSEMENT

Do special endorsements ever provide for the assignment of the policy to a mortgage holder?

There may also be special endorsements providing for the assignment of the policy to a mortgage holder when the insured places a mortgage on his house and also for the added cost of increased hazards such as longer periods of vacancy and the storing of inflammable materials.

STANDARD CLAUSES

You should analyze a standard form of fire insurance policy used in your state for clauses that are regularly included. The more important clauses of a standard fire insurance policy are briefly described here.

What effect will concealment or fraud have on a fire insurance contract?

Concealment and Fraud If there has been any willful concealment or misstatement of any material facts concerning the risks involved or the interest of the insured in the property, the policy is declared void.

EXAMPLE 5 Bob Hunter took out a fire insurance policy on his home. He concealed from the insurance agent the fact that he planned to open a small dry-cleaning plant in his basement. The policy would be void, and Bob could recover nothing if a fire happened after the cleaning plant was installed.

Vacancy If the risk or hazard insured against has been increased by any means within the control or knowledge of the insured, the policy will be suspended during the continuation of that risk. Until recently, the most common increase of risk resulted if the insured property was vacant for more than sixty consecutive days. A building was considered *vacant* if it was empty—if it did not contain goods or articles of furniture and if the owner was away and had no intention of returning. This limitation of time on lack of occupancy has now been lifted, particularly in protected areas.

VACANT

Removal If the policy covers personal property, the company is not liable for any loss if the property is removed from the premises specified in the policy.

EXAMPLE 6 Finch obtained a fire insurance policy which included coverage of personal property in his house. He loaned a chair from his livingroom to Smith for a special occasion. While the chair was at Smith's house, the house was damaged by fire, and the chair was destroyed. Finch's policy would not cover the chair while it was in Smith's home because it had been removed from the premises specified in the policy.

Cancellation Provision is made for the cancellation by either party on proper notice. If the insurer requests the cancellation, the premium is

The standard New York and New Jersey policies expressly provide that losses by theft from the insured premises during a fire are not covered by the contract of insurance.

Is a prorata share of the premium returned by the insurer if the policy is canceled by the insured? by the insurer?

returned *prorata*, according to the actual proportionate amount of insurance which the insured will not receive. If the insured requests such action, the premium to be returned is determined by using a short-term rate table. The amount of this premium will be less than the prorata amount.

PRORATA

EXAMPLE 7 Clint Furney insured his house against fire loss with the Mutual Insurance Company. The policy was paid up for three years, but six months after its issue Furney sold his house to John Frey. Furney could cancel his insurance and get back part of his premium from the company.

Assignment A fire insurance policy is a personal contract, thus there is a provision in the policy against assignment to another person without the consent of the insurer. As a practical matter, insurance companies are usually willing to rewrite the policy in the name of the new owner when real property is sold. From your study of contracts, you will recognize this as a novation.

Prorata Liability Many times a homeowner will have more than one policy of insurance on his house. In such a case there is a provision that the insurer will pay no greater percentage of the total loss than is represented by the insurer's policy in proportion to the total insurance carried by the insured. The different insurance companies prorate the loss among them. Under the prorata clause, the insured can recover the amount of his loss only once.

What is meant by prorating the loss?

EXAMPLE 8 If you had two fire insurance policies, one issued by the Eagle Company and the other by the Fore Company, each for $5,000, and you suffered a loss of $5,000, each company would pay half the damage, or $2,500.

Requirements in Case of Loss In the event that fire destroys your property, you must give the insurer immediate notice of the fire in writing. Within sixty days, you must send the insurer a proof of loss, giving full information about the loss.

RECOVERY FOR DAMAGES

A fire insurance policy covers loss resulting directly or proximately from an unfriendly fire. An *unfriendly,* or hostile, *fire* is one that becomes uncontrollable or escapes from the place where it is supposed to be. A bonfire or a fire in a furnace is a *friendly fire* unless it gets beyond control.

UNFRIENDLY FIRE

FRIENDLY FIRE

EXAMPLE 9 Finch, while starting a fire in the fireplace of his living room, accidentally dropped his glasses into the fire. Recovery for loss of the glasses would not be permitted. Had embers fallen from the fireplace to the rug and damaged it, however, a recovery would be allowed for that damage.

What is meant by proximate results of a fire?

Damages to property resulting from attempts to put out a fire or theft or breakages in attempting to remove insured goods to a safer location are *proximate results* of the fire and are covered by the insurance policy. The same is true of damage due to soot, smoke, water, or heat from a nearby burning building. The standard New York and New Jersey policies, however, expressly provide that losses by theft from the insured premises during a fire are not covered by the contract of insurance.

PROXIMATE RESULTS

EXAMPLE 10 A large fire was raging in a certain city. In order to keep the fire from spreading, it was necessary to demolish a number of buildings. It was held that the owners could collect on their own fire insurance policies for the losses suffered.

AUTOMOBILE INSURANCE

What potential losses may result from ownership or operation of an automobile?

One of the greatest potential sources of loss and liability you will probably face in the future is through the ownership or operation of an automobile. Not only do you face the possible loss of the automobile through fire or theft, but in addition you face the possibility of doing thousands of dollars' worth of damage to the property and personal well-being of other people.

If you are going to drive an automobile, you must protect yourself against these potential losses, not only for your own protection but also for the protection of the people you may possibly injure. Such protection is a personal and moral "must" and is legally required by *financial responsibility laws,* which have been passed in most states.

FINANCIAL RESPONSIBILITY LAWS

Higher premiums are usually charged for liability insurance if a car is to be driven by a person under twenty-five years of age.

KINDS OF POLICIES

The most common forms of insurance policies issued on automobiles are listed here.

Theft, Robbery, and Pilferage This policy usually covers losses arising from the theft, robbery, or pilferage of an automobile or its equipment or from damages to or destruction of such property caused by the theft, robbery, or pilferage. It does not cover losses due to the theft of articles left in a car, nor does it cover the loss of tools or repair equipment unless the entire car is stolen.

EXAMPLE 11 **The All Town Insurance Company issued a theft, robbery, and pilferage policy to Finch. During a trip Finch left his car outside a motel. In the morning he discovered that sample cases, a portable radio, and the car's battery and hub caps had been stolen. Finch was reimbursed for the loss of the battery and hub caps, but the company refused to pay for the loss of the sample cases and the portable radio. These losses were not covered by the policy.**

Collision Insurance This insurance policy protects you not only against actual collision but also against almost any property damage to your car. If, for instance, your car is damaged by going into a ditch, you are indemnified for the loss by collision insurance. Such insurance may be obtained at a much lower premium if you carry part of the risk yourself. This type of insurance is commonly called *deductible collision insurance*. Under a contract of this kind, you are personally responsible for all damages up to the amount stated. In a $50 deductible policy, any amount over $50 is borne by the insurance company. Under no circumstances, then, will you stand a loss of more than $50. Generally the higher the amount of the deductible, the lower the cost of the policy.

DEDUCTIBLE COLLISION INSURANCE

What is collision insurance? What protection does it provide?

Liability Insurance The most important insurance for the automobile owner to carry is liability insurance. *Liability insurance* protects you against claims for injury to the person or property of others. If you injure or kill somebody or if you damage the personal property of others, the claim against you may amount to many thousands of dollars.

LIABILITY INSURANCE

What is liability insurance? What protection does it provide?

A company issuing liability insurance does not undertake, under all circumstances, to pay third parties for damage that you may cause such parties. It merely agrees to pay if the circumstances are such that you would have to pay. In other words, the company steps into your shoes, fights the case if necessary, and makes settlement up to the limit of the policy if the case is lost after having been tried in court. This is provided under the *defense clause* by which the insurer agrees to defend the insured against any claims for damages.

DEFENSE CLAUSE

What is the purpose of the defense-clause in a liability insurance policy?

A new type of automobile insurance which is now required by several states and is being considered by other states is *no-fault insurance*. Under no-fault insurance, the insured may collect for medical and related expenses that result from an accident no matter who was legally responsible for the accident. This type of insurance, which will save the expense and time of legal action, applies only to personal injury and not to property damage.

NO-FAULT INSURANCE

When an accident occurs, it is your duty to notify your insurance company and to protest the claim of the injured in any manner that would be honest and justifiable if you had to pay your own damage. Failure to do this may void the policy.

EXAMPLE 12 **You had a collision with Fisher at a street intersection. The damage to your car was slight, but Fisher suffered a loss that amounted to $150. Although the accident was Fisher's fault rather than yours, you said, "I am carrying insurance, and I'll see that you are paid for your damage." The company would be justified in refusing settlement, and you might be left to fight the case yourself.**

Comprehensive Policy The protection provided by a *comprehensive policy* includes loss or damage to the motor vehicle insured if caused by fire, lightning, flood, hail, windstorm, riot, vandalism, theft, robbery, and pilferage. In case of loss, the insurance company's liability under a comprehensive policy is limited to the actual cash value of the damaged property at the time of the loss.

COMPREHENSIVE POLICY

What protection is provided the motorist by a comprehensive policy?

EXAMPLE 13 **Finch's car, which was covered by a comprehensive insurance policy, was stolen and presumed unrecoverable. Finch contended that the insurance company was liable for the replacement cost of the car. The company offered in settlement the actual cash market value of the automobile at the time of the theft. It was held that the insurance company was correct in its settlement.**

The insurance protection provided by this type of automobile policy covers losses due to fire or lightning and to the damage or destruction of the car by the collision, sinking, stranding, or burning of any conveyance on which it is being transported, such as a train, barge, or boat.

WHAT YOU SHOULD DO IN CASE OF AN ACCIDENT

1. Stop immediately.
2. Render aid to the injured while exercising extreme care to avoid further injury. It is best not to move an injured person until the doctor arrives.
3. If you are driving a car which belongs to someone else and the owner is not along, notify the owner at once.
4. Get the license number and the names of the driver, owner, and passengers of the other car. Give your name, address, and license number.
5. Get the names and addresses of all witnesses.
6. If a police officer is present, get his name and number.
7. Write a report of the accident to your insurance company. State statutes may require that you report the accident to some public official. This is particularly true if the damage exceeds an amount specified by statute.
8. Give no information regarding the accident to anyone but your insurance company's representative or the police, except as required by law; that is, license number, name and address of self, owner, and passengers in your car.

What steps should you take in case of an accident?

9. Do not admit any responsibility.

A comprehensive policy provides protection against almost every form of physical loss.

TERMINATION OF FIRE AND AUTOMOBILE POLICIES

Fire insurance and automobile insurance policies are terminated in much the same way. The most common way is the expiration of the policy. Fire insurance policies are usually written for a term of one or three years. At the end of that time, the policy expires and a new one must be written. The same is true of automobile policies, except that the term is usually limited to one year.

It is common practice for an insurance agent, if he wishes to renew a policy, to make out a new policy three or four weeks before the expiration date of the old one and mail the new policy to the insured. This amounts to an offer on the part of the insurer to insure for another year on the terms stated in the policy. If the insured keeps the policy and pays, or promises to pay, the premium, there is an acceptance of the offer.

The first time an agent sends the insured a renewal policy the insured is not obliged to return the policy if he does not want the insurance. If he once accepts a tendered policy in this manner, an established course of dealings has been created, however, and in future years he must notify the agent and return the policy if he does not wish to be reinsured.

● Either fire or automobile insurance can be canceled by either party on proper notice. When the policy is canceled, the insured is entitled to a return of the unused part of his premium. If an automobile insurance policy has been canceled and the insured finds it difficult to obtain public liability insurance, he may be assigned to an insurance company that will provide him with the minimum public liability insurance required by his particular state. In this case, the insured is called an *assigned risk*.

How are fire and automobile insurance policies terminated? canceled?

ASSIGNED RISK

NOTE: *The bullet indicates that there may be a state statute that varies from the law discussed here.*

SUGGESTIONS FOR MINIMIZING LEGAL RISKS

1. Carefully follow the written instructions provided by the insurance company for reporting a loss, an accident, or a claim; otherwise, you run a risk that the company may decline to settle.

2. Fire loss is frequently due to carelessness on the part of persons using the property. Any means that will reduce carelessness on the premises will minimize legal risks and possible financial loss. Inspect the property periodically for possible fire hazards and evidences of carelessness.

3. An accident that results from the negligent and illegal driving of an automobile may result in both a civil suit for damages and an arrest and trial on a criminal charge. Automobile liability insurance does not cover the costs and possible fines and jail sentence of a criminal suit. Drive carefully at all times, and do not break the law; otherwise, you incur two possible risks, one of which is not insurable.

4. If you are an observer of an accident or a victim of an accident, be extremely careful about what you say to anyone except to a policeman, your doctor, your lawyer, or your insurance company representative. Any statements made to others may be used later against you in a lawsuit. If you are attempting to collect damages for injuries, your statements to persons other than those mentioned above may be used to nullify your claim for damages.

5. If you are injured in an accident, try to get the names and addresses of all witnesses to the accident and follow all legal requirements of your state in reporting the accident. Report all necessary information to your insurance company according to the written instructions provided by the insurance company.

 APPLYING YOUR LEARNING

QUESTIONS AND PROBLEMS

1. The purpose of property insurance, which includes fire insurance, is one of indemnification. What does this mean?
2. Fire insurance covers loss due to an actual hostile fire. What is meant by this?
3. List the risks that might be covered by a fire insurance policy.
4. Why is it desirable to have a standard form of fire insurance policy?
5. Name and explain briefly several of the clauses found in a standard-form policy of fire insurance.
6. What is meant by a coinsurance clause? Explain and illustrate.
7. What is the distinction between a representation and a warranty in an insurance contract?
8. How is a fire loss determined? Explain briefly.
9. Can a fire insurance policy be assigned without permission of the insurer? Explain.
10. For what reasons may an insurer avoid or cancel a fire insurance policy?
11. How is a fire insurance policy usually terminated?
12. Distinguish between automobile collision insurance and automobile liability insurance.

13. Give several illustrations of typical accidents that would be covered by collision insurance and liability insurance.
14. Does your state have a financial responsibility statute? If so, what are the major provisions of this law?
15. Explain what one should do if involved in an accident when driving one's own automobile.
16. What should one do if an accident occurs while driving an automobile that belongs to someone else and the owner is not along?
17. What possible legal risks might result from attempting to move a person who had been very seriously injured in an automobile accident? What should one do in a case of this kind?
18. How are automobile insurance policies usually terminated?
19. When must one notify an agent and return the insurance policy if one does not wish to be reinsured?
20. How should one go about canceling an insurance policy?

WHAT IS YOUR OPINION?

In each of the following cases, give your decision and state a legal principle that applies to the case.

1. Colt insured his stock of goods under a standard fire policy. Later, he removed his stock to another warehouse but did not notify the insurance company of the change. The second warehouse burned, destroying Colt's merchandise. Can Colt collect on his insurance policy?
2. Gedrow carried fire insurance on his furniture, which was damaged by water used by firemen in putting out a fire in Gedrow's house. Was Gedrow entitled to collect from the insurance company for damage to the furniture?
3. Kantor bought a house from Burke for $16,000, paying $6,000 in cash and giving Burke a mortgage for $10,000. Burke immediately insured the property against loss by fire under a five-year policy. Four years later Kantor paid off the entire mortgage. One month after this the house was destroyed by fire. Is Burke entitled to collect on the policy?
4. Posner insured his $12,000 house for $20,000. Six months after taking out the insurance, the house was completely destroyed by fire. How much will Posner recover from the insurance company?
5. Ladue, while backing his automobile out of the garage, damaged a fender on the automobile. He carried liability insurance. Was he entitled to collect damages from the insurance company? If he had carried collision insurance, would your answer have been the same?
6. Lauer had liability insurance on his automobile. His car was damaged as a result of being crowded off the road. Is he entitled to collect from his insurance company?
7. Keith sold a car to Bell for $800, terms $200 down, the balance plus interest to be paid in ten equal installments. Bell also paid $16 to cover the cost of the necessary fire and theft policy for the car, naming Keith as beneficiary. After Bell had fully paid for the car, it was destroyed by fire. Can Keith collect on the policy?

8. Wicks took out a liability insurance policy on his automobile, providing for $5,000 property damage, $10,000 for maximum injury to one person, and $20,000 maximum for all persons involved in an accident. An accident occurred in which three persons were injured. The combined judgments against Wicks in a lawsuit totaled $100,000. Do you think his insurance policy would cover the cost of the lawsuit?

9. In the preceding case, one automobile involved was less than a month old. It was purchased by one of the injured persons at a cost of $3,500. It was completely demolished in the accident. Does Wicks's insurance cover the damage to this car?

10. Wicks's own automobile, which was two years old, was completely demolished. The original cost was $3,200. Can Wicks collect from his insurance company for the present value of his car?

11. If Wicks lived in a state having compulsory financial-responsibility laws, is it likely that he could recover the value of his automobile? Why?

12. Stevens sold his house, on which he carried $10,000 fire insurance. At the time of sale, the policy still had two years to run; so Stevens transferred it to Wesson, the purchaser. Within a year the house burned; and the insurance company, learning that Wesson was the owner, refused to settle with him. Was the insurance company within its rights?

13. Fields, whose furniture was insured against fire, moved without notifying the insurance company from a frame dwelling to a brick building where the risk of loss from fire was less. A fire destroyed the furniture in the brick building. Was Fields covered by insurance after the move?

14. DeWolf telephoned an insurance company and asked that his house be insured against fire loss, giving the necessary information to the agent, who agreed to insure the house. The next day, and before the insurance policy was issued, fire damaged the house through no fault of DeWolf's. Is the insurance company liable?

15. Herbert had fire insurance on his house, which was damaged by the collapse of a nearby burning building. Was Herbert entitled to collect from his insurance company for the damage?

16. Ladd took out a fire insurance policy on his barn. He lighted a wisp of hay to burn out a hornet's nest; and some of the sparks fell on a pile of hay, setting the barn and the hay on fire. Can he collect the insurance?

17. Kapp, a merchant, carried a standard fire insurance policy on his stock of goods. During a fire in a nearby store, Kapp's merchandise was damaged by smoke and water. Can Kapp collect damages under his policy?

18. Kane's furniture was damaged by a fire as a result of his accidentally dropping a cigarette into a wastepaper basket. If Kane had fire insurance on the furniture, was he entitled to collect damages from the insurance company?

19. Rutland, who carried automobile liability insurance, operated his car so negligently as to damage a car belonging to Laury. The insurance company refused to pay Laury for the damage, claiming that Rutland was unduly negligent and that he was at fault. Is the insurance company legally liable?

THE LAW IN ACTION

1. The plaintiff brought an action for damage to a rug caused by a lighted cigarette falling off an ash tray. The cigarette had fallen to the floor and burned a hole in the rug before it was observed. The defendant contended that a cigarette is lighted by and under the control of an individual and thus would be classed as a friendly fire. Do you think the insurance company was liable for the damage to the rug? (Swerling v. Conn. Fire Ins. Co., 55 R.I. 252, 180 A 343)

2. The defendant company issued an automobile insurance policy to the plaintiff providing for coverage of any "loss of or damage to the automobile caused by larceny, robbery, or pilferage." The automobile covered was taken out after hours and without authority by the plaintiff's chauffeur and seriously damaged. The defendant refused to pay the claim, contending that the "joy riding" by the chauffeur did not constitute a theft. What do you think? (Block et al. v. Standard Insurance Co. of N.Y., 292 N.Y. 270)

KEY TO "WHAT'S THE LAW?" Page 335

1. *Allan and Tim are both right, but Jack is not right since fire insurance has no cash surrender value and therefore cannot be considered an investment.*
2. *The most common forms are theft, fire, collision, and liability. There might also be wind, flood, glass breakage, and possibly other special kinds.*

A DIGEST OF LEGAL CONCEPTS

1. The purpose of insurance is to spread the cost of large and infrequent losses among a large number of people.

2. In stock insurance companies, the shareholders who invest their money own the company. A portion of the profits of the company are paid to the shareholders in the form of dividends.

3. In mutual insurance companies, the policyholders insure themselves by paying premiums to the management, which, in turn, operates the company. Some profits are returned to the policyholders as policy dividends.

4. An insurance policy is a contract and, except as changed by special rules, follows the ordinary rules of contracts.

5. The offer in an insurance contract is usually made by the party desiring insurance by his filling out an application. The offer is accepted by the insurance company on approving the application and issuing a policy.

6. In fire, automobile, life, and casualty insurance, the insurance agent is usually authorized by his company to make a temporary acceptance of an application by issuing what is known as a binder.

7. The application for insurance is the document relied on by the insurance company to determine the nature and extent of the risk it is assuming. Any material misrepresentation made by the insured in the application may be the basis of voiding the policy.

8. The primary purpose of basic life insurance is to protect the family of the insured from the risk of loss of income arising from the death of the insured.

9. A secondary purpose of life insurance is to provide a systematic method of saving and investment whereby the insured can provide for his own future security.

10. Term insurance is insurance for protection only. It is issued for specified periods of time, and the premium is the price paid for the protection only. There is no investment feature in term insurance.

11. Ordinary and limited-payment life insurance policies acquire a cash surrender value which increases from year to year as the policy remains in force.

12. Endowment policies place their chief emphasis on investment. They provide a stipulated sum in cash at the end of a specified period.

13. All insurance policies that have an investment feature build up a cash surrender value. The cash surrender value represents the approximate amount of the investment over and above the cost of the risk assumed by the company.

14. Investment-type policies also usually have a loan value that is approximately the same amount as the cash surrender value.

15. The insured may change the beneficiary named in the policy only as specified in the policy itself.

16. To protect the insured, most life insurance policies have an incontestability clause.

17. A misstatement of the insured as to his age usually will not cause a cancellation of the policy but will give the insurer a right to demand additional premiums.

18. The person taking out a policy of life insurance and paying the premiums must have an insurable interest in the life of the insured at the time the policy is issued.

19. After a specified number of years, a life insurance policy becomes incontestable. This means that the insurer may no longer cancel a policy because of an insured's false statements when the policy was originally issued.

20. Fire insurance makes it possible for you, by paying a small premium regularly, to minimize your risk of a great financial loss that may never happen.

21. The insured must have an insurable interest in the property covered by the fire insurance policy at the time the loss occurs.

22. If the insured willfully misstates or conceals any material fact concerning the risks involved, a fire insurance policy may be voided.

23. If property insured is moved to a different location without the consent of the insurer, the insurer is not liable for any loss incurred in the new location.

24. A fire insurance policy is not assignable without the consent of the insurer.

25. Where property is covered by more than one fire insurance policy, the various insurers pay a proportionate part of the loss.

26. Negligence on the part of the insured does not ordinarily prevent him from collecting in case of fire loss.

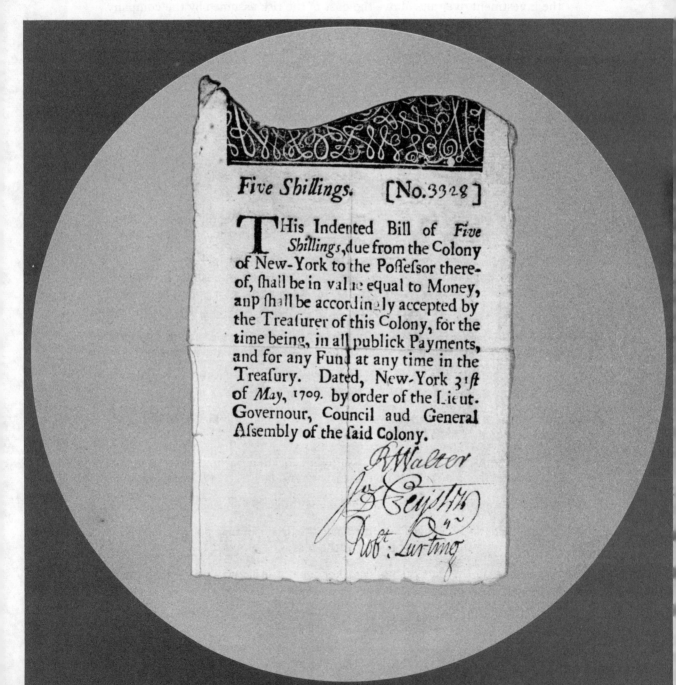

WHAT'S THE LAW?

1. *Petrof sold his used automobile to Lee on credit. Lee refused to pay the purchase price when he discovered that Petrof had made many fraudulent statements in promoting the sale. Could Lee use fraud as a defense if Petrof sued? If Petrof had assigned his rights to Eastman, could Eastman collect from Lee free of the defense of fraud?*

2. *Can you think of any way that Lee could have made a promise to pay that could be transferred free of defenses?*

◬ UNIT 37:
NATURE AND KINDS
OF COMMERCIAL PAPER

What is money? Why is it often referred to as a medium of exchange?

When you buy things, you need money. *Money* is often defined as "a measure of wealth." We might say, "Mr. Martin is a rich man. He has lots of money." We would be including all kinds of items—gold, silver, land, personal property, and money owed to Mr. Martin by others. This is a casual definition, but it comes very close to the concept that experts accept as the true meaning of money. We may also visualize money as something that we would accept in exchange for our property or services. This is why money is often referred to as a *medium of exchange*. The more valuable the medium of exchange, the more likely is it to be acceptable. At one time people readily accepted gold and silver as mediums of exchange. To eliminate the necessity of carefully weighing metals each time an exchange was made, responsible governments long ago began to coin gold and silver into units of certified weights, and thus standard symbols of money were developed. Because of the common use of coined valuable metals as money, we have often accepted a narrow definition of money as coined metal, usually gold and silver, upon which a government stamp has been impressed to indicate its value. Since March, 1933, paper money has by law been declared to be money in this country. Today, then, the definition of money as coined metal only is no longer valid.

MONEY

MEDIUM OF EXCHANGE

When did paper money become legal in the United States?

CREDIT IN BUSINESS TRANSACTIONS

You may well ask yourself, "Just why is a piece of paper acceptable in the purchase of goods? It has no physical value." If you look at a dollar bill, you will find that it is backed by the credit of the United States

The use of cash in business transactions can sometimes be very inconvenient.

government. Because the credit of the United States government is good, we are willing to accept its credit instruments in exchange for our services and goods. Money today, then, often consists of credit instruments. These government notes are usually referred to as "paper money."

Although paper money is much more convenient to use than coined metal, it is still not sufficient to meet our modern business and personal needs. There is not enough of it and paying cash is too slow. Think for a moment of the inconvenience of having to carry cash for a large purchase such as an automobile. Often people do not have such a large amount of cash readily available or feel that it is unsafe to carry large amounts of paper money with them.

KINDS OF CREDIT INSTRUMENTS

What are credit instruments? Is paper money considered a credit instrument?

Modern business needs not only credit but also credit instruments that are convenient and will circulate rapidly. These credit instruments are called *commercial paper* or *negotiable instruments*. They are written instruments of credit that can be transferred from one person to another by endorsement and delivery or by delivery alone.

COMMERCIAL PAPER

NEGOTIABLE INSTRUMENTS

In order to be a negotiable instrument, a written document must (1) be signed by the maker or drawer, (2) contain an unconditional promise or order to pay a certain sum in money, (3) be payable on demand or at a definite time, and (4) be payable to order or to bearer. U.C.C. Sec. 3-104(1)

A negotiable instrument may be a *draft* (bill of exchange) if it is an order for someone to pay money; a *check* if it is a draft drawn on a bank and payable on demand; a *certificate of deposit* if it is an acknowledgment by a bank of receipt of money with a promise to repay it; or a *promissory note* if it is a promise to repay money other than a certificate of deposit. U.C.C. Sec. 3-104(2)

DRAFT

CHECK

CERTIFICATE OF DEPOSIT

PROMISSORY NOTE

PROMISSORY NOTES

EXAMPLE 1 **Mr. Doolittle opens a new furniture store. He extends credit to his customers in order to sell more furniture. Most customers make a small** downpayment and agree to pay a specified amount each month. It may take a year or more for Mr. Doolittle to receive the full purchase price for his furniture sales. During this same period, he must buy more furniture to sell to other customers.

In a short time, Mr. Doolittle may have a great deal of money owed to him; but also he may run out of cash himself. Mr. Doolittle will then have to go to the bank and ask to borrow money in order to buy more goods. As security for the loan, he may offer to assign his right to collect from his customers, most often called *accounts receivable*. Mr. Gavin, the president of the bank, will probably answer: "We shall be glad to lend you the money, Mr. Doolittle. Before we can make the loan, however, we should like to examine your accounts receivable. We will send a representative over to look at them tomorrow and let you know about the loan next week." "But," exclaims Mr. Doolittle, "I need the money today. I have a shipment of new furniture that I must pay for."

ACCOUNTS RECEIVABLE

"I'm sorry," Mr. Gavin replies, "we cannot make the loan until we find out whether any of your customers have defenses to your claim."

You know from your study of contracts that Mr. Gavin is right. If the goods sold by Mr. Doolittle were defective or had been fraudulently represented or possibly returned for credit, the customers would have a defense against Mr. Doolittle's claim for the money. You also remember that, if a right to collect money is assigned, all defenses go right along with the assignment. So, any defenses good against Mr. Doolittle would be good against the bank. The bank will not make the loan until it has had time to check with the customers on the matter of defenses.

"Isn't there some way," you ask, "that Mr. Doolittle could get the money at once?" The answer is yes. If Mr. Doolittle had obtained negotiable promissory notes from his customers in payment for the goods instead of charging them on open account, he would be in a much better position to obtain a loan. U.C.C. Sec. 3-104(2)(d) After examining the notes to determine whether they were a good risk for the bank, Mr. Gavin would probably say, "These notes seem to be all right. Just endorse your name on the back, and we will give you the money." U.C.C. Sec. 3-202, Sec. 3-201

Commercial paper, or negotiable instruments, can be transferred from one person to another by endorsement and delivery or, under certain circumstances, by delivery alone.

What is the legal
significance of
the term
"negotiability?"

"What is the difference?" you ask. The difference is that these promissory notes are negotiable. When these notes are transferred to the bank, they are said to be *negotiated*. This act of negotiation has a definite legal significance. The customers who executed the notes can no longer use the defenses against the bank that they could have used against Mr. Doolittle. Negotiation in the proper way, to the proper parties, has the legal effect of cutting off defenses, that is, of preventing the person executing the note from using defenses that were good against the original party when the new owner sues for its collection. U.C.C. Sec. 3-202(1)

NEGOTIATED

What is the
distinguishing
characteristic
of a note?

Each note contains a promise to repay the money borrowed. This is the distinguishing thing about a note. It contains a promise to pay money.

$ 400.00 _____ Tyler, Texas, May 4, *19--*

_____Sixty days_____ *after date* I *promise to pay to*

the order of --------------------Thomas Ryan---------------------

Four hundred and no/100----------------------------- *Dollars*

at ____The Liberty National Bank_____

Value received

No. 55 *Due* July 3, 19-- *Vincent Cosenzo*

To better identify the parties connected with a promissory note, they are always called by specific names. The person who executes, or creates, a promissory note is called the *maker*. On his signature he accepts full responsibility for the payment of the note. If someone else signs the note on its face with the maker, he is called a *comaker*. The person to whom the maker promises to pay the money is called the *payee*. When the payee sells the note to someone else, the payee signs his name on the back. He is now called an *endorser*.

MAKER

COMAKER
PAYEE

ENDORSER

DRAFTS

In ordinary business language, a bill of exchange is called a *draft*. The most common example of a draft is an ordinary check. We use checks so often and they are so much a part of our personal and business lives that we seldom stop to think how complicated business transactions would be if we did not have them. U.C.C. Sec. 3-104

DRAFT

What is the most
common example
of a draft?

EXAMPLE 2 Mr. Stone owns and operates a store in the state of Texas. He buys some of his merchandise from a wholesaler in Los Angeles, some from a wholesaler in St. Paul, and the rest from other parts of the United States. Visualize, if you can, how difficult it would be for him to do business if there were no such thing as a bill of exchange such as a check. Each time he purchased goods, he would have to send an agent with cash to pay for the goods. This would be expensive, slow, and dangerous.

Today, by using a check or other form of bill of exchange, the transaction is simple. Mr. Stone sends each wholesaler a check. The checks are orders drawn on Mr. Stone's bank ordering the bank to pay the suppliers the designated sums

of money. Mr. Stone's bank, in turn, sends an order through regular banking channels to a bank in each supplier's city to settle the accounts. No money is shipped at all, except occasionally to settle accounts between banks.

What names are given to the parties to a draft? Distinguish among them.

The person who executes, or "draws," a bill of exchange is called the *drawer*. He corresponds to the maker on a note. He is the one who, as on a check, makes a demand on a bank or any other party for the payment of money to a third party.

DRAWER

The drawer of a bill of exchange orders someone else to pay. The person who is ordered to pay is called the *drawee*. A bank is the drawee of all checks drawn on accounts held by the bank.

DRAWEE

The *payee* on a bill of exchange is the same as the payee on a note. He is the person to whom the money is to be paid.

The payee and all subsequent persons receiving the instrument by delivery or by endorsement and delivery are *holders*.

HOLDER

The *endorser* of a bill of exchange is the same as the endorser of a note.

ENDORSER

How does the drawee of a draft indicate the fact that he will pay the draft when it becomes due?

If the drawee agrees to pay the bill of exchange, he writes "Accepted" on the face of the instrument and signs his name. He now has become the *acceptor*. The acceptor, once he has accepted, is the person primarily liable to pay the instrument. When the bank is the acceptor of a check, the name of the bank is generally stamped on the face of the check.

ACCEPTOR

SUGGESTIONS FOR MINIMIZING LEGAL RISKS

1. Giving a negotiable instrument in payment of a financial obligation is frequently desirable because the canceled instrument serves as a receipt for the payment.
2. Accepting a negotiable instrument in payment of goods sold when the buyer is unable to pay immediately is frequently desirable because it gives the holder an instrument that he can readily convert into cash.
3. Prepare all your negotiable instruments carefully using ink, a typewriter, or a check protector, so that it will be virtually impossible for them to be altered by a future holder, finder, or thief.
4. If you have to hold negotiable instruments for a period of time until maturity, keep them in a protected place where they will not become lost, stolen, burned, or destroyed.

 APPLYING YOUR LEARNING

QUESTIONS AND PROBLEMS

1. How did the idea of using money as a medium of exchange develop?
2. Why is "paper money" not always satisfactory for modern business transactions?
3. What are some reasons for the development of negotiable instruments?

4. Name as many different types of negotiable instruments as you can. How many of these types have members of the class handled?
5. What is the difference between a draft and a promissory note? Name the parties in each.

WHAT IS YOUR OPINION?

In each of the following cases, give your decision and state a legal principle that applies to the case.

1. In payment of a wager on a baseball game, Jim Wilson accepted an IOU from Will Lincoln which said, "IOU $10." Wilson offered the IOU in payment of his grocery bill. Do you think the grocery-store owner would be likely to accept this type of payment? Why or why not?
2. Stanley Stevens, who lives in California, sent a check to Dick Bundy, who lives in New York. Can Bundy reasonably expect that the laws relating to the collection of the check will be the same in both states?
3. Gordon Jackson signed a pledge in favor of his church for $520, payable at $10 a week for the following 52 weeks. Could the church trustees assign this promise to the Beber Coal Company in payment of the church's coal bill? Or would the coal company prefer to have some other type of promise to pay?
4. William Bogert gave Henry Britton his check for $500 in payment for an automobile. Britton contends that he may consider the check a promissory note. Is he correct? If not a note, what is it?
5. Gavin West wrote a postal card to his friend Joe Hall, which said, "Would you pay Jack Hutchinson $25 next week?" If Hall at this time owed $25 to West, would the payment by Hall to Hutchinson cancel that debt to West? Would you call this postal card a negotiable instrument?

THE LAW IN ACTION

1. The treasurer of a bankrupt corporation had embezzled funds of the corporation, invested the funds in company stock, and then pledged the stock with the defendant bank to secure a personal loan. In the resulting bankruptcy action the bank claims that the stock is a negotiable instrument. Do you think this is correct? (Millard v. Green, 94 Conn. 597, 110 A. 177)
2. The defendant drew an instrument, negotiable in form, on himself, ordering himself to pay. In an action brought for the collection of the instrument, the question was raised as to whether this was a note or a draft. On the basis of your study of this part, what is your opinion? (Pavenstedt v. New York Life Insurance Co. 203 N.Y. 91, 96 N.E. 104)

KEY TO "WHAT'S THE LAW?" Page 351

1. *Yes, this is an ordinary contract to pay money; fraud is always a defense in an action of this kind. No, you learned from your study of the assignment of contractual rights that defenses go right along with an assignment of rights.*
2. *Yes, Lee could have executed a negotiable promissory note.*

WHAT'S THE LAW?

1. Samuel Fong accepted a promissory note from Val James in payment for 10 shares of American Carbide Corporation stock. The statement "Payable 30 days after the delivery of the stock" was written on the face of the note. Would this be a negotiable instrument?

2. Before the stock was delivered in the preceding case, James discovered that he had been defrauded in the transaction. If Fong brought an action to collect the note, could James use fraud as a defense?

◭ UNIT 38: ESSENTIALS OF COMMERCIAL PAPER

If the holder of commercial paper (a negotiable instrument) needs money, he can sell the instrument more readily than he could sell an ordinary written acknowledgment of a debt. This is because the buyer to whom the instrument is negotiated can collect it free of all personal defenses; whereas, in the assignment of an ordinary promise to pay money, all defenses go right along with the assignment. To achieve this special advantage, however, certain definite requirements as to physical form and content must be met. U.C.C. Sec. 3-104(1) & Sec. 3-401(1) These requirements will be covered in this unit. While you are reading, remember that the terms "commercial paper" and "negotiable instruments" may be used interchangeably.

REQUIREMENTS AS TO FORM AND CONTENT

FORM OF NEGOTIABLE INSTRUMENTS

Can an oral promise to pay a debt be negotiated?

The Instrument Must Be in Writing The promise, or order to pay, must be in writing. An oral promise, no matter how specific it may have been, cannot be negotiated. The writing may be handwriting, typewriting, printing, or any other means of writing that will make a mark. The person who writes his name on it as the maker or drawer of the instrument is liable on it. U.C.C. Sec. 3-104(1)

CONTENTS OF NEGOTIABLE INSTRUMENTS

If the maker of a note or the drawer of a draft wrote his signature in the text of the instrument rather than at the bottom of the note or draft, would he be liable on the instrument?

The Instrument Must Be Signed by the Maker or the Drawer A promissory note must be signed by the maker. A draft must be signed by the drawer. A signature may be anything that is placed on the instrument with the intention of its being a signature. The signature may be either written at the bottom or into the text as "I, John Brown, promise to pay . . ." U.C.C. Sec. 3-401

The very earliest negotiable instruments were required to be in writing and signed by the maker or drawer.

EXAMPLE 1 **The Gotham Loan Company received two notes as evidence of loans. One note was signed "Henry Richmond, agent"; the other was signed "Matthew Dumont, Treasurer of the Minton Discount House." In the case of the first note, Richmond was personally liable—not the firm for which he worked. The word "agent" was a mere term of description. The Minton Discount House was bound on the second note. Dumont had clearly indicated that he had signed for his employer.**

Does a qualified promise in a note or order in a draft affect the negotiability of the instrument?

The Instrument Must Contain an Unconditional Promise or Order   The promise in the note, or the order in the draft, must be unconditional. If either is qualified in any way, the instrument is not negotiable. U.C.C. Sec. 3-104(1)(b) & Sec. 3-105

EXAMPLE 2 **Scott Sullivan's uncle gave him a promissory note for $100. The note was complete and regular in every way except that written on it was the statement, "Payable only on Scott Sullivan's graduation from high school."**

What effect do statements requiring that certain things be done prior to payment have on the instrument?

This is a good promise to pay; and, if Scott graduates from high school, his uncle will owe him $100. The note is not negotiable, however, and never can be. It is conditioned on Scott's graduation. Even if Scott is graduated and meets the condition, the note is still not negotiable because on its face it is conditional. Statements requiring that certain things be done or that specific events take place prior to payment make the instrument a simple contract rather than negotiable paper.

The Instrument Must Contain Words of Negotiability   To be negotiable, the instrument must contain the words "to the order of" or "to bearer." These are the *words of negotiability*. U.C.C. Sec. 3-104(1)(d) If such words as "to the order of" are omitted, the instrument is not negotiable. U.C.C. Sec. 3-104 and 405

What are the words of negotiability?

WORDS OF NEGOTIABILITY

EXAMPLE 3 **Suppose that the note given to Scott did not contain the condition mentioned in Example 2. It read, however, only "I promise to pay Scott Sullivan," etc., without the words "order" or "bearer."**

Are instruments made out to fictitious persons considered negotiable bearer instruments?

The implication is that the uncle would pay Scott but no one else. Thus, the instrument is not negotiable. U.C.C. Sec. 3-104(1)(d), Sec. 3-110(1)

Instruments made out to fictitious persons are not to be considered as bearer instruments.

The Amount Must Be a Sum Certain in Money   A negotiable instrument must be payable in money. Usually, it can be payable in any money that has a known or established value. An instrument payable in a foreign

Would an instrument payable in a foreign currency or in money that is not legal tender be negotiable?

currency or any medium of exchange accepted by a domestic or foreign government is negotiable. U.C.C. Sec. 3-107

A note made payable in either money or commodities at the option of the holder is negotiable. However, if the note states that the maker has the right to choose whether he will make payment in money or commodities, it is nonnegotiable. In the first case the holder may demand payment in money if he so desires. In the second case, if the maker chooses to pay the note in commodities, the holder must accept payment in that form; the note is thus nonnegotiable.

One note was made payable in either money or commodities at the option of the holder; another was payable at the option of the maker. Which note, if either, is negotiable?

EXAMPLE 4   The following note was received by Gotham Loan Company from a farmer in return for a loan of $500 that the company had made to him: "Two months after date, I promise to pay to the order of Gotham Loan Company $500 or, at my option, 200 bags of potatoes. Ezra Millard."

This note is nonnegotiable because the holder does not have the option of demanding potatoes or cash. If the note had contained the words "at the option of the holder," it would have been negotiable.

The sum to be paid is said to be certain, even though the maker promises to pay it with interest in stated installments or with cost of collection or attorney's fees added if payment is not made at maturity. U.C.C. Sec. 3-106(1)

Interest may be allowed on notes as follows: (1) when agreed on between the parties to a loan (as in a note); (2) when a non-interest-bearing note has passed the due date (for the period between the due date and the date on which payment is made); (3) when the credit period of a purchase has expired for the number of days from the expiration date to the date paid.

When a note reads "with interest" but does not stipulate the rate to be charged, what rate of interest may be charged?

The legal rate of interest specified by state statutes may be charged when a note reads "with interest" but does not stipulate the rate to be charged. The *maximum contract rate* of interest is the highest rate permitted, and it must be agreed upon by both parties and stated in a contract. Statutes differ in setting the rates; many states provide that the maximum contract rate should be no higher than the legal rate. Any provision for payment of interest at a rate higher than the maximum permissible contract rate allowed by law is considered to be usury and is illegal.

MAXIMUM
CONTRACT RATE

An instrument must be payable at a definite time rather than at a fixed or determinable future time. What is the legal significance of this statement?

EXAMPLE 5   Suppose Sampson had agreed to pay 12 percent interest on a loan in a state in which the maximum permissible contract rate is 10 percent. The note would be considered a usurious note. In most states Sampson would be relieved from liability for all interest payments on the note. In several states he would be relieved from payment of the principal as well. In some states he would only be relieved from payment of interest above the legal rate.

The Time of Payment Must Be Certain   The time at which the instrument is payable must be definite, or the instrument must be payable on demand. An instrument payable only upon an event whose occurrence is uncertain is not payable at a definite time. U.C.C. Sec. 3-104(1)(c), Sec. 3-109

EXAMPLE 6   If Scott's uncle had given him a note containing the words "payable thirty days after my death," the note would not be negotiable because it was not payable at a definite time.

If the instrument is payable "on demand" or "at sight," it must be presented for payment within a reasonable length of time.

In Drafts, the Drawee Must Be Indicated   The rule that the drawee must be indicated applies to drafts only. If you are ordering someone to pay, that person must be named or indicated with reasonable certainty. If an instrument named the drawee as "National Bank, New York," and there were several National Banks in New York City, the paper would be non-negotiable because the drawee was not named with sufficient definiteness.

DELIVERY OF NEGOTIABLE INSTRUMENTS

When is a negotiable instrument considered delivered?

A negotiable instrument—unlike other contracts—must be delivered to be effective. A negotiable instrument is delivered when the one who issues it transfers ownership and gives up possession of it to a new owner. If the instrument is in circulation, however, it is presumed to have been properly delivered until evidence is introduced to prove that it was not.

EXAMPLE 7   **Robert McIntosh fully executed a promissory note payable to Rodney Hough and left it lying on his (Robert's) desk. Rodney came in when Robert was not at his desk, took the note, and carried it away with him. If Rodney later brought an action against Robert to collect the note, the very fact that this note had been fully executed and was in circulation would be evidence of proper delivery. Robert, however, would be permitted to introduce evidence to show that Rodney took the note wrongfully and that there was no legal delivery.**

If Rodney had properly negotiated the note to the Exchange Bank, which had no notice of the wrongful taking, and the Exchange Bank had brought an action for its collection, the bank could collect it. Robert would not be permitted to use the defense of improper delivery against the bank. The proper negotiation would cut off this defense.

NONESSENTIALS OF NEGOTIABLE INSTRUMENTS

Can an instrument still be negotiable if some explanation is added or some additional rights are given?

An instrument can still be negotiable even though some explanation is added or even though some additional rights are given as long as the additions do not make payment of the note conditional.

EXAMPLE 8   **Edward Street gave George O'Brien a promissory note that was complete and regular in every way but had added to it the following statement: "This note is secured by the pledge of 10 shares of Acme Corporation stock. The holder of this note is authorized to sell this security if the note is unpaid at the due date."**

The preceding note would be negotiable because the added statement does not make payment conditional. **U.C.C. Sec. 3-112**

Certain things may also be omitted without destroying the negotiable character of the note. Some of these are (1) the date;* (2) the consideration, or value, given by the maker or the drawer; (3) the place where the instrument is drawn; (4) the place where it is payable; and (5) the sum in figures. **U.C.C. Sec. 3-112 & 114**

Is the negotiability of an instrument affected by the fact that it is undated, antedated, or postdated?

* An instrument's negotiability is not affected if it is undated, antedated, or postdated. If an instrument is undated, the date agreed upon may be inserted by the holder. If it is antedated or postdated, the time it is payable is determined by the date stated, making the instrument payable on demand or at a fixed period in the future. U.C.C. Sec. 3-114

EXAMPLE 9 Young executed and mailed to O'Toole a check for $100 in payment of a debt. O'Toole refused to accept it because Young had neglected to indicate the sum in figures on the check. He claimed that this omission rendered the instrument nonnegotiable. O'Toole was wrong. The omission of the sum in figures does not affect the negotiability of the note.

An instrument may be issued with some of the contents left out with the understanding that these items are to be filled in later. Any holder has the implied authority to fill in these blanks in accordance with the agreed terms. When it is completely filled in as agreed upon, it is a good negotiable instrument. If the holder wrongfully fills in the spaces, either willfully or negligently, he may be held liable for any loss suffered by the maker. Innocent third parties who may later be holders, however, may hold the maker responsible for the full amount shown on the face of the instrument. U.C.C. Sec. 3-115, 407

THE HOLDER IN DUE COURSE

What is meant by a bona fide holder for value without notice?

A *holder in due course*, sometimes called a "bona fide holder for value without notice," is one who takes a negotiable instrument before maturity in good faith and for value, without notice of any defects in the instrument. Such a holder is entitled to all the rights and benefits under the instrument and is almost wholly free from the risk that the parties liable on the instrument may have a good defense to an action for collection of the money. U.C.C. Sec. 3-302 & 3-305

HOLDER IN DUE COURSE

ESSENTIAL REQUIREMENTS

A person may be a holder in due course only if the following requirements are fulfilled.

1. *That the instrument is complete and regular on its face.* This means that the instrument must contain all the essentials of a negotiable instrument. U.C.C. Sec. 3-104

EXAMPLE 10 Higgins obtained a note from Rand, the payee, on which the due date had been obviously altered. Higgins knew that Rand had obtained the note from the maker by threatening to expose the maker for his part in a dishonest transaction. The note was not paid, and Higgins sued the maker. It was held that Higgins could not collect on the note because he was subject to all the defenses that the maker could bring against Rand. Higgins was not a holder in due course, having acquired the note with the knowledge that the due date had been changed and that duress had been used by Rand, the transferor, in obtaining the note.

2. *That the person became the holder of the instrument before the maturity date.* If the paper was acquired when it was past due, the holder is not considered to be a holder in due course because the fact that the paper was not paid at maturity was notice that something might be wrong. The holder, therefore, was not justified in taking the paper. The holder of an overdue negotiable paper could be a holder in due course only if he did not have notice or knowledge that it was overdue. "The purchaser of an

What is considered a reasonable time within which a check drawn and payable within the United States should be presented for payment?

instrument has notice that an instrument is overdue if he has reason to know that any part of the principal amount is overdue . . . or that he is taking a demand instrument after demand has been made or more than a reasonable length of time after its issue. A reasonable time for a check drawn and payable within the states and territories of the United States and the District of Columbia is presumed to be thirty days." U.C.C. Sec. 3-304(3)

3. *That he took the instrument in good faith and gave value for it.* The acquisition of an instrument for a disproportionately small sum would raise a suspicion of bad faith unless the purchaser, as a reasonably prudent person, had investigated the circumstances responsible for the low offer. A holder takes the instrument for value to the extent that the agreed consideration has been performed or when he takes the instrument in payment of a claim against any person whether or not the claim is due. U.C.C. Sec. 3-302 and 303

4. *That, at the time the instrument was negotiated to him, he had no notice that there was anything wrong with the instrument or any defect in the title of the person negotiating it.* A person who takes an instrument with the knowledge or a suspicion that there is some defect in the transferor's title is considered to be acting in bad faith, even if he gives full value for the instrument. U.C.C. Sec. 3-302 & 304

EXAMPLE 11 Mitchell stopped at the Gotham Loan Company office and offered to transfer to them a note made out to him by Rosen. The note was a promise to pay $350, and Mitchell stated that he would sell it to Gotham for $50. Such circumstances would indicate a possible defect in the instrument, and Gotham has the duty to investigate before it decides to buy the note.

If the purchaser of a draft gave full value for the instrument after learning that it had been presented for acceptance and had been dishonored, would he be considered to be a holder in due course?

If the purchaser of a draft has notice that it has been presented for acceptance and has been dishonored, he is not considered to be a holder in due course. Any person, other than the payee, who derives title to an instrument through a holder in due course is himself a holder in due course. U.C.C. Sec. 3-304

Any holder who knows of a fraud before negotiating the instrument to a holder in due course will not be protected if he acquires the instrument again at a later date. He cannot, therefore, improve his position by taking it from a later holder in due course. U.C.C. Sec. 3-201(1)

A holder in due course must have received an instrument in good faith with no notice that there was anything wrong with the instrument or any defect in the title of the person negotiating it.

A holder or purchaser must assume responsibility for an instrument that is incomplete, bears evidence of forgery or alterations, or is so irregular that its validity, terms, ownership, or party who must pay could be questioned. U.C.C. Sec. 3-304(1)(a) & 3-306

DEFENSES TO NEGOTIABLE INSTRUMENTS

PERSONAL DEFENSES

When a negotiable instrument in proper form is negotiated to a holder in due course, all personal defenses are cut off. What is a personal defense?

A *personal defense* is a defense that arises because of some improper act or omission by a party to the instrument. These are the same acts or omissions that would create a defense to a simple contract.

PERSONAL
DEFENSE

The most common personal defenses are such things as lack of consideration, duress, fraud, nondelivery of a complete or an incomplete instrument, counterclaim, and anything else that would be a good defense to the enforcement of an ordinary contract. U.C.C. Sec. 3-306

EXAMPLE 12 Joseph Hartmann sold his sports car to George Ruben for $700. In order to close the sale, Hartmann told Ruben that the brakes had been relined two weeks earlier; but this was not a true statement. Ruben gave Hartmann a $700 promissory note as payment for the car. When the note became due, Ruben did not pay the face value of the note, stating that he had a legal right to deduct the cost of a brake-relining job from the original purchase price. Was Ruben within his rights to do so?

Yes, Ruben was right in his contention; and he could use this as a defense if Hartmann brought an action on the note.

If, however, Hartmann had negotiated the note to Lester Moses, a holder in due course, Moses could collect the full $700 from Ruben. Ruben's only remedy would be to sue Hartmann for the cost of the brake job. The defendant to an action on a negotiable instrument may raise against any holder the defense of "such misrepresentation as has induced the party to sign the instrument with neither knowledge nor reasonable opportunity to obtain knowledge of its character or its essential terms." U.C.C. Sec. 3-305(2)(c) Unless a person has the rights of a holder in due course, he takes the instrument subject to "all defenses of any party which would be available in an action on a simple contract." U.C.C. Sec. 3-306(b)

EXAMPLE 13 Gotham Loan Company sent its agent to the office of a customer who had requested a $1,000 loan. No one was in the office at the time, but on the applicant's desk was a note for $1,000, made out to the Gotham Loan Company and signed by the applicant. Should the agent take the note, without delivery by the applicant, it could be considered invalid between the maker and Gotham. However, should Gotham negotiate the note to a holder in due course, it would then be enforceable by such a holder.

An incomplete instrument that was lost by (or stolen from) the person who signed it has no standing if payment is demanded by the finder. The defense of lack of consideration is good only among immediate parties. If, however, an incomplete instrument is delivered by the maker or drawer and if the blanks are filled in by the payee, it is presumed that the instrument was completed in accordance with the intention of the maker. Any holder in due course may collect on the instrument. U.C.C. Sec. 3-406

EXAMPLE 14 **Kahn owed Nugent $35 for work Nugent had done on Kahn's car. Without taking time to fill in a check, Kahn merely signed the check, saying to Nugent: "You fill in the check; I'll be on my way." Nugent made out the check for $50 instead of the amount owed. It was then negotiated to an innocent third party, who presented it for payment at Kahn's bank. Kahn would be responsible to the holder for the full amount of the check, although he has a right of action against Nugent for the loss suffered.**

The law provides that the loss should fall upon the party whose conduct in signing blank paper has made the fraud possible, rather than upon the innocent purchaser. This conforms to the majority of decisions that show a willingness to permit the loss to fall upon the person who is so negligent as to invite alterations by subsequent holders. U.C.C. Sec. 3-406

What distinction is made between lack of delivery of a complete or an incomplete instrument? Are these defenses effective against a holder in due course?

There is no distinction made between lack of delivery of a complete or an incomplete instrument.

Both a complete and an incomplete instrument are to be treated as a personal defense only, not effective against a holder in due course. An instrument that has been materially altered may not be enforced by any person presenting it for payment. The maker, however, remains liable on the instrument according to its original provisions. U.C.C. Sec. 3-115, Sec. 3-305, Sec. 3-407

REMEMBER: The defenses to the collection of the instrument that are cut off by negotiation to a holder in due course are personal defenses, that is, defenses that arise from the act of some individual.

REAL DEFENSES

What is a real defense? How does it differ from a personal defense?

If the instrument itself is defective, the defect is called a *real,* or *absolute, defense;* and it is good against everyone, even a holder in due course. A real defense is a defense that is directed against the instrument itself. The contention is that no valid instrument ever came into existence; therefore, the instrument could not be real or genuine.

REAL DEFENSE

Some real defenses are forgery, material alteration, legal incompetency of the maker or drawee, and illegality created by statute. U.C.C. Sec. 3-305(2)

EXAMPLE 15 **The Gotham Loan Company issued a $500 check on an automobile loan. Barton altered the check to $800, endorsed it, and presented it for payment to an out-of-town bank. When the check was returned to Gotham's own bank for collection, it refused to honor it, noting the alteration. If Gotham were sued by the bank that cashed the check, it would have an obligation to pay only the amount for which the check was originally drawn, $500.**

What is meant by fraud in the execution of a negotiable instrument?

If a person signs a paper that is apparently not a negotiable instrument and if the paper is later fraudulently converted into a negotiable instrument, he cannot be held liable even by a holder in due course. *Fraud in the execution of an instrument* is an absolute defense. This type of fraud is distinguished from fraud as a personal defense, which relates to the circumstances surrounding the issuance of the instrument, not the instrument itself.

FRAUD IN THE EXECUTION OF AN INSTRUMENT

What is meant by fraud in the inducement of a negotiable instrument?

For example, if a person who was in no way negligent was induced by trickery to sign a note that he believed to be a lease or a duplicate bill of sale, he could present as a defense for nonpayment, good against any holder, the fraud that was perpetrated on him in the execution of the instrument. If, however, he had signed and delivered a note in payment of merchandise that was not of the quality represented by the seller, his defense for nonpayment would be *fraud in the inducement of the contract*. This defense would be good against anyone except a holder in due course.

FRAUD IN THE INDUCEMENT OF THE CONTRACT

SUGGESTIONS FOR MINIMIZING LEGAL RISKS

1. Try to obtain a negotiable instrument from delinquent debtors because it is usually easy to enforce payment on a negotiable instrument in case an action must be brought to force payment.
2. Carefully verify the amount on a negotiable instrument that has been received in payment of an existing obligation. Accepting, holding, or cashing a negotiable instrument that is less than the correct amount raises the potential risk of being unable to collect the balance due at a later date.
3. Carefully examine all negotiable instruments received to make sure that no qualifying words or statements that make payment conditional have been written on the face.

 ## APPLYING YOUR LEARNING

QUESTIONS AND PROBLEMS

1. Name the requisites of a negotiable instrument.
2. Does the signature of the maker of the note always have to be in handwriting? Explain.
3. What is meant by an unconditional promise to pay a certain sum?
4. What are the requirements for one to be a holder in due course?
5. Name some personal defenses that would not be good against a holder in due course.
6. Name some real defenses that are good against a holder in due course. Explain each one.

7. Why is it desirable to have an instrument that is negotiable?
8. Explain how negotiable instruments aid and stimulate business.
9. Explain what is meant by words of negotiability. Must all negotiable instruments contain words of negotiability?

WHAT IS YOUR OPINION?

In each of the following cases, give your decision and state a legal principle that applies to the case.

1. *On May 20, 19—, I promise to pay Glenn Cooper one hundred dollars.*
   (Signed) Ronald Howell.
   Is this a negotiable instrument? Explain why or why not.
2. *I promise to pay to the order of Lloyd Lockwood two hundred dollars when he completes the painting of my house.* *(Signed) Jud Linsey.*
   Is this a negotiable instrument? Explain why or why not.
3. Grisley offered Termain a promissory note for $100 for merchandise purchased. Although the terms of the sale provided for payment with a 30-day note, Termain refused to accept the note because it had been written in pencil. Could the holder of the note have collected the $100 in thirty days had he accepted it in payment?
4. David Olsen borrowed $800 from Robert Mathews and signed a 3-month note. Mathews negotiated the note to his bank. Later, Olsen did repair work on Mathews' house and had $80 due him. When the note came due, the bank presented the note to Olsen and demanded payment. Olsen refused and claimed that he was liable for only $720. Was the bank entitled to collect the $800 from Olsen?
5. Joe Crochett executed a promissory note for $200 payable to the order of Peter Mayer five days after the next full moon. If all other essentials are present, is the note negotiable?
6. Is the following note enforceable? negotiable?
   Portland, Oregon, May 6, 19—
   On twenty-first birthday of Ellis Marks, I promise to pay to him, or to his order, five hundred dollars. *(Signed) Merton Cass*
7. A draft was drawn to "The owner of the Lawrence Department Store, Fort Worth, Florida." Is the person to whom this draft is addressed indicated with sufficient certainty for the draft to be classed as a negotiable instrument?
8. Roberts gave his brother a promissory note for a birthday gift. When the note became due, Roberts refused to pay it, claiming he had received no consideration for it. What are the rights of the parties? Suppose Roberts' brother had transferred the note, for value, to another person who presented it for payment. Would your answer be the same?
9. Jerry Corbin gave a 30-day note for $500 to his nephew as a gift. The nephew sold the note to Fred Dubois, a holder in due course. At maturity, Corbin refused to pay the note when presented by Dubois, claiming lack of consideration as a defense. Is this a good defense?

10. Jack Donley, a minor, gave his $100 note to Ed Gage, in payment for a radio for his home. Ed Gage transferred the note to Joe MacKay, a holder in due course. Donley refused to pay the note when it was properly presented for payment by MacKay. Did Donley have a good defense against MacKay?

11. Paul Lynch forged Nick Markley's name as the maker of a promissory note. When the note became due, it was in the hands of Jim O'Hara, a holder in due course, who made proper presentment and demand of Markley. Was Markley obligated to pay O'Hara?

12. Herbert Mason executed a negotiable instrument in which he ordered Walter Felix to pay to the order of Gordon Farmer the sum of $500, to be payable from the sale of his apple crop. In an action against Mason, Felix claimed that the draft was not negotiable. Was his contention sound?

THE LAW IN ACTION

1. The defendant issued an instrument that acknowledged the receipt of $7,500 in specified United States government bonds. The instrument further stated that the defendant promised to return the bonds to the payee or her order in six months or, at the defendant's option, to pay the value of these bonds in cash. Was this a negotiable instrument? (Louisa National Bank v. Paintsville National Bank, 260 Ky. 327, 85 S.W. 2d 668)

2. An instrument contained the following statements: "Comanche Sand & Gravel Co. . . . This voucher when properly endorsed becomes a check on The Union Savings Bank & Trust Co." This was followed by the name of the payee, the amount, and the signature of the company treasurer. Was this a negotiable instrument? (Soldier Valley Savings Bank v. Comanche Sand & Gravel Co., 219 Iowa 614, 258 N.W. 879)

KEY TO "WHAT'S THE LAW?" Page 357

1. *No. This instrument is not unconditional. It is payable only after the delivery of the stock.*
2. *Yes. If there is no negotiation, the personal defenses to the collection of the instrument are not cut off.*

◬ UNIT 39: NEGOTIATION OF COMMERCIAL PAPER

When is an instrument said to be negotiated? When an instrument has been executed and handed to the payee, has negotiation taken place?

Commercial paper may be passed freely from one person or business to another in the same way as money. When a negotiable instrument is transferred from one person to another so that the person to whom the instrument is transferred (the transferee) becomes the holder or owner, the instrument is said to be *negotiated.* U.C.C. Sec. 3-202

NEGOTIATED

The term *holder* includes anyone who is legally in possession of the instrument. Not all holders are holders in due course.

HOLDER

When the maker of a note, or the drawer of a bill of exchange, executes the instrument and hands it to the payee, the instrument is said to be *issued.* At this point there has been no negotiation. We are considering only the structure of the instrument itself; and the instrument may be regarded as an ordinary contract between the maker, or drawer, and the payee. The instrument is negotiated when the payee transfers it in the proper manner to a holder. From this time on, any transfer in the proper manner to a subsequent holder is a further negotiation of the instrument. U.C.C. Sec. 3-301

ISSUED

REMEMBER: Negotiation does two things. (1) It transfers ownership of the instrument to the new holder and gives him certain rights, and (2) it imposes certain liabilities on the endorser. (The general nature of these liabilities will be examined in Unit 40.)

What are the two types of instruments that must be considered in negotiation so that a transfer in the proper manner may take place?

Your next question logically would be, "What is a transfer in the proper manner?" The answer to this question varies with the type of instrument. Again, you will recall that there are two types of negotiable instruments that must be considered. They are (1) instruments payable to bearer and (2) instruments payable to order. U.C.C. Sec. 3-202

Negotiable commercial paper is passed freely from one person to another or from one business to another in the same way as money.

NEGOTIATION OF BEARER INSTRUMENTS

How is a bearer instrument negotiated?

A *bearer instrument* is negotiated by delivery only. It is just that simple. The payee hands it to the holder with the intention of passing title to him, and the instrument has now been negotiated. U.C.C. Sec. 3-202(1) A common bearer instrument is a check made payable to the order of "cash" or "bearer." The Code rules that either of these words makes the instrument a bearer instrument.

BEARER INSTRUMENT

EXAMPLE 1 **Willie Wheeler purchased two football game tickets from Mac Prince. Willie handed Mac a check made payable to the order of "cash." This delivery constituted the proper negotiation of a bearer note to a holder.**

NEGOTIATION OF ORDER INSTRUMENTS

How is an order instrument negotiated?

Instruments payable to order mean just what they say; that is, they are payable when the named payee orders them to be paid. The named payee gives this order by a process called *endorsement*. The *order instrument* is negotiated by this endorsement, followed by delivery, as in the case of the bearer instrument. U.C.C. Sec. 3-202(1)

ENDORSEMENT ORDER INSTRUMENT

EXAMPLE 2 **If, in Example 1, Willie Wheeler had paid for the tickets by a check made payable to Mac Prince, the check would be an order instrument. If Prince used the check to pay for groceries at the corner grocery store, there would be no negotiation until Prince endorsed the check and handed it to the grocer.**

KINDS OF ENDORSEMENTS

When is an instrument said to be endorsed? What is the purpose of an endorsement? How may it be made?

An instrument is endorsed when the holder writes his name on it, thereby indicating his intent to transfer ownership to another. Endorsements may be written in ink, made on a typewriter, or even stamped with a rubber stamp. For convenience, the endorsement is usually placed on the back of the instrument. To be acceptable, the endorsement must be written for the entire amount stated on the instrument. U.C.C. Sec. 3-202

EXAMPLE 3   Gotham Loan Company receives numerous checks each day from persons making payments on their loans. To simplify and make uniform the endorsement of checks for deposit, the cashier uses a rubber stamp containing Gotham's endorsement.

There are five commonly used types of endorsements. They are (1) endorsements in blank, (2) full endorsements, (3) restrictive endorsements, (4) qualified endorsements, (5) accommodation endorsements. Each of these endorsements fulfills a special purpose.

Blank Endorsement   A *blank endorsement* is an endorsement made by the simple act of turning the instrument over and signing it on the back. By doing this, the payee on an order instrument is in effect saying, "From now on this instrument may be paid to anyone." Once endorsed in blank, the former order instrument is now a bearer instrument. It requires no further endorsement to pass title; so it can be further negotiated by delivery only. Where an instrument is made payable to a person under a misspelled name or one other than his own, he may endorse in that name or his own or both; but signature in both names may be required by a person paying or giving value for the instrument. U.C.C. Sec. 3-203 and 204(2)

How is a blank
endorsement
made?

What must be
done in order to
pass title to an
instrument
endorsed in
blank?

BLANK
ENDORSEMENT

EXAMPLE 4   In Example 2, the check given to the grocery man was endorsed in blank and is now a bearer instrument. It could be further negotiated by delivery only. If the grocery man attempted to negotiate it to his wholesaler, the wholesaler would most likely demand the endorsement of the grocery man. This is logical. He knows the grocery man, but he does not know Prince or Wheeler. If the check should not be paid when presented to the bank, he would expect the grocery man to make good.

An instrument endorsed in blank is payable to the bearer. If the instrument is lost or stolen and gets into the hands of an innocent holder for value, the new holder may recover on it. U.C.C. Sec. 3-204(2)

REMEMBER: Any bearer instrument may be endorsed to add the security of the transferor's signature, even though an endorsement is not necessary for a proper negotiation of a bearer instrument.

Full Endorsement   A *full endorsement* is an endorsement made by first writing on the back an order to pay to a specified person and then signing the instrument. When endorsed in this manner, the instrument remains an order instrument and must be endorsed by the specified person before it can be further negotiated. A full endorsement is sometimes called a special endorsement. U.C.C. Sec. 3-204(1)

How is a full
endorsement
made? What is
the advantage of
this type of
endorsement?

FULL
ENDORSEMENT

EXAMPLE 5   Suppose Charles Ingersoll had borrowed money from the Gotham Loan Company to repay a debt which he owed to Harold Draper, who lived in another city. Fearing that the check might get lost or stolen in the mail, Ingersoll endorsed it, "Pay to the order of Harold Draper. Charles Ingersoll." This endorsement would provide protection to the parties if the check should fall into the hands of a dishonest person.

BLANK ENDORSEMENT

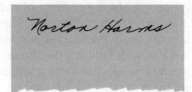

FULL ENDORSEMENT

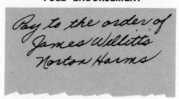

FULL RESTRICTIVE ENDORSEMENT

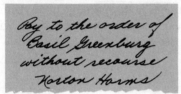

FULL QUALIFIED ENDORSEMENT

Pay to the order of
Basil Greenburg
without recourse
Norton Harms

ACCOMMODATION ENDORSEMENT

Norton Harms
Johnston Rollins

Restrictive Endorsement   A *restrictive endorsement* is one in which words have been added, in addition to the signature of the transferor, that restrict the further endorsement of the instrument. However, a restrictive endorsement does not prevent further transfer or negotiation of the instrument. U.C.C. Sec. 3-205 and 206(1)

RESTRICTIVE ENDORSEMENT

What is a restrictive endorsement? Does a restrictive endorsement prevent further negotiation of the instrument?

The endorsement "for deposit only" is a frequently used restrictive endorsement. A check endorsed this way may not be cashed. A restrictive endorsement can be in either full or blank form, depending upon the needs of the endorser. U.C.C. Sec. 3-206(3)

EXAMPLE 6   **Arthur Williamson received his monthly paycheck at the end of the month. He knew it would not be convenient for him to deposit the check for several days. To protect himself fully, he endorsed it: "For deposit only—Arthur Williamson." This is a restrictive endorsement. If the check should be stolen or if he should lose it, the only thing that could possibly be done with the check by any subsequent possessor would be to deposit it to Arthur's bank account.**

May one receiving under a restrictive endorsement be a holder in due course?

A restrictive holder would have the rights of any purchaser of negotiable paper, except that he must do with the instrument as the endorsement directs. This means that one receiving under a restrictive endorsement may be a holder in due course and may transfer to another the rights of a holder in due course. U.C.C. Sec. 3-206(4)

Qualified Endorsement   A *qualified endorsement* is one in which words have been added to the signature that limit or qualify the liability of the endorser. The endorsement, however, transfers title to the instrument. This form of endorsement is frequently used when the business paper is backed by a mortgage security or by collateral. In case of default by the maker, the endorsee is compelled to look for payment of the paper to the securities rather than to the endorser. The qualified endorser is relieved from liability on the paper by writing the words, "without recourse" above his name. The endorsement can be in either blank or full form.   U.C.C. Sec. 3-417(3)

What is a qualified endorsement? What is accomplished by using this type of endorsement?

EXAMPLE 7   Jack Wilson held a note signed by William Bradford in the amount of $500. Wilson knew that Bradford did not have the money and that he probably could not pay the note for six months and might not be able to pay the note at all. For this reason, he sold the note to Jerry Ward for $400 and endorsed it "Without recourse—Jack Wilson." By this endorsement he passed title to the note to Jerry Ward, but he did not warrant that Jerry could collect the money.

The holder of an instrument who negotiates it by a qualified endorsement, or by delivery only if it is a bearer instrument, does warrant (1) that the instrument is genuine, (2) that he owns it, (3) that all prior parties had the capacity to contract, and (4) that he has no knowledge of anything wrong with the instrument. He does not warrant that the instrument will be accepted or paid when presented. U.C.C. Sec. 3-417

What does the qualified endorser warrant by his endorsement?

The endorser who uses a qualified endorsement does not warrant that the instrument will be accepted or paid when presented.

Accommodation Endorsement   An *accommodation endorsement* is usually an endorsement in blank, although under special circumstances it might be any of the other forms illustrated and described. An accommodation endorser signs an instrument only to accommodate some other party and does so to add the security of his credit to the instrument. U.C.C. Sec. 3-415(1)

EXAMPLE 8   Warren Walker wished to borrow money from the First National Bank. Walker was known to be honest, but he did not have any property to pledge as security for the loan. His friend, Jasper Wilkinson, owned valuable property and was known to be financially sound. Wilkinson agreed to endorse his name on the back of the note and assume responsibility for its payment, just for Walker's accommodation.

How does an
accommodation
endorsement
differ in form
and purpose from
the other types
of endorsements?

Wilkinson would be an accommodation endorser and is liable for the payment of the note in the same manner as if he had negotiated it to the bank himself. Having endorsed the note as an accommodation without receiving any consideration, Wilkinson, of course, is not liable to the accommodated party (Walker). He is liable, however, to all subsequent holders, just as if he were a regular endorser. U.C.C. Sec. 3-415

SUGGESTIONS FOR MINIMIZING LEGAL RISKS

1. Do not accept negotiable instruments from a stranger without taking all possible precautions to verify his correct identity. Try to have him personally identified by someone you know.
2. If this is impossible, request a number of items showing his signature. Examine these carefully against a signature made in your presence. Recent letters addressed to the party delivered through the post office will ordinarily verify his most recent address. Insist that he endorse the instrument and place his address under the endorsement. If still in doubt about his identity, do not accept!
3. Examine all tendered negotiable instruments carefully to determine whether they contain words of negotiability. If they are bearer instruments, request that the persons tendering the instruments endorse them before you accept.

 APPLYING YOUR LEARNING

QUESTIONS AND PROBLEMS

1. Which type of negotiable instrument may be transferred by delivery only without endorsement?
2. Name several types of endorsements commonly used in the negotiation of credit instruments.
3. Why is it desirable to require an endorsement on all negotiable instruments?
4. What are the rights of a restrictive endorsee?
5. Why is a blank endorsement unsafe when the instrument is carried in the holder's pocket or sent through the mails?
6. What type of endorsement would give you the greatest protection if you were a holder of a negotiable instrument? the least protection? Explain.

WHAT IS YOUR OPINION?

In each of the following cases, give your decision and state a legal principle that applies to the case.

1. In order to obtain a loan from a bank, Michael Kuhns needed the signature of someone known to be reliable. Gene Landis endorsed the note, and Kuhns obtained the loan. On the due date, Kuhns failed to pay, and the bank sought to recover from the endorser. Landis claimed that he received nothing for his signature and therefore could not be held. Is Landis right?

2. Claude Laurent purchased a used car from Roger Pierce, giving his promissory note in payment. Pierce sold the note to the bank, using a full endorsement. When the bank presented the note to Laurent on the due date and demanded payment, he refused to pay, claiming that he had been induced to buy the car because of fraudulent statements made by Pierce. Did Laurent have a valid excuse for not paying the bank?

3. What kind of endorsement should a holder use in each of the following situations? (a) A check is being mailed to an out-of-town bank for deposit. (b) The holder is not sure of the financial responsibility of the maker of a note or other instrument he had received for value. (c) A note is given a contractor for work to be done on your house. (d) A check is presented for payment and is endorsed at the teller's window and in his presence.

4. Burns refused to accept a check from Edwards because it was endorsed with a rubber stamp. He contended that to be valid all endorsements on a check must be written in ink. Was his contention correct?

5. At various times Henry Selby, a merchant, endorsed the following checks and notes. Identify each type of endorsement.

   a. A note payable to the order of Henry Selby was endorsed on the back, "Henry Selby."

   b. Selby received a check that carried Luke Norwood's endorsement on the back. Selby transferred the check to Chase by writing on the back, "Without recourse, Henry Selby."

   c. Selby transferred a check that he had received from a customer to Murray, after endorsing the check, "Pay to the order of Frank Murray, Henry Selby."

   d. Selby sent several checks to the bank, endorsed as follows: "Pay to the Ridge National Bank for deposit only. Henry Selby."

6. Edwin Bennett was the maker of a $400 note and Angus Campbell was the payee. Angus Campbell transferred the note to Mark Farrell by a qualified endorsement. Mark Farrell sold it to the City Bank, using a blank (regular) endorsement. Because of lack of funds, Bennett refused to pay the note when it was properly presented to him by the City Bank. The bank gave proper notice of dishonor. Does the City Bank have any claim against Campbell? Does the City Bank have any claim against Farrell?

7. Ludlow, a teacher, agreed to endorse a check for a student who could not cash it at the local bank because of his age and the fact that he did not live in the town. After Ludlow had endorsed the check, the bank cashed it for the student. The check was returned for lack of sufficient funds, and the bank charged Ludlow's account for the amount. Ludlow claimed that he was not liable on the check because he had received no consideration for his endorsement. In case of suit, for whom should the court find?

THE LAW IN ACTION

1. The defendant, John Morrell & Company, endorsed certain checks as follows: "Pay to the order of the Sioux Falls National Bank for deposit only." The Sioux Falls National Bank sent the checks to the plaintiff bank for collection. What type of endorsement was made by the defendant? (First National Bank of Sioux City, Iowa v. John Morrell & Company, 53 S.D. 496, 221 N.W. 95)
2. The plaintiff bank purchased the order note involved in this case, along with many others, from another bank. At the time of sale, a contract was written listing the notes sold, but the notes were not endorsed until several weeks later. In the meantime, the plaintiff learned that the note in this case had been obtained from the defendant by fraud. The defendant claims that the note was not negotiated to the plaintiff until it was endorsed and, at that time, the plaintiff could not become a holder in due course because he knew of the fraud. Is the defendant correct? (Tennessee Valley Bank v. Williams, 246 Ala. 563, 21 So. 2d 686)

KEY TO "WHAT'S THE LAW?" Page 368

1. *Yes. Asa Harris may endorse the check with his own name and further negotiate it.*
2. *No. He warrants the genuineness of the instrument, the capacity of past parties, the legality of title, and his negotiation of the instrument in good faith.*

A DIGEST OF LEGAL CONCEPTS

1. Money is often referred to as a medium of exchange.

2. An assignment of an ordinary contract to pay money will not cut off any defenses that are good against the one making the assignment.

3. Checks, promissory notes, drafts, and paper money are common examples of negotiable instruments.

4. In ordinary language, a bill of exchange is often called a draft.

5. A negotiable instrument when properly negotiated to a holder in due course is collectible by him free of all personal defenses.

6. In a draft, one person, called the drawer, orders a second person, called the drawee, to pay money to a third person, called the payee.

7. A person who writes his name on the back of negotiable instruments is called an endorser. By his endorsement he both transfers title and makes certain warranties.

8. To be negotiable, an instrument must (a) be in writing, (b) be signed by the maker or the drawer, (c) contain an unconditional promise or order, (d) be payable to order or bearer, (e) be payable in money and for a definite amount, (f) be payable on demand or at a definite future time, and (g) if the instrument is a draft, name the drawee.

9. An oral order to pay money, no matter how specific, cannot be negotiated.

10. Payment of a negotiable instrument cannot be conditioned on the happening of an uncertain event.

11. The words "to the order of" and "to the bearer" are words of negotiation, and every negotiable instrument must contain one or the other.

12. An instrument promising or ordering the payment of some property other than money is not negotiable.

13. The amount of money must be definitely stated if the instrument is to be negotiable.

14. An instrument that does not indicate any time of payment is payable on demand.

15. The drawee on a draft must be definitely named or indicated.

16. Words on negotiable commercial paper that authorize the sale of securities if the instrument is unpaid do not affect its negotiability.

17. Where an instrument is issued with some space left blank, any holder is authorized to fill in the blanks according to the terms of the original contract.

18. A negotiable instrument must be delivered to be effective, but any instrument in circulation is presumed to have been delivered until proved otherwise.

19. An instrument payable in a foreign currency is negotiable. This also applies to money that is a medium of exchange authorized or adopted by a domestic or foreign government.

20. No distinction is made between lack of delivery of a complete or an incomplete instrument. In both cases it is to be treated as a personal defense only, not effective against a holder in due course.

21. To be a holder in due course a person must do the following:
    a. He must receive the instrument in good faith with no knowledge of any defects.
    b. He must have paid a valuable consideration for it.
    c. He must have received it before it was overdue.

22. A holder in due course takes a negotiable instrument free of all personal defenses.

23. Defects in the instrument itself are called real defenses and are good against a holder in due course.

24. An instrument that has been materially altered may not be enforced by any person presenting it for payment. However, the maker remains liable on the instrument according to its original provisions.

25. A defect in a negotiable instrument itself is an absolute defense—good even against a holder in due course.

WHAT'S THE LAW?

1. *Don Whitney bought George Kochman's tape recorder for $75 and paid for it with a check drawn on the Peoples Bank of Yorktown. George did not find it convenient to go to the bank with the check. He returned it to Don the next day, demanding cash instead. Could he collect on the check from Don Whitney without first presenting it to the bank for payment?*

2. *If George had presented the check to the bank for payment and payment had been refused, could George collect from Don?*

◭ UNIT 40: COLLECTING COMMERCIAL PAPER

You now know that if commercial paper is complete and regular on its face and it has been properly negotiated to a holder in due course, then it is collectible by the holder in due course, free of all personal defenses. "Collectible from whom?" you may well ask. It is the answer to this question that we shall seek in this part.

LIABILITY OF PARTIES

PRIMARY LIABILITY

What is meant by primary liability on an instrument? What two parties have primary liability?

Primary liability is an absolute liability to pay. A party with a primary liability has promised to pay the instrument without any reservations of any kind. There are two parties who have primary liability. They are (1) the maker of a promissory note, and (2) the acceptor, if any, of a bill of exchange. Each has personally promised to pay the obligation represented by the instrument without reservation. If there is a comaker on a note, he has a primary liability and is considered a maker whether he receives any consideration for his signature or not. U.C.C. Sec. 3-413(1)

Would a comaker on a note have a primary liability similar to that of a maker?

PRIMARY LIABILITY

SECONDARY LIABILITY

What is meant by secondary liability on an instrument? What two types of parties may have secondary liability?

Secondary liability is a liability to pay only after certain conditions are met. There are also two types of parties who may have secondary liability for the payment of an instrument. They are (1) the drawer of a bill of exchange, and (2) the endorser or endorsers of either a promissory note or a bill of exchange.

SECONDARY LIABILITY

The conditions that must be met before either the drawer or endorsers has a liability to pay are these: (1) the instrument must be properly presented to the primary party or drawee and payment demanded, (2) payment must have been refused by the primary party or be impossible (this refusal is called *dishonor*), and (3) notice of this refusal must be given to the secondary party within the time and in the manner prescribed by law. U.C.C. Sec. 3-413(2)

DISHONOR

WARRANTIES OF ENDORSERS

Endorsers of commercial paper make certain implied warranties. What are they?

By his endorsement, the endorser of a negotiable instrument impliedly warrants to his endorsee the following:

1. *The paper is genuine and is in all respects what it is represented to be.* Thus, if the maker's or acceptor's signature is forged, the endorser may be held responsible to a subsequent holder for payment of the instrument. U.C.C. Sec. 3-417(2)

2. *All prior parties had the capacity to enter into a legally binding contract.* If the maker or a prior endorser refuses to pay because he is a minor, a lunatic, or otherwise incompetent, the holder can collect from any endorser whose name follows that of the incompetent party on the paper.

3. *As the endorser, he has good title to the instrument.* U.C.C. Sec. 3-417(2)(a)

EXAMPLE 1 The Gotham Loan Company accepted a check from Chester in payment of his account. The check contained a blank endorsement by Harvey Sims. Gotham discovered that Chester had found the check on the street and that a stop-payment order had been issued by the real owner, Harvey Sims. Chester, by his endorsement, had warranted that he was the true owner of the instrument. He may be held liable on this warranty for any loss suffered by Gotham. U.C.C. Sec. 3-417(2)(a)

How can an endorser establish an exception to the warranty that he will pay the negotiable instrument if on due presentation it was not paid and if the proper proceedings had been taken by the holder?

4. *The instrument is a valid and existing obligation.* If the maker refuses to pay because of a subsequent material alteration, because of lack of execution, because the instrument is usurious, or because the instrument was given for a gambling debt, the holder can still recover against the endorser. U.C.C. Sec. 3-417(2)(c)

5. *As the endorser, he will pay the amount of the instrument to the holder or to any subsequent endorser who has been compelled to pay the instrument if, on due presentment, it was not paid and if the proper proceedings had been taken by the holder.* U.C.C. Sec. 3-414 An exception to this warranty is the endorser who has used the qualified endorsement with the words "without recourse" written above his name on the instrument. U.C.C. Sec. 3-417(3)

Warranties arising from or connected with the transfer of negotiable instruments run to every subsequent holder if the transfer is by endorsement. If the transfer is by delivery alone, the warranty applies to the immediate transferee only. U.C.C. Sec. 3-417

PRESENTMENT AND NOTICE OF DISHONOR

Neither presentment nor notice of dishonor is ever necessary in order to hold a maker of a note, or the acceptor of a draft, liable on his promise. Each already knows when the payment is due and that he and he alone

What effect does
proper
presentment and
notice of
dishonor have on
the potential
liability of the
drawer and
endorsers?

has the obligation to pay. If presentment and notice are not made, however, the drawer of a draft and any endorsers are released from liability to pay. U.C.C. Sec. 3-501

EXAMPLE 2 **You will recall from Example 8 in Unit 39 that Warren Walker was able to borrow money from the First National Bank only because his well-to-do friend Jasper Wilkinson endorsed the note for his accommodation. The bank lent the money on the credit of Wilkinson. The bank would be very careful to present the note properly to Walker for payment and properly notify Wilkinson if it was not paid when due. If the bank should be careless and fail to take these steps, then it would lose its right to collect from Wilkinson.**

Presentment The principal requirements for presentment by the holder of a negotiable instrument can be listed as follows:

1. Whenever possible the instrument must be presented on or before the day due if a time of payment is specified. U.C.C. Sec. 3-503(1)(a)

2. If the instrument is payable "on demand" and no date is specified, it must be presented for payment within a reasonable time after issue or, in the case of a draft, within a reasonable time after its last negotiation. U.C.C. Sec. 3-503(2)

3. It should be presented to the party primarily liable thereon or his agent; or, if that is not possible, to anyone who has the authority to make an acceptance or payment. U.C.C. Sec. 3-504(3) Presentment may be made by mail, through a clearinghouse, or at the place of acceptance or payment specified in the instrument or, if there be none, at the place of business or residence of the party primarily liable. U.C.C. Sec. 3-504(2)

What are the
principal
requirements for
presentment by a
holder?

Why is it
important that
the person paying
a negotiable
instrument get it
back at the time
of payment
together with any
collateral?

4. The party from whom payment is demanded can request to see the instrument, and, if payment is made, the instrument and any collateral must be handed over then and there. This is important because, if the party paying does not get the instrument back, it might show up later in the hands of a holder in due course and he would have to pay it again. Presentment and demand for payment are necessary only to fix the liability of the parties secondarily liable on the instrument, that is, the endorsers. U.C.C. Sec. 3-501(1)

If requested, the instrument must be shown to the party from whom payment is demanded, but it need be given to him only when payment is made.

EXAMPLE 3   Bill Knowlton endorsed a note as an accommodation to a business associate. When the note became due, the holder did not present it to the maker for payment. Several weeks later, when the note was dishonored, the holder attempted to hold Knowlton liable. Because the holder had failed to present the instrument for payment when due, neither Bill Knowlton nor any subsequent endorsers were liable.

Under what conditions is negotiable commercial paper considered dishonored?

Notice of Dishonor   A negotiable instrument is considered to be dishonored if it is not accepted when presented for acceptance, if it is not paid when presented for payment at maturity, or if presentment has been excused or waived and the instrument is past due and unpaid. U.C.C. Sec. 3-507(1)

EXAMPLE 4   A note was presented to Stanley Fowler for payment on the due date. Fowler refused to pay, claiming that it was a forgery. If this claim were true, the holder of the note would have to proceed against the endorsers on their implied warranties in order to secure payment. The note is considered dishonored because of Fowler's refusal to pay it.

To whom can the holder of a dishonored instrument look for payment?

Endorsers are liable to subsequent holders of the instrument if it is not paid by the maker when due or by a drawee or acceptor either at sight or when payment was promised. The holder of a dishonored instrument may seek payment from any or all of the endorsers that preceded him. U.C.C. Sec. 3-122(3)

So that the holder of dishonored negotiable paper may hold the drawer or the endorsers liable on the instrument, he must give notice of the dishonor to all of them. Any drawer or endorser to whom such notice is not given is relieved from liability. U.C.C. Sec. 3-501(2)

The following requirements of notice to an endorser or drawer must be complied with:

1. Notice that the instrument has been properly presented and payment has been refused may be oral or written. If notice of nonacceptance has been given, notice of nonpayment is unnecessary. U.C.C. Sec. 3-508(3)

2. A *protest* (a formal, written certificate of dishonor made by a person   PROTEST
authorized to certify dishonor by the law of the place where dishonor occurs) must be made at the place where the instrument was dishonored not later than the third business day after the dishonor. The costs of protest, together with the interest (from the due date of the instrument until the date of payment), are added to the amount to be paid. U.C.C. Sec. 3-509(1)

3. Notice of dishonor may be given by the holder of the instrument, by his agent, or by a notary public employed by the holder. U.C.C. Sec. 3-508(1)

4. When notice of dishonor is served by mail, it is considered as having been given when the notice is properly addressed, stamped, and deposited in the post office, even if the notice is lost in the mail. U.C.C. Sec. 3-508(4)

EXAMPLE 5   The Gotham Loan Company mailed notice of dishonor on a note that had been presented to Chilton and dishonored the same day. The notice was mailed to the three endorsers whose names appeared on the instrument. Although the notice was properly directed, two of the endorsers later claimed that they had never received the notice and sought to be discharged from their liability

A note payable at a bank is considered to be dishonored if funds sufficient to pay the holder are not on deposit on the due date.

on their warranties as endorsers. The court ruled that as long as the notices had been correctly stamped, addressed, and deposited with the post office, the endorsers would be considered to have been served with notice.

If no address is given on an instrument following the drawer's or endorser's name, where may the notice be sent?

If the drawer or the endorser places no address after his signature on an instrument, notice of dishonor must be sent to his home, to his place of business, to his temporary residence, or to the post office at which he usually receives his mail. Notice of dishonor actually received by the drawer or the endorser within the time allowed is good, no matter where it was sent. U.C.C. Sec. 3-508 & Sec. 1-201(26)

If notice of dishonor is to be given to a party living in the same community, when must the notice be received following dishonor?

Whether the holder and the parties whom he intends to hold liable live in the same community or in different communities, the holder must give personal notice or notice by mail in time so that the parties to be held will have been notified not later than the third business day after the dishonor. If sent otherwise than by mail, notice must be sent in time to reach the parties no later than they would have received it if it had been sent by mail. Any necessary notice must be given by a bank before midnight on the next banking day after dishonor or receipt of notice of dishonor. U.C.C. Sec. 3-508(2) This time requirement is known as the *midnight deadline.*

MIDNIGHT DEADLINE

If the parties live in different communities, when must the notice, if mailed, be received following dishonor?

EXAMPLE 6 **King, an endorser on a dishonored note held by the Gotham Loan Company, lived in a city only 10 miles from Gotham's office. A messenger employed by Gotham was asked to inform King of the dishonor on a trip he had to make through King's town. The messenger forgot to see King on his outgoing trip and did not stop to see him until five days later on his return trip. King may defend himself from all future obligation because of failure to receive notice within the time that he would have received it had regular mail service been used.**

What should the holder of a dishonored instrument do about giving notice?

The holder of a dishonored instrument usually gives notice of dishonor to the endorser who transferred the instrument to him. The endorser so notified has the same allowance of time for giving notice to the endorser ahead of him, and so on. The first person giving notice, however, is best protected by giving notice immediately to all prior endorsers of the instrument. U.C.C. Sec. 3-508

Presentment of the instrument is dispensed with if the holder has been unsuccessful in locating the maker or the acceptor or if the drawer or the endorsers have waived presentment. U.C.C. Sec. 3-511(1)(2)

An instrument payable at a bank is considered to be dishonored if funds sufficient to pay the holder are not on deposit on the due date.

EXAMPLE 7   A note made payable at the First National Bank, signed by James Rawlson and held by the Gotham Loan Company, was duly presented by Gotham for payment. No funds were on deposit at the bank at the time because Rawlson had closed out his account. The note is, therefore, considered dishonored, and Gotham may proceed against the endorsers, if any, on the note.

DISCHARGE OF NEGOTIABLE INSTRUMENTS

There are two things to be considered under this heading. They are (1) the discharge of the instrument itself and (2) the discharge of the individual parties.

DISCHARGE OF THE INSTRUMENT

How is a negotiable instrument discharged?

A negotiable instrument itself is discharged (1) by payment at or after maturity, (2) by the principal debtor's becoming the holder of the instrument at or after maturity, or (3) by the intentional cancellation of the instrument by the holder. U.C.C. Sec. 3-601

DISCHARGE OF A SECONDARY PARTY

How may a secondary party to a negotiable instrument be discharged?

A secondary party to an instrument may be discharged by any action of a holder that would tend to change the nature of the obligation originally assumed by the secondary party. U.C.C. Sec. 3-601(1)(f) and Sec. 3-407 This original obligation might be changed by specifically releasing the secondary party, either by canceling his name from the instrument or by canceling the name of a prior party. U.C.C. Sec. 3-605

EXAMPLE 8   Popovich was the third endorser on a note that he delivered to Wilkins for value. Wilkins, prior to further negotiation, crossed out the name of an endorser ahead of Popovich's name. Popovich was thus relieved of all liability because his right to depend upon one whose name was valid at the time the instrument transferred was denied.

The obligation of a secondary party may also be changed by the holder's extending the time of payment.

EXAMPLE 9   The maker of the note informed Wilkins, when the note was presented for payment, that he would pay the note if he could be given an additional thirty days. If Wilkins gave his agreement to the extension of time, this would automatically discharge Popovich and all other endorsers on the note.

If any presentment of notice of dishonor is delayed without excuse beyond the time when it is due, any endorser is discharged. The maker of the note, however, is not so discharged unless during the unreasonable delay the bank in which his funds are on deposit becomes insolvent and the maker is thus deprived of the means necessary to cover the instrument. In such a case the maker may discharge his liability by written assignment to the holder of his rights against the bank in respect to such funds. U.C.C. Sec. 3-502(1)

The holder must be careful about collecting on negotiable instruments. He must collect it strictly in accordance with the law if he expects to hold a secondary party to his promise to pay.

What is the effect on an endorser's liability for payment of a negotiable instrument if he writes "Demand and notice waived" above his endorsement?

An endorser who has written "Demand and notice waived," or words to the same effect, above his endorsement or across the face of the instrument is liable for payment without the necessity of presentment and notice of dishonor to bind him. Prior endorsers are excused from their liability to such an endorser. U.C.C. Sec. 3-511(2)(5)(6)

REMEMBER: The secondary party has promised to pay only according to the conditions of his contract. If the holder changes those terms in any way—for example, by releasing a prior party, by extending the time of payment, or by making any other change—the secondary party is released.

SUGGESTIONS FOR MINIMIZING LEGAL RISKS

1. Never sign a negotiable instrument as an accommodation party unless you are sure that the primary party has the ability to pay.
2. Never extend the time of payment on notes you hold that are secured by endorsements.
3. Keep a calendar of the maturity dates of all negotiable instruments held so that prompt and proper presentment can be made when the instruments become due.
4. In case of dishonor of negotiable instruments, give immediate notice of dishonor to all endorsers and drawers.

 ## APPLYING YOUR LEARNING

QUESTIONS AND PROBLEMS

1. What steps must a holder of a negotiable instrument take in order to fix the liability of endorsers?
2. What is meant by proper presentment?
3. Must presentment be made to the maker to hold him liable on a note? Explain.
4. Is it necessary to follow some special form in giving notice of dishonor of a note? Explain.
5. If notice of dishonor is mailed to an endorser or a drawer on a dishonored instrument, when does the notice take effect?
6. Under what circumstances will the holder be excused from giving notice of dishonor to prior endorsers or to a drawer?
7. What is meant by protest? How is it accomplished?

WHAT IS YOUR OPINION?

In each of the following cases, give your decision and state a legal principle that applies to the case.

1. Tom Harrison bought an automobile from the Acme Motor Company. In payment of the $600 purchase price, Tom gave the seller $100 in cash and his negotiable promissory note for $500 payable in ninety days. The Acme Motor Company endorsed the note and sold it to the Broadway Bank. If Tom did not pay when the note was presented to him for payment, would the Acme Motor Company have to pay? Could the bank hold the motor company without first demanding payment from Tom Harrison?

2. If, after Tom Harrison had failed to pay the note when it was presented to him on the due date, the Broadway Bank failed to give notice to the Acme Motor Company for one week, could the motor company then be held?

3. Suppose in the foregoing case that Tom Harrison asked the Broadway Bank for a 30-day extension of time and that the bank extended the time of payment for thirty additional days. Could the bank then hold the motor company if Tom did not pay at the end of the extended time?

4. Walter Stone gave a check to Roy Hayden. Hayden endorsed the check and cashed it at the Corner Grocery Store. The Corner Grocery Store kept the check for a week and then endorsed it and used it to pay the Wholesale Grocery Company. The Wholesale Grocery Company deposited it the day it was received. The check was dishonored and Hayden now claims that he was discharged from liability by the delay in presenting the check for payment. Do you agree?

5. Hand gave his son a note, payable on August 8, the boy's eighteenth birthday. On August 8 the young man presented it to his father for payment, but the father refused to pay it. What rights does the boy have against the maker?

6. Suppose, in the previous case, the son had negotiated the note to Parker for value. Parker knew nothing of the circumstances under which the note had been issued. On the due date he presented it to Hand for payment. Is Hand obligated to Parker on the instrument?

7. Lee employed Jackson, a real estate broker, to buy a tract of land for him. Lee gave Jackson $1,000 in cash and a $1,000 note made payable to "Jackson, on order," to be used as a down payment on the property. Jackson endorsed and transferred the note to Hull, a holder in due course. Hull sued on the note when payment was refused. Lee's defense was that Jackson had betrayed his trust by not using the note as directed. Explain.

8. Atkins forged the name of Sam Newman, a well-known merchant, to a $500 note. He then negotiated the note to William Kester, an innocent purchaser, for value. Kester sued Newman when payment was refused at maturity. Will Newman be required to pay the note?

9. Roger Hatfield was the holder of a negotiable note signed by Louis Simion as maker. Hatfield did not present the note to Simion for payment until one week after it was due. Simion now contends that he was relieved of liability by the delay in presenting the note for payment. Do you agree? Why or why not?

10. Trainer presented a note to Duke for payment on the due date. Duke had become insolvent and could not honor the note. There were four endorsers on the note, and Trainer gave notice of dishonor to the endorser immediately ahead of him. That endorser failed to give notice to the other endorsers. If Trainer cannot collect from the endorser to whom notice was given, may he then proceed against each of the others for payment?

THE LAW IN ACTION

1. The holder of a note extended the time of payment without the knowledge or consent of an accommodation maker of the note. The accommodation maker claims that he is discharged by this extension of time. Is he correct? Why? (Union Trust Co. v. McGinty, 212 Mass. 205, 98 N.E. 679)

2. The defendant drew a check for $337.91 on the Bank of Georgetown and gave it to the plaintiff payee. The plaintiff deposited the check at once. It was credited to his account and was charged against the defendant's account. The same day the bank was closed by the state banking examiner. Thereafter, the officers of the bank canceled the credit to the plaintiff's account, canceled the charge against the defendant's account, and returned the check to the plaintiff as dishonored. The plaintiff sued the defendant, and the defendant claims that the check was discharged by payment. Was the defendant correct? Why? (Boatright v. Rankin, 150 S.C. 374, 148 S.E. 214)

KEY TO "WHAT'S THE LAW?" Page 379

1. *No. The check must be presented to the bank and payment refused before Don would be liable.*
2. *Yes. The conditions in the answer above have now been met.*

WHAT'S THE LAW?

1. *George Dunegan drew a check on the Peoples Bank of Yorktown for $500, payable to Bob Smith. When Smith presented the check at the bank for payment, the bank refused to pay even though Dunegan had funds on deposit. Could Smith sue the bank for the amount of the check?*

---

2. *Paul Parker owns a business and his customers often pay by check. Sometimes Parker waits two weeks or more before presenting the checks at the bank. Is this poor practice?*

△ UNIT 41:
USE OF
COMMERCIAL PAPER

You learned earlier that the most common type of bill of exchange is an ordinary bank check. Let us look at bank checks a little more carefully.

CHECKS AND BANKING PRACTICE

CHECKS AS BILLS OF EXCHANGE

A *check* is a written order, drawn on a bank by a depositor, ordering the bank to pay on demand and unconditionally a definite sum of money to the bearer or to the order of a specified person. U.C.C. Sec. 3-104

CHECK

We have used a check as an example of a bill of exchange. It is not a typical bill of exchange, however, because there are some ways in which it differs from other types.

1. Checks are always payable on demand, and it is expected that demand for payment shall be made within a reasonable length of time. A *reasonable time* for presentment of a check is, with respect to the liability of the drawer, thirty days after date or after issue, whichever is later, and, with respect to the liability of an endorser, seven days after his endorsement. U.C.C. Sec. 3-503(2) A bank is permitted to pay a check presented more than six months after its date, but unless the check is certified, the bank is not required to do so. U.C.C. Sec. 4-404

REASONABLE TIME

Is a bank required to pay an uncertified check which is more than six months old?

2. If a check is not presented for payment within a reasonable time after its issue and if the bank has become insolvent during the delay, the drawer may discharge liability by written assignment of his rights against the bank to the holder of the check. The drawer is not, however, otherwise discharged of liability. U.C.C. Sec. 3-502(1) Today there is little chance that a bank

will become insolvent, and with the depositors' accounts insured by the federal government, there is little chance of loss to the depositor even if there is a delay in the presenting of the check for collection. This provision applies only to the drawer of a check. To hold the prior endorsers, a check must be presented for payment by the holder within seven days after the receipt of the check. U.C.C. Sec. 3-502

3. Checks are usually presented for payment rather than for acceptance. When a check is presented to a bank for acceptance rather than for payment, we call this acceptance by the bank a *certification*. The bank cashier writes or stamps "Certified" across the face of the check, together with the date and the signature of the bank. By so doing, the bank is promising to pay the check when it is presented for payment. The bank charges this check against the depositor's account at the time the certification is made. Certification is often requested by a merchant selling goods to a person whose credit standing is not known to him.

CERTIFICATION

What is meant by certification?

EXAMPLE 1 Buterbaugh received a certified check from Dukes, a customer, in payment of a bill of goods. He held the check for one week and then presented it for payment to the bank on which it was drawn. Because Dukes had become insolvent since the check was issued, the bank did not want to pay to Buterbaugh. However, the bank had to pay the check because it had certified it.

Who may present a check to a bank for certification? If a holder has a check certified, what effect has this on the liability of the drawer and endorsers?

A check may be presented to a bank for certification by either the drawer before the check is put in circulation, or the check may be presented for certification by the holder after it comes into his possession. If the holder causes the check to be certified, the drawer and all endorsers are discharged from any further liability and the holder must look to the bank only for payment of the check in the future. Unless otherwise agreed, a bank has no obligation to certify a check. U.C.C. Sec. 3-411

4. Checks are usually written on regular printed forms provided by the bank, but such forms are not required. As long as the instrument follows the requirements set forth by law, it will be legally considered a valid instrument. U.C.C. Sec. 3-104(1) and (2)(b)

Are printed check forms always required by a bank?

EXAMPLE 2 Hurd, a debtor from a nearby town, stopped at the offices of the Gotham Loan Company to make a payment. He had forgotten his checkbook, and the company had no blank checks available. Hurd wrote out a check on a piece of $8\frac{1}{2}$- by 11-inch typing paper, taking care to include the requisites of negotiability and the coded number assigned to him by his bank for identification. This would constitute a valid check when signed and delivered by Hurd.

What is the purpose of the encoded number on checks?

RELATIONSHIP BETWEEN BANK AND DEPOSITORS

In making a deposit, is the depositor lending his money to the bank?

When a depositor deposits his money in the bank, he is actually lending the money to the bank. In return, the bank impliedly promises to pay all checks drawn by the depositor if there is sufficient money in the depositor's account to cover the amount of the checks. This contractual obligation, which exists between the bank and its depositor only, does not extend to the holder. The holder of a check has no rights against the bank until the bank accepts the check either for certification or payment. U.C.C. Sec. 3-411 and Sec. 3-505

Who must bear
the loss where a
bank pays a
forged check? a
raised check?

Forged Checks   If a bank pays a forged check, it must bear the loss. It is the duty of the bank to know the signatures of its depositors. The bank must also bear the loss of the amount added if a check is changed from the original amount to a higher amount. This altered check may be referred to as a *raised check*. The intent to defraud and the creation of a liability must be proved. Signing another person's name without these two factors does not create a forgery.

RAISED CHECK

EXAMPLE 3   Greer applied for a $250 loan from the Gotham Loan Company and received its check for that amount. He raised the amount to $2,500, presented the check to a bank for payment, and received the money. Greer was guilty of forgery, having had the intent to defraud Gotham by making an alteration and by creating for it a liability that had not existed before.

The depositor has the responsibility of notifying the bank of a forgery within a reasonable time after receiving his monthly bank statement with his canceled checks. Failure to give notice will relieve the bank of liability.

A customer who does not discover and report his unauthorized signature or any alteration on the face or back of the item within one year from the time the statement of account and items are made available to him or does not discover and report any unauthorized endorsement three years from that time is precluded from asserting against the bank such unauthorized signature or endorsement or such alteration. U.C.C. Sec. 4-406(4)

EXAMPLE 4   In the preceding case, Gotham would have had an obligation to inform the bank at once after discovering that the $250 check had been raised. Any unreasonable delay in giving this information to the bank would relieve the bank of liability.

Because the bank alone inspects a check at the time of payment, it is liable for the payment of an altered check unless the alteration was made possible through the depositor's own carelessness. Even so, if the bank could have reasonably detected the alteration, it may be held liable. U.C.C. Sec. 3-406

EXAMPLE 5   A check was received from Thomas Cara by the Gotham Loan Company, where it was endorsed and transferred to Starr for value. Starr altered the check in a manner that was very obvious to anyone who might have looked at it. When the check was presented to the bank, the teller cashed it without question. The maker, Thomas Cara, could hold the bank responsible for this loss, even if he himself had been negligent in the manner in which he had made out the check. The teller had been guilty of gross negligence in his duty to both the bank and the depositor.

If a depositor is
so careless in
making out a
check that he
invites
alterations, will
the bank be held
liable for cashing
the altered
check?

With respect to liability on forged and raised checks, one court ruled: "The maker of a check is obligated to use all diligence in protecting it. The failure to use the most effectual protection against alterations is evidence of neglect, which renders him responsible for the fraudulent amount, the bank being liable only for the genuineness of the signature and the ordinary care in paying checks." Aware of this responsibility, most business firms today use check-writing machines and special check paper, which will immediately show any attempted alterations by the holder.

If an error is made in drawing a negotiable instrument, do not attempt to correct it. Mark the check "void" or destroy it, and draw up a new one.

Stopping Payment on a Check   The drawer of a check may change his mind before the check is presented for payment and order the bank not to pay it when presented. The bank is bound by this order to stop payment and has no right to pay the check after such an order is given. If the bank fails to heed the order and cashes the check, it is liable to the depositor for the amount paid. U.C.C. Sec. 4-403

How does one stop payment on a check?

Remember, however, that you cannot avoid liability on any check that is in the hands of a holder in due course, even by stopping payment. Also, if you stop payment on a check given in payment of an honest debt, you still owe the amount of the debt.

EXAMPLE 6   **Weston applied for a loan from the Gotham Loan Company, offering as credit reference a letter bearing the signature of one of the city's leading businessmen. Gotham granted the loan, issued a check for the amount to Weston, and then learned that the reference letter was a fraud and had not been written and signed by the man whose name was used. Gotham issued a stop-payment order to its bank on Weston's check. Since Gotham had a good and valid reason for issuing such an order, both it and the bank will be free of liability for damages in any action by Weston.**

The death of the drawer of a check does not revoke the authority of the bank to accept, pay, or collect an item or to account for proceeds of its collection until the bank knows of the fact of death and has a reasonable opportunity to act on it. Even with knowledge a bank may for ten days after the date of death pay or certify checks drawn on it prior to that date unless ordered to stop payment by a person claiming an interest in the account. U.C.C. Sec. 4-405

May a bank pay a check following the death of the drawer of the check?

EXAMPLE 7   **On April 1, Harding made out several checks which he mailed to various creditors in payment of their bills. On the evening of the same day, Harding died. When the checks were presented for payment during the next few days, Harding's bank paid them. The bank had a right to do so.**

What is considered a bad check?

Bad Checks   A *bad check* is one issued against a bank balance which is insufficient to cover or against a bank in which the drawer has no funds. Most states have statutes making it a larceny for a person to issue a check drawn on a bank in which he has no funds. Some states make it an offense for a person to issue a check on a bank in which he has insufficient funds.

BAD CHECK

A bank must not pay a check on which payment has been stopped. If it does so, it is liable to the depositor for the amount paid.

The payee has the obligation to inform the drawer of the nonpayment of the check, and of any state.

Failure of the drawer to make full payment of the check within the number of days allowed by statute will serve as presumption of guilt that the drawer did issue the check with full knowledge of all facts and with the intent to defraud.

EXAMPLE 8 **The Gotham Loan Company received Millard's check for $125, due on an installment note. After it was deposited, the check was returned to Gotham with the notation "Insufficient Funds." Gotham's collection department sent a registered letter to Millard, notifying him of the matter and of his responsibilities under the bad-check law. Should Millard fail to make the check good, a criminal complaint may be lodged against him through the state's prosecuting attorney.**

Bad-check laws are effectively used as a means of collection. When notified that they are subject to prosecution, most persons make every effort to pay the creditor the amount of the check.

BILLS OF EXCHANGE OTHER THAN CHECKS

DRAFTS

In ordinary business language, a bill of exchange is called a *draft*. A draft that is not a check is an unconditional written order, addressed by one person to another, requesting the latter to pay on demand (at sight) or at a fixed or determinable future time a certain sum of money to the order of a third person or to bearer, is a draft. U.C.C. Sec. 3-104

DRAFT

EXAMPLE 9 **The Gotham Loan Company owed $1,000 to Hilton of Daytona Beach, Florida. Yardley, who also lived in Daytona Beach, owed Gotham $1,000. Gotham prepared a draft and sent it to Hilton, with instructions that Hilton present it to Yardley for payment. Gotham notified Yardley of the issuance of the draft and requested Yardley to pay it and charge the payment to Gotham's account. Until payment is made on the draft, Gotham would remain liable to Hilton for the $1,000 it owes him.**

There are many specialized forms of drafts used to accomplish particular purposes. The draft used in this case was a sight draft.

Sight Drafts A *sight draft* is a written order on the drawee to pay on demand the amount named in the instrument. It is payable on presentation to the drawee. U.C.C. Sec. 3-409 A sight draft is often used as an instrument to collect money that a buyer owes to a seller as the result of the buyer's purchase of goods or to collect a debt that is due or overdue.

SIGHT DRAFT

How do sight drafts usually operate? What important function do they serve?

EXAMPLE 10 Cameron, a merchant in St. Louis, received an order from Emery, of Detroit. If Emery was not known to Cameron, the sale probably would be transacted in the following way: Cameron would ship the goods and then prepare a sight draft, drawn on Emery. He would deliver the draft to his bank in St. Louis for collection, with the bill of lading for the goods attached. The bank would then forward the draft and the bill of lading to its correspondent bank in Detroit (the destination of the goods) for collection. The Detroit bank would present the draft to Emery and, on receiving payment, would mark the draft "Paid" and deliver it to Emery with the attached bill of lading. The bill of lading entitles Emery to claim the goods from the transportation company. The Detroit bank would then notify the St. Louis bank that the draft had been honored (paid) and the amount credited to the bank. The St. Louis bank would notify Cameron that the draft had been collected and that his account had been credited with the amount of the draft, less the usual bank charges for collection.

Time Drafts *Time drafts* are frequently used when a seller extends a specified period of credit to a buyer who does not have ready funds at the time of the purchase. By receiving from the customer a signed acknowledgment of the debt (an accepted draft), the seller can obtain money on the draft if he needs funds for use in his business. The draft may be discounted or sold by the seller at his bank through endorsement and delivery. The bank then becomes the holder, entitled to payment on maturity of the draft. U.C.C. Sec. 3-503(1)(c)

TIME DRAFT

The drawee shows his willingness to obey the order and pay the draft by writing "Accepted," "Presented," or a similar word across the face of the draft and adding the date and his signature. This is known as *acceptance*. The drawee then becomes absolutely liable on the draft and the drawer's liability becomes that of an endorser. After acceptance of the draft, the drawee is known as the *acceptor*. U.C.C. Sec. 3-410

ACCEPTANCE

ACCEPTOR

EXAMPLE 11 Gotham Loan Company drew a draft on Cook for $650. The draft was mailed to Cook, who replied by letter that he was accepting the draft and was returning it with his letter. In the event of a later dispute, the draft would not be considered to have been accepted. Cook's acceptance would have been valid only if it had been written on the draft itself.

Is a draft that is retained or destroyed considered to be accepted?

A draft that is retained or altered is considered dishonored, not accepted. U.C.C. Sec. 3-419(1)

Trade Acceptances A *trade acceptance* is a draft that is drawn by the seller on the purchaser and accepted by him. Trade acceptances were introduced in business by the Federal Reserve System and are very widely used. A trade acceptance differs from other drafts in that it is used only in the purchase and sale of goods.

TRADE ACCEPTANCE

What is a trade acceptance? How does it differ from other drafts?

EXAMPLE 12 Zambeck drew a trade acceptance on his employer for back salary due him, payable six months after date. The employer accepted the instrument. It was held that this paper had the legal force of an ordinary draft, not that of a trade acceptance, because it did not result from the purchase and sale of merchandise.

All specialized forms of drafts contain the requisites of negotiable instruments; the variations are only to meet the needs of specific business transactions.

EXAMPLE 13 Craig Wyatt, who lived in New York, contracted to sell ten shares of The Boiler Plate Corporation stock to John Heath, who lived in Chicago. To fully protect both parties in the performance of the contract, Wyatt drew a draft on Heath, pinned the draft to the shares of stock, and mailed both to a Chicago bank. The bank called Heath and asked him to come in, pay the draft, and pick up his stock. By handling the matter in this way, Heath does not have to pay until the stock is available for delivery; and the bank, as an agent of Wyatt, does not deliver the stock until the draft is paid. In this way, both parties are protected.

EXAMPLE 14 William Watson sold an order of furs to Virgil Anderson in July. It was understood by both parties that the furs were to be delivered in September for the fall market. Watson was willing to extend credit to Anderson for three months because he knew that Anderson would not have the money until he resold the furs. Watson, however, needed money. To solve this problem, Watson drew a draft on Anderson, payable in ninety days. This draft he sent to Anderson. Anderson accepted the draft and returned it to Watson. Watson then negotiated the draft to his bank at a discount and received his money.

OTHER NEGOTIABLE INSTRUMENTS

Traveler's checks *Traveler's checks* are drafts drawn by a reliable financial organization. They may be purchased from banks and other institutions. For one who travels extensively, traveler's checks are a particularly convenient and safe form in which to carry money. They are safe because anyone finding or stealing them cannot use them. Only the purchaser who signed the checks may cash them. If he loses them, they will be replaced.

TRAVELER'S CHECK

When he wishes to cash one of the checks, the purchaser countersigns it in the presence of the person who is converting it into cash or accepting it in payment of a purchase.

Traveler's checks are more acceptable than personal checks, are easily negotiable, and are accepted virtually all over the world.

Money Orders *Money orders*, both postal and express, are acceptable in situations where a personal check would not be given credit. Whether or not they are issued by banks, they serve as checks. They may not be so freely transferable as are other credit instruments because they may be negotiated by endorsement only once.

MONEY ORDER

Certificates of Deposit A *certificate of deposit* is a negotiable instrument issued by a bank to a depositor acknowledging the receipt of a deposit of money with a promise to repay with interest on demand or on a fixed date. The certificate of deposit is in legal effect a promissory note signed by a bank against which checks cannot be drawn.

CERTIFICATE OF DEPOSIT

How does a certificate of deposit differ from a bank checking or savings account?

SUGGESTIONS FOR MINIMIZING LEGAL RISKS

1. Never use a pencil to draw a check unless you plan to cash it immediately in your bank. Even then it is better to use ink. It would be very difficult for you to prove forgery in case an altered check had been drawn in pencil. The bank would be relieved of liability without adequate proof of forgery.
2. A check drawn payable to "Cash" or "Bearer" or endorsed in blank can be cashed by anyone. Use these forms only when you plan to cash a check immediately in your bank.
3. Use ink to draw and fill in all blank spaces on a check, note, or draft, so that nothing can be added to or inserted before or following your writing of the instrument. You take a serious risk in permitting anyone to have a signed instrument that leaves blank the payee or the amount. Any holder may legally fill in these blanks and negotiate the instrument.
4. If an error is made in drawing a negotiable instrument of any kind, do not attempt to correct it. Mark it "Void" or destroy it.
5. To avoid possible loss, cash all checks as soon as possible after receipt, because unreasonable delay in presentment is calculated from the date of the check rather than the date of last negotiation.

APPLYING YOUR LEARNING

QUESTIONS AND PROBLEMS

1. How do checks differ from other bills of exchange?
2. Can a holder insist that a bank cash a check? Why?
3. What is considered a reasonable time for presentation of a check for payment? Explain.
4. Is the drawer of a check relieved of all responsibility because of an unreasonable delay in the presentment of a check for payment? Explain.
5. Name several reasons why a check should be cashed promptly.
6. Does stopping payment of a check relieve the drawer of liability for the original transaction for which the check was issued? Explain.
7. Why are traveler's checks a good investment for the traveler?
8. Distinguish between sight drafts and time drafts.

WHAT IS YOUR OPINION?

In each of the following cases, give your decision and state a legal principle that applies to the case.

1. Paul Reynolds received from his bank a statement of his account and his canceled checks, among which he found one for $50 on which his name had been forged. Could Reynolds hold the bank liable for $50?

2. Elmer Hudson received a check from Harvey Grant for $500. For no very good reason, the bank refused to pay it. Can Hudson sue the bank? Does he have a claim against Grant? Explain.

3. On October 1, Lee Duncan discovered that he had overlooked cashing a check that he had received in May of that year. Thinking it was worthless, he threw it in the wastebasket. Should he have done so? Explain.

4. Phillip Corbett forged Leon Couse's name to a check, payable to bearer, and passed it on by mere delivery to Joe Birch, who knew nothing of the forgery. Birch passed the check on to Morton Nelson, and Nelson took it to the bank where payment was refused. State what each holder in due course could do about it.

5. Grover requested his bank to stop payment on a certified check that he had drawn. The bank refused to do so, although the check had not been presented for payment at the time that the request was made. Was the bank justified in its refusal to honor Grover's request?

THE LAW IN ACTION

1. The defendant, Cramer, gave a check drawn on a local bank to the plaintiff. The plaintiff held the check for six weeks and then deposited it in an out-of-town bank. By the time the check reached the bank on which it was drawn, the bank had failed. The defendant had ample funds in his account at all times to pay the check. The check was returned to the defendant and he refused to pay it, claiming that he was discharged by the plaintiff's delay in presenting the check for payment. Was the defendant correct? (Sulsberger & Sons Co. v. Cramer, App. Div. 114, 155 N.Y.S. 775)

2. J. W. Albright and his son, Paul Albright, were in business together. In the past they had often borrowed money from the plaintiff bank. Each time they had executed a promissory note signed by both father and son. In this case, the son had presented a note, supposedly signed by both, collected the money, and left town. The signature of the father was a forgery. Could the bank collect from the father? (First National Bank of Shoemakersville v. Albright, 111 Pa. Sup. Ct. 392, 170 A. 370)

KEY TO "WHAT'S THE LAW?" Page 388

1. *No. The bank would not be liable because there is no contractual obligation between the bank and the holder. Smith, as a holder, would have to contact Dunegan, with whom the bank had a contractual obligation.*

2. *This is poor business practice for obvious reasons. Under the law, if Parker should hold any checks for more than thirty days, the drawers of these checks would be relieved of any liability for loss caused by the delay in demanding payment.*

WHAT'S THE LAW?

1. *Joe Seiver was in business. He wished to borrow money to buy new merchandise for resale. Do you think he will be able to borrow money? If so, would he most likely go to a commercial bank, an industrial bank, or a credit union?*

2. *Ron Fisher wanted to buy an automobile for his personal use and needed to borrow money to pay for it. Do you think he will be able to get a loan for this purpose? If so, to what kind of bank would he be most likely to go?*

▲ UNIT 42: MAKING PERSONAL LOANS

How is borrowing money closely related to buying on the installment plan?

The borrowing of money is very closely related to buying on the installment plan, and many of the rules for establishing credit apply with equal force to each. Installment buying was discussed in Part 6, and it might be well to review the features of that subject at this time. In this unit, however, we shall confine our discussion to the borrowing of money.

EXAMPLE 1 **Dick Maurer wanted to purchase a new pool table for his game room. He was short of money, but he had been promised a job at the Superette. The Sporting Goods Store offered pool tables for sale at $380 each. A customer could pay $10 down and $10 per week until the balance is paid. Dick's friend, Jack Bala, had a used pool table for sale for $160 cash. If Dick could obtain a $160 loan, he could buy a pool table at a lower price and pay off his loan in about half the time.**

There are many reasons why you may some day wish to borrow small amounts of money. The principal reasons, however, may be classified as follows:

1. You may need money to meet some emergency. The emergency might be to meet a pressing debt, to pay medical expenses, to make repairs on your home, or to meet an insurance premium.

2. You may be able to make money by getting a greatly reduced price by paying cash for an article you plan to buy, or you may be able to pay off an existing loan at a discount.

3. You may wish to buy some article that you need or desire, such as an automobile, a television set, or a refrigerator.

4. You may want to borrow because you are in sound financial condition and wish to indulge yourself in some luxury or take a vacation.

Whatever your reason for borrowing, you will most likely borrow from an institution that makes a business of lending small funds.

Most people borrow from institutions which are in the business of lending funds.

MONEYLENDING INSTITUTIONS

What are the most common moneylending institutions which make small loans?

The most common moneylending institutions making small loans are (1) commercial banks, (2) industrial banks, (3) small-loan, or personal finance, companies, (4) credit unions, and (5) pawnbrokers. As you remember from our discussion of the Truth in Lending Act in Unit 21, these institutions are now required to inform the borrower of interest charges in dollars and as an annual percentage rate.

COMMERCIAL BANKS

The bank in your hometown with which you, or members of your family, do business is probably a *commercial bank*. It is an institution that carries on the traditional type of banking business. It encourages all the people in the community to save and deposit money in both savings or checking accounts. Traditionally, also, it makes loans to people who want to buy or build houses or other types of buildings. These loans are usually secured by mortgages placed on the real estate bought.

COMMERCIAL BANK

Commercial banks also make large loans to business firms; and these loans are secured by such things as a pledge of stocks or bonds, inventories, accounts receivable, and other things. Traditionally, then, commercial banks make large, secured loans.

It is only in recent years that commercial banks have commenced to offer their services to the borrower of small funds. This service is being extended very rapidly, however; and you may well find that a commercial bank is a very desirable place to obtain a small loan.

The operation of the small-loan department of a commercial bank is very similar to that of other small-loan institutions. There are, however, a few distinguishing differences. Commercial banks are lending someone else's money; and they are, therefore, strictly regulated as to the amount of risk they may take. Since they usually lend money only to individuals who are good credit risks, they can sometimes offer lower rates of interest.

Why are commercial banks strictly regulated?

The interest rates in a commercial bank are usually fixed on a yearly basis, even though the loan is to be repaid by the month. The rate often charged is as much as $7\frac{1}{2}$ percent a year. You will remember from our discussion of true interest rates in Unit 21, however, that, because part of the loan is being returned every month, this $7\frac{1}{2}$ percent discount really amounts to almost 15 percent on a yearly basis. You must remember, however, that small loans, repayable monthly, require a great deal of book work; and the rate of interest must be higher than in a regular commercial loan that requires but a fraction of the time to handle the account.

How can you easily convert the discount interest rate to an approximate annual rate?

EXAMPLE 2   If, in Example 1, Dick was competent to contract and had a good credit standing, he might get a loan from the small-loan department of a commercial bank. He might find, however, that a commercial bank would not lend him the money, not because it did not trust him, but because it did not think his earning capacity would justify the loan. It is possible, however, that an industrial bank might be willing to take the extra risk and lend Dick the money.

INDUSTRIAL BANKS

Industrial banks are organized under regular or special banking laws, but they are organized for the major purpose of investing their funds in personal loans.

INDUSTRIAL BANK

They solicit savings and deposits just as other banks do, and they make loans in much the same manner as the small-loan departments of commercial banks.

There may be special legislation in your state with regard to industrial banks. Many states, for example, prohibit them from using the term *bank* and regulate their organization under special statutes. Industrial banks have an enviable record for financial soundness, however, and may prove to be just the type of bank to make the loan you wish.

SMALL-LOAN, OR PERSONAL FINANCE, COMPANIES

Unlike commercial and industrial banks, *personal finance companies* are organized solely for the purpose of lending money. These companies do not borrow other people's money through deposits or savings accounts. They lend only their own money. They raise money through the sale of stock or the issuing of bonds if they are a corporation, or they lend the personal assets of the owners if the finance company is a partnership or sole proprietorship.

PERSONAL FINANCE COMPANY

Why can personal finance companies take greater risks than a bank?

Because the personal finance company is lending its own money and not that of someone else, it can take greater risks than a bank. You may often be able to get a loan through a personal finance company when your credit risk would be too great for a loan from a bank. This means, naturally, that you may have to pay a greater rate of interest for the added risk.

REMEMBER: The interest you pay is proportional to the risk taken and the expenses incurred by the lending institution.

How is interest on personal finance company loans usually calculated?

Legitimate moneylending institutions are closely regulated by statutes, and it is not often that the interest they charge is out of line with their risks and expenses. Personal finance companies usually charge interest on a monthly basis, and the interest one pays is usually calculated each month on the basis of the unpaid balance.

EXAMPLE 3 Dick might find that, even though a commercial bank would not lend him money, a small-loan company would. The loan company might be willing and able to take the greater risk in return for a higher rate of interest. It might still be to Dick's advantage to borrow the $160 and pay the higher interest because he could then buy the used pool table for cash at a great saving.

CREDIT UNIONS

CREDIT UNION

What are credit unions?

Credit unions, or mutual benefit loan companies, are cooperative money-lending institutions. They are usually, but not always, operated by the members of some group, such as the employees of a given company, a lodge, a labor union, or some other association.

Credit unions operate under charters issued either by the state or by the federal government. The purpose of a credit union is to serve the members of its own group.

EXAMPLE 4 The employees of the Walton Manufacturing Company decide to organize a credit union. Some of the employees have some savings that they want to invest. Some other employees want to borrow small sums to make purchases or to pay bills. By cooperating and pooling their efforts, the employees can organize a credit union with a minimum of expense. As a result, those who invest their savings get a higher return and those who borrow can do so at a lower rate.

PAWNBROKERS

PAWNBROKER

What is a pledge as applied to a pawnbroker's loan?

Pawnbrokers make very small loans and accept personal property as a pledge to secure the repayment of the loan. Because the pawnbroker's loan is often not paid and he must sell the pledged chattel to get his money, pawnbrokers are in the retail business as well as in the business of making small loans. Like other financial institutions, pawnbrokers are closely regulated by the state. Because of the great risk involved, they are allowed to charge a very high rate of interest.

Pawnbrokers make very small loans and accept personal property as a pledge to secure the repayment of the loan.

PROCEDURE IN OBTAINING A PERSONAL LOAN

Small loans are of two types, but the procedure in obtaining a loan is similar in both types. The first type is a *loan secured by a chattel mortgage* and is similar to the process of buying on a conditional sales contract.

EXAMPLE 5   Joe Stone wishes to buy an automobile, and he expects to pay for it by means of monthly payments. The automobile dealer is willing to finance the car for him, but Joe believes he can do better by borrowing from a local bank. A bank or a small-loan company might lend him the money and take a chattel mortgage on the new car as security for the loan.

The second type of loan is an *unsecured loan*. The lender makes the loan on the basis of the good character, credit standing, and ability of the borrower to pay. Sometimes the lender might demand a cosigner. Most people hesitate to ask a friend to sign a note with them, however, and cosigner loans are being used less today than they were a few years ago.

UNSECURED LOAN

In either type of loan, however, the process usually begins with filing an application for a loan with a representative of the bank called an *interviewer,* or *loan counselor.* These interviewers are chosen because of their ability to judge character and estimate the ability of the applicant to pay. The importance of this interview cannot be overemphasized because it is on the basis of the interview that many loans are made. The following are some credit characteristics that determine whether or not the loan will be made:

LOAN COUNSELOR

How does one go about getting a small loan?

1. The borrower must be a good moral risk. He must have a good reputation for paying his bills and a genuine desire to pay his debts as they mature.
2. The borrower must have a job or other source of regular income. Sometimes the nature of the job and its permanence are more important than the amount of his wages.
3. The regularity of his income, the amount of his debts, the property he owns, and the savings he has accumulated are all important.
4. The borrower must be competent to contract. His family status is important, and the number of persons dependent on him for support is considered.
5. What the money is to be used for, the length of time required to repay it, and the security that can be offered are all important.

After the application is filed and the applicant is interviewed, the lender will usually want a little time to check references and credit. If these prove satisfactory, the loan will ordinarily be made within a day or so.

STANDARD PROVISIONS

The usual provisions of a small-loan contract have already been discussed, but by way of summary we might review them.

Small loans are usually repaid in monthly installments. In some loans, the full amount of the loan is turned over to the borrower, and the amount of the interest is added to each month's installment payment. In others,

APPLICATION FOR PERSONAL LOAN

I hereby make application for a loan of $ 1,000 for (Purpose of loan) car purchase

repayable in 12 monthly installments beginning Please indicate preference ☒ One Month From Date of Loan ☐ On the Following Date _____

Name: Launor P. Kerry   Age: 25 Married: yes Number of Dependents: none

Name: Mary Keats Kerry   Place of Birth: Rising Sun, Iowa
NAME OF HUSBAND OR WIFE

Home Address: 12 Mangatuck Drive, Sunnydale, Long Island   Phone: 813-2262

Previous Address: One Grassy Terrace, Rising Sun, Iowa   Soc. Sec. No.: 202-16-6123

Nearest Relative (Not living with you): Mrs. Peter Kerry (mother)

Address: One Grassy Terrace, Rising Sun, Iowa

Do you belong to any military organization? No If Yes, indicate branch: _____ Draft status if any: 4-F

Landlord's Name: Homer Gratz   Address: 195 Tenney Blvd., Sunnydale, L.I.

Years at present address: 2⅓ Rent per month: $185 Yrs. at previous address: 22

Employer's Name: John B. Rosen   Address: 2110-19 East 63 St., Garden City, L.I.

Monthly Salary $ 900 Position: foreman   Badge Number: none

Years employed here: 2 Name of Superior: Henry Boakum Phone: 819-1976

Other Income: amount per month $ 750 Source: wife's salary

Previous Employer: (Name and address if with present employer less than two years) _____

Bank Accounts (Checking) _____ Regular ☐ Special ☒ Sunnydale National   Sunnydale
                                                      NAME   BRANCH   CITY

(Savings): Long Island Savings and Loan Association   Sunnydale
                          NAME   BRANCH   CITY

Life Insurance Carried: $ 10,000 Beneficiary: wife

Charge Accounts: Friendly Drug, R.H. Department Store

Loans or Installment Debts Outstanding (ALL):

Creditor	Street Address	City	Loan Balance:	Monthly Payment:
Acme Appliances, Inc., 15 Baines Terrace, Sunnydale, L.I.			$185	$20

I authorize you to obtain such information as you may require concerning the statements made in this application and being duly sworn do declare that all replies to the above questions are true and accurate and agree that the application shall remain your property whether or not the loan is granted.

I AGREE TO NOTIFY THE BANK OF ANY MATERIAL CHANGE IN THE ABOVE STATEMENT

Nathan Gratz (WITNESS)   _Launor P. Kerry_ (APPLICANT'S SIGNATURE)

Dated at Sunnydale on September 9, 19--

CO-MAKER'S STATEMENT

I have read the accompanying application. I am agreeable to becoming a Co-Maker with the applicant in signing the note which will evidence the loan if granted. I am aware of the responsibility which I will assume in signing the note as I am also aware that you will rely on the truth of the following statement in considering the credit risk relative to the requested loan.

Name: Horace Gruley   Age: 47 Married: yes Number of Dependents: 7

Name: Martha Smith Gruley   Place of Birth: Grometown, Pennsylvania
NAME OF HUSBAND OR WIFE

Home Address: 135 Summit Way, Verona, New Jersey   Phone: 221-7959

Previous Address: 1 New Street, Grometown, Pennsylvania

Nearest Relative (Not living with you): Samuel Gruley (brother)

Address: 120 Dolan Terrace, Syosset, Long Island

Do you belong to any military organization? No If Yes, indicate branch: _____ Draft status if any: _____

Landlord's Name: None   Address: _____

Years at present address: 20 Rent per month: _____ Yrs. at previous address: _____

Employer's Name: New Jersey Hot Shoppes   Address: 113 Broadway, Newark, New Jersey

Monthly Salary $ 1,500 Position: Manager   Badge Number: _____

Years employed here: 20 Name of Superior: Oscar Mann Phone: 621-1234

Remarks: To my knowledge, Kerry is stable, honest, thoroughly reliable.

I authorize you to obtain such information as you may require concerning the statements made in this application and being duly sworn do declare that all replies to the above questions are true and accurate and agree that the application shall remain your property whether or not the loan is granted.

I AGREE TO NOTIFY THE BANK OF ANY MATERIAL CHANGE IN THE ABOVE STATEMENT

Mr. John Kaster (WITNESS)   _Horace Gruley_ (CO-MAKER'S SIGNATURE)

Dated at Verona on September 12, 19--

the loan is *discounted;* that is, the amount of the interest is subtracted from **DISCOUNTED** the amount of the loan at the time the loan is approved, and the borrower receives only the difference. If, for example, the amount of a one-year loan is $100 and the interest is to be 6 percent, the borrower would receive $94, the amount less the discount.

In what different ways may the interest on a loan be charged?

Interest is charged in different ways by different institutions. Banks usually charge interst by the year and generally use the discount method, whereas small-loan companies usually charge their interest by the month on the unpaid balance. All maximum interest rates are fixed by state statute for each type of loan.

Sometimes other charges are added, but the borrower should look on these charges with suspicion. There may, however, be legitimate "package" loans, in which additional charges for insurance on the mortgaged chattel and personal insurance on the buyer may be added.

SUGGESTIONS FOR MINIMIZING LEGAL RISKS

1. Being able to borrow money when you need it is important in both personal and business relationships. Build a reputation for ability and willingness to meet financial obligations when due. To do otherwise invites potential future financial and legal risks should you need to make a loan to save your business or meet an emergency.

2. Even though you are anxious to obtain a loan, be strictly accurate and honest in filing an application for the loan. Trying to obtain a loan by means of misstatements of any kind can lead to future difficulties when you attempt to obtain a loan when the need may be even more urgent.

3. Deal only with licensed lending agencies, and be sure that the interest rate charged does not exceed the maximum allowed by your state.

4. If repayments are made in installments, get a receipt showing the amount charged as interest and the amount applied to the principal. File these receipts carefully as evidence of payments on the principal and for possible use for income tax purposes.

5. Do not make repayments to anyone representing himself as an agent or collector for the lender unless you have positive proof that he is a duly appointed agent acting within his authority. Get and file a written receipt for all payments made to an agent.

 APPLYING YOUR LEARNING

QUESTIONS AND PROBLEMS

1. To whom are loans usually made by an industrial bank? If there is an industrial bank in your community, inquire regarding the interest rates usually charged for small loans.

2. By whom are credit unions usually operated? for what purpose?

3. Make some inquiries to determine whether there are any credit unions in your community. If so, who sponsors them?

4. What are the advantages and disadvantages of obtaining a loan from a pawnbroker?

5. What is meant by a secured loan? an unsecured loan? Illustrate each by a typical example.

6. What information does the interviewer look for in discussing a potential loan with a prospective borrower?

WHAT IS YOUR OPINION?

In each of the following cases, give your decision and state a legal principle that applies to the case.

1. Bill Lake needed a loan in a hurry to pay for an airplane ticket to attend the funeral of his father who had lived in a distant state. Bill applied for a loan at his commercial bank. The bank was willing to lend him $200 at 6 percent, discounted in advance, with repayment to be made in ten equal installments. How much money did Bill receive from the bank? How much interest was charged?

2. Chester Mills lived in a state that had adopted some of the provisions of a small loans law allowing the charging of $2\frac{1}{2}$ percent interest on the unpaid balance on loans up to $300. Chester wanted to borrow $50. He thought that he should be given a lower rate of interest since his loan was small. Do you agree that costs on small loans should be less than on larger loans? Explain your decision.

3. Sam Merrell urgently needed to borrow $75 to pay a doctor's bill. The licensed small-loan lender said he would lend him the money at the legal interest rate if Sam would buy a turkey worth $5 from him for $20 for Sam's Thanksgiving dinner. Do you think this would be a usurious agreement if Sam paid the $20? Why? If Sam believes this to be in violation of the spirit of the law, what should he do about it? If it is a violation, what would happen to the lender's license.

4. Floyd Wynn wanted to purchase a used car for not more than $500. He was married, owned his own home, was out of debt but short of cash, had a steady job and a reputation for paying his debts on time. How should Floyd proceed in order to get a loan of $500 that would be the least costly in interest charges? What are his best sources considering your own community?

5. Donald McBride also wants to purchase a used car, paying not over $500. He is single, nineteen years of age, and is working on his first job, which pays $50 a week. How should Donald proceed to get the loan? What are his best sources considering your own community?

6. Donald approached one used-car dealer who made him this offer: He could arrange a loan if Donald would pay $50 for investigation fees, $175 for insurance, $25 for legal fees in case Donald defaulted in his payments, and would agree to buy four new tires from the dealer at $25 each. Do you believe that Donald should consider this offer? Why or why not?

THE LAW IN ACTION

1. Martorano borrowed money from the Capital Finance Corporation. To secure the loan, Martorano executed a chattel mortgage on his automobile. The Capital Finance Corporation required Martorano to take out insurance on the car before they would make the loan. The cost of the insurance plus the maximum legal charges for making the loan were deducted from the amount of the loan. When sued for nonpayment of the loan, Martorano protested on the grounds that the contract was illegal because of the extra charge arising from the insurance requirement. Do you agree? (Martorano v. Capital Finance Corp., 289 N.Y. 21)

2. Krim purchased an automobile, and the financing of the purchase price was made through the defendant bank. Krim's note is now alleged by Krim to be usurious because it was an amount greater than the purchase price plus the interest and charges allowed by law. The bank contends that the note was given to the dealer and that the bank had then properly purchased the note at a discount. If this was true, this would not be usury. If it was shown instead that the dealer was in reality only an agent of the bank and had written up the purchase price to hide the excess interest charges, would this be usury? (Krim v. Morris Plan Industrial Bank, 173 Misc. 141, 17 N.Y.S. 2d 472)

KEY TO "WHAT'S THE LAW?" Page 397

1. *Yes. He would be more likely to borrow from a commercial bank.*
2. *Yes. Most likely, he would go to an industrial bank since this is neither a commercial transaction, a small loan, nor a loan secured by a pledge.*

A DIGEST OF LEGAL CONCEPTS

1. The maker of a promissory note promises to pay the note without qualification when it is due. This type of liability is known as primary liability.

2. The acceptor of a bill of exchange (draft) promises to pay the bill in accordance with the terms of his acceptance. He also has primary liability.

3. The endorser of either a draft or a promissory note and the drawer of a draft promise to make good if (a) the instrument is presented properly for payment, (b) payment by a primary party is refused, and (c) the endorser or drawer is properly notified of the refusal.

4. Drawers of drafts and all endorsers are called *secondary parties*.

5. A draft must be presented to the drawee for payment before secondary parties can be held liable.

6. Promissory notes must be presented to the maker before endorsers can be held liable.

7. No presentment for payment is necessary to charge the maker of a promissory note.

8. No presentment for payment is necessary to charge the acceptor of a draft.

9. A negotiable instrument must be presented on or before the day due if a time of payment is specified.

10. If the instrument is payable "on demand" and no date is specified, it must be presented for payment within a reasonable time after issue.

11. A negotiable instrument is dishonored if it is not accepted when presented for acceptance, if it is not paid when presented for payment at maturity, or if presentment has been excused or waived and the instrument is past due and unpaid.

12. An instrument payable at a bank is considered to be dishonored if funds sufficient to pay the holder are not on deposit on the due date.

13. Secondary parties are discharged from liability if the instrument is not properly presented to the primary parties for acceptance or payment or if notice of dishonor is not given to the secondary parties as prescribed by law.

14. A check is a draft that is drawn on a bank payable on demand.

15. A check must be presented for certification or payment not later than thirty days after date or after issue, whichever is later. Failure to do so releases the drawer from loss caused by the delay.

16. To hold an endorser liable on a check, the holder of the check must present it for payment within seven days after the endorsement.

17. A bank has no contractual obligation to the holder of an unpaid or uncertified check.

18. A bank may for ten days after the date of death of a depositor pay or certify checks drawn by him prior to that date, unless ordered to stop payment by a person claiming an interest in the account.

19. The drawer of a check should stop payment on it when it becomes lost; when a mistake has been made in the amount or the party to whom it has been passed; or if its issuance was the result of fraud, duress, or undue influence.

20. The drawee of a draft is under no legal obligation to pay it when it is presented to him.

21. A draft payable after sight must be accepted in order to create a legal liability on the part of the drawee to pay it. If this is not done, the draft would never become due.

22. The acceptance of a draft by the drawee is indicated by him by writing "Accepted," "Presented," or a similar word across the face of the draft. He then becomes absolutely liable on the draft.

23. A draft that is retained by the drawee or altered is considered dishonored.

24. A bank does have a contractual obligation to the depositor. If the bank refuses to pay a check under circumstances that would amount to a breach of contract, the depositor may have a claim against the bank.

25. Banking laws prohibit cashing of checks that would cause an overdraft.

PART 15: Renting, Owning, and Transferring Real Property

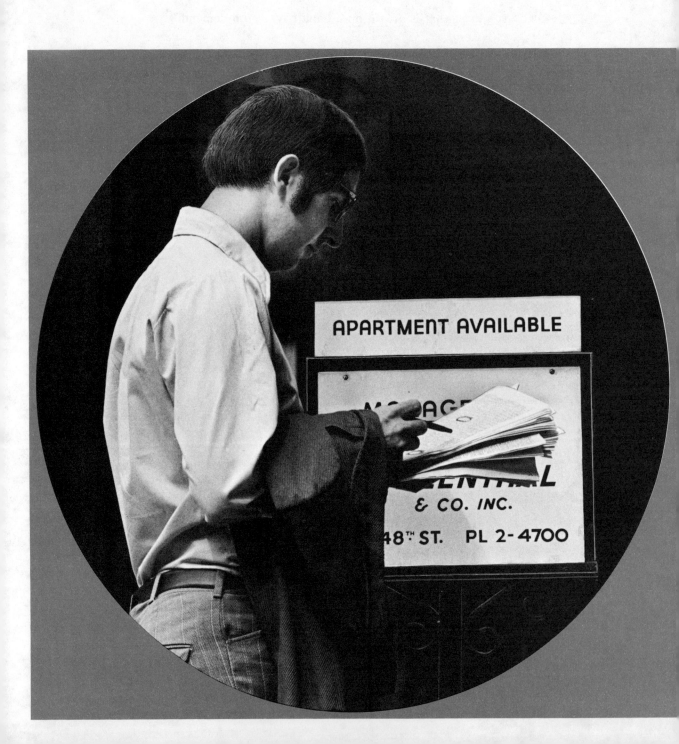

WHAT'S THE LAW?

1. *Don Burdick rented a house and lot from Dick Stoner on a month-to-month basis. The week after Burdick moved in, Stoner began parking his automobile in the backyard. Does he have any right to do this?*

---

2. *Roy Koontz leased an unfurnished apartment in the Mayflower Apartments for one year. Two days after he moved in, the plaster fell off the ceiling in the bedroom. Can Koontz demand that the landlord repair the ceiling?*

▲ UNIT 43: RENTING REAL PROPERTY

The cost of maintaining a home is one of the biggest items in the average family budget. It is usually estimated that approximately 25 percent of the average family income is spent on housing.

If you rent real property you are a *tenant*. If you rent real property to someone else, you are a *landlord*. The law that deals with the relationship between the two is known as the law of landlord and tenant. Most of the legal problems involved in landlord and tenant relationships can be anticipated in advance and properly provided for by contract.

TENANT
LANDLORD

The contract you make with your landlord, usually called a *lease*, is one of the most important of your everyday agreements. In a lease, the tenant is known as the *lessee;* the landlord, as the *lessor*. The lease needs your most careful attention. A knowledge of the legal problems involved, plus forethought and planning, will pay dividends in contracts of this kind.

LEASE

LESSEE
LESSOR

TYPES OF TENANCIES

Your contract with your landlord will most probably be for either a tenancy for years or a periodic tenancy. A *tenancy for years* is a right to occupy the property for a stated period of time. It may be one year, two years, five years, or even ninety-nine years. It could also be for one week, one month, or six months. However long the period, the time when it will come to an end is clearly indicated.

TENANCY FOR YEARS

A *periodic tenancy* may also be by the week, by the month, or by the year; however, in a periodic tenancy, week, month, or year is used only to show how the rent is to be paid. If you rent a house at $50 a week, it is a week-to-week tenancy. If you rent at $150 a month, it is a month-to-month tenancy, and so on. Nothing is said in the contract concerning how long you will continue to rent.

PERIODIC TENANCY

What are the various types of tenancies?

TENANCY FOR YEARS

Technically and historically, a tenant for years owns the property for the specified period of years. Even though that concept is often changed by statute and/or by contract, it is still the basis of the landlord and tenant relationship in a tenancy for years. You should keep this in mind because it will help you understand some of the usual provisions in a lease. Furthermore, it should serve as a warning to get all the terms of your agreement with your landlord written into your lease. Otherwise, you might find yourself bound to the responsibilities of owning a piece of property when you only intended to rent it.

The contract that creates an estate for years is known as a lease; it conveys ownership for a stated period of years, and it implies that the lessee acquires the usual rights and obligations of ownership.

REMEMBER: It can be very dangerous to buy a standard lease form and fill in the blanks without careful study; the parties signing may find themselves bound in ways that neither of them intended. A lease for less than a year can be oral, but it is never wise to enter into an oral lease. If the lease is for more than a year, the Statute of Frauds requires that it be in writing.

When must a lease be in writing?

A minor's contract to rent real property is voidable and unenforceable at the election of the minor. Should the minor be married, however, he is said to have been emancipated from his minor's rights and may be held to his agreement.

Is a lease signed by a minor ever enforceable?

EXAMPLE 1 **At the time of their marriage, both Robson and his wife were below the age of majority in their state. They had signed a one-year lease for an apartment. The landlord would be permitted to treat the Robsons like any other tenants. By virtue of their marriage, they had been emancipated from the safeguards surrounding minors.**

General Covenants The basic right the tenant wants is possession and a continued occupancy free from interference or annoyances. The landlord wants rent and possession of his property in good condition at the term's end. Every lease contains covenants providing for these items.

What is meant by the general covenants in a lease?

Decoration and Repairs The landlord has no obligation to decorate or maintain the premises unless it is so provided in the lease or by statute or local ordinance. He must however make those repairs necessary to keep the premises fit to live in. This obligation is known as *implied warranty of habitability*. Basically the tenant owns the property for the stated period, and, as temporary owner, he has the obligation of maintaining the premises and making repairs that are not the obligation of the landlord.

IMPLIED WARRANTY OF HABITABILITY

Can one hold the landlord liable for keeping the property decorated and in repair?

If you rented only a small apartment in a large building, you would have control of your apartment only. The landlord would have control of the entry, stairs, halls, basement, and so on. It would be the landlord's implied duty to maintain these parts of the premises.

You should always have a complete understanding with your landlord on these points before you sign a lease. The safest thing to do is to get everything written into the lease and not leave anything to be implied.

Before you sign a lease, be sure you have a complete understanding with your landlord about who is to make repairs.

● There are also some state statutes and local ordinances that relate to the maintenance and repair of multiple-family dwellings. The health and safety of its citizens are important to the state.

The tenant, for his part, must return the premises to the landlord in as good a condition as he received it, reasonable wear and tear excepted. Anything more than reasonable wear and tear is called *waste*. If the tenant has been guilty of waste, he must pay the landlord for the damage done.

What is meant by reasonable wear and tear? waste?

WASTE

EXAMPLE 2 While renting a house in Public Circle, Zentner placed an electric heater in one of the rooms. Because the thermostat was out of order, the heater became red hot and burned a hole in the floor. This damage was a result of negligence, and not ordinary wear and tear. Zentner will be held responsible.

May a tenant sublet his apartment if there is no covenant against subletting?

Subletting If the landlord does not want the tenant to *sublet*, or rent his interest in the property to another person, he must put a covenant against subletting in the lease. Otherwise, the tenant may sublet, but the tenant must retain all liability for the property.

SUBLET

EXAMPLE 3 The Olsons held a three year lease on a house in Vinnet. The house was near a college campus where Debbie Olson went to school. One summer while the lease was still in effect the Olsons went on vacation. A friend of Olson's, John Bennis, was hired by the college for the summer, so the Olsons sublet the house to Bennis and his family. In the fall the Olsons returned to their house and Bennis and his family moved back to their permanent home.

Renewals A tenancy for years absolutely ends at the expiration of the stated period unless there are provisions in the lease or statutory provisions to the contrary. It would be a hardship on either party if neither knew what the other was going to do prior to the end of the term.

● To prevent this hardship, many states have statutes that require each to give notice to the other a specified time before the end of the term. It is also quite common to have a provision pertaining to renewals written into the lease itself. This provision for renewal is usually only a covenant, however. If the landlord refuses to renew, the tenant's rights are for breach of contract only, although under some circumstances he might have an action for specific performance.

Why do some states have laws requiring notice to be given concerning renewals?

NOTE: *The bullet indicates that there may be a state statute that varies from the law discussed here.*

Holding Over by the Tenant   At the end of the lease term the landlord may evict the tenant if the tenant remains in possession. In many cases, however, the tenant remains in possession, becoming a *tenant by sufferance*. If he continues to pay rent and all goes on as before, a question is raised as to the relationship between the landlord and tenant under this new arrangement.

TENANT BY SUFFERANCE

EXAMPLE 4   The Robsons' lease specified that they were to occupy the apartment for one year, starting July 5. The lease required that they inform the landlord three months prior to July 5 of the following year should they decide to vacate the apartment at the end of the period. Neither Robson nor his wife gave the landlord prior notice of the termination of the lease, as required. The Robsons became tenants by sufferance.

Who is a tenant by sufferance? What are the rights of a landlord in relation to such a person?

Today, courts take different points of view about tenants by sufferance. Some courts say that if a tenant remains even one day after the expiration of his lease without justifiable cause,* the landlord may, if he desires, regard the tenancy as renewed on the same terms as the original lease for a period equal to that of the original term. If the original agreement was for more than one year, however, only a tenancy from year to year would be created as a result of a tenant's holdover. Other courts say that the tenant by sufferance becomes a month-to-month tenant.

By accepting rent from the tenant after the lease has expired, the landlord is deemed either to have renewed his lease with the tenant or to have accepted a month-to-month arrangement. He is not then permitted to change his mind and eject the tenant as a trespasser until the expiration of the renewed period.

EXAMPLE 5   Suppose, in the above case, Robson's landlord notified him of his intention to terminate the lease on July 5. Robson, however, sent the landlord a check for rent for the month following the end of the leasehold. The landlord cashed the check. This act by the landlord renewed Robson's tenancy, and the family could remain even though the landlord had others waiting for a vacancy.

REMEMBER: To be on the safe side, the parties should provide in the lease itself what the effect of holding over shall be.

Security Deposit   Many times, the landlord will require a money deposit as security for the payment of the rent or repairs for damages done by the tenant. This *security deposit* often is equal to one or two months' rent. Whether the security deposit may be used as rent is determined by the landlord.

SECURITY DEPOSIT

What is a security deposit?

EXAMPLE 6   Paul Malone leased an apartment from Julius Madden for one year. The lease provided that Malone was to deposit security equal to two months' rent with Madden and that the money was (1) to be applied to the payment of the last two months' rent, (2) to be applied by Madden to any unpaid rent, or (3) to be used to repair any damage caused by Malone during his occupancy of the premises.

*Justifiable cause for holding over, which will excuse the tenant from being bound by a renewal of the lease, has been held by the courts to exist in cases of death or serious illness in the family of the tenant at the time when the lease terminates or when temporary legal restrictions on moving or similar restraints prevail.

This would not be Madden's money, and he could not use it as his own. He is a trustee only and must keep the money to be used as provided.

Destruction by Fire   Modern statutes usually provide that if the property is destroyed by fire, the lease is terminated. The termination is usually left to the parties, however; and, if the landlord wishes to rebuild and the tenant wishes to continue, they may do so.

Termination of the Lease   By its very nature, a tenancy for years comes to an end at the termination of the specified term. The lease is a contract, and the parties may provide for any other methods of termination they wish. For example, a tenant whose employment may oblige him to move to another locality on short notice may obtain from his landlord an agreement that, if such a move becomes necessary, the lease will come to an end. This provision is especially important to servicemen who, because of their induction into service or call to duty, must relinquish their leases. Practically all leases provide for this emergency and make possible the release of the serviceman from his lease liability without penalty. Many communities provide for this relief for servicemen by statute.

Rent Control Laws   These laws have been enacted in many large communities because of the shortage of housing. Emergency protections for the tenant and obligations of the landlord, independent of the lease, have been brought under control first by federal statute and then by state statute. These states have materially modified and controlled the rights and duties of landlord and tenant.

Antidiscrimination Laws   In housing (especially in the selection of tenants), as well as in other areas involving the interrelation of people, landlords have been bound by antidiscrimination statutes. Laws such as the Civil Rights Act place special emphasis on human need and right.

PERIODIC TENANCIES

Periodic tenancies are ordinary rental contracts in which you agree simply to rent a given house for so much a month or so much a week. Occasionally, you might informally rent from year to year, but not often.

PERIODIC TENANCY

Year-to-Year Agreements   Tenancies from year to year are often confused with tenancies for years.

Modern statutes in all states provide that proper notice must be given before a tenant can be evicted by a landlord.

A tenancy from year to year is created when the lease provides for the payment of an annual rent without stating a definite period over which the lease is to extend. Such leases usually give the tenant the right to pay the annual rent in monthly installments. This type of lease continues from year to year, unless either the landlord or the tenant gives advance notice of intention to terminate the lease at the end of the year. What constitutes sufficient notice varies from state to state, the usual time being three months unless otherwise provided in the lease.

EXAMPLE 7   Albert Kingston agreed to rent Zenas Clark's house for $2,400 a year. Nothing else was mentioned. Neither party stipulated the time of rental. This situation would be a year-to-year tenancy and would continue as long as Albert paid the rent and stayed in possession.

EXAMPLE 8   If Albert Kingston had agreed to rent Zenas Clark's house for one year at a rental of $2,400 for the year, it would be a tenancy for years. In this case, the period of time—that is, one year—is clearly stated. At the end of the year, the tenancy automatically comes to an end.

It is important to distinguish between these two tenancies. If the tenant from year to year holds over, even for one day into the second year, he automatically renews his obligation for another year. In a tenancy for years, if the tenant holds over, he may be a tenant by sufferance. As you will recall, some courts will consider his new arrangement with the landlord as a monthly agreement, and others as a renewal of the lease for one year.

What is a month-to-month rental agreement?

Month-to-Month Agreements   A fairly common type of rental contract is a *month-to-month agreement*. Usually it is entered into rather informally, although it should have more attention than it usually gets.

MONTH-TO-MONTH AGREEMENT

EXAMPLE 9   William Hockensmith rents the Shaffer home for $250 per month and moves in. The agreement is oral, and nothing is said about the length of contract. This is a month-to-month tenancy. If Hockensmith holds over at the end of each month, an automatic renewal period takes place.

REMOVAL OF FIXTURES BY A TENANT

What must be considered by a judge in deciding a case involving a dispute over fixtures?

One of the most troublesome problems that arises in the leasing or purchasing of real property is in regard to fixtures. Some judges have defined *fixtures* as personal property that is attached to real property in such a way that it can be readily removed. Other judges have defined fixtures as personal property that is attached to real property in such a way that it cannot be removed. The two following examples are typical of the interpretations placed on articles that are classified as fixtures.

FIXTURE

EXAMPLE 10   Phil Torrey rented a house from Alex Tower. Torrey did not like the electric-light fixtures in the house, so he replaced them with some of his own. At the end of his tenancy, Torrey insisted that the new fixtures were his and that he could remove them and take them with him. Tower, however, contended that they had become part of the real property and could not be removed.

EXAMPLE 11   Paul Snyder bought a house from Elmer Valle. When Snyder looked at the house before he made his offer, there were attached to the house window shades, storm windows, awnings, a dishwasher, and a stove. When Snyder took possession, he found that Valle had removed all these items. Valle claimed that they were all items of personal property that he could remove and take with him.

There is no absolute answer to either one of these problems. In deciding lawsuits growing out of problems of this kind, judges usually consider the following things: (1) the manner and completeness of the attachment; (2) how completely the item had been attached to the real property; and (3) the intention of the parties at the time the attachment was made.

EXAMPLE 12 **Tom Brill had built several bookshelves in his apartment with the written permission of the landlord. When Brill moved, the landlord permitted him to remove the shelves, with an obligation to fill in any holes left by the nails or screws used to attach the shelves to the wall.**

When fixtures are installed in such a way that removal would definitely deface the appearance of a room or building, the fixtures become part of the real property and may not be removed.

EXAMPLE 13 **Besides the bookshelves, Brill received permission to install a breakfast nook, building it into the room in such a way as to make it an integral part of the room itself. This installation would be considered real property, and Brill would have no right to remove it at the expiration of his lease.**

REMEMBER: Never attach any item of personal property to real property until you have an agreement with the landlord allowing you to remove it. Make sure that there is complete understanding with all parties who might be concerned before any attachment is made. Usually, tenants may remove things they attach if they can do so without damage to the real property.

When you make an offer to buy real property, write into your offer every item that you expect to go with the house, no matter how small.

SUGGESTIONS FOR MINIMIZING LEGAL RISKS

Tenants . . .

1. Be sure that the premises meet your needs.
2. Negotiate a written lease that will be entirely satisfactory to you. Try to anticipate your future needs and desires.
3. Read and reread the lease. Do not sign it until you understand it thoroughly.
4. It is wise to record the lease if it involves property of considerable value with a high rental charge.
5. If you may be called on to move to another community before the expiration of the lease, have a definite understanding about subletting or assigning the lease.
6. Have a definite understanding as to the effect of holding over.

7. If the premises are used by the general public, it is desirable to carry public-liability insurance.

8. Be sure that you understand the effect of default in rental payment on the due date.

 ## △ APPLYING YOUR LEARNING

QUESTIONS AND PROBLEMS

1. What are reasons for the difficulties that frequently develop between landlord and tenant?

2. What is the difference between a tenancy for years and a tenancy from year to year?

3. Define a tenancy for years; a periodic tenancy.

4. What are some potential risks of entering into an oral lease?

5. Is a lease signed by a minor ever enforceable? Explain.

6. List several covenants or specific agreements that you would try to insist on having in a lease if you were to rent a house or apartment, beginning next week.

7. When a tenant holds over without a specific covenant in the lease covering this possibility, how may the landlord interpret this act?

8. Who is a tenant by sufferance? What are the rights of a landlord in relation to such a person?

9. What is an implied warranty of habitability?

10. How is a lease terminated?

11. Why is it difficult to give an acceptable definition of fixtures?

12. What must be considered by a judge in deciding a case involving a dispute over fixtures?

13. How can you avoid future trouble over an interpretation of fixtures?

WHAT IS YOUR OPINION?

In each of the following cases, give your decision and state a legal principle that applies to the case.

1. Rhodes leased a house for one year. When his lease expired, he said nothing but continued to pay the rent and occupy the premises for three more months. Rhodes then moved and refused to pay any more rent after he moved. The landlord was unable to lease the house for the balance of the year. Does the landlord have a claim against Rhodes for additional rent?

2. Morse signed a three-year lease for Land's house at a rental of $1,080 a year, payable monthly in advance. After living in the house for one year, Morse assigned his unexpired lease to Meeker and notified Land. Meeker failed to pay the rent for three months. Was Land legally entitled to collect from Morse?

3. Earl Moylan signed a one-year lease for an unfurnished apartment. The apartment was in very bad condition, and Moylan assumed that the landlord would repair it and put it in a habitable living condition. When the day arrived for Moylan to take possession, he found that nothing had been done to the apartment. May Moylan force the landlord to make needed repairs?

4. Rutnik rented an apartment in an apartment house from Russo for one year at $135 a month, subject to termination by either party by giving sixty days' written notice. Nothing was said in the lease about painting and repairs. A small fire in Rutnik's apartment smoked up the woodwork and walls so that the apartment needed redecorating. Rutnik sought to have Russo redecorate the apartment. Russo refused. Can Rutnik force Russo to redecorate?

5. The elevator in Russo's apartment house was declared unsafe by a public official responsible for inspecting apartment houses. This forced Rutnik and his family to climb sixteen floors to their apartment. Russo refused to replace the elevator. Because Rutnik had a heart condition, his doctor advised him to move. Rutnik moved out one week after the elevator was declared unsafe, and Russo sued Rutnik for two months' rent. Do you think Russo will succeed?

6. Schepp leased a house and lot for two years from Tracy. Nothing was said in the lease about subletting the property. Three months later Schepp was transferred by his employer to another city; so Schepp sublet the house to Shell, who had two children. Tracy tried to restrain Schepp from subletting to Shell because he was afraid the children might damage the property. Do you think that Tracy can restrain Schepp from subletting? Is Schepp still liable to Tracy for the rent?

7. Klinger rented a house to Seltzer for ten months at a monthly cost of $210. After three months, Seltzer moved, claiming that he had never signed a written lease and was not, therefore, liable to Klinger. Klinger sued for the rent for the remaining seven months during which the house remained unoccupied. Judgment for whom?

8. Hopkins owned a six-family house that was fully rented. The tenants complained that the hallway was not properly lighted and that the front steps were broken and in dangerous condition. Hopkins refused to make repairs, contending that it was the responsibility of the tenants to do so. The tenants attempted by court action to force Hopkins to make the necessary repairs. Should they succeed?

9. Yager signed a one-year lease for an apartment in the Executive Suites. During the winter, ice and snow piled up over the front entrance to the building and the janitor made no effort to remove it. Yager slipped and fell on the ice, suffering serious injury to his back. He sued the landlord for his injuries. The landlord defended himself, saying that he had no responsibility to clear ice and snow from the premises. What will be the outcome of this case?

10. Shaw, a minor, married and rented a small house for himself and his wife under a two-year lease. After living in the house for only six months, Shaw and his wife separated and he notified the landlord of

his intention to terminate the lease. The landlord insisted that Shaw was bound by the lease and that, if Shaw moved, he would sue him for the remaining eighteen months' rent. Will he succeed in this action?

11. On May 1, 1971, Burr signed a two-year lease, agreeing to pay $100 a month rent for an apartment owned by Decker. On July 1, 1972, Burr assigned his lease to Dart and gave proper notice to Decker. Dart lived in the apartment until February 1, 1973, and then moved out, being two months in arrears on his rent. The apartment then remained unoccupied until May 1, 1973. Decker, the landlord, sued Burr for $500, the rent due for the last five months of the lease. Is Burr liable for this rent?

12. Presley orally leased an apartment from Crosby for an indefinite period. The rent was to be $150 a month payable in advance on the first of each month. Presley lost his job and decided to move in with his parents. He paid his rent on the first of the month but gave notice to the landlord on the fifteenth of the month of his intention to move. He vacated the premises before the end of the month. Crosby now insists that Presley still owes him $150. Does Crosby have a valid claim for an additional month's rent?

THE LAW IN ACTION

1. The defendant leased real property from Brown for one year at a rental of $450 a year, payable in quarterly installments. The defendant failed to pay the second installment, and the plaintiff brought an action to put the defendant out for nonpayment of rent. The defendant contended that he owned the property for one year and that the only action the plaintiff could bring was for the rent. Was the defendant correct? (Brown's Administrator v. Bragg, 22 Ind. 122)

2. The plaintiff and the defendant entered into a lease agreement whereby the defendant was to lease the property in question for $2\frac{1}{2}$ years at a yearly rental of $3,000. The written lease was invalid because it was not properly signed, and the defendant moved out after a year and a half. The plaintiff brought this action for the rent for the second half of the second year, contending that there was year-to-year tenancy and that, by holding over into the second year, the defendant became obligated to pay a full second year's rent. Was he correct? (Coudert v. Cohn, 118 N.Y. 309, 23 N.E. 298)

KEY TO "WHAT'S THE LAW?" Page 409

1. *No. The tenant has the right to the exclusive possession of the property.*
2. *Yes. The landlord must keep the premises fit for habitation.*

WHAT'S THE LAW?

1. *August Dietz argued, "Buy a house. Once it is paid for, you can live rent-free for the rest of your life." Frank Machak argued, "Renting a house is much cheaper than buying one." Who is right?*

2. *Sam Kerner bought a house and received a warranty deed to the property. This, he felt, protected him fully from any loss due to a defect in the title. Do you agree or not?*

▲ UNIT 44: OWNING REAL PROPERTY

What are the advantages of owning a home? the disadvantages?

To rent or to buy? There are advantages to renting a house, and there are advantages to owning your own home. When you make payments in buying a house, you are making some investment; eventually, the house will belong to you. After your house is paid for, however, there are still costs to be met. Taxes and insurance have to be paid and repairs have to be made. If you had invested your money in something else, it would be paying you interest. Over a long period of years, the costs of renting and buying are not materially different.

ACQUIRING OWNERSHIP

What is a real estate broker? In most instances, who does the real estate broker represent?

Most property is bought and sold through real estate brokers. Buyers and sellers can deal directly, but finding the right buyer for your property when you want to sell or finding the right property when you want to buy is sometimes a problem. The broker, in most cases, is an agent of the seller. If you are the buyer, you should make it clear before you buy that the broker is to look to the seller for his commission. Whether the buyer and the seller get together by themselves or through a real estate broker, the same general procedure is followed in closing the transaction.

CONTRACT OF SALE

What is a contract of sale? In most cases, who makes the offer in the sale of real estate?

The first step in buying a house is a *contract of sale* entered into between the buyer and the seller. Under the provision of the Statute of Frauds, all contracts for the sale of an interest in real property must be in writing to be enforceable. The buyer, in most cases, makes the formal offer; and an acceptance is given by the seller if the offer meets with his approval.

CONTRACT OF SALE

It might not be worth much, but if it is real property, a contract for its sale must be in writing.

One of the important items in any contract for the sale of real estate is the *closing date*, the date on which the purchase price will be paid and the title will pass to the buyer.

CLOSING DATE

PASSING OF TITLE

The most important thing to be done before the closing date is for the buyer to satisfy himself that the seller has good title to the property. This is done by means of a *title search*. The attorney making the title search provides the buyer with an *abstract of title* containing a history of the property, a listing of all previous encumbrances and evidence of their settlement, a list of all present liens and encumbrances, unpaid taxes, and other matters of importance to the security of the buyer.

TITLE SEARCH
ABSTRACT OF TITLE

What is meant by the closing date? title search? abstract of title?

EXAMPLE 1 **Henry Mischel, the purchaser of a house recently completed, requested his attorney to make a title search. The search disclosed that an unpaid judgment had been recorded against the seller in connection with an automobile accident in which the court had found him guilty of negligence. Mischel's attorney insisted that the seller pay off the judgment before Mischel accepted a deed to the property.**

The abstract itself does not prove ownership. The lawyer who presents the abstract of title is not insuring the title; he is merely giving you his opinion that the title is good. If you want title insurance, you must go to a title insurance company. *Title insurance* pays the property's value in the event a prior claim is uncovered.

TITLE INSURANCE

What is title insurance?

Assuming that the title is found to be good, the parties get together on the day set for the final closing, and the seller delivers to the buyer the deed to the property.

DEEDS

The *deed* indicates the sale of the property; title passes to the buyer the moment the deed is delivered to him. His lawyer will then cause the deed to be recorded in the proper public office as required by law. The recording gives notice to the public that the buyer now owns the property.

DEED

When does title pass in the sale of real property?

What is the effect of recording the deed?

Types of Deeds There are two general types of deeds, although each type may have several specialized forms. The *quitclaim deed* purports to sell whatever interest the seller may have in the property but does not warrant that he has any interest. It merely releases a party's rights to the property.

QUITCLAIM DEED

EXAMPLE 2 Charles Dubois learned that several years ago the seller of the house he had purchased had given a neighbor the right to cut across the rear of the property. Dubois did not wish to continue this easement on his property. In return for a small consideration, the neighbor gave up his right by signing a quitclaim deed.

A *warranty deed* not only passes title to whatever interest the seller has in the property but also warrants that the seller's title is good. This warranty is the personal promise of the seller that the title is good and that, if this later proves to be untrue, the seller will make good any loss that the buyer suffers.

WARRANTY DEED

What are the general types of deeds?

A carefully drawn abstract of title will show every transaction pertaining to a parcel of land, dating back to the grant from the original owner.

MORTGAGES

Very few people have enough money in cash to pay the full purchase price at the time they buy. You should never sign a contract promising to buy a house until you are sure you can borrow the money with which to pay for it. If you do, you should always insert a provision in your offer that your offer is conditioned on your ability to arrange for a loan.

At the time you borrow the money you will be required by the lender to sign a promissory note or bond promising to repay the money. In addition, you will be required to sign a mortgage to secure the repayment of the note. In this document the lender will be referred to as the *mortgagee* and you, as the borrower, will be referred to as the *mortgagor*. The *mortgage* gives to the lender the right to have the property seized and sold if the mortgage loan is unpaid within the specified period of time. This right is known as the mortgagee's *right of lien*. The money received at the sale is used to pay off the loan. This action to have the property seized and sold is called *foreclosure*. If the proceeds from the sale of property resulting from the forced sale are not sufficient to pay the mortgage, the mortgagee, if he holds a bond on the property, may sue the mortgagor for the balance.

When borrowing money to pay for a house, it is customary to give the lender a note or bond and a mortgage. What added protection does the bond furnish the lender?

MORTGAGEE

MORTGAGOR
MORTGAGE

RIGHT OF LIEN

FORECLOSURE

In a modern mortgage foreclosure, the mortgaged property is sold to the highest bidder under the direction of the court. The mortgagee does not just step in and take the land.

Modern mortgages may contain many covenants giving to the lender the right to have the property foreclosed for other reasons, such as failure to pay the taxes or interest or failure to keep the property properly insured.

Mortgage loans are customarily made to provide for the repayment of the loan in monthly installments, a part of each installment being credited to the payment of interest and the balance credited toward reducing the balance on the loan. When the mortgage loan has been paid, the lender executes a document called a *satisfaction piece*. This cancels the mortgage and removes the mortgage lien from the property.

SATISFACTION PIECE

What purpose does recording a mortgage serve?

Mortgages, like deeds, should be recorded. By recording, the holder of the mortgage gives notice to the public that he has a claim against the property. In most states, if he does not record his mortgage, the mortgagee may not claim the property against the claims of other creditors.

EXAMPLE 3 Steven Nagel borrowed $10,000 from the Gotham Loan Company, giving a first mortgage on his house as security. The mortgage clerk at Gotham forgot to have Nagel's mortgage recorded in the county office. Nagel subsequently sold his property to Weiss, whose attorney found no record of the mortgage when making the title search. Weiss will take the property free of the mortgage, and Gotham must collect the $10,000 loan by suit against Nagel on the note.

After the mortgage loan has been repaid and a satisfaction piece executed, the satisfaction piece also should be recorded to show that the mortgage has been discharged.

LIMITATIONS ON USE OF PROPERTY

What rights does one acquire by ownership of land?

Ownership of land means that you have certain rights in it. Basically, these are (1) the right to use the land during your lifetime, (2) the right to exclude others from using it, (3) the right to leave the property to your heirs when you die, and (4) the right to sell the property to someone else during your lifetime if you wish. There are some limitations on your use, however. These limitations may be imposed by public authorities or may arise out of contract.

LIMITATIONS IMPOSED BY PUBLIC AUTHORITIES

What limitations may public authorities put on the use of your land?

Zoning Laws The use you make of your land may affect the rights of other people. If this use seriously damages the property of your neighbors, you may be prevented by law from continuing that type of use.

EXAMPLE 4 **Cal Frank owned a house on a 100-foot city lot in a middle-class neighborhood. He decided to raise chickens in his backyard for food and a hobby. His neighbors objected vehemently, claiming that such a project would lower the property value of their street.**

What is a nuisance? To which courts may a person apply for a discontinuance of a nuisance?

The neighbors would have every right to object. This action of Frank's would in law be called a *nuisance,* which might be defined as "an annoyance that does harm." Determining whether a given use of property is legally a nuisance is difficult. It must be determined by the facts of each case. Loud noises, constant vibrations, smoke, dust, obnoxious odors, and the like, which unreasonably interfere with the enjoyment of property by adjacent landowners, are said to be nuisances, as are the loud playing of a television set late at night, bright lights on a lawn, unsanitary conditions on the property. Those subjected to such situations may seek removal of the nuisances in courts of equity.   NUISANCE

EXAMPLE 5 **Andy Clayton directed a local dance band which often conducted rehearsals at the Clayton home late at night. Residents in the neighborhood asked Clayton to terminate band practice at a reasonable hour. When he refused to do so, his neighbors entered a complaint in a court of equity. The final result was an injunction which required The Clayton Dance Band to cease and desist rehearsals at eleven o'clock at night.**

The value of all the property in a given neighborhood will be kept at a higher level if all the property is used in about the same way. It is for this reason that most cities have *zoning laws,* which prescribe the use that may be made of property in specified areas. One area, for example, might be zoned for one-family houses only, another for multiple-family dwellings; another for stores; and another for factories.   ZONING LAW

EXAMPLE 6 **The Lingenfelters purchased a new home. Shortly after moving into the new residence, they learned that a private land developer had purchased five acres of adjoining property and planned to build a new shopping center complex. Lingenfelter reviewed the zoning laws of the area and discovered that commercial construction of any kind was prohibited within a 20-block area. The land developer would probably be denied a construction license because of the zoning restriction.**

What is police power as it relates to government regulation of real property?

Health and Public Safety Regulations City ordinances dealing with health and public safety may include fire-prevention laws; required inspections of plumbing, electric wiring, heating equipment, and general soundness of construction; and regulations dealing with public health. This right of government to regulate the use of real property for the public welfare, morals, and health is known as *police power.*   POLICE POWER

Eminent Domain The right of the government (federal and state) to take private land with or without the consent of the owner for public use is called the right of *eminent domain.* It is under this right of eminent domain   EMINENT DOMAIN

You may not use your property in such a way as to endanger your neighbors.

that private land can be taken for such things as public buildings, highways, school buildings, power projects, housing projects, parks, and many other public uses. The private owner is paid for the land taken. Usually, a price can be agreed on by the two parties. If they cannot agree, an action in court is commenced; then the court must determine the value.

Air Rights   Before the advent of the air age, landowners had exclusive possession of property from the surface up to the sky and down to the center of the earth. The right to air above property has been limited by court decisions in the interest of aviation, permitting free navigation of the air without fear of trespass actions. Today, an owner is said to own to a height over his land within which he has reasonable control. This is usually interpreted to be only a few feet above the highest structure.

Subterranean and Riparian Rights   The exclusive rights of an owner below the land surface, or *subterranean rights,* are still said to extend to the center of the earth. Property owners sometimes sell subterranean rights if their property is in an area where mines or wells are operated.

SUBTERRANEAN RIGHT

The rights of a person through whose lands a natural watercourse runs are known as *riparian rights.* The owner of such land may use the water and may build a wharf and have access to navigable water. However, he does not have title to the water or to the fish that swim in the water. Thus, the owner may not pollute waters flowing through his land, nor may he divert streams from their natural channels to the detriment of landowners or otherwise unreasonably diminish the flow of water in the streams. If the stream is not navigable and does not adjoin navigable waters, the owner of the adjoining land has title to the soil to the middle of the stream.

RIPARIAN RIGHT

What is meant by subterranean rights? riparian rights?

EXAMPLE 7   The Franklin Tool Corporation drew water for manufacturing use from a stream that flowed through its property. Siefert, who owned property farther upstream, dammed the stream, cutting off all flow into the plant's property. The corporation secured an injunction against Siefert, requiring him to remove the dam and stop interfering with the natural flow of the stream.

When water freezes, the ice is considered to be a part of the land and belongs to the owner of the land adjoining the stream. Owners on opposite banks of the same stream have ownership to the ice to the midpoint of the stream unless their deeds state otherwise.

LIMITATIONS ARISING OUT OF CONTRACT

Restrictions in the Deed   Restrictions in deeds may require that all the houses in a given subdivision cost not less than a certain amount to build, that all houses be set not less than a specified number of feet from the street, or that they all have basements. Such restrictions are possible when all the land so restricted originally belonged to one person.

What is meant by restrictions in a deed?

EXAMPLE 8   Tom Olivo owned a 40-acre farm located at the city limits. He decided to subdivide his farm into building lots and sell them to prospective builders. He laid out streets and blocks, dividing each block into building lots. As he owned all the lots, he could sell them subject to any building restrictions he wished. These restrictions would be written into the deed of each lot sold. He knew that prospective buyers would pay a higher price for the lots by reason of the protection afforded by the restrictions.

Easements and Licenses   An *easement* is a right to make some use of land belonging to another. Most often it is a right to cross someone else's land at a particular place. It may also be a right to erect poles and suspend power lines over land or to lay pipelines beneath the surface. An easement is a property interest, and once established it cannot be terminated without the consent of the owner of the right. Usually, it is a right that is bought and paid for, either in money or by some other consideration.

EASEMENT

EXAMPLE 9   A driveway extended from the street between the property owned by the Hestons and that owned by their neighbors. By consent of both parties, one-half of the driveway was constructed on Heston's land and one-half on the neighbor's land. Therefore, each owner had an easement in a part of the other's land in the use of this driveway. Neither could close off his part of the driveway without affecting the rights of the other.

A *license* is a right to do something on the land of another that would otherwise be unlawful. A good example would be hunting or fishing or the painting of a sign on a farmer's barn. A license does not convey a right or interest in the land; it merely grants the privilege of use in the manner and for the purpose agreed upon by the owner.

LICENSE

SPECIAL TYPES OF HOME OWNERSHIP

MOBILE HOMES

Mobile homes, sometimes called trailers, are becoming increasingly popular and represent a sizable segment of dwellings in this country. They offer certain advantages which have made them desirable in many areas and to certain people. Unless placed on permanent foundations and given other special treatment, mobile homes are said to be personal property and therefore do not come within the jurisdiction of real estate tax boards.

What are some advantages of mobile-home ownership?

Most states have passed legislation requiring special fees to be paid by trailer residents. These fees, in addition to the usual highway license, provide income from the mobile-home owners for use in providing schools and other services enjoyed by all citizens.

EXAMPLE 10   Joseph Spevak purchased a mobile home for $9,000 and parked it on a designated site in compliance with zoning regulations. A small home nearby was assessed by the local tax office at a valuation of $7,500, which included the land. Spevak's children attended public school, and the family received the benefits provided those living in the area but, unlike their neighbor, did not have to pay real property taxes. Their only expense was a small annual registration fee charged mobile-home owners, plus a small rental for their parking privileges.

There are certain disadvantages to mobile-home ownership. Residents of mobile homes are not considered by other citizens as stable elements of the community. Although this objection is gradually being overcome, some property owners are reluctant to accept mobile-home owners as contributing members of a community.

What are some disadvantages of mobile-home ownership?

Mobile homes depreciate in value rapidly. The resale value of such an investment is not nearly as high as the same amount invested in real estate.

EXAMPLE 11   Although the Spevaks had made an investment of $9,000 in their mobile home, they found that after ten years' use it would bring them less than half that amount if sold or traded on a new model. The same amount of money invested in real estate could have shown an increase in valuation over the same ten years.

Owners of mobile homes are required to observe many statutes adopted in most states for the regulation of mobile homes, both as dwellings and as moving vehicles. The states are gradually adding more restrictions and obligations each year for the regulations of mobile homes. When mobile homes are moved from one state to another, special fees must be paid by the owners and inspections must be made by the authorities. Failure to obtain permission to transport such vehicles before passing through a state can lead to arrest and fines. The fees charged are determined by the size of the home being transported. Because of their small size, certain types of mobile homes used as vacation trailers are accorded special privilege in this respect. Complying with the laws of the states traversed while the mobile home is being moved from state to state can be expensive.

EXAMPLE 12   Spevak accepted a position with a new firm in a city many miles from his present location. He contracted a company which specialized in the transport of mobile homes. A representative of the company informed Spevak that the usual charge for moving a unit the size of his would be approximately fifty-two cents per mile. This did not include special licenses, tolls for bridges, thruways, or other added fees. Spevak would have to decide whether it would be to his advantage to move the mobile home to the new location or to sell it and make other provisions for his family after the move to the other city.

COOPERATIVES

Cooperative ownership of apartment residences begins with the formation of a corporation which builds or buys an apartment building with a number of living units. The corporation usually places a mortgage on the land for the purpose of constructing the building. Prospective tenants purchase shares of stock and thus the capital necessary to complete the apartment building is raised. The purchase of a specified number of shares

What is meant by proprietary lease?

gives a prospective tenant the right to a *proprietary lease,* which is a long-term lease issued by the corporation. Such a lease gives the tenant all the usual rights of ownership. He has the right of possession of his apartment, for which he makes regular payments to the corporation of his share of operating expenses, mortgage debt and reduction, and taxes. The amount levied against each tenant is determined by the number of shares of stock held. The large apartments are held by those owning a greater number of shares. Tenants provide their own electrical appliances, floor coverings, and interior maintenance. **PROPRIETARY LEASE**

What are the usual features of cooperative apartment leasing?

The disadvantage of cooperatives is the possibility of mortgage foreclosure, in which case the tenant may lose his rights. In such a case a receiver is appointed for the operation of the apartment project for the benefit of the mortgagee, and each tenant is required to either pay a proportionate share of the mortgage or pay full rental for his apartment as a means of liquidating the mortgage.

CONDOMINIUMS

Another concept in apartment ownership is the *condominium.* Under this type of ownership, the co-owner purchases a unit and receives a deed that gives him absolute ownership of the apartment unit that he has purchased, together with an undivided interest or share in the ownership of those parts of the ground and structure that are not under the supervision or care of one individual. These include the roof, stairways, yard, swimming pool, elevators, heating system, and the like. **CONDOMINIUM**

How does condominium apartment ownership operate? What are the advantages of condominium ownership? the disadvantages?

The owner of a condominium has a legal status similar to that of a home or cooperative owner. He has exclusive ownership of his unit and, with certain restrictions, may decorate and occupy the premises as he wishes. The advantage of a condominium over a cooperative is that the owner is not faced with the possibility of foreclosure affecting the entire building. The only foreclosure that might threaten him would be of a mortgage covering his own investment, and that, of course, is always under his own control and not affected by limited occupancy of other units or by faulty management.

SUGGESTIONS FOR MINIMIZING LEGAL RISKS

Purchasers . . .

1. Carefully examine the property before entering into a contract to determine whether the property will meet your present and future needs. Obtain the advice of an expert if necessary. Do not be in a hurry.
2. Select an able attorney who is known for his reasonable fees and his ability in handling real estate matters to assist you in your purchase.
3. Get the advice of your attorney as to legal restrictions, covenants, zoning laws, or easements that could interfere with use of the property.

4. Have your attorney examine the owner's title for possible defects, recorded liens, recorded leases, unpaid taxes, mortgages, or other encumbrances.

5. Consult your attorney as to the way the deed should name the owner if both husband and wife are owners. This is very important in case of later divorce, sale, or death.

6. If payment of the loan is to be in installments, carefully read the note and mortgage to determine the effect of a default in payment.

7. Record the deed as soon as possible.

APPLYING YOUR LEARNING

QUESTIONS AND PROBLEMS

1. What precautions should one take in his dealings with a real estate broker or agent?

2. What should the buyer do between the contract of sale and the closing date?

3. Explain the differences between a warranty deed and a quitclaim deed.

4. Does a warranty deed guarantee that you will get a good title to the property?

5. Does a deed give you absolute rights to do as you please with your property? Explain.

6. What is meant by the mortgage? mortgagee's right of lien? foreclosure?

7. What is the purpose of a satisfaction piece? What should be done with this document on receipt?

8. What is meant by zoning laws? the right of eminent domain?

9. What property right does the owner of land have in the air above his land?

10. What is an easement? a license?

11. What are some of the legal obligations of the owner of a mobile home?

12. Are mobile homes considered real property? How are they taxed?

13. Discuss the comparative advantages and disadvantages of owning, renting, and living in a mobile home.

14. What advantage does a condominium offer over a cooperative in multifamily dwellings?

WHAT IS YOUR OPINION?

In each of the following cases, give your decision and state a legal principle that applies to the case.

1. Kerr bought 10 acres of land bordering on a river from Adams, who gave a quitclaim deed to the land. Later, Kerr discovered that a former owner of the land had sold and assigned the water rights to the land to an owner of an industrial plant, thereby defeating Kerr's plans for using the property. Kerr sued Adams for damages. Can Kerr recover?

2. The state needs the land owned by Unright for a highway. May the land be obtained for such purpose if Unright refuses to sell it?

3. Volmer, a contractor, made an agreement with White to build at the rear of White's house a brick building to be used as an automobile repair shop. Before the building was started, a city ordinance was passed making it illegal to operate such a business in that particular area. Was this contract terminated by the passage of this ordinance?

4. Monette held a mortgage on Duke's house and land. This mortgage had been properly recorded in the county clerk's office. Later, Morrow purchased the property from Duke, not knowing about the mortgage. Did Morrow get a clear title to the property?

5. Norton orally agreed to purchase a summer cottage from Prince for $2,000. On tendering a certified check for the amount, Prince refused to execute a deed, stating that the agreement was not binding because it was not in writing. Can Norton force Prince to execute the deed?

6. Prindle entered into a written contract to purchase a house and lot from Sanders for $10,000. Before the closing date arrived, Prindle saw a better house which he could buy for $8,000; so he notified Sanders that he had changed his mind. If Prindle refuses to purchase the house, what are Sanders' legal rights?

7. The Polk Ice Company owned a long strip of land adjoining Saratoga Lake. Anticipating a great demand for ice during the coming summer, the company started cutting ice from a point far beyond the middle of the lake. A property owner ordered the company to stop cutting ice so close to his shore. What are the rights of the ice company and the other party?

8. The Harding Social Club purchased a house adjoining the Community Church. Equipment was installed in the house for the entertainment of members, including a public-address system to be used for dances. The members held regular dances every Wednesday evening, during which time the church held midweek services. The music was so loud that the church service had to be called off. May the church members enjoin the operation of the public-address system by their neighbors?

9. Kinder entered into an agreement to purchase a building lot in a new development. The deed contained a provision that any house built on the lot must cost at least $25,000. Kinder wanted to build a $17,000 house. Can Kinder be restrained from building the $17,000 house?

10. Carr lent $8,500 to Dahl, receiving from Dahl a note for that amount secured by a mortgage on his house. The note was not paid at maturity, and Carr foreclosed on the realty. The property brought only $5,000 when sold under order of the court. What may Carr do to collect the $3,500 still due him? If the property at the foreclosure sale had brought more than the amount due Carr, to whom would the money remaining after Carr was paid belong?

11. Three weeks after Welch purchased a vacant city lot, he discovered that a street-paving assessment levied eight months previously was still unpaid. Was Welch liable for paying the assessment to the city?

12. Welter had a $5,000 properly recorded mortgage on real estate owned

by Mestler. Mestler sold the property to Monroe. Did Welter still have a mortgage on the property?

13. Weber owned a plot of ground adjacent to the Kebberly Airport and in direct line with the main runway. He planned to build a three-story airport motel on his ground but was refused permission when he sought a building permit. Weber appealed the building inspector's decision to the courts, claiming that as long as he stayed within the boundary line of his own property he had the legal right to build the motel. What will be the decision in this case?

14. Samfred purchased a lake-front cottage from Smyth, who owned a large farm adjoining the lake. In order to get to the cottage from the main highway, it was necessary to pass over Smyth's land. Samfred entered into a written agreement with Smyth giving him a right of way over Smyth's land. Five years later Smyth died, and the farm was sold to Toohey. Toohey refused to let Samfred cross his land. Samfred brought suit against Toohey on the grounds that he has a right to cross the land. Do you think that Samfred will succeed? Why?

THE LAW IN ACTION

1. Mary B. Taggart executed a deed naming the plaintiff, Boyd, as recipient. She placed the deed in a strongbox in her own home, where it was found after her death. Boyd claimed title to the property. Do you think title passed to Boyd by this deed? Why or why not? (Boyd v. Slayback, 63 Cal. 493)

2. The plaintiff, Tordello, held an unrecorded mortgage on property owned by Ellison. Ellison executed a second mortgage and gave it to Jones, who had it recorded at once. If Jones did not know of the first mortgage, would he have the first claim on the property? If Jones knew of the first mortgage, who would have first claim? (Tordello v. Ellison, 132 Wash. 20, 231 Pac. 9)

KEY TO "WHAT'S THE LAW?" Page 419

1. *Dietz is not right because there are always some expenses that might be considered "rent." These would be such things as taxes, repairs, and insurance. Machak may or may not be right.*

2. *No. A warranty is only as good as the person giving it.*

WHAT'S THE LAW?

1. *Barry Ratuer desired to make a gift of his property to his nephew, Steve Welch, the gift to take effect at Barry's death but not before. He did not want to go to the trouble, however, of drawing a formal will. Can he do this without making a will?*

2. *Dennis Murphy carefully drafted his own will, typed it neatly, signed it, and filed it with his important papers. Would this be an effective will or not?*

◬ UNIT 45: TRANSFERRING PROPERTY BY WILL

A *will* is a document executed by a person during his lifetime that provides for the disposition of his property at his death. You, as the owner of property, may use it as you choose while you are alive or sell it. **WILL**

You can give your property away during your lifetime by simply delivering the property to the person whom you wish to have it. This is an *executed gift.* But the only way that you can make a gift that is to take effect at your death is to make a will; otherwise, your property will be distributed at your death according to the law. **EXECUTED GIFT**

What is an executed gift?

EXAMPLE 1 **Allan Tuthill's Aunt Margaret liked him very much. Many times during her lifetime she had said to him in the presence of other people, "When I die, I want you to have my house." She died without making a will, however. Would Allan get the house?**

No. It would become a part of the aunt's estate and would go, along with the rest of her estate, to her legal heirs. "This doesn't seem right," you may say. "The aunt wanted Allan to have the house." That may be true; nevertheless, the law is very particular on this point.

REQUISITES OF A WILL

CAPACITY OF THE TESTATOR

The capacity of the testator is one of the most important considerations in determining the validity of any will. *Testator* is the name given to a man who makes a will; a woman who makes a will is called a *testatrix.* Anyone who is above the minimum age set by statute, owns property, and has the contractual capacity to dispose of it can make a will. **TESTATOR TESTATRIX**

To whom is the name testator applied? testatrix?

A person must be of sound mind in order to make a valid will.

Soundness of Mind   Many wills are questioned on the basis of the soundness of the testator's mind at the time he executed the will. As in contracts, the testator must have sufficient mental capacity to understand the nature and extent of his property and the nature and effect of the document he is signing.

EXAMPLE 2   Edward Mullins called for an attorney during his last illness and dictated to him the provisions which he wished to have included in his will. The attorney prepared a will which Mullins signed. After the man's death, disappointed heirs might dispute the validity of the will on the grounds that the testator did not know what he was doing when he dictated the terms of the will.

Freedom From Undue Influence   For the reasons mentioned in the preceding paragraph, wills are often questioned on the grounds of undue influence. Here, again, it is important to have witnesses who are able to testify that the will was made free from all constraint and by the testator's own free will. When a person comes under the influence of another to the degree that he is unable to express his real intentions in a will, it may be declared invalid. The court must distinguish between undue influence and the kindnesses, attention, advice, guidance, and friendliness shown toward the testator by the one named in the will.

What is meant by the testator's own free will?

EXAMPLE 3   Steward Jergen suffered a heart attack which confined him to the hospital for several weeks before his death. Jergen's brother, who had greatly influenced his life since childhood, persuaded him to draw up a new will making him the sole heir to his estate. The will was declared void by the probate court* on the grounds that the brother had exerted undue influence on Jergen because of his physical condition and his relationship to him.

PROBATE COURT

FORM OF WILL

A will can be very simple. It needs only to identify definitely the testator, to identify clearly the testator's property and the persons to whom he wishes it to go, and to be properly signed and witnessed. It must conform

*A probate court, also known as a surrogate's court or an orphan's court, is one in which wills are probated, or proved, after the death of the testator. The probating of a will is the legal procedure followed in establishing or proving that the document is the last will of the deceased.

Is the form and
content of wills
uniform in all
states?

exactly to statutory requirements, however; and it should at least be checked by a lawyer before it is signed.

The law of wills varies a little from state to state, but the following general requisites are found in all states.

Last Will and Testament

I, Scott Brick

of the City of Chicago

County of Cook **State of** Illinois

being of sound and disposing mind and memory, and considering the uncertainty of this life, do make,

publish and declare this to be my last **Will** *and* **Testament** *as follows, hereby revoking all other*

and former Wills by me at any time made.

First, after my lawful debts are paid, I give Boys' Camping Association of Chicago, Illinois, $7,500 in cash. And to my mother, Mrs. Abraham Brick, the balance of my estate remaining after the above bequest has been distributed.

Likewise, I make, *constitute and appoint* Henry Skillon, 2910 North Tenth Street, Port Deposit, Maryland

to be *the* **execut** or *of this, my last Will and Testament,*

In Witness Whereof, *I have hereunto subscribed my name and affixed my seal, the*

third *day of* May *, in the year one thousand*

nine hundred and seventy-three

Scott Brick

WE, whose names are hereto subscribed, do certify that

the testat or *, subscribed* his *name to this instrument in our presence, and in the presence of*

each of us, and at the same time he *declared in our presence and hearing that the same was*

his *last Will and Testament, and requested us, and each of us, to sign our names thereto as*

witnesses to the execution thereof, and which we hereby do in the presence of the testat or *and of*

each other, this third *day of* May 19 73 *, the day of the date of the said*

Will, and write opposite our names our respective places of residence.

Pauline Grier *residing at* 420 Chester Drive
Chicago, Illinois

Joseph Carter *residing at* 325 Grand Avenue
Chicago, Illinois

Must be in Writing   With very minor exceptions, a will must be in writing. A will is an important document transferring title to valuable property. It must be in writing to be properly proved in court and to be recorded in the public record. It may be handwritten or typewritten.

The will offered for probate must be the original copy, not a carbon. It must not be torn, mutilated, or show any signs of burning; such conditions may be accepted as evidence of the testator's intent to revoke the instrument.

A will should contain no erasures or alterations of any kind.

EXAMPLE 4   A will was offered for probate by the executor of Gerald Cook's estate. On close examination it was found that the will had been torn in half and later mended with cellulose tape. The court refused to accept the will for probate, questioning its validity and suggesting the possibility that the testator had deliberately destroyed the will.

● Some states have statutes that provide for the distribution of only a limited amount of personal property by a *nuncupative,* or *oral,* will. The circumstances under which such a will may be used, however, are very limited. The circumstances are usually confined to emergency situations, such as soldiers and sailors in battle and to mariners at sea.

Must be Properly Signed   Every will must be signed in such a way as to identify the will as that of the testator. In some states a will must be signed at the end as required by statute, but in other states it is held to be valid if a signature is found anywhere in the will. The signing must take place in the presence of witnesses.

● **Must be Witnessed**   The law specifies the number of witnesses who must be present at the signing. Usually the number is two, although in some states it is three. Following the testator's signing, the witnesses must then sign in the presence of the testator and of each other.

EXAMPLE 5   In a state requiring three witnesses on a will, Sullivan made a will and had two persons sign it as witnesses. The will was refused for probate because it had not been prepared in conformity with the state law. Sullivan was considered to have died intestate, that is, without a will.   INTESTATE

Since the witnesses will be called upon to attest to the genuineness of the testator's signature, it is advisable that witnesses be young adults.

May beneficiaries named in a will be witnesses to the will?

Persons named as beneficiaries in a will may not be witnesses. The failure to observe this provision may result in their being disinherited.

CHANGING OR REVOKING A WILL

If you wish to change a simple will, the best thing to do is to write an entirely new will. If the will is long and involved, however, and only some minor change or addition is needed, it may be added to the original by means of a *codicil,* or supplement, that is added to the original document or drawn up on a separate piece of paper. In either case, however, it must be prepared with all the formalities of the will itself.   CODICIL

What is a codicil? When is it usually used?

NOTE: *The bullet indicates that there may be a state statute that varies from the law discussed here.*

EXAMPLE 6 William Black prepared a will in which he left his entire estate to his wife, providing that the estate should go to their child should his wife die before him. Two years later, another child was born to the Blacks. To provide for this second child, Black drew up a codicil and attached it to the original will. To be valid and enforceable, the codicil had to be properly signed and witnessed, as was done when the will itself was prepared.

REMEMBER: If a new will is written, it should clearly state that it revokes all former wills. All former wills should be destroyed so as to remove all doubt as to which one is to be effective.

In the absence of a new will, statutes usually provide that to revoke a will you must tear it up, burn it, or so mutilate it that it is clearly destroyed.

CARRYING OUT THE PROVISIONS OF A WILL

A properly drawn will always names an executor (or executrix). The *executor* (male) or *executrix* (female) is a person named to execute or carry out the terms of the will. As soon as the testator dies, title to all the testator's property is automatically assigned to the executor by operation of law. It is then the duty of the executor to dispose of the property as provided in the will.

What is the responsibility of the executor or executrix?

EXECUTOR
EXECUTRIX

As soon as the testator dies, his will is filed for probate. The first job of the probate court is to establish the validity of the will. If no one contests, or opposes, the probating of the will, this can be a simple matter. Sometimes, however, heirs who are left out of the will may contest it, and long litigation may result.

After the will is properly proved, or probated, the judge authorizes the executor to take charge of the property and distribute it according to the terms of the will. The executor remains under the supervision of the court, however, and must receive the approval of the court in everything he does.

A will may be set aside by the court if undue influence is proved to have been exercised in its making.

After the estate is distributed, the executor is discharged by the court and the estate is declared closed.

If the executor cannot serve because of death, illness, or other reasons, the court will appoint an administrator to perform the duties that the executor was expected to perform. When an administrator is appointed under these circumstances, he must distribute the assets of the estate according to the provisions of the will.

EXAMPLE 7   In his will Tenser named Lovett as executor of his estate, to serve without bond. Lovett died a few months before Tenser. Unless Tenser had named another executor in the will, the court, on Tenser's death, would appoint a competent person, acceptable to all parties, to act as the administrator of the estate.

WHEN A PERSON DIES WITHOUT MAKING A WILL

A person who dies without making a will is said to have died intestate, and his property is distributed according to the laws of descent in his particular state. The estate is handled in exactly the same way as in the case of a will, except that the probate court appoints an *administrator* (or *administratrix*) to look after the estate. The duties of an administrator are comparable to those of an executor, except that he must distribute the estate according to the law of the state.

How do the duties of an administrator differ from those of an executor?

ADMINISTRATOR
ADMINISTRATRIX

Distribution of Intestate Property   The property of one who dies intestate goes to his heirs; and, conversely, a man's heirs are those who take his property at his death. Finding out just who these heirs are is sometimes a problem, but the laws of most states are rather precise on this matter. All that is necessary is to look at your own state statutes.

● Generally, when an intestate leaves children only, the children take the property in equal parts. If any children are deceased, their heirs take their share of the estate. (This varies from state to state.)

A wife always has an interest in her deceased husband's property, whether he leaves a will or not. At common law, the interest of the wife was called a dower interest and was a life estate in one-third of the real property owned by the husband during the marriage. Under modern statutes, the *dower right* of the widow remains in many states; but it has been modified in most of them and has been replaced by a statutory share of the estate in some. In most states (and you should check your own state statutes on this), a surviving wife, or husband, gets one-third of all the estate and the children get the remaining two-thirds.

What is meant by dower rights?

DOWER RIGHT

At common law, the husband acquires a life interest in all the inheritable realty of his wife, providing children had been born alive to them even though they may have died before the mother. This is known as a husband's *curtesy right*. This right has been abolished in many states, giving instead to the husband an absolute estate, that is, making him an heir of his wife.

What is meant by curtesy right?

CURTESY RIGHT

● Modern state statues vary somewhat in cases in which the intestate leaves a wife but no children. Such cases follow the pattern of one-third to one-half of the estate going to the surviving wife or husband, and the balance going to the parents of the intestate or the parents' descendants.

SUGGESTIONS FOR MINIMIZING LEGAL RISKS

1. An attorney should be consulted when one draws a will, as the terms of the writing must be clear and definite. Real property should be clearly described, and personal property should be carefully identified.
2. Where the testator's property is considerable and valuable, all possible precautions for minimizing risks should be taken. Some of these precautions might be to have the will drawn by an experienced attorney; preferably read aloud by the testator or attorney in the presence of the witnesses; formally acknowledged by the testator as his will; properly signed, attested, and witnessed according to the laws of the state. In addition, the signatures of the witnesses should be notarized.
3. The executed original copy of the will should be placed in the hands of the executor; deposited with the attorney who drew the will; or, at the very least, placed in a safe-deposit box or some equally protected place.
4. Several copies of the will should be made and deposited in a safe place or places, and this fact should be made know to some of the principal heirs.
5. All subsequent codicils should be accurately dated and should be drawn with all the formality of the original will.
6. In these days of frequent automobile and airplane accidents, many times both husband and wife, and sometimes children, lose their lives in what is known as a *common disaster*. The order in which death occurs may affect the distribution of the testator's property. To minimize this possible risk, the will can be so drawn that the distribution of property to take effect in case of a common disaster can be specified by agreement.

 APPLYING YOUR LEARNING

QUESTIONS AND PROBLEMS

1. What is a will? Who may make a will?
2. What factors are considered in determining whether the testator has the capacity to make a valid will?
3. Name and explain the required form of a will.
4. Are there any age requirements for a person making a will? Explain.
5. How does the old saying "A person who tries to serve as his own attorney usually has a fool for a client" apply to the making of one's own will?
6. How should a person proceed to change his will?
7. How should a person revoke his previous will?

8. How is a will probated? What is the name of the special court used for this purpose in your state?
9. What happens when one dies without leaving a will?
10. How is property distributed under the laws of descent in your state?

WHAT IS YOUR OPINION?

In each of the following cases, give your decision and state a legal principle that applies to the case.

1. After Turner's death, two wills that he had made were found. One was dated May 20, 1971, and the other was dated June 17, 1972. Which of the wills should be accepted by the court in settling the estate?
2. When Abbey died, he left his wife and three children as survivors. Was his wife entitled to the entire estate if he did not leave a will?
3. Addis signed his typewritten will and had Bollin, a friend, sign it as a witness. Was this a valid will?
4. Bogart made out his will according to the laws of his state. Six months later he decided to leave a favorite uncle $2,000 from his estate. He orally notified the executor named in his will to be sure to see that his Uncle Henry got $2,000 on his death, but he did not change his will. Is the executor allowed to give Bogart's uncle the $2,000?
5. Baker was an elderly man of considerable means. He became seriously ill and decided to make his will. He called for his attorney, but he was very indefinite about the extent of his property and the correct names of the relatives he wanted to benefit under the will. Do you think that Baker was competent to make a valid will?
6. Bailey became enraged at his son and tore up the original copy of his will which had included a generous bequest to the son. He subsequently made a new will, leaving his son only $1. Following Bailey's death, the son tried to have the will set aside in favor of the previous will, a copy of which was found among Bailey's papers. Do you think the son will succeed in having the new will set aside?
7. Chaplin died without leaving a will. Surviving were his wife and two children. His estate amounted to $20,000. Under the laws of descent in your state, how would the property be distributed?
8. Clancy, whose wife was deceased, died without leaving a will. His only known relatives included his aged mother and one sister. Under the laws of descent in your state, how would Clancy's property be divided?
9. Goff asked his cousin Blair to witness the signing of his will. Blair had been named a beneficiary in the will. When Goff died, the will was contested on the grounds that it had not been properly witnessed. Will Blair receive his legacy under the will?
10. Avery drew up his own will and had it typed with lines indicated for signatures of witnesses. Avery visited his neighbor, Bacon, and asked him to sign the will as a witness. He then visited his neighbor, Cahill, and asked him to sign as a witness. Following Cahill's signature, Avery then signed the will. Has Avery executed a valid will?

THE LAW IN ACTION

1. The deceased testator of the will in question left all his property to his second wife and her relatives and nothing to his children. There was evidence to show that the wife was much stronger physically and mentally than the husband, that she had driven the sons away from home by continuous ill treatment, that the testator had told friends that he wished to leave his property to his sons but that "Margaret wouldn't allow him to," and that she had used every effort to influence her husband in the execution of his will. Are these items that should be considered by the court in determining whether the will was executed by the testator freely and of his own desire? Explain. (In re Tyner's Estate, 97 Minn., 181, 106 N.W. 898)

2. The will in question in this case was written on a printed blank that provided for the signature of the testator on dotted lines at the bottom of the last page. The state statutes provided that all wills should be signed at the end thereof. The testator and the witnesses did not sign at the place specified; but, instead, their signatures appeared on the back, in a space provided for marking the folded document for identification and filing. Do you think this will is valid? (Albright et al. v. North et al., 146 Cal. 455, 80 Pac. 700)

KEY TO "WHAT'S THE LAW?" Page 431

1. *No. He cannot make this type of gift without making a will.*
2. *No. There are no witnesses, and there may be other defects in the will.*

A DIGEST OF LEGAL CONCEPTS

1. A landlord conveys a right to use land and the buildings thereon to the tenant by means of a special contract called a lease.

2. A tenancy for years gives the tenant a right to occupy property for a fixed period of time.

3. A periodic tenancy gives a right to the tenant to occupy property for an indefinite period of time. A periodic tenancy may be from week to week, month to month, or year to year.

4. Technically, an estate or tenancy for years gives to the tenant an ownership of the property for the stated period. In actual practice today, however, the landlord and tenant usually write into their lease provisions that materially change this technical meaning.

5. The basic rights of a tenant in leased property are the right of possession and the right of continued occupancy free from interference or annoyances.

6. The basic rights of the landlord are the right to collect his rent and the right to recover possession of his property free of waste at the end of the term agreed on by the landlord and tenant.

7. Unless it is so provided in the lease or by statute or local ordinance, the landlord is only obliged to keep the property habitable.

8. Unless there is a provision in the lease prohibiting it, the tenant may assign the lease or sublet the property to another.

9. To evict a tenant, the landlord must bring an action in court.

10. A lease may be terminated by the expiration of a specified period of time, by mutual agreement, by abandonment and repossession by the landlord, by destruction of the property, by nonpayment of rent, or by eviction by court order.

11. Fixtures are items of personal property that are attached to real property.

12. The facts that are considered by courts in determining whether a fixture has become a part of the real property are (a) the manner of attachment, (b) how completely the item has been appropriated to the real property, and (c) the intention of the parties at the time the attachment was made.

13. When a tenant installs fixtures in such a way that removal would definitely deface the appearance of the property, the fixtures become part of the real property and may not be removed.

14. Real property consists of land and the things that are firmly attached to land.

15. The first formal step leading to a conveyance of real property is the signing by both parties of a written contract of sale.

16. The prospective purchaser of real property must determine for himself whether the seller has good title to the property by examining an abstract of title, which consists of short statements pertaining to every document of record that affects the title to the land.

17. Title to real property passes when a properly executed deed is delivered to the new owner with the intention of passing title.

18. There are two general types of deeds—quitclaim deeds and warranty deeds.

19. A quitclaim deed conveys any title or interest that the seller may have, but it makes no warranties.

20. A warranty deed not only conveys the title or interest of the seller but also warrants that the seller's title is good.

21. The owner of land is said to own the air rights over his property to a height a few feet above the highest structure erected on the land. His rights below the land surface are said to extend to the center of the earth.

22. Zoning laws restrict the real property in a specified zone or area to specific uses.

23. Eminent domain is the right of a government to take private real property for public use.

24. A mortgage gives to the holder of the mortgage (the mortgagee) a right to have the real property covered by the mortgage seized and sold for the nonpayment of the mortgage debt.

25. Deeds and mortgages are recorded in order to give notice to the world that these documents and the interests they represent exist.

26. A valid will must be drawn strictly in accordance with the statutes of the particular state in which the will was drawn up.

PART 16: Business Organizations

△ UNIT 46: FORMING, OPERATING, AND DISSOLVING PARTNERSHIPS

Robert Burke was the sole owner of a hamburger stand. He operated it himself with the aid of one employee named James Cady, who sometimes acted as an agent. Robert owned the simplest type or form of business organization; that is, a *single*, or individual or sole, *proprietorship*.

What is a sole proprietorship?

SINGLE PROPRIETORSHIP

EXAMPLE 1 **Robert's business prospered. He had a good location, he gave good service, and he had more customers than he could handle in his small hamburger stand. Robert had the extra space on his lot needed to build an addition that would add three times the present space. His volume of business seemed to warrant the expansion. However, he did not have the money to build. Also, the added investment would make it advisable to keep the stand open twenty-four hours a day because there were many night workers in the area. Robert could hire more employees; but he felt that if he made the expansion, he should have someone to share the responsibility of ownership with him.**

Now suppose that about this time Robert's helper, James Cady, inherited $10,000 that he wanted to invest. The logical solution to Robert's problem would be to suggest to James that he join Robert as a partner.

A *partnership* is created when two or more competent parties agree to combine their assets, labor, or skills, or all of these, for the purpose of carrying on a lawful business, with the understanding that the profits and losses arising from the undertaking will be shared between them.

PARTNERSHIP

What is a partnership?

A partnership is defined in the Uniform Partnership Act, Section 6(1) as "an association of two or more persons to carry on as co-owners a business for profit." The most important reasons for entering into a partnership are given in Example 1. Others are listed in the chart on the next page. Study it carefully, and compare different types of organizations.

The Uniform Partnership Act has been adopted in most states. The act restates much of the common law of partnerships. In addition, it has some new provisions not found in the common law that tend to make the law more precise and up to date.

COMPARISON OF ADVANTAGES AND DISADVANTAGES OF SINGLE PROPRIETORSHIP, PARTNERSHIP, AND CORPORATION

TYPE OF ORGANIZATION	ADVANTAGES	DISADVANTAGES
Single Proprietorship	All profits retained by owner Unified control Less taxation than a corporation Adaptable to situation Can obtain family assistance Responsibility fixed on the individual	Limited capital Bears all losses Unlimited liability Concentrated management Expansion difficult Legally and actually, proprietorship destroyed by death of proprietor
Partnership	More capital Partners share losses Easier to expand More credit Better chance for specialization Better supervision	Death dissolves the partnership Profits divided Unlimited liability Each partner is fully liable Bickering between partners Mutual agency
Corporation	Capital not limited Continuity of life Limited liability Employ specialists Legally separate from owners	Special or double taxation Government regulation Restricted charter Harder to organize

What are the advantages of the partnership type of business organization? the disadvantages?

FORMATION OF A PARTNERSHIP

CREATED BY CONTRACT

What is the name given to the contract that states the terms of the partnership agreement?

The formation of a partnership requires merely a valid agreement entered into by the interested parties. Such a contract is usually entered into by express agreement, although it may be in whole or in part implied. If the partnership is to continue for a year or more, it must be in writing in order to satisfy the requirements of the Statute of Frauds. The partnership agreement is known as the *articles of copartnership*.

ARTICLES OF COPARTNERSHIP

EXAMPLE 2 Hatcher and Hammer agreed at a meeting one day to open a peanut and popcorn stand near the university campus. Each man was to invest $100 and divide the work time evenly according to each man's circumstances. Hatcher and Hammer's agreement constituted a partnership even without a written contract.

EXAMPLE 3 The Goodrich brothers decided to go into business selling men's clothing. They drew up an elaborate partnership agreement. In what way was this different from that of the peanut and popcorn stand partnership arrangement?

There are so many possible points involved in connection with a partnership that the agreement should be clearly and fully expressed. It should preferably be in writing. Some of the important items to be covered are (1) the parties to the agreement; (2) the specific nature, scope, and limits of the business; (3) the duration of the business; (4) the amount of the original investment and provisions for future investment; (5) provisions regarding salaries, withdrawal of funds, interest on investment, and the division of profits; and possibly (6) some provision regarding terms under which a partner may withdraw from the firm.

What are some of the important items usually included in a written partnership agreement?

Should a minor enter into a partnership agreement, he may withdraw at any time before becoming of age or within a reasonable time thereafter. However, a minor will not be permitted to withdraw his investment if such withdrawal might jeopardize the interests of creditors of the partnership.

EXAMPLE 4 **Clark and French formed a partnership, each contributing $5,000 capital. Clark, a minor, announced his withdrawal three months after the start of the business. When creditors learned of his intention to withdraw, they demanded the payment of all existing accounts before any capital was returned to Clark. Clark would have to abide by these demands.**

● **Partnership Name**   The partners may call their firm by any name they choose, subject to the following limitations: (1) They may not use the same name as some other firm if doing so would cause confusion in the minds of the public. (2) If the firm name does not contain the names of the partners, most states require that a statement shall be filed in a specified public office giving the name of the firm and the names of the partners connected with it. This is particularly true if a new firm with new partners continues to use an old firm name after dissolution. (3) If the firm name adds to the names of the partners "& Company," most states require that the "& Company" shall indicate an actual person.

If the firm name has "& Company" after the names of the partners, what does this addition usually indicate?

When a partnership is sued, against whom is legal action taken?

At common law, legal action against another must be taken in the name of the individual partner, not in the name of the firm. Similarly, when a partnership is sued, it is the individual members who are sued, not the partnership per se. Real property may be held either in the names of the partners, or in the name of the firm.

NOTE: *The bullet indicates that there may be a state statute that varies from the law discussed here.*

One partner may not use partnership property for nonpartnership purposes without the consent of the other partner or partners.

KINDS OF PARTNERS

There are five types of partners—general, secret, silent, dormant, and limited. Each of these partners is a co-owner of the business and has some liability for the firm's debts.

General Partner Every partnership must have at least one general partner. In most firms all the partners are general partners. A *general partner* is one who takes an active part in the management of the firm and who is publicly known as a partner. A general partner has unlimited liability for the firm's debts.

What type of
partner must be
associated
with every
partnership?

GENERAL
PARTNER

Secret Partner A *secret partner* is one who is active in the management of the firm but whose connection with the firm is kept secret from the public. A secret partner also has unlimited liability for the firm's debts.

SECRET
PARTNER

Silent Partner A *silent partner* is one who takes no active part in the management of the firm. A silent partner is known publicly as a partner, and he has unlimited liability for the firm's debts.

SILENT
PARTNER

EXAMPLE 5 **Hager and Dodge, general partners, were in the luggage manufacturing business. Hamilton offered to invest in the partnership on equal terms with the other partners, to receive his share of the profits, but to take no active part in the management of the firm because of his ignorance of matters surrounding the luggage industry. This new arrangement, if acceptable to Hager and Dodge, would give the investor the status of a silent partner.**

Dormant Partner A *dormant partner* is one who takes no active part in the management of the firm and whose connection with the firm is kept a secret from the public. A dormant partner, however, has unlimited liability for the firm's debts.

Can creditors
hold dormant,
silent, or secret
partners liable on
the firm's
contracts?

DORMANT
PARTNER

EXAMPLE 6 **Suppose Hager and Dodge were in need of more capital and agreed to admit a wealthy acquaintance to the partnership. The new partner's contribution to the business was only the money invested. He did not participate in the management of the firm nor was his name publicly associated with the name of the firm. He would be considered a dormant partner; his only incentive in becoming a partner would be the sharing of the profits earned.**

Limited Partner A *limited partner* is one whose liability extends no further than the amount of his investment. This liability arrangement is known as *limited liability* and must be stated in the partnership agreement. A limited partner may be active and unknown or inactive and known or unknown, but he may not be active and known, since he may not then have limited liability.

LIMITED
PARTNER

LIMITED
LIABILITY

NONOWNER "PARTNERS"

A "partner" who is not a co-owner is known as an ostensible partner. An *ostensible partner* is a person held out as a partner with his consent when actually he has no relationship to the firm. If third persons have relied on this false representation, he may be held liable for the firm's debts, and the firm may be bound by his actions. His relationship with the firm is much like that of an agent by estoppel.

What are
ostensible
partners?

OSTENSIBLE
PARTNER

By what other names are ostensible partners known?

Ostensible partners are also known as *partners by estoppel, nominal partners,* or *partners by implication.*

EXAMPLE 7   Fred Hill had two sons, James and Donald. Fred permitted his two sons to carry on a partnership under the name of "Fred Hill & Sons," even though Fred actually had no connection with the firm. Fred could be held as an ostensible partner by persons who had relied on Fred's credit.

The party seeking to hold another as a partner must show that he has in good faith reasonably relied upon and been not only misled but also injured by the latter's representation. Uniform Partnership Act Sec. 16(1)

OPERATION OF A PARTNERSHIP

RIGHTS OF PARTNERS

Each partner is a co-owner of the business, and his rights are those that an owner would naturally have.

How are disagreements among partners about ordinary business affairs resolved?

To Share in Management   Each partner has a right to share in the management of the firm. Unless it is provided otherwise in the partnership agreement, each partner has an equal voice in management and may bind the firm on any matter that is within the scope of the partnership business. In case of disagreement as to an ordinary business matter, the decision of the majority is final.

REMEMBER: As a practical matter, partners must get along together. If they cannot agree, then the partnership must be dissolved. If there are only two partners, there is no majority, for any action by one partner can be undone by a counteraction of the other partner.

EXAMPLE 8   Tom Duff and Louis Duff were brothers and partners in a business. Tom had a son, Albert, who worked for the firm. Albert was shiftless and lazy, and he would not attend to business. Every week or so his Uncle Louis would become angry and discharge Albert. A day or so later, Albert's father, Tom, would rehire him. Each partner was within his rights in his action, but this did not create a friendly atmosphere in which to do business. Eventually the partnership had to be dissolved.

Partners have an equal voice in the management of the partnership business. They must get along well together if the business is to be successful.

To Inspect the Firm's Books Each partner has a right to inspect and make copies of the books of the firm. Usually, one partner will be assigned the responsibility of keeping the books, but he must keep them at a specified place and open to the inspection of the other partners at all times. If any partner is excluded from access to the books of the firm, it may be grounds for dissolution of the partnership. The law provides that "partners shall render on demand true and full information of all things affecting the partnership to any partner or the legal representative of any deceased partner or partner under legal disability." Uniform Partnership Act Sec. 20

To Share in the Profits Unless there is an agreement to the contrary, partners share equally in the profits, regardless of their contribution to the firm's capital or the time devoted by each to the business. This sharing of profits is such a fundamental right of a partner that any individual who shares in the profits of a business is presumed to be a partner until evidence is presented to show that he is not. A person may receive a share of the profits and not be declared a partner if the share is paid (1) in repayment of a debt, (2) as wages to an employee or rent to a landlord, (3) as an annuity to the widow of a deceased partner, (4) as interest on a loan, or (5) as consideration for the sale of the goodwill of a business. Uniform Partnership Act Sec. 7(4)

When may a person receive a share of the profits of a partnership and not be declared a partner?

EXAMPLE 9 **A serious illness required Hager to remain at home for a month. During his absence, work piled up in the shop of Hager and Dodge. Dodge had to work night and day to fulfill the contract obligations of the firm. Although it was unfair for Dodge to put in these long hours, he would receive no greater remuneration for his work than would Hager, who was at home. Had provision been made in the articles of copartnership for such a contingency, a more equitable arrangement would have resulted.**

DUTIES AND RESPONSIBILITIES OF PARTNERS

Partners must be able to trust one another. Each is an agent of the others and has duties comparable to those of an agent. Each partner must (1) always act in good faith and in the best interests of the firm, (2) be loyal to the firm and put the firm's interest ahead of his own (he cannot make a secret profit at the expense of the firm), and (3) always use his best skill and judgment in looking after the firm's affairs.

A partner is always liable to the other members of the firm for his share of the firm's debts. Uniform Partnership Act Sec. 18(b) Partners share losses in the same proportion that they share profits. If one partner is forced by creditors to pay all the firm's debts, he, in turn, has a right against the other partners for the payment of their share.

What are the duties and responsibilities of partners?

EXAMPLE 10 **During Hager's illness, Dodge paid for a shipment of merchandise using his own money. Dodge has an implied right to receive Hager's contribution toward the expense. Hager will be obligated to pay his share of the amount paid.**

RELATIONSHIP TO THIRD PERSONS

Each partner is an agent for the firm. The basic rule is that each partner may bind the firm by any act that is within the apparent scope of the firm's business. Any act of a partner that is outside the apparent scope of the firm's business is not binding on the firm.

If the business is a trading firm, a partner has the right to borrow money on the firm's credit and to secure the loan by a pledge or a mortgage on the firm's property. Uniform Partnership Act Sec. 11

The law states, "The act of every partner, including the execution in the partnership name of any instrument, for apparently carrying on in the usual way the business of the partnership . . . binds the partnership." This rule of *apparent authority* is borrowed directly from the law of agency.

APPARENT AUTHORITY

LIABILITY OF PARTNERS FOR FIRM'S DEBTS

How do partners share in the firm's losses?

Each partner has an unlimited liability for all the debts of the partnership that are incurred while he is a partner, even to the extent of his personal assets.

General Liability   A partner is jointly liable with his copartners on contracts entered into by any member of the firm acting within the actual or apparent scope of the firm's business. He is *jointly and severally liable* on torts; that is, the injured party, at his option, may sue all the partners or one or more of them. Uniform Partnership Act Sec. 13 and 14 This may startle you a little, and well it should. This is the biggest single drawback to the partnership form of business organization.

What is the general liability of a partner for all the debts of the partnership?

JOINT AND SEVERAL LIABILITY

REMEMBER: This risk of unlimited liability makes it doubly important for you to consider with care the selection of any future partners.

EXAMPLE 11   **Suppose Dodge borrowed money from the bank to buy new equipment for the firm, although Hager did not believe additional equipment was needed. Since the money had been borrowed by Dodge in the name of the firm and for firm use, Hager would also be liable on the debt. If the firm's assets were not sufficient to repay the debt, the creditors could demand payment from the personal assets of either partner.**

New Partner Liability   When a new partner is taken into an existing partnership, the new partner is liable for all the existing debts of the firm, but only to the extent of his investment. The new partner has no personal liability for the old debts. Uniform Partnership Act Sec. 17

EXAMPLE 12   **Max Leigh and Ray LeFleur were partners. They took in John McArdle as a partner in their firm, McArdle making a capital contribution of $10,000. The firm was badly in debt at the time and owed $25,000. The old creditors could demand McArdle's $10,000 contribution to the firm's capital, but they could not hold McArdle liable for anything more.**

Retiring Partner Liability   When a partner withdraws from a firm, the partners usually make some kind of agreement among themselves with regard to the payment of the existing firm debts. This agreement, however, is not binding on existing creditors. The retiring partner remains liable for all the debts created while he was a member of the firm until they are paid. He also is liable for all new debts created after he retires until actual notice of his retirement is given to all old creditors and general notice by publication (*constructive notice*) is given to all possible new creditors who knew of his former relationship with the firm.

What is meant by constructive notice of retirement?

CONSTRUCTIVE NOTICE

DISSOLUTION OF A PARTNERSHIP

The *dissolution* of a partnership is a change in the relation of the partners caused by any partner ceasing to be associated in the carrying on of the business. This is to be distinguished from the winding up of the business. When a partner dies or voluntarily withdraws from the firm, the firm is dissolved. The firm may also be dissolved by court decree. The partners then are no longer carrying on as co-owners of a business for profit. Dissolution occurs at once; that is, the moment one partner ceases to be associated with the firm.

What is meant by dissolution of the partnership?

DISSOLUTION

GROUNDS FOR DISSOLUTION

The business operations, however, cannot be terminated on a moment's notice. It takes time to wind up the firm's affairs and bring it formally to an end. During this winding-up period, the partners are not carrying on a going business; they are bringing it to an end. Some of the specific things that cause a change in the relationship, and thus bring about a dissolution, are described in the following paragraphs.

Expiration of Specified Period If, in the original partnership agreement, the partners agreed that the firm would terminate at a specified time, then, when that time arrives, the firm is dissolved. Uniform Partnership Act Sec. 31(1)(a) This does not necessarily mean that the partnership needs to be discontinued. If the partners agree to continue the firm, either expressly or by implication, they may do so.

Subsequent Agreement Like any other contract, a partnership agreement may be changed at any time by the will of all the partners (*mutual agreement*). They must, of course, respect the rights of the creditors and those with whom they may have executory contract agreements.

MUTUAL AGREEMENT

Admission of a New Partner If a new partner is admitted to the firm, the relationship of the old partners is changed. The old firm is dissolved and a new one is formed. A person cannot buy another's interest in a partnership, thus becoming a partner without the consent of the other members of the firm.

Withdrawal of a Partner When one partner withdraws or is expelled from the firm by other partners, there is a change in the relationship and the old firm is dissolved. If the remaining partners choose to do so, they may continue in business together in a new partnership, or they may wind up the affairs of the firm and go out of business.

Death of a Partner When one partner dies, the effect on the firm is just the same as when a partner voluntarily withdraws—that is, the partnership is dissolved.

The death of a partner terminates the partnership.

LIQUIDATING PARTNERS The surviving partners who wind up the affairs of the firm after the death of a member are referred to as *liquidating partners*. It becomes their obligation to liquidate the business; that is, to estimate the deceased partner's share of the firm's assets after all the debts have been paid. These assets are turned over to the executor of the deceased partner's estate. The articles of copartnership usually indicate what steps shall be taken by surviving partners in such cases. Surviving partners are usually given the right to purchase the deceased member's share, thus having assurance of the continuance of the business as a new partnership.

LIQUIDATING PARTNER

What are liquidating partners?

EXAMPLE 13 **Two partners operated a motel and restaurant. The business was operating at an excellent profit when one of the partners suddenly died. The articles of copartnership stipulated that the surviving partner would have the right to purchase the other's share from the estate for an amount determined to be reasonable by a group of examiners. In this way the business continued as a new partnership, and the surviving partner was not obligated to liquidate the business.**

How is a partnership affected by insolvency? bankruptcy?

Bankruptcy of the Firm or of a Partner When the firm is bankrupt or only one member is bankrupt, the general effect is the same. There is no longer the relationship that existed before, so the firm is dissolved. Bankruptcy of the firm or one of the partners causes the dissolution of the firm; insolvency alone does not. Uniform Partnership Act Sec. 31(5)

Should one of the partners become involved in a legal suit related to his personal affairs, a judgment against him might result in a forced sale of his interest in the partnership business and thus result in a dissolution of the firm.

Dissolution by Court Decree Any partner always has the power to dissolve the partnership. If he does so in violation of the partnership agreement, however, he will be liable to the other partners for breach of contract. Many times a partner may honestly believe that the best interests of the firm demand a dissolution, but he is afraid to exercise his power to dissolve for fear of being sued. Under these circumstances, he may bring an action asking the court to order dissolution. The court may order dissolution when (1) a partner becomes insane or otherwise incompetent; (2) a partner has been guilty of such conduct that it is impossible or impracticable to continue carrying on a business with him; (3) the business can be carried on only at a loss; (4) other circumstances render a dissolution advisable.

EXAMPLE 14   Joseph Hill and Harry Jamison were partners in the wholesale hardware business. It was discovered by Hill that Jamison had been selling merchandise from the store and pocketing the money received. Careful investigation showed that several thousand dollars had been taken from the business in this way. Hill would have the legal right to demand dissolution of the partnership and the return of all money pocketed by his partner. Should Jamison refuse to accept this proposal, Hill would have the right to seek a court order providing for a full accounting of the firm's finances and property and its final dissolution.

EFFECT OF DISSOLUTION

Remember that dissolution is just a change in relationship. It does not necessarily bring the business to an end. If partners are added or withdrawn and the other partners want to continue in business together, there must be an accounting of the old firm's affairs and new financial arrangements must be made with regard to the new firm. A new agreement must be drawn up regarding the conduct of the new firm. Public notice must usually be given in order to relieve retiring partners from liability on any new debts created by the new firm.

What is the effect of dissolution of a business?

Distribution of Assets   An accounting of the firm's financial affairs is necessary to determine how the firm's assets are to be distributed. The rules for the distribution of the firm's assets are the same, no matter what the reason for dissolution. In case the business is continued, however, the remaining partners leave their share in the firm and continue as before.

The liabilities of the firm rank and are paid in the following order: (1) those owing to creditors other than partners; (2) money, other than capital, lent by one partner to the firm; (3) the capital contribution of the partners; and (4) profits owed to the partners.

When both the firm and one or more partners are insolvent, what is the distribution order for the firm's assets and for the personal assets of the individual insolvent partners?

If the firm is insolvent, all the assets go to pay the creditors; in addition, individual partners are liable for any unpaid balance that the sale of the assets will not cover. If both the firm and one or more partners are insolvent, the firm's creditors have first claim on the partnership assets, but the personal creditors of the individual insolvent partners have first claim on the insolvent partners' personal assets.

EXAMPLE 15   The firm of Mayer & Noble is insolvent. Noble is also insolvent. The firm owes debts of $10,000 and has assets of $7,500. Noble owes debts of $500 and has assets of only $100. The firm's creditors could get all the $7,500 worth of assets belonging to the firm, and Noble's personal creditors could claim no part of these assets. However, Noble's personal creditors could claim all of Noble's $100 worth of assets, and the firm's creditors could get no part of these assets.

SUGGESTIONS FOR MINIMIZING LEGAL RISKS

Becoming a partner . . .

1. Before entering into a partnership, be sure that you can get along with all the intended associates. If not personally acquainted with all of them, get a number of confidential reports on their moral backgrounds, personal habits, and personal relationships from former associates and responsible persons who have known them for a number of years.
2. Investigate the financial history and background of intended associates through a credit agency. Determine whether there are any unpaid judgments or any records of dishonesty in their case histories.
3. The partners can minimize many risks by frankly discussing possible eventualities leading to potential disagreements and risks before forming the partnership. A written copartnership agreement carefully drawn by an attorney incorporating provisions for meeting these foreseen eventualities will be helpful in reducing possible disagreements and risks to a minimum.
4. It is desirable to have a written agreement giving partners the prior right to buy out the interest of a partner who desires to sell, retire, or leave the partnership under any possible contingency. This eliminates the necessity of a forced liquidation and possible financial loss for this reason.
5. If the partners plan to lease premises for the conduct of the firm's business, it is important to provide for a long-term lease with options for renewal, with exclusive right to operate a certain type of business in the building, and with an agreement as to fixtures. The firm should also try to protect itself from having the lease wiped out by a mortgage foreclosure on the building or some other eventuality.

 APPLYING YOUR LEARNING

QUESTIONS AND PROBLEMS

1. Why is a partnership form of organization sometimes preferable to a sole proprietorship?
2. May a minor who is a partner in a business withdraw from the firm at any time? May a minor withdraw his investment from a partnership of which he is a member? Explain.
3. What advantages can you see for having the partnership agreement in writing? Under what conditions must it be in writing?
4. What are some limitations that must be considered in the selection of a firm name?
5. Name and define the five basic kinds of partners.

6. What are the rights of the partners in their relationships with one another?

7. May a partner bind the partnership in dealing with third parties under these conditions:
   a. Purchasing goods for use in the partnership business?
   b. Hiring a mechanic to repair one of the firm's trucks?
   c. Borrowing money from a bank in the firm's name for use in the course of business?
   d. Borrowing money from a bank in the firm's name to use for a pleasure trip for himself and family?
   e. Purchasing an airplane in the firm's name to use personally for pleasure trips?

8. What is the liability of a new partner for the existing debts of the firm? Can he be held personally liable for the old debts of the firm?

9. What is the liability of a retiring partner for existing firm debts? for future firm debts? How can he limit his liability for future firm debts?

10. What things will bring about the dissolution of a partnership?

11. When can a partnership be dissolved by court decree?

12. What are the rules for the distribution of the firm's assets when the firm goes out of business?

13. During the prolonged illness of one partner, the other partner ran the business himself, putting in many extra hours of work. Was the partner who was ill entitled to any part of the profits earned by the business during his illness? Explain fully.

14. What is one partner's liability for torts committed by his copartners or contracts entered into by any of his copartners while acting within the actual or apparent scope of the business of the firm?

WHAT IS YOUR OPINION?

In each of the following cases, give your decision and state a legal principle that applies to the case.

1. Prince, Pringle, and Gruber are partners in a retail store selling musical instruments. Pringle and Gruber wish to have the store advertise over the local radio. Prince objects. Do Pringle and Gruber have the legal right to bind the firm to a radio advertising contract?

2. From his own personal funds, Sandler, a partner, paid the telephone bill owed by the partnership. Is the partnership liable or not liable for reimbursing Sandler?

3. The partnership of Hill, Perkins, and Moore failed. A creditor sought to hold Moore personally liable for a partnership debt incurred before Moore joined the partnership. Is Moore liable or not liable?

4. Steiner invested $15,000 and Werner invested $10,000 in their partnership. The partnership agreement stated nothing concerning the distribution of the profits. If the profits for the first year amounted to $4,500, how much should each partner receive? Explain why.

5. Watts, a general partner, was in charge of purchasing all merchandise for his partnership. A manufacturer gave Watts 5 percent commission on the goods Watts purchased from him for the partnership. When the other partners learned about the commission, they demanded that Watts turn over to the partnership all commissions that he had received. Was the partnership entitled to the commissions?

6. Miner and Nelson were partners in a retail shoe business. According to the partnership agreement, each was to give his full time to the firm business. Nelson became ill for a period of six months, and Miner had to take complete charge of the business and frequently worked extra time to operate the business. Miner demanded extra pay for his services. May he legally obtain it?

7. Aldrich and Scott were partners. The articles of copartnership provided that Scott was to receive one-half of the profits but was not to be responsible for any losses. What was the effect of this provision on Aldrich? on third parties doing business with the firm?

8. Van Ness was the owner of a large business property. He rented a store in the building to Roberts and agreed to accept as rent 20 percent of the net profits of the business. Did this agreement make him a partner?

9. Davis, of the firm of Davis and Fitzgerald, made a contract with Prince for partnership purposes. Davis was guilty of fraud in the making of the contract. Fitzgerald was entirely ignorant of the matter. Prince sued Davis and Fitzgerald. Is the firm liable?

10. Mendel and Moxley are general partners. Mendel signed the firm name to a contract for advertising. The partnership agreement stated that Moxley, not Mendel, had that authority. Is the partnership liable on the contract?

11. Snead, a general partner, signed the firm name to a contract selling the partnership as a whole. Are the other partners liable or not liable on the contract?

12. Waugh, Wells, and Thomas formed a partnership to sell pianos at retail for a period of ten years. Four years later, with the increase in popularity of the radio, Waugh and Wells wished to change the business to that of selling radios at retail. Thomas objected to such a change. Did the majority have the right to make the change?

13. Welsh, Young, and Hooper are partners. Welsh and Young wish to admit Rhodes as a partner, but Hooper objects. Do Welsh and Young have a legal right to admit Rhodes?

14. Girard withdrew from the partnership firm of Girard and Lilly. By mutual agreement, Lilly assumed full responsibility for all existing debts. Later, Lilly went into bankruptcy. Merrill, a creditor who held a claim against the old firm, tried to recover from Girard. Is Girard liable to Merrill?

15. Nolan and Kerper are partners. According to the partnership agreement, Nolan was to be the salesman and Kerper the buyer for the firm. Nolan purchased merchandise for the firm from Oliver. Oliver sought to hold the partnership liable. Can he do so?

16. Becker and Wyant, partners, agreed in writing to give Abeles, an employee, a certain percentage of the profits of the business for his services. Does this agreement make Abeles a partner to Becker and Wyant? Is he obligated to third persons?

17. Fecher and Walker were partners in a firm selling merchandise. Walker personally was judged a bankrupt. What effect, if any, did Walker's bankruptcy have on the partnership?

18. Dale was admitted into the partnership firm of Peters and Helmer. At the time of Dale's admission as a partner, the firm was indebted to several creditors including Mahn. The firm thereafter became insolvent, and the assets of the partnership and the old partners were insufficient to pay the partnership debts. Mahn sought to hold Dale personally liable for the deficit in his claim. Could he do so?

THE LAW IN ACTION

1. The plaintiff brought this action as the president of the National Paving Brick Association of America. This association consisted of a group of paving-brick manufacturers who were banded together for the purpose of promoting the sale of paving brick. It was the hope of the members that each would profit individually from the efforts of the association, but the association itself carried on no business for profit. The liability of the defendant depended upon whether the National Paving Brick Association of America was a partnership. What do you think? (Blair v. Southern Clay Manufacturing Company, 173 Tenn. 571, 121 S.W. 2d 570)

2. The defendants were partners doing business under the name of Kline's. They operated a clothing store in a building leased from the plaintiff. This action was brought for the collection of an increase in rent as provided by the terms of the lease. The defendants contended that the lease was not binding because it was signed by only one of the partners. Is this a correct contention? (Lawer v. Kline, 39 Wyo. 285, 270 P. 1077)

KEY TO "WHAT'S THE LAW?" Page 443

1. *The profits should be divided equally in the absence of an agreement to do otherwise.*
2. *No. This was sharing the profits as interest on a loan.*

WHAT'S THE LAW?

1. *Eugene Nathan, Sherman Evans, and John Wysocki decided to organize a corporation. The three men could not agree on a name for the corporation, so Nathan suggested that they wait until after the corporation's first month of operation before selecting a name. Could this be done?*

---

2. *A corporation bought three automobiles for the use of the members of the firm. One member contended that one of these cars belonged to him because he owned one-third of the stock. Is he correct?*

▲ UNIT 47: FORMING, OPERATING, AND DISSOLVING CORPORATIONS

Although partnerships and sole proprietorships are excellent forms of organization for many small businesses, they have their limitations. A corporation may at times fit the needs of a small business better.

EXAMPLE 1 Suppose that we again consider Robert Burke, James Cady, and the hamburger stand in Unit 46. The business does well as a partnership, and Robert and James consider further expansion. They believe there is an opportunity to make more profit by opening several more hamburger stands in good locations. Again, they are faced with the problem of raising money. Several people are interested in investing small amounts in the business; but these new investors do not want to take any part in the management, and they do not want to assume the unlimited liability of being partners. Robert and James might well consider the possibility of forming a corporation.

Why do large business concerns favor the corporate form of organization?

In a large business enterprise a corporate form of organization is almost a necessity. Our modern economic structure frequently requires large business organizations that need investments of millions of dollars of capital. These large business enterprises require the investment of money by thousands of persons. A partnership form of organization would be impractical, with thousands of partners all trying to run the business at once. Our modern form of corporate organization has been developed to meet the needs of these giant enterprises.

FORMATION OF A CORPORATION

Define
corporation in
everyday
language.

A *corporation* has been defined as "an artificial person created by statute." CORPORATION
This definition does not make much sense standing by itself.

In a partnership, you will remember, it is the partners themselves who
are important. It is the partners who have legal life and capacity, and it
is the partners who are liable for the debts of the firm. A corporation, on
the other hand, organized under the authorization of an appropriate
statute, is given a life and existence of its own, separate and distinct from
that of the individual members. It is this new person, created by the state,
that does business, makes contracts, creates debts, has the liability for
paying them, can sue and be sued in its own name, acquires and disposes
of personal and real property, and does all the other things that a natural
person might do if he were engaged in the same type of business.

EXAMPLE 2 As a partnership, the firm Hager and Dodge was in reality the
merger of the capital and talents of two men in a going business. As a corporation,
the two men will lose their identity as persons operating a business. The business
itself will be the person. The former partners will be the owners, or part owners,
of this newly created legal entity. As such, the new organization will be operated
in its own name and will be regarded in almost all respects as a true person.

When were
corporations first
made possible by
state statute in
the United
States? When did
England adopt
the corporate
form of
organization?

The first state to provide for the corporate type of business organization
was New York State, which, in 1811, passed a law making corporations
valid business organizations. Other states soon followed the action of New
York State, providing procedures for the creation, regulation, and taxing
of corporations chartered within their own states. England followed the
United States in the adoption of the corporate form of business organization, when, in 1855, corporations were recognized by an act of Parliament. Today, the corporation is the type of business structure selected
by most new business ventures anticipating growth and long-term existence.

A corporation cannot come into existence by itself. It must be organized
by natural persons who take the necessary steps for bringing it into legal
existence. These persons who organize the corporation are called *promoters*. PROMOTER

A corporation is
regarded in almost
all respects as a
person and, as
such, can be sued
in its own name.

STATUTORY PROCEDURE

Each state has its own laws (*General Corporation Codes*) under which corporations may be organized. These laws set forth the exact steps that must be taken in order to form a corporation. The procedure may vary a little, but usually the requirements conform to the following pattern

1. A specified number of persons, usually three, must sign and file the proper papers.

2. An application for incorporation, referred to as the *articles of incorporation,* is drawn up, signed, and filed with the proper state official. This application must usually contain the name, object, duration, capital structure, place of business, and proposed directors of the corporation to be formed.

3. If the articles of incorporation conform to all the requirements of the law and are approved by the state, they become the *charter* from which all authority flows.

GENERAL CORPORATION CODE

What are the articles of incorporation?

ARTICLES OF INCORPORATION

CHARTER

KINDS OF CORPORATIONS

Corporations may be classified into public or private corporations, stock and nonstock corporations, and domestic and foreign corporations. *Public corporations* include incorporated political units, such as towns, villages, cities, school districts, and the like. These public corporations are conducted according to regulations based on the laws of the state.

PUBLIC CORPORATION

EXAMPLE 3 The village of Diamondville was made up of many people who lived in the general area known by this name. There was a village improvement association but no actual legal entity to represent the people, make laws, levy taxes, and collect fines. By popular vote, the people of the community applied for a corporate charter for their village from the state legislature.

Private corporations may be classified into profit and nonprofit corporations. *Profit corporations,* private corporations organized for the purpose of making money, are found in virtually every major field of economic activity—transportation, mining, manufacturing, business, financial, and service fields. These corporations are regulated by the laws of the state in which they operate. If they are engaged in interstate commerce, they are also regulated by federal regulations.

PRIVATE CORPORATION

PROFIT CORPORATION

Distinguish between public and private corporations.

Any corporation formed for business purposes is operating for a profit and has a capital stock. A bank, a railroad, and a trading and manufacturing firm are *stock corporations.*

STOCK CORPORATION

Distinguish between stock and nonstock corporations.

Nonprofit corporations such as the Red Cross are formed for educational, religious, charitable, or social purposes.

NONPROFIT CORPORATION

A nonprofit corporation in which membership is acquired by agreement rather than by acquisition of stock is also a *nonstock corporation.* Many nonprofit fraternal organizations are nonstock corporations.

NONSTOCK CORPORATION

Corporations may also be classed as domestic and foreign. In the state in which it is incorporated, the corporation is considered a *domestic corporation.* In all other states in which it may operate, the corporation is considered a *foreign corporation.* As long as a foreign corporation complies with the laws of the states in which it operates, it will be permitted to operate.

DOMESTIC CORPORATION

FOREIGN CORPORATION

Distinguish between domestic and foreign corporations.

Certificate of Incorporation
of
MIDLAND AIRCRAFT COMPANY, INC.

We, the undersigned, desiring to form a corporation, for profit, under the general corporation laws of the State of New Jersey, do hereby make, subscribe, acknowledge, and file this certificate for that purpose, as follows:

FIRST: The name of the proposed corporation is: the Midland Aircraft Company, Inc.

SECOND: The principal office of the corporation is to be located in the city of Newark, county of Essex.

THIRD: Ralph Lodge, with offices located at 370 Broad Street, Newark, New Jersey, is the registered agent on whom process may be served.

FOURTH: The purposes for which the corporation is to be formed are: the manufacture of aircraft parts and research into scientific navigational equipment.

FIFTH: The amount of capital stock of the corporation shall be two hundred thousand ($200,000) dollars divided into 1,000 shares of preferred stock, par value $100 per share, and 10,000 shares of common stock, par value $10 per share.

SIXTH: The names and the post office addresses of the three directors of the corporation, who are also subscribers to this Certificate of Incorporation, and the number of shares of common stock that each agrees to subscribe for, are:

Steve Clark, 174 Broad Street, Newark, 2,000 shares

Allan King, 732 Renner Avenue, Newark, 2,000 shares

Frederick Herberts, 211 Park Place, Newark, 2,000 shares

SEVENTH: All the subscribers to this certificate are of full age; a majority of them are citizens of the United States, and at least one of them is a resident of the State of New Jersey.

In witness whereof, we have made, signed, and acknowledged this certificate this fifth day of July, 19--.

(Signed) *Steve Clark*

(Signed) *Allan King*

(Signed) *Frederick Herberts*

State of New Jersey⎫
County of Essex ⎭

Personally appeared before me, the undersigned, a Notary Public, in and for said county, this 5th day of July, 19--, Steve Clark, Allan King, Frederick Herberts, to me known and known to me to be the persons described in and who executed the foregoing instrument, and they duly severally acknowledged to me that they executed the same for the uses and purpose therein mentioned. Witness my hand and official seal on the day and year last aforesaid.

Arthur Moore
Notary Public

(Seal)

OPERATION OF A CORPORATION

Ownership of an interest in a corporation is acquired by the purchase of shares of stock. The number of shares you own indicates the extent of your ownership. U.C.C. Sec. 8-102 As the owner of shares of stock, you are a *stockholder*, or shareholder, and have a right to share in the management,

STOCKHOLDER

How does one acquire an ownership interest in a corporation? a share in the management of the corporation?

but in a special way. That way is to attend an annual meeting of shareholders and vote for the directors of your choice. Once elected, the *board of directors* has the exclusive right to manage the company for the next year. If the shareholders do not like the way the directors manage the corporation, they may elect new and different directors at the next annual meeting. In the meantime, however, the stockholders may not interfere with the directors' management.

BOARD OF DIRECTORS

It is the duty of the directors to direct the overall general policy of the corporation. Immediately after their election, the directors meet to organize the board and to select *officers*. The officers are entrusted with the everyday operation of the company. The directors meet at stated times throughout the year for the purpose of giving general directions to the officers, checking on the general welfare of the corporation, and declaring dividends if earned. Unless a director is also an officer, he takes no part in the active operation of the business. In fact, a director as such has no authority to do anything outside of a board of directors meeting.

OFFICER

Who decides whether or not the stockholders will receive any dividends on their stock?

How may the directors become liable to the stockholders for corporate losses?

The directors are entrusted with the general welfare of the corporation by the stockholders. They are not personally responsible for any acts performed in the conduct of the corporation business, provided they were prudent and used reasonable care and diligence in their decisions. They are liable to the stockholders, however, for all losses caused by their neglect of duty, by fraud, and by exceeding their authority.

EXAMPLE 4 One of the board members of Hager and Dodge, Inc., owned a section of real estate for which he had paid $10,000. After private consultation with members of the board, he offered to sell the tract to the corporation for $25,000, agreeing to divide part of the profits among the board members. If the members agreed to this, they would make themselves personally liable to the stockholders for the secret profits made at the firm's expense.

What are the duties of the officers of the corporation?

The officers have the responsibility of running the business. They, in turn, hire employees and manage the firm as the directors' general agents.

POWERS OF A CORPORATION

All corporations operating under charters granted by state authority are permitted only such rights and powers as are expressly conferred on them by the charter and those that may be reasonably implied from such express powers.

What are the necessary rights and powers of a corporation?

The necessary rights and powers of a corporation are (1) to have a corporate seal and name, (2) to sue and be sued in its corporate name, (3) to acquire and dispose of such property as is necessary for the conduct of the business of the corporation, including the right to own real estate, (4) to make such contracts as may be necessary to its corporate existence or purpose, (5) to collect money due it, to settle disputed claims, and to pay its debts, (6) to elect and to remove its officers, (7) to make bylaws for the regulation of the business of the corporation, and (8) to engage in a specific type of business.

EXAMPLE 5   Green sued Del Boccio, an officer of the Capetown Ship Company, about certain shipbuilding materials belonging to the corporation. Since the corporation, not Del Boccio, should have been sued, the case was dismissed. The corporation is a legal entity, a complete being, distinct and separate from the corporation's incorporators, stockholders, directors, officers, and employees.

Acts in Excess of Powers (Ultra Vires Acts)   Any act or contract of a corporation beyond its express or implied powers is said to be *ultra vires.* Ultra vires acts do not bind the corporation. If, however, the ultra vires contract has been fully performed by both parties, neither can rescind the agreement and recover what was given under it.

ULTRA VIRES

What are ultra vires acts?

EXAMPLE 6   The officers of the Diamondville Tool Company contracted with a manufacturer to assemble television receivers in its plant. This contract was outside either the express or implied powers granted in the corporation charter. After the contract had been executed, the manufacturer attempted to get back the money paid Diamondville on the grounds that the contract was ultra vires. As the contract had been fully performed by both sides, the demand for the return of the money would fail.

DISSOLUTION OF A CORPORATION

The dissolution of a corporation is also quite different from that of a partnership. You will remember that a partnership is dissolved any time there is a change in the relationship of the partners. This is not true of a corporation. One of the purposes of organizing a corporation is to avoid this instability of organization. The owners—that is, the stockholders—may freely sell their shares of stock to others, and their doing so will have no effect on the corporate structure.

CANCELLATION OF CHARTER

Corporations come into existence by the issuance of a charter. They are dissolved by the reverse process of canceling that charter. This may happen in several ways.

By Expiration of Charter   In many states charters are issued for a specified number of years. When the specified time expires, the corporate existence comes to an end. When that happens, the last elected directors become *trustees* of the corporate assets until the corporation is reorganized or the business is wound up and the assets distributed.

TRUSTEE

The life of a corporation is sometimes limited to the time required for the completion of a certain project. In most cases, however, the charter provides for the perpetual existence of the corporation.

EXAMPLE 7   The Armament Corporation owned a subsidiary corporation that had been formed to carry on five years of research in connection with government contracts held by the company. The corporation had been chartered for five years. At the end of five years, whether the project was completed or not, the charter would have expired. A petition for an extension or a new charter would have to be made should it be necessary for the organization to be continued.

A corporation may be dissolved by court order because of fraudulent advertising.

By Surrender of Charter State laws usually provide that a corporation may be terminated by a surrender of its charter to the state. The unanimous consent of the stockholders or the vote of the directors and two-thirds of the stockholders is usually required for such dissolution.

By Decree of Court Many times, it is impossible to find all or a substantial part of the stockholders, and a court action may be necessary to terminate the corporation. Some states have special statutes that allow the state to cancel charters when the corporation has been out of business for a number of years.

By Consolidation When two or more corporations decide to consolidate and form a new corporation, the stockholders of the corporations involved must vote their approval and obtain the consent of the state for the consolidation. The old corporations are dissolved and a new one is formed.

By Reorganization Sometimes a corporation can improve its financial condition by reorganizing and forming a new corporation. It is necessary to get the approval of creditors and the security holders for this reorganization. The new corporation then usually takes over the business of the old corporation.

In what ways may the charter be canceled?

FEATURES OF A CORPORATION

Let us examine some of the desirable and undesirable features of this type of organization. There are many advantages to a corporation as a form of business organization. There are also disadvantages.

DESIRABLE FEATURES

Limited Liability If a partnership becomes insolvent, any partner may be held for all the debts of the firm. If a corporation becomes insolvent or bankrupt, a stockholder may not be held for the debts of the firm. All the stockholder will lose is the money he has invested in the stock. Creditors may not go beyond the corporation's own assets in enforcing payment of valid debts of the corporation. This is *limited liability*.

EXAMPLE 8   As members of a partnership, Hager and Dodge were personally liable for partnership debts. This liability might cause them to lose their homes, savings, and all other personal assets. The new corporate form of organization would give them security even if the business were to become bankrupt. This is one of the most important reasons for incorporation.

Larger Capital   We mentioned earlier that our modern giant industries require the investment of many millions of dollars. These millions must be obtained from thousands of different people. This can be done by means of a corporation.

Continuous Existence   No one knows how long a partnership will last. Its existence is very unstable. Any change in the relationship between partners will bring about a dissolution. That is not true of a corporation.

A corporation can outlive those who form it. The death or disability of one or more of the owners (stockholders) will not jeopardize its existence. A corporation ceases to exist when its charter expires or is repealed, surrendered, or forfeited.

Transferability of Shares   Again, one of the primary purposes achieved by incorporation is to create transferable shares of ownership. These shares of stock may be bought and sold at any time. This makes it easier for the corporation to raise money, and it gives a stability of organization.

Centralized Management   Partners have an equal voice in the active management of the firm. This may cause problems in case of disagreement and may bring about a dissolution of the firm. In a corporation this difficulty cannot arise. The corporation is controlled by the vote of the owners, who are the stockholders, rather than by a few partners. The stockholders' wishes, expressed by majority vote, are carried out by the board of directors through the officers.

EXAMPLE 9   On a few occasions, Hugh Hager and John Dodge had serious disagreements about important decisions relating to the management of the business. Dodge once threatened to withdraw from the partnership, thereby terminating the partnership. As a stockholder, Dodge would not have so much power. The votes of all the stockholders would be needed to determine the corporation's future.

What are the principal advantages of the corporate form of organization?

Also, the larger organization makes it possible for the corporation to hire specialists for the management of various phases of its operation.

UNDESIRABLE FEATURES

Before you decide that a corporation is best for all purposes, you must look at the disadvantages.

Taxation   A corporation is usually subject to special taxes that do not apply to partnerships. There are good reasons for this, because there are additional expenses to the state in supervising and regulating corporations.

Also, if you organize your business as a corporation, you will have to pay double taxes because the corporation's profits will be taxed, and your dividends as a stockholder will also be taxed.

Regulation Corporations are granted special privileges by the state in allowing them to incorporate. In return, they are subject to more regulations than a partnership. Corporations must make more reports to the state, and they must keep their books open for inspection by various people to a greater extent than is necessary in partnership operation.

EXAMPLE 10 **As a partnership, Hager and Dodge made all financial arrangements with their bank. With the creation of a corporation, the former partners found that they would be selling stock and floating bonds, all of which would be under the jurisdiction of the Securities and Exchange Commission and state agencies. Thus, the two men would no longer have the full decision as to financing that they had as a partnership operation.**

What are some undesirable features of a corporate form of organization?

Scope of the Business The scope of a partnership's business is limited only by the partners themselves. Anything they agree among themselves to do, they may do. A corporation may engage in only those business activities that are specified in its charter, either expressly or by implication. Today, however, corporation charters usually grant very broad powers to the corporation. Also, courts will usually allow a rather wide range of implied powers. Major changes in the nature of the corporation's business, however, must have the approval of the percentage of the stockholders, usually two-thirds, provided for in the charter.

How is the scope of a corporation's operations limited?

Lack of Owner Management In a partnership, the owners actively manage the business. In a corporation, the personal touch of owner management is lacking. Stockholders who are not always familiar with the operating problems of the corporation may make unwise decisions when voting at the annual stockholders' meetings.

SUGGESTIONS FOR MINIMIZING LEGAL RISKS

Forming a corporation . . .

1. Make a very careful study of the advantages, disadvantages, legal consequences, tax advantages, and special license requirements of the following types of businesses as they apply to your state: (1) individual proprietorship, (2) partnership, (3) limited partnership, and (4) corporation.

2. Obtain the advice of a competent attorney and tax consultant in an attempt to determine present and future advantages of the corporate form of organization as they are reflected by economic and legislative trends in your state.

3. As management skill is the key factor in the success of a corporation, it is imperative that a plan for providing effective and efficient management be seriously considered and eventually provided.

4. If a closely held corporation is considered, it is important that the other shareholders, who will also be directors and possibly officers in the corporation, are in complete agreement with you as to fundamental policies and proposed management plans.
5. If possible, determine in advance whether it will be possible to obtain all necessary permits, licenses, leases or required premises, desired corporate name, and needed capital.

 APPLYING YOUR LEARNING

QUESTIONS AND PROBLEMS

1. Name the different kinds of corporations. Explain briefly the distinguishing features of each.
2. What do the promoters do in the organization of a corporation?
3. What are the usual steps followed in the organization of a corporation?
4. How does the operation of a corporation differ from that of a partnership?
5. How are the directors of the corporation elected? What is their function?
6. How are the officers appointed? the employees hired?
7. In what ways may a corporation be dissolved?
8. List the data contained in an application for incorporation.
9. What is a corporation charter? How is it obtained?
10. A director, acting as an individual and not with the other members of the board, signed a contract in the name of the corporation. Can he be held personally liable on the agreement? Explain.
11. Name several corporations that are doing business in your locality. Give some reasons why these particular companies were organized as corporations.
12. May the stockholders or the directors of a corporation dissolve the corporation at any time before the expiration of the time limit specified in the charter?

WHAT IS YOUR OPINION?

In each of the following cases, give your decision and state a legal principle that applies to the case.

1. The Acme Corporation, when sued by Sanders, stated that it could not be sued because it was an artificial person created by law. Is this a good defense?
2. A corporation that was chartered for the purpose of manufacturing and selling farm machinery purchased three vacant lots adjacent to its manufacturing plant in order to display samples of its products. Did the corporation have the legal right to make such a purchase?

3. Plant and Waters had operated their business for several years as a partnership. Waters convinced Plant that it would be a good idea to convert the business to a corporation. Plant agreed; so they changed the name of the firm to Plant and Waters, Incorporated. They did nothing further, although they told their customers and creditors that they had formed a corporation. How will the court judge their status in case of a lawsuit?

4. Howard Chester, a director of the Fallstown Manufacturing Company, entered into an agreement with the Nelson Power Tool Company whereby he was to receive a commission on all purchases that his company made from the power tool company. When the other directors learned of this arrangement, they sued Chester for all commissions he had received as a result of the agreement. What should the judgment of the court be?

5. James Cullins, a holder of a majority of issued stock, designated his nephew as secretary-treasurer of the corporation. Certain minority stockholders objected claiming that Cullins did not have the authority to make the appointment. They took court action to enforce their objections. For whom would the judgment be?

6. The directors of a steel corporation voted to manufacture radios as a sideline. The state dissolved the corporation. The company sued. For whom would the judgment be?

7. A corporation, in its charter, was authorized to manufacture and sell radios. At a regular meeting of the stockholders, a majority voted to change over to the manufacture of airplane engines. Does the corporation have the power to change the nature of its business merely by a majority vote of the stockholders?

8. The directors of the Oliver Corporation voted to merge with the West Corporation. Does Roberts, a stockholder of the Oliver Corporation, have a right to prevent the merger because the stockholders were not given an opportunity to vote on the matter?

9. Pitcher was a member of a social club that had been incorporated as a nonprofit corporation. Without authorization of the club directors or officers, Pitcher ordered a new television set to be installed at the club. When the bill arrived for the television set, the club refused to pay for the set. Is the club within its rights in refusing to pay for the set?

THE LAW IN ACTION

1. In this case a question was raised as to the validity of the charter issued by the state to a corporation. The defendant contended that it was within the powers of the state to set up the requirements of a corporate charter and that it was also within the power of the state, acting through the courts, to determine whether those requirements had been met. Do you agree with these contentions? Why? (People v. Ford et al., 294 Ill. 319, 128 N.E. 479)

2. In its charter, the Philadelphia Electric Company stated as its purpose, "supplying heating, lighting, and power by electricity to the public." The company did supply electric power, but also began to sell electrical appliances. In an action brought against the electric company, it was contended that selling electrical appliances was an ultra vires act. Do you agree? (Commonwealth of Pennsylvania ex rel. Baldridge, Attorney General v. Philadelphia Electric Co., 300 Pa. 577, 151 A. 344)

KEY TO "WHAT'S THE LAW?" Page 457
1. *No. The application for incorporation must include the name of the corporation.*
2. *No. The corporation and its shareholders are different persons.*

WHAT'S THE LAW?

1. *Perth, Ross, and Brooks, incorporators of Power Machinery, Inc., each subscribed to 20 percent of the firm's stock. The stock has a par value of $100 a share; each of them owned 100 shares. They arranged for their stock to be issued on the payment of $50 a share. If the corporation became insolvent, could creditors collect the additional $50 per share?*

2. *If Brooks held preferred stock and the others held common stock, would his liability for the unpaid balance be greater than theirs?*

◢ UNIT 48: CORPORATE OWNERSHIP

Although we speak of a corporation as something that has existence in tangible form, actually no one ever saw a corporation and no one ever will see one. It is really a product of the legal imagination—an artificial person created by the state—with many of the rights, powers, duties, and liabilities of a natural person. To function as a legal entity and to be in business, a corporation needs capital. This is obtained by selling membership in the corporation by placing on sale units, or shares, of stock.

EVIDENCE OF OWNERSHIP

An owner's interest in a corporation is represented by transferable shares of stock.

EXAMPLE 1 If Robert Burke and James Cady decide to change the organization of their hamburger business from a partnership to a corporation, one of the first things they will have to decide is how much money the new business will need. They may decide that, to expand as they wish, $200,000 is needed. To raise the $200,000, they may decide to sell 2,000 shares of stock at $100 a share. They may decide to sell their present hamburger stand to the new corporation for $50,000 and take 500 shares of the new stock in payment. The remaining 1,500 shares they may decide to sell to other people for $150,000. This new money is additional capital to be used in the building of new hamburger stands.

Where can you learn how many shares of stock a corporation plans to issue?

The number of shares a corporation plans to issue and the price per share if par value stock is issued are specified in the articles of incorporation. This is necessary because prospective creditors of the corporation have a right to know how much money the corporation had at the time it commenced business.

Creditors of a corporation have the right to know how much money the corporation had at the time it commenced business.

KINDS OF STOCK

There are different kinds of stock issued by corporations. Stock may be par value stock, or it may be no par value stock. It may also be common stock, preferred stock, treasury stock, or watered stock.

Par Value Stock   Where the value of the stock is stated in the articles of incorporation, the stock is said to be *par value stock*. Thus, if a share of stock is said to have a par value of $100, it means that $100 was paid to the corporation for the share. In Example 1, Robert and James issued 2,000 shares of stock having a par value of $100 a share. If par value stock is issued by the corporation for less than the stated par value, the stockholder owes the corporation the difference between par and the price he paid for it. The stockholder who has purchased stock from a corporation and has paid the full par value for it may subsequently dispose of it at any price he pleases.

No Par Value Stock   Sometimes stock is issued as *no par value stock*. This means that it does not have any stated value. The corporation can sell no par value stock for any price it chooses, and the purchaser cannot be held for any additional purchase price. Most states require, however, that corporations make known to the public the amount of money actually raised by the sale of no par value stock. This, again, is for the protection of the future creditors. The creditors need to know how much money the corporation had with which to begin business. Remember that the creditors can look only to the corporation for payment; therefore, they are entitled to know something about the corporation's finances.

Common Stock   The most usual form of stock issued by a corporation is *common stock*, which represents the interest of the stockholders in the net worth of the corporation. It does not guarantee to its holders the right to profits. The return is based on the earnings of the corporation and is usually the amount remaining after the preferred stock holders have received the amount guaranteed them.

The control of a corporation, evidenced by the voting power of the stockholders, is in the hands of the holders of the common stock.

EXAMPLE 2 **Landen was the owner of 100 shares of common stock in Hager and Dodge, Inc. At the end of the first year of operations, dividends were paid only to the holders of preferred stock. Landen insisted that he and the other holders of common stock were entitled to a similar dividend. His arguments will avail him nothing if there were no additional earnings that could be distributed.**

Preferred Stock *Preferred stock* gives to the owner some special preference over the rights of holders of common stock. The usual preferences are (1) the right to have their investment returned first in case of dissolution; and (2) the right to have a certain rate of income paid to them before any of the profits are distributed to holders of common stock in the form of dividends. The preferences to be given are stated in the articles of incorporation and in the stock certificates. Special types of preferred stock are sometimes issued to make them more attractive to purchasers.

PREFERRED STOCK

CUMULATIVE AND NONCUMULATIVE *Cumulative preferred stock* means that, if the guaranteed dividends are not paid on the stock in any one year, they will be paid in following years before any dividends are paid to common stock holders.

CUMULATIVE PREFERRED STOCK

Noncumulative preferred stock means that, if the guaranteed dividend is not earned by the corporation in any one year, then the right of the stockholder to the dividend is lost; it is not carried over to the next year.

NONCUMULATIVE PREFERRED STOCK

Distinguish between cumulative preferred stock and noncumulative preferred stock.

EXAMPLE 3 **Hiller held 100 shares of preferred stock in Air Plastics, Inc. After dividends had been skipped for two years, the firm showed a large profit which would be available for dividend payment for the third year. Hiller sought payment of all dividends that had been missed over the past years. Since back payment of dividends was not provided in the articles of incorporation, Hiller was entitled only to the current year's dividends.**

PARTICIPATING AND NONPARTICIPATING *Participating preferred stock* gives to the holder the right to share in extra earnings along with the common stock holder after he has received his fixed rate of dividend.

PARTICIPATING PREFERRED STOCK

Distinguish between participating preferred stock and nonparticipating preferred stock.

EXAMPLE 4 **Carlin Electronics, Inc., had a good year. After paying the preferred stock holders a 6 percent dividend as specified in the articles of incorporation, the corporation had enough money to pay a 6 percent dividend to all the common stock holders and still had earnings that could be used to pay even greater dividends. If the preferred stock was participating stock, the preferred stock holders would share equally with the common stock holders in the distribution of the extra dividends. If the preferred stock was nonparticipating, all the extra dividends would go to the common stock holders.**

NONPARTICIPATING PREFERRED STOCK

Treasury Stock Legally issued stock that is presented to the corporation as a gift or repurchased by it is called *treasury stock*. Only surplus funds may be used for the purchase of treasury stock. The stock may be resold at a reasonable price agreed upon by the board of directors. Dividends are not paid on the stock while held by the corporation.

TREASURY STOCK

A corporation may guarantee to repurchase the stock from subscribers upon request to overcome sales resistance. Such stock becomes treasury stock. When a corporation is in financial difficulties, stockholders sometimes donate a portion of their shares as treasury stock. These shares are then resold in order to assist in refinancing the firm.

How may a corporation acquire treasury stock?

Watered Stock Stock issued for insufficient value or for no value at all is referred to as *watered stock*. Stock is said to be watered when it is issued as a bonus; when it is issued as fully paid, but actually at less than its par value; or when it is issued for property or for services greatly overvalued.

WATERED STOCK

EXAMPLE 5 **A member of the board of directors of Air Plastics, Inc., suggested that each officer of the firm be given a bonus of 100 shares of the company's stock for the loyalty he has shown the company. Unless such a bonus had been rightfully earned and was owed to the officers, the stock presented to them would be watered stock.**

DIVIDENDS

What are dividends?

Dividends are profits distributed to the stockholders. They are generally payable when the board of directors declares them. A dividend must be a given percent or a fixed amount for each share.

DIVIDEND

EXAMPLE 6 **During its second year of operation, Air Plastics, Inc., earned a profit which enabled the board of directors to declare a $20,000 dividend to its common stock holders. Each share of common stock will be entitled to an amount determined by dividing the total number of shares of common stock outstanding into the $20,000 to be distributed.**

A dividend can be declared only from profits or from earned surplus. When a dividend is declared, it becomes a corporation liability, payment of which can be enforced by the stockholders. The dividend belongs to the stockholders, who are the owners of record on a date designated by the board. A dividend is usually in the form of cash or stock.

EXAMPLE 7 **During Electronics Unlimited Corporation's fourth year of operations, new products, outstanding management, and excellent research resulted in substantial profit improvement for the corporation. As a result, the board of directors declared a dividend to all stockholders of record on July 7. Everyone owning Electronics Unlimited shares on July 7 will participate in the dividend, even though they might sell their stock before the dividend is actually distributed.**

STOCK PURCHASES

You, as a purchaser of corporation stock, may possibly buy the stock direct from the corporation, or you may buy it from individual owners of stock.

Purchase by Original Subscription All stock is originally sold by the corporation itself. At the time the corporation is being organized, the promoters will seek subscriptions from interested persons. These *stock subscriptions* are contracts to take stock when the corporation completes its organization and is authorized by the state to sell stock to the public. These subscriptions are similar to any contract to sell, and the subscriber does not become a stockholder until the organization is completed and a *stock certificate* is issued to him. The corporation may continue to sell shares after its incorporation is complete up to the number of shares authorized in its charter.

STOCK SUBSCRIPTION

What are stock subscriptions? When are they requested? by whom?

STOCK CERTIFICATE

Purchase From Existing Stockholders Most corporations do not have unissued stock on hand. If all their authorized stock has been issued, then, in order to buy a share of stock, you must find a stockholder who is willing to sell. You may be able to find such a stockholder yourself and buy direct, but usually it is necessary to buy such stock through a stockbroker. The *stockbroker* is in business to get buyers and sellers of stocks together. If you have stock to sell, you usually list it for sale with a broker. U.C.C. Sec. 8-303

STOCKBROKER

STOCK TRANSFERS

How would you transfer or assign stock?

Like any other form of personal property, stock may be transferred or assigned. To be binding on the corporation, however, the transfer must be recorded in the corporate books. The ownership of the stock certificate is essential to owning an interest in the corporation, and the shareholder's interest cannot be transferred without the certificate.

How may a new stock certificate be obtained to replace a lost certificate?

Lost Stock Certificates A stockholder who loses a certificate of stock should notify the corporation promptly. The corporation then will issue a new certificate. The stockholder generally is required to file a bond to protect the corporation against any claims that may be made by a person who comes into possession of the lost stock certificate. U.C.C. Sec. 8-405

EXAMPLE 8 **Kessler, who owned common stock in the Diamondville Tool Company, found that it was quoted on the stock exchange at a price that would net him a profit of $8 per share if he sold his stock at once. But when he looked for his stock certificate, it was missing; he had either misplaced or lost it. He had to notify the company and await issuance of a new certificate, during which time the price of Diamondville Tool common stock dropped to a price that removed any chance of his making a profit from selling his shares.**

GOVERNMENT CONTROLS

It is not always easy for the prospective buyer of corporate stock to evaluate the financial condition of the corporation offering stock for sale. This condition has led to many frauds on investors in the past. To help prevent these frauds in the sale of worthless stock, both the federal and state governments now actively regulate the sale of corporate stock. The federal government regulates transactions in securities through the Securities and Exchange Commission and the U.S. Postal Service. Many states have their own corporation commissions established under so-called *blue-sky laws*. Under these laws, which vary only slightly from state to state, the seller must make a public statement of responsibility, disclose the general financial condition of the corporation, and make a full accounting of the use to which the proceeds of the new stock issue are to be put by the corporation. These facts are submitted to a designated state official or security commission. Both criminal and civil penalties are provided in the event that a violation of the law is uncovered.

BLUE-SKY LAW

By what act was the Securities and Exchange Commission established? When?

Federal Regulation The *Securities and Exchange Commission,* established by the *Securities Act of 1933* and subsequent amendments, is the most

SECURITIES AND EXCHANGE COMMISSION

important federal agency regulating the sale of stock. This commission does not guarantee securities registered with it, but it attempts to make information available to prospective buyers that will aid them in protecting themselves. It regulates the sale of all securities sold in interstate commerce as well as all stock exchanges doing an interstate business. It requires the registration of the stock before it is offered for sale and also requires that proper information shall be furnished in the form of a *prospectus.*

What are some of the duties and responsibilities of the Securities and Exchange Commission?

PROSPECTUS

The U.S. Postal Service also regulates stock transactions under its power to prevent the perpetration of frauds through the use of the mails.

What part does the Post Office Department play in the regulation of stock transactions?

If you cannot get adequate, accurate information about the stocks you propose to buy, you should seek information from the Securities and Exchange Commission. If you have been defrauded in the sale of stock by mail, you should report the matter to the U.S. Postal Service for investigation by postal inspectors.

● **State Regulation** Many states have enacted blue-sky laws designed to regulate the sale of securities within the state, so that investors will be protected from fraudulent stock-selling schemes. Permission may be granted to a corporation to sell stock within the state after satisfactory compliance with the state requirements. Failure to comply, however, may result in a fine, or imprisonment, or both.

Stock exchanges and brokerage concerns also set up their own regulations and rules for the sale of securities. These regulations tend to protect the purchaser of securities who buys through these agencies. These agencies must conform to state and federal regulations.

STOCKHOLDER RIGHTS AND RESPONSIBILITIES

RIGHTS OF STOCKHOLDERS

A stockholder has the following basic rights: (1) the right to receive a stock certificate, (2) the right to have his stock registered in his name, (3) the right to receive dividends, (4) the right to vote at stockholders' meetings, (5) the right to inspect the books, (6) the right to sell his stock, (7) the right to buy new issues of stock, and (8) the right to share in the assets of the corporation on dissolution.

What are the basic rights of a stockholder?

Right to a Certificate A subscriber of stock has a right to receive a stock certificate from the corporation showing the number of shares he owns. If a purchaser buys from another stockholder, he has a right to the seller's certificate properly endorsed. The corporation usually cancels the seller's certificate and issues a new certificate that is registered in the purchaser's name.

Right to Registration The owner of a stock certificate has a right to have it registered on the books of the corporation in accordance with the charter and bylaws. It is only after he becomes a *stockholder of record* that the stockholder acquires the true rights of a shareholder; therefore, registration of his stock certificate is very important. U.C.C. Sec. 8-102(1), Sec. 8-302

STOCKHOLDER OF RECORD

NOTE: *The bullet indicates that there may be a state statute that varies from the law discussed here.*

Right to Dividends   The stockholder is an owner of the corporation; therefore, he has a fundamental right to share in its profits. His right to dividends, however, is subject to some restrictions. He has no right to dividends until dividends have been declared by the directors. The directors have the responsibility of managing the finances of the corporation. If they feel that the company has not made enough money to pay a dividend in a certain year, it is their duty not to declare any dividends for that year. *Dividends can be declared only out of profits.* Even where there are profits, if the directors honestly feel that the overall interest of the corporation requires the retaining of the dividends in the company, the directors may retain them and declare no dividends.

When dividends are declared on certain classes of stock, all stockholders of that class have a right to demand their dividends. Only a stockholder who is a shareholder of record may demand dividends.

Right to Vote   The right to vote at stockhoiders' meetings is a fundamental right of a shareholder. Sometimes, however, the right to vote is given up in return for special privileges in the payment of dividends or distribution of assets. The holders of preferred stock usually do not have voting rights.

A stockholder may exercise his right to vote by attending the annual meeting and casting his vote himself, or he may give his right to vote to someone else by signing a paper called a *proxy*. Stockholders whose names still appear on the books of the corporation are entitled to vote even though they have transferred their stock.

What is a proxy?

PROXY

Right to Inspect the Books   As an owner, a shareholder has a right to know something about the financial structure of the corporation. There was a time when a stockholder had the right to inspect all the corporation's books, just like a partner. Business expedience today, however, requires that a stockholder must limit his right of inspection. Most state laws require, nevertheless, that certain books, such as stock books and transfer records, be kept at certain places and open to the inspection of the stockholders.

May a stockholder inspect all the books of a corporation?

EXAMPLE 9   **In an effort to determine whether a certain person was actually a holder of common stock with the right to vote for new directors, Parker, a stockholder of the Diamondville Tool Company, retained an attorney to examine the corporate stock books. Parker has the right to appoint a competent agent to do this for him, and the right may not be denied.**

Right to Transfer Ownership   A share of stock in a corporation is personal property and may be bought and sold like other personal property. The new buyer must make proper application according to the company rules to be able to have his purchase registered on the books of the company.

Corporations sometimes attempt to restrict the resale of shares of stock. If there is good reason for such limitation, the limitation may be valid; otherwise limitations are usually declared contrary to public policy and may be waived in a court of law.

The corporation and its shareholders are different persons, and the shareholders are not liable for the debts of the corporation.

EXAMPLE 10   A group of physicians formed a corporation to operate a wholesale drug company. In their articles of incorporation, they limited the ownership of stock in the corporation to physicians because they believed in that way the company would be operated according to the high standards of the medical profession. This might well be a proper limitation, and any shareholder might be required to sell his stock only to another physician.

Right to Buy New Stock Issues   If new issues of stock are authorized, each stockholder has a right to buy his proportionate share of the new issue. This makes it possible for him to retain the same percentage of ownership that he had before.

EXAMPLE 11   Riggs owned 5 percent of the capital stock of the Diamondville Tool Company. If the stockholders vote to increase the capital stock, Riggs would have the right to buy 5 percent of the shares added to the stock. This right is given to a stockholder to preserve his proportionate share in the accumulated surplus of the corporation.

Right to Share in the Assets on Dissolution of the Corporation   When a corporation is dissolved, all outstanding debts must be paid first out of the assets. If the holders of preferred stock are specifically given such a preference, their investment is returned next. If there is enough money left, the investment of the holders of common stock is then returned. If there is not enough money to repay the holders of common stock all their money, each has a right to his proportionate share. If, after the return of all investments, there is still money remaining, it is distributed as profits are usually distributed.

Upon dissolution of the corporation, how are the assets usually distributed?

LIABILITY OF STOCKHOLDERS

It is usually stated that stockholders have no liability for the debts of the corporation. This is substantially correct, but it needs qualification.

Liability for Unpaid Subscriptions You will remember that sometimes corporations issue shares of par value stock for less than par value. The original subscriber who receives such stock remains liable for the balance of the purchase price. Sometimes this unpaid balance is collectible by the corporation, but it may always be collected by the creditors if needed to pay the corporate debts.

EXAMPLE 12 **Fisk subscribed for $1,000 worth of the Diamondville Tool Company common stock, paid $100 with the subscription, but failed to pay the balance due. Should Diamondville become insolvent, the creditors of the corporation could recover the $900 balance plus interest at the legal rate for the period during which Fisk had been in default on his payment.**

Dividends can be declared only from profits or from earned surplus. If a dividend should be declared out of capital, could the stockholders be held liable for the amount of the dividend? If the answer is "yes," then, to whom?

General Liability for Corporation Debts One of the most important single reasons for the incorporation of a business is to free the owners from liability for the firm's debts. Unless exceptions are made by statute, a stockholder is not liable for the corporation's debts beyond the amount of his investment. Sometimes special statutes may place a liability on the shareholders for the payment of wages of employees; but, as insolvency laws usually give employees preferences against the corporation's assets, this shareholder's potential liability is not large. However, an unlawful distribution of any assets of a corporation makes each stockholder liable to the creditors of the corporation for the amount involved. Thus, if a dividend was declared and distributed out of capital because no profits were available, the stockholders would be liable to the creditors for the amount received.

SUGGESTIONS FOR MINIMIZING LEGAL RISKS

Investing in stocks . . .

1. Purchase stocks through reputable persons or brokers only after thorough investigation and on competent advice and adequate information about the stocks.
2. Do not invest heavily in speculative stocks unless you can afford to lose your investment.
3. Register your stock certificates promptly; otherwise, you will not acquire the rights of a stockholder of record.
4. Exercise your voting rights to ensure that you have a voice in the management of the company.
5. Advise the company of your change of address in order to receive notices, reports, and dividends promptly.
6. Keep stock certificates in a protected place with other important papers.

◭ APPLYING YOUR LEARNING

QUESTIONS AND PROBLEMS

1. Explain the difference between par value stock and no par value stock.
2. Explain what is meant by common stock and preferred stock.
3. What are the usual preferences available to holders of preferred stocks?
4. What are the names and characteristics of the most common special forms of preferred stocks?
5. From what sources can one purchase shares of stock?
6. What possible liability does a stockholder have who buys par value stock from a corporation for less than par value?
7. What types of protection are available to the prospective stock purchaser? How can one avail oneself of this protection?
8. What are the basic rights of a stockholder? Explain each briefly.
9. What potential liabilities does a stockholder have when he acquires shares of stock?
10. What is treasury stock? watered stock?
11. Explain what is meant by blue-sky laws. For whose protection are they designed?

WHAT IS YOUR OPINION?

In each of the following cases, give your decision and state a legal principle that applies to the case.

1. Reinhart subscribed for $900 worth of stock in a corporation. He paid $550 on account. The corporation was declared bankrupt. In order to meet the corporation's liabilities, the receiver sought to collect the unpaid $350. Is Reinhart liable?
2. The A & B Corporation failed. Does Decker, a creditor, have a legal claim against Rice, who is a paid-up stockholder?
3. Richards, a large stockholder in the Atlas Machine Corporation, purchased a large quantity of equipment at a very low price from a competing company that was going out of business. The corporation refused to accept or pay for the equipment claiming that Richards had no right to bind it in any way. Is the company correct?
4. Snell, who owned 51 percent of the stock of the Atomic Corporation, died. Did Snell's death automatically terminate the corporation?
5. Warren, a stockholder in the Arcara Company, is ill and unable to attend a meeting of the stockholders of the company. Is it possible for him to have a vote on matters at the meeting?
6. Warner is a stockholder in the Brass Corporation and wishes to inspect the books to obtain a list of stockholders and the amount of stock each owns. Is he legally entitled to see such records?
7. Wiesner, who owns 60 percent of the stock of the Westover Corporation, was sued by the Black Company for a debt of $900 owed that company by Westover. Was Wiesner legally liable for the debt?

8. Willis, one of the five stockholders in the Rome Corporation, owns 80 percent of the stock. When the corporation dissolved, was Willis entitled to 80 percent of the assets that remained after all the debts of the corporation had been paid?

9. On May 12, 1967, Hires bought from Wing 200 shares of stock in the Woods Corporation. Hires did not have the stock transfer recorded on the books of the corporation. A dividend on these 200 shares was paid to Wing on July 6, 1967. Hires sued the corporation for the dividend. Was the corporation liable to Hires for the dividend?

10. The directors of a corporation issued stock having a par value of $50,000 in payment of property worth only $30,000. Discuss the rights and liabilities of the parties involved in this transaction.

11. Robert Darwin purchased fully paid-up stock from the Emerson Building Company at a price less than half its par value. A short time later, the corporation became insolvent, and the creditors sued Darwin for the difference between the amount paid for the stock and its par value. Was Darwin liable?

12. Sam Brown, the manager of Herberts and Allen, Inc., Department Store, caused the arrest of Gerald Kelly on suspicion of shoplifting. Kelly was acquitted of the charge. He sued the corporation. How should the case be decided?

THE LAW IN ACTION

1. The defendant signed an application for stock in the U.S.I. Realty Company, a corporation. An officer of the company signed the application to signify the acceptance of the corporation. Before any stock was issued, the corporation was adjudged a bankrupt. The trustee in bankruptcy brought this action to collect the purchase price of the stock. The defendant contends that an application for stock in an existing corporation follows the ordinary rules of contracts and that there was a failure of consideration because the corporation could not perform its part of the bargain. Do you agree? Why? (Stern v. Mayer, 166 Minn. 346, 207 N.W. 737)

2. The plaintiffs owned stock in the Ford Motor Company. This action was brought to force the directors of the corporation to declare a dividend. It was contended by the plaintiffs that the directors were building up undistributed reserves far in excess of the needs of the company and that they planned to use these funds to build a new plant. The purpose of the new plant was not to make more money for the stockholders but to benefit the buying public by reducing the price of cars. If true, would this be a proper action on the part of the directors? Why? (Dodge v. Ford Motor Company, 204 Mich. 459, 170 N.W. 668)

KEY TO "WHAT'S THE LAW?" Page 469

1. *Yes. Each subscriber to new issues of stock automatically promises to pay the par value of the stock he buys.*
2. *No. It would be the same.*

A DIGEST OF LEGAL CONCEPTS

1. Each partner is a co-owner of the partnership business, and his rights are those that an owner would naturally have.

2. These rights of a partner ordinarily are (a) a right to share in the management, (b) a right to inspect the books, (c) a right to share in the profits, and (d) a right to share in the distribution of the assets on dissolution.

3. Partners share losses in the same proportion that they share profits.

4. A partner is an agent of the firm when dealing with third persons in the name of the firm, and the ordinary rules of agency apply to his conduct.

5. Except for limited partners, every partner has an unlimited liability for all the debts of the partnership that are incurred while he is a partner.

6. New partners coming into the firm are liable for all the existing debts of the firm, but their liability is limited to the amount of their investment.

7. A partner who withdraws from a firm must give notice of his withdrawal to the former creditors. If he does not, he may be held for all the debts of the new firm.

8. Partners leaving a firm that continues in business remain liable for all debts incurred while they were partners unless the old creditors have agreed to release them.

9. A dissolution occurs when there is a change in the relationship of the partners caused by any partner ceasing to be associated in the carrying on of the business.

10. The assets of the firm are distributed following a dissolution in the following order: (a) debts to creditors, (b) debts owed to partners, (c) capital contributions of partners, and (d) profits.

11. A change of fundamental policy in the conduct of partnership affairs requires the consent of all partners.

12. The firm and each partner are liable for frauds or torts of a partner or of an agent acting within the scope of the business.

13. A partner owes the duty of utmost good faith and loyalty in the conduct of the partnership business.

14. A corporation has a life and existence of its own, separate and distinct from that of its owners, who are the stockholders.

15. A corporation comes into existence when a certificate of incorporation, or charter, is issued by the state following the proper filing of an application by the incorporators and the compliance with all necessary legal requirements.

16. In a corporation, the shareholders elect directors, who have the responsibility of establishing broad policies for the operation of the company.

17. The directors elect the officers of the company, who, in turn, are responsible for the actual operation of the corporation.

18. A corporation may be dissolved by the canceling of its charter by the state.

19. A corporation charter may be canceled by a surrender of the charter by the corporation, followed by acceptance by the state.

20. The desirable features of a corporation are (a) the limited liability enjoyed by its shareholders, (b) the greater ease of raising capital, (c) continuous existence, (d) ease of transferring shares of ownership, and (e) more efficient management.

21. The undesirable features of a corporation are (a) higher taxes, (b) more regulation by the state, (c) limitations specified in its charter, and (d) lack of personal owner management.

22. An owner's interest in a corporation is represented by transferable shares of stock.

23. An owner of stock is called a shareholder or stockholder.

24. A corporation, depending on the charter, may issue stock with a par value, or it may issue stock with no par value.

25. A large corporation usually issues both common stock and preferred stock.

26. Common stock represents ownership in the corporation, but it ordinarily gives no preferences or extra rights to the holder regarding profits.

27. Preferred stock also represents a share of ownership, but it gives the holder some special preferences in respect to the distribution of assets on dissolution and in the payment of dividends.

◮ LAW DICTIONARY

This law dictionary contains brief definitions of more than 500 legal terms. Some are concise restatements of more detailed definitions given elsewhere in the text. Some are new terms that are not defined in the text, but terms that may be encountered in your future business and legal relationships. Approximately five hundred other specialized terms defined in the text are not included in this dictionary because of limited space. For a thorough review of the vocabulary of business law, review the marginal terms in each of the forty-eight separate units as well as the entries in this dictionary.

Pronunciation: bāke, chãotic, câre, căt, cärt, ȧcross, ēat, ĕvade, ĕbb, runnẽr, īce, hĭt, ōak, ŏbey, ôrder, cŏt, lo͞ot, fo͝ot, ūnit, ûnite, ûrge, ŭp, ′ primary accent, ″ secondary accent

A

ABANDONMENT The relinquishment or surrender of a right or property with the intent not to reclaim.

ABET To encourage and aid another in an act of a criminal nature.

ABROGATE (ăb′ rō gāt) To annul or repeal; to abolish a law.

ABSCOND To flee secretly; to hide or absent oneself with intent to avoid legal process.

ABSTRACT OF TITLE A summary of the history of the title to land, including all conveyances, mortgages, liens, and other changes affecting a parcel of land.

ACCEPTANCE The act of the drawee of a bill of exchange which signifies he agrees to pay it; also, the bill itself after acceptance.

ACCEPTOR The drawee of a bill of exchange after he has agreed to pay it.

ACCESSION (ăk sĕsh′ ŭn) An increase in property that is produced by other property; the acquisition of title to all that one's own property produces.

ACCESSORY One who, though not present, aids a crime.

ACCOMMODATION PAPER A note or draft, including a check, that is drawn or endorsed by one person for another without consideration.

ACCORD An agreement between debtor and creditor as to the allowance or disallowance of their respective claims.

ACCORD AND SATISFACTION The substitution of another agreement for an existing claim and the full execution of the new agreement.

ACCOUNTING The science of accounts; a statement of receipts and payments in trust or contract relationships.

ACCRETION (ăh krē′ shŭn) The process of growth by natural enlargement, as an addition to land by a gradual deposit of soil along its borders.

ACKNOWLEDGMENT The act by which a party who has executed an instrument goes before a competent officer and swears that he did execute the instrument and that it is genuine.

ACQUITTAL A verdict of not guilty; the discharge by a court of a party charged with a crime.

ACT OF BANKRUPTCY Any act, as defined by the laws of bankruptcy, that will cause a person to be adjudged a bankrupt.

ACT OF GOD An accident due to a force beyond human control, such as a flood, an earthquake, or a tornado.

ACTION A lawsuit; a proceeding in a court for enforcement of a right.

ACTUAL DAMAGES Damages which an injured party to a contract can prove as a result of another party's failure to perform. Also, damages which can be factually proved, as contrasted with speculative damages.

ADEQUATE CONSIDERATION That which is equal, or reasonably proportioned, to the value of that for which it is given.

ADJECTIVE LAW The part of our law that deals with the supplying of remedies to reimburse an injured party when his rights have been interfered with.

ADJOURN (ăh jûrn′) To postpone action of a court or a body until a specified time.

ADJUDICATION (ăh jū″ dĭ kā′ shŭn) The act of a court in giving judgment in a lawsuit.

ADMINISTRATOR The person appointed by the court to settle the estate of one who died intestate, that is, without making a will.

AFFIDAVIT A signed, written statement sworn to before one who is authorized to take oaths.

AGENCY BY ESTOPPEL (e′ stäp ŭl) The creation of an agency by acts of the parties, leading third parties to believe that an agency agreement exists to their subsequent injury.

AGENCY COUPLED WITH INTEREST An agreement in which an agent has an interest in the subject matter of the agency.

AGENT One who acts for another in dealings with third parties.

AGENT'S RIGHT OF LIEN (lēn) An agent's right to retain possession of the principal's property if the principal fails to compensate him for his services or expenses related to the agency agreement.

ALIAS (ā′ lē ŭs) An assumed name; otherwise; different; another.

ALIBI A statement that the defendant was not present when the tort or crime was committed.

ALIEN (āl′ yĕn) A person who lives in one country but owes allegiance to another country.

ALIENATE (āl′ yĕn āt) To convey the title to property.

ALIMONY An allowance granted to a woman while she is seeking a legal separation from her husband or after the separation or a divorce has been granted.

ALLEGATION (al″ ĭ gā′ shun) A statement of fact made during a legal proceeding.

ALLONGE (ă lŭnj′) A strip of paper attached to a negotiable instrument for the writing of additional endorsements.

ALTERATION A change in the terms of a written contract or instrument.

AMALGAMATION (ă măl″ gĕ mā′ shŭn) The union of two incorporated companies or societies by the merging of one in the other.

AMBIGUOUS (ăm bĭg′ u ŭs) Doubtful and uncertain as to meaning.

AMENDMENTS Additions or changes made in a constitution.

ANNUITY An amount of money payable annually to the recipient until his death.

ANNUITY POLICY A policy that provides for the payment of a sum of money in fixed annual payments to the insured when he reaches a certain age.

ANNUL To make void, to cancel, or to destroy.

ANSWER A formal written statement containing the defense to an action; a reply to a charge.

ANTEDATED Dated earlier than the actual date.

ANTICIPATORY BREACH (ăn tĭs′ ĭ pà tō″ ri) The right under the law of contracts to sue on a contract before the time of performance if the promisor has already repudiated the contract.

APPARENT AUTHORITY The rights and powers that a third party may reasonably suppose the agent possesses and which bind the principal as to third parties.

APPEAL The referral, or attempt to refer, a case to a higher court for reexamination and review.

APPELLATE COURT (ă pĕl′ ăt) A higher court with the right to review cases sent up on appeal from a lower court.

APPRAISE To set a price or value upon something.

APPURTENANCE (ăh pĕrt′ nĕn[t]s) Any right with reference to land that goes with the land in a deed or lease.

ARBITRATION A method of settling disputes between parties by referring to third parties for settlement.

ARRAIGNMENT (ăh rān′ mĕnt) Calling a prisoner to the bar of a court to answer an indictment.

ARREARS Any money due and unpaid.

ARSON The deliberate and malicious burning of any structure.

ASSAULT A threat or attempt to injure a person by physical violence.

ASSENT To approve what has already been done or to agree to do as requested.

ASSIGN To transfer to another.

ASSIGNEE (ăs ī nē′) The person to whom property or other rights have been transferred or assigned.

ASSIGNMENT The transfer of any property right from one person to another; usually used in connection with the transfer of intangible rights, such as the right to collect money.

ASSIGNOR (ăs″ ĭ nôr′) The person who transfers or assigns property or rights to another.

ATTACHMENT Legal seizure, usually of goods.

ATTEST To certify as to the genuineness of a document; to bear witness to.

ATTORNEY IN FACT A person appointed by another to act for him.

AWARD The decision reached by arbitrators or referees.

B

BAIL Security given for the release from legal custody of a defendant with assurance that he shall appear when summoned by court.

BAILEE (bāl ē′) The one to whom personal property is delivered under a contract of bailment.

BAILMENT The delivery of goods to another for a certain purpose, the goods to be returned later.

BAILOR (bāl ôr′) The owner of personal property which has been temporarily transferred to another person in a bailment.

BANK DRAFT An order for payment of money drawn by an officer of a bank upon either his own bank or some other bank in which funds of his bank are deposited.

BANKRUPT One who has done some act or suffered some act to be done in consequence of which, under the laws of his country, he is liable to have his property seized and distributed among his creditors.

BARGAIN AND SALE DEED A deed which transfers title to property but makes no warranties with respect to the title or use of the property.

BARRED ACCOUNTS Accounts receivable which are not collectible, having been barred by the Statute of Limitations.

BARREN PROMISE A promise to do that which one is already bound to do.

BARTER The exchange of goods for other goods.

BATTERY The unlawful striking or touching of another person.

BENEFICIARY (běn ĭ fĭsh′ ē ĕr″ ē) One who is entitled to the proceeds of a life insurance policy; one who is entitled to the benefit of property held by another as trustee; one who receives a gift under a will.

BEQUEATH (bĭ kwēth′) To give personal property by will to another.

BEQUEST That which is left by a will; a legacy.

BILATERAL (bī lăt′ ĕ rĕl) A term used to indicate two promises or two obligations. Thus, in a bilateral contract there is a mutual obligation, consisting of a promise by each party that is binding on both parties.

BILL OF EXCHANGE A negotiable instrument drawn by one party ordering another to pay a certain sum of money to a third party named in the instrument. Bills of exchange are commonly called drafts.

BILL OF LADING A combination contract and receipt given by the common carrier to the person shipping certain goods.

BILL OF SALE A written contract transferring personal property from one person to another.

BINDER A memorandum given an insured when it is agreed that the contract of insurance is to be effective before the written contract is executed.

BLANK INDORSEMENT An indorsement in which the holder or payee does no more than sign his name on the instrument.

BLUE-SKY LAWS Statutes for the protection of the investing public from the sale of worthless securities.

BONA FIDE (bo′ nĭ fīd″) In good faith; honestly; without fraud or unfair dealing.

BOYCOTT A combination between persons to discontinue dealings with other persons who refuse to comply with their requests.

BREACH A violation of an agreement or obligation.

BRIEF The written or printed arguments and legal authorities furnished the court by lawyers.

BROKER (brō′ kĕr) An agent who carries on negotiations for a principal, acting as an intermediary between the principal and third parties in making contracts involving rights or property.

BUCKET SHOP TRANSACTIONS Stock sales in which there is no intent to deliver a stock certificate; classed as wagering contracts.

BULK SALE The sale of an entire business, occasionally made with the intent to defraud creditors.

BY-BIDDING In auction sales, the unethical and illegal practice of encouraging higher bids through the bidding of an accomplice of the seller or his agent.

BYLAWS The rules which a private corporation adopts for its internal regulation.

C

CAPITAL STOCK The total designated value of shares issued by a corporation.

CASHIER'S CHECK A check issued by the cashier of a bank and drawn against bank funds.

CASUALTY INSURANCE Insurance protecting a person from losses due to accident or disaster.

CAUSE OF ACTION The grounds for a lawsuit.

CAVEAT EMPTOR (kă′ vē ăt ĕmp′ tôr) Latin phrase meaning "Let the buyer beware."

CAVEAT VENDITOR (kă′ vē ăt věn′ dǐ tôr) Latin phrase meaning "Let the seller beware."

CERTIFICATE OF DEPOSIT A bank certificate stating that the person named has deposited a stated amount of money payable to his order.

CERTIFICATE OF STOCK A certificate issued by a corporation showing that a certain party has a specified number of shares of the corporation's stock.

CERTIFIED CHECK A check that has been accepted by the bank on which it was drawn and has been marked or certified to indicate such acceptance.

CHANCERY (chăn′ sēr ē) A court of equity as distinguished from a court of law.

CHARTER A grant by the state permitting a corporation to exist.

CHATTEL A piece of personal property.

CHATTEL MORTGAGE A mortgage on personal property.

CHATTEL REAL Personal property related so closely to real property that it is considered to be real property. Keys to doors in a house or building would be included in this term.

CIVIL ACTION An action at law in which a party seeks to recover damages resulting from the invasion of his legal rights.

CIVIL LAW A system of codified law based on Roman law, common on the continent of Europe. Or, used in a different context, that division of laws that deals with the rights and duties of private parties, as contrasted with criminal law.

CLIENT One who employs an attorney; one who seeks professional advice or assistance.

CODE An organized collection of laws.

CODICIL (kōd′ ǐ sǐl′′) A formal supplement to a will.

COLLATERAL SECURITY Additional obligations, usually stocks or bonds, pledged as security for a personal performance of an agreement.

COLLUSION A secret agreement designed to attain an unlawful objective or advantage.

COMMERCIAL PAPER Negotiable instruments obligating a maker or payor for the payment of money, as notes, drafts, etc.

COMMON CARRIER A carrier of freight or passengers operating under a franchise granted by state authority.

COMMON LAW The part of our law that comes from custom or precedent, usually referring to the long-established law of England that was based on the recorded decisions of the early law courts.

COMMUNITY PROPERTY By statute in some states, the right of a husband and wife to a one-half interest in the property acquired by either or both during their marriage.

COMPLAINT The plaintiff's statement of his cause of action.

COMPOSITION OF CREDITORS An agreement among creditors and with the debtor that the creditors will accept part of the debts in full settlement.

COMPROMISE A settlement reached by mutual agreement and concessions.

CONCURRENT Happening at the same time; acting together.

CONDEMN (kŏn děm′) To take land for public use; to pass sentence on a person who has been convicted of a crime.

CONDITION PRECEDENT (prěs′ ěd ěnt) In sales, a condition that must be fulfilled before title to goods passes to a buyer.

CONDITION SUBSEQUENT (sŭb′ sě kwěnt′′) In sales, a condition to be met after title has passed; as a money-back guarantee.

CONDITIONAL SALE A contract in which it is agreed that title to goods shall not pass from the seller to the buyer until the happening of a certain condition, usually the payment of the purchase price.

CONDOMINIUM (kän′′ dŭ mǐn′ ē ŭm) Absolute ownership of an apartment unit together with an undivided interest in the structural parts of a building and grounds not under the supervision and care of one individual.

CONFISCATION The appropriation by the state of private property for public use.

CONNECTING CARRIER A carrier designated by an initial carrier to deliver freight beyond the terminus of the initial carrier.

CONSANGUINITY (kŏn′′ săn′′ gwǐn′ ǐ tē) Blood relationship.

CONSIDERATION In contracts, the impelling influence that causes a contracting party to enter the contract; a benefit received by the promisor or a detriment suffered by the promisee.

CONSIGNMENT Goods directed by one person to another to be sold for the first person and credited to him by the second person.

CONSIGNOR One who directs goods to a consignee for sale.

CONSTRUCTIVE NOTICE Information or knowledge of a fact that a person should have because of custom or acquaintance with the law.

CONSUMER CREDIT PROTECTION ACT Federal legislation protecting consumers from obligations on contracts wherein all credit terms are not clearly disclosed.

CONTEMPT (kŏn těmpt′) Conduct in or toward a court which tends to impair the respect due the court or tends to interfere with the due administration of law.

CONTRACT TO SELL GOODS A contract whereby the seller agrees to transfer the ownership of goods to the buyer for a consideration called the price.

CONVERSION The unlawful assumption of ownership or destruction of property of another.

CONVEYANCE The transfer of title to real property; the instrument used to transfer title to real property.

COOPERATIVE APARTMENT In real property, a proprietary lease on an apartment unit giving the tenant the rights of ownership and use.

COPYRIGHT A right granted to an author, photographer, artist, or the agent of any one of these by the government to publish and sell exclusively an artistic or literary work for twenty-eight years.

CORPUS DELICTI (kôr′ pŭs dē lĭk′ tī) The body (material substance) upon which a crime has been committed, the actual facts that must be proven to establish that any specific crime has been committed.

COSTS An allowance granted by the court to a successful party to a suit to reimburse him for his expenses in conducting the suit.

COUNTERCLAIM A claim set up to offset another claim.

COUNTEROFFER An offer made by the offeree to the offeror in answer to the original offer made by the offeror.

COURT OF EQUITY A court in which rules of equity rather than rules of law are supplied, giving relief where money damages will not be adequate.

COVENANT (kŭv′ ĕ nŭnt) An agreement under seal; a promise in a sealed contract.

COVER After a breach of contract by a seller, a purchase of goods in good faith by the buyer as a substitute for those not delivered by the seller.

CRIME A wrong which the government recognizes as injurious to the public; a violation of a public law.

CURTESY (kûr′ tĕ sĭ) The estate to which by common law a man is entitled on the death of his wife, provided they have had children born alive who might have been capable of inheriting the estate.

D

DAMAGES The money recovered by court action for injury or loss caused by another.

DAYS OF GRACE Additional days in which to complete a contract after maturity.

DE FACTO (dē făk′ tō) As a matter of fact; from the fact.

DE JURE (dē joo′ rē) By right; by lawful title.

DECEDENT (dĭ sē′ dĕnt) A deceased person.

DECEIT A fraudulent misrepresentation or contrivance by which a person is misled to his injury.

DECLARATION The statement by the plaintiff setting forth his cause of action.

DECREE An order made by the court in a suit in equity.

DEED A formal written document granting the right to real property.

DEFAULT A neglect or failure to act.

DEFENDANT The person sued in a civil action; the person charged with a crime in a criminal action.

DEFENSE The answer to a cause of action or indictment.

DEL CREDERE (dĕl krĕd′ ĕr e) A term used to describe an agent who guarantees payment for goods which he sells in his principal's name.

DELEGATION The transfer of an obligation from one person to another, usually the substitution of one debtor for another.

DEMAND A request for payment of a claim.

DEMURRAGE (dē mûr′ ĭj) Compensation for delay of a vessel or railroad car beyond the time allowed for loading, unloading, or departing.

DEMURRER (dē mûr′ ēr) The formal mode of disputing in sufficiency in law of the other side's pleading.

DEPONENT (dĭ pō′ nĕnt) One who makes a sworn statement.

DEPOSITION The testimony of a witness given under oath for use in the trial of a case.

DESCENT The passing of an estate by inheritance and not by will.

DEVISE (dĭ vīz′) A gift of real property contained in a will.

DICTUM An opinion expressed by a court which is not necessary in deciding the question that is currently before the court.

DISAFFIRM To repudiate a voidable contract.

DISCHARGE The act by which a person is freed from performing a legal obligation.

DISHONOR To refuse to pay a negotiable instrument when due.

DIVISIBLE CONTRACT A contract consisting of two or more separate and distinct obligations, none of which is dependent or interrelated with the other.

DOUBLE JEOPARDY A subsequent trial of a person for a crime of which he has already been found not guilty in a previous trial.

DOWER (dŏw′ ēr) The provision made by law for a widow out of her late husband's real property.

DRAWEE The party named in a draft on whom demand for payment is to be made.

DUE PROCESS OF LAW The right to the protections and privileges afforded by constitutions, statutes, and courts.

DURESS (do͞o rĕs) Restraint or compulsion, usually by threat or fear of injury.

DUTIES Obligations that are the correlative of rights; also taxes, such as customs duties.

E

EARNEST The payment of part of the purchase price to bind a sale.

EASEMENT The right of an owner of land to use the land of another in a limited way.

EMANCIPATE To set free. A minor is emancipated from parental obligation when facts prove that parents no longer exert influence on a grown child, as when a minor is given parental authority to act before reaching his majority.

EMBEZZLEMENT The fraudulent appropriation of goods or money by one to whom they were entrusted.

EMBLEMENTS (ĕm′ blĕ mĕntz) Products of the earth produced annually by labor and industry.

EMINENT DOMAIN (dŏ mān′) The right of the government to appropriate private property for some public use.

ENACT To make or establish a law.

ENCUMBRANCE (ĭn cŭm′ brŭn[t]s) A lien or claim attached to property.

ENDORSE To sign a negotiable instrument on the back for the purpose of transferring it to another person.

ENDORSEMENT A name, with or without other words, written on the back of a negotiable paper.

ENDORSER Person who writes his name on the back of an instrument.

ENEMY ALIENS Aliens who are subjects of a hostile country.

ENTIRE CONTRACT A contract consisting of two or more obligations each of which is dependent and closely related to the other.

EQUAL DIGNITIES RULE A rule stating that a contract between a principal and an agent must be of equal formality as contracts that the agent is empowered to make for the principal with third parties.

EQUAL PAY RULE Federal legislation guaranteeing women workers engaged in interstate commerce the same wage or salary paid men in the same job classification.

EQUITY A branch of law granting relief when there is no adequate relief otherwise available.

EQUITY OF REDEMPTION The right of the mortgagor to reclaim his property after the time of payment has expired.

ESCHEAT (ĭs[h] chēt′) The reversion of property to the state if the property holder dies without legal heirs.

ESCROW (ĕs′ krō) A written document held by a third person until a prescribed condition comes about.

ESTATE An interest in property.

ESTATE FOR LIFE An estate created by dead or grant giving ownership during the lifetime of the holder but ceasing at the end of his life.

ESTATE IN COMMON An estate owned by two or more persons whose individual title rights pass to persons named in each one's will or to each one's heirs.

ESTATE IN FEE SIMPLE Absolute inheritance clear of any limitations that would prevent heirs from inheriting.

ESTOPPEL (e′ stäp ŭl) A rule of law that precludes the denying of certain facts by a man or conditions arising from his previous conduct, allegations, or admissions.

EVICTION Dispossession by process of law.

EVIDENCE Proof, either written or unwritten, of the allegations in issue between parties; that which is used to induce belief in the minds of the jury or of the court.

EX POST FACTO LAW A law that renders criminal an act that was not criminal at the time it was committed; these laws are prohibited by the Constitution.

EXECUTED That which has been fully performed.

EXECUTION The performance of an act, or the completion of an instrument; a writ directing an officer to enforce a judgment.

EXECUTOR (ĭg zĕk′ [y]ŭt ŭr) The party named in a will to carry out the terms of the will.

EXECUTORY (ĭg zĕk′ [y]e tŏr″ ē) Relating to that which is yet to be performed.

EXPRESS WARRANTY Any statement of fact or any promise by the seller that would have the natural tendency to induce the buyer to purchase the goods.

EXTRADITION The surrender by one government to another of a person charged with a crime.

F

FACSIMILE (făk sĭm′ ĭ lē) An exact reproduction or copy.

FACT A thing done or existing. Whether a thing was done or does exist is a question of fact for the jury. If the facts are proved, the matter of the rights and liabilities of the parties is a matter of law for the court.

FACTOR An agent appointed to sell goods sent to him on a commission basis.

FEDERAL EMPLOYER'S LIABILITY ACT Federal legislation removing the common-law defenses against employers' liability and outlining a common carrier's liability when engaged in interstate commerce.

FEDERAL FAIR LABOR STANDARDS ACT Federal legislation regulating hours worked, wages, and child labor.

FEE SIMPLE Fully owned lands.

FELONY A crime usually punishable by imprisonment in a state or federal prison.

FIDUCIARY (fĭ do͞o′ shĕ ĕr″ ē) A person who possesses rights and powers to be exercised for the benefit of another person; a trustee.

FIRM All members of a partnership taken collectively; the name or title under which a partnership transacts business.

FIXTURE An article of personal property physically attached to real property.

FORECLOSURE A legal proceeding to apply mortgaged property to the payment of a mortgage.

FORFEITURE The loss of some privilege or right, usually as a penalty for some illegal act or some negligence or breach of contract.

FORGERY The act of falsely making or materially altering a document with intent to defraud.

FRANCHISE A special privilege conferred by law.

FRAUD The gain of an advantage to another's detriment by deceitful or unfair means.

FREIGHT Goods which one party entrusts to another for transportation.

FRIENDLY FIRE A fire which burns within its intended boundaries.

FULL COVENANT AND WARRANTY DEED A deed in which the seller conveys property to a buyer, also giving special warranties known as covenants.

FULLY INSURED Under social security a person who has made contributory payments for a required period, thereby giving the worker and his family full coverage under the act, is fully insured.

FUNGIBLE GOODS (fŭn′ jĭ bl) Movable goods composed of like units which can be estimated and replaced by like units according to weight, measure, and number.

FUTURE GOODS In sales law, goods not yet in existence or manufactured.

G

GARNISHMENT A court order authorizing the attachment (taking) of property, usually wages, in order to satisfy an unpaid claim.

GENERAL RELEASE A statement in writing and under seal terminating an existing obligation between two parties.

GIFT A voluntary transfer of property without consideration.

GOOD FAITH An honest intention not to take advantage of another.

GOODS Tangible personal property; articles of merchandise; chattels.

GOODWILL The advantage or benefit that is acquired by a business, beyond the capital or stock used therein, resulting from having a body of regular customers and a good reputation.

GRAND JURY A jury that hears evidence prior to an actual trial to determine whether a criminal charge should be brought against an individual.

GRANT The transfer of title to real property by means of a deed.

GRATUITOUS (grŭ t[y]û′ ŭt ŭs) Without value or legal consideration.

GUARANTEE (găr″ ăn te′) A contract whereby one party agrees to answer for the debt or default of another.

GUARDIAN One having legal custody of the property or the person of a minor or incompetent.

H

HABEAS CORPUS (hā′ bē ăs kôr′ pŭs) A writ issued by a court ordering a person who detains another in custody to bring that person before the court to determine if the detention is legal.

HEIR One who inherits by right of relationship.

HOLDER IN DUE COURSE One who has taken a negotiable instrument in good faith and for value without any knowledge that there is anything irregular about the instrument.

HOLDING OVER The act of retaining possession, without the landlord's consent, of leased property after the term of the lease has expired.

HOLOGRAPHIC WILL (hăl″ ŭ grăf′ ĭk) A will written in the testator's handwriting.

HOMEOWNER'S POLICY A single policy protecting a homeowner from all risks of loss and liability related to ownership and occupancy of a home.

HONOR To accept and pay a bill of exchange, note, or check.

HOSTILE FIRE A fire ignited from causes outside the control of the insured or through his negligence.

I

IMMATERIAL Unimportant; without significance.

IMMEDIATE PARTIES The parties whose names appear on the face of a negotiable instrument.

IMPLIED AUTHORITY Authority of an agent to perform acts incidental to the duties of the agency.

IMPLIED CONTRACT A contract created by the acts of the parties rather than by their oral or written agreements.

IMPLIED WARRANTY A warranty that is proved by the acts of the seller or by surrounding circumstances rather than by words spoken or written.

INCAPACITY Legal disability, such as infancy, want of authority, or other personal disability, to make binding agreements.

INCIDENTAL BENEFICIARY One who indirectly benefits from the performance of a contract without the specific intention of the contracting parties.

INCUMBRANCE A mortgage, lien, or claim on real property.

INDEMNITY An agreement that one party will secure another party against loss or damage due to the happening of a specified event.

INDENTURE (ĭn dĕn′ chĕr) A sealed agreement between two or more parties.

INDICTMENT (ĭn dīt′ mĕnt) A formal charge of a crime of a public nature handed up by a grand jury.

INJUNCTION A court order forbidding the doing of a specified act.

INLAND BILL A bill of exchange drawn and payable in the same state.

INSOLVENCY A state wherein one does not have sufficient property for the full payment of his debts or is unable to pay his debts as they become due.

INSURABLE INTEREST Interest of one person in the life or property of another from which he derives a benefit and would suffer a financial loss if the property were destroyed or the life were to end.

INTANGIBLE PROPERTY Property not perceptible to the senses; generally rights rather than goods.

INTERSTATE COMMERCE Traffic, intercourse, commercial trading, or the transportation of persons or property between different states.

INTESTATE One who dies without leaving a will.

INTRASTATE COMMERCE Commerce that is begun, carried on, and completed wholly within the limits of a single state.

INVALID Of no legal force; void.

INVASION OF PRIVACY An act that deprives a citizen of his right to privacy and his freedom from invasion of his personal life.

INVOLUNTARY BANKRUPTCY Bankruptcy in which creditors petition the court in an effort to have a debtor declared bankrupt.

IPSO FACTO (ĭp′ sō făk′ tō) Of itself; by the fact itself.

IRREVOCABLE (ĭr rĕv′ ăh kă bl) Not able to be revoked or rescinded legally.

ISSUE Direct descendants; children.

J

JETTISON (jĕt′ ĭ sŭn) To throw overboard part of the cargo of a ship in time of peril.

JOINT CONTRACTS Contracts in which two or more persons hold themselves liable for performance.

JOINT ESTATE An estate owned by two or more persons whose interest will go to the surviving owners at the death of anyone named in the deed.

JOINT TENANTS Two or more tenants holding land under conditions whereby the survivor takes the whole interest.

JUDGMENT The official decision of a court.

JUDGMENT BY DEFAULT A judgment rendered in favor of a plaintiff on his evidence alone because of the failure of the defendant to answer the summons or appear.

JUDICIAL DECISION A court's interpretation of the common law, statutes, and constitutions accepted as the law.

JURISDICTION (joor ĭs dĭk′ shŭn) The legal authority of a court to try a case.

JURY Body of persons selected to determine the truth in questions of fact in either civil or criminal cases.

L

LAISSEZ-FAIRE (lĕ′ sā′ fâr′) A policy of noninterference.

LARCENY The wrongful taking and carrying away of personal property of another.

LEASE A contract granting the use of certain real property to another for a specified period in consideration for the payment of rent.

LEGACY A gift of personal property as designated by will.

LEGAL TENDER Money, according to law, which must be accepted in payment of a debt.

LEVY The legal seizure of property in order to raise money to satisfy an unpaid judgment, fine, or tax.

LIBEL A slanderous or untruthful written or printed statement that reflects upon a person's reputation or character.

LICENSE Permission to do or to refrain from doing some act.

LIEN (lēn) A right to retain certain property as security for a claim or debt.

LIFE ESTATE The right of a person to use or receive the income from property for life.

LIQUIDATED DAMAGES An amount agreed upon that is to be paid in case of a breach of contract.

LITIGANTS (lĭt′ ĭ gănts) involved in a lawsuit.

LITIGATION (lĭt ŭ gā′ shŭn) A contest in a court of justice for the purpose of enforcing a right.

LOAN SHARK STATUTES Laws protecting borrowers and debtors against unfair threats of creditors in their efforts to collect overdue accounts.

LOCUS SIGILLI (lō′ kŭs sĭ jĭl′ ĭ) Latin phrase meaning "the place of the seal." Also indicated by the abbreviation L.S. Required in the execution of contracts for the sale of interest in real property and others. Not required in all states.

L.S. Abbreviation for locus sigilli, "the place of the seal"; the seal.

LUNATIC (lū′ nătĭc) One who has lost his reason.

M

MAJORITY Legal age, usually twenty-one years.

MAKER One obligated as the payor on a promissory note; the one promising to pay.

MALFEASANCE (măl fēz ĕn[t]s) The commission of an unlawful act.

MALPRACTICE In medicine, improper and negligent treatment resulting in injury or physical discomfort to a patient under a physician's care.

MANDAMUS (măn dā′ mŭs) A court order demanding the performance of an act or certain acts as required by law. The writ may be directed to an individual, government official, or corporation.

MARTIAL LAW A system of law which governs the army and navy. In war or serious emergency, it may be declared to govern the civilian population.

MATERIAL ALTERATION Any change in an instrument that affects the rights of the parties.

MATURITY The time when a bill becomes due.

MECHANIC'S LIEN (mē kăn′ ĭks lēn) Claim created by law to ensure that the cost of labor and materials used in repairing or erecting a building shall be paid before the owner of the property is released from liability.

MEDIATION (mēd″ ē ā′ shŭn) The intervention of a third party to dispute of two contending parties.

MEDICARE Health insurance protection, consisting of both medical and hospital benefits, available to all Americans sixty-five years of age and older under social security.

MEMORANDUM A note or instrument stating something that the parties desire to fix in memory by the aid of written evidence.

MERCHANTABLE QUALITY Goods of a quality that can be resold under the same description at ordinary market prices.

MERGE To absorb one right into another; to combine a contract with a superior one.

MINOR Also called infant, one under the age of legal maturity, which is usually twenty-one years of age.

MISDEMEANOR (mĭs″ dĕ mēn′ ĕr) A minor criminal offense of less serious nature than a felony.

MISREPRESENTATION A false statement of fact, innocently made, without any intent to deceive.

MISTRIAL A trial which has been declared void because of errors in law or fact arising during the prosecution of the case. A mistrial creates the necessity of a new trial before a different jury.

MONOPOLIES Business agreements which, because of their exclusive control of an operation, result in the restraint of competition and free trade.

MORATORIUM (mȧwr″ ŭ tōr′ ē ŭm) A period of time during which a debtor has the legal right to delay the payment of an overdue account.

MORTGAGE (mȧwr′ gĭj) A lien given on property as security for a loan.

N

NECESSARIES Things indispensable or things proper and useful for the sustenance of human life. This is a relative term, and its meaning will contract or expand according to the situation and social condition of the person referred to.

NEGLIGENCE (nĕg′ lĭ jŭn[t]s) The failure to exercise the degree of care required by law.

NEGOTIABILITY (nē gō″ shĭ ȧ bĭl′ ĭ tĭ) The characteristic of commercial paper (a note, draft, check, etc.) whereby it may be transferred to another person who then becomes the legal holder.

NOMINAL DAMAGES A small award given to one whose legal right has been violated but who sustained no actual loss.

NOMINAL PARTNER A person who is not a partner but who holds himself out as a partner or permits others to do so.

NON COMPOS MENTIS (nŏn kŏm′ pōs mĕn′ tĭs) Not of sound mind; insane.

NOTARY PUBLIC A public official who certifies under his seal various documents such as deeds and affidavits. He has the power to present and formally protest notes and bills of exchange.

NOTICE OF PROTEST A formal notice that a bill of exchange or note has been dishonored.

NOVATION The substitution of a new debt or obligation for an old one, which cancels the latter.

NUISANCE (nū′ sȧns) Anything that endangers life or health, gives offense to the senses, violates the laws of decency, or obstructs the reasonable and comfortable use of property.

NUNCUPATIVE WILL (nŭn′ kyoo pāt″ ĭv) An oral will made and declared in the presence of witnesses by the testator during his last illness.

O

OATH A solemn affirmation that statements made or to be made are true; testimony in court is given under oath.

OFFER A proposal by one person to another, intended to create a legal duty on its acceptance by the person to whom it is made.

OFFEREE (ôf′ ĕr ē) One who receives an offer.

OFFEROR (ôf′ ĕr ôr) The person who makes an offer.

OPEN POLICY A contract of insurance in which the amount recoverable is determined by the amount of the loss.

OPTION The right, usually obtained for a consideration, to purchase anything within a specified time at a stated price.

ORDER BILL OF LADING A receipt for goods shipped, issued by a carrier and containing a promise by the carrier not to redeliver the goods to anyone until the original order bill, properly endorsed, is presented to the carrier.

ORDINANCE The legislative act of a municipal corporation; a law, statute, or decree.

OUTLAWED A claim barred by the Statute of Limitations; something outside the protection of the law.

P

PANEL A list of persons summoned to act as jurors at a particular sitting.

PAROL (pŭ rȧwl′) By word of mouth; oral, verbal.

PAROLE (pŭ rōl′) The conditional release of a prisoner before the full expiration of his regular sentence.

PATENT A right granted by the government to an inventor or his agent to manufacture and sell a patented article for a period of seventeen years.

PAWNBROKER A person licensed to lend money on goods pledged to him.

PAYEE The party, named in commercial paper, to whom payment is to be made.

PER SE (pŭr sā′) In, through, or by itself.

PERCOLATING WATERS Water originating from springs and subterranean streams.

PERJURY A false statement made while testifying under oath in court, made willfully concerning some material point.

PERSONALTY (pŭrs′ nŭl tē) Personal property as distinguished from real property.

PETIT JURY (pĕt′ ē) The trial jury that has the duty of determining the facts at issue after hearing the evidence presented in open court by each party; called a petit jury because the number of jurors is usually smaller than in a grand jury.

PICKETING In labor law, the stationing of union members, usually with placards and signs, in such a way as to convey the union's grievances to the public or to management.

PLAINTIFF The party who brings an action in court against another party.

PLEA (plē) The answer of a person to a complaint or charge against him.

PLEADINGS The written statement of claims and defenses of the parties involved in a court action.

PLEDGE A bailment of goods as security for a debt or other obligation.

POLICE POWER The power to govern; the power to enact laws for the protection of the public health, welfare, morals, and safety.

POLLING THE JURY Asking each juror individually in open court if the verdict of the jury as announced by the foreman was agreed to by him.

POSSESSION Physical control of property, without regard to title and ownership.

POST-MORTEM (mōr′ tĕm) Occurring after death.

POSTDATED To date an instrument as of a later date than the one on which it was made.

POWER OF ATTORNEY A written instrument which empowers one person to act for or represent another in specified matters.

PRECEDENT (prē sēd′ ĕnt) adj., (prĕs′ ê dĕnt) n. A principal legal decision cited as having an effect upon an action being presented in a court of law or equity.

PREMIUM The price paid for insurance.

PRESENTMENT The exhibition of a note and demand for payment; also the presentation of a draft or bill of exchange to a drawee with a request for payment or acceptance.

PRIMA FACIE (prī′ mȧ fā′ shĭ ē) Legally sufficient for proof unless rebutted or contradicted.

PRINCIPAL In agency, one who appoints and directs the activities of an agent.

PRINCIPLE As of law, a fundamental truth or doctrine that is almost universally accepted.

PRO RATA (prō rā′ tȧ) Proportionately.

PRORATE To divide into shares according to interests.

PROBATE (prō′ bāt) The legal procedure of proving or establishing a will.

PROBATE COURT A specialized court having the responsibility for the administration of the estates of deceased persons or persons who are under the jurisdiction of the court by reason of some incapacity. Sometimes called a surrogate court or a widows' and orphans' court.

PROFESSIONAL OPINION An opinion based upon expert knowledge and judgment, usually accepted as a fact in actions on contracts, as the opinion of a medical doctor, a master mechanic, a jeweler, etc.

PROOF The establishment of a fact by evidence.

PROOF OF CLAIM A written statement, under oath, setting forth one's claim to share in a bankrupt's estate.

PROSECUTE To proceed against a person by legal means.

PROTEST (prō′ tĕst) A statement by a notary public that an instrument has been refused payment at maturity.

PROXY A document by which one person authorizes another to act for him.

PUBLIC OFFER An offer made publicly in situations in which the offeree's identity or location is unknown to the offeror.

PUBLIC POLICY That principle of law which holds that no person may lawfully perform an act that has a tendency to be injurious to the public.

PUBLIC UTILITY A private corporation having certain powers of a public nature to enable it to discharge its duties for the public benefit.

PUFFING Expressions of opinion of a seller regarded by the courts as merely persuasive and not as actionable statements of fact.

PUNITIVE DAMAGES (pū′ nĭ tĭv) Damages, in excess of actual damages incurred by the plaintiff, awarded as a measure of punishment for the defendant's wrongful and malicious acts.

Q

QUASI (kwā′ sī) Almost; bearing some resemblance to but not having all the requisites.

QUASI CONTRACT A contract implied by law, not by fact; not a contract in the true sense because it lacks the element of mutual assent.

QUIET POSSESSION Undisturbed possession; as used in the law of sales, the right to hold goods free and clear of the claims of all other persons.

QUITCLAIM A deed granting any interest that the grantor may have in the property, without covenants.

QUORUM (kwôr′ ŭm) The minimum number of persons who must be present to transact business.

R

RATIFICATION The subsequent approval of an act that previously had not been binding.

REALTY (rē′ ăl tē) Real property, as distinguished from personal property; land and anything permanently attached thereto.

REBATE A discount or reduction; a return of part of a debt after full payment has been made.

RECEIVER A person legally appointed to receive and hold in trust property that is or may be subject to litigation.

RECLAMATION The right of an owner to the return of property in the possession of a bankrupt but not subject to claims of creditors.

REDEMPTION (rē dĕm′ shŭn) The act of buying back one's property after it has been sold.

REDRESS To correct; to make right.

REFEREE A person appointed by a court to hear and decide a disputed matter.

REIMBURSE To pay back; to make equivalent return or restoration for something paid, expended, or lost.

RELEASE The giving up, or surrender, of a claim or right of action; an instrument evidencing such a surrender.

REMEDY The legal means to recover a right or to redress a wrong.

REMOTE PARTY Person or persons other than the original and immediate parties to an agreement.

REPLEVIN (rĭ plĕv′ ĭn) A court action for the purpose of recovering possession of personal property wrongfully taken or held.

REPRIEVE (rĭ prēv′) To suspend the execution of a sentence for a time.

REPUDIATE (rĭ pūd′ ē āt″) To reject; to renounce a right or obligation.

RESCIND (rē sĭnd′) To cancel; to annul; to avoid.

RESCISSION The annulling of a contract by mutual consent of the parties involved or by court decision as a result of breach by one of the parties.

RESTRAINING INJUNCTION A decree of a court of equity ordering a party to cease and desist from certain acts.

RESTRAINT OF TRADE Contracts or combinations designed to eliminate or stifle competition, effect a monopoly, or artificially maintain prices.

REVERT To fall back into the possession of the former proprietor.

REVOCATION (rĕv″ ŭ kā′ shŭn) The act of recalling a power conferred previously.

RIDER In insurance, an attached writing which modifies or supplements the printed policy.

RIGHT OF PRIVACY The right of a person to be protected from intrusion and invasion of his personal life by unauthorized persons and agencies. In hotels, the right of privacy means a guest's right to use his room without fear of intrusion by others.

RIGHT OF RESCISSION A right granted a contracting party to disavow contract obligations under certain prescribed conditions.

RIGHT TO WORK LAW A law in force in some states that prohibits compulsory union membership. It bans, in effect, the union shop as well as the closed shop.

RIGHTFUL POSSESSION The possession of personal property with either express or implied authority from the owner.

RIPARIAN RIGHTS (rī pâr′ ĭ ăn) The rights of an owner of land abutting a stream or other body of water to the use of water and to water and ice he may wish to remove from the body of water.

ROMAN CODE A comprehensive system of laws established by Emperor Justinian and the emperors who followed him for the better administration of the vast Roman Empire.

S

SALE A contract whereby property is transferred from one person, called the seller, to another person, called the buyer, for a consideration, called the price.

SALE WITH A LIEN RESERVED A sale of goods in which title passes to the buyer and possession is retained by the seller, usually as security for payment; as a layaway sale.

SATISFACTION PIECE A written acknowledgment that a claim between plaintiff and defendant has been satisfied.

SEAL A particular sign adopted and used by an individual to attest in the most formal manner the execution of an instrument.

SECURITY INTEREST An interest in personal property which secures payment or performance of an obligation.

SETOFF A counterclaim or cross action that a defendant sets up against the claim of the plaintiff.

SHERMAN ANTITRUST ACT A congressional act passed in 1890 providing free trade without suppression of competition.

SIGHT DRAFT A written order on the drawee to pay on demand the amount named in the instrument.

SINE DIE (sī' nė dī' ē) Literally, *without a day;* indefinitely.

SINE QUA NON (sī' nė kwā nŏn') Meaning *without which it is not;* an indispensable requisite.

SINKING FUND An amount set aside for the payment of the interest and principal of a loan.

SOCIAL LEGISLATION Laws passed to improve the welfare of the masses, especially working people and those with small incomes.

SOCIAL SECURITY ACT A federal act providing financial assistance to retired workers at ages sixty-two and sixty-five, to widows at age sixty, and to insured workers who are totally disabled at any age.

SOLVENCY The state of being able to pay one's debts as they become due.

SOVEREIGN A person, body, or state in which independent and supreme authority is vested.

SPECIALTY A contract under seal.

SPECIFIC PERFORMANCE The performance of an agreement according to the exact terms originally agreed upon.

SPECULATIVE DAMAGES damages which have not actually been inflicted and cannot be proved.

SQUATTER One who settles upon the land of another without permission.

SS (sĭl' ĭsĕt) The abbreviation for the Latin word scilicet, meaning *that is to say;* to wit, namely.

STATION IN LIFE An expression used to aid in the determination of what constitutes necessaries for particular individuals whose social or economic position may vary from the average.

STATUS QUO The existing state of things.

STATUTE A law enacted by a legislature.

STATUTE OF FRAUDS A law requiring written evidence to support certain contracts if they are to be enforced in court.

STATUTE OF LIMITATIONS A law that prevents bringing an action if that action is not begun within a specified time.

STIPULATION An article or material condition in a contract.

STOPPAGE IN TRANSIT The right of an unpaid seller to stop goods in transit and order the carrier to hold the goods for the benefit of the unpaid seller, in cases in which the buyer becomes insolvent after the goods have been shipped.

STRAIGHT BILL OF LADING A receipt for goods shipped, issued by a carrier to a shipper and containing the contractual terms under which the goods are received for shipment.

SUBPOENA (sŭb pē' nȧ) An order or writ commanding a person to appear and testify in a legal action or proceeding.

SUBROGATION The substitution of one person for another with reference to a lawful claim or right.

SUBSTANTIAL PERFORMANCE A principle of law that allows the collection of the full contract price, less damages for any breach, when a contract has been essentially fully performed and in good faith, even though there has been some slight defect in the performance.

SUBSTANTIVE LAW (sŭb' stăn tĭve) That part of our laws that deals with the determination of rights and duties.

SUMMONS A notice issued from a court requiring a person to appear therein to answer the complaint of a plaintiff within a specified time.

SURETY One who promises to answer for a debt on behalf of a second person to a third person.

SURROGATE The name given in some states to the judge who has the administration of probate matters.

SYNDICATE An association of individuals formed to conduct a specific business transaction.

T

TAFT-HARTLEY ACT The Labor-Management Relations Act of 1947, providing for the mediation of labor-management disputes.

TALESMAN A person who is ordered to report for jury duty.

TANGIBLE Occupying space; able to be touched; palpable.

TENANT One who has temporary possession of and interest in the land of another.

TENDER An unconditional offer to deliver money or other personal property in pursuance of a contract.

TENURE (tĕn′ ŭr) A manner in which lands are held; the services a tenant owes the landlord.

TESTATOR (tĕs′ tāt″ ŭr) A person who makes a will.

TESTIMONY (tĕs′ tĭ mō′ nĭ) The spoken or written declaration of a witness given under oath.

THIRD PARTY BENEFICIARY One who receives a benefit as the result of a valid agreement made expressly to benefit him.

TIME IS OF THE ESSENCE An expression applicable to those agreements in which time of performance is critical in the carrying out of the agreement.

TITLE The right of ownership often evidenced by a certificate of title, bill of sale, or similar documentation.

TITLE POLICY A policy of insurance protecting the owner of real property from any damages resulting from a defect in his deed, or title.

TORT A private or civil wrong arising from something other than a breach of contract.

TORTIOUS BAILEE (tôr′ shŭs) One who has possession of another's property either illegally or .without the owner's permission.

TRADEMARK A mark or symbol a manufacturer places on goods he produces.

TRANSCRIPT An official copy of certain proceedings in a court.

TREASURY STOCK Stock of a corporation issued by it and later reacquired.

TRESPASS An injury done to the person, property, or right of another individual, with force or violence, either actual or implied in law.

TRUST A property interest held by one person for the benefit of another.

TRUST RECEIPT A document issued by a borrower of money, stating that the borrower holds title to certain named goods as a trustee for the benefit of the lender.

TRUSTEE A person who holds property in trust.

TRUTH IN ADVERTISING Federal legislation regulating advertising of credit terms and time-payment costs in consumer sales.

TRUTH IN LENDING ACT Federal legislation regulating consumer purchases on credit and consumer loans.

U

ULTRA VIRES ACT (ul′ trȧ vī′ rēz) An act by a corporation that is beyond its express or implied powers.

UMPIRE One who decides a question in dispute.

UNCONSCIONABLE AGREEMENTS (ŭn känch′ ŭ nŭ bŭl) Contracts which the courts refuse to enforce due to obvious unfair practices wrought upon victimized buyers.

UNDERWRITER One who insures another against some risk; an insurer, usually an insurance company.

UNDIVIDED INTEREST The title rights of two or more persons in personal property, as an airplane, wherein each has a fractional right to the entire property, rather than title to a specific part of the co-owned property.

UNEMPLOYMENT COMPENSATION Guaranteed payments to unemployed workers under state law.

UNIFORM PARTNERSHIP ACT An act adopted by many states for the purpose of giving uniformity to the regulation of partnership businesses.

UNILATERAL (u″ nĭ lăt′ ŭ rŭl) Having relation to only one of two or more persons, things, promises, actions, or obligations.

UNPAID SELLER'S LIEN The right of an unpaid seller who is still in possession of the goods to hold the goods until the purchase price has been paid, when the sale is for cash; or when the sale is on credit, but the credit terms have expired; or when the buyer has become insolvent.

UNWRITTEN LAW The portion of the law not found in constitutions, statutes, or ordinances. Most of the unwritten law is found in reports of cases.

USURY (ūzh′ ĕ rē) A charge for the use of money beyond the rate of interest set by law.

V

VALID Having legal force; lawful or binding.

VALID TENDER An offer by one obligated on an instrument to pay the one having possession and title to an instrument.

VALIDITY The quality of being good in law.

VALUED POLICY A contract of insurance in which the parties have agreed on a specific sum as the amount recoverable in event of a loss.

VENDEE A buyer or purchaser.

VENDOR A seller.

VENIRE (vŭ nī′ [u]rē) A judge's writ or order summoning a jury for court trial.

VENUE (vĕn′ ū) The geographical area over which the court has jurisdiction.

VERBAL Oral, or by word of mouth.

VERBATIM (vĕr″ bā′ tŭm) Word for word.

VERDICT The official finding of fact by the jury.

VERIFY To determine, fix, or establish a fact. In court the fact is determined under oath.

VERSUS Against; abbreviated as vs. or v.

VESTED Established; fixed; settled; something that should be maintained.

VOCATIONAL EDUCATION ACT Federal legislation providing skill training to workers unemployed due to changing demands for skilled workers in industry.

VOCATIONAL REHABILITATION ACT Legislation providing handicapped persons with education and other assistance in preparation for job opportunities within their mental and physical limitations.

VOID Of no legal effect or force.

VOIDABLE Capable of being voided or nullified, usually at the election of one party to a contract.

VOUCHER A document that evidences a transaction; a receipt.

W

WAGER A bet; an agreement that one will gain or lose in accordance with the determination or happening of an event.

WAGES The agreed compensation paid by an employer to an employee for work done.

WAIVER The surrender of some right, claim, or privilege granted by law.

WARD A minor in the custody of a guardian.

WAREHOUSEMAN A person whose business is to store goods for other persons.

WARRANT (wŏr′ ănt) To guarantee; an order of a court authorizing an arrest.

WARRANTY An agreement to be responsible if a thing is not as represented; the covenant of the grantor of real property and of his heirs that the grantee will have title to the property.

WARRANTY OF TITLE A guarantee of the full rights of ownership, implied by law, by a seller to the buyer.

WATERED STOCK Stock issued for insufficient values, or for no value at all.

WILL A document drawn in conformity with the laws of a state indicating how property is to be disposed of after the death of the testator.

WILLFUL Intentional; deliberate.

WORDS OF NEGOTIABILITY Words required to give an instrument the quality of negotiability: "to the order of," or "to bearer."

WRIT Anything written; a judicial process by which a person is summoned to appear; a legal instrument to enforce obedience to the orders and sentences of the court.

WRONG The infringement of a right.

Z

ZONING LAW An ordinance restricting or permitting certain uses of land in specified areas.

▲ INDEX